ORDEAL OF THE UNION

VOLUMES I AND II
ORDEAL OF THE UNION

VOLUMES III AND IV
THE EMERGENCE OF LINCOLN

The Emergence of Lincoln

ABRAHAM LINCOLN IN 1858

(From an ambrotype taken by Mr. T. P. Pierson on August 25, 1858, at Macomb, Illinois)

The Emergence of Lincoln

VOLUME II ... PROLOGUE TO CIVIL WAR 1859·1861

by ALLAN NEVINS

New York · CHARLES SCRIBNER'S SONS · *London*

CONTENTS

ILLUSTRATIONS

The Emergence of Lincoln

1

Plotters North and South

A RAINBOW of resurgent prosperity was now bent against the storm clouds of sectional dissension. Indeed, the Manichean dualism of the period was never better illustrated than during the summer and fall of 1859. On every hand a restoration of economic activity was visible. Although the depression had continued with slowly lessening force until the beginning of the year, and though the flour-milling, coal-mining, and ironmaking industries continued to suffer severely, spring had brought a steady brightening of business prospects. The New England cotton, woolen, and shoe factories began running almost full time; lumbering showed a revival in Michigan and Wisconsin; railroad traffic increased, and a midsummer agreement by leading roads upon more remunerative rates was hailed with pleasure in financial circles.[1] As French, Austrians, and Italians fought in Lombardy, agriculture found a stimulant in the new war.[2] Wages of laborers rose, securities sold at quotations which made their low level just after the panic seem incredible, and real estate in the large cities found a brisker market. When importers and exporters cast up the totals of the year, they found them larger than in any twelvemonth of the nation's history except 1857.[3]

Yet all the while the sectional quarrel, like a cancer gnawing at the viscera of some outwardly healthy man, furnished constant spasms of pain and fever. When Congress was in session the inflammation was at its worst, but it never quite ceased. In the very issue in which Greeley's *Tribune* hailed the return of good times, it declared that no soft words could annihilate the fact that the predominant sentiments of North and South were irreconcilably hostile, and the chasm between them was inexorably widening.[4] It was even so. As summer brought news of Magenta and Solferino, as the demand for cotton and grain increased,

1 *Bankers' Magazine*, August, 1859, p. 159.
2 Greeley, travelling 270 miles from Chicago to Quincy in 1859, found Illinois steadily growing. "There are new blocks in her cities, new dwellings in every village, new breakings on this or that edge of almost every prairie." N. Y. *Weekly Tribune*, May 28, 1850.
3 *Wages in U. S. From Colonial Times*, 254; *Statistical Abstract*.
4 N. Y. *Weekly Tribune*, May 7, 1859.

3

as smoke thickened over industrial towns and money jingled on the planter's desk, citizens began looking ahead to the Presidential contest. Republicans scanned the future with confidence. But thousands of Southerners declared, with John Cuningham of Charleston, that if such a man as Seward were elected, the Union would become intolerable for the cotton States and all that was dear to them would best flourish under a separate nationality.[5]

One of the fundamental tasks of reviving business was to knit the country together by rail and steam. John W. Garrett, the young Baltimore businessman who was made president of the Baltimore & Ohio late in 1858, was drafting plans for expansion. In the West, he meant to acquire the railroads between Marietta and St. Louis, and throw a branch into Pittsburgh; in the East, he intended to construct splendid port facilities in Baltimore.[6] John Murray Forbes, supported by Baring Brothers and wealthy New Englanders, had made possible the completion of the Hannibal & St. Joseph across northern Missouri in 1859.[7] J. Edgar Thomson was strengthening the Pennsylvania and its allied line the Pittsburgh, Fort Wayne, & Chicago; Forbes gave the Chicago, Burlington & Quincy complete control of the roads linking the three cities of its name; the railway from Chicago to Fond du Lac was completed in 1859; and in Alabama, Mississippi, and Louisiana men were making plans to utilize the Congressional land grants of 1856–57.[8] The thickening network of railroads, their mileage practically doubling in 1855–61, was creating a national market for manufactures in place of the old myriad of local markets.[9,10]

But while unity was being promoted by economic forces—while textile production was demanding larger and larger central mills;[11] while the patents of Lyman Blake and the enterprise of Gordon McKay foreshadowed the day when great central shoe factories would replace local shoemakers; while dozens of American products, from pens to pianos, gained trade names known all over the country—unity was being undermined by political forces. And while economic forces moved slowly, political forces moved with terrible speed.

Certain clouds hardly larger than a man's hand appeared on the horizon early in 1859. Ominously, the name of John Brown of Ossawatomie had cropped up again in the news from Kansas. He had left that Territory in the fall of 1856, shocking old friends in the east by his gray, gnarled look and his intense mental

5 Cuningham to Hammond, April 18, 1859; Hammond Papers, LC.
6 Hungerford, *Baltimore & Ohio*, I, 345.
7 J. W. Starr, *One Hundred Years of Amer. Railroading*, 181; H. G. Pearson, *An Amer. Railroad Builder*, 92, 93.
8 *Bankers' Magazine*, February, 1859, pp. 606, 607.
9 The fateful meeting of Cornelius Cole, Judah, and others above the hardware store of Huntington & Hopkins in Sacramento to organize the Central Pacific took place early in 1861. Cornelia Phillips, *Cole*, 111.
10 Oscar Lewis, *The Big Four*, Ch. I; N. Y. *Weekly Tribune*, June 9, 1860.
11 Clark, *Manufactures in U. S. 1607–1860*, pp. 560, 574.

fixity. In the next three years his actions were destined to affect American affairs profoundly.

[I]

John Brown was fifty-nine years old in May, 1859. He was no ordinary man. All who saw him, whether friends or foes, were struck by his iron will, his consuming inner fire, and his intense though erratic devotion to causes outside himself. Great as were his faults, he united a certain elevation of character with the traits of a born leader. His intimates—members of his family, employees, his picked Kansas band, the eastern conspirators soon to befriend him in a desperate venture—regarded him with deferential admiration. His business partners (who all rued the partnership) knew that it was hopeless to argue with his stubborn convictions. Proslavery settlers in Kansas, upon whom his murder of five men on the Pottawatomie had created a deep impression, breathed more easily when he left the Territory. He was the product partly of inheritance. He came of stern Puritan stock, but of unhappy immediate antecedents. His father Owen, a man of strong religious and abolitionist convictions, was an industrious, respected citizen of his chosen Ohio community for more than fifty years, becoming a trustee of Oberlin and accumulating a substantial estate; but his mother Ruth Mills Brown, like his maternal grandmother, died insane. John Brown was the product also of a peculiarly hard, failure-ridden life.[12]

A man of scanty schooling, speculative, of nomadic tastes and marked business incapacity, he made repeated migrations in a fruitless effort to better himself. From northeastern Ohio, where he made his start in life, he went for ten years to northwestern Pennsylvania; then back to Ohio again; then to Virginia, to look into the possibility of settlement; then to Springfield, Massachusetts, on wool business; and then to upper New York. He tried calling after calling; managing tanneries, land speculation, breeding racehorses, surveying, selling cattle and sheep, wool factorage, and farming. Once he even contemplated winemaking. His large family—for his first wife bore him seven children, his second, thirteen—were reared in hand-to-mouth fashion. His character seemed full of contradictions. Usually rigidly honest, he sometimes showed a financial irresponsibility that approached dishonesty; a man of principle, he could be a provoking opportunist; kindly and philanthropic, he had a vein of harsh cruelty. All this,

12 Oswald Garrison Villard's *John Brown Fifty Years After* is exhaustive and judicious. Hill Peebles Wilson relentlessly states the adverse case in *John Brown, Soldier of Fortune: a Critique,* while Robert Penn Warren in *John Brown, the Making of a Martyr* attempts a balanced view. Of the older biographies Richard J. Hinton's *John Brown and His Men* is much the best. F. B. Sanborn's biography is not only inaccurate but suppresses vital particulars and mangles documents. James C. Malin's *John Brown and the Legend of '56* is indispensable. I have used collections of papers relating to John Brown in at least a dozen libraries from Boston to Topeka.

with his self-righteous stubbornness and utter intractability, pointed to some psychogenic malady.

All our evidence on his early years shows that he was an exemplary husband, father, and citizen, public-spirited and industrious though incompetent in affairs.

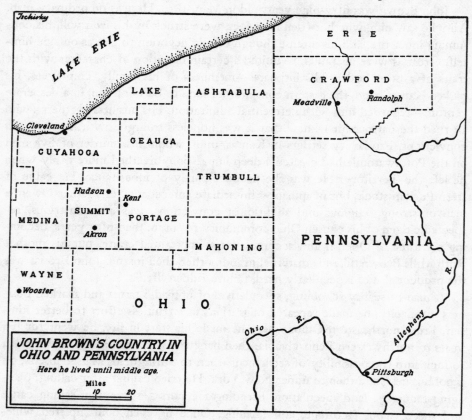

JOHN BROWN'S COUNTRY IN
OHIO AND PENNSYLVANIA
Here he lived until middle age.
Miles
0   10   20

Of devout Congregational stock, he believed in predestination, foreordination, and providential interpositions, and prayed daily with family and apprentices. He had cherished in youth, he said later, a strong desire for death—doubtless a wish to be united with God. He showed a rigid probity. A journeyman who lived with him in Hudson, Ohio, for some years, testifies that he was stern in ferreting out dishonest employees, but with an eye to reformation rather than punishment. He took pride in good workmanship. A customer might come ten miles for five pounds of sole leather, yet if Brown detected the least particle of moisture in his stock, he sent the man home empty-handed. He was highly charitable. Once he learned that a neighboring family was destitute; he sought out the neighbor, struck a bargain with him for work the following summer, and made him take food and clothing as pay in advance. He studiously kept the Sabbath, but on other days he toiled hard. He abhorred fishing and hunting as a waste of time. His conversation was often jocose and mirthful, but never vulgar, and always studded with Biblical texts. He liked to argue stubbornly with others, and was eager to gain information from all comers. He despised any man who agreed with him at all points, respecting only those who had ideas of their own. On certain principles, however, he was unyielding. If a stranger entered the community, his first questions were whether the man observed Sunday, supported the gospel and common schools, and opposed slavery. If he failed on any point, Brown regarded him with suspicion.

His own early record on slavery was that of a moderate abolitionist. As a boy he had been shocked and grieved by a Northern innkeeper's maltreatment of a Negro lad his own age. In early manhood he had frequently concealed fugitive slaves. Indeed, a friend who knew him well in Ohio testifies that he repeatedly saw Brown come in at night with several blacks whom he had piloted all the way from the Ohio River; and a woman neighbor thought that he spent time and money on fugitives that might better have gone to the neglected education of his own children. In 1834, he proposed to his brother Frederick that the two enlist helpers and start a school for Negro children in Randolph, Pennsylvania, but the scheme came to nothing. While at first Brown seems to have been a nonresistant of the Garrisonian type, in 1850, helping some free and fugitive Negroes of western Massachusetts organize a League of Gileadites for mutual protection, he preached them a fighting doctrine.[13]

As he grew older, as the world gave him hard buffets, as his lack of business system and foresight plunged him into failure after failure, and as his sceptical temper weakened his religious dogmas, his character changed. One disaster was especially severe; the crash of the Franklin Land Company (1837), in connection with which he had made excessive realty purchases near Franklin Mills, Ohio. His affairs in 1837–41 (which were gloomy depression years after the panic of 1837 anyhow) fell into utter confusion. Struggling in a morass of debt, he lost his reputation for probity. In 1839, he persuaded an agent of the New England Woolen Company of Connecticut to let him have $2,800 for buying wool in Ohio. He converted the money to his own uses, and escaped punishment only because the corporation was lenient—perhaps also because he gave pledges of payment which he never wholly carried out. To reimburse some Ohio sureties who had put their names on one of his bonds or notes, he pledged them his rights to a certain piece of property; then, when this property was conveyed to him,

13 The *Ohio State Arch. and Hist. Quarterly* has printed valuable articles on Brown in Vol. XXX by C. B. Galbreath; in Vol. LXVII by Mary Land; and in Vol. LVIII by Louis Filler. Other aspects of his career are examined by Floyd C. Shoemaker in *Missouri Hist. Review*, XXVI, and by Ernest C. Miller in *Pennsylvania History*, XV.

he secretly recorded the deed and raised money on it by a mortgage. In 1840, he made an abortive effort to obtain a thousand acres in a tract of Virginia land belonging to Oberlin College. His business misfortunes, combative temper, and failure to meet clear legal obligations had resulted in one controversy after another, so that between 1820 and 1845 he figured in twenty-one lawsuits in Portage County, Ohio. One case was specially embarrassing; the Bank of Wooster, suing him for a check which he had drawn on the Leather Manufacturers Bank of New York when he had no account there, recovered $917.65.

It was thus as a failure, a man who had lost part of his early integrity as well as his faith in organized Christianity, a soured, hardened reformer who took refuge from his own deficiencies in fighting the wrongs of others, that Brown in 1855 reestablished his family on the farm at North Elba in the Adirondacks that he had obtained from Gerrit Smith, and saw his sons off to Kansas, himself soon to follow. His purpose was not to resist border ruffians, but to engage in farming and surveying. The Browns migrated to the frontier, like countless other families, to get a fresh start in life. It was only when the sons reported that many Missourians were hostile that John Brown collected arms and money for possible battle. That incisive Kansas historian, James C. Malin, tells us that Brown was not an idealist longing to liberate the prairies; that through years of toil, error, and frustration he had rather become a restless trader moving from place to place in one business after another, constantly pursuing that will-of-the-wisp, a spectacular stroke which would make his fortune. He tells us that Brown's murder of five men on Pottawatomie Creek in May, 1856, probably had nothing to do with slavery, but was an act of political assassination.

This may be true, and yet not all the truth. Brown apparently remained a convinced hater of slavery, who had steeped himself in abolitionist literature and who regarded slaveholders as criminals. He remained, also, a man with a sense of mission—one on whom the finger of the Lord had been laid for some great object. Such a man was easily kindled by the heroic struggle of the free State men in Kansas.

The old veins of Puritan idealism and reformative zeal were still to be found in his nature; but a vein of the ruthlessness peculiar to fanatics, and especially fanatics gnarled by failure, had asserted a dominant place. The cranky scepticism which now kept him from any formal church allegiance perhaps chiefly concerned the New Testament. It is significant that in the many religious letters of his last year he makes but one reference to Christ, and none to Christian mercy. His belief in the harsh, implacable Jehovah of the Old Testament, however, remained unchanged. Charity and forgiveness had no place in his creed. When executed, he refused to let a Virginia minister go to the scaffold, for these ministers believed in slavery, and (said he) "my knees will not bend in prayer with them while their hands are stained with the blood of souls." He left a final injunction to his children to be good haters—to abhor that sum of all villainies, slavery. To him, the Missourians who mustered along the Kaw in 1856–57 were as the Philistines who camped between Sokoh and Azekah; he was as Gideon against the Midianites; he was like the Samson who slew thirty citizens of Ascalon. The scarred, warped, self-tortured man who supervised the murders on the Pottawatomie told Mahala Doyle, whose husband and sons he killed, that if a man stood between him and what he thought right, he would take that man's life as coolly as he would eat breakfast.

"Always restless," wrote poor Mahala Doyle. "With an eye like a snake, he looks like a demon."

We are thus brought to the question of mental aberration, a subject on which much evidence is available. Most of it lies in affidavits in the papers of Governor Henry A. Wise of Virginia, sent him by people who knew Brown well. It can be summed up in a sentence written by Dr. W. W. Durbin of Canfield, Ohio, whose acquaintance was of long standing and who wrote emphatically: "I am fully satisfied he is and has been a crazy man for years." These affidavits are supplemented by other evidence. The word "monomania" is used with significant frequency. When Brown paid his last visit to Boston in May, 1859, that shrewd businessman John Murray Forbes noted "the little touch of insanity" about his glittering gray-blue eyes, an impression not lessened by Brown's loud insistence that only bayonets and bullets could settle the Kansas issue—though Kansas was then at peace. A correspondent of the Chicago *Tribune* declared in 1860 that many who knew Brown in Kansas believed that the slaying of his son Frederick had "made him a monomaniac on the subject of slavery"; and that, denying any motive of revenge, he labored under "a religious hallucination to the effect that he was the appointed instrument for putting an end to human slavery." [14]

In the parlance of the day, he had a tendency toward monomania. Endowed with a narrow, intense, dogmatic mind, he fastened it upon one subject with a fervor which shut out all other considerations. But how early did this tendency appear? Was it upon slavery alone that he was a monomaniac? If so, we might doubt the analysis, for by 1860 the country had a multitude of monomaniacs upon slavery. But evidence appears of inordinate preoccupation with one topic after another before he turned to slavery. He was subject to extravagant religious fixations. In 1852, worried because his son John did not exhibit piety, he spent

14 For testimony from many sources relating to Brown's sanity see material in the Villard Collection, Columbia University Library; John Brown Papers, LC; and State Executive Docs., Va. State Library. For a modern treatment of pertinent medical questions see Charles Berg's *Clinical Psychology;* E. H. Williams, *The Doctor in Court.* The author has been advised on this subject by Dr. Joseph Collins of New York and Dr. Bradford Murphey of Denver.

an entire month writing a letter of pamphlet length to him, composed largely of scriptural quotations. We might question the sanity of a nearly penniless man with a large family who devotes a month to such an exhortation—which proved futile. He seems in 1836-37 to have shown a similar fixity of interest in land speculation. And while no final judgment is possible, his wool ventures may also point to psychogenic disorders amounting to mental disease.

That they did so was the belief of Aaron Erickson, a shrewd, well-educated wool dealer of western New York who saw much of Brown in the years when he engaged in sheep growing and wool selling. Brown in 1844 had gone into partnership with Simon Perkins, Jr., of Akron, in the sheep business. Two years later, Perkins & Brown had established an agency in Springfield, Massachusetts, for the sale of wool, with Brown in charge. In August, 1846, a Springfield meeting issued a call for a wool-growers' convention in Steubenville, Ohio, the following year. It was duly held, with Alexander Campbell, founder of the Campbellite sect, as chairman. Brown was present, and delivered a shrewd, practical address on the preparation of wool for the market. He had gained a standing among farmers and stockmen by contributions to the *Ohio Cultivator* and other publications, and by a well-esteemed cure for bots in sheep. The Steubenville meeting adopted a report complaining that textile manufacturers and dealers generally did not properly grade wool, but paid for fine and medium qualities on a low-grade basis; thus endorsing a crusade long carried on by Brown.

Erickson had heard of this crusade; he had heard of local meetings in Ohio at which Brown had declared with rhadamanthine unction that his great mission in life was to right this wrong. Believing the existing system fair, Erickson concluded that the man was some unscrupulous sharper imposing on the farmers' credulity. After Brown had opened the Springfield agency, Erickson had taken pains to meet him. He had been instantly disarmed of his suspicions. Instead of a swindler, he found a man whose frank character, simple manners, and childlike ignorance of his great project stamped him a Dr. Primrose, a deluded visionary. He had convinced himself, Erickson writes, of a total fallacy.

Sometime later, Erickson called again at the Springfield headquarters, finding Brown in high elation. The Perkins & Brown agency, designated as an eastern depot by the Steubenville meeting and supported by the *Prairie Farmer*, had received large consignments of wool from its western friends. Once more Brown showed intense fervor in proclaiming his mission of doing justice to the growers. Once more he praised his own grading system, which Erickson thought manifestly bad. The visitor seized an opportunity, when Brown's back was turned, of transposing three fleeces; and when he pointed to them, Brown emphatically maintained the accuracy of his classification. The reformer, writes Erickson, had valued the finer grades about fifty percent above true market quotations, and the coarser grades about twenty-five percent below. He was deaf to warnings that he had underestimated these lower grades, which would be snapped up by buyers. When he persisted in his course, they were quickly bought at ruinous prices, while the finer fleeces remained a drug on the market. Some farmers interposed before the wool was all sold, states Erickson, bringing a lawsuit which cost Perkins & Brown heavy damages.

Talking of a manufacturers' conspiracy, Brown in 1849 decided to ship his best grades to England. Fine British wools were then being imported despite the tariff; and Brown no sooner shipped two hundred thousand pounds abroad than a Massachusetts manufacturer who had unsuccessfully offered sixty cents a pound at home brought a consignment back from London at a cost, freight and duty included, of fifty-two cents. The loss on this venture may have reached $40,000, and Perkins & Brown went into liquidation. "These," Erickson writes, "were the acts of an insane man." This whole wool agency business constitutes an intricate chapter. Much evidence on it has been lost, and Brown's supporters thought his general position sound. But that at least one astute judge believed him a monomaniac on wool grades and prices is certain.[15]

Medical science has long since discarded the term monomania. It might now classify Brown's aberrations under the head of reasoning insanity, which is a branch of paranoia; that is, of mental disease marked by systematized delusions, but accompanied in many instances by great logical acumen. Such a man may mingle with others and most people will never suspect his disorder. One form of the disease is called litigious paranoia, the victim engaging in many lawsuits; another form is ambitious paranoia, in which the subject feels called to exalted missions. On all subjects but one the patient may appear eminently sane. It is perhaps significant in this connection that a son of one of Brown's partners states: "J. B. saw everything large; felt himself equal to anything; . . . and would accept no suggestions, advice, or direction from anyone." If Brown was a paranoiac, he had moved by 1857 to a feverish absorption in the idea of guerrilla warfare upon slavery. As he did so, the sectional crisis reached a pitch which rendered the acts of such a cool, determined, fanatical leader potentially dangerous.

And Brown intervened in precisely the way that was calculated to do the gravest damage to sectional concord. The steps leading toward his intervention may be briefly exhibited in a series of scenes, all dramatic enough.

15 Brown's wool ventures deserve a separate monograph. While his business mismanagement was deplorable, much may be said for his effort to protect the wool growers. Many papers on the subject are in the Brown collections of the Boston Public Library, Columbia University Library, and Ohio Arch. and Hist. Society. Files of the *Prairie Farmer* are useful.

[II]

Scene First: Concord, Massachusetts, on a February night in 1857. The Town House is ablaze with lights. A hundred citizens and more stamp in, taking off scarves and mittens in the grateful heat from the big stove. They glance curiously over their shoulders as tall lanky Frank B. Sanborn, a young Harvard graduate whom Emerson had brought to the town as head of the academy, escorts down the aisle a worn but wiry man of medium height, with clean-shaven face, burning eyes, and grimly set mouth. Some townsfolk know that John Brown had come by the noon train, had lunched at Mrs. Thoreau's house with Henry and the boarders, and later had chatted with Emerson, who called on an errand. He begins to speak in a metallic, clipped voice, with positive gestures, about the Kansas troubles. He tells of the outrages committed by the border ruffians, of the murder of his son Frederick, and of the interference by Missourians in elections. Attacking the peace party in Kansas, he declares that the Territory needs men who will fight, and needs money too—for war is expensive where food, clothing, and arms must be carted for long distances. He shakes the chain that his son John wore when dragged for miles by Federal dragoons under a hot sun to prison. He also utters some telling epigrams. When he says that the proslavery marauders "had a perfect right to be hanged," Emerson and Thoreau exchange appreciative glances. His declaration that he and his five remaining sons will never stop battling against slavery brings a murmur of approval, and the townspeople march out into the chill night air manifestly impressed.[16]

This Concord address is one of many which Brown makes in his fund-raising tour of New York and New England in late winter and spring of 1857. Naturally, he says nothing of the coldblooded murders which he had instigated on the Pottawatomie the previous May; nothing of other homicides by free State men, and nothing of the fact that the volunteer company he left in Kansas had (under his instructions) made a horse-stealing raid into Missouri.[17] It is only the crimes of proslavery men that he lists. The time is well chosen for his appeal. The Dred Scott decision, the appointment of Walker as governor, the publication of

16 Authorities differ on details. Emerson's *Journals*, followed by Townsend Scudder in *Concord: American Town*, fixes the date of this meeting in February; F. B. Sanborn's *Recollections*, I, 108 ff., followed by Villard, places it in March. Edward Emerson's note to the *Journals* obviously confuses some parts of John Brown's two appearances in Concord. Scudder says Sanborn was on leave in Boston, while Sanborn says he was living in Concord. Such details are inconsequential. As evidence of the impression Brown made, see Thoreau's "Plea for Captain John Brown." Mr. Boyd B. Stutler, owner of valuable John Brown material, believes that the Concord meeting took place about February 18.
17 Villard, *Brown*, 261.

TO THE FRIENDS OF FREEDOM.

The undersigned, whose individual means were exceedingly limited when he first engaged in the struggle for Liberty in Kansas, being now still more destitute and no less anxious than in time past to continue his efforts to sustain that cause, is induced to make this earnest appeal to the Friends of Freedom throughout the United States, in the firm belief that his call will not go unheeded. I ask all honest lovers of *Liberty and Human Rights, both male and female,* to hold up my hands by contributions of pecuniary aid, either as counties, cities, towns villages, societies, churches or individuals.

I will endeavor to make a judicious and faithful application of all such means as I may be supplied with. Contributions may be sent in drafts to W. H. D. CALLENDER, Cashier State Bank, Hartford, Ct. It is my intention to visit as many places *as I can* during my stay in the States, provided I am first informed of the disposition of the inhabitants to aid me *in my efforts,* as well as to receive my visit. Information may be communicated to me (care of Massasoit House) at Springfield, Mass. Will editors of newspapers friendly to the cause kindly second the measure, and also give this some half dozen insertions? Will either gentlemen or ladies, or both, who love the cause, volunteer to take up the business? It is with *no little sacrifice of personal feeling* that I appear in this manner before the public.

JOHN BROWN.

John Brown's Circular Preceding His Eastern Tour of 1857

13

Geary's attacks on the slavery party, have excited widespread Northern apprehension. Brown meets one important rebuff. He and Sanborn spend an afternoon with ex-Governor Reeder at Easton, Pennsylvania, trying to persuade him to go

for being suspected of favouring Free State Men   Page 4ᵗʰ
He is known as Ottawa Jones, or John T Jones.

In last cost   Free State called Stonton
I visited a beautiful little town, on the North side of the Osage
or Mariderine as sometimes called; from which every inhabitant
had fled for fear of their lives after having built a strong Block house
or wooden fort at a heavy expence for their protection. Many of
them had left their effects liable to be destroyed or carried off
not being able to remove them. This was a most gloomy scene &
like a visit to a vast Sepulchre

Deserted houses, & Cornfields were to be found in almost every direction
South from the Kansas river.   by a boddy 400 Ruffians
I saw the burning of Osawatomie, Aug 30ᵗʰ & of Franklin after
Gov Geary had been some time in the territory; & might have easily pre
—vented it. It would not have cost the U S. One Dollar to have saved
Franklin.

*　　　　I saw three mangled bodies two of which were dead*
& one alive with Twenty Buck shot & Bullet holes in him; after the
two murdered men had lain on the ground to be worked at by Flies
for some 18 Hours. One of those young men was my own Son.
*　　　saw   about the head*
I a Mr Porter who I will know; all bruised, & with her throat partly
cut, after being draged sick from the House of Ottawa Jones, & thrown
over the bank of the Ottawa Creek for dead: about the first of Sept

From John Brown's Notes for A Speech

to Kansas as agent of the Massachusetts Kansas Committee, and to take the Kansas leadership away from moderate Charles Robinson. "I will serve as commander of field forces in guerrilla warfare," promises Brown. Reeder warily declines. Elsewhere, however, the fanatical leader has better success.[18]

18　Brown had issued a well-printed circular, of which the Chicago Historical Society has a copy. It states that he intends to visit as many places as possible in his tour of the East

Wherever he goes—Philadelphia, New York, Syracuse, Worcester, Boston—the gaunt, weather-beaten warrior pleads for money and arms; everywhere he denounces the Kansas peace party and predicts that war will again burst forth on the plains.[19] He induces the Massachusetts Kansas Committee (which includes the manufacturer George L. Stearns, the reformer Dr. Samuel Gridley Howe, and Sanborn) to give him custody of two hundred Sharps rifles at Tabor, Iowa, with four thousand ball cartridges and thirty-one thousand percussion caps, and to vote him $500 for their care. The same body grants another $500 to him for the relief of Kansas. The National Kansas Committee in New York appropriates $5,000 to him in aid of defensive measures, but this results in an actual transfer of only $150 to his pockets.[20] In Boston, various men, including Amos A. Lawrence and Wendell Phillips, give him $1,000 to complete the purchase of the farm at North Elba, New York, where his wife and some of the children reside. While the total of monetary donations falls far short of his goal of $25,000, it is nevertheless considerable.[21]

Scene Second: A village drugstore in Collinsville, Connecticut, one February morning in 1857. A group are gathered about Brown, congratulating him on his Kansas lecture the night before, and asking for additional information. He launches into the story of his encounter at Black Jack with a little force led by Henry Clay Pate, captain of Missouri militia and deputy Federal marshal. Brown, boasting that with nine brave followers he had captured twenty-odd well-armed border ruffians, draws a vivid picture. "We came up at daylight to those blackjack oaks at the spring," he says. "It is on the Santa Fé trail. I ordered my men to get ready to attack. Pate and his crew were lurking in a ravine; plenty of bushes and trees for cover. I moved around to their flank, and drew in to close quarters. The sun was well up then and getting hot. The grass was dry; I remember thinking how it would look spattered with blood. Suddenly one of those border ruffians stood up with a white handkerchief on a long rod."

The listeners gape. Then they draw back as Brown whips from his bootleg a handsomely mounted bowie knife. "Look—this was Pate's. His Virginia friends gave it to him when he left for Kansas." Several men, including a blacksmith named Charles Blair, feel its keen edge. "If I had a lot of these blades fastened to poles about six feet long," says Brown, ruminatively, "they would make good weapons for our freestate settlers to keep in their cabins." The group chorusses

---

"provided I am first informed of the disposition of the inhabitants *to aid me in my efforts.* . . ." He was so pressed for money that he wrote H. N. Rust offering to sell a captured sabre, for "I am literally driven to beg: which is very humiliating." Brown Papers, Chicago Hist. Soc.

19 Sanborn, *Recollections*, I, 117.
20 Villard, 274–276; Sanborn, I, 118, 119.
21 R. J. Hinton, *John Brown and His Men*, 143–145.

assent. With an air of sudden decision he turns to Blair. "You're a forge-master," he remarks. "You can make good edge tools. What would you charge to make five hundred or a thousand of these pikes?" Blair considers a moment. "Well," he ventures, "I could probably make you five hundred at a dollar and a quarter apiece, or a thousand at a dollar apiece." "I want them made," says Brown in his terse way; and a little later a contract is signed.[22]

Obviously, this order for pikes has curious aspects. With rifles and revolvers so abundant in Kansas, why an order for a thousand spears? They might be useful for men who could not handle firearms—say colored men, but not for hardy frontier folk. Why give the order to a Connecticut blacksmith, when an Iowan could fabricate them just as well? Delivery is to be made July 1, 1857, but Brown is able to supply only $500 on the contract, and though Blair buys the materials, no weapons are shipped this summer.

It is also curious that Brown holds conferences this spring and summer with an Englishman now resident in New York, Hugh Forbes, who, at one time a silk merchant in Siena, had taken up arms with Garibaldi in the disastrous campaigns of 1848–49. A middle-aged man of considerable ability as linguist, drillmaster, and military engineer, Forbes is a radical idealist of the Mazzini school, loves conspiracy, and is hungry for better employment than his odd jobs as fencing-master and translator and reporter for the *Tribune*. He and Brown talk eagerly of methods of guerrilla warfare. In fact, the two exchange ideas, and if we may believe Forbes, hammer them together in what they call "The Well-Matured Plan." The Englishman agrees to serve at $100 a month instructing a volunteer company which Brown intends to raise, providing a handbook of tactics (*The Manual of the Patriotic Volunteer*, based on an earlier book), writing a tract to persuade American soldiers never to support wrong against right, and doing other work. When authorized to draw upon one of Brown's supporters for $600, he does so within the month.[23] Partly as a result of his talks with Forbes, Brown is making some curious notes in his memorandum book. For example, he writes of the "valuable hints" for guerrilla warfare in a life of Wellington, adding: "*See also* same book Page 235 these words Deep and narrow defiles where 300 men would suffice to check an *army*." [24]

22 *Mason Report* (36th Cong., 1st Sess., Senate Rept. No. 278), 121–199; Sanborn, I, 104. Brown made final payment for the pikes by a draft from Troy, N. Y., June 7, 1859; Brown Papers, Chicago Hist. Soc.

23 A Hartford gentleman, W. H. D. Callender, supplied this sum; Villard, 286.

24 All statements by the adventurer Forbes require verification. He arrived in New York in 1850, and in 1851 delivered anti-Catholic lectures in the city. His tactical handbook was based on his *Manual of the Patriotic Volunteer* published in one volume in New York in 1854 and in two volumes in 1856. That with his military experience (treated in G. M. Trevelyan's volumes on Garibaldi), versatility, and dash he made an impression on Brown's thinking is indubitable. Hinton in *Brown and His Men*, 146–152, treats him rather favorably; Villard, 285, 317 ff., very unfavorably.

In truth, Brown's talk to certain eastern supporters of defensive operations in Kansas is a blind. He is contemplating offensive activity, not merely in Kansas but in some part of the Southern Appalachians; perhaps the Shenandoah, perhaps further south. He believes that hundreds of slaves will rise at the first blow. He intends to place the thousand pikes in their hands, and to use the two hundred revolvers which Stearns bought for him from the Massachusetts Arms Company in hand-to-hand fighting.[25] Perhaps already he is scheming a dash at the Harper's Ferry arsenal, destroying what arms he cannot carry off.

How long he has revolved his plan for moving a well-armed force into the Appalachian country, making raids into slave areas, and destroying slavery by rendering it unsafe, we do not know. If we may credit the autobiography of Frederick Douglass, he had confided to that Negro leader in 1847 his belief that he could put a well-trained force into western Virginia, support them there, run off large numbers of slaves, keep the bravest while sending the weaker north by the underground railroad, and thus so undermine the institution that it would topple in ruins.[26] Once seized with an idea, he is not the man to let it go. Early in August, 1857, he reaches Tabor, Iowa, where two days later Forbes arrives. They agree that their volunteer company will need a school of instruction. Forbes presently goes back east to choose a place; Brown goes on to Kansas to raise recruits and money.

Scene Third: A blazing campfire at night on the open prairie near Topeka in November, 1857. Chill winds howl about, as Brown piles fuel on the embers. Four roughly dressed men sit near, their knapsacks and blankets affording partial shelter. These first recruits of Brown's irregular company are fairly typical of the whole lot, a body of reckless, adventurous young drifters with a few true idealists. Physically the most striking is Aaron D. Stevens, a six-footer with magnificent chest and limbs and handsome face. He had run away from a Massachusetts home to fight in the Mexican War, had got into a drunken riot at Taos and struck an officer, and had been sentenced to three years in jail at Fort Leaven-

25 Villard, *Brown*, 289.
26 Frederick Douglass, *Life and Times* (London, 1882), 238–240. Brown knew how to dissemble his purposes. When the National Kansas Aid Committee, sitting in New York in January, 1857, showed some inquisitiveness, he pretended to take offense. The secretary, H. B. Hurd, asked what he thought a pro forma question: "If you get the arms and money you desire will you invade Missouri or any slave territory?" Brown replied with asperity: "I do not expose my plans. No one knows them but myself, except perhaps one. I will not be interrogated; if you wish to give me anything, I want you to give it freely. I have no other purpose but to serve the cause of liberty." The committee, which had previously understood that Brown intended to arm some Kansas settlers who would not be called out except to protect the free State population, became suspicious. He got his vote of $5,000 only for defensive purposes. At the same time Brown was giving his abolitionist friends a fuller view. Gerrit Smith, Frank Sanborn, and T. W. Higginson knew that he intended violence, and that this violence might aid their disunionist schemes. H. B. Hurd, March 19, 1860, to Stearns; Stearns Papers, Kansas State Hist. Soc.

worth, whence he escaped to join the free State men. The most talkative, an incessant chatterer, is John E. Cook, an impulsive Connecticut Yankee in his late twenties, one-time law clerk in Ogden Hoffman's office in New York. Fresh-faced and youthful looking, he has never quite grown up. Intellectually the most distinguished is John Henry Kagi, an Ohioan of Swiss-English descent, whose speech gives evidence of a quick mind and superior education. Only twenty-two, this ardent young man, a devoted abolitionist, has been a schoolteacher, is proficient in Latin, French, and mathematics, has studied law, and has helped report the debates in the recent Kentucky constitutional convention. He talks with the skill of a trained debater.[27]

The four treat Brown with deep respect. They know that he has other recruits, but they wish to learn his plans; and they inquire where they are to serve.

Brown tells them that the whole company is to go back east to drill. The Territory is quiet, and winter campaigning is impossible anyhow. His sons, with various other volunteers—Realf, Parsons, Tidd—will travel with them. He hands Cook a draft for $82.50. "Get this cashed in Lawrence tomorrow. We'll all meet again at Tabor in Iowa. Then I'll tell you just what we are going to do. If you want hard fighting you'll get plenty of it."

And at Tabor, as ten men gather about him, Brown's face wears a look of awakened resolution. "Our ultimate destination," he says, "is Virginia." [28]

Scene Fourth: The town of Chatham in Upper Canada, not far from Detroit, on a Saturday in May, 1858. It is a bustling city of six thousand, with one long shopping thoroughfare, King Street, wharves on the Thames from which ships ply to all the Great Lakes ports, and prosperous industries—flour mills, wood-working establishments, iron foundries, wagon shops. It is also a center for refugee slaves, who constitute one-third the population. The streets are full of them; and, as even unskilled Negroes earn $1.25 a day, while many are artisans and farmers, they seem well dressed and happy. At least one colored man has a bachelor's degree from Oberlin.[29] On this May 8, a number of Negroes and whites are at a Negro schoolhouse in Princess Street, where they say they are organizing a Masonic lodge.

Inside the schoolhouse, as ten o'clock strikes, the eyes of the eleven white and thirty-four colored men present are fixed on John Brown. He nods to a delegate named Jackson, who raps for order. The first business is the election of officers. A colored minister from Detroit, W. C. Munroe, is made president, and Kagi, an impressive figure with his long dark hair, large eyes, and fine forehead,

27 Hinton knew these recruits and in *John Brown and His Men* gives excellent sketches; for fuller material see Villard, 678–687.
28 See Cook's pamphlet "Confession" published in November, 1859.
29 Chatham is fully described in the N. Y. *Weekly Tribune*, October 24, 1857.

is chosen secretary. A colored physician, Dr. Martin R. Delany, later to hold in the Civil War the highest rank, that of major, given to any colored man, moves that John Brown address them on the purpose of the meeting. Rising, the fiery-eyed leader begins to talk. He remarks that for more than twenty years the idea of giving freedom to the slaves has obsessed him. He describes how, when he visited Europe in 1851, including Waterloo, he inspected fortifications and especially earthworks.

"I have formed a plan of action," Brown asserts. All over the South, he explains, slaves are eager to escape from bondage. He wishes to strike a blow from some point in the mountain chain which thrusts diagonally down from Maryland and Virginia into Tennessee and north Alabama. He believes that slaves will rise all over the South and struggle to reach his standard; he will welcome them and put arms in their hands; they will entrench themselves, and make sudden descents into the plantation country on each side.

"But what if troops are brought against you?" asks one listener.

A small force will be sufficient to defend these Thermopylae ravines, responds Brown. We shall defeat the green State militia if they march against us. If United States troops come, we shall defeat them too. I hope, however, that little bloodshed will be necessary. If the slaveholders resist us, we shall carry them back as hostages, holding them to guarantee proper treatment of any of our own men who may be taken prisoners. We shall soon be too strong to attack, for I expect the able-bodied free negroes of the North to flock to my banner, and all the Southern slaves who can escape will do the same. Gradually we shall build up a powerful state. Our freedmen will go to work tilling farms and running workshops; they will organize schools and churches. We shall not molest slaveholders who do not interfere with us, but of course we shall treat all enemies who attack us alike. I am confident that we can maintain ourselves, and can defy any enemy. John Brown draws himself more erect and gesticulates more emphatically. Thus, he concludes, the slave States will finally be compelled to emancipate the people they are holding in bondage, and we shall put an end to that accursed institution. That done, we shall reorganize our mountain state on a new basis, and elect a fresh set of officers.[30]

The next business is the adoption of a constitution for the proposed state, and the choice of a commander-in-chief, secretary of state, and secretary of war. Brown has his document ready, and after an oath of secrecy is taken by every member, it is read. "Whereas," its preamble began, "slavery throughout its entire existence in the United States is none other than a most barbarous, unprovoked, and unjustifiable war of one portion of its citizens upon another portion . . ." On motion of Kagi, the provisional constitution is adopted, and that

30 See Realf's report of the speech, Villard, 331, 332; *Mason Report,* 96, 97.

afternoon, with congratulatory speeches, is signed. At an evening session Brown is elected commander-in-chief and Kagi secretary of war, while the next day a white recruit named Richard Realf is named secretary of state.

Monomania has reached its climax, for this Chatham gathering marks a full crystallization of Brown's plans. In every feature the scheme is preposterous: the idea that slaves are ready for wholesale revolt; the idea that State and national forces can be resisted; the idea that a temporary new commonwealth can be created. Yet there is method in Brown's madness. The preamble of his constitution is a declaration of war which justifies the killing of slaveholders, the liberation of slaves, the confiscation of other property, and the ravaging of enemy lands. It does more than justify the fomenting of slave insurrections; it assumes that a universal and incessant slave insurrection is under way, and that only brute force is restraining it within bounds. Rejecting the American Constitution, Brown is establishing his own government and laws, under which he will be free to commit any act of belligerent violence. As he wages war against the slaveholders, the States, and the nation, his robberies will be called the confiscation of enemy property, his kidnappings will be termed the seizure of enemy hostages, and his murders will be denominated legitimate military operations. His knowledge of what had happened in Haiti when a war of races began does not daunt him, for he believes that without the shedding of blood there can be no remission of Southern sins, and that, as he has told Emerson, it is better that a whole generation of men, women, and children should pass away by violence than that slavery should endure.

[III]

By the spring of 1858—and this fact is of cardinal importance—a group of New England and New York abolitionists approved Brown's mad plan for an attack, at some unnamed point, upon the South. In February, staying with Gerrit Smith at Peterboro, New York, he had unfolded his scheme to that wealthy reformer and his wife, to his old friend Frank Sanborn, and to Captain Charles Stewart, a veteran of Wellington's army in Spain. When they protested that failure was certain, Brown made it clear he would go forward whether they aided him or not. Sanborn tells us that they decided to lend assistance rather out of their regard for the Kansas fighter than from any hope of immediate success; but this, as we shall see, by no means covers their motivation. They were thinking of a remote success rather than of any immediate victory. Proceeding to Boston, John Brown early in March communicated his scheme in outline to Theodore Parker, Samuel G. Howe, and George L. Stearns. Thomas Wentworth Higginson at Worcester knew all about it, and so did Frederick Douglass. What they did not know was just where Brown would "raise the mill," as he put it. But they formed a secret committee of six which advised Brown and raised a considerable sum of money for him.

Why did these abolitionists lend their aid to the fanatic who, fatuously overrating his strength and underestimating that of the South and the nation, intended to hurl himself against the Gibraltar of slavery? Partly, because the stalwart courage of the man awed them. He loomed up in their vision like another William Tell or Robert Bruce. Holding the conviction they held upon the wickedness of slavery, they could not let him rush into desperate battle without a helping hand. Partly, too, because they believed that he did have one chance in a dozen of instant success. The abolitionists constantly exaggerated the intellectual capacity and fighting power of the slaves; they constantly deluded themselves that widespread slave insurrections were possible in the South. Above all, however, they helped him in the hope of achieving a remoter object; he would fail, but in failing he would start a civil war in which slavery would perish.[31]

For years, many of the abolitionists had wished for civil war—we have quoted Wendell Phillips and Theodore Parker in wishful predictions; even the pacifist Garrison had predicted civil war. Some abolitionists had not merely hoped that it would start in Kansas, but had labored to blow the spark into flame. Just after Frémont's defeat in 1856, Thomas Wentworth Higginson had written Gerrit Smith that he desired "to start a *private* organization of picked men, who shall be ready to go to Kansas in case of need, to aid the people against *any* opponent, State or Federal." It would not be expedient to form a large organization in the East because of the cost of transportation. "But it is essential to involve *every* State in the war that is to be." His plan therefore would be to enlist a hundred men in Massachusetts and perhaps fifty each in the other New England States; drill and organize them; and then, when trouble began in Kansas, use them as "a nucleus of an Army of Reinforcement." As his movement grew he would extend it to other States. He had talked his plan over with "all the best men," who approved it but were disposed to leave the leadership to him:[32]

Some of us here (Republicans and Garrisonians) are planning a *Convention* to be held here, which shall consider the idea of Disunion between Free and Slave States, *as a practical problem which the times are pressing on us.* . . .

31 Sanborn had read a lecture on John Brown before the Concord School in March, 1857, the MS of which is in the Chicago Hist. Soc. He declared that if the country was to have a war over slavery, it needed such old men and young men as Brown. Many abolitionists wanted slave insurrections. The abolitionist and disunion convention which met at Cleveland in the fall of 1857 adopted a resolution declaring that the slaves ought to strike down their masters by force whenever the blow could be effective. *Ann. Rept. Amer. Anti-Slavery Soc.*, 1858, pp. 181, 182.
32 November 22, 1856; Gerrit Smith Papers, Univ. of Syracuse.

about Fort Scott and Trading Post, did sporadic troubles between proslavery men and freesoilers ("jayhawkers") continue. They had reached a climax in the late spring of 1858, in the horrifying Marais des Cygnes massacre, in which a hotblooded Georgian named Charles A. Hamilton, heading a band of border desperadoes, marched eleven prisoners into a ravine, drew them up in line, and opened fire, killing five and wounding more. Fortunately, an attempt at retaliation by the principal jayhawker chieftain, James Montgomery, resulted in nothing worse than a little incendiarism at Fort Scott. Thereupon, Governor Denver undertook a pacificatory tour through the region, making speeches and using his personal influence to compose old feuds. By July, a period of comparative repose had opened. Freesoilers who desired to see it prolonged heard of Brown's arrival with uneasiness and dread.[35]

Inevitably, Brown swung to any area of fever and violence as the needle swings to its pole; inevitably, he exaggerated whatever trouble existed; and inevitably, he preached an eye for an eye and a tooth for a tooth. On July 23, he wrote his family from a poor, narrow, hot little cabin at Trading Post near the Missouri line, where for a week he and about ten of his men had stayed on the same quarter section where the Marais des Cygnes murders had been committed. Every few days, he inaccurately declared, some new murder was committed; deserted houses and farms lay in every direction; the atmosphere was one of uncertainty and fear.[36] A fortnight later, he boasted to his son John of the consternation which his arrival had created among the Missourians. "Which of the passions most predominated, fear or rage, I do not pretend to say." A prolonged attack of malarial fever helped keep him inactive until autumn. Recovering with the cool weather, he was ready, as he wrote Kagi, to take the field with Montgomery in a renewal of guerrilla operations; and he soon validated this statement by going far beyond anything that Montgomery had contemplated.[37]

First, he joined Montgomery and about a hundred others in a descent upon Fort Scott to liberate a free State prisoner there, the attack ending in the death of a storekeeper and the seizure as loot of about $7,000 worth of goods. Montgomery later declared that he had taken the leadership of this expedition because Brown was bent upon burning the entire town to the ground, and killing anybody who resisted. Immediately thereafter, Brown executed a raid into Missouri to free all the slaves he could reach. One object in this, according to his follower

35 Spring, *Kansas*, 244-251; Robinson, *The Kansas Conflict*, 391-395.
36 John Brown Papers, Ohio Arch. and Hist. Soc.
37 Charles Robinson later wrote with bitterness that while his forces took great care to commit no crimes, Brown's murders and thefts had "put all our people under suspicion." By lies and disguises he escaped unhurt; innocent men suffered the penalty. "While our free state colonies were trying to convert the whites from the South and make them sound free state men, John Brown thought it better to murder them." Undated fragment, Robinson Papers, Kansas State Hist. Soc.

Cook, was to illustrate the feasibility of his grand scheme so that it would be easier to raise in the East the funds that he needed.[38]

This raid, an indefensibly lawless outrage upon inoffensive citizens, created a sensation North and South. On the night of December 20–21, Brown invaded Missouri with two bands; he leading eight or nine men, while the former dragoon Stevens headed eight. Brown's group attacked the homes of two planters, seized their slaves, stole some watches and personal trinkets, and carried off livestock, harness, clothing, and miscellaneous articles. Stevens's expedition forced entry into a house, looted it, stole livestock, and carried away a slave. Worst of all, Stevens shot the owner of this house dead. The morning of December 21 found Brown safe in Kansas again, with eleven Negroes, two white prisoners, and a large booty of spoils. Sheltering his force that day in a heavily wooded ravine, he moved northward as soon as darkness fell. On Christmas Eve the Negroes were at Ossawatomie, to which point Brown, after delaying near Fort Scott for a time, followed them on January 11. Late that month, he and the slaves set out on their long journey to Canada. He might have lingered in Kansas if the warfare for which he hoped had broken out along the Missouri border; but although the countryside sprang to arms, and for a time general bloodshed was feared, the frantic efforts of Montgomery and other responsible leaders to preserve the peace proved successful. He had good reason for leaving, in that he found his outrage emphatically condemned by the very settlers whom he had hoped to excite to battle. He had miscalculated sentiment.[39]

The opinion of decent Kansans, in fact, was registered in no uncertain terms. A correspondent of the Lawrence *Herald of Freedom* expressed consternation at finding free State men guilty of the same villainies for which they had arraigned the border ruffians. Montgomery, whom Brown urged to fight, turned the other way. A prominent free State settler, William Hutchinson, sought out Brown near Trading Post to expostulate. "We are settlers—you are not," he said. "You can strike the blow and leave; the retaliatory blow falls on us. We are at peace with Missouri. Our legislature is a free State legislature; even in the disturbed counties of Bourbon and Linn free State men are in the majority. Without peace we can have no immigration. No Southern immigrants are coming, and your agitation only keeps out our Northern friends." This man found, as did others, that Brown was engrossed in the monomania of "my work," "my great duty," "my mission." Another settler and old friend of Brown's, Augustus Wattles, also took him to task. Brown replied that he had considered the matter

38 Villard, 367; Cook's "Confession" (pamphlet).
39 A few Kansans took the view that, as one wrote the N. Y. *Tribune*, the raid was needed to punish Missouri crimes, give free State settlers confidence, prevent further flights from the country, and teach border ruffians to stay at home. Dated Moneka, Kansas, December 22, 1858.

well and would now leave Kansas. "I consider it my duty to draw the scene of excitement to some other part of the country." [40]

Yet the fact that as Brown carried his slaves into free soil he found ready helpers did not escape the Southern press, which resounded with denunciation of his act. To the law, he was a dangerous felon. President Buchanan offered a reward for his capture; the Missouri governor rumbled threats; the newly appointed governor of Kansas, Samuel Medary, not only did the same but asked the legislature to take some action. Nevertheless, as Brown and his charges worked their way across the north-central states to Ontario, he met with no real obstacle. At one point in Kansas, his band successfully charged through a posse from Atchison, and at another evaded a larger force. In Iowa, his party stopped at various underground stations; at Des Moines, the editor of the *Register* paid their ferriage across the river; at Grinnell, three Congregational ministers led the townsfolk in extending succor, while the founder, Josiah B. Grinnell, provided an ample store of supplies and money and hired a boxcar to carry them to Chicago. In that city, the detective Allan Pinkerton raised more than $500 for them, and procured a well-stocked car to Detroit. In short, although every reader of the press knew that Brown had organized a robbery and been party to a murder, and although the presidential reward of $250 for his capture was an attraction, he crossed State after State with impunity. Such was the public sentiment upon Kansas and the protection of escaped Negroes that no officer of the law cared to touch him. [41]

John Brown's self-confident sense of a special mission could not but be increased by the applause which he met outside Kansas. He made two speeches at Grinnell, and moved freely about Chicago; he and Kagi lectured in Cleveland, where Artemus Ward praised his pluck in the *Plain Dealer;* and on March 12 he saw his colored wards marshaled aboard the Detroit ferryboat to Windsor. Proceeding to Rochester and Boston, he was petted as a hero. The Northern press had published a self-exculpatory letter in which he weirdly distorted the facts of his raid, and most Northern editors accepted it at face value. [42] Gerrit Smith told an applauding audience that, of all men, he thought John Brown the nearest approach to a perfect Christian. The South found something more than

40 Villard, 373, 375.

41 The oft-made statements that Missouri posted a reward and that all rewards aggregated $3,500 have no basis. Brown wrote an exultant letter to his son from Winterset, Iowa, on December 13, 1857, mentioning that he had nine young men whom he was placing in the military school at Springdale, Ia.

42 The perversions were egregious. He wrote that he heard that a family of Negroes was to be sold, and had gone to liberate them; the sale was a fiction. We "took certain property," he confessed; they took a great deal. He declared they had returned some property; this the owners denied. His force had killed one white man "who fought against the liberation"; this man was slain defending his cabin. For text of letter see N. Y. *Weekly Tribune,* February 12, 1859.

Northern insolence in the protection of such an assailant of its peculiar institution; it found a threat to its safety. It noted, too, that the effort of the free State legislature to outlaw slavery in Kansas and the use of Kansas as a base for raiding a slave State, occurring almost simultaneously, could be cited as arguments for a Federal slave code in the Territories.

The threat to slavery was greater than the South realized, for it knew nothing of the plan of Brown and the abolitionist committee for a direct blow. The eastern conspirators were deeply impressed by their hero's success. While Gerrit Smith pledged him $400, the Boston group raised more than $4,000, nearly all of it given with a clear knowledge that it would be used in a new and larger effort. Dr. Howe delightedly wrote John Murray Forbes that Brown was staying at a hotel in Beach Street, and that any man who wanted $3,500 had only to go and try to take the old fellow. "He knows more about the question of practical emancipation than anyone whom I have seen." The emotional hysteria of those abolitionists, who totally disregarded both the property rights of Southerners and the tremendous difficulties of race-adjustment bound up in any plan of emancipation, had always been dangerous. Now a cabal of them had found in this implacable Puritan warrior from the Kansas border, robbed by his exalted mental state of all ability to calculate risks or observe ordinary canons of right and wrong, a fearfully dangerous instrument.

[V]

Such was the antagonism between North and South that perils and irritations now came not as single spies, but in battalions. While John Brown was spiriting his captured slaves off to Canada, the South was watching with anger the movement to circulate in vast numbers a free, or nearly free, edition of Helper's *Impending Crisis*. Regarding the book with abhorrence, Southern leaders did not fail to note the prediction of the New York *Tribune* that its general circulation would lead to a speedy extinction of slavery, at least in the border States. Just how, asked slaveholders? By setting class against class, by firing all the materials for a social conflagration, by arousing the slaves to a bloody revolt? The fund required was raised with considerable difficulty. A long list of Northern freesoilers contributed $100 apiece, while an anonymous Southern clergyman gave $250 through Cassius M. Clay. Copies were soon passing from hand to hand in the North and border area.[43] Nor did the South fail to find other provocations.

43 The main aim of Republican leaders was to convert Northern Democrats rather than to reach border men. We agree, one wrote Lyman Trumbull, that arduous labor will be required to carry Pennsylvania, Illinois, and Indiana in 1860; the book will help. W. M. Chace, October 19, 1857; Trumbull Papers.

This spring brought on the much-advertised trials of the "Oberlin rescuers," which proved again that the Fugitive Slave Law could no more be enforced in northern Ohio than in New England. The previous September, two Kentuckians had appeared in the college town of Oberlin, an abolitionist center since the middle thirties, in search of a runaway.[44] They would have encountered trouble anywhere in the Western Reserve, but in this particular community they struck a hornets' nest. The fugitive was no sooner captured than a body of excited citizens from Oberlin and the neighboring town of Wellington seized him and hurried him off to Canada. The frustrated Kentuckians appealed to the Federal authorities. Indictments were found against thirty-seven of the rescuers, and the ensuing trials in the Federal court in Cleveland proved one of the *causes célèbres* of Ohio history. A counterattack was opened on the Kentuckians, the grand jury of Lorain County indicting them under State law as kidnappers. Since they were indispensable as witnesses in the Federal case, the Federal Marshal locked them up to prevent their being arrested and detained elsewhere. Rival county and Federal posses glared at each other in the courthouse grounds; a great Cleveland massmeeting on May 24, with the venerable Joshua Giddings presiding and Governor Salmon P. Chase (full of Presidential ambitions) the chief speaker, cheered resolutions declaring the Fugitive Slave Law null and void; and a tumultuous procession marched through the streets to demonstrate in front of the jail. The rescuers were continuously feted; visitors thronged to their cells, letters of sympathy and funds for expenses poured in, and they were showered with presents.[45] The first sentences were ridiculously light, all the Wellington defendants gaining release in April with fines of $25 and costs apiece, superadded to a day in jail. Only by a narrow vote of three to two did the State Supreme Court decide against releasing the Oberlin prisoners on a writ of *habeas corpus*.

By late spring, despite the earnest attitude of the Federal authorities, it was plain that the case against the rescuers still in jail could never be pressed to a successful termination. The extreme penalty thus far meted out was sixty days in prison and $600 fine. When the Kentucky "kidnappers" were put upon trial, their counsel, fearing that the court would sentence them to heavy terms, proposed a compromise. In virtue of this arrangement, the men still under Federal indictment were freed by a *nolle prosequi*, while the State proceedings against the Kentuckians were dropped. Northern Ohio held gay celebrations. While the Cleveland *Leader* announced that the rescuers of Oberlin were returning home in triumph, a hundred guns were fired on the public square.

44 Many antislavery students and some teachers had migrated to Oberlin from Lane Seminary in Cincinnati. Arthur Tappan and other abolitionists had made gifts; the college admitted colored students; and it scattered antislavery lecturers through the region. Henry Howe, *Hist. Collections of Ohio*, II, 126.
45 Cleveland *Leader*, May 25-28, 1859.

Manifestly, this episode was certain to excite Southern indignation. The national government, with law, justice, and the facts on its side, said slaveholders, had been mocked by Ohio's higher-law fanatics. Nobody denied that John was a fugitive slave, that the Kentuckian legally owned him, or that the Federal statute of 1850 applied. But, since the spring of 1857, Ohio had a law which made it an indictable misdemeanor to arrest, imprison, or forcibly carry away any free person of color. The spirit in which the Western Reserve would interpret this law was suggested by Judge Carpenter of the Lorain County court: "The constitution of Ohio inhibits slavery and regards all persons as free and equal except criminals." Various Ohio newspapers termed the Federal law wicked, abominable, and anti-Christian; and the *Leader*, threatening with the halter all "men-thieves who dare to pollute our soil," remarked that it would save trouble if they would bring along some Kentucky hemp in addition to their manacles.[46]

Throughout part of the North, the Fugitive Slave Act was now largely unenforceable, for State after State had passed laws making recovery difficult or impossible. The obstructive areas with "personal liberty" statutes eventually included all New England, Pennsylvania, and the four Mid-Western States of Ohio, Indiana, Michigan, and Wisconsin. When the first conflicts occurred between the Federal and State authorities, Northern sentiment proved defiant. In Wisconsin, the State Supreme Court declared the Fugitive Slave Act unconstitutional and discharged an editor named Sherman M. Booth for helping to rescue a runaway black. The Federal Supreme Court then took jurisdiction, and Taney pronounced its unanimous judgment in one of the most powerful of all his opinions. The central issue did not concern slavery or the enforcement of a particular statute on fugitives, but the supremacy of the national government within its own sphere. Taney pointed out that unless Federal jurisdiction were sustained in Federal areas, the general government could not meet the grand and indispensable purposes for which it had been established; and impartial journals commended his stand.

Yet extreme Republican sheets assailed it as an encroachment on the reserved rights of the States, even Bryant's *Evening Post* taking this view; and the Wisconsin legislature responded with a *brutum fulmen*. On March 17, 1859, only ten days after Taney spoke, it accused the Supreme Court of an arbitrary act of power, and declared that the several States, being sovereign and independent,

46 Cleveland *Leader*, July 7, 1859, *et seq.*; W. C. Cochran, *Colls. Western Reserve Hist. Soc.*, 1920, pp. 118–157, 197–207; J. R. Shipheard, *History of the Oberlin-Wellington Rescue, passim*. The press of northern Ohio reviled the prosecution in the harshest terms. It termed the presiding judge a Jeffreys, the jury a set of broken-down party hacks, and the Federal attorney a man of infamous character. See the *Ohio State Journal*, Cleveland *Leader*, and *Portage County Democrat* for April–July, 1859.

had the right to judge of infractions of the Constitution. It was a State's duty, said the legislature, to offer a positive defiance to all unauthorized acts done under color of constitutional interpretation. This was the very doctrine of 1798. Nor did the quarrel of State and nation stop with mere words. The Federal authorities once more arrested Booth; the editor once more asked the State courts for a writ of *habeas corpus;* and they once more liberated him. Thus, in fighting the Fugitive Slave Law, the Republicans went to the verge of nullification, even while their leaders were denouncing the Southerners as the arch-nullifiers of the country.[47]

The fanatic never sees his own inconsistencies. Though antislavery journals continually arraigned Southerners for their intolerance, no more dishonorable example of political lynching could be found than the removal of Judge Edward G. Loring in Massachusetts in 1858. An upright, capable magistrate, he was forced from the Suffolk County bench by the legislature because he had sat as Federal Commissioner in the Burns rendition case of 1854; "in defiance of the moral sentiment of Massachusetts," ran the address. In fine, he was removed because, in the face of angry public antagonism, he had faithfully done his duty as a Federal officer. Enlightened editors of Massachusetts, without regard to party, condemned the action as arbitrary and vindictive. The Boston *Traveller* and the *Journal,* for example, termed it disgraceful. In other parts of the North comment was scathing, the *National Intelligencer* remarking that the Bay State should have given Loring not a stigma but a statue. A later generation of New England historians was to admit that even South Carolina, which always honored the dissident J. L. Petigru, had placed no such stain upon her escutcheon.[48]

The press throughout Buchanan's administration was full of stories of Northern defiance of the law for recovering fugitive property. In Indianapolis, a slave belonging to a Kentuckian became the center of spirited legal clashes between a State judge and Federal commissioner, incidental to which the owner was arrested on the familiar kidnapping charge. At New London, Connecticut, a fleeing Negro was seized to be returned South; a police magistrate at the head of a mob asked the man if he wished to reenter slavery, and bade him go on his way. At Ottawa, Illinois, in the fall of 1859, a slave who had fled from Missouri was brought before Judge John D. Caton, on a writ of *habeas corpus.* Caton, pleading with a hostile crowd not to violate the law, remanded him to the custody of the Federal deputy marshal of the southern district of Illinois. He might as well have spoken to the Mississippi in flood-time; the mob seized

47 Arthur C. Cole, *The Irrepressible Conflict,* 274; Warren, *Supreme Court* (1926 ed.), I, 336; Carl Schurz, *Reminiscences,* II, 105 ff.; *National Intelligencer,* April 2, 1859; N. Y. *Weekly Tribune,* June 4, 1859.
48 See press quotations in *National Intelligencer,* March 23, 1858.

the fugitive and carried him to safety. Later a Federal marshal appeared in Ottawa, arrested the ringleaders, and lodged them in jail in Chicago, where they were tried, found guilty, and sentenced; but this did not restore the slave. That same fall, William Dennison, a Miami University graduate, made a successful run for governor of Ohio. He declared that if elected he would permit no slave to be returned South, "and if I cannot prevent it in any other way, as commander-in-chief of the military of the State I will employ the bayonet—so help me God!" [49]

These were galling injuries which the South suffered in Brown's triumphant slave-stealing foray, in the preparations for scattering Helper's attack upon slavery broadcast, and in the occasional breakdown of the Fugitive Slave Law. All the while, the radical Northern press augmented its fire upon the special Southern institution. Scores of journals seldom mentioned slavery without opprobrious epithets, or slaveholders without a sneer. When Henry Wilson was reelected early in 1859, Edmund Quincy rejoiced, not because he was a good Senator but because "it gives vexation and rage to the enemy." Enemy! Some Southern Congressmen, as Charles Francis Adams shortly observed, were spoiling for a fight; but so were Northerners like Wendell Phillips, who said he would thank God if the South would defy Massachusetts to the sword and the musket. Greeley, visiting Kansas early in 1859, denounced the "slave power" with stinging epithets. Carl Schurz, delivering an oration in Faneuil Hall, assailed the slaveholding system for despotic tendencies and termed the Fugitive Slave Law an abomination. Southerners noted that few Northern journals ever spoke of

49 *National Intelligencer*, December 8, 1857; N. Y. *Weekly Tribune*, October 9, 1858; Washington *Constitution*, October 21, 1859. In April, 1859, the arrest of a colored man in Pennsylvania as the property of a Virginian precipitated the movement to carry a personal liberty bill through the legislature, then in session. It should in all fairness to the North be added that newspaper accounts gave an exaggerated impression of the number of rescues. They reported all escapes; they seldom reported recaptures. Douglas said in 1860 that nine-tenths of the Southern complaints were unfounded. "As far as Illinois is concerned, I am prepared to say that in nineteen cases out of twenty where a fugitive slave enters Illinois, he is arrested and returned without any judicial process whatever. Those portions of the State which border on the Kentucky and Missouri lines are in harmony with their neighbors on the other side, and a fugitive slave is returned as regularly as a stolen horse." He added that in the Northwest it was seldom that a rescue was not followed by penalties of the law. "And then civil suits are brought to pay for the slave, and not only the damage, but smart-money granted." *Cong. Globe*, December 11, 1860. The exaggerated impression was eagerly accepted, however, in the Lower South.

A Kentuckian who wrote an able pamphlet on the subject ("South Carolina, Disunion, and a Mississippi Valley Confederacy") pointed out that the Lower South lost very few slaves; he doubted if South Carolina had lost ten in as many years. It was the border States which suffered, and their sufferings had been greatly overstated. "A slight application of the *lex talionis* would soon compel Ohio to repeal her obnoxious legislation. She is the only one of our three near neighbors who has resorted to such statutes. Indiana and Illinois have habitually performed their duty to us in this particular. A large majority of our recaptured fugitives have been taken by their owners or by the citizens of those States, without the aid of any officers of the law." See Appendix V of this work.

the beneficent side of slavery; but when early this year Pierce Butler held his sale of more than four hundred slaves at the Savannah race course, the detailed description penned by a correspondent of the New York *Tribune* was quoted far and wide.[50]

It is not strange that the South now believed the North incapable of a fair attitude toward an institution which Southerners had inherited, of justice to Southern fears, or of helpfulness. A passenger on a Potomac steamer in 1859 heard a Virginian address a newsboy who had New York *Tribunes* for sale. "Don't you know better than to sell that paper here? Take it and put it in the stove. If you don't I'll cut the heart out of you!" It is not strange that moderate men in both sections began to feel genuine despair. Washington Hunt wrote from northern New York to his friend William C. Rives: [51]

It becomes a very important practical question, which cannot be long postponed, by what means the honest and conservative men of the North and South can be brought together so as to unite their strength in the approaching Presidential election. Many of the leading politicians in both sections are evidently disposed to prolong the strife and inflame the people, by adhering to extreme issues on the slavery question. . . . There must be an end of this unnatural and hateful warfare between the North and the South.

[VI]

If the South found solid ground for suspicion and resentment, so did the North. The Southern demand for territorial expansion in the Caribbean seemed made for the strengthening of an eventual Southern Confederacy; the crusade for reopening the slave trade and importing hordes of barbarous Negroes seemed made for capturing western Territories with an expanding slave population; the demand for a Congressional slave code seemed made to fortify territorial slavery against any adverse majority. If the North was nullifying the Fugitive Slave Act, the South was nullifying the law against the foreign slave trade. If the North seemed bent on expanding freesoil institutions all over the West, the South seemed bent on expanding slavery throughout Gulf and Caribbean. If the North took a one-sided view of slavery, so did the South; and while Virginia officers arrested men on the charge of circulating Helper's book, a Kentucky mob sacked the *Free South* office in Newport on the Ohio.

"Is it not already clear," demanded the New York *Tribune*, "that the 'irrepressible conflict' affirmed by Mr. Seward is . . . a sober and present reality?

50 Quincy Papers, January 17, 1859; Schurz, *Works*, I, 48–72; London *Times*, April 13, 1859. The account of the Butler sale (*Tribune*, March 9, 1859) was a masterly report, whose accuracy was never impugned. All such sales were blots on American civilization—but slavery had less repugnant aspects.
51 May 19, 1859; Rives Papers.

Is it not plain that we are already in effect two nations, held together by the ties of tradition and interest, but at heart and in life as hostile as the Romans and Carthaginians of old?" [52]

While the agitation for reopening the African slave trade seemed growing, Northern sentiment was aghast at the thought that the traffic might already reach significant proportions. In this spring of 1859, the Southern Commercial Convention, meeting at Vicksburg, significantly reversed its stand on the subject. It voted three to one for the repeal of all laws prohibiting the foreign slave trade, State or Federal, and some members were hot for a declaration that the Federal prohibitions ought to be flouted as unconstitutional.[53] The convention had no sooner adjourned than an African Labor Supply Association, with the tireless De Bow as president, was organized to conduct a crusade for repeal.[54] Additional journals, such as the Richmond *Whig*, were demanding a renewal of the trade. Yancey and De Bow, in a widely publicized correspondence, called for the removal of the Act of 1820 from the statute books; for the government, declared Yancey, should have no concern with slavery except to protect it.[55]

Although part of this might be bravado, a deeper significance had to be attached to speeches of the most eminent Southern leaders. Alexander H. Stephens, retiring from Congress and, as he thought, from all public life, was tendered an impressive dinner at Augusta this summer. In his carefully prepared speech he asserted that the revival of the slave trade might be considered a necessity if the institutions of the South were to expand. States could not be made without people, and slave States could not be made without Negroes; unless the South had more Africans, it could not colonize more territory and might as well give up its race with the North. In the same month (July, 1859) Jefferson Davis made a defiant address to the Democratic State Convention at Jackson, Mississippi. He pronounced the law of 1820 insulting to the South, and added that he deemed it unconstitutional. It would be best, he thought, to leave the importation of Africans to the decision of the various States; he would oppose it for Mississippi, but other States might do as they pleased. What had been the result of the Federal law? "It has magnified the horrors of the middle passage; it has led to an alliance with Great Britain, by which we are bound to keep a naval squadron on the deadly coast of Africa . . . under the false plea

---

52 N. Y. *Weekly Tribune*, May 7, 1859.
53 Moderate Southerners complained that these conventions had ceased to be commercial and had become political. The Vicksburg gathering was convoked by a committee of radicals including De Bow, J. J. McRae, and Yancey, and was sharply attacked by such conservative journals as the New Orleans *Picayune* and Savannah *Republican*. See quotations in *National Intelligencer*, April 9, 1859, H. Wender, *Southern Commercial Conventions*.
54 Vicksburg *True Southron*, May 14, 1859.
55 Correspondence, N. Y. *Weekly Tribune*, August 13, 1859.

for humanity; it has destroyed a lucrative trade for ivory, oil, and gold dust
. . . and transferred it to our commercial rivals, the British." [56]

To be sure, the Administration maintained its strong opposition to the slave
trade, and, under constant British proddings, even increased its measures of
enforcement. During the fall of 1859 it strengthened the squadron off the African
coast to a total of one hundred and sixteen guns, borne by four sloops and four
steamers. The latter, being of light draught, could penetrate shallow coastal
reaches and were therefore specially useful in pursuit. Simultaneously, the
African base was removed from Puerto Praya to São Paulo de Loando, much
nearer the main seat of the slave traffic. Four armed cruisers were on station
in the vicinity of Cuba to pick up slavers which escaped through the African
cordon. But the Administration was so feeble in most respects, so sensitive to
Southern opinion, and so frigid in its attitude toward British requests for cooperation, that Northerners placed little reliance upon its continued vigilance. Moreover, if such a man as Jefferson Davis entered the White House in 1861, the trade
might well flourish.

And how great were the clandestine importations already? Some thought
them large. The New Orleans *Delta*, an advocate of the trade, had announced
early in 1858 that a depot had been established on Pearl River in Mississippi,
where cargoes of Africans were landed and sold. The slavers, it added, generally
used the French flag. The Richmond, Texas, *Reporter* in the spring of 1859
carried an advertisement, signed only by initials, of four hundred likely Africans,
lately landed on the Texas coast, and to be sold on reasonable terms. That summer, a correspondent of the New York *Herald* declared that the running of
African cargoes into secluded inlets and bays was reaching wide proportions,
and the New York correspondent of the London *Daily News*, without corroborative data, made the same assertion. The *Herald* quoted Senator Douglas as
saying that within a year and a half seventy vessels, with more than fifteen
thousand slaves, had reached the Florida coast, and as predicting that a dozen
more would discharge Africans between Pensacola and Key West during the
summer. This latter prediction he had made on the authority of an interested
Southern Senator. [57]

Such statements were supported by John C. Underwood, a large Virginia
landowne who had lately removed to New York. A graduate of Hamilton College and an attorney and scientific farmer, Underwood had many Southern
connections. Returning in early summer from an extended Southern tour, he
declared that the slave trade was so brisk that the arrival of cargoes of blacks in
unguarded Southern waters had become a frequent event. Why, then, was so

56 Rowland, IV, 61–88.
57 N. Y. *Herald*, September 3, 1859.

little known of the traffic? Because, Underwood explained, many Southern journals were attached to the trading interest; editors of others feared the brutal men engaged; and public sentiment favored the crime wherever planters were hungry for cheap labor. Many people in the Gulf States were denouncing the law as a protective tariff which enabled the slave-breeders of Virginia and the borderland to grow rich by charging $1,000–$1,500 for slaves who might be brought from the Congo for $100–$300. Then, too, sectional loyalty and the omnipresent hostility to the North made many observers keep still.[58]

Actually, these reports of clandestine shipments seem to have been decidedly exaggerated. No clear evidence exists that Douglas made the statements attributed to him, and if he did, he was deceived. The Pensacola *Tribune* called the *Herald* report a Munchausen absurdity. The Federal marshals for both the northern and southern districts of Florida, vigilant men with watchful deputies throughout the State, believed that not a single African had been landed there.[59] The New York *Journal of Commerce*, taking pains to inquire into the reports, published letters from three independent and informed sources in Florida, each declaring the stories of importations false. From other Southern intelligence, the *Journal* found good reason to conclude that the only ship which had landed negroes in the country during the past thirty years was the *Wanderer*, and that the Africans whom Douglas had seen were from this vessel.[60] President Buchanan had detective work done by a special agent in Florida, who found no basis for the tales of importations. Yancey, writing just after the opening of the Civil War, stated his belief that not more than five hundred Africans had been brought into the United States since 1807, and that these had been imported during 1859–61 rather as a political than a commercial transaction.[61]

Majority opinion in the South as a whole, moreover, was unquestionably against any revival of the trade. W. L. Yancey admitted as much. Even in South Carolina, we have the testimony of Judge Magrath that only a small minority were agitating for a revival, that the overwhelming majority of citizens were opposed, and that it was the noisy violence of the advocates that made the State seem greatly divided. Governor A. B. Moore of Alabama, running for re-election, condemned the movement both on grounds of public policy and as a cause of division among the Southern people. So did Robert Toombs, speaking at

58 Underwood in N. Y. *Weekly Tribune*, July 23, 1858.
59 Washington *Constitution*, September 20, 1859.
60 Quoted in *Idem*, August 30, 1859.
61 August 11, 1861, to A. Alison; Yancey Papers, Ala. State Lib. On the other hand, John S. Kendall, in his article on "New Orleans' 'Peculiar Institution'" in *La. Hist. Quart.*, XXIII, 864–866, declares that contraband slave traffic with Cuba, and less extensively, with Africa, was "heavy," slave ships slipping into quiet bayous on the Gulf coast to discharge their cargoes. And William H. Russell in *My Diary North and South*, I, 270–272, describes newly imported Negroes whom he saw in Alabama.

Augusta soon after the dinner to Stephens; and he added that prohibition was in harmony with the judgment and sentiment of the country. When Buchanan paid a visit to Raleigh, Secretary Jacob Thompson took occasion to condemn the scheme as the work of a class of reckless men, which would prove an evil for the South "in the Union or out of it." Houston, Wise, and all the border State leaders were resolutely antagonistic. Meanwhile, a finer voice than that of any politician had fallen upon the South, grave, melodious, and inspiring, when Justice Campbell of the Supreme Court, in charges to Federal grand juries in Louisiana and Alabama, reminded citizens that the suppression of the slave trade had enlisted the most enlightened, humane, and just men of all the nations of Christendom. He told them that in every civilized state the laws condemned this foul traffic, and that the people of the nation would take no backward step from a policy so right and high.[62]

Nevertheless, a large body of Southerners agreed with De Bow, Keitt, Hammond, and A. G. Brown that determined effort could in time effect a repeal of the Federal prohibition. In repeated speeches these men called upon the small farmers who wanted Negroes to join hands with the large planters who desired to widen the base of slavery; arguing that with a rich expanding supply of slaves they could consolidate their hold upon the border States, and win new Caribbean realms for their cherished institution.

Beyond doubt, a considerable number of extremists went further. Their aims could be summed up in a sentence: They meant to have explicit Congressional sanction for obtaining slaves from Africa and placing them in all the Territories. What A. G. Brown said bluntly, the adroit A. H. Stephens suggested by indirection. Antislavery newspapers this summer sounded the alarm. No careful scrutinizer of the times, they warned, could doubt that Democratic success in 1860 would be followed by a double *coup de main;* the legalization of the foreign slave trade, and the enactment of a territorial slave code. These measures might not be expressly incorporated in the Charleston platform, for the Lower South still preferred to finesse its cards until it could make sure of winning the rubber —but they were being planned by determined leaders.[63]

Frenetic as this program seemed, Senator A. G. Brown informed Douglas that in the Charleston convention the South would insist upon precisely these demands. Our section, he wrote on September 10, will call for "a platform explicitly declaring that slave property is entitled, in the Territories and on the

---

62 Magrath to Hammond, July 21, 1859, Hammond Papers, LC; Moore's letter in N. O. *Picayune*, July 2, 1859; Toombs's speech, Washington *Constitution*, September 22, 1859; Campbell's charges of July 30, 1858, and April 12, 1859, in *National Intelligencer*, January 11, August 25, 1859. Though Wise was against the slave trade, he was for the territorial slave code; *Harper's Magazine*, 1859, p. 555.
63 N. Y. *Weekly Tribune*, July 23, 1859.

high seas, to the same protection that is given to any other and every other species of property. Failing to get it, she will retire from the convention. The South will demand of the Congress that it afford protection to her people in their lives, liberty, and property. If Congress refuses . . . we will as our right resist the Government and throw off its authority." [64] Nor was this the bluster of an isolated Sir Lucius O'Trigger. Shrewd observers knew that behind at least half of Brown's program, and in many instances all of it, stood Rhett, Miles, and Pickens of South Carolina, Jefferson Davis, John J. McRae, and J. J. Pettus of Mississippi, Mason, Pryor, and Muscoe R. H. Garnett of Virginia, Howell Cobb and Senator Iverson of Georgia, C. C. Clay and Yancey of Alabama, and Slidell of Louisiana. They knew that these men were supported by such influential journals as the Charleston *Mercury* and *Standard*, New Orleans *Delta*, Mobile *Tribune*, Montgomery *Advertiser*, and Jackson *Mississippian*. Some of these sheets were steadily proclaiming their readiness to break up the Union if Congress refused to enact a territorial slave code.

We have seen that Yancey and Rhett had conferred in detail early in 1858. Now, in midsummer of 1859, after an exchange of letters, they carried their campaign into a more active phase. In an Independence Day speech at Grahamville, South Carolina, his first public appearance in half a dozen years, Rhett urged the South to make the coming Presidential campaign a final struggle against Northern tyrannies, demanding its full rights in the Territories or an end of the Union. Yancey spoke at Columbia and other towns, laying down a defiant program. Southern men should go to the Charleston convention, he said, prepared to quit it and organize a new party unless full protection were promised slavery in the Territories; and if a Republican were elected, the South should withdraw before he could be inaugurated. While Rhett promulgated these ideas in his Charleston *Mercury*, Yancey turned homeward to subsidize the Montgomery *Advertiser* and begin his struggle for control of the Democratic Party in Alabama.

This double-barrelled ultimatum of Southern radicals, the slave trade and slave code, seemed so preposterous that many sober observers North and South quickly concluded that it must cloak an ulterior motive. Behind it, they said, lurked a desire for disunion or at least a readiness to accept it. Jefferson Davis seemed extreme enough when, in his before-mentioned address to the Democratic Convention of Mississippi on July 6, 1859, he said that if the existing laws did not protect slavery in the Territories the South must insist on special legislation; argued for the acquisition of Cuba; and called for the dissolution of the Union if any President were elected on Seward's "irrepressible conflict" platform. Altogether, his chip-on-shoulder speech was full of ultimatums to the North. Still more reckless were the Rhett-Yancey-Ruffin group, steadily speaking and laboring for secession. The time has come, Yancey said at Charlotte, North Carolina, this summer, to strike for independence. "We have eight millions of people educated to the use of arms, trained to self-reliance, with a thorough knowledge of governmental principles, with as much real spirit and manhood as was ever possessed by any people. We have unity of production, unity of institutions, and a compact country. We have the great product without which the world cannot do. We are rich in all the elements of prosperity." If three millions had won freedom from Britain, demanded Yancey, could not eight millions win freedom from the North? [65]

The Buchanan Administration, anxious now to pursue a middle-of-the-road course, temporarily opposed both demands of the Southern radicals. It had a new voice in the Washington *Constitution*, successor to the *Union*. Under pressure from the Directory, George W. Bowman, a Pennsylvania journalist who had become superintendent of printing, had bought the paper in March, 1859, changed its name, employed William M. Browne, an English-born writer for the New York *Journal of Commerce*, as leader-writer, and invigorated its editorial policy. The *Constitution* became a steam calliope with five keys: economy, administrative reform, protection of the people against special privilege, expansion, and suppression of the "dead" slavery question. "Constitution" Browne plied a lively pen and received assiduous help from the heads of the Directory, Black, Cobb, and Thompson. The paper scored the slave-trade movement. As for a territorial code, it argued that new legislation was unnecessary, for the Federal courts would apply the same laws to slave property as to other possessions; that it was unwise to draw any distinction between different sorts of property; and that if one demand for special laws were carried through, others would arise. Some grumbler would allege that the territorial laws against murder were too lenient to afford protection; somebody else would call the laws against arson weak. Congress would soon be intervening along a broad ambit. The proper course was to look to the judiciary for aid—and if necessary, the courts could ask for Federal troops.[66] A sagacious stand; but would Buchanan maintain it, once Howell Cobb and Jacob Thompson yielded to the Southern thrust?

No Northerner was more emphatic in pointing to the spectre of disunion which lurked behind the "slave-trade, slave-code" demands than were certain Southern watchers on the Union battlements. Yancey's neighbor, Benjamin

65 Yancey's Columbia speech, Charleston *Mercury*, July 14, 1859; Du Bose, *Yancey*, 439–441; Yancey to Samuel Reid, July 3, 1861, on the *Advertiser* subsidy, Yancey Papers, Ala. State Lib. South Carolina moderates attacked the program, Senator Chesnut declaring a slave code unnecessary. Laura White, *Rhett*, 155–157.
66 Washington *Constitution*, August 20, 1859 and ff.

Fitzpatrick, pronounced the idea of "positive protection" a baneful abstraction.[67] In Yancey's home city, the Montgomery *Confederation* spoke of a dissembled purpose. "Is there any sane man living in this broad land who believes that the laws prohibiting the African slave trade can be repealed? That Congress will intervene and discriminate in favor of slavery and slave property in the Territories, and pass a system of laws specially designed for its defense and protection? No man would be so wanting in candor as to pretend that he had any such idea. Then, are we to stake the existence of the Union upon the issue of these two propositions, that we admit at the outset are foregone propositions?" [68] Sam Houston wrote the Galveston *Union* this summer that the very existence of the country was threatened by the three dogmas of Nullification, Secession, and Disunion, "which are in vogue with many men who claim to be friends of the South, but are in reality demagogues, who live on agitation, hoping to be elevated by the confusion of the times." The men who urged revival of the slave trade were trying to fasten on the land a horrible piece of barbarism. "In my opinion, all these devices are intended to bring about disunion." [69] Senator Hammond, who blew alternately very hot and very cold, penned a denunciation of the South for countenancing the *Echo* verdict and the *Wanderer* importations. His section had put herself in the same lawbreaking category with the North.[70]

Then she has demanded, what may in a very abstract sense be her right, but what practically is as absurd to ask for as a railroad to the moon (and everybody knows it), a Congressional slave code for the Territories. This is *sheer faction*. Another suicidal stab, and all in six or eight months. She seems to have surrendered—*prostituted* herself all at once to every sort of adventurer—Cuban filibusters, slave trade felons, and political aspirants of the basest and *silliest* order. Who would have thought it? *I am ashamed of her*. I have constantly blushed for her during the late session. Such folly—such madness—I never expected from the South. It makes things look very blue. It is insuring Seward's election on the Rochester platform.

Nevertheless, the radicals held their ground. In the autumn of 1859 an avowed disunionist, John J. Pettus, was chosen governor of Mississippi. Another, the wealthy, cultivated, and implacably secessionist William Henry Gist, had the previous year been made governor of South Carolina. A third, Andrew B. Moore, who had sat for two years in the governor's chair in Alabama, was now chosen for his second term. Scattered all over the South, men who openly or covertly wished to see a great slaveholding republic come into existence looked toward 1860 as their year of opportunity. As they thought of the boiling

67 August 30, 1859; C. C. Clay Papers.
68 Quoted in Washington *Constitution*, August 3, 1859.
69 Quoted in Warsaw, Illinois, *City Bulletin*, July 25, 1859.
70 To W. G. Simms, April 22, 1859; Hammond Papers, LC.

excitement of the Presidential campaign, the prospect that a Republican might be chosen to the White House, and the certainty that in that event many would say "Now or never," their spirits rose.

The country was coming back to prosperity. It was also moving inexorably toward disruption. Yet two final hopes remained. One was that the Democratic Party, the only great organized bond of union not yet parted, would somehow place a strong leader, respected by all sections, in the Presidential chair. The other was that a new Union party, composed of the Whigs, the remaining Know-Nothings, and moderate Democrats and Republicans, might organize to elect such a man as Crittenden of Kentucky or Bates of Missouri. The time has come to examine a party situation as interesting as any in the history of the nation, and to see how a bright possibility of strengthening the Union was raised to view just before an unpredictable catastrophe took all conservative men by surprise.

The Last Hope of Adjustment

IF THE Democrats were to win again in 1860, they must quietly ignore the demand for territorial protection of slavery which would hurry the party to a yawning grave. Voters of every Northern State would flock to the Republican guidons if the slaveholding radicals dictated such a requirement. But who would lead the party along a safe path that would hold Northern votes without repelling those of the South? It would not be Buchanan. In September, 1859, he wrote a letter avowing his final determination not to be a candidate for reelection. His high office beckoned to a number of ambitious politicians. While people followed with intent gaze the new gold rush to the Pike's Peak region, while they watched Napoleon III gather his Italian garlands, while they saw Palmerston overthrow the Derby ministry, while they read George Eliot's *Adam Bede*, and while industry and employment revived, newspapers were busy "hoisting the flag" of various aspirants, and politicians were forming committees and raising funds. It was the Democratic organization which provided most of the drama.

Observers were struck by the fact that Southern leaders were far hotter than Northerners in pursuit of the Democratic nomination. Since Polk, the party had named no man from below the Potomac, but now word had traversed the slave States that it was their turn. Though Howell Cobb was widely regarded as a failure in the Treasury, his Georgia followers were planning to send to Charleston a delegation that would give him devoted support. If most politicians thought Jefferson Davis too much a martinet, too moody and metaphysical to be a good candidate, he too had his loyal band. A. H. Stephens was publicly issuing disclaimers but he was privately receptive.[1] Yancey and Houston, both impossible, had their eyes on the prize. The temperamental James L. Hammond, who under happier circumstances would have made a good Vice-President, believed he had a chance for the White House. "If I had the stomach and nerves and muscle of Cobb or Toombs I would get it easy enough," he wrote. "By common consent, I am universally regarded as *dignus imperate*." [2] In brief, as

1 Von Abele, *Stephens*, 179, 180.
2 To M. C. M. Hammond, April 10, 1859; Hammond Papers, LC.

Hammond put it, there were at least twenty men in the South looking for the nomination, and forgetting their public duties in their anxiety to get it.[3]

Some of them were put out of the running this summer by their enemies or their own indiscretions. Henry A. Wise, brilliant and erratic, permitted the New York *Herald* to publish a letter to a friend which made his opponents rub their hands with glee.

He indulged in a baseless fling against the President as secretly a candidate, using the patronage to promote his fortunes. He assailed Tammany, and proposed steps to force a factional split in the New York delegation. He took up the "positive protection" cry. Above all, he proclaimed a remorseless vendetta against Douglas, whose platform he described as a short cut to all the ends of Black Republicanism. The South would not tolerate the Little Giant's ideas, declared the Virginia governor. "If he runs as an independent candidate, and Seward runs, and I am nominated at Charleston, I can beat them both." If Douglas got the regular nomination and the South named an independent candidate, the election would go to the House. "Where, then, would Mr. Douglas be? The lowest candidate on the list. If I have the popular strength you suppose, it will itself fix the nomination. Get that and I am confident of success." [4]

At one stroke Wise had heightened the active enmity of the Administration, the Tammany men, and the Douglas Democrats, while the rank egotism of his epistle offended everybody. "He has written one letter too much," remarked the St. Louis *News*. "Smothered by his own gas," was the verdict of the Pittsburgh *Post*.

Slidell, meanwhile, had been put out of the contest in different fashion. This unscrupulous intriguer, always close to the ear of Buchanan, had made countless enemies by his crafty ways and malignant temper. While all Douglas men hated him for his implacable warfare on their chieftain, the Soulé faction in his own State lusted for his political life. The spring of 1859 gave them their chance. Slidell rested under the stigma of the Houmas Grant scandal, and Northern journals never ceased to attack him for the juggle by which he had gotten this Louisiana grab through Congress to his alleged personal profit, under the dark cover of a bill relating to Missouri lands. He met the Yankee assaults stoically. But when in April the New Orleans *Delta* published a mass of letters relating to the subject, and other Southern newspapers took them up, he emitted a groan of agony. At the same time, Soulé organized a thrust against his dictatorship. A great mass meeting in New Orleans, with eighty-seven prominent organizers, heard Soulé declare that the time had come for revolt against Slidell's "unprincipled gang of political speculators and blacklegs"; that his contemptible oli-

3 To W. G. Simms, March 13, 1859; Hammond Papers, LC.
4 N. Y. *Herald*, August 4, Washington *Constitution*, August 6, 1859.

garchy, "incrustated on all sorts of Federal and State spoils," must no longer be allowed to make legislatures and party conventions open marts for the sale of votes; and that men who smuggled through laws for their own pecuniary interests must be forced out of public life.[5] The revolt was carried into the State convention at Baton Rouge near the end of May. Slidell, staggered in his own State, was more discredited than ever in the nation at large.

Three Democratic leaders stood well in advance of all others as possible nominees at Charleston. The least able, R. M. T. Hunter, was in some ways the most available, for, if he was a mediocrity, he was a hard-working, likeable man of fairly moderate views who had offended few outside of Virginia. Though when Southern institutions were under fire he would fly to their defense as readily as the proud Davis or the blustering A. G. Brown, his nature was essentially cautious and conciliatory. In guiding the tariff of 1857 through the Senate, he had made many Northern friends. Moreover, he had long experience, for he had been in Congressional life since the late eighteen-thirties. Vice-President Breckinridge, who modestly insisted that he was not a candidate but was obviously as willing as Barkis, possessed still wider popularity. An urbane, polished gentleman, with plenty of common sense backed by moderation and tact, he had been fittingly chosen, though a Democrat, to deliver the funeral oration over Clay, and had easily carried Clay's Ashland district for Congress. In presiding over the Senate he had shown judicial poise. When, at the beginning of 1859, the Senate had moved to its new chamber, he injected into the farewell address a stirring appeal for the Union.[6] Greatest of all, looming head and shoulders above other aspirants in intellectual power, energy, fighting edge, was Douglas, the storm center of the Party. The Democratic South had many sons; the Democratic North had an Achilles with no helping Patroclus and no rival.

Since his deposition from the Territorial Committee, Douglas was more than ever a fighting leader. Returning to Chicago from a late spring visit to inspect some family properties in Mississippi, he determined to utter a plain warning to the Southern fire-eaters. As he journeyed on to Washington, he shaped a letter which, dated June 22 and addressed to the editor of a Dubuque newspaper, created a national sensation. He announced that he would be a candidate for nomination on a platform embodying the principles of the Kansas-Nebraska Act and the Cincinnati Convention, but would repudiate the party if it adopted extreme dogmas. If the Charleston gathering should reject time-honored Democratic principles and substitute "such new issues as the revival of the African slave trade, or a Congressional slave code for the Territories, or the doctrine that the Constitution of the United States either establishes or prohibits slavery

5 See *National Intelligencer*, April 14, 1859, for details.
6 *Cong. Globe*, 35th Cong., 2d Sess., 202–204, January 4, 1859.

in the Territories beyond the power of the people legally to control it as other property, it is due to candor to say that in such an event I could not accept the nomination if tendered to me." Nor, obviously, could he support any candidate who did accept it.

This display of manly independence won the applause of most Northern Democrats and many Republicans. The New York *Times* praised it warmly, declaring that if Douglas had small chance of nomination it was because he was too strong a man; the Philadelphia *Press* said that, while doing no injustice to the South, the letter offered the party a prospect of victory in every free State.[7] Greeley's *Tribune* hailed the statement as a proclamation of independence from the tyranny and assumed infallibility of national conventions.[8] It was much more than this, however. It was an announcement that the Northern Democrats would flatly refuse to follow the lead of the Southern ultras in 1860. A few friends of Douglas believed that he had committed a tactical error. Pugh of Ohio, for example, one of his staunchest aides, then and later asserted that he had played into the hands of his enemies; that he had given the whole pack of anti-Douglas men an opportunity to make a rush upon Charleston with the intention of placing the denounced doctrines in the platform, and thus preventing his selection.[9] Actually, the pack needed no pretext; they had already gathered for their man-hunt. Douglas had said what the party crisis demanded, vindicating with promptness the moral position of the millions of Democrats north of the Ohio—and many below that river, for his mail was filled with vigorous letters promising support even in the Deep South.[10]

In great part, the letter was an attempt to appeal over the heads of the Southern radicals to the sober-minded rank and file of the party in the slave area. Though the Charleston *Courier* called it an insult to the South, and the Administration organ deplored it as a blow to party unity, actually it was but a courteous statement of the only terms on which continued party unity was possible. Even in Alabama and Louisiana, in eastern Tennessee and northern Georgia, many of the rank and file were with Douglas.[11] Could they assert themselves against the Slidells, Rhetts, and Davises? As part of his propagandist campaign, the Little Giant issued his speech on popular sovereignty in the debate of February 23 as a pamphlet, with an appendix of statements by Davis, Brown, Quitman, and others praising the principle. It was circulated by hundreds of thousands—with such effect, indeed, that a rumor sprang up that A. G. Brown had prearranged the debate in order to give Douglas a triumph over his opponents.[12]

7 Both editorials in Phila. *Weekly Press*, July 2, 1859.
8 N. Y. *Weekly Tribune*, July 2, 1859.
9 *Cong. Globe*, 36th Cong., 1st Sess., 2246; May 22, 1860.
10 Milton, *Eve of Conflict*, 372; Douglas Papers, *passim*.
11 John W. Womack, Eutaw, Alabama, 1859, n.d., in McClernand **Papers**.
12 Milton, *Eve of Conflict*, 379.

The response of the Southern ultras and of the Directory associated with Buchanan was prompt. These men had put themselves in a position where they could not yield to Douglas without a fatal loss of prestige. The old ambiguity on popular sovereignty had become impossible; the party had to accept or reject the Freeport Doctrine; and Douglas's letter dramatized the fact that a vital issue of principle must be resolved before a candidate was chosen. Had the radicals been acting on a non-political plane they might have ignored abstractions, accepted the situation in the Territories where the Kansas settlers *had* proved their power to exclude slavery, and cloaked their defeat in a mere readoption of the platform of 1856. A wise and courageous President would have supported such a compromise with the Dred Scott decision; compromise alone could avert party disaster in 1860. Unfortunately, the Southern radicals were acting on a plane of practical politics. They had aroused popular fears and prejudices which they must satisfy or their political careers would be forfeit. In Mississippi, for example, Jefferson Davis and A. G. Brown were at bottom eager rivals, bidding against each other with defiances of the North.[13] As for the President, his virtues included neither sagacity nor bravery. His confidence in Cobb, Floyd, and Jacob Thompson was undiminished, and he constantly corresponded or talked with Slidell, who saw the only safety of his section in a Southern Rights leadership of the party.

Throughout the summer and early fall of 1859, the Administration's attacks on Douglas were as flagitious as in the previous year. Slidell spurred Buchanan on with charges that the Illinoisan was intolerably arrogant, a would-be party dictator.[14] Floyd, going to the Virginia springs for his health, consorted with the wealthier type of Southerner and reported to the President their faith that the Administration was completely right and that the squatter sovereigns of the prairies were utterly impossible. The Southern people are behind you, wrote Floyd. "You have only to dictate your policy and to excommunicate all who fail or refuse to sustain it, to organize the party, and assure harmonious action sufficient to carry whatever their united strength can accomplish." [15] The Washington *Constitution* was tirelessly abusive. Republishing every misrepresentation or criticism uttered by Northern marplots or Southern fanatics, it maintained its own stream of denunciation; and other pensioned newspapers throughout the country followed this lead. Still, month by month, the heads of officeholders friendly to Douglas or lukewarm in the Administration cause continued to roll.

The grand object now was to deprive Douglas of every possible Northern delegate at Charleston. In New England, where the party had little strength except as it was nourished by Federal offices and contracts, the Administration

13 S. P. McCutchen, "A. G. Brown," MS Dissertation, Univ. of Chicago.
14 John Slidell, July 3, etc., 1859; Buchanan Papers.
15 From Red Sweet Springs, September 5, 1859; Buchanan Papers.

ruled with an iron hand. Such lieutenants as Caleb Cushing, B. F. Hallett, and Isaac Toucey kept the party file leaders on the alert. Jobholding or jobhunting Democrats ran the newspapers, staffed the post offices, and manipulated State committees and conventions. In the Middle Atlantic States the Administration grip was weaker. Such willing agents as Daniel S. Dickinson and William Bigler could transmit orders to thousands of placemen, but the organization leaders were conscious of a groundswell of public opinion in opposition to Southern domination. Revolt against the Directory had progressed far in New York, where Dean Richmond of Buffalo, vice-president of the New York Central and chairman of the State committee, agreed with Henry J. Raymond that Douglas alone could carry the North. It had progressed far in Pennsylvania, where Forney's *Press* daily cheered on the struggle against the Buchanan regime. Freest of all from Washington controls was the Middle West. From Ohio, where Senator Pugh and Henry B. Payne upheld Douglas's hands, to Iowa, where Augustus Caesar Dodge and other moderate Democrats relied on him to recapture the State from the Republicans, the Administration was in low repute.

Yet everywhere the Directory exerted itself mightily. Even in Illinois, the bolters of the previous year were instigated to raise a clamorous opposition, and to call a convention to send anti-Douglas delegates to Charleston. Many conservative Democrats saw that this attempt to kill Douglas's chances by machine manipulation—by efforts to wheedle, bribe, and threaten, particularly effective in New England and the border region—was a costly luxury for the Southern wing of the party; that if he were implacably assailed for now holding opinions which he had entertained without change for at least ten years (and opinions well understood when a majority of Southern delegates voted for him at the Cincinnati convention), the effect on Democratic fortunes would be calamitous. But Slidell, Cobb, Floyd, and Thompson had imbued the President with their vindictive hostility. Defending his removals, Buchanan wrote a friend:

I cannot retain in an important position any man who preaches rebellion against the Supreme Court of the United States. A party founded on this principle is purely revolutionary. Let a territorial legislature confiscate the property of an American citizen;—such a law has been already declared unconstitutional by the Judiciary and must of course produce a collision between Federal and Territorial authority. Never before in this country has there been a general party founded on the principle of repudiating a judgment of the Supreme Court. The attempt to resist such a decision was made in individual States, as in the case of Olmstead in Pennsylvania; but was indignantly put down. Now Seward and the Black Republicans resist this decision on the ground that Congress has the right to prohibit slavery; and Douglas and his followers resist it on the ground that a Territorial Legislature possess this right.

If the power existed the latter would be the worst mode in which it could be exercised. In Congress it could be debated by Representatives from the whole country and might be successfully resisted. Not so before a territorial legislature on the frontiers. Besides, one legislature might prohibit and another might introduce slavery and so the people be kept in a state of constant excitement on this subject.[16]

A singularly prejudiced statement this, in its unfounded talk of rebellion and confiscation; a singularly confused statement in its suggestion that the way to get rid of "constant excitement" over slavery was to let slaves into all the Territories. And Buchanan added a singularly inept prophecy. "The issue in 1860," he wrote, "beyond all question will be between the Republicans who refuse to yield obedience to the decision, and the Democrats who sustain it and in doing so will sustain the cause of law, property and order. *On this line we shall win.*" He actually thought the North could be swept for the Dred Scott decision!

Buchanan, in fine, was with the radical proslavery men on every issue except revival of the slave trade. He was with them in opposing any bar against slavery in the Territories, any bar against expansion in Cuba and Mexico, any bar against new slave States. In a letter to Slidell on June 24, 1859, he even intimated his support of a Congressional slave code, if needed for "the rights of property consecrated by the Constitution of the United States." [17] He was against the principal Northern Democrat with all his power, sneering at him as a man who would not condescend to accept a nomination unless the party first erected just the platform he wanted. As the agitation for a slave code continued to overspread the South, making progress even in the border States partly as a "logical" deduction from the Dred Scott decision and partly as promising new territorial markets for slaves, the anti-Douglas front gained solidity.

[I]

The Little Giant, spending most of the summer in Washington, saw that organization of his forces was imperative. Before autumn, a group of friends led by A. D. Banks had opened headquarters for him in New York. A committee which included Moses Taylor, John Jacob Astor, Dean Richmond, August Belmont, and Walter Sherman, with other wealthy men, began raising an initial campaign fund. George Sanders besought Douglas to cultivate the good will of Senator Green of Missouri. James B. Steedman was active in Ohio, with Washington McLean and the Cincinnati *Enquirer* taking a friendly attitude; Lanphier and Sheahan were busy as ever in Illinois; and that staunch Unionist, John Forsyth, made the Mobile *Register* an efficient exponent of Douglasite doctrines. As the Douglas forces picked up delegates here and there in New England, and

16 To M. Johnson, September 19, 1859; Buchanan Papers, NYHS.
17 June 24, 1859; Buchanan Papers.

in New York despite the opposition of Dickinson took forty-five of the seventy delegates, they gathered confidence. The Illinoisan could count on most of the Middle West, and his hopes grew.[18]

To help rally his forces and give Democrats of the South a fair exposition of his doctrines, Douglas astonished the country by publishing in the September issue of *Harper's Magazine* a copyrighted twenty-page discussion of "Popular Sovereignty in the Territories: the Dividing Line between Federal and Local Authority." [19] It became the sensation of the hour. Written in a heavy, involved style quite unlike Douglas's lucid, hard-hitting speeches, and loaded with erudition, it was hard reading for most politicians; yet no other article of the decade was so widely discussed. It had been prepared with a thoroughness which would have done credit to Lincoln; Douglas had borrowed from the Library of Congress the works of Calhoun, the *Federalist*, five volumes of Bancroft, Elliott's *Debates*, Carey's *Slave Trade, Domestic and Foreign*, and other treatises. Ostensibly directed against both Republicans and positive-protection Democrats, it concentrated its fire on the latter. Widely summarized in newspapers and issued in pamphlet form, it attained national currency. "You have made the most of a bad cause," A. G. Brown wrote the author.[20]

Douglas began by describing the various schools of Democratic thought upon the issue of slavery in the Territories. He then launched into an argument, mainly upon historical grounds, for his own view that the people of a Territory were free to form and regulate their own institutions. He did not go into the vital questions of precisely *how* and *when* the people should act upon slavery, but implied that they had the power to do so from the moment that they became "a distinct political community." One passage, as Lincoln noted, indicated a rough guess that the number of inhabitants needed to deal with slavery lay between ten and twenty thousand. He did not restate the Freeport Doctrine, but strongly implied his faith in it. He did not say precisely what the functions of the courts touching slavery should be, but he plainly intimated that the popular will should be the court of last resort.[21] Altogether, the article politely renewed his defi-

18 Milton, *Eve of Conflict*, 384, 385.
19 William A. Seaver of New York had given a dinner party in the summer of 1859 where Douglas met Fletcher Harper, Park Benjamin, Paul Morphy, J. W. Forney, and others; the article followed. Douglas tried to keep the paper a secret, but word of its preparation leaked out. He took pride in it, and was pleased by its national circulation in the magazine. Douglas to Seaver, July 17, 1859; Douglas Papers, Ill. State Hist. Library.
20 Milton, *Eve of Conflict*, 389.
21 Kellogg of Illinois had introduced a bill at the previous session for what he called genuine popular sovereignty. It provided that the people of the Territories should elect their governors, secretaries, judges, marshals, and all other officers; and that Congress should put its legislative power in the Territories in abeyance in favor of popular rights. This recalled Chase's amendment to the Nebraska bill. The Chicago *Tribune* termed the bill "Republican Popular Sovereignty—the pure metal, with a clear and always recognizable ring!" June 28, 1859.

ance of the Administration and the South. In its historical portions, it traced the dividing line between local and central governments from colonial days down to the Dred Scott decision. At every stage since Jamestown, Douglas argued, the planters and shapers of the nation had insisted that the people should make their own local laws and mould their own institutions, subject only to the Constitution, first of the British Empire, and later of the United States. He quoted the admission of Taney himself in the Dred Scott decision: "No word can be found in the Constitution which gives Congress a greater power over slave property . . . than property of any other description"—and property in the Territories had always been controlled by local legislatures and sentiment.

Argument of this sort was open to forcible rebuttal, and Republican editors, led by Bryant, Greeley, and Bowles, had no difficulty in citing history to their own purpose—to show Congressional supremacy over the question.[22] Lincoln, too, summed up Douglas's inconsistency in an epigram: "Slavery may be legally excluded from a Territory in which it may legally remain." The main quarrel of the Senator, however, was with his Democratic colleagues. His article evoked sterner attacks than ever from such journals as the Jackson *Mississippian*, Richmond *Enquirer*, Charleston *Mercury*, and Memphis *Avalanche*, all declaring that the South could never accept him. And since the Administration could not afford to keep silent, its readiest writer, Jere Black, was chosen to fire an immediate salvo in reply.

The five-column article of the Attorney-General, published in the Washington *Constitution* on September 10, was simultaneously issued as a pamphlet, while many Administration newspapers reprinted it in full. Black's arguments were constitutional, not historical, and as such were familiar. His main thesis was simply that the Constitution regarded as sacred all the rights which a citizen might legally acquire in any State, and if a man gained property in a State and carried it into a Territory, he could not then be deprived of it. What was most notable in his legalistic presentation was its strong proslavery tone and its virulently anti-Douglas trappings. Black spoke of slavery precisely as Howell Cobb and Jacob Thompson spoke of it, as a positive good. "Here, then, is a species of property which is of transcendent importance to the material interests of the South—which the people of that region think it right and meritorious in the

22 For example, Douglas had written that in Jefferson's plan for the Northwest, the article prohibiting slavery after 1800 was rejected by the Continental Congress. True; but the States had voted 6 to 3, the delegates 16 to 7, in favor of it, and it failed of the required majority of seven States only because neither New Jersey nor Delaware had enough delegates present to cast a ballot. The Ordinance of 1787 did exclude slavery from the Northwest Territory, and the first Congress under the Constitution accepted the Ordinance. Republicans reiterated their familiar contention that as Congress would estop the transportation of explosives, harmful drugs, and intoxicants into a Territory, it could forbid the entry of property so dangerous to peace, order, and prosperity as slaves.

eyes of God and good men to hold—which is sanctioned by the general sense of all mankind among whom it has existed—which was legal only a short time ago in all the States of the Union, and which was then treated as sacred by any one of them—which is guaranteed to the owner as much as any other property is guaranteed by the Constitution"; such was his language.

Acrid and contemptuous references to Douglas studded the essay, which accused the Illinoisan of raising a new issue and stirring up the bitter waters of strife. In making this accusation, Black did not mention the attempt to foist Lecompton upon Kansas in which the Administration had been so signally defeated. He did not speak of the Southern demand for positive protection which was now rending the party asunder, nor did he take any Southern extremist to task for opinions far less defensible than Douglas's.

Other pamphlets appeared on both sides. By far the ablest came from the pen of Reverdy Johnson, who was heard with the more interest because as counsel for Sanford he had helped bring about Taney's decision upon Dred Scott. In his "Remarks On Popular Sovereignty," he unequivocally took Douglas's side.

What would be the consequence of accepting Black's view that the territorial legislature had no power to shape local institutions? asked the former Attorney-General. The cards, dice, and roulette wheels used in gambling were legal property in some States; was the legislature of a Territory to have no power to exclude gambling? Polygamy might be legal in one State; could the husband take ten wives into a Territory? And then, as to slavery itself, how absurd would be the result of the doctrine that the statutes of the State of origin controlled that species of property! "An emigrant from one State might sell each slave single, whilst one from another could not sell at all, or sell if the sale separated man and wife, parent and child. In one case slaves would be liable to execution for debt in the lifetime of the owner, in the other not. In one the children of a slave might belong to her owner, in the other not. . . . In one the mode of feeding, working, and clothing might be prescribed, in the other not." Adopt Black's interpretation, remarked Reverdy Johnson, and the statute book of a Territory would be a singular volume. Its title would be, The Statutes and Other Laws of the Territory; open it, and readers would find the enactments of Massachusetts, Virginia, Georgia, and other States, with a note that they applied respectively to the citizens who had emigrated from each State.

Johnson also argued that if the Dred Scott decision meant anything, it was that Congress had no power whatever over slavery in the Territories; neither power to prohibit nor to establish it. And if Congress had no authority to prohibit or establish, how could it legislate to protect slave property? When Buchanan had told Congress that, under the Dred Scott decision, slavery existed by virtue of the Constitution, he made an unfounded assertion, for no such doctrine was to be found in the decision either in words or by fair inference. "All that the court decided . . . was that the Constitution did not prohibit the institution, and that it gave no power to Congress to prohibit it." This was the opinion of a man whose reputation in constitutional law far exceeded Jeremiah Black's.

As the debate continued, it became acrimonious. Douglas was incensed by passages in Black's article bearing upon his public conduct, and especially by the charge that he had completely revolutionized his political opinions in the course of eighteen months. An important election was at hand in Ohio; handed Black's argument when traveling to Wooster, he made a vituperative reply. At Columbus and Cincinnati he spoke more calmly. Once more, he said, the Administration was endeavoring to drive him from the party. Attorney-General Black had been the agent of the cabal about Buchanan when, in 1858, he had sent letters abusing Douglas to Democrats all over Illinois. Now he was its catspaw again. This effort to thrust him into exile would fail; "the thing cannot be done." Returning east, he began to write a full-length rejoinder to Black, but was prostrated first by inflammatory rheumatism and then by bilious fever. His illness rapidly became so alarming that friends and opponents alike besieged his door to express sympathy, while several times rumors of his death flew about Washington. Happily, by mid-November he was recovering.[23]

The Ohio speeches provoked a fresh clamor of denunciation in the South. Douglas, declared Representative Eli Shorter of Alabama, was great in talent, in oratory, in ambition—and in treason to the South and the party. Numerous Southerners swore they would just as soon vote for Seward or Joshua Giddings as for the Illinoisan. The Democrats of Noxubee County in Georgia announced their rejection of Douglas, even if the Charleston convention nominated him. If the Dred Scott decision is to be trampled into the dust, wailed the Memphis *Avalanche,* for heaven's sake let the infamous outrage be committed in the name of Black Republicanism instead of the Democracy. The Mobile *Tribune,* Montgomery *Advertiser,* and Atlanta *Intelligencer,* spurning the Northwestern wing of the party, and branding Douglas as a hypocrite and marplot, demanded every jot and tittle of territorial rights. If the South should fail of full protection for slavery when asked, declared the *Intelligencer,* "she will then fall back upon her own resources, seize the sword of independence, and fight for the laws of the land and our rights." [24]

It was Douglas against the field—but Administration enmity and Southern rejection of the Freeport Doctrine made his chances dubious. Nor was his

23 Washington *Constitution,* September 10–27; Phila. *Press,* November 25; Mobile *Register,* November 23, 1859, etc.
24 *National Intelligencer,* quoted in N. Y. *Weekly Tribune,* October 15, 1859.

candidacy without other elements of weakness, rooted in his personality and record. In the border area, he had never been much liked by thoughtful, conservative men like Bayard, Letcher, and Guthrie. While he had many friends in New England, shrewd politicians of the Caleb Cushing-B. F. Hallett stripe were affected not merely by Administration pressures but by a sense that he was unsafe, and so took an adverse stand. Throughout the rest of the North he possessed immense power, the main body of Middle Western Democrats positively idolizing him. Even there, however, many sober men had always distrusted his flamboyant attitudes, bellicosity, and impetuosity. The main body of the Northern party still hoped that he might carry everything before him, and believed that in any frontal collision with the Southern wing his forensic power and personal force would be irresistible. But the chance of Democratic success more and more depended on the choice of some such trustworthy if uninspiring compromise nominee as Hunter.[25]

[II]

On the Republican side, Seward and his aide Thurlow Weed, as efficient a political combination as any in American history—as Jackson and Van Buren, or McKinley and Hanna—were actively at work for the nomination, Weed pulling wires, enlisting editors, keeping in *rapport* with such New York leaders as E. D. Morgan and Preston King, and planning the capture of State delegations. Seward spent the summer in Europe. Before going abroad, he visited Cameron at Harrisburg, shook hands with the whole legislature, dropped encouraging words on the tariff, and departed with some half-promises of support. The little Senator, with his careless rural dress, bubbling loquacity, and burning ambition, was hailed in New York City with music, cheers, and feasting—"the next President." Far down the bay he was accompanied by a vessel full of friends, waving, huzzaing, and singing.[26] He stood preeminent among aspirants for the nomination—but half a dozen powerful elements distrusted or disliked him.

The Ohio governor was equally ardent and equally hopeful. Chase, like Seward, had been talked of in 1856, and he too belonged to the radical antislavery wing of the party. Carl Schurz spent the night at his house, breakfasted with him and his pretty daughter Kate, and heard him express a frank desire to be the next President. "You will be a delegate to the convention, Mr. Schurz," he said in effect. "What do you think?" And Schurz replied with

25 Cf. John Appleton's letters to Buchanan on political situation, September 1859; Buchanan Papers.
26 Thurlow Weed, *Memoir*, 256, 257; R. H. Luthin, *The First Lincoln Campaign*, Ch. 2; Frederic Bancroft, *Seward*, I, 493–495.

blunt candor: "If the Republican Convention at Chicago have courage enough to nominate an advanced antislavery man, they will nominate Seward; if not, they will not nominate you." But Chase was not abashed; he could not see why antislavery men should not place him ahead of Seward. What of his long labors for the Liberty Party and Free Soil Party? What of his ten years' experience as Senator and governor? Throughout the fall of 1859 and the ensuing winter, he and his friends, with the *Ohio State Journal* as organ, were ceaselessly busy.[27]

As in the Democratic Party many were turning to the hope of some compromise figure, so a growing number of Republicans began to study Edward Bates of Missouri. The staid, white-bearded, mild-eyed old jurist, past sixty-five but still vigorous, had never identified himself with the new party. In principle he was still an old-line Whig; but he was ready to accept a Republican nomination on terms that would permit other Whigs, freesoil Democrats, and moderate Know-Nothings to join hands behind him. The three Blairs believed that they might rally an irresistible coalition around him. Their platform would embrace the containment of slavery, a homestead bill, internal improvements, the colonization of negroes outside the United States, and a Pacific railroad.

In the spring of 1859, Frank Blair and Schuyler Colfax, dining with Bates, ascertained that he would stand firm against any expansion of slavery and that he sympathized with Blair's hope to abolish slavery in Missouri. They assured him that Seward could not get the nomination. Bates rose to their proposals, which contemplated not so much a Republican as an Opposition Party—a People's Party, for which, wrote Gratz Brown, the Republicans, Whigs, Americans, and Honest Democrats could all vote.[28]

The immediate result was the publication of a long letter by Bates (written before the dinner conference, but now first brought forth) assailing Buchanan's policies, expounding old Whig doctrines on the tariff, river and harbor improvements, and railroad aid, and deprecating the agitation of the slavery issue. The question of slavery extension he did not discuss. Greeley's *Tribune*, praising the letter as just and sagacious, intimated that if he *had* treated this issue, he would have taken a correct stand. Bates's candidacy had two great and obvious weaknesses. It assumed that the slavery agitation *could* be stopped—and all those who saw that it could not distrusted his stand; and it involved the practical creation of a new party, from which radical Republicans would be certain to depart with wrath and clamor. Nevertheless, the Blairs, laboring diligently, enlisted Orville H. Browning, Henry Winter Davis, and Tom Corwin in at least tentative support. Browning shortly talked to his friend Lincoln in Springfield on the subject:

27 Pike, *First Blows;* Schurz, *Reminiscences,* II, 171 ff.; Hart, *Chase,* 179–181.
28 Bates, *Diary* (ed. Howard K. Beale), 11; Luthin, *op. cit.,* 55.

February 8 (1860). . . . At night Lincoln came to my room and we had a free talk about the Presidency. He thinks I may be right in supposing Mr. Bates to be the strongest and best man we can run—that he can get votes even in this county that he cannot get—and that there is a large class of voters in all the free states that would go for Mr. Bates, and for no other man. He says it is not improbable that by the time the national convention meets in Chicago he may be of opinion that the very best thing that can be done will be to nominate Mr. Bates.

Of the less prominent aspirants for the Republican nomination, Lincoln displayed the shrewdest type of activity. Having stated the issue of slavery-restriction so forcibly in the Douglas-Lincoln debates that all influential free-soilers began to watch him carefully, he intended to maintain the position he had won. As his comment on Bates indicated, this old-time follower of Henry Clay believed that a moderate rather than radical candidate was needed in 1860. At the same time, he realized that the party must win essentially on its Northern strength without regard to the South, and that if it sacrificed freesoil principle in order to woo border votes, Cotton Whigs, and weak-kneed Democrats, it would meet well-merited defeat. On such a basis, he wrote Nathan Sargent, the Republicans would probably carry Maryland—and would certainly lose every other State. They would gain nothing in the South and fail in the North.[29] Or, as he put it in another widely publicized letter of May, 1859, he would support a fusion of Republican and other opposition elements only if it could be had on Republican terms. In the selection of a candidate, compromise was possible. He would even go to the South for an able, patriotic man who would stand on Republican ground.

"But," Lincoln declared, "I am against letting down the Republican standard a hair's-breadth." [30] Bravely spoken! At the same time, while privately making modest assertions that he was unfit, he was keeping his name and views before the voters and cultivating political friends.

He bought title to a German newspaper in Springfield, the *Staats-Anzeiger*. He abandoned his distaste for social formalities to give parties for politicians. He made an Independence Day speech at Atlanta, Illinois. He corresponded with Schuyler Colfax, giving sagacious advice; the party must not campaign in one State for some idea popular just there, but unpopular in other States and divisive in the national convention.[31] In midsummer of 1859 he made a nine-day trip to Iowa and Kansas on business, delivering by request a political speech at Council Bluffs. Here, discussing the slavery question at length, he again insisted that the Republican Party retain its definite principles and national organiza-

29 Gilbert A. Tracy, *Uncollected Letters of Abraham Lincoln*, 111-113.
30 To Theodore Canisius, May 17, 1859; *Works*, I, 534, 535
31 To Schuyler Colfax, July 6, 1859; *Works*, I, 535.

tion.[32] The friendly *Nonpareil* termed his speech masterly and unanswerable, while even the hostile *Bugle* admitted that he had been quite a lion in western Iowa. Invited by Republican leaders to speak in half a dozen States from Minnesota to New York and New Hampshire, he agreed to make addresses in Ohio (replying to Douglas) and Wisconsin.

The Ohio speeches were of sufficient importance to obtain wide notice. In Columbus, where the *Ohio State Journal* had announced Lincoln as a man of "great renown and national reputation," he spoke on September 16 from the steps of the capitol for two hours. Next day in Dayton he made a speech of similar length at the courthouse, even the Democratic *Daily Empire* admitting that he "is a very seductive reasoner." At a rally that night, ex-Representative Robert C. Schenck called him the proper man for the Republican Presidential nomination. On his arrival in Cincinnati, where he spoke on Saturday evening, the seventeenth, he met an enthusiastic reception. His audience, according to Murat Halstead's *Commercial*, was three or four thousand. The hostile *Enquirer* carried a good Sunday morning report of the speech, and the *Gazette* on Monday printed its full text. Facing his Cincinnati hearers, he had modestly remarked: "This is the first time in my life that I have appeared before an audience in so great a city as this. I therefore make my appearance under some degree of embarrassment." It was evident to thoughtful readers, however, that the State was entertaining one of the most vigorous political thinkers of the time. And of readers he had a great many. Robert Hitt of the Chicago *Press and Tribune* accompanied Lincoln to report his utterances in shorthand; the New York *Times* paid careful attention to his tour; and the New York *Tribune*, to which Greeley now returned from California, printed nearly a column of matter from the Columbus address.

Taking the Ohio speeches together, Lincoln made a number of forcible points. (1) He insisted that the central purpose of the Republican Party was eminently conservative; it proposed only to bring slavery back to its original place in the American scheme and keep it there, asking for no other change than that which the framers of the government had anticipated with respect to it. (2) He brilliantly exposed the logical weakness of the Freeport Doctrine, pointing out again how it declared that an institution might lawfully be driven from a place where it might lawfully exist. (3) Douglas, he said, assumed that slavery was one of the little, unimportant matters, of no more consequence in a Territory than the question whether men should grow tobacco or raise horned cattle; a matter of dollars and cents, with no moral implications. The Little Giant assumed that the first comers to a Territory might properly plant there something which the millions who came thereafter could never dig up; some-

32 Baringer, *Lincoln's Rise to Power*, 90–93.

thing which deeply affected the family of older States. It was not so. (4) This non-moral view of slavery, he remarked in Columbus, was a sapping and mining operation, breaking down public opinion. Once men were converted to the view that no wrong inhered in slavery and that whoever wanted it might have it, then both territorial expansion and fresh importations would become possible. Men would be ready for Jeff Davis, Stephens, and their friends to sound the bugle for revival of the slave trade, pouring a flood of slavery over the free States. (5) In Cincinnati he appealed to the freesoil Democrats to come into the Republican Party as their only ark of refuge. He did so by ostensibly speaking to Kentuckians, telling them that if they wished to make slavery permanently safe and extend it over new lands, they should hasten to nominate Douglas.

In their homely, lucid combination of logic with historical citations, the Ohio speeches were the best refutation of the *Harper's* article which had yet appeared. As in all of Lincoln's utterances, however, appeals to principle dominated mere debating points. All his arguments were woven about two main themes. One concerned ideas:

Mr. Clay many, many years ago . . . told an audience that if they would repress all tendencies to liberty and ultimate emancipation, they must go back to the era of our independence and muzzle the cannon which thundered its annual joyous return on the Fourth of July; they must blow out the moral lights around us. . . . I call attention to the fact that in a preeminent degree these popular sovereigns are at this work: blowing out the moral lights around us; teaching that the negro is no longer a man, but a brute; that the Declaration has nothing to do with him; that he ranks with the crocodile and the reptile; that man, with body and soul, is a matter of dollars and cents. I suggest to this portion of Ohio Republicans, or Democrats . . . that there is now going on among you a steady process of debauching public opinion on this subject.

The other theme concerned action:

This government is expressly charged with the duty of providing for the general welfare. We believe that the spreading out and perpetuity of slavery impairs the general welfare. . . . I say that we must not interfere with the institution of slavery in the States where it exists, because the Constitution forbids it, and the general welfare does not require us to do so. We must not withhold an efficient fugitive-slave law, because the Constitution requires us, as I understand it, not to withhold such a law. But we must prevent the out-spreading of the institution. . . . We must prevent the revival of the African slave-trade, and the enacting by Congress of a territorial slave code. We must prevent each of these things being done by either Congresses or courts. The people of these United States are the rightful masters of both Congresses and courts, not to overthrow the Constitution, but to overthrow the men who pervert the Constitution.

Moncure D. Conway went to the Cincinnati meeting, held in a public square in bright moonlight. He listened to the steady battering flow of logic from the gaunt, hollow-cheeked, sad-eyed Illinoisan, whose strong features wore such a bronzed, thought-carved, kindly look that he seemed to fit Robert Browning's description of a German savant—three parts sublime to one grotesque. Conway was struck by Lincoln's voice, every intonation expressing liveliness, earnestness, and shrewdness. He thought the man's personality charming in its total lack of pretense—simple, direct, and humorous. When Lincoln said, "Slavery is wrong!" Conway heard the Kentuckians in the audience murmur and hiss. Lincoln instantly elaborated: "I acknowledge that you must maintain your platform just there, if at all. . . . But your hisses will not blow down the walls of justice." [33]

As the New York *Tribune* printed its quotations from the Columbus and Cincinnati speeches, and the Chicago *Press and Tribune* and *Illinois State Journal* published both in full, Lincoln tarried in Indianapolis on his way home to deliver a two-hour address to an enthusiastic audience.[34] Again, using the Ohio arguments, he produced a notable impression. The end of September found him in Milwaukee, addressing the Wisconsin State Agricultural Society; a non-political discourse remarkable chiefly for the vigor with which he demolished the mudsill theory of society. Who were the mudsills? In the free States, he said, most people were neither exclusively hirers nor hired, but a mixed body working partly for themselves and partly for others; no hired laborer was fixed to that condition for life; and free labor was deemed compatible with the highest education attainable.[35] He made another impromptu speech in Milwaukee, and on his return addressed audiences at Beloit and Janesville. The *Gazette* of the last-named town, admitting that his oratorical style was plain and his gestures were awkward, added that the power of his intellect made itself felt not only while the speech was being delivered, but afterward; that his arguments and hits would be long remembered; and that his audience would retain "a vivid recollection of that tall, gaunt form, stooping over towards his hearers, his countenance full of humor or frowning with scorn, as he lays bare" the absurd positions of his opponents.[36]

Of all the speeches delivered in 1859, Lincoln's showed the shrewdest thought, the most irrefutable logic, and the greatest moral power. That fact did

33 Conway, *Autobiography*, I, 317, 318; "Personal Recollections of Abraham Lincoln" in *Fortnightly Review*, I (1865), 56 ff. Lincoln's written version of his speech makes no reference to hisses, but does contain his flat statement to the Kentuckians: "I think slavery is wrong, morally and politically."
34 N. Y. *Weekly Tribune*, September 24, October 1, 1859.
35 Lincoln, *Works*, I, 576–584.
36 Quoted in Baringer, *Lincoln's Rise to Power*, 110.

not escape some party leaders who recalled his similar primacy in 1858. He kept in touch with Norman B. Judd and Secretary Jesse Fell of the Illinois Republican organization. Content with a dark-horse position, he took pains to praise Seward, Chase, Cameron, Bates, and other leaders, sought no delegates outside Illinois, allowed the impression to grow that he might be content with a Vice-Presidential nomination, and labored for party harmony on a platform genuinely embodying principle. He was far from being a prominent figure. When the Philadelphia *Press* this fall listed forty-five men who had been named for the Presidency, he was not among them. Yet the Chicago *Tribune*, asserting its preference for him, declared that the Northwestern Republicans would insist upon placing him at the head of the ticket.[37]

[III]

Douglas was a moderate leader—his popular sovereignty position was an effort to reconcile Northern and Southern views and keep the Democratic Party national. Lincoln was a moderate leader—he was ready even to accept a Southern candidate in order to make the Republican Party less sectional. The groping attempt of the Blairs, Gratz Brown, and Schuyler Colfax to lift Edward Bates to leadership of a Republican-Opposition Party was a moderate movement. The great mass of reflective Americans, at least outside New England and the cotton kingdom, were in apprehensive mood; only moderation, they believed, could save the country. Throughout the border States, meanwhile, a vigorous attempt was being made to organize moderate men behind a more realistic, generous, and patriotic approach to State and national problems. Dark was the outlook in areas dominated by slave-code men in the Deep South and radical antislavery men in the North; but a gleam of sunshine lighted up the broad region from Maryland to Missouri.

"Recent political results in Virginia, Kentucky, North Carolina, and Tennessee," exulted the Mobile *Register*, John Forsyth's moderate paper, "conclusively show that at least in these important central States of the Union, which constitute the northern division of the slaveholding section, the prevailing sentiment of the people is sound, wholesome, and true to those broad national principles which look to the peace and harmony of the Confederacy, and to the sinking of the slavery agitation." [38]

The attempt to create an Opposition Party in this region was half a movement against fanaticism and disruption, half a movement for long-overdue attention to internal reform and development. The resources of the borderland

37 Phila. *Press*, November 28, 1859; Chicago *Tribune*, November 19, 1859.
38 Quoted in *National Intelligencer*, August 24, 1859.

were wasting away while men quarrelled over slavery instead of planning more railways, more canals, better seaports and river ports, a fairer tax system, and free public schools. As historic friends of internal improvements and business enterprise, the old-time Whigs could best take up the demand for new attitudes. This rebirth of the opposition in the upper slave States began with the Lecompton schism. The hope for some effective Southern front against the triumphant Democrats, slight just after the election of 1856, had revived when the Democrats quarrelled and the Administration became demoralized. A strong body of Southern Whigs and Know-Nothings disapproved of the attempt to force the Lecompton constitution on Kansas. The speech of Crittenden of Kentucky against it, and the still more spirited denunciation by Bell of Tennessee, terming it fraught with evils tending to the destruction of the Union, were lustily applauded.

Leaders began to confer and exchange letters. Nathan Sargent of Washington (remembered for his graphic memoirs of the long era from Monroe to Fillmore) and A. H. H. Stuart of Virginia (Fillmore's Secretary of the Interior, now a Know-Nothing member of the State Senate) were especially active in shaping plans for a new party—a conservative, national, Union-exalting party, which should thrust aside the slavery issue, denounce all secessionists, push a broad program of internal improvements, and on constructive grounds overthrow the Democrats. These two men talked or wrote to Bell, Crittenden, Washington Hunt, Tom Corwin, ex-Senator W. A. Graham and George E. Badger of North Carolina, and such former Representatives as Kenneth Rayner of North Carolina, Henry W. Hoffman of Maryland, and L. M. Kennett of Missouri. William C. Rives of Virginia, heartily sympathizing with the movement, used his pen to forward it.[39]

So rapidly did the project of an Opposition Party develop that, by the winter of 1858–59, an impressive group of leaders believed that they might combine the disjointed conservative elements of the nation, displace the Republicans as the chief anti-Democratic Party, head off the "radical" Seward, and elect a statesman of nationalist convictions.[40] Theirs must be a new party; it could not be the Republican Party reorganized, for the Republicans could hardly carry a Northern State *without* a slavery-containment plank, while the Opposition could not carry any border State *with* it.[41] In the closing days of 1858, representative Opposition men of thirteen States met, canvassed their prospects, and resolved to nominate a moderate Union leader in 1860.

39 A. C. Cole, *The Whig Party in the South,* 330 ff.; Rives Papers, 1859.
40 Nathan Sargent, October 31, 1858; Stuart Papers, LC.
41 George D. Prentice of Louisville wrote Orville Browning that the Southern Opposition could never support the Republican Party on a platform forbidding any further extension of slave territory. January 9, 1860; Browning Papers.

Many thought that if they held an early convention the Republicans would have to fall in behind them. Sargent was especially sanguine. Suppose we name Crittenden and Washington Hunt, or Edward Bates and Senator Solomon Foot of Vermont, he asked; what can the Republicans do but ratify the ticket? The early months of 1859 found the new gospel converting followers. In February, the State Council of Maryland Know-Nothings congratulated voters on the prospect for a union of all conservative elements, and called for a national Opposition convention in 1860. In March, the Whig General Committee of New York City applauded letters from William A. Graham and D. D. Barnard explaining the need for a great Opposition Party. A. H. H. Stuart was organizing Virginians, and proposing an Opposition newspaper of national range.[42]

In several States the crusade gained strength from a demand for internal reform and development. Virginians of the Shenandoah and the West still had serious grievances against the Tidewater. The State constitution, as revised in 1850, showed a decided favoritism to slaveholders, for it exempted from taxation all slaves under twelve, while upon others it placed an average valuation of $300 which was notoriously too low. Because of insufficient revenues, and the high cost of improvements which benefitted chiefly the Tidewater region, the State debt had reached a disturbing level. It was necessary to raise more money. Western Virginia wished the slaveholders taxed more heavily; the Tidewater discussed instead a tax upon wages and salaries—that is, upon free workers. Senator Hunter had just said that "the master at the South, who owns the labor, wields the power of the government, and does justice to all." To freemen of the western counties it seemed plain that while he did wield the rod of power, his justice was something less than even-handed.

In North Carolina the Opposition, with Rayner, Badger, and Graham as spokesmen, meanwhile declared for internal improvements, a better support of education, and—most appealing of all—a just system of State taxation. At last, many North Carolinians were awakening to a realization that the revenue system grossly favored the wealthy slaveholders. Negroes paid nothing but a poll tax, which varied from county to county but was always low. Land taxation, by contrast, might reach one percent of real value. In the Fayetteville area, land worth $2,400 was taxed $24, while two slaves worth that amount bore a burden of only $5.82. Inasmuch as the eastern part of the State contained a heavy majority of the Negroes, the issue aroused sharp sectional feeling. The Tidewater counties, protesting that they already paid two-thirds of the State levies, declared that if slaves were taxed by value, the burden would become intolerable. The western spokesmen, estimating that the three hundred thousand slaves were worth $600 on the average, or $180,000,000 in all, contended that

42 February 18, 1859, Stuart Papers, LC; *National Intelligencer*, March 17, 1859.

the chief slaveholding districts paid nothing like their due share. Newspapers on both sides of the *ad valorem* proposal mentioned Hinton Rowan Helper's suggestion that the slaveless majority in the South should tax Negroes to the point where they became unprofitable. Beyond question, a good many small farmers were growing restive and critical as they looked at their slaveholding neighbors. The system of representation, too, seemed unfair to the upland counties; it had a mixed foundation, resting upon taxation and Federal numbers, and a few hardy reformers proposed a pure white basis. The Democrats were for maintaining the existing socio-economic system, and the Opposition was hot to change it.[43]

In Kentucky, the Opposition held its convention in Louisville February 22, 1859, with the venerable Robert P. Letcher in the chair. Nominating candidates, it drew an indictment of the Democrats as essentially a disunion party, who embraced many avowed secessionists, and many of whose national leaders had threatened rebellion if Frémont were elected in 1856. Ample proof exists, declared the resolutions, of "the general diffusion of the disunion sentiment within the great body of the party at the South." A week later, the Tennessee Opposition met in Nashville. Ex-Governor Neil S. Brown presided and John Bell, who had just left the Senate, spoke. The ten-plank platform constituted an attempt to combine old Whig tenets with the more legitimate Know-Nothing doctrine. It called for stern maintenance of the Union; a tariff with specific duties wherever applicable, discriminating in favor of American industry; the acquisition of Cuba whenever this was consonant with national honor; a stiffening of the laws on naturalization and voting; and such a disposition of the public lands as would give Tennessee and other old States a proportionate share with the western States and Territories. This platform, on which John Netherland stood for governor, was widely published East and West.[44]

Meanwhile, in Virginia the Opposition under A. H. H. Stuart, John Minor Botts, and W. C. Rives was gathering its forces to defeat the radical Democrats under Henry A. Wise, Roger A. Pryor, James A. Seddon, and Edmund Ruffin. For several reasons the contest attracted national attention. It would indicate whether Virginia would favor extreme or moderate action in the Charleston convention, would show whether the Shenendoah-Western Virginia or Tidewater-Piedmont sections were likely to dominate the State, and would throw light on the question whether the proslavery pamphleteering of Ruffin and George Fitzhugh had affected public sentiment. The Opposition convention, held August 22 with Stuart in control, adopted resolutions which followed the principles of Clay and Webster. Calling for a revenue tariff with incidental

43 See Wilmington *Weekly Journal*, March–April, 1860; Fayetteville *Observer*, 1859–60.
44 *National Intelligencer*, March 15, April 5, 1859.

protection to industry, it assailed the Democratic Party for permitting factories and furnaces to close, crops to lie unsold, and labor to languish for want of action to stimulate manufactures and afford a home market for products of the farm. It declared against any disposition of the public lands not general in character and equal in benefits to all the States. It also demanded a livelier prosecution of internal improvements. Why should the trans-Allegheny region remain isolated from the rest of the State? Why should Norfolk not be made a port rivaling Baltimore and Philadelphia? The convention pronounced its inflexible antagonism to the reopening of the slave trade. Attacking the Democratic Party for measures which had irritated sectional feeling, it appealed for an end to the whole dolorous slavery quarrel.[45]

The leaders of this Opposition movement were men of character and some intellectual eminence. Crittenden, a veteran champion of conservatism and the Union, was beloved wherever known. His repugnance to the slave-trade and slave-code demands was shared by most Kentuckians. Bell's retirement from the Senate had been widely deplored as removing a pillar of moderation. A wealthy slaveholder, a loyal Tennesseean whose life paralleled the history of the State, this old-time Jacksonian turned Whig had always detested extremists both North and South. He had never failed to fight for his convictions. In Tyler's Cabinet he had opposed a spoils appointment so implacably that the President, giving way, had remarked: "Bell, I know you are honest, but I think you are obstinate." Combating Douglas's Nebraska bill as the violation of a compact to which Southern honor had been pledged, he had predicted with prophetic force the calamities flowing from its passage. He had assailed Lecompton in defiance of instructions from the Tennessee legislature. His final Senate speech, opposing Buchanan's Cuban scheme, showed all his grasp and prudent outlook, many deeming it the best argument made on the subject. Stuart, too, was a leader of principle; and John Minor Botts had been a rugged fighter ever since 1836, when, a young Congressman from the Richmond district, he had supported J. Q. Adams in battling against the gag rule. Later he had denounced the annexation of Texas.

It was not true that, as many Southerners said, Crittenden, Bell, and Stuart were harlotting with the Republicans. It was not true that, as the Nashville *Union* bitterly alleged, many leaders of the border Opposition had a positive dislike for their proslavery brethren of the South, and that the Kentucky and Tennessee elections would decide whether the Opposition in these States could move forward to a coalition with the Republicans in 1860.[46] Actually, the

45 C. H. Ambler, *Sectionalism in Virginia*, Ch. 10; H. T. Shanks, *Sectionalist Movement in Virginia*, Chs. 3, 4; Richmond *Whig*, July–September, 1859.
46 Nashville *Union*, July 31, 1859.

marshals of the Opposition hoped to found a party midway between Republicans and Southern Democrats.

Their object was to force an abandonment of extreme proslavery or antislavery positions in national affairs. They did believe, however, that a multitude of conservative Republicans, Democrats, and Know-Nothings might throng to this bright new standard. Even in the Deep South not a few men cried them Godspeed. In Alabama, for example, James H. Clanton of Montgomery, an attorney, legislator, and militia officer, sprung from a wealthy planting family and sometimes called the Chevalier Bayard of his State, took precisely the Opposition point of view. Like John Forsyth of the Mobile *Register*, he constantly denounced secession, but unlike Forsyth, he had no antagonism to protective tariffs, internal improvements, and centralization of power. In due course he was to become an elector on the Bell-Everett ticket. The Selma *Reporter* called for an Opposition convention. In Louisiana, fourteen members of the legislature signed an appeal in March for a revival of the Whig Party on the principles of Clay.[47]

Moderation made the Opposition a powerful aggregate in Kentucky, Tennessee, North Carolina, and Virginia. Moderation made Edward Bates an imposing figure in Missouri, the St. Louis *Evening News* declaring him its candidate for the Presidency (with Crittenden or Everett second choice), and the St. Louis *Democrat* asserting that he and Bell alone of the Southern Opposition could be elected. Moderation led the Virginia Democracy to select John Letcher for governor who, a dozen years earlier, had expressed strong views on the evils of slavery. Moderation inspired Senator Green of Missouri, wrung by the quarrel within the Democratic ranks, to propose a plan for uniting the Buchanan and Douglas wings: Douglas to be reinstated in the party, all discussion of intervention or non-intervention in the Territories to be dropped, and Kansas to be admitted by the next Congress. That a decided majority of the American people wanted such compromises and adjustments as would assure general peace, there could be no question.[48]

Naturally, Republicans of the radical type, believing in the milk of the word, denounced the movement for a union of the Northern and Southern Opposition. Bryant's *Evening Post*, declaring that the basic issue was slavery in the Territories and the basic tenet was antagonism to slavery extension, assailed the idea

47 William Garrett, *Reminiscences of Public Men in Alabama*, 632–645.
48 Bates, *Diary*, 41–45; Washington *States* quoted in *National Intelligencer*, May 12, 1859. Secretary Floyd recognized the strength of the moderates. "You have power in the South," he wrote Buchanan, September 5, 1859; "and this was never stronger than it is today. The efforts to form extreme parties even this summer have signally failed. Nothing could be more pitiable than the abortive efforts of Governor Adams on the slave trade question. . . . So too with a movement gotten up for the peaceful colonization of Sonora, a sort of varioloid form of filibustering." Buchanan Papers.

of any fusion. Who would dilute our tonic medicine to dishwater, it demanded? Naturally, the few true-blue Know-Nothings left were sceptical. The New York *Express*, their chief eastern organ, thought that the slightest aroma of Republicanism would kill Bell, Bates, Botts, and their friends in the South. It was evident that, as the Know-Nothing organization continued to disintegrate, many slave State members—including half a dozen Congressmen—were joining the Democratic ranks. But commercial elements were catching at the new hope. The Philadelphia *North American*, a mercantile journal, recommended that Republicans, Whigs, and Know-Nothings, uniting in a spirit of forbearance, frown down the men who wished to prescribe rigid platform tests.

[IV]

The October elections in 1859, watched with interest as forecasting the trends in 1860, had two spectacular results. They were another stinging repudiation of the Administration, suggesting that the people were disgusted with President, Cabinet, and policy. They were also a demonstration of the strength of conservatism, North and South.

The Republicans carried Ohio by seventeen thousand majority, taking control of both branches of the legislature. The Democrats had known they were beaten before they began. Senator Pugh had disgustedly written in the spring that his own county, which once gave the party forty-five hundred votes above all opponents, was going the way of Berks in Pennsylvania: "Buchanan has lost, for us, these famous strongholds which the enemy was never able to storm—to what taunts is he not entitled?" [49] In Iowa, the Republicans carried the governorship, legislature, and other offices. They swept Minnesota, electing both Representatives and making sure of a Senator in place of Shields. Their most telling triumph, however, was in Pennsylvania. Here a coalition which was predominantly Republican, though it included Know-Nothings and anti-Lecompton Democrats, won Philadelphia, Pittsburgh, and most other cities, seized the legislature, and piled up a majority of nearly eighteen thousand in the State. So much for Buchanan's dream of winning Pennsylvania on the Dred Scott issue! In New Jersey, the Democratic candidate for governor was defeated.

These elections meant that the Republicans in the Senate would be strengthened by James W. Grimes, Salmon P. Chase, and M. S. Wilkinson, shortly sent thither by Iowa, Ohio, and Minnesota. They meant more Republican governors controlling the State Houses in the critical days to come. Above all, they meant that the party possessed a bright opportunity in the campaign

49 June 5, 1859; C. C. Clay Papers, LC.

of 1860. The national platform was largely written this year in various State platforms. In Minnesota, for example, the Republicans declared against any expansion of slavery into the Territories, and any reopening of the slave trade, denounced the Administration for the defeat of the Homestead bill, called for efficient national aid to a Pacific railroad, and favored rivers and harbors improvement. In Pennsylvania, the coalition emphasized the tariff so heavily that such newspapers as the New York *Herald* and *Journal of Commerce* traced its victory to that demand. Though this interpretation was challenged by the *Tribune*, which pointed out that the Wilmot-Grow district, never much interested in the tariff, had been swept from its old Democratic moorings, Greeley too declared the tariff a potent factor. The Republican Party had numbers, it had the spirit of victory, and it had appealing new doctrines.

Upon the question whether the Republican gains were a blow to Douglas, opinion was much divided. His friends of the New York *Times* put the best face upon the situation by contending that as the Democrats could not win in 1860 without Pennsylvania, Ohio, and Illinois, and that as Douglas alone could reverse the tide in these and other Northern States, his nomination was therefore imperative. But could even he change the current? In Iowa, Minnesota, and Ohio, the Democrats had stood squarely upon a popular sovereignty platform, striving to cast off the dead weight of Buchanan's unpopularity— and yet they had met defeat. Both Southern Democrats and Republicans asserted that Douglas had been repudiated in his own section. "The truth is," remarked the Warsaw (Illinois) *Bulletin*, "all this talk about Douglas's popularity in the West and Northwest is sheer gammon, and the result of the elections proves it most conclusively." [50] Judicious observers might conclude that internecine war had almost fatally weakened the Democratic Party, that only a restoration of unity under Douglas's leadership could save the critical Northern States, and that the march of freesoil Democrats into the Republican Party was so strong that even the Little Giant would have to fight his hardest battle to hold the Northwest.

In parts of the cotton kingdom the current of intransigence flowed strong. The Democrats carried Mississippi three to one, doubled their majority of two years earlier in Georgia, and swept Florida. This area was becoming a one-party region. Yet, taking the slaveholding States as a whole, the surprising fact was the strength of the conservatives.

A strong Opposition showing had been foreshadowed by the early election in Virginia. John Letcher's nomination by the Democrats was itself a victory for moderation, bitterly disappointing Wise and his radicals. The Opposition Party named for governor a Tidewater man, W. L. Goggin, who had opposed

50 Warsaw *Bulletin*, October 17; Washington *Constitution*, October 19, 1859.

the admission of Texas, supported the Compromise of 1850, and aligned himself since with Stuart and Botts. By a close vote Letcher won, losing every Congressional district but two east of the Blue Ridge and carrying all but one west of it.

No doubt could exist that despite a recent recantation of his criticisms of slavery, he owed his margin to his refusal to extol the institution or support its extension and to his fervent attachment to the Union. While antagonists accused him of warring on the foundation interests of the State and trying to abolitionize western Virginia, the Wheeling *Intelligencer* denied that slavery was a foundation and appealed to the white workingmen and farmers of the uplands to reject such an assumption. The geographical cleavage in the election foreshadowed the future partition of the State. A victory for Goggin himself, popular in the slaveholding counties, would not have been a more emphatic rebuke to the fire-eaters. The Richmond *Whig* pointed out that after nominating a man of former freesoil views, strong in freesoil districts, the Democratic Party had won by a margin of only 5,570 as against Buchanan's majority of nearly 26,000, three years earlier.[51]

The election of Alexander R. Boteler to Congress especially heartened the Virginia Opposition. The scion of an aristocratic family which owned "Fountain Rock" at Shepherdstown, a graduate of Princeton, united by marriage with the Stocktons of New Jersey, he had moved from the Whigs through the Know-Nothings into the Opposition. His success gave the Union an eloquent defender, destined to make for it within two years what S. S. Cox pronounced one of the two most eloquent speeches ever delivered in Congress.[52] The journalist "Porte Crayon" (D. H. Strother), a son of the district, congratulated him on overthrowing a despicable regime, while William C. Rives was delighted at the prospect of having a sterling old-time Whig in Washington to maintain communications between the Virginia Opposition and their brethren in other sections. If the moderates of the border kept their ranks firm, and if the Opposition in the North showed a true national spirit, prophesied Rives, Virginia might well be won back to her ancient principles in 1860.[53]

In Kentucky and Tennessee, the Opposition made an equally impressive showing. Sensible men in these States realized that if secession precipitated war, the border would find brother fighting brother, and would be trampled under contending armies. Though the Democrats elected Beriah Magoffin (himself a moderate man) governor of Kentucky with 76,187 votes, the Opposition nominee, Joshua F. Bell, was close behind him with 67,271. In Tennessee, a

51 Ambler, Ch. 10; Shanks, Ch. 4.
52 S. S. Cox, *Three Decades*, 93.
53 Rives, June 4, D. H. Strother, June 15, 1859; Boteler Papers, Duke Univ.

radical proslavery Democrat, Isham Harris, ran against the Opposition leader, John Netherland. Here the result was still closer; Harris polled just over 76,000 votes, Netherland just over 68,000. Between them, Kentucky and Tennessee elected eleven (some said twelve) Opposition Congressmen. At least two of them, Francis Bristow and Emerson Etheridge, both former Whigs, were men of ability. The party did particularly well in Tennessee, where it chose seven out of the ten members of Congress; and jubilee meetings in Nashville and Memphis celebrated the result. John Bell's star rose higher than ever.[54]

While the New Orleans district elected a Know-Nothing of staunch Unionist views, John Edward Bouligny, to Congress, and the Opposition polled a respectable vote elsewhere in Louisiana, in Texas the moderates swept the board. With State officers and two Representatives to be elected, the Democrats were soundly trounced. Sam Houston, running for governor as an Independent Democrat, defeated the regular party nominee, 33,335 to 27,500. One of the Congressional seats went to A. J. Hamilton, another Independent Democrat of rigid Union views. The regular Democrat, John H. Reagan, was reelected in the first district after proclaiming his unflinching enmity to all proslavery extremists. He denounced filibustering. He attacked the slave-trade proposals. He called the disunionists of the Lower South wanton troublemakers. They ranted about the evils of Northern aggression and the violations of the Fugitive Slave Law, he said, ignoring the fact that it was the border States alone which really suffered. Yet from Maryland to Missouri the border people, proud and courageous as they were, opposed disunion, filibustering, and the foreign slave trade, and labored for peace and concord. "These facts show that it is for revolution and conquest, and not merely for the resistance of Northern aggression, that our agitators are at work." He would labor staunchly for the preservation of Southern rights. "But I will not advocate a destruction of our government as a matter of policy, or those revolutionary measures, based upon crime, which look to such a result. It is time that we should all see where we are drifting, to what the times are tending, and determine whether we are ready for revolution, with all its attendant insecurities to life and property, and with all its hazards to civil and religious liberty." [55]

Altogether, the Opposition vote in the border region, the Southwest, and

54 Election figures from N. Y. *Tribune Political Textbook for 1860.* The Washington *Union* (August 11, 1859) viewed the Tennessee battle as John Bell's fight. "Whatever influences large wealth, high social distinction, extensive and powerful political and family connections, elevated personal character, and the *prestige* of associations in public life with the most illustrious statesmen whom this country has produced, could exert in favor of a presidential candidate, have been thoroughly employed for many months for the purpose of carrying the State for the opposition."

55 J. H. Reagan, "Address to the Voters of the First Congressional District."

parts of the Lower South showed an impressive antagonism to extremist ideas.[56] It was obvious that the Republican victories in the Northwest and Pennsylvania were attributable to the revolt of freesoil Democrats against Buchanan and the appeal of new economic ideas. At least three-quarters of the nation opposed radical proslavery or antislavery ideas. Only in a few States of New England had abolitionist principles taken deep hold, and only in a few States of the cotton kingdom could State Rights extremists claim a majority. If the Opposition Party was given effective organization and leadership, it might play a decisive role in the coming campaign. Douglas, as reported by Nathan Sargent, told Democratic friends that if moderate voters united on Bates, he would defeat any man the other parties put into the field. As yet, Bates, Bell, Stuart, and Sargent had ground for hoping to capture the whole moderate wing of the Republicans. They were encouraged by such Republicans as two former Congressmen, S. F. Vinton of Ohio and S. A. Purviance of Pennsylvania.[57] As yet, Pugh, Green, and other Democrats had grounds for hoping to effect a reunion in their party.

Much depended on unforeseeable events. It was a time for generosity. If some national leader suddenly caught men's imaginations as Clay had known how to do! If some bright act lifted men's gaze above that sullen abstraction of slavery in the Territories! Then the crisis of 1860 might be passed. If, on the contrary, the nation's luck was bad, if ill-temper exploded into violence, then all hopes might be dashed.

[V]

Violence was an American tradition. In mid-October the country was startled by news that, for the first time in its history, a Senator had been slain in a duel. The victim was one of Douglas's ablest lieutenants, David C. Broderick.

California had just witnessed a campaign of alarming bitterness, the most passionate ever known on the Pacific Coast. Broderick was leader of the popular sovereignty Democrats, and Gwin of the Administration forces. Dozens of orators stumped the land from the Sierra to the sea. The two antagonists stooped to savage recriminations. On September 7 the election brought more than a hundred thousand voters to the polls. The Administration Democrats won, but by a closer margin than they liked. Broderick still had four years to serve in the Senate, and his abilities and prestige were both growing. His enemies

---

56 In Alabama, according to the Mobile *Daily Advertiser*, good leadership might have made a strong battle. If the Opposition had fought on old Whig principles, it might have carried Mobile, while in Montgomery an excellent chance for victory "was literally thrown away—sacrificed at the shrine of ultraism."

57 Nathan Sargent, February 18, 27, August 28, 1859; Stuart Papers, LC.

marked him for destruction. David S. Terry, a hot-tempered man of Southern origin, challenged the Senator to a duel; they met before a crowd of spectators; and Broderick fell, mortally wounded. California and the Douglas forces were deprived of a talented, aggressive leader. As a free State, California should have stood with the Northwest, but now she would send delegates to Charleston to support a proslavery candidate on a slave-code platform. "They have killed me," Broderick gasped on his deathbed, "because I was opposed to the extension of slavery and a corrupt Administration." [58]

Would further acts of violence occur? Would some unforeseen accident interrupt the growing movement for moderation and reconciliation? "Nobody who has watched history in the making," wrote Harold Nicolson after the second World War, "can doubt the immense part played in human affairs by the element of chance." America was a land of the unexpected, and the situation was one in which some blind stroke of fate, falling on excited nerves, might have malign consequences.

For the moment, in the autumn of 1859, the state of the country seemed fairly serene. Crops were excellent; wheat, corn, and cotton were bringing high prices; and business continued to improve. The iron mills were finding Western and Southern customers as railroad-building revived. On August 30, Edwin F. Drake struck oil at Titusville, and the ensuing rush to Pennsylvania's fields of black gold gave instant vigor to the petroleum industry. Businessmen everywhere were laying plans which assumed a peaceful national future. Nobody anticipated that a catastrophic lightning bolt might fall upon the land.

One of the most energetic of these businessmen, as we have seen, was John W. Garrett of the Baltimore & Ohio, planning an integrated trunk line from the Atlantic to St. Louis and extending the use of sleeping cars and other innovations. October 17, 1859, found him and other officers busy with their usual tasks. A telegram, filed at Monocacy at 7:05 A.M., brought them news which some at first thought incredible. It came from a conductor:

"Express train bound east under my charge was stopped this morning at Harper's Ferry by armed abolitionists. They have possession of the bridge and of the arms and armory of the United States. Myself and baggagemaster have been fired at. . . . They say they have come to free the slaves, and intend to do so at all hazards." [59]

58 Jeremiah Lynch, *A Senator of the Fifties*, 199-226; A. E. Wagstaff, *David S. Terry*, *passim*; N. Y. *Weekly Tribune*, October 15, 1859. Terry had previously wounded a vigilante agent (1856) with a bowie knife. Later he entered the Confederate army and fought bravely. In 1889, assaulting Justice Field of the Federal Supreme Court, he was shot dead by Field's bodyguard. Quite a chapter in American morals and manners is bound up in his career.

59 Edward Hungerford, *Story of the Baltimore and Ohio RR.*, I, 332-336.

3

John Brown at Harper's Ferry

WORDS MAY excite mankind, but it is the violent act which raises emotions to fever heat. Newspaper polemics and party broadsides can never crystallize popular sentiment like a dramatic blow—the Boston massacre, the destruction of the *Maine*, the sinking of the *Lusitania*. In both the North and South by 1859, feeling was deeply stirred, nerves were tense, and anger lay near the surface. Any sudden clash—the quick frenzy of some street mob, or a new Brooks-Sumner affair in Congress—might fall on latent passions like a spark on tinder. What would kindle Northern emotions most quickly? The slaying of some devoted man in an effort to liberate a slave. What would enrage the South to an implacable temper? Any attempt to foment, arm, and support a slave insurrection, with its peril to property, wives, children, and the entire social fabric for whose safety many Southerners felt a sharp and sleepless apprehension.

[I]

From Maryland Heights, just north of Harper's Ferry, a strikingly beautiful landscape extended to the south and west. Jefferson, in his *Notes on Virginia*, had called it "stupendous," adding: "This scene is worth a voyage across the Atlantic." In the foreground flowed the silvery Potomac, studded by islets, its high banks green in summer with foliage, its current rippling and boiling as it poured southeastward through its cleft in the Blue Ridge. It was flanked by a canal along which, now and then, lazily passed a horse-drawn barge. Here was the river highway which Washington had dreamed of making a link between the Atlantic and the Ohio-Mississippi system. Looking across it to the southward, an observer on the Heights could see the narrower Shenandoah winding through its rich valley to join the Potomac. The two streams enclosed a high, narrow neck of land, a hill or bluff, its sides washed by the converging waters, its crest dotted with houses, and the brief stretch of level ground at its toe occupied by a village and some workshops. The village was Harper's Ferry. The substantial shops, looking like factories, were the Federal armory for arms

70

manufacture, the arsenal for housing military stores, and, some distance away, the rifle works. Among them they usually employed several hundred hands and could fabricate ten thousand stand of arms a year.

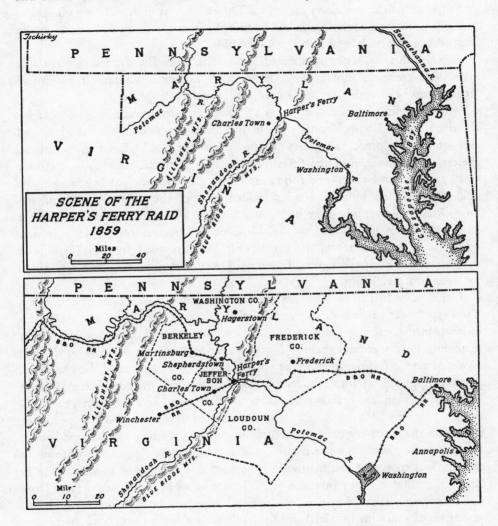

At this point, the Baltimore & Ohio Railroad crossed the Potomac on a bridge about nine hundred feet in length, a sturdy structure supported by five heavy piers and covered by a strong wooden roof. The glistening tracks of a little branch railroad led up the Shenandoah Valley to Winchester. Harper's Ferry was only about eighty miles from Baltimore by rail, and a little less than sixty miles from Washington by turnpike, but its mountain setting gave it an air of remoteness. The village itself, with its railway offices, hotels, stores, cheap eating-houses, frame cottages, and gaunt national shops, was not attractive. All the buildings lined two confluent streets, Potomac Street beside one river and Shenandoah Street along the other. The effect was drab and straggling. But the village seemed negligible in the beautiful panorama of swift streams, white sand-spits and islands, and richly wooded hills.

To this district, a chosen base of operations, John Brown, two sons, and a friend had come on July 3, 1859, the taciturn leader calling himself Smith and letting men believe that he was a land-seeker and cattle-buyer.[1]

After a brief search, he had rented a rough two-story farmhouse owned by the heirs of Dr. Booth Kennedy about five miles from town on the Maryland side of the Potomac, a rickety cabin across the road affording additional shelter. Here the men of the little force he had recruited trickled in, until by early fall he had twenty-one followers in all. Of his principal lieutenants, the able, high-minded John H. Kagi remained most of the summer in Chambersburg, Pennsylvania, where he had useful tasks to perform; the reckless former dragoon, Aaron D. Stevens, who had killed a Missouri farmer in a former raid, was at the farmhouse; and the boyish, loose-tongued John E. Cook took up quarters in Harper's Ferry. The sons, Owen and Oliver, were soon joined by their brother, Watson.

Great pains had to be taken, as the band increased, to keep them concealed. Two quick-witted girls of Brown's family, his daughter Anne and daughter-in-law Martha, each in her seventeenth year, arrived to keep house and divert suspicion. Both were delightfully ingenuous and observant. Anne, who showed a vein of poetic feeling, later wrote appealing sketches of some of the company, notably Kagi, whose idealistic temper pleased her, and the adolescent William Thompson, with his yellow hair, innocent blue eyes, and diffident yet affectionate manner. "My evenings," she recorded, "were spent on the porch or sitting on the stairs *watching*, and listening to the katydids and whippoorwills. I used to enjoy watching the fireflies, and looking at the lights and shadows on the fine old trees and the mountain ridges on fine moonlight nights." Late in September, fifteen heavy boxes of "tools" were brought down to the farm from Chambersburg, containing one hundred and ninety-eight Sharps rifles with appurtenances, and nine hundred and fifty pikes. As the men occupied themselves studying tactics under Stevens upstairs, browning the rifle barrels, making belts and pistol holsters, playing checkers, reading the Baltimore *Sun* and a thumbed copy of Paine's *Age of Reason*, and arguing, the girls mounted sentinel. If a

1 Brown, wiry and alert as ever, had grown a long beard, largely because his quarrel with Forbes and the approach of his scheme to its climax made a disguise desirable. See pencil note by R. J. Hinton in G. W. Brown's *Reminiscences of Old John Brown*, Hinton Papers.

caller approached at mealtime, he was detained outside until the men, seizing dishes, food, and tablecloth, could vanish upstairs.[2]

The fierce-eyed, iron-jawed chieftain, adjuring everyone to constant caution and vigilance, awaited the best hour to strike. When he arrived, he had almost completely matured his plan. It was not what many writers have stated. He did *not* intend to make a sudden raid and then retreat to some mountain bastion. He meant by a sudden blow to take Harper's Ferry, thus (as his daughter put it) striking terror to the slaveholders about; to send agents among the surrounding plantations, rallying the slaves; to hold the town for at least a short time, expecting as many helpers, white and black, from the district as assailants; to prepare for rapid movement *southward*; and, as he moved, to continue sending out armed bands to free more slaves, secure provisions and hostages, and destroy slaveholding morale. He would follow the Appalachians into Tennessee and even Alabama, the heart of the South, making forays into the plains on either side. He had told Forbes that on the first night of the stroke he thought he might get from two to five hundred Negro adherents. As for the militia and regular army, he contemptuously judged them by the specimens he had seen in Kansas. His daughter writes that he deemed them "an inefficient lot." A crazy plan? At any rate, he believed in it intensely. An Ohio friend had expostulated with him in 1858:

He replied that with a hundred men he could free Kansas and Missouri too, and could march them to Washington and turn the President and Cabinet out of doors. . . . He seemed unable to think of anything else or talk of anything else. This affiant attempted to quiet him and get him into conversation upon other matters, but without success. The Kansas difficulties, the death of his son, and slavery were the only things of which he could be induced to speak. His whole manner and conversation was that of a monomaniac, and upon matters in regard to which he held the conversation, this affiant regarded him as altogether insane; such was his opinion at the time.[3]

News of his proposed attempt to deal a bloody stroke at some Southern community and set a slave revolt ablaze was being awaited with varying degrees of knowledge by his abolitionist backers: Gerrit Smith, George L. Stearns, Theodore Parker, Frank B. Sanborn, Thomas Wentworth Higginson, S. G. Howe, Frederick Douglass, and others. Visiting New England in May, Brown had held frequent meetings with the secret conspiratorial committee; had spoken again in Concord Town House, where he impressed Bronson Alcott and Rockwood Hoar as well as Emerson; and had received a little more than $4,000, of which Sanborn says that at least $3,800 was given with a clear understanding of its

2 Undated MS, Hinton Papers; Warren, *John Brown*, 323-325.
3 James W. Weld, Richfield, Ohio, undated affidavit of 1859; Villard Papers, Columbia Univ. See also Realf's testimony, *Mason Committee Report*, 96 ff.

future use. Indeed, he intimated frankly to all his intention of levying a blow for freedom, running off as many slaves as he could, and making slavery insecure. Higginson and Douglass knew that he intended to strike at Harper's Ferry.[4]

Servile insurrection, armed strife, wide and continued bloodshed—these were inherent elements of Brown's wild scheme, and he and his fellow-conspirators of the North knew it. In an effort to delude others (and perhaps himself) he had tried to confuse the issue. He had said that his well-controlled blow would *forestall* an inevitable, uncontrollable, and horribly vengeful revolt in the future. He had also told Higginson that he would not foment a slave rebellion at all, but merely get together families and bands of fugitives who would then defend themselves. This was a distinction without a difference. Any widespread attempt by slaves to escape would be insurrection, would be treated by masters and government as such, and would involve fierce combat. What Brown called defensive warfare by slave bands would be called offensive warfare by all Southern whites. According to his follower Realf, Brown spoke of killing no slaveholder, and yet in the same breath talked of fighting off individual opponents, militia, and the Federal army—which meant general killing. It was not for nothing that he had given careful study to the tactics of Toussaint l'Ouverture and Garibaldi. If Gerrit Smith, Sanborn, and the rest did not comprehend that his enterprise would bring on an implacable conflict and a heavy effusion of blood, they were much less acute men than the world esteemed them. The greater Brown's success, the bloodier would be the fighting of whites and blacks, raiders and troops.

The fact was that Higginson and some others actually wanted civil war, and hoped that Brown's raid would precipitate it. For a clergyman, young Higginson had a bloodthirsty mind; for while visiting Kansas in the spring of 1856 he had approved of the killings on the Pottawatomie, and he now avowed himself ready to see slavery extinguished in gore. Brown had told Gerrit Smith, Sanborn, and Higginson how many weapons he had and how he meant to use them. He had written Sanborn: "I expect to effect a mighty conquest, even though it be like the last victory of Samson." Of the conspirators, Parker, Stearns, and Howe knew less about the details of the scheme, and Parker, mortally stricken, had departed for Europe. They were aware, however, that he planned shortly to launch his great scheme of slave-liberation.

For the selection of Harper's Ferry as the point of attack, Brown alone was responsible. He had hesitated as to the place of his stroke, for a time believing that it should be in the Deep South—Anne Brown says that he mentioned Baton Rouge. But he had rejected this idea on grounds of humanity, believing

---

4 Sanborn, *John Brown*, 423; Alcott, *Journals*, May 8, 1859.
5 Sanborn, *Recollections*, I, 150; Higginson, *Cheerful Yesterdays*, 207.

that the "ferocity" of the slaves in the Lower South might prompt them to a wholesale massacre. His notion of the fierce rebelliousness of slaves in the cotton kingdom had been derived from abolitionist publications. Moreover, Harper's Ferry seemed a better point in that he hoped for helpers from Pennsylvania and western Maryland and Virginia. Frederick Douglass had vehemently protested against the choice on strategic grounds, declaring that the town would prove a perfect trap where concentrating forces would swiftly recover the arsenal, cut off the raiders, and kill or capture them. But Brown was immovable.

Members of the attacking party expressed similar fears when Brown first explained the plan to them after they had gathered at the Kennedy farmhouse. Until then, they had believed that he intended merely to repeat on a more ambitious scale the slave-running coup executed in Missouri the previous year. Hearing the leader announce that they were to take the town, garrison the arsenal, armory, and rifle works, and hold them, the men were aghast. A majority, including Brown's three sons, protested that failure was inevitable. The dispute grew heated. "In September it nearly broke up the camp," Charles P. Tidd, a Maine lad who had shared in the Missouri raid, later testified. But the sanguine Cook, busy familiarizing himself with the town, supported the plan; Kagi accepted it, believing they would get out of the pent-up village before troops could be mobilized; and Stevens acquiesced. When Brown told the men that since a majority opposed him he would resign and they could choose another leader, this ultimatum brought them to his side. Several, however, believed they were going to certain death—and one described his own end.[6]

John Brown's whole course showed that, despite statements made by some biographers, he had given up the idea of a swift retreat to some mountain fortress. In the first place, no impregnable eyries, no deep hidden fastnesses, exist anywhere near Harper's Ferry. The district bounded by Winchester, Hagerstown, Frederick, and Fairfax is everywhere passable; it contains no steep cliffs, no chasms, no swamps, no unknown caverns; troops could move through it at will. During the Civil War they did quarter it in every direction, and stormed Maryland Heights opposite the Ferry with ease. Three expert topographical engineers, writing a dozen years later of the mountainous country of Maryland between the Potomac and Pennsylvania, stated that it, "so far from being wild and uninhabitable, contains some of the finest roads and most desirable farms in the State, much of the region being characterized by hills of moderate height whose rounded summits are covered with verdure." The two Virginia and two Maryland counties which environ Harper's Ferry were a rich grain country with

6 Higginson, *op. cit.,* 228, 229; Hinton, *John Brown,* 258, 259; Sanborn, *Recollections,* I, 182–184; letter by Charlestown, Virginia, correspondent in N. Y. *Weekly Tribune,* November 12, 1859.

a combined population in 1860 of one hundred twelve thousand, three hundred people. No real hiding places were available.[7]

In the second place, Brown never even made a reconnaissance of the surrounding country to familiarize himself with hidden paths and spots of refuge. He knew the road north to Chambersburg, and that was about all. And thirdly, he made no effort in advance to stock or fortify any hill area. To retreat to the Allegheny ridge, some twenty-five miles to the west, without food and water, would have been madness. Any leader contemplating a stand in some recess there would have made a cache of arms and provisions. It is significant that, just before his attack, Brown moved his main stock of weapons—to what point? Not to the hills, but to a schoolhouse about a mile from the Ferry.

Obviously, this military tyro believed that he could hold Harper's Ferry for some time. He expected to be successful in gaining widespread support, and to push forward down the Appalachian chain. If by any chance he was unsuccessful, he might retreat northward into Pennsylvania.

Two factors gave him a certain amount of confidence. He knew upper Maryland and Virginia to be full of people who disliked slavery, the citizens who later held Maryland firm in the Union and who detached West Virginia as a new State; and he believed many would flock to his aid. He was deceived by his Kansas experience into thinking that any border country was a region of sharp antagonism between slaveholding and freesoil elements. At an early date he had taken some steps to inform himself about the antislavery families of Bedford, Chambersburg, Gettysburg, and Carlisle in Pennsylvania, of the Hagerstown district in Maryland, and of the Martinsburg area in Virginia. As the second factor, he believed great numbers of slaves would flock to him. Here he was deceived by abolitionist literature, which represented the negroes as a highly intelligent body, chafing under their yoke and eager to rise. He knew that the lonely Allegheny chain was a favorite route for escaping slaves, much used by the intrepid underground leaders of rescue work. He knew that in Jamaica and Guiana runaway blacks, the Maroons, had maintained impregnable settlements in upland valleys and plateaus not for decades but for generations, treating with the Crown officers as an independent power. Abolitionist literature was full of accounts of these heroic Maroons.[8]

Once established in Harper's Ferry, he thought he could arm a large number of white and colored recruits from the arsenal. He could destroy or barricade

7 S. J. Martenet, H. F. Walling, and O. W. Gray, *New Topographical Atlas of the State of Maryland and District of Columbia* (1873), 5 ff.

8 See letter of Anne Brown (Adams), May 23, 1893, to Hinton; Hinton Papers. Brown's instructions for collecting data on antislavery families are in his letter of April 8, 1858, to his son John; Brown Papers, Ohio Arch. and Hist. Soc. For articles on the Maroons see Henry Brougham, *Edinburgh Review*, II, 376 ff., and T. W. Higginson, *Atlantic*, V, 213 ff., 549 ff.

the two bridges; taking hostages, he could use them in negotiating with attackers, and when ready, he could move forward. He later told one of the prisoners he took just why he chose Harper's Ferry: "I knew there were a great many guns there that would be of service to me, and if I could conquer Virginia, the balance of the Southern States would nearly conquer themselves, there being such a large number of slaves in them." One of his men, Jeremiah Anderson, wrote a brother late in September that they expected to win a victory at Harper's Ferry and push through Virginia and on southward, inciting the slaves to rise and carrying them forward in a growing body. When himself captured, Brown told Governor Wise that he had expected ample assistance once he put the ball in motion. From what States? asked Wise. "From more than you'd believe if I should name them all," replied Brown, "but I *expected* more from Virginia, Tennessee, and the Carolinas than from any others." [9]

Here, perhaps, lay the paranoiac flaw in John Brown's mind, the key to his type of reasoning insanity. On all subjects but one—slavery and the possibility of ending it by a sudden stroke which would provoke a broadening wave of slave uprisings as a rock thrown into a pond sends forth widening ripples—he was sane. (An admirer was later to call him the stone tossed by God into the black pool of slavery.) He talked and acted with great coherence and even acuteness; he laid ordinary plans rationally; he maintained his domination over his followers, and was later to impress Governor Wise as exceptionally clear-headed and logical. But on this special question of the readiness of slavery to crumble at a blow, his monomania, as Amos A. Lawrence termed it, or his paranoia, as a modern alienist would define it, rendered him irresponsible. This it was that made him seem to some observers increasingly speculative and impulsive, a gambler on chance; from this paranoia, too, sprang his sense of a God-given mission, in which Providence would carry him to success even through seeming failure. When his confident blow met a sharp check, he was certain to grow confused. Hence the conclusion of his ablest biographer that he seemed to be losing the power of quick, effective decisions.[10]

That his fanaticism and violence of speech on slavery had increased is unquestionable. Speaking in Kansas the previous March, he declared that his son had been shot down like a dog for no reason save that he was a free State man. The killing of Frederick Brown was certainly murder but it had not been without provocation, for he had helped to slay the five men on the Pottawatomie, and he was tending stolen horses when he was assassinated. Brown had boasted to his Cleveland audience how he had taught his young men to dispatch adherents

9 *Mason Report*, 1–12; Sanborn, *Recollections*, I, 184, 185.
10 Villard, *John Brown*, 424. Brown's Negro follower Osborne P. Anderson writes in *A Voice From Harper's Ferry*, 36, of the raid: "Capt. Brown was all activity, though I could not help thinking that at times he appeared somewhat puzzled."

of slavery, and had said that, if necessary, he would execute more of them; he would drive them into the ground like fence stakes, where they would remain permanent settlers. He felt that he was *at war* with slaveholders, and that his private war justified shootings and confiscations. To his recent Missouri raid he pinned an exaggerated significance. The fact that it had spread alarm far and wide, had sent some slaveowners fleeing into Arkansas and had led others to mount a close guard, convinced him that a stroke in some more strategic quarter might bring slavery down in ruins. He had forgotten how glad free State men were to see him leave, and how quickly peace had descended upon the Kansas-Missouri border as soon as he departed.

Not a figure out of Cromwell's time, as some have said, a warped religious fanatic; not one of the old Puritans or Covenanters, ready to harry for conscience's sake and to hold with Clarendon's hero that stone dead hath no brother. Let us say rather that he had the strength and weakness, the sincerity and cunning, of a gnarled Western pioneer who through inheritance and prolonged hardship had fallen prey to reasoning insanity. Such a man was certain to move forward relentlessly.

As September ended, the two young women went home. A late recruit arrived, F. J. Meriam of Boston, whose gift of $600 in gold to the treasury ended all financial embarrassments. The last arms were fetched in. On October 10, Kagi quitted Chambersburg for the farm. All was in readiness.

[II]

About eight o'clock on the night of Sunday, October 16, Brown ordered his troop to march upon the Ferry. Two by two, armed with a Sharps rifle and two revolvers apiece, seventeen men swung down the lonely road, while Brown himself drove a one-horse wagon with some pikes, a crowbar, and a sledge hammer. Three men were left at the farm. The moonless gloom, the chill damp air, the sombre silence of the column, broken only by the creaking of the vehicle and the rustle of dead leaves and grass underfoot, gave some of the marchers a funeral impression. As they came within sight of the town lights, nerves grew tauter. Cook and Tidd turned aside to cut the telegraph wires; the others pushed on.[11]

With a brisk rush, the force deployed across the railroad-and-wagon bridge,

11 Had Secretary of War Floyd exercised due vigilance the march would never have begun. On August 25, he had received an anonymous letter of warning dated Cincinnati, August 20, saying that Brown would invade Virginia at Harper's Ferry in a few weeks. Text of letter in *Mason Report*, 250. Its author was David J. Gue, who had received secret information; Gue, *History of Iowa*, II, 26–30. Floyd dismissed it as a hoax. The night of the attack was overcast, ending in rain. Anderson (*A Voice from Harper's Ferry*, 28 ff.) says the company "marched along as solemnly as a funeral procession."

seized the bridge watchman, and left two men as guards. The end of the Shenandoah bridge was similarly secured, and two sentinels were posted. Turning up Potomac Street, the force pinioned the watchman at the armory gate and quickly took possession of both armory and arsenal. Brown and others then hurried to the rifle works, half a mile up the Shenandoah, took possession, and placed Kagi and two privates in charge. Here another watchman was captured.

All the Federal property, including several million dollars' worth of arms and munitions, was now in John Brown's hands. His next step was to send a detachment of six men about five miles into Virginia to seize as his first hostage Colonel Lewis W. Washington, great-grandnephew of the President and a prosperous planter. That gentleman was forced to surrender a sword which Frederick the Great had reputedly given to General Washington, his carriage, wagon, and horses were taken, and four of his bewildered slaves were collected. Another farmer, John H. Allstadt, his son, and six of his Negroes were similarly aroused from sleep. The whole body were brought down to the arsenal, where the slaves were given pikes and told to guard Washington and the Allstadts. Telegraph wires had now been cut both east and west of town.

At about one o'clock in the morning, the express train from Wheeling to Baltimore arrived at Harper's Ferry, stopped, and was ready to proceed across the bridge when Conductor Phelps learned that the track was obstructed. The engineer and another employee walked forward to investigate, were fired upon, and hastily backed the train to the platform again. At this point the first bloodshed occurred. Hayward Shepherd, a free Negro working as station baggage master, went to the bridge to look for the night watchman there, was fatally wounded by Brown's men, and was carried inside the station to die. The shots, the long delay of the puffing train, the hum of the bewildered passengers (who guessed some labor trouble was afoot), the noise of the Washington-Allstadt cavalcade, and the unusual bustle about the arsenal, attracted attention. Citizens began to stir, and as dawn broke, one of them, Thomas Boerley, was also fatally shot. A number of employees, innocently entering the armory yard for the day's work, were added to the list of prisoners.

Meanwhile, John Brown was waiting for Negro and white recruits to pour in; "when I strike the bees will swarm," he had told Douglass, and Cook had given him misleading assurances of a rising. Slaves from the Maryland side were supposed to report to Owen Brown at the schoolhouse and take arms there; slaves from the Virginia side were to report to Oliver Brown at the Shenandoah bridge and Kagi at the rifle works, receiving arms from the arsenal. Had the bees swarmed, had a large-scale insurrection begun, Brown expected to establish a commanding position at the armory, holding both ends of the Potomac and Shenandoah bridges; to parley with any assailants, demanding an exchange of slaves for his hostages; and as he gained force, to go on. Only if an overwhelming force came up would he retreat northward. But he had done nothing to prepare defenses out of town, and the rapidity with which troops arrived left him utterly nonplussed.

For as day broke cold and gray, the alarm was spreading swiftly. A slow-witted physician of the town, brought out by the shot that wounded Shepherd, first attended the dying man and then waited till dawn to act. But he finally saddled a horse, roused the outlying parts of Harper's Ferry, set the Lutheran churchbell clanging, hurried a messenger to Shepherdstown, and himself rode with all speed to Charlestown. On the alarm of this tardy Paul Revere, the Jefferson Guards of Charlestown fell hastily into line with any weapons they could pick up. Meanwhile, before five o'clock that morning Brown had foolishly let the Baltimore express push on. It quickly carried news of the raid to Monocacy. Thence word was hurried to Frederick, where shouting men by about ten o'clock mustered a volunteer company into line. Farmers from all the surrounding area caught up firearms and clattered toward the Ferry. In Baltimore, the telegram which the train conductor sent from Monocacy was at first treated with incredulity. When in midmorning Garrett saw it, however, he immediately notified President Buchanan, Governor Wise, and the commander of the Maryland militia that a slave revolt, with whites assisting, was under way.

Before eleven o'clock, general firing began at Harper's Ferry, townsmen and farmers engaging the raiders. Noon saw the Jefferson Guards seizing the Potomac bridge, while a swiftly mustered volunteer company from Charlestown, accoutered with muskets, shotguns, and squirrel rifles, occupied the heights back of the Ferry, and swept down from them to capture the Shenandoah bridge. The celerity with which these farmers and villagers moved was as creditable as the skill with which they seized the key points. Brown was now trapped.

Seeing that his position was hopeless, he determined to negotiate a truce. But the first man he sent out for the purpose was taken prisoner, held for a time at the Galt House, and soon afterwards killed by the excited mob. A little later, Watson Brown and Stevens were sent out under a flag, but were promptly fired upon; Watson dragged himself back to shelter mortally wounded, while Stevens, also hurt, was taken prisoner. Early in the afternoon the rifle works on the Shenandoah were stormed by a small party. Of the little garrison, the brilliant Kagi was killed, another man mortally wounded, and the third seized.

All that day and night the alarm spread through Maryland, northern Virginia, and the District of Columbia. In Baltimore, a half-dozen militia companies were ordered under arms. A special train was assembled, thousands poured to the Camden Station, and in midafternoon it pulled out amid deafening cheers of the populace. Along the line of the B. & O., crowds were gathering to hear the news. In Martinsburg, a company formed chiefly of railway employees was hurriedly mustered. It reached Harper's Ferry about four o'clock, just after the beloved mayor of that town, Fontaine Beckham, had been killed by one of Brown's men. Deploying through the armory yard from the rear, it drove the remaining raiders, with a handful of prisoners, into the small fire-engine house. Forces from Sheperdstown were at that moment arriving on the Shenandoah side of Harper's Ferry to join the Charlestown men on the bridge. Other companies were on their way from Frederick and Winchester. As night fell, the arriving troops thronged the town. John E. Cook, of the small rear guard of raiders left in Maryland, looking down from a hilltop, saw John Brown's party closely beleaguered and under constant fire. Summoned to surrender, the bewildered and desperate Brown offered to liberate his hostages if he were allowed to escape across the Potomac bridge, but these terms were of course rejected.[12]

While the Maryland and Virginia militia thus sprang to arms, Federal troops were on their way. Nowhere was the excitement that Monday afternoon greater than in Washington. The mayor put the whole police force on duty, stationed guards on every road into the capital, and conferred with citizens who thronged his office. Before one-thirty, President Buchanan ordered three companies of artillery from Old Point Comfort to the scene of action, and then directed the ninety-odd marines at Washington Barracks to move. Garrett, learning of these measures, told the White House they were inadequate, for his information indicated that seven hundred determined whites and Negroes held the arsenal. First reports in Baltimore had put the insurrectionists at several hundred, who were gaining reinforcements from the surrounding district, and rumor magnified the figures. The President, duly impressed, held a hurried conference with Secretary Floyd, Brevet-Colonel Robert E. Lee of the Second Cavalry, and Lieutenant J. E. B. Stuart of the First Cavalry. These officers were instructed to proceed at once to Harper's Ferry, where Lee would take command. Late that night they reached the town, took charge of the newly arrived company of marines, and deployed them to strengthen the militia surrounding the engine house. Lee would have attacked at once but for fear of killing some of the hostages.

Headlines were blazing that night throughout the East. "Negro Insurrection at Harper's Ferry!" ran the typical caption. As yet the outside world did not know the identity of the leader. No dispatch published on Monday in Washington, Baltimore, or New York bore Brown's name. Instead, one Anderson or Andrews, a gray-bearded stranger, was reported in charge. Not until evening

12 This account is based on the books of Villard, Hinton, Sanborn, H. P. Wilson and R. P. Warren on John Brown; on reports in the Baltimore *Sun*, N. Y. *Herald* and *Tribune*, and Washington *Constitution;* on the *Mason Report;* and on statements by J. T. Allstadt and others in Villard Papers, Columbia Univ.

did Harper's Ferry dispatches reveal that the raiders had rendezvoused at a farm rented by Captain Brown of Kansas notoriety, and thus make it possible to spread his name in Tuesday's journals.[13]

Brown's losses during the day had been severe. His sons Oliver and Watson had been mortally wounded. The reckless ex-dragoon, A. D. Stevens, had been wounded and captured, "Captain" W. H. Leeman had been slain, and others killed or taken. The free Negro, Dangerfield Newby, had been the first of the raiders to die. He had a greater object in fighting than anyone else, for his wife and seven children were in bondage in Virginia, and feared sale farther south. "Oh, Dear Dangerfield," his wife had written, "come this fall without fail, money or no money I want to see you so much: that is one bright hope I have before me." Shot twice, he expired instantly. Cook and the rear guard, including Owen Brown, had gotten away—at least for the time being.[14]

Inside the engine house that night, pitch dark and intensely cold, Oliver Brown died in great agony; a young Canadian, Stewart Taylor, lay dead; and Watson Brown drew his last heavy breaths. Three unwounded raiders with their leader and eleven prisoners watched the hours drag by. The gaunt, haggard old man, exhausted by a day of fighting without a morsel of food, fingered the sword which the Prussian monarch had given Washington, the mocking symbol of a very different attempt at revolution. He listened impassively to the clank of arms outside. He bade Oliver to bear up and to die like a man. This long vigil in the gloomy building with its three great barred doors, the forces of the land gathering for his doom, was the Gethsemane of Brown's life. Small wonder that, momentarily giving way, he essayed a few words of lame self-justification to his hostages. "Gentlemen," he said, "if you knew of my past history you would not blame me for being here. I went to Kansas a peaceable man, and the pro-slavery people from Kentucky and Virginia hunted me down like a wolf. I lost one of my sons there." It was the last time in his life that he would take an unheroic attitude.

Lee had resolved to carry the engine house at dawn at the point of the bayonet, not firing lest he injure the hostages. At five o'clock on Tuesday morning, chill and misty, all the military companies were ordered under arms, an imposing display. The soldiers cleared spectators from the streets surrounding the government buildings, and the ninety-odd marines, who had encircled the engine house all night, were drawn up inside the arsenal enclosure. Storming parties, armed with heavy sledges, were formed. The engine house, perhaps thirty-five feet in length and thirty in depth, was a heavy brick structure with

13 Baltimore *Sun*, Washington *States*, N. Y. *Times, Herald, Tribune*, October 17, 18, 19, 1859.
14 Villard, *John Brown*, 415.

three large double doors in front, each of strong oak planking, girt with iron and studded with nails. Arched windows high above the doors afforded light but no means of ingress. Brown had barricaded and loopholed the doors, inside one of which stood a fire engine. As the sun rose, Lee beckoned Jeb Stuart to his side. A son of the Shenandoah, a West Pointer, this tall, bearded young man, not yet twenty-seven, was already an experienced Indian fighter. He was to take a note, said Lee, to the raiders. If they came out and surrendered, they would be protected from harm and handed over to the proper legal authorities. If they refused, the marines would come in and take them. Stuart was to demand an answer, yes or no; he was not to parley; if it was no, he was to leap aside, and the two storming parties, twenty-four of the biggest, strongest leathernecks at hand, would charge at a run.[15]

A moment later Stuart was at the right-hand door. It opened a crack, and the white beard and fierce troubled eyes of John Brown (whom he recognized from Kansas days) appeared. Reading the note deliberately, Brown began to talk; he would surrender only on terms that would allow his party a safe head start from pursuers. One of the men inside and perhaps others wished to give up, while several prisoners begged for Lee to parley. But cutting Brown short, Jeb Stuart leaped from the door and gave the signal by waving his cap.

Instantly the storming parties sprang forward, some men battering at the doors with sledges while others pried at them with hammers. The little garrison inside fired with carbines, the smoke wreathing through loopholes and cracks. Seeing that hammers were useless, Lieutenant Israel Green ordered a double file to attack with a heavy ladder. A few powerful efforts shattered the right-hand door at the bottom, the planks buckling upward. As the troops and spectators raised a wild yell, Green threw himself through the opening, and with marines at his heels rushed inside. Colonel Washington coolly pointed to Brown, who knelt firing, and said, "This is Ossawatomie." Two marines fell, one shot through the body and the other in the face. A general melee followed. One raider was pinned to the wall by a bayonet, and another, cowering under a fire engine, was run through; both were mortally wounded. Green aimed a blow at Brown with his light dress sword which did little harm. Then, plunging, he almost lifted him from the floor by a savage thrust which failed, as his weapon struck a belt or buckle and bent double. As the leader fell, Green beat him with the hilt until he sank unconscious. A minute later, the dead and wounded were all lying on the grass outside, while Lee gave orders for their attendance.

Within thirty-six hours after it commenced, Brown's attempt to detonate a slave revolt, enlist and arm a force of colored men, and establish a base to which hundreds of adherents could flock, had been utterly defeated. Ten of his crew

15 John W. Thomason, Jr., *Jeb Stuart*, 47–57.

had been killed or fatally injured, five were prisoners, and the others had escaped, some temporarily, some for good. He himself, less seriously hurt than was at first believed, was lodged in Charlestown jail, whither Governor Wise and others repaired to interrogate him. He had only himself to blame for the swift debacle. He had made no thorough plan of action, had hesitated at the crucial moment, and had miscalculated the time required to mobilize a sufficient force to pin him down.

In any event, however, his rash scheme would quickly have failed. One historian has suggested that he might have fared better in an area containing more slaves. This is erroneous, for in any Southern district the whites would have risen with instant power, while the blacks would have been both unwilling and unable to aid him. Another has written that if after taking the arsenal he had fled to the mountains, he could have placed his force in a position where starvation alone could have conquered them.[16] The quick efficiency of the marines shows that this is a wild overstatement. Though he could have resisted longer, his men would have been dislodged by mortar and bayonet within a few days; no mountains near Harper's Ferry were wild enough to afford safety, and the larger the body of slaves in his train the greater would have been his vulnerability —for the slaves had to be fed, and they were too ignorant and undisciplined to make fighters. Ignorant of military science, he had never learned that guerrilla bands succeed only with the help of mobility, celerity, compact unity, surprise, and numerous fit hiding places or strong points.

Is it not evident that he knew he would probably fail, but that his very failure would deepen the antislavery sentiment of the North as no success could? He had written of dying for the cause, and had told Sanborn that God had honored him with a chance for mighty and soul-satisfying rewards.[17] This much is certain: he believed that his attempt, victorious or defeated, would bring the struggle over slavery to a crisis. It would test the ripeness of the slaves for rebellion; it would show the South that at least a few Northerners were ready to die in striking at the institution; it would give antislavery men everywhere an example of desperate action. It would thus succeed even while failing. In so far as he grasped these ideas, Brown was making no mad attempt. He was quick to see the possibilities opening from Lieutenant Green's failure to kill him on the spot. Dying on the scaffold, in full national view, he would meet the end of a martyr. Except in the one respect in which systematized delusion flawed his mind, he retained a piercing vision; the foresight of a man "cool, collected, and indomitable," as Governor Wise of Virginia was soon to write.

16 Allen Johnson, *DAB*, III, 133, 134; Channing, *United States*, VI, 222.
17 Sanborn, *Recollections*, I, 150. Brown had often said to his men: "We have only one life to live, and one to die; and if we lose our lives it will perhaps do more for the cause than our lives would be worth in any other way." Owen Brown, quoted in Sanborn, 183.

[III]

The excitement and anger of the South were proportionate to its belief that many Northerners thirsted for an uprising of the slaves. Exaggerated reports of the power and ramifications of the conspiracy filled the press. Having accepted the early stories of an attack by hundreds of armed men, Virginians and Marylanders clung to an exaggerated notion of the outbreak. While Lee immediately withdrew his marines, the surrounding region remained in a state of deep apprehension. Many feared that a force of Yankee invaders—from Pennsylvania, from Ohio, from other points—was about to rescue Brown. Rumors flew about of confederate bands and clandestine shipments of arms. While citizens improvised local defense companies, scouts were sent into the mountains to hunt escaped raiders and look for other troublemakers. Strangers were eyed with suspicion and sometimes arrested. Farther South, men looked to their arms, tightened the slave patrols, and drilled the militia companies. On large plantations the discipline became stricter. The raid of twenty-two men on one Virginia town had sent a spasm of uneasiness, resentment, and precautionary zeal from the Potomac to the Gulf.

Although this alarm was largely irrational, it was not wholly so. It is true that slaves about Harper's Ferry showed no disposition to accept Brown's invitation to revolt, and that many negroes felt the warmest loyalty to their masters. *Harper's Weekly* spread on its front page a sentimental picture of a Southern planter arming his slaves to resist invasion. The Civil War was to show that amid the stress of battle slave risings were almost unknown, and practically no violence was offered the white folk by their dependents. But the South believed it was living on volcanic soil—and in one sense it was right. We cannot too often repeat that slavery was not only a labor system but a mode of racial adjustment; that the Southern majority had resolved to freeze this adjustment as it stood; and that countless Negroes secretly opposed this determination. Should news of a Northern attempt at slave liberation be diffused by the efficient grapevine telegraph, it might have a profoundly disturbing effect. Slaves might feel little impulse to rebel; they *would* feel disposed to question their status. They would feel the emotions of a prisoner who, half-resigned to his walls, suddenly catches the faint sound of men battering on the outer gates. Since the news of Brown's raid could not be stifled, it had to be met by disciplinary measures.[18]

18 Evidence of widespread restlessness among slaves in 1856, verging on revolt, is abundant. The Northern and Southern press printed numerous stories on the upheaval. Robert Bunch, British consul in Charleston, wrote in December that plans had been discovered for a great slave insurrection, with Nashville as headquarters, embracing Kentucky, Tennessee, Louisiana, and Georgia. To prevent alarm and avoid unfriendly Northern comment, Southern news-

From the hour of the raid, the South denounced it as not merely a crime involving robbery, murder, and treason, but a fearful effort to cut the ligaments of society in fifteen sovereign States.[19] Much of the North viewed it very differently. It was a crime, assuredly—but a crime with extenuating circumstances, committed by a man holding a noble purpose. A hundred journals agreed with Bryant's *Evening Post* that Brown had been driven to madness by the outrages of proslavery men on the soil of Kansas. A hundred others agreed with the New York *Tribune* that he and his men "dared and died for what they felt to be right, though in a manner which seems to us fatally wrong."

Inevitably, the trial of Brown and his associates commanded the eager attention of the whole nation, and gave him an opportunity to arouse the sympathy of millions by a display of heroic firmness and devoted self-sacrifice. From the first, he acted in the knowledge that he stood upon a great stage. Not once did he exhibit any weakness. He was questioned by bystanders when first laid on the lawn in front of the engine house; questioned again in the paymaster's office by Governor Wise, Senator J. M. Mason, Representative Vallandigham of Ohio, Jeb Stuart, and others; questioned once more at a preliminary examination in the magistrate's court of Charlestown on October 25; and then, after being indicted on the triple charge of conspiracy with Negroes to produce insurrection, murder, and treason to the Commonwealth, was brought to trial in the Circuit Court of Virginia.[20] His statements showed general consistency (we cannot be sure that apparent inconsistencies are not attributable to bad reporting) and unbroken composure.

All his words breathed conviction that whatever he had done to free slaves was right, that he deserved credit for the humane treatment of townsmen and hostages, and that he should be given the respect due a prisoner of war. At the same time, he displayed a basic confusion as to his central object. His first utterances when taken doubtless contained less rationalization of his course than those made later. To Governor Wise, Representative Vallandigham, and others

---

papers had said little, but Bunch learned that many Negroes had been executed and several whites arrested. The consul in Richmond, G. P. R. James, sent word of the same movement. He believed that it was vague and disjointed but general, extending from Delaware to Texas, and that its wide diffusion and the implication of some whites indicated a Northern origin. He, too, heard that many Negroes had been executed, and one white man had been flogged to death. Foreign Office dispatches, November, December, 1856, January, 1857.

19 Yet many Southerners found their condemnation tinged with another feeling. Edmund Ruffin wrote of Brown on October 26: "It is impossible for me not to respect his thorough devotion to his bad cause, and the undaunted courage with which he has sustained it, through all losses and hazards." MS Diary.

20 The Virginia law of treason covered the levying of war against the State, the giving of comfort to its enemies, and the establishment of any other government within its bounds, the punishment being death.

he said that he did not intend to excite a slave revolt, but did intend to gather up large bodies of slaves and set them free; he did not intend to fight, burn, or destroy, but did intend to fight off resisting Southerners. As if this did not mean insurrection and bloody warfare! He let out one statement that frankly implied his expectation of a widespread servile rebellion—his before-quoted remark to Wise that if he could conquer Virginia, the other States "would nearly conquer themselves, there being such a large number of slaves in them."

Judge Richard Parker, presiding over the Charlestown courtroom in which Brown's trial began on October 25, combined dignity with a judicial spirit. Two capable attorneys were assigned to defend the prisoner, and others came from the North to assist them. From first to last, Brown had five different lawyers at his command. Order was strictly preserved—the courthouse yard bristled with bayonets. Though Brown, who at first seemed weak and haggard, complaining that his wounds enfeebled him and impaired his hearing, asked for a brief delay, the court ordered the case to proceed forthwith. On the second day, one of the defending counsel read a letter from a citizen of Akron, stating that Brown and his family had lived in that county for years, that insanity was hereditary in their line, that his mother's sister had died insane, and that two nephews and a niece of his mother were at that moment under restraint. The raider, while admitting that his mother's family was tainted with insanity, was incensed. Raising himself from the cot on which he lay, he told the court that he regarded the move as a miserable artifice on the part of friends who ought to treat him as responsible for his actions. He believed himself of perfectly sound mind—and the court dropped the matter.

The seven-day trial, moving with efficient speed, brought out much interesting testimony. Colonel Washington declared that although Brown had complained of the mortal wounding of his son Watson under a flag of truce, he had made no threats to the prisoners and uttered no vindictive word. Another prisoner, J. A. Brua, said that once only during the night vigil had Brown seemed to show temper. Allstadt described the listlessness and indifference of the Negroes, passive pawns in the game played for their future. He believed that in the final struggle it was Brown's shot which had killed a marine, while Lieutenant Green thought that this bullet had gone wild.[21] Conductor Phelps of the midnight express train and Armistead Ball, master machinist at the arsenal, testified that the leader had told them that his object was to free slaves and destroy slavery, not to hurt the whites. According to Ball, Brown had spoken of his determination to seize the arms and munitions of the government to enable the negroes to defend themselves against their masters, and had called on the officers

21 Full testimony on this point in N. Y. *Weekly Tribune*, November 5, 1859.

of the armory to give up their stored weapons. A. M. Kitzmiller, in charge of the arsenal when it was attacked, heard the raider say that his object was to free the slaves and, if necessary, fight the proslavery men for that purpose.

From this and other evidence it was plain that Brown had been both deluded and confused. He had clung to the delusion that large numbers of slaves would peacefully flock to his standard, that many antislavery whites in western Maryland and Virginia would come to his aid, and that Southerners would let themselves be kept at bay by his imposing force and by fears for the safety of his hostages. He had held the confused idea that war is not war when waged against a bad institution, that an attack is not an attack when called a defensive action, and that wholesale slave liberation could be distinguished from wholesale slave insurrection. On slavery his mind was distorted. Yet throughout the trial he gave every impression of composure, shrewdness, and balance. Lying wrapped in a blanket, his eyes often closed, from time to time he started up, grim as a cornered wolf, to snap out a sharp question or deliver a curt, dry speech. He never lost his coolness, never offered an apology, and was defiant only when deeply aroused, manifesting in general a civil, courteous demeanor. When questioned he spoke frankly, and when granted small favors expressed his gratitude.[22] He interrupted the proceedings several times, but only to speak to important points. Given the unusual privilege of helping cross-examine witnesses, he used it sagaciously.

No one could deny that the prisoner received a thoroughly fair trial. Of the three Northern counsel, George H. Hoyt of Athol, Massachusetts, who arrived the third day, took the leading place. When defense attorneys moved that the prosecution be confined to one of the three counts, Judge Parker's adverse ruling was in accordance with legal procedure, and was later upheld by the Virginia Court of Appeals. On the murder charge, Brown's counsel tried to show that he had been free from malice aforethought and had killed only in self-defense. On the treason charge, they argued that since he had never sworn allegiance to the Commonwealth of Virginia, he could not be held guilty of treasonable action. On the charge of fomenting insurrection, they declared that he had merely abducted slaves, a very different matter. Of the two prosecuting attorneys, only one counted. Andrew Hunter, an able, aggressive Virginian of distinguished bearing, pushed his case with relentless energy, fighting for every possible advantage. Sharing the exasperation of the Southern people, he called for justice at double-quick time, expressed fear that the prisoner Aaron Stevens, who had suffered terrible wounds, might die before he could be hanged, and was disappointed at the end when the case had to be continued over Sunday.

22 *Harper's Weekly*, November 12, 1859.

Before pronouncing judgment on November 2, Judge Parker (the jury having held Brown guilty on all three counts) asked the prisoner if he had anything to say. This was Brown's culminating opportunity. He had seized every chance of protesting that he had merely done the will of God, obeying the Biblical injunction to remember them that are in bonds as bound with them. Now, rising slowly and speaking with distinct utterance, he addressed himself not so much to the court as to a vast unseen audience beyond. In a five-minute discourse he made a truly noble statement:

I see a book kissed, which I suppose to be the Bible, or at least the New Testament, which teaches me that all things whatsoever that men should do to me, I should do even so to them. . . . I endeavored to act up to that instruction. I say I am yet too young to understand that God is any respecter of persons. I believe that to have interfered as I have done, as I have always freely admitted I have done, in behalf of his despised poor, I did no wrong, but right. Now, if it is deemed necessary that I should forfeit my life for the furtherance of the ends of justice, and mingle my blood further with the blood of my children and with the blood of millions in this slave country whose rights are disregarded by wicked, cruel, and unjust enactments, I say, let it be done.

He also made three statements as to his purposes: that he had intended only to carry slaves off to Canada, that he had not designed any slave insurrection or bloodshed, and that he had never tried to induce men to join him, merely accepting them as volunteers.

Millions in the North took these words at their face value. Emerson was later to compare Brown's speech with Lincoln's Gettysburg Address. A modern biographer has asserted that it must forever remain on the list of great American utterances.[23] The fact was, however, that all three statements contravened the truth. Brown had not intended quietly to push north with a small group of slaves; he had intended to induce large bodies of slaves to join him, to arm them, to push south, to organize them into a state, if possible, and to make this state impregnable. His constitution for his proposed state of liberated slaves could not be explained away. His Missouri raid had not been bloodless, for one man had been slain; and this Virginia undertaking was not simply a larger raid for spiriting slaves northward—it was an entirely different kind of enterprise. Had he intended to repeat his Missouri venture he would have fled with his handful of captured slaves at dawn on Monday. Finally, his assertion that all his men had joined of their own accord was false. He had recruited most of them with various inducements, among them the chance of station and rewards in his provi-

23 Emerson, *Works* (Concord ed.), VIII, 125. Emerson's two addresses on Brown are more admirable as expressions of his idealism than as accurate essays. Calling Brown the founder of liberty in Kansas, he contributed mightily to the legend of the man. Villard's statement (*John Brown,* 497) is more just. Brown's parting words will be remembered along with Vanzetti's, and for much the same reasons.

sional government; he had led them (largely impulsive, pliable young fellows) from step to step; and he had finally precipitated them into criminal acts from which they would originally have shrunk.[24]

The full measure of Brown's distortion of truth can be illustrated by comparing his courtroom appeal with what he had privately told Frederick Douglass early in 1858. He denounced slavery "in look and language fierce and bitter," writes Douglass; he "thought that slaveholders had forfeited the right to live"; he believed that neither moral suasion nor political action would ever abolish the system. While he did not wish an insurrection, "his plan did contemplate the creating of an armed force, which should act in the very heart of the South." He was "not averse to the shedding of blood"; he thought that the practice of carrying arms would give colored people a sense of their manhood; they must "fight for their freedom" in order to gain self-respect. When Douglass suggested that the slaveholders might be converted, he angrily replied that these proud folk "would never be induced to give up their slaves, until they felt a big stick about their heads." Nearly three weeks after his courtroom statement, he wrote a letter to the public prosecutor to explain the discrepancy between a statement he had made in the paymaster's office that he did not intend to carry off slaves and free them, and his subsequent statement that his whole object was to carry off slaves. The latter assertion was true, he wrote, but required more explanation. He meant to place the slaves in a condition to defend their liberties, if they would, but not to run them out of the slave States. That is, he meant to carry them into his new state. But this brings us back again to the fact that what Brown called defensive fighting would have seemed to any slaveholding community an aggressive operation; and that to organize liberated slaves in some grand defensive body was essentially to take them out of the slave States.

John Brown, no doubt partly self-deluded, was striking the pose of a blameless as well as heroic figure for the benefit of his unseen audience of Northern millions. If he could not be the Spartacus of a new freedmen's state, he could be the martyred Stephen of a new gospel. Given a month in prison between sentence and execution, he made the most of it in eloquent letters and interviews. He *was* heroic—but not blameless.

24 Brown contradicted himself on several points in his last weeks. He insisted that he did not value the armory weapons, having plenty of his own. But Armistead Ball, master machinist at the Ferry, and one of Brown's prisoners, testified that Brown had said he was determined to seize the arms of the government to enable the slaves to defend themselves, and had called on him and others to deliver up the government stores. At his first examination Brown was asked respecting the slaves: "Your intention was to carry them off and free them?" He replied: "Not at all." Later he insisted that he *did* mean to carry them off. As a commentary on his statement that his followers had come to him voluntarily, see his daughter Anne's admission: "Father had hard work to induce a few men who did follow him to go there." Undated MS. Hinton Papers. But of the man's fundamental sincerity in wishing to help the poor and oppressed there is no question whatever.

[IV]

Was putting him to death expedient? Reflective men, North and South, saw that the consequences of making him a martyr might be highly unfortunate for the Union. Numerous letters fell upon Governor Wise's desk begging him on humanitarian grounds to spare Brown's life, and with them came many which urged him to deny the abolitionists any opportunity to canonize a saint. Amos A. Lawrence, who now repented the aid he had given Brown, advised the governor to deal leniently with the man. "From his blood would spring an army of martyrs, all eager to die in the cause of human liberty." Following the trial, Lawrence wrote "Governor" Robinson of Kansas: "If they hang old Brown, Virginia will be a free State sooner than they expect." [25] Mayor Fernando Wood of New York informed Wise that his firmness was highly applauded. "Now, my friend, dare you do a bold thing, and 'temper justice with mercy'? Have you nerve enough to send Brown to the State Prison instead of hanging him? Brown is looked upon here as the mere crazy or foolhardy emissary of other men. Circumstances create a sympathy for him even with the most ultra friends of the South."

Many antislavery leaders, contrariwise, were eager for a scaffold scene which they could exploit with revivalist fervor. While the trial proceeded, Henry Ward Beecher admonished his flock not to pray for Brown's release. "Let Virginia make him a martyr. . . . His soul was noble; his work miserable. But a cord and gibbet would redeem all that, and round up Brown's failure with a heroic success." [26]

Quite aware of the perils of the situation, knowing as well as anybody that "glorious is the martyr's gore," Wise also knew that he could assign plausible grounds for his staying a death sentence in the evidence of Brown's dementia. The traits the leader exhibited at the trial—his intense egotism, his belief in his providential mission, his display of a persecution complex when he denounced his Virginia attorneys, his distortions of fact—pointed to the "monomania," the reasoning insanity, of which various observers had accused him. His behavior in Kansas pointed as strongly to an irrational element in his nature. Amos Lawrence gave the governor his emphatic conviction: "Brown is a Puritan whose mind has become disordered by hardship and illness." John Brown's brother, Jeremiah, certified in writing that after talking with John about two years earlier, "I had no doubt he had become insane upon the subject of slavery, and gave him to understand this was my opinion of him." Jeremiah had such

25 William Lawrence, *Amos A. Lawrence*, 134, 135.
26 Warren, *John Brown*, 415-417.

"knowledge of him, when once intensely absorbed in any one subject," as made him sure that the Harper's Ferry raid was an insane act. We have spoken of the similar affidavits by reputable, informed people, chiefly relatives and former neighbors. Brown's attorney, Hoyt, collected no fewer than nineteen.[27]

But Virginia paid the penalty in this hour for having elected a hopelessly erratic governor. Most States now and then put men devoid of judgment into their gubernatorial chairs; but they seldom suffer as the Old Dominion was to do from its error in electing the learned, the patrician, the eloquent, and the brilliant fool (a man, writes Forney, who "rioted in the eccentricity of his genius") now directing her affairs. Wise's folly combined with Brown's mania to make the raid a great turning point in American history. On one side, he magnified the event to whip up excitement all over the South, firing men's fears and tempers. On the other, he insisted upon an execution which gave the North an antislavery martyr.[28]

Wise, believing it just possible that 1860 might see him elected President, did his utmost to dramatize both the raid and his own dauntless resourcefulness in meeting it. He helped give currency to alarmist reports of fresh Northern invasions. He repeatedly mobilized bodies of militia, marching and counter-marching troops to sustain the excitement. He did everything to foment a legend that the raid sprang from a portentous Northern conspiracy, probably with organized Republican support behind it, and offered a dire threat to the South. At the same time, he gave the Northern legend of martyrdom its opportunity to expand into a pillar of fire by night and of smoke by day. Confinement of Brown in an asylum for the criminal insane would have satisfied the demands of justice, protected public safety, and prevented any idealization of the man and his offense. Instead, Wise placed him on a pedestal for the ages.

The governor momentarily wavered. Eight days after sentence was pronounced he instructed Dr. Stribling, the expert superintendent of the State

27 Brown's attorney, Hoyt, visiting Washington, talked with Montgomery Blair, who told him that he thought Governor Wise would probably welcome a demonstration of Brown's insanity. An article which had appeared in the Richmond *Inquirer* looked to Blair like an inspired invitation for affidavits. At once Hoyt went on to Ohio to see what could be gathered up in the shape of statements. Blair was positive that Senator Mason and other fire-eaters would make every effort to use the affair to break up the Union, and was anxious to block their schemes. See letters of Hoyt November 14, 16, 1859, to J. W. L. Barnes, Hinton Papers.
28 One measure of Wise's folly is found in his statement of 1856 that, if Frémont were elected, he would arm and equip 50,000 men the next morning ready for revolution. L. G. Tyler, *Life and Times of the Tylers*, II, 523. Another is found in his belief that "a preparation of the Southern States in full panoply of arms," and "a prompt, bold, defiant, armed attitude," in 1860–61, "would have prevented war." Wise, *Seven Decades*, 250. Wise declared in his message to the legislature on December 5, 1859, that imprisonment would have been martyrdom no less than hanging; that Brown's state of health would have been heralded weekly from the jail, visitors would have come with affected reverence to see him, and the work of his hands would have been sought as holy relics. To this the answer, as Villard states (pp. 505, 506), is that prison rules could have been adopted to block publicity and visits.

lunatic asylum at Staunton, to examine Brown and report before the date of execution. Then, on reflection, he cancelled the order. For one reason, before Hoyt's affidavits reached him the Court of Appeals had confirmed the sentence, thus closing the door to a legal presentation of the plea of insanity. For another, Wise convinced himself that the prisoner was exceptionally quick, logical, composed, and shrewd mentally. "Did I believe him insane," the governor told a caller just before the execution, "if I could even entertain a rational doubt of his perfect sanity, I would stay his execution even at this hour. All Virginia should not prevent me. I would sooner sever this arm at the shoulder than permit his execution. But I have no such belief, no such doubt." It can be said that Wise did not have the benefit of modern knowledge of mental derangement. It can also be said that an important legal precedent would have supported him in refusing to treat Brown as insane. In 1843, the private secretary of Sir Robert Peel had been murdered by a paranoiac named McNaghten. The appeal judges, passing on McNaghten, made a famous deliverance in the House of Lords on criminal responsibility in this type of insanity. They held that since the man might be regarded as quite sane except on the subject of his "monomania," he should be held accountable for his acts. This was precisely the line Wise followed in deciding that Brown knew the quality of his acts and should therefore be hanged. Modern science, however, holds that the paranoiac is not partially but wholly insane and should be so treated. And on grounds of mere expediency, as the New York *Journal of Commerce* counselled, Wise should have seized the opportunity of depriving the antislavery fanatic of the martyrdom for which he longed.[29]

As John Bigelow wrote, it was much easier to put John Brown upon a scaffold than to get him down again.

[V]

The fact that skillful management by the Virginia authorities might have reduced John Brown's attempt to the level of a reckless, crazy adventure was demonstrated by the conduct of the Northern conspirators abetting him. Almost

---

29 One fiery Virginian, Roger A. Pryor, believed that imprisonment would have been the wiser course. Wise's statements show that he was not (as some have said) influenced by public clamor in his decision. Yet plenty of public clamor there was. "The miserable old traitor and murderer belongs to the gallows," declared the Richmond *Whig*. That Wise had no qualifications for passing on Brown's sanity is clear. Writes Dr. E. H. Williams in *The Doctor in Court*, p. 100: "Insanity is a complex disease, the most difficult of all diseases to understand; so much so that even a regular medical education simply lays foundation knowledge for special study of this condition. The amount of knowledge about it that any layman can acquire, even from the Bench, is limited." Yet Wise made his judgment on the basis of some brief conversations.

with one accord they broke for cover. The pusillanimous behavior of Samuel G. Howe, Gerrit Smith, and others placed them in lamentable contrast to the iron strength of their champion. They had hoped for some easy, resounding success; instead, when news came of the killing of innocent men, the seizure of Federal property, and the arming of slaves, all terminating in surrender, they realized that they faced hard penalties. The rich Gerrit Smith, enjoying the role of abolitionist so long as it meant simply the expenditure of money, time, and talk to gain applause, had never done anything that called for Garrisonian courage. Now, as clamor broke out in the press, he fell into a panic, hastily burned all letters bearing on Brown's plans, sent his son-in-law to Boston and Ohio to destroy evidence there, talked wildly of impending ruin, and suffered a physical and nervous collapse. He was well past sixty. Sleepless nights of excitement and fear culminated in temporary insanity. Five days after Brown's trial ended he was removed to the State asylum at Utica, where he stayed nearly two months. When discharged, he was too ill to appear before any investigating committee, but not to pour out lying denials of his connection with any conspiracy.[30]

The equally terror-stricken Howe fled to Canada, accompanied by the half-reluctant George Stearns. According to Mrs. Stearns, Howe was "possessed with a dread that threatened to overwhelm his reason"; he came to Stearns, declared he would go insane if they did not both go North at once, and persuaded his friend to take care of him. "How well do I remember his agitation, walking up and down the room," writes Mrs. Stearns, who calls her husband's consent an act of heroic self-abnegation.[31] Howe had given Brown a Smith & Wesson revolver to use in fighting.[32] Frank Sanborn heard with alarm that a number of his letters had been captured at the Kennedy farm. He instantly destroyed compromising papers, and picking up Stearns at Medford, drove into Boston to consult the abolitionist lawyer John A. Andrew. Andrew told them they might be suddenly arrested and extradited to Virginia. Late the next day Sanborn was in Quebec, where he stayed for a week. When he heard that Andrew had revised his opinion, and believed that if indicted he would be tried in Massachusetts, he returned to Concord—only to make a new flight to Canada some weeks later, when the United States Senate voted his arrest. By November 10, three weeks before the date set for the execution, he was urging that something be done (by other men) to effect Brown's escape.

Edwin Morton, who as Sanborn's classmate and Gerrit Smith's household companion knew the inside of the conspiracy, hastily took refuge in England. Frederick Douglass, after seeing to the concealment of his papers, hurried by

30 Harlow, *Gerrit Smith*, 421–425.
31 Undated MS in Hinton Papers.
32 Sanborn, *Recollections*, I, 182.

way of Canada to the same haven. It can be said in his behalf that he had never believed in the Harper's Ferry raid, that he had for some time intended an English trip, and that he sent a letter to a Rochester newspaper with a frank confession: "I have always been more distinguished for running than fighting, and tried by the Harper's-Ferry-Insurrection test, I am most miserably deficient in courage." The only important conspirator who stood his ground was Thomas Wentworth Higginson. Rejoicing in his mistaken view that Harper's Ferry was the most formidable slave insurrection in our history, this militant minister remained in Worcester, joining Wendell Phillips, John A. Andrew, and others in providing counsel for Brown.[33]

An inglorious record! Several conspirators, notably the religious Gerrit Smith, must have felt that a heavy responsibility for the death of innocent men at Harper's Ferry lay on their souls, but none admitted it. Not one, except Higginson, had the manliness to express regret that the conspirators were not at Brown's side when he fought. Nor were the attempts of these safe-distance helpers to organize Brown's rescue at all creditable. Hoyt, sent from Boston ostensibly as Brown's lawyer, was actually a spy and plotter. One of his objects was to get hold of the raider's papers lest they incriminate the Yankee group. He made a nervous search for these "relics," and tried to snatch them and other property of Brown's from under the eyes of the Virginia authorities—unavailingly as regarded the "records." He also tried to arrange a jail delivery. This rescue would have involved more bloodshed, including the possible slaying or wounding of the sheriff and jailor, both kindly, humane men.[34] Brown himself had the good sense to reject the scheme. My death, he declared again and again, is worth infinitely more for the cause than my life. It was with good reason that Hoyt was compelled to leave Charlestown by the excited citizens of that place. Going to Washington, he characteristically urged his friends to stir up a newspaper clamor over his expulsion.

[VI]

In his last weeks John Brown rose to a height of moral grandeur which went far toward redeeming his name from the terrible blots which he had placed upon it. Caught up by exaltation of spirit in his confidence of a vast posthumous influence, he displayed neither grief for the two sons killed at his side nor fear of approaching death. Moving as a man who fulfilled a mighty destiny, he impressed all observers by his unshaken courage and serene equanimity. He believed that he had done right; he felt certain that God reigned and would yet

33 *Letters and Journals of T. W. Higginson*, 84–88.
34 George H. Hoyt, November 11, 13, 14, 16, etc., to Barnes *et al.*; Hinton Papers.

overmaster all opposition to his divine decrees. He realized that he was now holding the center of the stage in a historic scene watched by the nation and millions overseas. "Already," he wrote his family during the trial, "dear friends at a distance with kindly sympathy are cheering me with the assurance that *posterity* at least will do me justice." [35]

The Virginia authorities generously permitted him to write anyone he pleased, and he displayed in his letters a spiritual power, couched in a style as simple and forcible as Bunyan's, which was destined to impress multitudes of readers. His only suffering was lest his kindred should feel humiliated by his scaffold death. The burden of his message, the same in all his epistles, may be summed up in two sentences addressed to his wife. "I will say here that the sacrifices *you*; and I, have been called to make in behalf of the *cause we love*, the *cause of God; and of humanity*: do not seem to me as at all too great. I have been *whipt* as the saying *is*; but I am sure I can recover all the lost capital occasioned by that disaster; by only hanging a few moments by the neck; and I feel quite determined to make the utmost possible out of a defeat." [36] Remembering his ancestor Peter Brown, who came over in the *Mayflower*, and his grandfather, who died in the Revolution, he was anxious to display a fortitude worthy of his sires. On his last Sunday he wrote his sisters that he had experienced a perfect consolation and peace. In great part, beyond doubt, this arose from a belief that his death would aid "the crushed Millions who 'have no comforters.' " [37]

At eleven o'clock on the morning of December 2, a bright, warm day, Brown was brought out of his Charlestown jail. Drawn up on the street were the glittering ranks of six companies of Virginia infantry and a troop of horse, commanded by Major-General W. B. Taliaferro with his entire staff. At the door stood an open wagon with a pine box containing a heavy oak coffin. Brown climbed into the vehicle, seated himself beside his jailor on the box, and surveyed the soldiery with interest. Closely flanked by two files of riflemen, the wagon creaked slowly off to the forty-acre field chosen for the execution. Here were additional troops, massed in a hollow square with cannon commanding the scaffold, a precaution against any attempt at rescue. From the field, the beautiful undulating country and distant Blue Ridge were in full view, the

---

35 Villard, *John Brown,* 537. As early as November 24, the New York *Independent* was urging that special ceremonies be held all over the East to make the day of the execution memorable. "What is it that will be hung up on the gallows in the gaze of all men?" it asked. "Not John Brown, but Slavery!"

36 *Ibid.,* 540.

37 November 22, 1859, to Mary and Martha Brown; Brown Papers, Chicago Hist. Soc. Brown on the morning of his execution handed a jail guard his famous prophecy, now also in the Chicago Hist. Soc. It announced: "I John Brown am now quite *certain* that the crimes of this *guilty land:* will never be purged *away;* but with Blood. I had *as I now think:* vainly flattered myself that without *very much* bloodshed; it might be done."

mountain crests bright in the sun, while through several lower valleys the night mists were still pouring like slow silvery torrents. Clusters of spectators were to be seen on various eminences about the grounds. When Brown reached the spot, he inquired why none but the military were allowed there, saying: "I am sorry citizens have been kept out."

He had refused to permit any minister who approved slavery to accompany him to the gallows, and no friend was allowed at his side. Several notable figures were scattered through the concourse. One, accompanying the detachment of cadets from the Virginia Military Institute, brave in their uniforms of gray trousers and red flannel shirts, was Professor Thomas J. Jackson; one, a militia-man from Richmond, was the actor John Wilkes Booth; one, a newspaper editor in the same city, was a son of Governor Wise who would soon lay down his life on the battlefield. Another, given place among the V.M.I. corps, and carrying his musket with soldierly erectness, was the agricultural reformer and disunionist agitator Edmund Ruffin. Fixing his eyes intently on the doomed man, Ruffin was impressed by his firmness, dignity, and impassive silence.[38]

The prisoner climbed the scaffold with readiness and even alacrity, the first man on its platform. Shaking hands with the jailor and sheriff, he bade them farewell, and stood erect as a large hood of white linen, with an aperture for the halter, was drawn over his head. The rope was knotted about his neck. When the jailor asked him to step on the trap, he replied, "You must lead me—I cannot see," and was properly placed. All seemed ready. Then occurred an awful delay as the last-arriving troops marched and countermarched to take their appointed places. It was a striking sight, as eight long minutes ticked away, to see the old man straight and unmoving on the trap, his dark clothing in contrast with his blood-red slippers and the long white hood. To him, as to onlookers, those minutes must have seemed an age. The jailor asked if he were tired. "No, not tired," came the answer, "but don't keep me waiting longer than is necessary." Then, as the soldiery came to a stand, the sheriff brought his hatchet down upon the rope sustaining the trap. In the preternatural stillness which had settled upon the field, the screech of the hinges and thud of falling planks struck heavily on all ears.

The voice of Colonel J. T. L. Preston of the V.M.I. rang out: "So perish all such enemies of Virginia! All such enemies of the Union! All foes of the human race!"

38 Ruffin, MS Diary, December 2, 1859; letter of December 4, 1859, Ruffin Papers, Univ. of N. C. An important duty of the V.M.I. cadets was to guard the arsenal at Lexington. Their vigilance had been increased when in December, 1856, a request was received from Buchan, about twenty-five miles away, for arms to meet an anticipated slave revolt. W. Couper, *One Hundred Years at V.M.I.*, I, 318, 319.

4

"Drifting Into Destruction"

WHILE John Brown was being hanged; while the noonday sun shone down upon the far-sweeping Blue Ridge, the two winding rivers, the immobile lines of riflemen and horse, and the grim gallows; while the commanding officer proclaimed that the majesty of Virginia law had been satisfied, a mounting emotion swept the whole land from St. Croix to the Florida keys. Next day, the telegraph told how deep an imprint Brown's act and fate had laid upon the feeling of millions.

In many Northern communities, such as the Concord of Franklin Pierce and the Chicago of Douglas, bells were tolled at the hour of execution; in some, minute guns were fired; in still others, crowded public meetings were held. In Philadelphia, a gathering offered prayers for Brown, heard the Rev. W. H. Furness read letters from him, and applauded a speech by Lucretia Mott. In New York, Dr. George B. Cheever, author of *God Against Slavery*, addressed an audience at his Church of the Pilgrims. A crowd filling Tremont Temple in Boston heard a discourse by William Lloyd Garrison. In Albany, while a hundred guns were fired, meetings continued all afternoon and evening; in Syracuse, the city hall was packed with citizens who met for three hours of speechmaking; in Cleveland, buildings were hung with black, and a leading minister spoke to five thousand people. Newspapers everywhere appeared in augmented editions.[1]

Had Wise acted foolishly in making a martyr? He must have been prepared for the instant voice of the abolitionists. Emerson termed Brown a new saint in the calendar; Thoreau described him as an angel of light; Longfellow, on the day of execution, entered in his diary, "The date of a new revolution, quite as much needed as the old one." Dr. Cheever's sermon the following Sunday treated Brown as an incarnation of God's protest against slavery. But the significant fact

---

[1] In Oberlin citizens erected a monument to three negroes: Lewis Leary, killed in following Brown, and Shields Green and John Copeland, who had been hanged. Copeland's letters to his family made a great impression in the North. He would rather die a rebel than live a slave, he declared, and hoped his name might be preserved with that of Crispus Attucks. "Believe me when I tell you, that though shut up in prison and under sentence of death, I have spent some very happy hours here." Hinton Papers.

was that men whose opinions fell far short of abolitionism spoke in similar terms. Wrote William Cullen Bryant: "History, forgetting the errors of his judgment in the contemplation of his unfaltering courage, of his dignified and manly deportment in the face of death, and of the nobleness of his aims, will record his name among those of its martyrs and heroes." Young William Dean Howells, writing his father from the capital of Ohio, predicted for the raider a great place in history: "Brown has become an idea, a thousand times purer and better and loftier than the Republican idea." Charles Eliot Norton, explaining to an English friend how the bitterness of the Virginia press, the hurry of the trial, the noble manliness of Brown under condemnation, his speech, his letters from prison, the visit from his wife, and, at last, his death, had wrought up popular emotion to the highest pitch, predicted that it would not die away: [2]

I have seen nothing like it. We get up excitements easily enough . . . ; but this was different. The heart of the people was fairly reached, and an impression has been made upon it which will be permanent and produce results long hence. . . . The events of this last month or two (including under the word events the impression made by Brown's character) have done more to confirm the opposition to slavery at the North . . . than anything which has ever happened before, than all the antislavery tracts and novels that ever were written.

A great legend had been created in the North; a legend that was to place its mark on political thought, influence multitudes at the ballot box, and within two years send armies into battle singing "John Brown's Body." In the aura of that legend the real man was transfigured, and his crimes were palliated by his favorite text: "Without the shedding of blood there is no remission of sins." To be sure, conservative men in thousands denounced his raid. Washington Hunt termed it an infernal performance; Edward Everett confessed himself disgusted and alarmed; Richard Henry Dana, Jr., spoke of the man's insanity. Even Henry Wilson wrote that he knew of no Republican who did not condemn the John Brown blow, or at least regret it. Whittier, as a non-resistant Quaker, a believer in moral warfare alone, of course deplored such violence. Yet most Northerners believed that the man's character was noble, that his errors were those of a fanatic, and that if his act condemned himself, it also condemned slavery. It is the heaviest blow yet struck against the institution, said some; it brings the end of slavery ten years nearer, said others.[3]

Within a few weeks, Brown was being canonized. In Kansas, the *Herald of Freedom* disgustedly commented that his conduct in the Territory was being gilded and garlanded, his murders on the Pottawatomie were being praised, and his unreal "victories" over proslavery men were being grossly exaggerated;

2 Mildred Howells, *Life in Letters of W. D. Howells,* I, 26; Norton, *Letters,* I, 197, 198.
3 Winthrop Papers, November 13, February 8, 1860.

that, in short, his erratic and often vicious course was being treated as splendid. In the East, the most powerful of editors wrote that though his acts were lawless, they were not really criminal. The essence of crime, Greeley argued, is selfish gratification; but Brown had sacrificed his life and those of his sons to benefit a despised race and deliver from bitter degradation those whom he had never seen. This was also the verdict of the Springfield *Republican*.

"We can conceive of no event," it remarked, "that could so deepen the moral hostility of the people of the free states to slavery as this execution. This is not because the acts of Brown are generally approved, for they are not. It is because the nature and spirit of the man are seen to be great and noble. . . . His death will be the result of his own folly, to be sure, but that will not prevent his being considered a martyr to his hatred of oppression, and all who sympathize with him in that sentiment will find their hatred grow stronger." [4]

Swiftly the legend grew. Lithographed portraits were soon circulated all over the North. One weekly magazine gave its subscribers free copies of a large nine-color chromo depicting five of the most crucial scenes in Brown's life.[5] James Redpath hurried a popular and highly mendacious biography through the press, and compiled a five-hundred-and-fourteen-page volume of the better speeches, poems, and other effusions following Brown's death (*Echoes of Harper's Ferry*), which sold widely at $1.25 a copy.[6] Within six months, more than $6,000 was raised by popular subscription for Brown's family. After the burial of the body at North Elba, New York, where Wendell Phillips spoke eloquently, his grave became an object of pilgrimage. On the next Independence Day, nearly a thousand people assembled there to hear speakers reaffirm Brown's principles.[7] His deed had caught the attention of Europe. Britons paid their tribute, and Victor Hugo proposed an epitaph: "Pro Christo sicut Christus."

For many, a great movement of the age had found in Brown its Arnold of Winkelried, its Hampden, its Nathan Hale—a more spotted hero than these but one as ruggedly devoted. To abolitionists, to many freesoilers, and to radicals of all types, countries, and future times, his was now a name which raised spirits

---

4 *Herald of Freedom*, December 15-30; N. Y. *Weekly Tribune*, December 3, 1859; Merriam, *Bowles*, I, 252, 253.
5 *The Philadelphia Weekly*; critical of Brown in general effect.
6 Redpath was assisted in writing his biography by Richard J. Hinton, who had lived in Kansas, and who later produced a superior biography himself. The book was being advertised before Brown's execution and quickly sold thirty-five thousand copies. It outrageously falsified the Kansas story, declaring that Brown had nothing to do with the Pottawatomie murders, and treating him as one of the liberators of Kansas. Until F. B. Sanborn issued his equally distorted *Life and Letters of John Brown* in 1885, Redpath's book was the chief vehicle of the Brown legend, which was more fable than truth. Three British publishers brought out editions.
7 Thaddeus Hyatt, N. Y. *Tribune*, July 28, 1860.

from the vasty deep.[8] Like Cranmer and Algernon Sidney, men said, he had been executed because he embodied a sublime idea. Nor should we forget that to another group, destined to grow important, his services were unforgettable—the Negroes. When his remains reached Philadelphia on the way north, the city

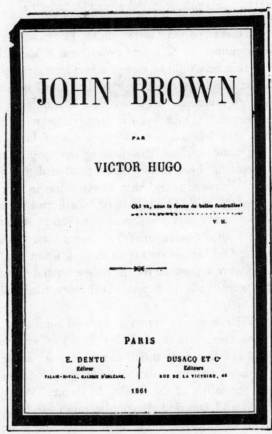

JOHN BROWN

PAR

VICTOR HUGO

Oh! va, nous te ferons de belles funérailles!

V. H.

PARIS

E. DENTU
Éditeur
PALAIS-ROYAL, GALERIE D'ORLÉANS.

DUSACQ ET Cⁱᵉ
Éditeurs
RUE DE LA VICTOIRE, 46

1861

Victor Hugo's Tribute to John Brown Contained an Imaginative Sketch
of the Execution by the Poet.

was astonished to see the station choked by a spontaneous outpouring of free colored people, poor, meanly clad, and ignorant, but showing the deepest emotion and frantically eager to lay their tributes on his coffin.

8 In 1948 the author, after lecturing to a group of German editors, chatted with them about American history. Did they know the name of Charles Sumner? Nein. Had they ever heard of William H. Seward? Nein. Of Stephen A. Douglas? They were doubtful. Of John Brown? "Oh, ja! ja!" they exclaimed with eager smiles; his name was famous.

[I]

It was just as inevitable that a very different legend of John Brown should spring up in the South. The bitter resentment aroused by his raid, felt by slave-holders and slaveless alike, embraced all Northerners suspected of being his helpers and abettors.

Suspicion fell not merely upon Gerrit Smith, Higginson, and other actual conspirators, but upon numerous Northern politicians. A Virginian advertised in the Richmond *Whig* that he would be one of a hundred men to pay $10,000 for the delivery of Joshua Giddings dead, or half that sum for his head.[9] At first, many Southerners were reluctant to believe that any but the more malignant abolitionists would express sympathy for treason, servile insurrection, and murder. Then, when they learned that Emerson, Longfellow, and Bryant had penned panegyrics of their assailant, that leading newspapers and hundreds of ministers were apotheosizing him, their tempers hardened. An observant young Tennesseean, John W. Burgess, found that a revolution in sentiment occurred during the month after the raid. The tolling of Northern bells and half-staffing of Northern flags for Brown's execution were accepted as evidence of a wicked desire to destroy the South. Governor Wise's son noted the same change in Virginia. People of the Old Dominion began to look upon the Yankees as men who hated them, who were willing to see them assassinated at midnight by their own slaves and who were ready to support still more formidable invasions of Southern soil.[10]

The activities of Wise in giving credence to wild rumors of fresh Northern invasions, in deploying large bodies of militia, and in temporarily suspending travel on certain railways, had done much to whip up an artificial antagonism. John Minor Botts condemned his policy in scathing language. It had struck blows which cracked the fabric of the Union, he wrote. "Whether designed or not, it has exasperated and frenzied the public mind—it has begotten an ill-feeling, antipathy, and hostility between members of the same political community, that every good man and patriot must deprecate, and that it becomes

9   That is more than my head is worth, said Giddings, who added that he would let the Virginians have it at that quotation—after he was through with it. He at once added a lecture on Brown to his repertory. Joshua Giddings to his children, November 9, 25, 1859; Giddings Papers.

10   Burgess, *Civil War and Constitution*, I, 36; John S. Wise, *End of an Era*, 135. Ruffin, a shrewd observer, thought that Wise gained strength from his errors and follies. "Before the Harper's Ferry affair, he had but little support in Virginia (and none elsewhere) for the presidency, which he was seeking so boldly and shamelessly. But his conduct in and since the affair, though very blameable for indiscretion, has given him more popularity than all he ever acquired for his real worth and ability, or his praiseworthy public services." *Diary*, February 6, 1860. One of Robert Toombs's closest friends believed that Harper's Ferry turned the scale with him, convincing him that secession was a necessity. Reed, *Brothers' War*, 264.

the . . . representatives of the people to do all in their power to smooth down and rectify."

That wealthy Calhounite Democrat and former Congressman, James A. Seddon, who was spending the winter in Louisiana, believed equally that Wise had done tremendous mischief. Instead of treating the Harper's Ferry affair as the work of a few fanatics or the crime of a squad of ruffians, he had elevated the perpetrators to the station of political offenders and had done his utmost to make them appear champions of Northern sentiment. Throughout the South, others, taking their cue from the Virginia executive, had joined him in trying to convert the squalid foray into a grand political transaction and to arouse hostility toward all Northerners. In short, wrote Seddon, the foolish governor, mad for the Presidential nomination, "has conjured a devil neither he nor perhaps any other can lay, and, arraying the roused pride and animosities of both sections against each other, has brought on a *real crisis* of imminent peril to both." Seddon did not deplore this, as Botts did, from love of the Union. He deplored it because he thought the raid should have been used to strengthen the Democratic Party both North and South, bringing Northern members into better comradeship with Southerners, and because he feared that this premature cry of "Wolf! Wolf!" would leave disillusionment in its wake, rendering the South more apathetic toward the "practical disunion" which Seddon wanted.

It was natural that a great part of the Southern press should interpret John Brown's raid as evidence that the abolitionists would arm new bands of assailants, and that their section must now live under daily menace of attack. The scope of the conspiracy was vastly exaggerated. When maps of several Southern States were found in Brown's baggage, with marks indicating certain counties in which the colored people exceeded the whites, many jumped to the conclusion that abolition agents had been sent to these areas or would soon go thither.[11]

Indeed, the captured papers indicated that Brown had dispatched an emissary, one Lawrence Thatcher, to make a Southern tour and determine the best places for blows against slavery; and that Thatcher had reported, early in October, that Tennessee and Arkansas were exceptionally favorable ground, for the slaves were ripe for action and few whites were strongly attached to the institution. Governor Isham Harris of Tennessee regarded the report as proof of a widely ramified plot.[12] It was easy to quote—or misquote—statements by the abolitionist leaders. Garrison had written in the *Liberator* three years earlier that it was far more important to send Sharps rifles to the Southern slaves than to Kansas. "If every border ruffian invading Kansas deserves to be shot, much more does every slave-

11 *De Bow's Review*, XXIX, 71.
12 *National Intelligencer*, November 16, Baltimore *Weekly Sun*, November 19, 1859.

holder, by the same rule; for the former is guilty only of attempting political subjection to his will, while the latter is the destroyer of all human rights, and there is none to deliver. Who will go for arming our slave population?" [13] Giddings had declared that he looked forward to the hour of servile revolt, "when the torch of the incendiary shall light up the towns and cities of the South, and blot out the last vestiges of slavery."

Unfortunately, the Republican Party was now widely misidentified with the abolitionists. Though most Republicans reprehended Brown's deed, the South was no longer in any mood to make the vital distinction between those who wished to contain slavery and those who wished its immediate extirpation. Howell Cobb, declining in a letter of October 31 to speak in New York, called the raid a practical result of Republican abuse of the South and talk of an irrepressible conflict. Much of the Democratic press in both sections took up the hue and cry.

Thus the Administration organ, the Washington *Constitution*, which could have raised a moderating voice, burst out in a series of articles on Seward's responsibility for the raid. It remarked in the first article that while the South had accepted the irrepressible conflict speech as a declaration of war upon its equality, peace, and safety, nobody had supposed that the initial blow would be struck so quickly. The anonymous letter of warning to Secretary Floyd was construed as evidence that widespread arrangements had been made for the outbreak. Later articles quoted Giddings and others, declared that the Republican Party was the implacable enemy of the South, and accused Seward of doing more than anyone else to consolidate antislavery feeling into a political organization pledged to war upon the rights of fifteen sovereign States.[14] The New York *Herald*, reprinting Seward's "bloody and brutal" speech entire, saw a connection clear as sunlight between it and the bloody and brutal acts committed on the Potomac.[15] The New York *Daily News* spoke in similar vein. A Democratic group in New York City, the Fifth Avenue Hotel Committee, even circulated the accusation that Seward had known in advance of the raid and kept silent about it.[16] The *Democratic Review* in its October issue arraigned Seward along with Wendell Phillips, Giddings, and Gerrit Smith as more guilty than Brown himself for the Harper's Ferry murders.

The unhappiest single result of the raid, in a practical sense, was this intensification of Southern hatred and suspicion of the Republican Party. It was uni-

13   Garrison, *Garrison*, III, 439. A non-resistant, Garrison was against arming anybody.
14   Washington *Constitution*, October 20, 21, 22, 1859.
15   N. Y. *Herald*, October 19, 1859.
16   N. Y. *Weekly Tribune*, December 10, 1859. A slight basis of fact existed for the story of the Fifth Avenue Committee. Brown's associate Forbes declared that he had discussed Brown's general scheme with Seward; but we cannot trust Forbes.

versally called the Black Republican Party, its leaders were increasingly characterized as enemies of Southern institutions, and its doctrine of non-interference in the States but exclusion of slavery from the Territories was vituperatively distorted into a doctrine of warfare upon slavery everywhere. A resident of Plaquemines, Louisiana, wrote Lyman Trumbull that absurd misrepresentations of Northern feeling were being daily and weekly thrown before the Southern people in an inflammatory phraseology which could not but work mischievous results.[17]

When the mild Amos A. Lawrence (an old Cotton Whig, an enemy of abolitionists, a man shocked by Harper's Ferry) wrote Wise to ask mercy for Brown, he received a sharp rebuke. The governor expressed the view that Brown's folly was the fruit of the excited preaching and arms-shipping which Lawrence and other Yankees had used to sway the result in Kansas—that Lawrence and his friends had instigated John Brown to his crime.[18] Jefferson Davis was typical of hundreds of Southern leaders now proclaiming that Republican hostility knew no limit. At first, he said, the antislavery agitation had been a thrust for political power; then it had assumed a social form; and now it had reached the pitch of revolution and civil war. He asserted that Brown's raid represented an attempt "by extensive combinations among the non-slaveholding States" to levy war against Virginia and stigmatized the Republican Party as one "organized on the basis of making war" against the South.[19]

In an effort on the part of some to reassure the South, and of others to turn public sentiment against the Republicans, Northern conservatives hastily arranged Union meetings in many cities. Such gatherings, however, simply confirmed the South in its fears and prejudices, while irritating honest-minded Northerners. Many orators took an apprehensive view; John A. Dix told the New York meeting that Brown's invasion was the product of a "vast" conspiracy that was but scotched, not killed. Many speakers cried encouragement to Southern disunionists; Charles O'Conor said that if the North continued to elect fanatics to Congress, he would not blame the South for seceding.[20] Franklin Pierce sent a letter to the Portsmouth meeting which laid unfortunate emphasis on the continuing nature of the peril. The Republicans, he wrote, had long been ready to scuttle the Union, and now seemed prepared to condone murder and

17 Paul Selby, former Illinoisan, November 28, 1859; Trumbull Papers.
18 Anon., *William Winston Seaton*, 321–323.
19 *Cong. Globe*, 36th Cong., 1st Sess., 1942.
20 N. Y. *Weekly Tribune*, December 24, 1859. The effort in many Union meetings, and in such newspapers as the N. Y. *Herald*, Washington *Constitution*, and Boston *Courier* to hold Republicans responsible for the raid cost the party few votes in November. N. P. Banks was reelected governor of Massachusetts on the Republican ticket by more than twenty thousand plurality, while in the election of minor state officers in New York the party made marked gains.

treason. "The amazing, dangerous, and unconstitutional aggression on the part of the North against the people and institutions of the South which has been kept up through so many years . . . must cease, or the relations which have been the basis of our prosperity, power, and glory must be terminated." [21] No Southern agitator could have been more alarming as to the future. A wealthy Philadelphian was writing William C. Rives: "I cannot think the South can endure many such attacks; I can hardly hope the North will protect them from them"—as if attacks were to become a regular feature of national life.[22]

The Union meetings gave no reassurance because they could give no guarantees. They demonstrated what was obvious, that right-thinking Northerners deplored any outrage; but who could check wrong-thinking Northerners? The conservative Senator Dixon of Connecticut was struck, in talking with Hunter of Virginia, usually the calmest of men, by his perturbed words and despondent manner. When, asked the Virginian, would the growth of radical abolitionism stop? Would Garrison and Wendell Phillips ultimately win all Northern opinion to their views? Was the irrepressible conflict not at hand, and in a shape more violent than Seward had envisaged? Communicating these inquiries to Gideon Welles, Dixon warned him that disunion, long dreaded, might be near now that Southern leaders were holding it up not as an evil to be deprecated, but as a good to be desired.[23]

Outwardly, the Faneuil Hall meeting, addressed by Caleb Cushing and Edward Everett, was impressive; so was the Academy of Music meeting in New York, with speeches by Mayor Tiemann, John A. Dix, and Washington Hunt; so were meetings in other commercial centers. They struck many Southerners, however, as ridiculous. Men who had sowed the wind were now affecting astonishment at the whirlwind harvest. They struck other Southerners as insincere: if Brown's insurrection had succeeded, would not Everett and Hunt have sung a different tune? Their effect on Northern freesoilers of principle was equally bad. The willingness of some Democratic speakers to defend slavery as morally right created disgust. When the eminent attorney O'Conor said that slavery was benign in its influence on whites and blacks, was a necessity created by nature herself, and must be perpetuated, he exacerbated the feeling he should have quieted. Republican editors were quick to declare these Union-saving assemblages a double hypocrisy. On one side, they were a partisan attempt to use John Brown's irresponsible raid to besmear the Republican organization. On the other, they were an effort of Northern merchants to truckle to the Atlanta *Daily Confederacy* and other agencies which had gotten up blacklists of offen-

21 December 26, 1859; Pierce Papers, LC.
22 J. L. Fisher, November 29, 1859; Rives Papers, LC.
23 December 17, 1859; Welles Papers, LC.

sive Yankee firms, and to keep slaveowners in a mood to buy A. T. Stewart's silks and Ben Whitlock's extended brandy.

In short, emotion North and South had now passed the point at which moderate utterances could have an emollient influence. If they pleased one side they seemed provocative to the other.[24]

As the wave of anger and fear, throwing up its surf of hysteria, rolled across the South, it had a variety of unpleasant immediate effects. Intolerance was accentuated. From this hour it became treason in most Southern areas to breathe a word against slavery. Newspapers far and wide published warnings that the section was infested by abolitionists, trying to imbue both races with their doctrines. The Montgomery *Mail* was especially fearful of peddlers and colporteurs, slipping about among the plantations to corrupt the slaves. The safest course, it said, was to arrest such men and hang them upon conviction of anything like sedition. Forsyth's Mobile *Register* protested against such dangerous teachings —behind every bush a Catiline!—but they had their effect.[25] The publication of letters from Brown's valise which indicated that he had considered operations at various Southern points brought Wise a flock of agitated inquiries. We have several abolitionists near here, wrote citizens of Center, North Carolina, including a Wesleyan minister from Ohio; is he one of Brown's agents? We have a Yankee schoolteacher named Forbes, stated people of Cold Spring, Louisiana; he looks suspicious; does he belong to Brown's gang? Two Northern book agents, one selling a volume on the Indians and the other a treatise on Christ and his apostles, were seized at Salisbury, North Carolina, threatened with tar and feathers, and driven from the State. "Do you know Old Brown?" demanded the mob.[26] To be sure, underground agents did exist—but they were few.

24 Philip S. Foner, *Business and Slavery*, 156–164. The Southern blacklists, an attempt at commercial proscription, lent themselves to blackmail. Various offices calling themselves Southern business agencies were opened in Northern cities, and invited patronage on an implied-threat basis. William P. Gilman & Company of Richmond, for example, proposed to publish a directory of sound Northern firms, which could get their names entered by paying not less than $50. The Atlanta *Confederacy* published black-and-white lists for the benefit of Georgia merchants, while the Charleston *Mercury* threatened to list all Charleston merchants doing business with a New York firm whose partners attended Beecher's church. The alacrity of many Northern merchants to attend Union meetings, and to get their names signed to the printed call for such gatherings, was attributed by unkind folk to business considerations. *Annual Report, Am. Antislavery Society, 1860*, 197–199.

25 Mobile *Register*, November 29, 1859. The idea that they might have to defend their women and children against slaves armed by the North made many Southerners savage. T. J. Jackson, the future "Stonewall," said that in dealing with any new raiders they should raise the black flag of no quarter, for in the end that would prove true humanity and mercy. Mary Anna Jackson, *Life and Letters of T. J. Jackson*, 308–310.

26 Hartford *Press*, December 12, 1859. Newspapers were soon chronicling scores of instances in which well-behaved residents of Southern communities had been forced to flee; innocent book venders and notions peddlers had been threatened and even attacked for no offense but speaking with a Yankee twang; schoolteachers, intent only on teaching, and ministers devoted to the gospel had been warned to leave because their education had been

For some weeks the panic and anger grew. The protests of such responsible Unionists as Herschel Johnson, John Minor Botts, and B. H. Hill seemed unavailing. The British consul in Charleston reported on December 9 that a veritable reign of terror had opened in the Lower South. Suspect men were being torn from their homes, tarred and feathered, ridden upon rails, or cruelly whipped; and, as a result, Northern businessmen, drummers, and tourists, finding their letters opened in the post offices and all talk about slavery sternly prohibited, were leaving for home.[27] More than one person, added the consul, had been hanged for uttering obnoxious sentiments. The consul in New York complained of the hard case of a Scotch-Irishman in Augusta, Georgia, who, after suing a local firm and obtaining judgment, was warned out of town as an abolitionist, and at two in the morning seized by a mob and thrown into jail. As he had done no wrong, a courageous lawyer released him—but he had to leave. In Virginia, various postmasters, such as R. H. Glass of Lynchburg, informed the New York *Tribune* that they would no longer distribute the journal. In Arkansas, after reports spread that the John Brown conspirators intended to stage another raid from some point on the Arkansas River, and after panic-stricken inhabitants arrested various abolition agents and shot one alleged Negro-

gained at Northern colleges; mechanics of British or New England origin had been tarred and feathered on some groundless accusation. In December, it was stated that thirty-two men, agents of New York and Boston houses, had arrived in Washington on one day, reporting sentiment in the South so hostile that it was no longer safe for them to pursue their work as commercial travellers. The temper of Southern communities is illustrated by two newspaper utterances. "We regard every man in our midst an enemy to the institutions of the South," declared the Atlanta *Confederacy*, "who does not boldly declare that he believes African slavery to be a social, moral, and political blessing." When a meeting was held at Boggy Swamp, S. C., to expel two Northern tutors from the district, the Kingstree *Star* commented: "Nothing definite is known of their abolitionist or insurrectionary sentiments, but being from the North, and, therefore, necessarily imbued with doctrines hostile to our institutions, their presence in this section has been obnoxious, and, at any rate, very suspicious." Quoted in *Annual Report Am. Antislavery Society, 1860*, pp. 167, 168.

27 "The time has come," wrote the Washington correspondent of the New Orleans *Picayune*, "when no Northern man, whatever his business, can safely travel in the Southern states, unless he has means of showing that his objects are not unfriendly. Many who have business in the South come here to obtain credentials. A proper passport system must be devised and adopted, in order to secure the South from Abolition intruders and spies." New Orleans *Picayune*, January 11, 1860. Many old friendships were now feeling a severe strain. Philip St. George Cooke of Virginia and A. J. Davis of New York, for example, both interested in art, had seen each other whenever possible and maintained a genial correspondence. But just after Christmas Cooke warned his friend that the South was in earnest. "If your Conservative Party at the North does not *put down* and *put out* the accursed and pestiferous abolition faction, they will speedily bring about a dissolution of our hitherto glorious Union! Able men of all parties have come to this conclusion at the South, and as we see no hopes of such a result at the North, we are arming . . . as rapidly as possible." He expected to turn his peaceful lawn into a drillground for soldiers. What hellish madness!—but the South must defend itself against this insane crusade, led by the vilest of the Northern population. A. J. Davis Papers, Metropolitan Museum, N. Y.

stealer, a plot for a general slave escape was discovered in Washington County and some white men were seized as participants.[28]

One of the unhappiest episodes occurred in Kentucky. Here, at Berea on the fringe of the bluegrass district, Cassius M. Clay had established an antislavery community, and through the activities of an abolitionist minister, John G. Fee, and others, the Berea School had been founded for the education of white children and Negroes. Just before Christmas, a mob which included prosperous and influential men, riding from house to house, ordered Fee and his associates to leave Kentucky within ten days under threat of death; when the governor refused to interfere, a dozen families were stripped of their property and lost their means of livelihood.[29] Fee's offense was that, being in New York at the time of the raid, he had delivered a sermon in which he said (like Whittier in "Brown of Ossawatomie") that the country needed more John Browns, armed not with guns but spiritual weapons. The slaveholders of the county, hearing of this, had met, appointed a committee, and passed resolutions warning the antislavery folk of Berea to quit the State.[30]

One unfortunate result of the Southern furore was a heightened rigor in the treatment of the Negro. It was a bitter irony that Brown's effort to aid them should have made their lot harsher. The tension that caught at the nerves of slaveholders found expression in stricter patrols, a closer watch on recreation and much petty tyrannizing. Legislatures of various States hastened to debate bills (which we summarize later) to hedge free Negroes within narrow bounds, or drive them back into slavery; the theory being that, as the Montgomery *Mail* put it, "their anomalous position is an eyesore to the slaves and an annoyance to the white population." [31] British consuls were shocked by the passions of the hour. In Louisiana, Consul William Mure, under instructions from the Foreign Office, prepared to expostulate against the new law requiring that all free Negroes on ships arriving from abroad must be held in jail until the vessel was ready to depart. When he spoke to two legislators who had opposed the law, however, they advised him not to offer any petition while such excitement reigned, for a protest might retard repeal for years. In Georgia, a British sailor, a Negro named Brodie, was thrown into jail on a charge of enticing a slave to run away, tried before the mayor's court at Darien, illegally sentenced to be sold into slavery, and hurriedly sent to unknown western points. It was impossible to

28 See John Bunch, January 25, 1860, F.O. 115/230; E. M. Archibald, January 16, 1860, F.O. 115/230; Little Rock *True Democrat*, November–December, 1859; E. L. Harvin, "Arkansas and Crisis 1860–61," M.A. Essay, Univ. of Texas Lib.
29 Cincinnati *Commercial*, December 31, 1859, gives full documents.
30 Fee, *Autobiography*, 147, 148; Coleman, *Slavery Times in Kentucky*, 112, 321, 322.
31 *Annual Report Am. Antislavery Society, 1860*, 206–225.

find him. On a trumped-up charge, he had been enslaved for life. Worse still was the case of a colored British seaman at Charleston. A runaway slave hid himself in this man's berth; the sailor denied any knowledge of him; but Judge T. J. Withers of General Sessions sentenced him to death. When J. L. Petigru persuaded the governor to commute the sentence, the judge evinced great chagrin.[32]

Amid this general fever, disunionist excitation blazed up with renewed vigor. Such leaders as Ruffin, who got a consignment of Brown's pikes from Harper's Ferry and distributed them as evidence of what he termed the fanatical hatred in the North, plucked up hope. Talking with Letcher in Richmond on December 17, Ruffin, after finding that even the moderate governor-elect thought it impossible any longer to preserve the rights of the South within the Union, urged him to call a convention in Virginia and to propose a general convention of all the Southern States. Rhett and Yancey were jubilant over the outlook. "Never before, since the Declaration of Independence, has the South been more united in sentiment and feeling," rejoiced the Sumter (South Carolina) *Watchman* the day before Christmas. Ruffin was for immediate secession by any State that could act, but most radicals thought this premature. The first step, they held, was to effect a firm alliance of the Southern States for future action.[33]

Various leaders and legislatures expressly formulated the idea of Southern solidarity. The Georgia house resolved that any blow at slavery in a sister State vitally affected the interests and honor of Georgia, and that the Southern people were bound by such a close community of feeling that they must stand or fall together. The State senate, in language shaped by the moderate Benjamin H. Hill, contented itself with praising the energetic action of Buchanan and Wise.[34] In Louisiana, the brilliant Henry W. Allen, who had studied at Harvard and traveled widely in Europe, presented resolutions declaring that the universal sympathy manifested by the Black Republican Party for the murderers of Harper's Ferry gave evidence of deep-seated hostility to all the slaveholding States, and if a Black Republican were elected to the Presidency, Louisiana

32 William Mure, February 16, 1860, F.O. 115/230. E. Molyneux, March 8, 1860, F.O. 115/230. John Bunch, January 7, 1860, F.O. 115/230.
33 Edmund Ruffin, *Diary*, December 16, 1859–January 4, 1860. A significant letter appeared in the N. Y. *Express*, Know-Nothing organ. Signed R. S. P., it quoted a conservative lover of the Union who had just arrived in Washington from New Orleans, traversing Alabama, Georgia, and South Carolina, and visiting Montgomery and Columbia while the legislatures were in session. "He says in his whole route he has not met a single individual who does not advocate an immediate secession, and the formation of a Southern confederacy. He says all attempts to reason or argue are useless; they will not listen. For once, and the first time, he says, in his life, he almost despairs." Quoted in N. Y. *Tribune*, December 10, 1859. This was exaggerated—but it was perhaps possible for a man seeing only restricted circles to get this impression.
34 *House Journal; Senate Journal*, November 5, 1859, p. 47.

would consider this a ground for dissolving the Union.[35] Though not passed, the resolutions were widely supported. Alabama, affirming the right of any State to secede and declaring she would take part in a convention of slaveholding States, provided for calling her own convention if a Republican were elected President —for she would never submit to the foul domination of a sectional Northern party. Florida, too, resolved that the choice of a Republican President, committed to interfere with slavery, would justify the rupture of the Union.[36]

It was natural for South Carolina and Mississippi to go farthest of all. The States of Calhoun and Rhett, A. G. Brown and Jefferson Davis, hold the leadership in disunion sentiment.

Governor William H. Gist of South Carolina, a wealthy lawyer-planter, hot-tempered (he had killed his man in a duel), rigid (an ardent Methodist and pro-hibitionist), and hostile to the Union (he had demanded separate secession in 1851), was quick to see his opportunity. He told the legislature that the whole North was arrayed against the slaveholding area, that Harper's Ferry had marked the crossing of the Rubicon, and that it was hopeless to look to the Democratic Party for protection—it was a pasteboard ship tossed by ocean storms. Resolutions were introduced by Christopher G. Memminger, lawyer and financial expert of Charleston, now turning from conservatism to radicalism. They recalled that South Carolina by her ordinance of 1832 had affirmed the right to secede, asserted that the assaults upon Southern rights had continued with increasing violence, called upon the slaveholding States to meet for concerted action, and directed the governor to send a commissioner to Virginia to press for joint measures of defense. These resolutions were received with acclaim. Already, many public gatherings had been called to organize local vigilance committees, while a number of previously cautious newspapers had become extreme. A vote on still more radical resolves indicated that not less than fifty-three percent of the senate and forty-three percent of the house stood for disunion. As Memminger's proposals passed, and the governor named him commissioner to Richmond, Mississippi accepted the plan for a Southern convention, suggested that delegates meet in Atlanta early in June, and sent a commissioner of her own to Virginia.[37]

Forthwith, the governors of South Carolina, Alabama, and Mississippi began exchanging letters. Where, Gist asked Moore of Alabama, shall our convention

35 New Orleans *Picayune*, January 21, 1860.
36 *Acts of Alabama* 1859-60, 685-687. The Alabama legislature, immediately after the raid, authorized the organization of a volunteer corps in each county to the total of eight thousand men and set aside $200,000 for equipping them. Denham, *Secessionist Movement in Alabama*, 77. Letter of mother of E. Kirby Smith, St. Augustine, January 11, 1860; Smith Papers, Univ. of N. C.
37 Harold Schultz, "South Carolina and National Politics, 1852-60," Ph.D. Dissertation, Duke Univ.; Ames, *State Documents*, 69, 70; Capers, *Memminger*.

be held?—as our three States alone seem ready, must it not be within our borders? [38] Forthwith, too, the radicals in Congress began conferring as never before, talking, planning, and spurring each other on. Representative Porcher Miles of South Carolina gave special attention to the Virginia members. "If," he wrote Memminger, "you can only urge our Carolina view in such a manner as to imbue Virginia with it . . . we may soon hope to see the fruit of your addresses in . . . a Southern Confederacy." [39]

Some strange scenes marked the startling shift of public sentiment in both sections as 1859 closed. In the North, pulpits were still resounding with laudation of John Brown, hawkers were selling John Brown biographies, and halls were vibrating with antislavery oratory. In border cities, pathetic bands of free Negroes, exiles from harsh Southern laws, were succored by private charity as they passed on their way to Canada. In Southern towns and cities, people were meeting to adopt rules for boycotting Northern merchandise, young men and women were agreeing to wear nothing but homespun, and vigilance committees were warning commercial travellers to turn home. In Richmond, a tumultuous crowd gathered at the station to welcome one hundred and sixty medical students, who had left Philadelphia in a body upon assurances that they could receive training in the medical colleges of the South. "Let Virginia call home her sons!" exclaimed Governor Wise. On many a Southern field, militia and volunteers were training; for Alabama this winter appropriated $200,000, Mississippi $150,000, and South Carolina $100,000 for military contingencies. Everywhere, men found excitement pervasive, emotion mounting, and premonition rising of momentous events just ahead. [40]

[II]

The opening of Congress on December 9, 1859, brought no reassurance to the nation, for many shared the fear of ex-President Tyler that a contest over the speakership and the debates of both houses would only add fuel to the general blaze. This first session of the Thirty-sixth Congress, destined to last until the summer heat of 1860 smote the capital, found Minnesota and Oregon added to the American constellation. Each had sent eastward a man of whom more would be heard, Minnesota giving William Windom a place in the House, and Oregon awarding Joseph Lane, an able secessionist orator of North Carolina birth, unscrupulous and imperious, a seat in the Senate. While the upper chamber

38 March 29, 1860; Governor's Papers, Alabama Dept. Archives and History.
39 January 10, 1860; Memminger Papers, Univ. of N. C.
40 Clement Eaton, "The Resistance of the South to Northern Radicalism," *New England Quarterly*, VIII, 215.

was safely Democratic, the House was closely divided. The Republicans counted one hundred and nine members, the Democrats one hundred and one, and the Know-Nothings and Whigs, chiefly from the South, twenty-seven. It would require one hundred and nineteen votes to organize the House. This meant that either the Republicans, who wanted John Sherman for Speaker, or the Democrats, whose caucus nominated Thomas S. Bocock, would have to engineer an alliance with the American-Whig group to succeed. Battle and stratagem lay ahead.

The Senate had profited from some recent losses of the House, for it now had the brilliant oratory of Toombs and the sturdy force of Andrew Johnson. There were giants still in the upper chamber—Douglas, Trumbull, Seward, Davis, and Crittenden; there were lesser men of impressive stature—Wilson, Wade, Chandler, Fessenden, and Benjamin. There were intellectual grotesques, commanding in some ways, absurd and dangerous in others—Sumner for the North and Hammond for the South.

And some striking new figures appeared in the Senate. Iowa, as we have noted, sent James W. Grimes, a Dartmouth graduate and man of culture. While active as farmer, lawyer, and railroad promoter, he was a skillful politician who had done more than anybody else to make his State Republican.[41] From Rhode Island came Henry B. Anthony, charming, kindly, and cultivated, who for twenty years had edited the influential Providence *Journal*. South Carolina gave a seat to James Chesnut, Jr., a quiet-mannered attorney, educated at Princeton and in the law office of J. L. Petigru, who displayed a persuasive gift of speech. From Texas an alarming newcomer strode down the aisle, Louis T. Wigfall. Before Harper's Ferry, the Texans had seemed securely under the control of such unionists as Sam Houston and Reagan. After the raid, however, the legislature met in an ugly mood, seized upon Wigfall as the most advanced Southern Rights man in sight, and, knowing that he was peculiarly obnoxious to Houston, sent him to Washington. The change which had placed A. O. P. Nicholson in John Bell's seat was equally significant.

Republican newspapers could boast that in the House, at least, their stripling party already had a greater intellectual strength than the Democrats. The Northwestern group were particularly strong. Here was Tom Corwin, who had sat in the Senate and held the second office in the Cabinet; despite his sixty-odd years and ripe experience, a man still vigorous. Here were Owen Lovejoy and Elihu B. Washburne of Illinois, Schuyler Colfax of Indiana, and Cadwallader C.

41 Grimes became a boon companion of Fessenden of Maine, and Justin S. Morrill heard them in their rooms repeat Shakespeare, Pope, and Burns to each other almost by the hour. Parker, *Morrill*, 115.

Washburn of Wisconsin. Before long, William A. Howard of Michigan would arrive from the Detroit district. The New England delegation contained nearly as many able men. Eyes turned expectantly to Charles Francis Adams, who had spent most of the interval since his Free Soil campaign editing the ten volumes of John Adams's papers and writing a biography. He owed his nomination and election largely to the personal aid of Charles Sumner. Massachusetts had returned Anson Burlingame and Henry L. Dawes to the House, while Maine had sent back Israel Washburn, making three brothers from one yeoman Androscoggin Valley family. Vermont had reelected Justin S. Morrill. From New York came Roscoe Conkling, all fire, party zealotry, and well-preened vanity; from Pennsylvania, Galusha A. Grow and "honest" John Covode; and from New Jersey, William Pennington.

The member from the middle States who carried most weight, however, was Thaddeus Stevens, club-footed, shaggy-haired veteran of old renown. "I am old and lazy," he wrote his friend Giddings, when actually he thirsted for battle.[42] Two rough witticisms in this session became famous. Smarting from interruption in an argument, he snorted: "I yield to the gentleman from Virginia for a few feeble remarks." Entering the House while an election contest was being debated, and being told that both men were rascals, he commented as he reached for a ballot: "Yes, but which is *our* rascal?"

On the Democratic side, Alexander H. Stephens, Orr, and the generous-hearted John A. Quitman were all missed sorely. The place of the much-lamented Harris of Illinois, Douglasite leader in the fight against Lecompton, was taken by the clever, flippant John A. McClernand. Some striking Southern figures compelled notice. William W. Boyce of South Carolina extorted even from the New York *Tribune* a handsome compliment—"a thinker, a reasoner, a scholar"; J. L. M. Curry of Alabama, who had vision and heart as well as intellectual power, was the brains of the Alabama delegation; L. Q. C. Lamar was an exceptional parliamentarian as well as a man of philosophic depth; and Roger A. Pryor of Virginia, youthful and self-confident, brought a reputation as a fiery editor. The impetuous, lovable Keitt was conspicuous.

On both sides, the extremists were in the saddle. How could it be otherwise? Before Harper's Ferry, moderate doctrines had seemed in the ascendant; the Opposition Party, basis for a future Constitutional Union Party, had shown astonishing strength in the October elections; and Crittenden, Bell, Rives, and Everett hoped for a rapidly growing body of followers. Now in Virginia worried groups were talking of Wise's military measures; on Charleston drill grounds gray-haired men were clattering arms alongside boys who thirsted for action; amid the Alabama cottonfields, officers were selecting two young men

42 November 4, 1859; Giddings Papers.

from each county to attend at State expense the private military academies. In the North, an editorial writer for the *Tribune* was declaring that the Seventh Regiment alone could conquer the Old Dominion; Edmund Quincy was sneering at Louisiana and South Carolina as militarily helpless; the Republican press was ablaze with stories of Southern intolerance. "The Reign of Terror" was a headline which some editors kept standing for items of violence or repression.

With defiant mien, Southern members in hotel lobbies unfolded the *Union*, the *Mercury*, or the *Picayune* to accounts of Yankee provocations. As days passed into weeks, they had plenty to read. The annual convention of New York antislavery forces, held at Albany early in 1860, surpassed itself in vehemence. Slaveholders were denounced as robbers, adulterers, pirates, and murderers. The first resolution declared that in the irresistible conflict being waged against despotism, men could find a glorious assurance that the deliverance of enslaved millions drew nigh. Wendell Phillips was soon telling a Brooklyn audience that slavery should be destroyed, law or no law, Constitution or no Constitution; and that if a Democrat were elected President, war would break out along the Southern mountains.[43] Tokens multiplied that the Fugitive Slave Law had become unenforceable. A runaway Negro who reached New York smuggled aboard a Norfolk schooner had the help, in making his escape to a safe area, of attorneys and magistrates.

Meanwhile, Northern members with equally defiant mien opened the *Evening Post*, the *Republican*, or the *Press* to stories of Southern misdeeds. They, too, had plenty to read. They could study tales of lashing and lynching. Cassius M. Clay, defying the Kentuckians who chased Fee and other Berea men from the State, was asserting that, if necessary, he and his family would flee to some natural stronghold and sell their lives dearly. In North Carolina, Daniel Worth, a minister of fine character and imposing presence, was sentenced to a year in jail on a charge of circulating incendiary books; and onlookers lamented that he was not publicly flogged, as the law permitted. "We shall stripe him yet!" one exclaimed.

On the opening day in the Senate, after prayer and the swearing in of new members, Mason of Virginia arose with his usual stiff dignity. He offered a resolution, he said, which the clerk would read. From the desk came a voice: "Resolved, that a committee be appointed to inquire into the facts attending the late invasion and seizure of the armory and arsenal of the United States at Harper's Ferry, in Virginia, by a band of armed men."

Assuredly, there was truth in what Thoreau had written of John Brown after the execution: "I meet him at every turn. He is more alive than ever he was."

43 N. Y. *Weekly Tribune*, February 4, March 24, 1860.

[III]

In keeping with his character, Buchanan in his annual message of December, 1859, treated the Harper's Ferry affair in admonitory but soothing terms. The raid, he remarked, was important only because it excited Southern fears (which he did not share) that still more dangerous outrages would follow. Good citizens in both sections, he urged, should cultivate mutual forbearance, and allay the demoniac spirit of internecine strife. As an old public functionary, he appealed to the spirit of the wise statesmen of the preceding generation, under whom he had commenced his service, declaring that his dearest earthly wish was to leave the country tranquil, united, and powerful.

A happy sentiment! Yet the light of patriotic generalities paled when brought beside the deep red flame kindled by clashing material and political interests. In one part of the message, Buchanan declared that the Supreme Court had established the right of every citizen to take slave property into the Territories "and to have it protected there under the Federal Constitution." An interesting phrase, whose authorship could probably be traced to Cobb and Jacob Thompson. Just what did Buchanan mean by "have it protected?"—protected by a slave code passed by Congress? Douglas Democrats would have something to say on that. At this very moment, the Republican national committee, calling the party convention at Chicago in May, declared that it would oppose to the last the doctrine that the Constitution of its own force carried slavery into all the Territories.[44]

At once, the House plunged into a convulsive two months' battle over the speakership. The contest began on the first day when, as Republicans rallied behind John Sherman, Representative J. B. Clark of Missouri brought forward a resolution declaring that no man who had endorsed the insurrectionary doctrines of Helper's *Impending Crisis* was fit to be Speaker. Sherman was among the sixty-eight Representatives who had signed a circular asking for funds to scatter a hundred thousand copies of the compendium of that volume throughout the land. In vain did he now assert that he had never read Helper's book. In vain did he offer a letter from Francis P. Blair, Sr., explaining why many leading Republicans had joined in recommending the compendium before it was printed. Helper had brought the book to Silver Spring for examination. After ploughing through it, Blair had told the author that it was objectionable in many passages, and had obtained his written promise to excise or modify the harsh language. On the strength of this pledge, many Representatives had signed the circular—

44 Buchanan's phrase deeply angered Republicans and outraged Douglas's followers. Representative John A. McClernand called the message "a national calamity"; January 3, 1860, Lanphier Papers.

READ! READ! READ!

In the year 1857, an individual named Hinton Rowan Helper, who had been forced to leave his native State, North Carolina, in disgrace, published a book, of which he was the reputed author, entitled "The Impending Crisis." The book recommended direct warfare on Southern society, "be the consequences what they might." It was so extravagant in tone, and so diabolical in its designs, that it was at first generally supposed to be the work of a fool or a madman. No one could believe that any sane or civilized person really entertained any such devilish purposes as it professed.—What, however, was the surprise of the public when the book was actually adopted by the Republican party as a campaign document, and its atrocious principles endorsed by SIXTY-EIGHT Republican members of Congress and *all the influential members of the party!* Below will be found an abstract of the principles it advocated, taken from the large edition of the work, published by A. B. BURDICK, No. 145 Nassau street, N. Y., 1860, and the names of their endorsers, &c :

1. We unhesitatingly declare ourselves in favor of the immediate and unconditional ABOLITION OF SLAVERY.—*Page 26.*

2. "We cannot be TOO HASTY in carrying out our designs."—*Page 33.*

3. "No man can be a true patriot with-

The Mottoes on Our Banner.

1. Thorough organization and independent political action on the part of non-slaveholding whites of the South.

2. Ineligibility of slaveholders; never another vote to the trafficker in human flesh.

3. No co-operation with slaveholders in politics, no fellowship with them in religion no affiliation with them in society.

4. No patronage to slaveholding merchants; no bequest to slave waiting hotels; no fees to slaveholding lawyers; no employment to slaveholding physicians; no audience to slaveholding parsons.—*Pages 155 and 156.*

5. No recognition to pro-slavery men, except as ruffians, outlaws, and criminals.

6. Immediate DEATH to SLAVERY, or if not immediate, unqualified proscription of its advocate during the period of its existence.—*Pages 155 and 156.*

7. Thus, terror engenderers of the South, have we fully and frankly defined our position: we have no modifications to propose, no compromises to offer, nothing to retract, Frown, sirs, fret, foam, prepare your weapons, threat, strike, shoot, stab, bring on civil war, dissolve the Union, nay, annihilac the solar system if you will—do all this, more, less, better, worse, anything—do what you will, sirs, you can neither foil nor intimidate us; our purpose is as firmly fixed as the eternal pillars of Heaven; we have determined to ABOLISH SLAVERY, AND SO HELP US GOD, ABOLISH IT WE WILL.—*Page 187.*

to me a work of *great merit*, rich, yet accurate in statistical information and logical analysis, and I do not doubt that it will exert a great influence on the public mind, in favor of *the cause of Truth and Justice.*

I am, gentlemen, very respectfully,

Your ob't servant,

W. H. SEWARD.

We, the undersigned, members of the House of Representatives of the National Congress, do cordially endorse the opinion and approve the enterprise set forth in the foregoing circular:—

Schuyler Colfax,
Owen Lovejoy,
Edwin B. Morgan,
Joshua R. Giddings,
Calvin C. Chaffee,
Wm. A. Howard,
John Sherman,
Daniel W. Gooch,
Justin S. Morril,
J. A. Bingham,
E. B. Washburne,
Edward Dodd,
John Covode,
Sam'l G. Andrews,
Sidney Dean,
Emory B. Pottle,
John F. Potter,
J. F. Farnsworth,
R. E. Fenton,
Mason W. Tappan,
T. Davis, (Iowa)
Homer E. Royce,
A. S. Murray,

Anson Burlingame,
Amos P. Granger,
Galusha A. Grow,
Edward Wade,
William H. Kelsey,
Henry Waldon,
Geo. W. Palmer,
Henry L. Dawes,
I. Washburn, Jr.
Wm. Kellogg,
Benjamin Stanton,
Cydnor B. Tompkins,
Cad. C. Washburne,
Abraham B. Olin,
Nath'l B. Durfee,
DeWitt C. Leach,
T. Davis, (Mass.)
C. L. Knapp,
Philemon Bliss,
Charles Case,
James Pike,
Isaac D. Clawson,
Robert B. Hall,

Name	Amount
Greeley, Horace, New York city,	100
Greenleaf, R. C. Boston, Mass.	50
Harris, Edward, Woonsocket, R. I.	100
Henrick, Benjamin S. New York city,	50
Helper, H. R. New York city,	25
Hurlbut, F. Brooklyn, N. Y.	100
Jay, John, New York city,	25
Ketcham, Edgar, New York city,	25
McCauley, Wm. Wilmington, Del.	10
Marble, Nathan, Port Byron, N. Y.	10
May, Samuel, Boston, Ms.	100
Morgan, Edwin D. Albany, N. Y.	100
Neamite, John, Lowell, Ms.	10
Norton, John T. Farmington, Ct.	100
Parsons, J. C. New York,	10
Pinner, M., Kansas City, Mo.	100
Plumly, Benjamin Rush, Philadelphia, Pa.	30
Randolph, Evan, Philadelphia, Pa.	
Republicans of Pottsville and N. Coventry, Pa. $40. Crown Point, N. Y., $11,	51
Republicans of Shawnee Mound, $20. South Bend, Ind. $10,	
Roberts, W. S. New York city,	30
Robinson, Hanson, New Castle Co. Del.	10
Ryerson, David, Newton, N. J.	20
Sherman, S. N. Ogdensburgh, N. Y.	64
Smith, Gerrit, Peterboro, N. Y.	33
Spring, Marcus, Eaglewood, N. J.	20
Stoner, John A. Smyrna, N. Y.	10
Stranahan, J. S. T. Brooklyn, N. Y.,	100
Tappan, Lewis, Brooklyn, N. Y.,	100
Thompson, Wm. B., Philadelphia, Pa.,	100
Tweedy, Edmund, Newport, R. I.,	10
Wadsworth, James S., New York City,	100
Wakeman, Abram, New York City,	100
Weed, Thurlow, Albany, N. Y.,	100
White, Aaron, Thompson, Conn.	10
Wright, E. N. and James A., Philadelphia, Pa.	50
Wood, Bradford R., Albany, N. Y.,	100
A. A., $50; B. H., $50; C. C., $10; D. D., $10; E. $20; F. F., $25, North Carolina,	165
S.F. M., Wilmington, Del,	10
A friend, by S. E. Sewell, Boston, Mass., $10; E. B., Brooklyn, N. Y., $25	35
Total,	**2,518**

Democratic Propaganda Against the Republican Endorsers of Helper's Book.

and then some deplorable paragraphs slipped through. This explanation did not mollify the Southerners. We are entitled to know, declared Leake of Virginia, whether we are to select a Speaker who, whilst we are discharging our public duties in Washington, is inciting our slaves at home to apply the torch to our dwellings, and the knife to the throats of our wives and children.

The Southern uproar over a book which probably few members had seen, much less read, was somewhat exaggerated. We have seen that the original volume contained much indefensible billingsgate directed at "slaveocrats," and a few suggestions of violent action.[45] But in general it was a dry, statistical, and factual body of comparisons between the results of free and slave labor. It was as exciting as Euclid, and as fiery as a ledger. Moreover, it was addressed wholly to the whites—the non-slaveholding whites—of the South. Not being intended for Negroes, it would not interest even those who could comprehend it, while its plan of Negro deportation would anger them and their abolitionist friends. It was unfortunate that the compendium contained offensive matter, including a passage headed "Revolution Must Free the Slaves." But all attempts to connect it with John Brown and slave insurrections were wide of the mark.

House debate had been disorderly for years, but never with the deep, searing hatred which now manifested itself. On the second day, Thaddeus Stevens accused the South of trying to intimidate the free States; you have succeeded fifty times, he said, but now you will fail. Crawford of Georgia strode forward to confront him. Your Union meetings are hypocrisy, he said; you pretend to respect our rights, yet continually plan war; when will you let us alone? As excited groups collected behind each champion, a collision seemed imminent.

Next day the House met in a chastened spirit. "A few more such scenes as we had on this floor yesterday," exclaimed Morris of Illinois, "and we will hear the crack of the revolver, and see the gleam of the brandished blade." Tempers soon grew edged again, however, and on December 9 an affray was barely averted. Logan of Illinois was understood by Kellogg of that State to use the expression "a spaniel coward"; the two rushed at each other, and amid general uproar were parted with difficulty. Both on the floor and in the lobbies, talk of civil war was now frequent. Try to stir up insurrection in our midst, or to force us back into the Union once we decide to secede, said Bonham of South Carolina, and we shall welcome you Yankees to bloody graves.

More was at stake in the speakership contest than a mere question of prestige, for the make-up of the committees depended upon the choice. Having won the advantage in the elections of 1858–59, Republicans felt entitled to make the most of it. No mere expert in rules will do, insisted Thaddeus Stevens; the Speaker must have nerve and iron fidelity to *our* principles. Democrats could not face

45 Helper, *The Impending Crisis*, 128, 139, 149, 158.

with indifference the threat that their opponents would set up committees to investigate the situation in Kansas, the foreign slave trade, Federal expenditures, and, most painful of all, accusations of departmental mismanagement.

Yet it was certainly true that, in organizing the Senate, Southern Democrats had set an example of flagrant partisanship. The sixty-six members of the Senate represented eighteen free States with a white population of about twenty millions, and fifteen slaveholding States with about seven million white inhabitants. Of the twenty-two standing committees among which business was distributed, however, the chairmanships of sixteen went to slaveholding States, and of the six others to Northern Democrats politically sympathetic with the South. Not one really important Senate committee was allowed either a Northern chairman or a majority of Northern members. This sectional partisanship was denounced by no less prominent a Northern Democrat than Pugh of Ohio, who warned his Southern brethren that if they wished to put down the agitation over slavery, they must forego such transparent tactics. If the South is to rule the Senate, said Republicans, the rich and populous North has a right to rule the House.[46]

Partly because committee control would be so important during the Presidential campaign and afterwards, and partly because of heightened sectional animosities, this eight weeks' struggle differed sharply from the speakership contest of 1855; it was more desperate, more violent, and, above all, more clearly stamped as the effort of a minority to coerce the whole House and make obstruction a political weapon. The slave State Democrats were willing to block the wheels of government until March 4, 1861—until a new House had been elected and seated—if they could not have their way. Their strategy came nearer to an introduction of Latin American methods into Washington affairs than any previous event in our history. Even Jefferson Davis was ready for an indefinite paralysis of Congress, writing a friend that as the South had little to hope and much to deprecate from its action, no legislation at all might be their best estate.

46 See Cleveland *Leader*, December 23, 1859, for typical comment. The Foreign Affairs Committee in the Senate was presided over by James M. Mason, old-time messmate and disciple of Calhoun, and a firm believer in the necessity for Southern separation. The chairman of the Territories Committee was Green of Missouri, whose name was gall and wormwood to Western Democrats who could never forget how he had planned and executed the overthrow of Benton and stepped into Douglas's place as head of this key group; tall, spare, intellectual looking, he was an incisive spokesman for the Buchanan Democrats. Clay of Alabama was head of the Commerce Committee, Yulee of Florida of the Post Office Committee, Bayard of Delaware of the Judiciary Committee, Brown of Mississippi of the Committee on the Federal District, Mallory of Florida of the Naval Affairs Committee. Why, Republicans asked, should the South complain that one chamber was led by its opponents? The slaveholding States still controlled the Presidency, Vice-Presidency, Supreme Court, and machinery of the Senate. A single county in Ohio—Hamilton—had more voters than all Florida, yet Florida boasted of two important Senate chairmanships and Ohio had none. The Democrats of the Northwest had once been a powerful body; they could now declare that because of such Southern measures as Lecompton, they had lost most of their members in both Senate and House.

Some Northern sympathizers believed that a deadlock might frighten their section into surrender. "Don't organize," George Sanders telegraphed the secessionists Keitt and Porcher Miles on December 16; "earnest revolution going on all over the North adjourn Congress until after holidays and all come here." [47]

Representative Clark's resolution for the exclusion of any person who had endorsed Helper's book was unprecedented in character, a breach of parliamentary practice, and in violation of the Act of 1789. When it was dropped, a substitute of somewhat similar tenor was offered and lost by a tie vote. Democratic members thereupon claimed unlimited freedom of debate. They obstructed a resolution to shut off all discussion until after the election of a Speaker. They obstructed a proposal to take at least three ballots daily; even one ballot. They obstructed a plan for limiting each speaker to one thirty-minute utterance on any pending question. They flatly refused to permit adoption of a rule for electing the Speaker by plurality, which had twice before been accepted to break a deadlock, and which for weeks seemed to offer the only escape. Meanwhile, the Administration Democrats made long and vituperative speeches, offered endless chains of dilatory motions (to adjourn, to be excused from voting, to call the *ayes* and *nays*, and so on), and did everything in their power to create confusion. Fifty-eight of them, all from slaveholding States, signed a pledge of mutual union in resisting by every weapon of parliamentary tactics the adoption of a plurality rule. This rule-or-ruin group constituted an iron-bound body to prevent the strongest party from taking effective action. With 114 or 115 votes usually needed to elect a Speaker, Sherman could muster 110 or 111, but no more.

The obstructionists thus held the House at a standstill, permitting votes only when they believed them perfectly safe. In the first week, they allowed three ballots for Speaker; in the second, seven; in the third, when they were trying to make combinations with other groups, eleven; in the fourth, when these combinations failed, three; in the fifth and sixth, five each; in the seventh, none; and in the eighth and ninth, again five each. Altogether, they permitted forty-four votes in forty days of actual session. During a similar period in 1855, no fewer than one hundred and thirty ballots had been taken. With good reason, McPherson of Pennsylvania later said that the Administration men, organizing a conspiracy, had approached the verge of revolution.[48] The Republicans, meanwhile, showed a praiseworthy moderation. They held no caucus meetings, displayed little discipline, and were so ready to let their most conservative men do nearly all the talking that the radicals chafed. An Iowa member, Samuel R. Curtis, found the taunts of the Southerners almost insupportable and longed to retort

47 Jefferson Davis, January 1, 1860, De Leon Papers, South Caroliniana Library; Sanders, December 16, 1859, Miles Papers, Univ. of N. C.
48 *Cong. Globe*, 36th Cong., 1st Sess., February 24, 1860.

in kind. "But our friends generally advise a cool, quiet indifference," he wrote in his journal, "believing the [Southern] object is to keep up such a feeling as will drive stragglers into the Democratic lines." [49] Tom Corwin's good-natured utterances had a mollifying effect.

Restraint was imperative, for at times a spark would have set loose an explosion. The Clerk, his indecision approaching imbecility, was utterly unable to control the vociferous assemblage. Again and again, when he declined to put motions that would have restored discipline, members longed for another John Quincy Adams to arise, as Adams had done in the deadlock of 1839, to take control and lead the House in self-organization. Henry A. Wise's ejaculation of that time might have been reechoed: "Now we are a mob!" Until its constitutional officers were installed the House *was* a mob, and an inflammable one.

On the floor, angry harangues, denunciations, and charges, emphasized by bursts of hand-clapping, foot-stamping, and raucous laughter. In the galleries, applause and hissing from the motley crowd of onlookers—loafers, clerks, politicians, handsomely dressed ladies and gentlemen. In the lobbies, a seething, murmuring, ugly-tempered mass of hangers-on; everywhere, at times, language that would have disgraced a barroom. Recurrently, speakers lashed out in passages that threatened to precipitate a general affray. Once, two Indianans, Dunn and Davis, exchanged the lie amid a general uproar; once, Haskin of New York ridiculing McRae of Mississippi as a circus rider brought on an approach to mob fighting. Roger A. Pryor made insolent speeches in polished language; Keitt turned on his stage thunder; and Reuben Davis declared that he was for hanging Seward and others who avowed what he called murderous sentiments. "The Capitol resounds with the cry of dissolution," wrote Senator Grimes to his wife, "and the cry is echoed throughout the city."

Practically all members were now armed with deadly weapons. In both chambers, Senator Hammond said, "the only persons who do not have a revolver and a knife are those who have two revolvers." For a time a New England Representative, a former clergyman, came unarmed, but finally he too bought a pistol. A Louisiana Congressman threatened to fetch his double-barrelled shotgun into the House. Supporters of both parties in the galleries also bore lethal weapons, and were ready to use them.[50] A single shot or blow might have brought on a melee which would have shocked the civilized world and perhaps have dissolved the government.

One Southern spectator wrote Alexander H. Stephens that he expected to see bloody fighting before the House was organized. A good many slave State members, he declared, "are willing to fight the question out, and to settle it

48 MS Journal, December 8, 1859; Illinois State Hist. Library.
50 *Cong. Globe*, 36th Cong., 1st Sess., December 7, 8, 1859, January 5, 12, 1860, etc.

right there; and some are even anxious. Deplorable as this is, it is nevertheless true. I can't help wishing the Union were dissolved and we had a Southern confederacy." [51] These were the Southerners who impressed Charles Francis Adams, Jr., as spoiling for a war; but this was a mistaken interpretation, for their temper was much less aggressive than it seemed. Fear—honest fear of the future—was really at the root of much of the bluster. The Southerners had a general fear of losing their rights, a deadly fear of servile rebellion, and a growing fear of Northern onslaughts. A few subtle men, listening to the speeches, thought that their brave words concealed a gnawing apprehension. [52]

However compounded of resentment, aggressiveness, braggadocio, and fear, the current temper made some kind of violent denouement all too possible. Reports circulated that Governor Wise had promised, if fighting began, to send Virginia troops to seize the capital and impound the national funds and papers. The impetuous governor had certainly used Brown's raid as an excuse to arm and drill the militia, spending more than $250,000, quartering large bodies of soldiery on the inhabitants, and enforcing martial law. "More than fifty thousand stand of arms already distributed," ex-President Tyler had written on December 6. Wise's alarmist inflation of the raid had done much to place Virginia on a military footing—and, had fighting broken out in the capital, he might have been foolish enough to march on the city. [53]

It is certain that another governor, Gist of South Carolina, promised armed support to the Congressmen of his State if they offered forcible resistance to the seating of such a Speaker as John Sherman. Declaring that, though he preferred a peaceable solution, he was prepared to wade in blood rather than submit to a degrading inequality, he privately assured them: "If . . . you upon consultation decide to make the issue of force in Washington, write or telegraph me, and I will have a regiment in or near Washington in the shortest possible time." [54]

The country was perhaps nearer to bloodshed in these tense weeks than it knew. In the South particularly, popular feeling rose as the press published reports of the speeches. Just before Christmas, the Virginia legislature passed resolutions extending sympathy to the Representatives of the State in the struggle in which they were engaged, and recommending, in view of the public danger, a union of all elements opposed to the Black Republicans. [55] As January dragged on with Congress still deadlocked, business became alarmed. Men directing the large financial houses predicted that, unless early organization of

51 J. Hanly Smith, January 14, 1860; Stephens Papers, LC.
52 S. R. Curtis MS Journal, December 6, 1859.
53 See J. M. Botts, "Letter to Opposition Members" (pamphlet); Hunter Corr., 281.
54 To W. P. Miles, December 20, 1859; Miles Papers, Univ. of N. C.
55 Printed circular, December 23, 1859.

the House restored confidence, the country would suffer a panic worse than that of 1857.[56]

[IV]

Then, at the end of January, to the nation's intense relief, the paralyzing contest terminated. With only 109 Republicans and 86 Administration men in a House of 230 sitting members, neither side could elect a man without gaining a considerable number of Know-Nothings or Whigs. At one moment, on the thirty-ninth ballot, it seemed that the Democrats were about to triumph. Joining hands with the "South Americans," they mustered one hundred and twelve votes for William N. H. Smith, a North Carolina Know-Nothing. As last-minute pledges on the popular sovereignty issue were given, some Douglas Democrats changed their votes to place themselves in Smith's column: Pendleton of Ohio, Montgomery of Pennsylvania, Morris of Illinois, and others. Amid cheers over their decision, pages raced down from the Clerk's desk to report that Smith had a majority of one and was elected! Triumphant Democrats placed the news on the House telegraph.

The Republicans, however, still had a card to play. Instantly, the tall, slender form of John Sherman rose above the clamorous groups. For seven weeks, while his name led the balloting, he had cast no vote. "Mr. Clerk," he said calmly, "call my name." The Clerk did so. Sherman responded, "Mr. Corwin!" The vote was tied. As several members again changed their votes, the Clerk announced the final result: Smith 112, Sherman 106, scattering 10, with no choice.[57]

It was now the turn of the Republicans to strike a blow. On January 30, Sherman withdrew to clear the track for a coalition nominee. It was unfortunate that he had to do so, for he would have made an excellent Speaker. A quiet, moderate, businesslike man, who since entering the House in 1855 had devoted his main attention to financial subjects, he no more sympathized with abolitionism than his brother William Tecumseh, who wrote him from New Orleans that abolitionist ideas would mean disunion, war, and anarchy. "You ask why I signed the recommendation of the Helper book," John wrote his brother. "It was a thoughtless, foolish, and unfortunate act." [58] During the debates, Sherman had reemphasized his opposition to any interference with slavery inside the States, and had assured his Southern colleagues that the Republicans had come to Washington filled with condemnation of the John Brown raid.

56 J. W. Bryce, Phila., January 20, 1860; Boteler Papers, Duke Univ.
57 *Cong. Globe*, 36th Cong., 1st Sess., January 28, 1860; N. Y. *Herald, Tribune,* Washington *Constitution,* January 29, 30, 1860.
58 *The Sherman Letters,* 78, 79.

Now, as he gave way, a coalition slate comprising William Pennington of New Jersey for Speaker, John W. Forney for Clerk, and Thomas H. Ford of Ohio for printer, was brought forward. Pennington, a new member of hazy political affiliations, long a Whig, had been elected to his seat by a People's Party. On the forty-fourth ballot, taken February 1, he obtained one hundred and seventeen votes and a majority. He was to prove one of the worst-equipped and most incompetent Speakers in the nation's history.

Both sides could take some satisfaction in what one member termed a dogfall result. The Democrats could boast that they had blocked Sherman and forced their opponents to turn to an old-time Whig who supported the Fugitive Slave Law just as it stood. The Republicans could say that they had chosen a determined upholder of Congressional exclusion of slavery from the Territories. The major advantage, however, lay with the Republicans.

Pennington, aligning himself with that party, accepted with little change the roster of committees which Sherman had drawn up in anticipation of his own election. He made Sherman chairman of the powerful Ways and Means Committee, and placed Justin S. Morrill in that key group to write new tariff legislation. He made Owen Lovejoy, a champion of homestead legislation, chairman of the Public Lands Committee. He named the veteran Galusha A. Grow head of the Committee on Territories. Well might Republicans give the new Speaker a serenading party, with champagne flowing freely at Willard's Hotel. Well might John Sherman stand up there to assert that, since the decisive vote, stocks had advanced, cotton ruled firm at eleven cents, slave property was as valuable as ever, and the public mind was serene. The Republicans had elected a Speaker, and the Union was safe. So will it be, he predicted, when they have elected a President.[59]

Nevertheless, passionate scenes were still enacted on the floor. Early in April, a violent speech by Lovejoy aroused the anger of Southerners to a high pitch. Pryor interrupted him; friends of the two men sprang forward to support them; and for a moment a battle seemed imminent. Crawford, who declared that not a dozen overseers in Georgia would submit to such language as Lovejoy used, was minded to shout: "Gentlemen will take parties for a cotillion." By a mighty effort he kept calm. "I never said a word to anybody," he wrote Stephens, "but quietly cocked my revolver in my pocket and took my position in the midst of the mob, and as coolly as I write it to you now, I had made up my mind to sell out my blood at the highest possible price." For several days the excitement constantly threatened an explosion. If some member had lost his self-control, the ensuing melee might have precipitated civil war.

59 N. Y. *Weekly Tribune*, February 11, 1860. Elihu Washburne was made chairman of the Commerce Committee, Schuyler Colfax of Post Offices, and Corwin of Foreign Affairs.

[V]

The currents of sectional antagonism which flowed from the House were reinforced by similar impulses from a quarreling Senate. Mason's resolution for an inquiry into Harper's Ferry had no sooner been offered than Lyman Trumbull was on his feet to demand an investigation into the pillaging of the arsenal at Liberty, Missouri, in 1855, by a band arming for the invasion of Kansas. This was a gratuitous gesture, for the facts of the Missouri episode were well known. After Trumbull had irritated Southerners by alluding to the "shrieks" of Virginia, Hale of New Hampshire deepened their resentment by declaring that some judges of the Supreme Court were base tools of the slave power, that Federal trials under the Fugitive Slave Law were the most monstrous perversions of justice in the history of the English-speaking peoples, and that Northern forbearance had been stretched to its utmost limits. If the first attack in the House had come from the South, in the Senate it came (with far less provocation) from the North.

Republican spokesmen, one after another, spiritedly denied any connection with or sympathy for John Brown. Trumbull, for example, declared that no man who was unprepared to destroy the government and society itself could justify such a criminal act. Yet even as these men spoke, Jefferson Davis, Chesnut, Yulee, C. C. Clay, and other Southerners insisted that the raid was the logical result of Republican teachings. They scornfully rejected the idea that a few pale words of Republican censure could weigh against the memorial meetings and minute guns which had honored Brown on the day of his death. What had given birth to his violence and Helper's incendiarism? It was the nefarious spirit of multitudes of Northern Republicans, who, shouted Chesnut, are constantly scattering firebrands among us. Southerners harked back not only to the irrepressible conflict address, but to Seward's speech of 1855 in which, pointing to three million slaves as a sullen, half-hostile force, he had said that a servile rebellion is always the most hideous form of war, and that the outside world always sympathized with slaves in revolt.[60]

Conditional threats of secession were taking on increased emphasis in Senate as well as House, and were all too plainly an expression of hardening sentiment. It was not difficult to detect the note of apprehension underlying these utterances. We say, declaimed Chesnut, that we can no longer tolerate the present dangers; "we will sunder the Union, pull it to pieces, column, base, and tower, before we submit to be crushed by a government which is our own as well as yours." Clay of Alabama predicted that few if any Southern States would sub-

60 *Cong. Globe*, 36th Cong., 1st Sess., 129.

mit to the installation of a Republican President. Senators Toombs, Iverson, and Clingman all asserted that the triumph of a Northern party would mean the disruption of the Union. Hunter, always inarticulate, voiced his emotions in an absurd figure of speech. The Union was a mighty arch, held together by the concentrated strength and mutual support of its parts—"and the very keystone of this arch consists of the black marble cap of African slavery; knock that out, and the mighty fabric, with all that it upholds, topples and tumbles to its fall." In the House, Albert Rust was declaring that the people of Arkansas loved the Union. "But, sir, when it is perverted and prostituted into an instrument of wrong, injustice, insult, and oppression, . . . we will oppose and resist it, though it should be rent into as many fragments as there are States composing it." Jefferson Davis expressed the feeling of radicals: "The power of resistance consists, in no small degree, in meeting the enemy at the outer gate." [61]

That there was no danger of immediate action, however, was demonstrated by the failure of Memminger's mission to Virginia. The agent of South Carolina, received with due ceremony, delivered a four-hour address to the Richmond legislature on January 19, 1860. He urged the Old Dominion to join other States in a convention to discuss means of protecting their rights and property. South Carolina, he said, would abide by the will of her sisters. "If our pace be too fast for some, we are content to walk slower; our earnest wish is that all may keep together." While the address was heard with attention, and the legislature voted to publish and distribute ten thousand copies, no strong disposition to act appeared. Not wishing to embarrass the deliberations, Memminger returned to South Carolina on February 10. He reported to Governor Gist that the Virginians were hesitant because they felt that Southern rights might yet be preserved within the Union, and feared that the proposed convention would prove precipitate.

In the end, the Virginia legislature resolved that it was inexpedient to appoint deputies to a conference. Most other Southern States showed a similar reluctance (Mississippi alone selecting delegates), and the gathering vanished into oblivion. On this point, conservatism still won the day. Gist, indeed, had to write Governor Hicks of Maryland that he never desired secession so long as the rights of the South in the Union were respected and her equality was recognized.[62]

61 *Idem*, 37, 124, 272, etc.
62 A group of former Whigs and other Opposition members of the Virginia legislature addressed a letter to John Minor Botts, January 14, 1860, declaring themselves disturbed by the manifestation of a design to prepare Virginia for Civil War, and to use the John Brown raid as a pretext for early hostilities. Botts replied to the group in a pamphlet of fifteen pages of fine type, denouncing the efforts of Wise and the Virginia radicals to exaggerate current difficulties. In Richmond, he wrote later, these men had created an uproar that had rarely been paralleled even in Paris and that had spread all over the State. See Botts, *The Great Rebellion*, 177, 178; Shanks, *Secession Movement in Virginia*, 62 ff.,

In the running Congressional debate, the repercussions of the John Brown raid happily counted for less than had been anticipated. The investigating committee under Senator Mason, sitting behind closed doors, accumulated a mass of evidence but none of it implicated the Republican Party. Gerrit Smith, T. W. Higginson, George L. Stearns, and the others involved were abolitionists pure and simple. The committee failed to make any deep impression on public opinion. When Frank B. Sanborn and several others whom it summoned to Washington to testify refused to move, the Senate voted their arrest as contumacious witnesses.[63] Early in April, a deputy Federal marshal and deputy sergeant-at-arms of the Senate, acting under a warrant issued by the Vice-President, appeared in Concord to seize Sanborn. As they tried to force the struggling young man into a carriage, a menacing crowd gathered, while Judge Rockwood Hoar hurriedly wrote out a writ of personal replevin. The case promptly came before the State supreme court under Chief Justice Lemuel Shaw. That tribunal held unanimously that no authority existed for the arrest, and that Sanborn should be discharged. All spring, vehement disclaimers of John Brown by most Republican chieftains continued, and a repudiation of his acts was shortly to be written into the Republican platform.

Yet the fact of a powerful change in Southern feeling since the raid could not be ignored. It was not founded on any growing desire for disunion *per se;* it was not attributable—far from it—to any rising response to the demands for a territorial slave code and a reopening of the foreign slave trade. It was a change founded on fear; fear, since Harper's Ferry and the Northern response thereto, of assaults from without and uprisings from within which would undermine their precarious social and economic system and initiate a series of revolutionary changes. The best Southerners knew in their hearts that the system was full of objectionable features. Thoughtful men were well aware that they could no more hold the system frozen and changeless than they could immobilize the Mississippi River. Committed to the pretense that slavery was untouchable and unchangeable, they saw the tides of world-wide social progress surging at their bastions. They realized that Harper's Ferry, unimportant in itself, was a symbol; that John Brown's pikes were so many flaming glaives brandished in the heavens. They were afraid; afraid of the future, which down to the night of the

---

85 ff. For Memminger's mission, see Charleston *Courier*, February–March, 1860; "South Carolina Mission to Virginia," *De Bow's Review*, IV, 751–777; Miles Papers, Univ. of N. C. Gist's letter is in the Charleston *Mercury*, February 17, 1860.

63 Stearns more courageously appeared before the Senate committee on February 24, 1860, and did not mollify Southerners by his outspoken statement that he believed John Brown the representative man of the 19th century as Washington was of the 18th. "The Harper's Ferry affair and the capacity for self-government shown by the Italians in 1859 were the great events of the age," he remarked. N. Y. *Weekly Tribune*, March 3, 1860.

raid had still seemed far away, but which the morning after was knocking imperiously at their gates. How could they forget those levins of a coming tempest, and how arrest the future? Only by forsaking the Union—only by isolation. A tie with the North and the world was a tie with irresistible social progress.

This widespread fear, struggling with the deep-seated love of the Union and with the hope that some rational adjustment could yet be worked out (for optimism was one of the cardinal traits of American life), produced a seething maelstrom of ideas and emotions. How far even the more radical States yet stood from any desire for an irrevocable break was illustrated by the course of Alabama.

Outwardly, the Alabamians seemed bent on militant action. The State Democratic convention, meeting in Mobile on January 11, 1860, with Yancey its leading spirit, passed with a remarkable approach to unanimity resolutions declaring that the South should maintain the principles of the Dred Scott decision, that the delegates in Charleston should present these resolutions, and that if they were not accepted in substance, the delegation should withdraw. Yancey, after a struggle of twelve years, had succeeded in committing the Alabama party to support of Calhoun's resolutions of 1848. On February 24, the Alabama legislature adopted resolutions—and here again Yancey's master hand was visible—directing the governor, in the event of a Republican victory in November, to call an immediate State convention to determine what steps Alabama should take to protect herself.[64] Yet these steps did not point to a general intention to break with the Union if a Republican were constitutionally elected President; they did not even point to a general desire to break with the Douglas Democrats.

Many voted for the conditional instructions to withdraw at Charleston simply as a threat, believing that the fear of Democratic ruin would bring about concessions by the Douglas men to the demands of the South. If the threat failed—well, the delegation might disregard its instructions. Much the same threat had been made by the Alabama State convention in 1848, but the delegates had meekly fallen into line behind Cass. Many also believed that even if the Alabama representatives did bolt at Charleston, this would break up neither the party nor the Union. In some fashion or other the party would reunite before the

64 A desperate struggle had been under way in Alabama between the forces of Yancey and of Douglas. The chief Yancey organ was the Montgomery *Advertiser*; the chief Douglas organ, John Forsyth's Mobile *Register*. The Montgomery *Confederation*, which wished the Lecompton issue forever buried, was ready to support Douglas on the Cincinnati platform and a noncommital reassertion of the Dred Scott decision. John J. Seibels, editor, to Douglas, January 17, 1860, Douglas Papers. The *Southern Advocate*, published in North Alabama, took the same stand. The Yancey wing stood for the slave-code doctrine; the Seibels-Forsyth wing for a reassertion of the Cincinnati platform. As we shall see later, the Yancey forces won. Murphy, *Alabama and the Charleston Convention of 1860*, 245 ff.

campaign got well under way; and if it did not, the fact that three or four parties were in the field would mean no electoral majority for anybody, a choice of President by the House, and a probable Southern victory. As for the legislative resolutions providing for a State convention to decide upon the question of secession, here too defiance of the North was more apparent than real. "Many who voted for the call," testifies an Alabamian familiar with the spirit of the time, "were ready to deny that occasion existed for extreme action, and in the event of the meeting of a convention, would be ready to resort to any delay by which the passions of the hour could be assuaged and the dreaded spectre of disunion be exorcised." [65]

Nobody, in fact, as 1860 opened, could predict how far the South would go in the fateful months just ahead. The men most uneasy were those who realized that, in a time of revolutionary crisis, the extremists always gain ground at the expense of the moderates. Crittenden, Bell, Rives, Botts, and other border State men of the Opposition were trying hard to rally and organize the conservative groups. Declaring the country on the verge of ruin, carrying on an active correspondence with Washington Hunt, Letcher, John P. Kennedy, Amos A. Lawrence, and others of their type, Crittenden led in issuing a January call for the establishment of a national constitutional party to combat both the Democrats and Republicans. He implored Alexander H. Stephens to aid him in the movement, which he thought was favored by the feeling of the whole country.[66]

At the same time, Southern radicals made no concealment of their determination to push forward as fast and far as circumstances permitted. Another correspondent of Stephens, Representative Martin J. Crawford of Georgia, asserted that his fellow-Southerners in the House were prepared for decisive measures. "All the members say that they have no doubt their people are ready to dissolve, not only extreme men but men from the border States, in fact they talk stronger than we do." [67] The South, declared Pryor of Virginia, "is bracing her energies for the inevitable struggle." The more intransigent governors—Moore of Alabama, Perry of Florida, Joseph E. Brown of Georgia, Gist of South Carolina, McWillie of Mississippi—continued to issue exhortations to resistance.

Everywhere in the South, men were torn between old loyalties and new fears. From letters and diaries significant testimony of their agony of spirit can be disinterred. Typical of innumerable others is the statement of a North Carolina Unionist, William A. Walsh, that, long as he had stood by the national cause, the Northern applause for John Brown and Helper had shaken him, and that unless the slaveholding areas were made safe from further assaults, he was

65 Hodgson, *Cradle of the Confederacy*, Ch. 15.
66 January 13, 1860; Stuart Collection, 1860.
67 Washington, December 13, 1859; Stephens Paper, LC.

willing to take the chance of every probable evil that might flow from disunion. A majority in his county, he believed, would still accept an honorable compromise, but a large minority was already determined upon secession by fair means or foul.[68] In the South Carolina senate, another staunch Unionist, E. J. Moses, announced that while he had never expected his feelings to change, he was at last ready for secession; for he did not believe that peace, safety, or honor could longer be found in a yoke with the North. Only one Unionist newspaper was now left in South Carolina, Benjamin F. Perry's *Southern Patriot* at Greenville; and only two effective speakers in the legislature, Perry and M. P. O'Connor, took the Unionist side in debate.[69]

The passions of the hour were strongly affecting the emotions of Southern women. Though that good soldier, E. Kirby Smith, serving in the West, was still a hearty nationalist, his mother wrote him from St. Augustine in terms used by countless others:

The whole country is in a state of fearful agitation—disunion! disunion! is the cry with our Southern friends, it is boldly spoken of by the fireside, in public, in all places it is the absorbing subject. The aggressions of the North and the insults to which we are subjected in their papers their treasonable acts how can it be otherwise if our rights as guaranteed by the Constitution are trampled under foot defiantly—disunion must follow. Southern men and Southern women will not sit down with folded hands if the masses elect a Black Republican President. There are no doubt noble Patriots, lovers of Country and respecters of law among them, but they are as sprinklings in the multitude. These are fearful times. What will be the end I know not. . . . I feel confident that your sword will be offered to the land of your birth—was not the stampede of the Southern students from Northern colleges a beautiful thing—how I honor those youths—I have the blood of a soldier of the Revolution in my veins, and it warms up as I think how the noble fabric of this building has been desecrated.[70]

It is not remarkable that Caleb Cushing, whose legal work took him to Washington, used New Year's Day to make a gloomy report to ex-President Pierce. "We seem to be drifting into destruction before our eyes, in utter helplessness. The Administration is utterly depopularized; the President is embarrassed with insoluble questions; Congress is paralyzed by party spirit; and everybody seems to despair of any help from man, though many are looking vaguely for they knew not what interposition from Providence."[71]

We have spoken of the Southern realization that a tie with the North and the world was a tie with irresistible social progress. A good many Americans

68 December 12, 1859; L. C. Branch Papers, Duke Univ.
69 Kibler, *Perry*, Ch. 16; M. D. O'Connor, *Life of M. P. O'Connor*.
70 January 11, 1860; E. Kirby Smith Papers, Univ. of N. C.
71 January 1, 1860; Pierce Photostats, LC.

were now hearing of *The Origin of Species*, just published in England. The Darwinian age, not only in biology but in the social sphere, was opening. Faith in evolution was henceforth to be mightily reinforced. Slavery could not be detached or shielded from the forces of the time; and how, in the year of grace 1860, did slavery look against the background of an evolving world civilization? For beyond all question, beneath the issue of union or disunion, war or peace, lay the complex problem of slavery.

5

Slavery in a World Setting

IN THE summer of 1860, Augustus Baldwin Longstreet, former judge, author, and head of South Carolina College, drove to Somerset House in London, scene of the Fourth International Statistical Congress, to which Secretary Cobb had appointed him a delegate. The American minister, Dallas, was present. They had just applauded Prince Albert's opening address when a voice abruptly addressed the chair. Lord Brougham was saying in an ironical tone that as a veteran reformer he wished to call the attention of Mr. Dallas to the fact that one delegate was a Negro, Dr. Delany, born in the United States but now a resident of Canada. As the audience clapped, Delany got up, thanked Brougham, and begged to assure the congress that he was a *man*.

Thereupon, as Dallas glowered, Longstreet stalked out of the assemblage with affronted dignity. A great commotion followed. The venerable Brougham, wishing to soothe Dallas's feelings, called on the minister but was turned from his door. Lord Lansdowne, for the government, tendered regrets. The greatest reformer of all, Lord Shaftesbury, wrote that Brougham's conduct had been foolish and unwarranted. Though friends urged Longstreet to return to the congress, he sternly refused. Before leaving London, he not only sent Cobb a long letter of explanation but published in the *Morning Chronicle* a paper upholding slavery and pouring out against the free society of Britain the same arguments that Southerners often used against the North.[1]

The infirm, eccentric Brougham had offered the American representatives a sad insult; but then the United States was in a sad position before other lands.

[I]

It was all too true, as Bryant wrote and Lincoln said, that slavery placed American principles in a false light to the outside world. "How it moves the pride and curls the lip of European despotism!" wrote Bryant. "How it strikes

1 Wade, *Longstreet*, 325, 326; *Diary of G. M. Dallas*, 407–410.

down the power and crushes the hopes of the struggling friends of freedom all over the world!" [2] In 1859, Lord John Russell brought out the first volume of his life of Charles James Fox. Although in treating the Revolution he paid tribute to the founders of the republic, he noted certain defects of the American system; above all, slavery—a blot which oceans could not wash away. No boasts of wealth, literary power, and refinement of manners, he wrote, could make men overlook the vices and crimes which American slavery begat.

Fortunately, declared Russell, this blot must vanish. "Neither the philosophical dogma of the authors of the Constitution, nor the strict pedantry of law, can stifle the cry of outraged humanity, nor still the currents of human sympathy, nor arrest forever the decrees of Eternal Justice." Such moralizing stung many Americans like a whiplash. So did the Earl of Carlisle's introduction to *Uncle Tom's Cabin*. So did the news in 1859 that citizens of the Swiss canton of Vaud were raising money to purchase freedom for American slaves. And so did word early in 1860 that an emancipation committee had been formed in London, addressed at its first meeting by the Haitian minister, to put Britain on guard against proslavery visitors, protest against any communion between British religious bodies and American proslavery churches, and diffuse information on slavery.

The fact that the antislavery movement, as a world force, was bound up with the world-wide struggle for democracy, was clear to all who studied European opinion. In Britain, France, and other lands the eighteenth-century aristocracy, with some philanthropic exceptions, had been relatively indifferent to slavery; titles and wealth had long protected the slave trade. In France, the Revolution, an uprising of the masses, had given birth to a powerful if short-lived emancipationist movement. The British crusade which outlawed the slave trade and brought about abolition in the colonies had been organized mainly by middle-class Quakers, Methodists, other Dissenters, and Radicals. Taken up by artisans, tradesmen, and writers, it had finally become an overwhelming mass movement before which the government gave way. Few national acts in history have exhibited such a disinterested benevolence as British emancipation; and it, like the stoppage of the slave ships, had been forced upon the governing class by an irresistible pressure from below.

Whatever friendliness to slavery remained in Britain, France, Holland, and other European lands was found chiefly in aristocratic circles, and in wealthy trading groups connected with the old West Indian planting interest. It was no accident that in France such students of democracy as Tocqueville and Edouard Laboulaye were emancipationists. The liberal elements in England represented by Bright, Cobden, Forster, and John Stuart Mill, by the London *Daily*

2 Nevins, *Evening Post*, 253.

News and the *Spectator*, were keenly absorbed in the antislavery movement in America. An address of "Democrats of England," nearly two thousand in number, had been sent in 1853 to "Democrats of the United States":

Brace up your hearts to extinguish slavery as soon as it can be done *with safety*, and you will at once have double resolution, double moral power, to reanimate the swooning liberties of Europe. Fail us not, we pray you! but urge your government to all active aid which can be prudently and wisely given, and that without delay. Strengthen your own liberties, fulfill your providential destiny, and earn the glory of rescuing fallen Europe—a glory which *our* government does not know how to appreciate or achieve.[3]

The voice of one great European democrat claimed attention on the morrow of John Brown's execution—Victor Hugo. The fame of the French poet was now at its height. From his exile under the British flag, he had protested against the tyranny of Napoleon III and every other form of European oppression. The day Brown died, he wrote the London *Daily News* a letter which was republished in every nation of the civilized globe, even Russia. As was his habit, he grew over-rhetorical. "There is something more terrible than Cain slaying Abel," he declared; "it is Washington slaying Spartacus." But, expressing the devotion of freedom-loving Europeans to the transatlantic republic, his letter was moving in its appeal from the America of 1860 to the America of the Founders. The transaction just closed, he wrote, took place not, alas, in Turkey, but in the brightest free community of the globe:

Such things are not done with impunity, in the face of the civilized world. The universal conscience of mankind is an ever-watchful eye. . . . At this moment the gaze of Europe is fixed on America. . . . The more one loves, admires, reveres the Republic, the more heartsick one feels at such a catastrophe. No matter how intense may be the indignation of the generous Northern States, the Southern States associate them with the disgrace of this murder. All of us, whosoever we may be, for whom the democratic cause is a common country, feel ourselves in a manner compromised and hurt. . . . When we say to ourselves that the republic is a glory of the human race, that she is the queen of an entire world, and that she bears on her brow a radiant light of freedom we affirm that John Brown will not die, for we recoil, horror-struck, from the idea of so great a crime committed by so great a people.

3 N. Y. *Tribune*, September 20, 1853. The *Edinburgh Review*, discussing slavery and the slave trade in its issue for October, 1858, emphasized the fact that in proportion as the South placed restrictions on the press, and discouraged free thought and speech, it must grow less liberal. In the North, meanwhile, the lower type of mercantile spirit was inimical to public service. "No consideration, however, is more plain than that of the high merit and hopeful greatness of the genuine republicans throughout the Union." The British and Americans must stand together for democracy. "Never were we and they more bound to each other in a common duty and a common sentiment than now. . . . We are thinking of the free millions who regard labor and social organization in the light of the century in which they live."

American slavery was one of the stubborn obstacles to the progress of democracy throughout the world. Harriet Martineau had said so in the eighteen-
thirties, James Silk Buckingham said so in the eighteen-forties, and Alexander
Mackay said so in the eighteen-fifties. Laboulaye and Fredrika Bremer were emphatic in this assertion—the latter adding, however, that the curse of slavery
might eventually be made a world blessing if large numbers of American-taught
Negroes could be returned to Africa to give that land freedom and progress.
Every reactionary abroad, even admitting the need of home reforms, could ask
whether it was well to discard existing institutions for the ideas of a slaveholding
America; for the practices of a democracy which, as one Englishman put it, sold
wives and children into perpetual exile from distracted husbands and mothers.
As slavery was defended in the United States by men who pointed to the slums
of Lawrence, Manchester, and Lyons, so social and political ills in Europe were
defended by men who pointed to the evils of Southern slavery. By simple logic
(as the Civil War soon proved), European liberals and American freesoilers were
partners in a grand common cause.

Intelligent British opinion (better informed than Continental criticism) recognized the complexity of the American problem, the fact that slavery was
inherited from the era of European domination, and the defensibility of the
system as a transitional status. The *Westminster Review*, in various articles, reminded Britons that they had done much to fasten slavery upon the South; that
an immense part of Southern wealth was invested in slave labor; that if four million black people dwelt in England the British would feel differently about the
race problem; and that the apprehension of the Southerner for his property, the
lives of his family, and all that made existence comfortable and honorable, was
excusable. It accused the North and Europe of complicity with the slaveholders
in accepting profits from forced labor.[4] The *North British Review*, too, was
aware of the many difficulties attending emancipation. Much, in its opinion,
would depend on the gradual advance of the Negro. He had arrived in America
with only a barbaric culture, but already climate, religious instruction, and intercourse with the whites had made him entirely different from his African con-
geners. His intellectual curiosity, above all, had been aroused; nothing that
America could do would prevent him from acquiring knowledge, and knowledge must ultimately mean freedom.[5]

This magazine had little faith in compensated emancipation. While Britain

4 Vol. 59, p. 153; January–April, 1853, 127, 128, 140 ff.
5 Vol. 27 (1857), 442 ff. As early as 1854, *Fraser's Magazine* warned the South not to
count on British support in secession. The *Quarterly Review*, three years later, predicted
that if war came the South would be defeated—and defeated in part by global sentiment;
for "a bad cause cannot prevail against the sympathy and reason of the whole civilized
world."

had been able to afford it because her slaveholders were a small body, North-erners could not and would not buy up the slave rights of fifteen States. Nor had the review any faith in colonization schemes. The problem, it believed, would be solved by gradual elevation of the Negro in association with the white, by the influence of industrialism, always incompatible with brutish slave labor, and by the force of world opinion.

Olmsted's proposals for the gradual extinction of slavery made a sharp im-pression in Britain. Dickens praised his book in *Household Words*, urging a return to Jefferson's doctrine of gradual emancipation.[6] The *Westminster Re-view* pointed out that Olmsted's plan was far more constructive than Helper's proposals for a vindictive class warfare. Articles in the *Spectator*, *Saturday Re-view*, *Fraser's*, and other periodicals indicate that Olmsted's ideas were more widely accepted than those of any other student. As the years passed, a rising note of impatience crept into liberal British commentaries.[7] Let the Southern planters put aside their exaggerated fears, urged many critics. A writer in the *Westminster Review* pointed to West Indian experience as disproving their pre-dictions of impoverishment, black supremacy, racial amalgamation, and ceaseless social strife. In Jamaica and other islands, the immense colored majority had made no vengeful use of its preponderance; the Negroes were more prosperous and enterprising than before emancipation; strife had diminished. As for amal-gamation, the author—who urged a gradual liberation in America—thought that less of it would occur under freedom than under slavery. Unprincipled whites would not have such easy access to colored women; religion would do more to elevate morality; and the marriage bond among Negroes would be respected.[8]

Other British writers suggested that the first step toward emancipation, after restricting slavery within existing bounds, would be to abolish the internal slave trade—the very life of the system. If the sale of slaves from border States were forbidden, the Lower South would be deprived of about thirty thousand Negroes annually. Already the cost of Negro labor had cut into plantation profits; and without new hands, the cotton kingdom would have to turn toward a more variegated agriculture, demanding better-skilled labor. The next step would be to stop all dealings in slaves. The odious conception of human property would be eradicated, the Negro would become a man instead of a chattel, and a

6 *Household Words*, Vol. 14, August 23, 1856.
7 The London *Times* was reckoned particularly tolerant of slavery. But its editorial comment on the New York *Tribune* report of Pierce Butler's sale of slaves at Savannah on March 2-3, 1859, which it reprinted, was scathing. The whole melancholy drama of slave life, it remarked, was here exhibited; the ruin of a speculative Southern gentleman, the woe of the slaves, the grasping character of their buyers. "If anyone wishes to see how low the white man can be brought by unlimited power to use human beings for gain, let him read the lifelike description of the Southern planters, and see into what a class the increase of the cotton trade has changed the gentlemen of the Carolinas and Georgia."
8 *Westminster Review*, January–April, 1853, 152 ff.

scheme could be worked out by which the Negro could be paid for unusual exertions and given other opportunities to earn money, his savings being appropriated to buy his freedom. The more diligent, intelligent Negroes would gain liberty first, while the stupid and lazy continued in a state of serfdom. Thus the difficulty of dealing with a horde of semi-civilized Africans would gradually disappear. So ran the argument of various Britons.[9]

Of two important British books on slavery in the late eighteen-fifties, that of William Chambers was pessimistic, that of James Stirling hopeful. Chambers, depicting the institution in *American Slavery and Colour* as both a social wrong and a wasteful, inefficient economic arrangement, feared there were but two remedies: insurrection or war. Stirling, whose *Letters From the Slave States* was fairer, believed that rising economic forces would overthrow the system. As trade and industry grew and one-crop agriculture declined, slavery would be abolished as unprofitable. Both men thought slavery doomed. So, indeed, did all British writers. And all liberals continued to express a hope that the republic would soon vindicate its moral position. Calling slavery a pestilential marsh which infected the world air, the *North British Review* declared: "America will see reflected in European opinion the coming doom of the accursed evil, and will be ashamed of the foul blot that makes Europe point the finger of scorn at her professions of liberty." [10]

French opinion, too, oversimplifying the problem, manifested a growing impatience. The geographer Elisée Reclus, who had traveled in America, contributed a denunciatory essay to the *Revue des Deux Mondes* just after Lincoln's election, attacking slave law in particular. Cucheval Clarigny, a French librarian and essayist who had been horrified by radical Southern pronouncements on the perpetuity and expansibility of slavery, wrote a more burning attack in the same review. He was specially severe on Southern censorship and terrorism.[11] Sir Willoughby Jones, who translated Clarigny in a widely circulated pamphlet, was equally critical of the Southern attitude. It was safer for a Frenchman to profess sympathy with Louis Capet in 1793, he wrote, than for a citizen of Charleston to take the side of a maltreated Negro in 1860.

[II]

Many fair-minded men, looking at the clock of the world, hoped that it might be telling the last decades of slavery in western lands. In half a century

9 *Westminster Review*, Vol. 75 (1861), 166, 167; *North British Review*, Vol. 27 (1857), 435 ff.
10 Vol. 27 (1857), 435 ff. Marshall Hall's *Facts of the Twofold Slavery of the U. S.* (1856), which proposed a scheme of self-emancipation, also attracted notice.
11 Clarigny in *Revue*, December 1; Reclus, December 15, 1860.

SLAVERY IN THE
WESTERN HEMISPHERE
1820

Slave states

SLAVERY IN THE
WESTERN HEMISPHERE
1860

Slave states

UNITED
STATES
1863

CANADA

ATLANTIC

PACIFIC

MEXICO
1829

BR.
HONDURAS
1834

CUBA
1886

BAHAMA IS. (BR.) 1753
1834

HAITI, 1793
DOMINICAN REP.
PUERTO RICO, 1872

HONDURAS
1823

JAMAICA, 1834
(BR.)

NETH., 1863

GUADELOUPE (FR.), 1848
MARTINIQUE (FR.), 1848
BARBADOS (BR.), 1834
TRINIDAD (BR.), 1834

GUATEMALA, 1823
SALVADOR, 1823
NICARAGUA, 1823
COSTA RICA, 1823

VENEZUELA
1854

COLOMBIA
1852

BR.
GUIANA
1848

ECUADOR
1854

PERU
1855

BRAZIL
1888

OCEAN

BOLIVIA
1851

1843
PARAGUAY

CHILE
1823

1846
URUGUAY

ARGENTINA
1853

OCEAN

Tschirky

139

the clock had registered a sweeping change. Men still living in 1860 could recall the time when slavery or serfdom had seemed the rule throughout most of the globe. Chief Justice Taney might well remember a day when the British, French, Dutch, Portuguese, and Danish combined had forty factories on the African coast for the shipment of slaves; when Yankee slave ships dotted the Atlantic; when Spanish America and the Portuguese, Dutch, and French colonies, with many under the British flag, were strongholds of slavery; and when the institution yet existed in considerable parts of the North—for New Jersey, the last State, did not act until 1804. But stroke by stroke, the bell of the world clock had rung the knell of slavery and the slave trade as institutions which the Western World could tolerate.

Two strokes had rung out in 1780, when Massachusetts by the memorable words in her constitution declaring all men "born free and equal" extinguished slavery, and when the Pennsylvania legislature provided that all children born thereafter to slave parents should be free, though holding the position of servants until twenty-eight.[12] Another stroke sounded when, in 1787, Congress passed the Ordinance forbidding slavery northwest of the Ohio. The negroes of Haiti gained freedom and independence in 1804.

Then, as the South American colonies broke away from Spain, slavery (never strong except on the northern and northeastern shores of the continent) was abolished in one new republic after another. Chile had only a handful of negroes. Her struggle for independence began in 1810, and the first Congress decreed emancipation. In Buenos Aires, the more numerous colored population was signally versatile and energetic, carrying on many crafts; and the state no sooner gained practical independence than it provided that all children born to slaves after January 21, 1813, should be free.[13] Colombia, which had more than two hundred thousand blacks and mulattoes, took similar action, decreeing that all children born after July 16, 1821, should be liberated on attaining their eighteenth year. In Mexico, negroes were comparatively few. In view of her nearness to the United States, however, her abolition of slavery in 1829, eight years after independence, was another telling stroke on the world bell.[14]

Immediately afterward came a more resounding peal when on August 28,

12 Emory Washburn, *Mass. Hist. Soc. Proc.*, May, 1857; *Laws of Pa.*, II, 246.
13 Sir Woodbine Parish, *Buenos Aires and the Provinces of the Rio de la Plata;* F. A. Kirkpatrick, *A History of the Argentine Republic.* For Latin American slavery in general, see the *Hispanic American Historical Review*, XIII, 151–196, and XXIV, 363–431, 547–559. Light is thrown on the matter by Charles E. Akers, *A History of South America*, and A. Curtis Wilgus, ed., *South American Dictators.* It must never be forgotten that Latin American humanitarians did much more for the negro than for the impoverished and maltreated Indians and *mestizos.*
14 Bancroft, *Mexico;* Priestley, *The Mexican Nation;* and Ralph Roeder, *Juarez and his Mexico.* On slavery in Colombia, see Eduardo Posada, *La Esclavitud en Colombia, o leyes de manumision;* J. Fred Rippy, ed., Hennar and Arrubla's *History of Colombia.*

1833, as a result of the long crusade of Clarkson, Wilberforce, Zachary Macaulay, and others, the law abolishing slavery in all British possessions received royal assent. Originally, a seven-year transitional period was fixed but it was soon abbreviated, so that all slaves became completely free in 1838. The disappearance of slavery in Jamaica, Trinidad, Barbados, and neighboring islands with a dense black population, in Guiana, South Africa, Mauritius, and other areas, was important not only in itself but as making similar action in the French, Dutch, and other colonies eventually certain.[15] Slavery had lingered on in Paraguay. A law of 1842 for gradual emancipation struck it at the root, and it rapidly withered away. France, unable to lag far behind Britain, moved just after the revolution of 1848, when her provisional government decreed immediate colonial emancipation. Next came Venezuela, where negroes and mulattoes composed nearly a third of the people; perhaps more. The land of Bolivar, by a law of March 24, 1854, conceded liberty and equal rights to all inhabitants. Once more the world clock struck in 1858, when Portugal enacted that all slaves in her possessions should be placed in a system of tutelage, and become free in twenty years. In Macao and Angola, the Lisbon authorities abolished slavery outright.

Thus in half a century many living Americans had seen slavery wither away on three continents. In civilized regions of the globe it had been driven back into four redoubts: Brazil, Cuba and its neighbor Puerto Rico, Dutch Guiana and adjacent islands, and the American South. In the South itself, down to 1830 and even afterward, large elements had responded generously to the tendency of the age. Slavery was sternly criticized. The debates on it in Virginia showed a potent opposition; in Maryland and Virginia the number of free negroes increased faster than that of slaves, reaching eighty-four thousand in Maryland and fifty-eight thousand in Virginia by 1860; and many slaves were permitted broad privileges. But the Southern impulse ebbed.

Year after year, the two great antislavery societies, those of Britain and America, chronicled the progress of a movement that went forward fitfully but seldom slipped backward. Two parts of the globe that in 1858–60 attracted hope-

---

15 On slavery in the Guianas see James Rodway, *Guiana: British, Dutch, and French,* especially Ch. 6; J. F. H. Mourie, *La Guyane Française,* 280 ff.; Anthony Trollope, *The West Indies and the Spanish Main* (1859). Much was made by proslavery men in America of the introduction of African and East Indian apprentices or indentured workers into the British and French colonies after the abolition of slavery; and the French system in especial permitted gross abuses. But Rodway declares that the coolie improved his lot in America, and was well protected. "Having thrown off the fetters of caste, he has become more independent than he once was at home. The system may be a five years' bondage in one sense, yet in another it is such freedom as was never before known by these people." P. 205. On slavery in Venezuela, see Miguel Tejera, *Historia de Venezuela,* 231; J. M. Spence, *The Land of Bolivar,* I, 142. See also Charles H. Washburne, *History of Paraguay,* I, 348, 349; Harris G. Warren, *Paraguay;* Eduardo Acevedo, *Manuel de Historia Uruguaya;* Luis Goldames, *Chile.*

ful attention were the Dutch West Indies and Russia. The Netherlands held about forty thousand slaves in Surinam (Dutch Guiana) and a few thousand in Curacao, St. Eustatius, and St. Martin. Emancipation, backed by a growing sentiment in Holland, had been discussed for years. Inspired by *Uncle Tom's Cabin*, some young men of Amsterdam in 1853 had formed an abolition society. For a time, the planters and their mercantile friends had obstinately resisted the pressure. But after French emancipation, many landholders, seeing that with free British Guiana on one side and free French Guiana on the other slaves would constantly desert, themselves called for action. By the late fifties, the ministry was ready to move, and for several years presented the States-General with plans for compensated emancipation. Though in 1860 the project still hung fire, it was certain of success—which actually came in 1863; the only question was of details. Meanwhile, in 1859, slavery was abolished outright in the Dutch East Indies. Many slaveholders, according to the Hong Kong *Register*, refused compensation, while others accepted it only to transfer the money to the freedmen.[16]

As for Russia, her press reported that by the summer of 1858 thirty-eight governments, containing about ten million male serfs, had commenced the formation of committees of emancipation; and the Czar was speeding the nobility forward in a reform which, he said, must come peacefully from above lest it come bloodily from below.[17] Russian serfdom was a very different system indeed from American slavery—but to strike one kind of shackle from toilers in the Muscovite domains was to hearten those who wished to strike fetters from the bondsmen of the New World.

[III]

Why was it that the South, as its own antislavery energies flagged after 1830, stood in such evident contrast with the remainder of the world, and especially with Latin America? Some of the reasons have already been indicated, but others require a brief explanation. The Southerners, many of whom were sensitively concerned with Northern and British opinion, had certain defensive considerations to urge. If pressed by critics, they replied that the slavery problem had unique features in the United States, where special reasons existed for continuing the institution.

That they were correct, and that slavery in the United States differed

16   *Anti-Slavery Reporter* (London), March 1, 1855. On Dutch emancipation, see Ackersdyck, "Mouvement des Idees Economiques; Progres des Reformes; État de la Question Coloniale et de l'Esclavage en Hollande," pamphlet, Utrecht, 1861. See also N. Y. *Tribune*, October 17, 1857; *Report*, Paris Anti-Slavery Conference, 1867, pp. 75–78. In Dr. Morton E. Kahn, *Djuka: the Bush Negroes of Dutch Guiana* (1931) readers will find much on the culture of a primitive people who received comparatively little from the whites.
17   *Ann. Report Am. Antislavery Soc.* 1858–59, p. 129–132.

sharply from slavery in Mexico, Venezuela, or Peru, is unquestionable. In those countries, the Indian and *mestizo* (that is, mixed Indian and white) populations far outnumbered the pure whites.[18] Indeed, the largest single element in Mexico and Venezuela was the *mestizo* element. So it was, also, in Colombia. In Peru, the largest single group was the pure-blooded Indians, with the *mestizos* next. In all three republics, as in the Guianas, people of Indian or part-Indian blood felt no reluctance to intermarry with Negroes or mulattoes. Economically, socially, and culturally, the Indian, *mestizo*, and negro were all on a fairly even footing. For that matter, even the pure-blooded Spaniard of the lower classes was often ready to take a Negro or mulatto woman in marriage. It was therefore natural to make the road to manumission easy, and widespread manumission led to general emancipation. The freedman became a freeman.

Why should a Mexican Indian, still following his ancient way of life, his possessions few, his education tribal, his social status lowly, hinder the liberation of a black slave? Aside from a small white ruling class, society in the greater part of Spanish America was comparatively level and devoid of racial antipathies; the intermarriage of different stocks was natural, and the transition from slavery to freedom could be accomplished without friction. Formal abolition of slavery was also facilitated in various Latin-American countries by the fact that great masses remained in peonage, midway between slavery and freedom. This was notably the situation in Mexico, where the Spanish conquerors had instituted a system of forced labor, and in Peru, where the *mita* served the same purpose. J. Fred Rippy writes of Latin America as a whole: "Debt peonage or some other system differing from serfdom was prevalent in the majority of nations until after 1900."

Inherited Latin traditions and legal and religious concepts, moreover, simplified the processes of manumission, intermarriage, and emancipation.

Long before the Moorish conquests, before even Hannibal's invasions, the people of what are now Spain and Portugal had been familiar with their African neighbors, had intermingled with them, and had learned to attach no excessive importance to the color line. The burnished livery of the sun carried little if any stigma. The peninsular peoples shared, too, in the ancient Greco-Roman concept of the slave; a concept based on the fact that in the ancient world most slaves were white, that they fell into slavery through conquest, economic misfortune, or some other accident, and that servile status implied no natural infe-

18 The term *mestizo* usually meant a half-breed of white and negro, or white and Indian, parents. The term *zambo* was applied to the issue of negro and Indian unions. But no exact and unvarying meaning can be attached to any of the names applied to persons of mixed blood, whether mulatto, *mestizo, zambo, zambo preto, chino,* or *cholo.* A table of these names with some of their general meanings may be found in A. Wyatt Tilby, *Britain in the Tropics, 1527–1910,* 59.

riority.[19] The codification of Spanish traditional law under Alfonso the Wise (1263–1265) accepted the principle that men are naturally equal and that slavery is contrary to the law of nature. Slavery in the ancient world was cruel beyond any comparison with the American system; the picture of it given by Cato, Juvenal, Seneca, and Caesar (who after the capture of the Aduatuci sold fifty-three thousand prisoners into slavery on the spot) is revolting in the extreme. Tacitus states that the Romans lived in constant fear of slave revolt. But it was primarily white slavery. Many slaves possessed talent and skill; friendships between master and slave were often close—Cicero's letters were edited by his manumitted slave Tiro; and when a slave was admired, loved, or pitied, he could be freed without the slightest difficulty.[20]

Spain, Portugal, and the Latin-American lands had largely inherited this Roman tradition of slavery. The two leading facts in the legal position of the Roman slave had a potent influence on Hispanic-American thinking. One was that the slave was absolutely under the control of his master, who possessed a power of use, punishment, and life or death without accountability to any higher authority. The other was that the slave, if capable, well-behaved, or appealing, enjoyed a fair prospect of liberation, and, when manumitted, often achieved Roman citizenship with all accompanying civil rights. Spanish and Portuguese law mitigated the first principle, though on Cuban sugar plantations in the eighteen-fifties countless slaves were treated with a brutality that might have shocked Tiberius, and many were callously worked to death. Spanish and Portuguese law preserved and extended the second principle, holding open the road to freedom. We must, however, be on our guard against accepting written codes as representing social realities. The evidence is strong that in parts of Latin America the laws were ignored or violated.[21] Nevertheless, the statutes did

19 Tannenbaum, *Slave and Citizen: the Negro in the Americas*, 45. Negro slaves had become common in Spain and Portugal by the close of the fifteenth century, and very numerous by 1650. Lisbon, indeed, at that date had more negroes than whites. H. Morse Stephens, *Portugal*; Tannenbaum, *Slave and Citizen*, 44. Marriage between whites and negroes had taken place from the beginning without hindrance. Elizabeth Donnan, *Documents Illustrative of the Hist. of the Slave Trade to America*, I, 29.

20 Fowler, *Social Life at Rome in the Age of Cicero*, 204–236.

21 *Journal of Negro Hist.*, VI, 183 ff.; XXIX, 7 ff. Cruelty of slavery in Cuba and Puerto Rico is proved by a mountain of evidence. On paper, the Spanish laws were relatively good; in practice, slavery was much harsher than in the South, was attended by a much heavier mortality (placed by some writers at five percent a year), and left the slaves in a much more barbarous condition. The Cuban and Puerto Rican abolitionists who wrote *The Abolition of Slavery in Cuba and Puerto Rico* (N. Y., 1865; p. 34) declare the better laws a dead letter. They state of Cuba that "were it possible to make public all the data existing in the offices of the *Sindicos*, the Christian world would be horrified at such an enormous sum of cruelties committed against that poor and defenseless class." Puerto Rico in 1860 had 41,736 slaves against 300,430 whites and 241,015 free colored people. Cuba in 1862 had 368,550 slaves, as against 764,750 whites, 221,417 free colored people and 34,050 slaves. In Brazil, however, slavery was milder than in the Lower South. Lord Brougham was correct when he told Dallas's clerk that negroes had a better status in Brazil than in the United States.

facilitate manumission, social custom encouraged it, tax gatherers imposed no obstacle, and a procedure was developed by which slaves might buy their freedom in installments. Once liberated, the slave mingled with the Indian, *mestizo*, black, or mulatto population on terms of full equality.[22]

The church, too, accepting the traditions of its environment, lent aid to assimilation. It would be erroneous to say that Catholicism *per se* was more hostile to slavery than Protestantism, for much evidence can be adduced for an opposite conclusion. In Britain and the United States the antislavery crusade was a child of Protestantism. The Catholic Church was not more friendly to the Negro in Maryland or Louisiana than the Protestant sects; it was a slaveholding church (Southern monasteries owning bondsmen), which the Protestant churches were not. A Catholic historian writes that the slave system among American Catholics reflected on the whole the patterns of thought prevalent in the community, and that the church condemned the principles of Garrisonian abolitionism as conflicting with Catholic ethics and ideals.[23] In Latin America, however, the church threw itself on the side of forces that labored for manumission, social equality, emancipation, and intermarriage. Emphasizing the spiritual integrity of every individual, teaching that all human beings are children of God, urging that marriage and the family be held sacred, and instituting religious fraternities among slaves, the church made full use of its favorable social environment. The Indians, Negroes, Caucasians, and people of mixed blood were taught to regard each other as brethren in Christ.

Very different, and much more difficult, was the situation in the South. The population had but two elements, white and colored, master and slave. Since the aborigines had died out or disappeared beyond the Mississippi, no large Indian or half-breed population existed to break down lines of color and caste and act as a racial solvent. The norms of education, intellectual discipline, comfort, skill, and social responsibility attained by the whites were a pole apart from those to which the Negro, in Africa or America, had been used; no such flattening-out of standards had occurred as in Latin America. No system of peonage existed (at any rate outside New Mexico) as a halfway house between slavery and freedom. One might be developed, but that would require time. The whole tradition of the white American respecting slavery was not merely alien to the Greco-Roman tradition, but antipathetic toward it. It was the tradition of a stock which, whether among the folk of the ancient Teutonic forests, the Danish and Norse sea rovers, or the modern English-speaking peoples, had always regarded slavery as a badge of degradation. To sink into servitude, in the opinion of this stock, was the ultimate humiliation; to raise Gurth or Sambo from it required a heroic effort.

22 Tannenbaum, *Slave and Citizen*, 53, 54.
23 Rice, *American Catholic Opinion in the Slavery Controversy*, 60, 85.

It was the tradition, too, of a people which associated slavery almost exclusively with the Negro race, and which—however mistakenly—found it natural to think of that race in terms of natural inferiority. In the United States the line of slavery coincided with a marked color line, a line of apparent substandard capacities, a line drawn by inherited beliefs respecting the baseness of any people who let themselves become enchained—and hence an almost impassable social line. In Latin-American countries no such coincidence existed. The Indian, *mestizo*, Negro, and mulatto recognized no important differentiation as regarded color, capacity, attainments, or traditional dignity. The ordinary Spaniard or Portuguese, with perhaps a Moorish pigmentation, founded his immense pride of race on other considerations.[24]

The Southerner was hostile to large-scale manumission and emancipation because he felt that racial equality might end in race mixture; the Latin American felt no such hostility because he accepted racial amalgamation. A South Carolinian or Mississippian would have said that his view proved him a better man than the Mexican or Venezuelan. The Venezuelan would have said that *his* view proved him the better man. The fact was that they were different men, made so by an immense complex of inheritances and pressures. The special character of society in the United States made the problem of slavery incomparably more difficult than in Latin countries.

How great a gulf existed, again, between the Southern States and the typical West Indian colony! The English and Dutch planters felt as sharp a racial exclusiveness as the Southern slaveholders. But in most islands they were a handful of men lost in a black sea. These tropical holdings never built up distinctively white civilizations which required protection and perpetuation as such. Once Jamaica was filled with slaves, the whites never represented much more than two percent of the inhabitants. In Barbados and St. Kitts, which of the British islands had the largest white elements, the figure was usually six or seven percent; elsewhere it was below five percent. Emancipation, therefore, involved no great social or cultural revolution. Its effects, disastrous at first but later beneficent, were primarily economic. The Dutch islands were from eighty to ninety percent colored, while in Martinique and Guadeloupe the French amounted to but two or three percent of the whole. Where the disproportion of races was so great, there could be no such grim problem of race adjustment as that which appalled the South.[25]

---

24 G. Freyre, *The Masters and the Slaves*, 11, 40, 185–277.
25 Cf. W. W. Macmillan, *Warning from the West Indies*. Oceans of ink were spent on the controversy whether Jamaica had benefited or suffered from emancipation. The best conclusion is that a decline in prosperity had been incipient before emancipation, attributable mainly to the one-crop system and to absentee landlordism. Under the new order a hundred thousand negro farmers successfully tilled their own holdings, rejecting the long hours of

No, Southerners might well assert that the question of liberation was far more difficult in the fifteen slave States than in any other part of the globe; so perplexing that it demanded the utmost caution. The successive strokes of the world clock registered the trend of the age. In the long run, the spirit of modern industrial society, liberalism, and the humanitarian movement must prove irresistible. But then why not a little patience? And nothing was to be learned from superficial comparisons with simpler lands. The extreme difficulty of the Southern situation arose in part from the advanced nature of Southern civilization; the high pride of Southerners in their inheritance and achievements accentuating the gap between the races. "The question," as Robert Toombs said, "is not whether we could not be more prosperous and happy with these three and a half million slaves in Africa, and their places filled with an equal number of hardy, intelligent, and enterprising citizens of the superior race; but it is simply whether, while we have them among us, we would be more prosperous with them in freedom or in bondage." [26] More prosperous, that is, spiritually, culturally, socially, and materially.

What *was* the Southern feeling about slavery? Most Southerners had a sense, to begin with, that this was *their* problem; that they had to live with it and plan for it; that it was their business and nobody else's; and that they could deal with it better if they were not hectored and reproached by ignorant onlookers. They had a belief, in the second place, that, while they might do much voluntarily to improve slavery, they would do nothing under compulsion. No self-respecting individual or community cares to be driven to any course of action. As the Northern and foreign clamor grew, Southern obstinacy grew with it.[27] The South felt a strong conviction, in the third place, that Northern emphasis on the moral aspects of slavery distorted the problem, insulted the Southern people, and gave the critics an air of ethical superiority as false as it was offensive.

Liberal-minded Southerners did not deny that slavery had moral implications. But they knew that its social and economic aspects were as important as its moral

---

toil for low wages offered on the white plantations. John Bigelow, *Jamaica in 1850*. The termination of the protection which British sugar-planters had enjoyed in the home market, effected by the free trade legislation of 1846, was most damaging to the island industry. A. Wyatt Tilby, *Britain in the Tropics, 1527-1910*, 60, 61.

26 Phillips, *Toombs*, 165.

27 This was well expressed by W. L. Yancey. The South, he wrote, had at first viewed the warfare upon its rights and institutions by Europe and the North with contempt; then with indignation. "The inevitable effect of this moral warfare upon slavery, has been to force the adoption of a more rigid police over the intercourse of the slaves and a strict watchfulness over the movements of strangers through the slave population. Insulated from the world by their peculiar institution, denounced by the world as a degraded and corrupted race on account of his connection with it, the Southerner brightly rejects all opinions and schemes relative to it, which the world may proffer. Such a disposition is the natural consequence of insult, contumely, and wrong, long endured by our section." Undated essay, Yancey Papers, Ala. Dept. Arch. and Hist.

aspect, and that, in any scientific study of labor systems, Northern and European industrialism had dark moral blots which should be weighed against the evils of slavery. They resented the tendency of abolitionists to treat the moral issue as if it alone counted, or could be detached. Such an approach obscured the fact that the two cardinal goals in a proper race relationship—the best economic use of the Negro, and the establishment of the Negro on a plane where he could better himself and yet not break down the barriers to racial union—were more important than the satisfaction of an abstract moral demand.

Most intensely of all, even liberal Southerners felt that terrible dangers to their whole future might lurk in hasty action upon slavery. They saw that many Northerners wished to free the slaves and raise them (hundreds of miles from their own homes) to equality with the whites. They believed that such equality would lead in the immediate future to a breakdown of the plantation system, to harsh competition between the Negro and the small white farmer or artisan, and to a thousand social frictions. They believed it would lead in the distant future to that nightmare, wholesale racial amalgamation and the birth of a negroid South. Even to ameliorate slavery by hasty steps involved, in the Southern view, the risk of frightful evils. Much was to be said for legislation to legalize slave marriages and prevent the forcible break-up of families (though Southerners believed that such break-ups were less frequent than under Northern industrialism); much was to be said for tuition in reading, writing, and the mechanic arts; and much was to be said for letting industrious slaves earn their freedom, as the New Orleans merchant John McDonogh had done. Once this process of amelioration was started, however, how could it be prevented from rushing forward with accelerated speed? Where would it stop? Northern pressure and Negro demands would double-quick the march to complete freedom. Plans might be made for an intermediate tutelage, but, as in the British colonies, this would be cut short. Once let the camel get his head into the tent, and the whole animal would lunge inside.

From the prospect of these dangers, Southerners sprang back affrighted. Small farmers, clerks, and laborers, owning not a single slave, felt the perils of race adjustment quite as keenly as their richer neighbors. In most instances, they did not uphold slavery because they hoped to become slaveholders; they upheld it, rather, because they were appalled by the dangers of a premature forced march toward racial equality. And gradually many Southerners arrived at a conviction which in older days would have horrified them: If they could not persuade the North to let them alone in facing the problem, they would set up an independent Southern republic which could deal with slavery according to its own interest and conscience. Meanwhile, they would do what they could to strengthen their social system against its enemies.

[IV]

As slavery was increasingly menaced, so it must be increasingly buttressed. As the knocking on the prison gates became louder, more stringent precautions had to be taken against efforts to respond. The history of all forces of occupation is the same; while secure they can afford to be mild, but when menaced they become severe. The world movement against slavery produced a sense of crisis in the South, and, with it, panicky restrictions.

Already the slave was helpless. His status, a Southern historian writes, had been fixed to the satisfaction of masters by legislation in the years 1829–1835; the Negroes were prostrate, restrained at every point by law.[28] The institution, however, might be weakened in various ways; by benevolent owners, by the growth of industry and trade, by population changes, and by the spread of education. At various points, slavery by 1858 seemed crumbling away. In Delaware it was manifestly dying. Of the three counties, Sussex alone had many slaves, and lands there were worth only a fraction of their value in Kent and Newcastle. Exponents of gradual emancipation, led by the Milford *News,* were urging the legislature to pass a law freeing all slaves born or brought into the State at the ages of eighteen for women, twenty-one for men; this, they said, would attract a rush of immigration, stimulate industry, and raise realty by five millions at once. The chief argument against such a law was that slavery would soon perish without it. As prime field hands became worth $1,500, it paid better to smuggle them southward than to keep them.

The situation was not very different in Maryland, where nearly half the negroes had gained their liberty. At the slaveholders' convention in 1859, one planter declared that, if the existing trend continued, the State would glide into freedom within a quarter-century. Another asserted that it was impossible to hold slaves in the northern counties, for they would not do forced labor while Pennsylvania was a night's journey away. These counties *could* not keep negroes; and, while slaves were worth $1,500 in New Orleans, *would* not. The tone of the convention led the Richmond *Argus* to predict that Virginia's northern neighbor would be lost. "We shall soon cease to regard Maryland as a slave State practically. Politically, she has been dead to the South for a long time past."

In Missouri, freesoil population and ideas were growing apace. For every hundred thousand whites, the State in 1850 had fifteen thousand two hundred and nine colored people; in 1860 it had only eleven thousand one hundred and forty-three. The *Missouri Democrat* fought continuously for the free labor

28 Bassett, *Slavery in the State of North Carolina,* 108, 109.

cause, and John F. Hume's editorials, collected in a pamphlet entitled "Hints Toward Emancipation in Missouri," were widely distributed. B. Gratz Brown told the legislature in 1857 that a system of graduated emancipation was already

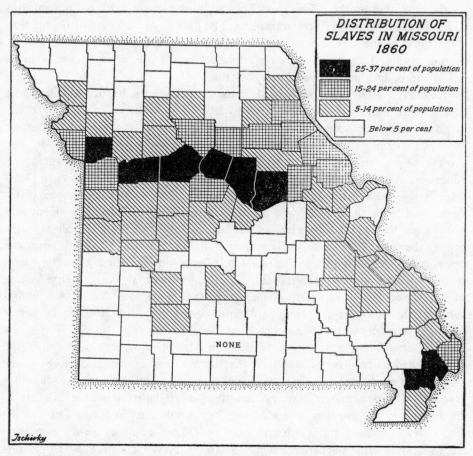

One Weak Point in Slavery. White population in Missouri more than trebled 1840–1860, rising from 322,000 to 1,063,500. Slave population failed to double, rising only from 58,000 to 115,000.

in effect; that every census showed the whites gaining steadily over the slaves; that a few years would find ninety-five largely slaveless counties pitted against a dozen heavily slaveholding counties; and that Missouri, marketing three-fourths of her exports through Northern cities and drawing two-thirds of her imports thence, had far more in common with the North than the South. James S. Rollins was almost elected governor that year on a free labor platform, declaring that emancipation might be left to the laws of latitude, climate, immigration, and production.[29]

Other danger points existed—in northern Kentucky; in western Virginia; in New Orleans, where the varied occupations of the port required intelligent labor, free Negroes thrived and the attorney George M. D. Hahn dared to denounce the institution; and in the German area of Texas. The astonishing rise in the value of Negroes was placing a heavy strain on slavery in some novel areas. Consul Bunch in Charleston noted that many rice planters were selling hands. "During the past winter," he wrote Lord Clarendon on March 4, 1857, "nearly all the slaves sold in the Charleston market have been purchased by Negro Traders from or for Mississippi and the Southwestern States; an entirely novel proceeding here, where Publick Opinion has, hitherto, been opposed to the removal of slaves from their own neighborhood." [30] In Mississippi, Texas, and other new States a $1,400 Negro could earn twelve percent or more on his value; in South Carolina, as in Missouri and Maryland, he might earn but three or four percent. Hence the tendency to dispose of hands to the richest cotton-growing districts; and hence the continued decay of slavery in the upper Carolinas from Greenville and Spartanburg to Asheville, where slavery did not pay at all. As these perils and stresses appeared, even before Harper's Ferry legislators set their pens to protective bills.[31]

Much of the restrictive legislation we have already reviewed. Louisiana went as far as any State. In 1857, it provided the death penalty for murder, rape, attempted rape or murder, insurrection, arson, or violent robbery by a slave. Any slave who struck any member of his master's family (or an overseer) hard enough to bring blood might be put to death. No slave was allowed to testify for or against a free Negro, except in cases involving servile insurrection. In 1859, free Negroes not native to the State were compelled after September 1 to choose between exile and reduction to slavery. No free Negro might keep billiard tables, coffee houses, or any establishment where spirits were sold; and free Negroes on vessels reaching Louisiana ports were to be kept in jail until the vessel was ready to leave. Slaves were forbidden to hire their own time in four

29 Wright, *The Free Negro in Maryland, 1634-1860:* Merkel, *The Anti-Slavery Controversy in Missouri, 1819-1865;* Hume, *The Abolitionists;* Brown, "Speech on Gradual Emancipation in Missouri" (pamphlet St. Louis, 1857); *Ann. Report Am. Antislavery Soc.,* 1860, pp. 209, 210.
30 FO 5/677.
31 In the western slave area of Texas many runaways escaped to Mexico. Texas slave laws were stringent, and in Washington on the Brazos, planters banded together to discourage the practice of letting slaves hire their own time. M. H. Ellis, "Social Conditions in Texas About 1850," MS, Univ. of Texas. The Charleston correspondent of the N. Y. *Tribune,* writing under date of November 7, 1860, states that a South Carolina slave cannot earn at home three percent interest on the high price he fetches; if he is sold, the money invested in State bonds or bank stock will earn eight or nine percent.

parishes where the practice had been common. Arkansas took equally harsh steps. Months before Harper's Ferry, in 1859, it prohibited any future emancipation of slaves, gave free Negroes the choice after January 1, 1860, of leaving the State or going into slavery, and forbade steamboats in Arkansas waters to carry or employ any free negro. Another law abolished imprisonment for criminal slaves, substituting up to one hundred lashes.[32]

Other States responded to the apprehensive movement. The free Negro was a menace to the institution of slavery, and must go or be kept in social fetters. The Alabama legislature in its session of 1859–60 forbade any manumission of slaves by will or bequest, or the removal of slaves from the State for the purpose of freeing them. It enacted another law permitting free persons of color to select a master or mistress, if the choice were made free from any undue influence, and become slaves.[33] The Montgomery *Mail* proclaimed it the universal sentiment of Alabamians that within two years not a single free Negro must be left. In Mississippi, the lower house carried an exile-or-slavery bill which was halted in the senate. In Georgia, both chambers voted a similar measure but the governor refused his signature. A widespread clamor for such action in North Carolina might have resulted in legislation but for the fact that a very respectable elite existed among the thirty thousand free colored folk. As it was, the increasing hostility to this so-called third class encouraged mob violence, and deterred kindly whites from helping them.[34] The Georgia legislature made it possible to indict any free Negro leading an idle, immoral, or profligate life, and to sell his labor; at the first offense for not more than two years, and, at the second, for life.

Even in the border States this attempt to rivet new armor upon the institution yielded some detestable proposals. The Missouri legislature, in March, 1860, laid before the governor a bill which prohibited the emancipation of any slave unless he or she were removed from the State within ninety days, and provided that all free adult Negroes who remained after the following September should be reduced to slavery. Special provision was made for free colored persons under eighteen. The governor, declaring that the measure was unconstitutional because it deprived persons of liberty without due process of law, and that the enforcement of any such law would cause a strong revulsion against slavery, vetoed it.

The Tennessee legislature debated a similar measure for banishing or enslaving the free Negroes. It gave Judge Catron of the Federal Supreme Court an opportunity to utter the same home truths spoken by the Missouri executive. Such an enactment, he asserted, would be cruel, shameful, and unconstitutional.

32 *Louisiana Acts of 1857*, No. 232; *Acts of 1859*, Nos. 16, 87; *Arkansas Acts of 1859*, Nos 151, 195, 225.
33 *Acts 1859–60*, Nos. 36, 71.
34 Johnson, *Ante-Bellum North Carolina*, 581, 611, 612.

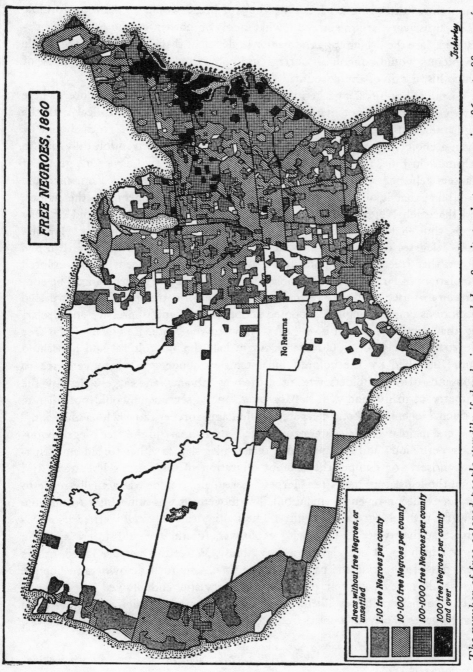

FREE NEGROES, 1860

Tschirky

No Returns

	Areas without free Negroes, or unsettled
	1-10 free Negroes per county
	10-100 free Negroes per county
	100-1000 free Negroes per county
	1000 free Negroes per county and over

The number of free colored people sturdily if slowly increased. In 1850, it stood at 434,000; in 1860, at 488,000, of whom about 250,000 were in the South.

The sight of the wretched exiles begging for bread would be the most forcible of all antislavery arguments. "In what nook or corner of the State," he demanded, "are the principles of humanity so deficient that a majority of the whole inhabitants would commit an outrage not committed in a Christian country of which history gives any account?" [35] The bill failed.

In the fall of 1858, a gathering of Marylanders of the Eastern Shore (where slavery was strong) not merely called for a State convention to deal with the regulation of the colored race, but suggested that all free Negroes should be given a choice between expulsion or enslavement. The convention duly met in Baltimore in June, 1859, and debated this suggestion for two days. One group of planters vehemently urged that the free colored population was a nuisance and an injury; that it ought to be abolished on terms advantageous to the whites; and that such Negroes as would not consent to leave should be sold on easy terms, thus enabling citizens of limited means to become slaveowners. Happily, most delegates were against any such heartless policy. The census of 1850 had shown that free Negroes constituted about forty-five percent of the colored population, and many were conspicuously industrious and enterprising. The convention majority decisively rejected the demands of extremists. In fact, it passed resolutions condemning the proposed action as cruel and oppressive and declaring that expulsion would be a heavy blow to the State. Removal of the free Negroes, it declared, would nearly cut in half the agricultural and household labor furnished by the colored inhabitants, produce great inconvenience to thousands of householders who used them as servants, and largely destroy the property of many landowners. Moreover, public sentiment would not tolerate it. Such a scheme, said one delegate, would damn forever those who adopted it. [36]

Yet a majority of delegates pronounced any increase in the free Negro population pernicious, and recommended that the legislature either forbid emancipation entirely, or compel the prompt migration of all persons liberated. And when the legislature met after Harper's Ferry, an attempt was actually made to pass an expulsion-or-enslavement bill. The movement was sufficiently formidable to alarm many Negroes and whites. The Baltimore *American* warned its advocates that they were playing with explosives, for they would arouse a public anger which might deal slavery a heavy blow. While the measure failed, others were passed reflecting the passions of the time. One forbade owners to liberate slaves unless they were transported out of Maryland, and allowed free Negroes to choose masters if they liked. Another created a commission to supervise the free Negroes in eleven counties, required them to provide homes for themselves,

---

35 *Ann. Report Am. Antislavery Soc.*, 1860, pp. 215, 216.
36 N. Y. *Tribune*, June 9-12, 1859; *National Era; Ann. Report Am. Antislavery Soc.*, 1860, 205-212.

and provided that those incapable of self-support, with their minor children, should be hired out. This regulatory law, however, was to be submitted to popular vote in the fall of 1860.[37]

These hard enactments produced a horrified impression in the North. They were the work not of excited mobs, but of gentlemen in glossy broadcloth and snowy linen, sitting at their desks in handsome marble capitols. "Barbarism Rampant" was the caption which the American Antislavery Society placed over a partial summary in its yearbook for 1860. The South seemed not merely unwilling to go forward; many leaders wished to move backward. Jefferson Davis was saying that the law against the slave trade in the District of Columbia was not only unconstitutional but abominable. Did he wish to see auctioneers again selling human chattels near the White House, as A. G. Brown wanted to see slave ships again plying the Atlantic?

So enlightened a leader as Edmund Ruffin was now denouncing manumission in any form, assailing the Virginia law which gave the Colonization Society $50 for every free Negro sent to Liberia, calling for the reduction of many free colored persons to bondage, and insisting that slaves be placed under a tighter discipline. He wished the emancipation of slaves by kindly masters (one, he wrote in 1858, had recently set three hundred free) completely stopped. He wished laws passed requiring that all free Negroes guilty of major crimes to be sold into slavery; that all who committed minor offenses should be hired out temporarily as slaves, and if the offense was repeated, be sold into lifelong slavery; and that all free Negroes leading an idle, improvident, and dissolute life should similarly be placed in bondage, to be made perpetual if they did not reform.[38]

The result, he believed, would be to remand at least three-fourths of the free colored folk of the Old Dominion to slavery. In addition, Ruffin argued for laws which would completely block all self-redemption from slavery. That is, he would terminate what he called the abusive system, in cities and towns, of giving slaves a money allowance in lieu of food and lodging; and the equally abusive practice of letting slaves hire themselves and act as if free. He recommended the entire exclusion or effectual punishment of all "abolitionist agents" operating within the borders of Virginia. In fine, Ruffin would convert slavery in Virginia (a State where Seward noted that slaves were well treated, and that many masters refused to call them anything but servants) into a system with Dante's legend, "All hope abandon," inscribed over its gate.[39]

37 *Ann. Report Am. Antislavery Soc.*, 1860, pp. 211, 212.
38 During the summer and fall of 1857, large meetings had been held in Virginia to pray the legislature to authorize a sweeping sale of all free negroes by auction. *Cong. Globe*, 35th Cong., 1st Sess., 294.
39 Cf. Ruffin's articles in Richmond *South*, 1858, *passim; Diary*, January 28, July 2, 1858.

Lincoln said at Springfield on June 28 that the condition of the Negroes in the United States had deteriorated sharply since the era of the fathers, "and their ultimate destiny has never appeared so hopeless as in the last three or four years."

And yet harshness was no real part of the temper of Americans of the South, who differed no whit from Americans of the North. The main excitant impulse was fear, and they wanted to protect the *institution*, not to penalize the individual. It was because the free Negro menaced the institution, because manumission undermined it, because all self-help systems for the slave corroded it, that proslavery men urged new legislation. Their object was not to surround slavery with an atmosphere of terror. It was to shore up an institution built on quicksand and battered by all the forces of world sentiment and emergent industrialism. Ruffin was personally the kindliest of masters. The unhappy fact was that it had become impossible to safeguard slavery without brutal violence to countless individuals; either the institution had to be given up, or the brutality committed. The legislators of Louisiana and Arkansas, of Alabama and Georgia, with humane men like Ruffin and the Eastern Shore planters of Maryland, had faced this alternative. They had chosen the institution. The Richmond *Examiner* stated their choice in unflinching language:

It is all an hallucination to suppose that we are ever going to get rid of slavery, or that it will ever be desirable to do so. It is a thing that we cannot do without; that is righteous, profitable, and permanent, and that belongs to Southern society as inherently, intrinsically, and durably as the white race itself. Southern men should act as if the canopy of heaven were inscribed with a covenant, in letters of fire, that the negro is here, and here forever—is our property, and ours forever—is never to be emancipated—is to be kept hard at work and in rigid subjection all his days.[40]

This has the ring of the Richmond publicist Fitzhugh, and would have been repudiated by many Southerners. But Jefferson Davis said, July 6, 1859: "There is not probably an intelligent mind among our own citizens who doubts either the moral or the legal right of the institution of African slavery." Senator A. G. Brown said September 14, 1858, that he wanted Cuban, Mexican, and Central American territory for slavery: "I would spread the blessings of slavery . . . to the uttermost ends of the earth." Such utterances treated slavery as permanent, and assumed that it must be defended at every point.

[V]

Terrorism was not the object; and yet, as the danger to the institution grew, terrorism came to be practiced. "There exists, at this moment," declared the

40 *Quoted in Ann. Report Am. Antislavery Soc.,* 1855, p. 128. Toombs had said in the debates of 1850: "This is a proslavery government. Slavery is stamped on its heart!"

New York *Tribune* in 1860, "throughout the Southern States, an actual Reign of Terror. No Northern man, whatever may be his character, his opinions, or his life, but simply because he is a Northern man, can visit that region without the certainty of being subjected to a mean espionage over all his actions, and a rigid watchfulness over all his expressions of opinion; with the risk of personal indignity, and danger even to life and limb."

The wave of apprehension that rolled across the South after Harper's Ferry naturally brought into activity the most reckless and violent members of ill-organized communities. Already, large Southern groups had been conditioned to yield an emotional response to activating shibboleths and signs. "Abolitionist," "Black Republican," "nigger-lover," and "slave-stealer" were terms which, loaded with bitter feeling, were applied with little discrimination to all Northerners. The Southern press had for years assailed "Yankee incendiaries" and "Garrisonian fanatics" in terms which made multitudes ready to believe that the North was filled with them. It is a basic principle of social psychology that mob action readily appears in situations in which two or more opposed races, or social classes, or religious or political elements, stand in uneasy equipoise—the resulting prejudices and fears quickly generating an explosive hatred. That situation existed in large parts of the South in 1859. Tension, conflict, and alarm were ready, on a slight impulse, to create a pathological state of mind—in many places, actual hysteria. Inhibitions of custom and reason would go down; mob action would come to the front. John Brown's raid supplied the requisite stimulus. When Governor Wise set his evil example, how would weaker men act?

In some Southern communities, the committees of safety and vigilance committees which sprang up in hundreds provided an orderly control; but in others, they acted as agents of a mob, usually of a confused and erratic rather than purposeful type. To the mob any Yankee was suspect, and any suspected man at least half guilty. A New Yorker, Dr. Meigs Case, who arrived in Salem, Alabama, in the late summer of 1859 to reorganize a female college there, was run out of the community when the Harper's Ferry excitement surged. In the same State a Connecticut minister named Alberton, an innocent book agent, was imprisoned, threatened with hanging, and frightened into mental derangement. In Arkansas, an Illinois schoolteacher was given thirty-six hours to depart. From all over the South, as we have seen, scores of drummers, evangelists, itinerant mechanics, and notion peddlers fled northward. Men were tarred and feathered, and a few were hanged.[41]

Fundamentally this was not, as the New York *Tribune* suggested it was, an expression of sectional antagonism; a hatred of the Northerner "simply because

41 *The New "Reign of Terror" in the Slaveholding States, 1859–60* (Anon. 1860). Beyond doubt the terrorism was exaggerated; but it was sufficient to deepen the Northern belief that the South was engaged in a sweeping denial of civil liberties. Cf. Russell B. Nye, *Fettered Freedom: Civil Liberties and the Slavery Controversy, 1830–1860, passim.*

he is a Northerner." Nor was it an expression of brutal proclivities, of which the South had no more than the North. It was an attempt to defend the institution of slavery as the one tolerable solution of the race problem which the South knew. For a generation, the Southern public had been made increasingly responsive to certain stereotyped stimuli. The terms slavery, abolition, freesoil, Southern rights, servile revolt, and popular sovereignty had been filled with a deep emotional content. For ten years, the Southern masses had been interconditioned to the psychology of a crisis. Ever since Calhoun said that he knew but the South, and the South in danger, the section had taken on an increasing fixation of interest. It had become, like publics of all nations at such times—like Americans in 1775–76, when New England saw plenty of mob action—more credulous, excitable, and primitive. It would be easy to make too much of the hundreds of instances of Southern violence. What was really significant was the social psychology beneath them. It was a psychology which was erecting an iron wall around the special Southern institution, as Spain, Japan, and Russia have at various times tried to erect iron walls around equally special ways of life.

By the beginning of 1860, Republican newspapers—the New York and the Chicago *Tribune*, the Springfield *Republican*, the Cleveland *Leader*—were being stopped in Southern post offices. Even *Harper's Weekly*, full of compliments to the South, was being excluded in some communities because of the private antislavery views of its editor, George William Curtis. In Virginia, a Doddridge County postmaster asked Governor Wise what he should do with such journals as Greeley's. The governor replied on November 26, 1859, that when mail reached its local destination, Federal control over it ceased; the State alone could determine whether citizens should receive it; and postmasters were bound under heavy penalties to obey a State law which required them to extract from the mails any publication or writing which incited negroes to rebel or inculcated resistance to the rights of masters. Postmaster-General Holt accepted this doctrine, writing another Virginia postmaster that Wise had correctly stated the facts. Inevitably, Southern postal officials were soon halting a great variety of Northern publications. Even religious periodicals were stopped, and *Frank Leslie's* innocuous pages were impounded.

The embargo on newspapers, books, and magazines spread so rapidly that by 1860 the Springfield *Republican* observed that nearly all Northern journals had been excluded except the New York *Herald* and New York *Observer*, "the one the organ of proslavery diabolism and the other of proslavery piety." [42] The Montgomery *Mail* suggested, early in 1860, an *auto da fé* of the sermons of the

42 *Ann. Report Am. Antislavery Soc.*, 1860, 192 ff.

English divine Charles Spurgeon, and, when a pile of his books had been duly burnt, it commented approvingly that if the pharisaical author should ever find his way into central Alabama, the editors hoped that a stout cord would speedily be placed around his eloquent throat.[43]

On many points Southerners would have denied, quite correctly, that they were a static community. They had progressive leaders in agriculture, in political thought, in letters, and in industry. But dominant elements insisted that the slavery system must be static and even retrogressive; and to maintain the status, they countenanced tendencies which fettered progress in many departments of Southern life. Their intolerance was akin to that later created in totalitarian states of one overruling dogma. They stood for something approaching a one-party system; for an increasingly rigid control of all implements of education, publicity, and propaganda; for police agencies of patrol and espionage; and even for the use of violence against dissenters. The faster the Western world in general marched, the closer had to be the Southern lock-step. E. L. Godkin, traversing the South, found a former governor of Mississippi, a grave, wise gentleman, ready to use the halter to stop discussion:

. . . He could see no harm in lynch law when directed against abolitionists or Frémonters. He considered it a necessity of the case. He declared that he looked upon the freesoil party as more dangerous and objectionable than the rank abolitionists, because more harmful and insidious. To restrict slavery within certain limits looked a more harmless proposition than to abolish it outright, but in reality was just as fatal. Room for the expansion of the "institution" was, he said, an absolute necessity for the South. If the slaves became massed together, insubordination would be the result, and it would be impossible to keep them in subjection. Even now, he declared, many men could not lie down quietly at night, though the blacks were scattered over a wide extent of territory, and though they still bore a reasonable numerical proportion to the whites. What would it be if the whites found themselves in a miserable minority; and if the blacks, crowded together in a confined area, began to discover the strength which lay in numbers? This day, he knew, would come some time or other, even if the South had it all their own way; but it would not, and should not, come in his own time; and as to the future, it should take care of itself. If each generation did its duty, it might be staved off for a long time.[44]

[VI]

As the South thus lowered its portcullis, locked its gates, and manned its battlements, hope that really constructive proposals would be received for solv-

43 February 17, 1860.
44 London *Daily News*, January 29, 1857.

ing the combined problems of slavery and race adjustment died away. The North had been gravely remiss in failing to make such proposals. Down to the Kansas struggle, perhaps down to Harper's Ferry, a statesmanlike plan, solidly supported, for compensated emancipation combined with such a diffusion of the negro population as would have reduced the tensions of racial readjustment, might gradually have enlisted a large Southern allegiance. John Brown's raid coffined all hope of such a happy consummation.

Did the hope ever really exist? Probably hundreds of thousands of Southerners, in the aggregate, took a realistic view of slavery, believing it a social curse and an economic handicap. Though most of them kept quiet, every traveler in the South found these men. Olmsted conversed with them in Virginia, Alabama, and other States.[45] Godkin talked in Louisiana with a slaveholder who feelingly described the incubus which the institution laid upon farmers and small planters. He expatiated upon the fact that if he could use the capital which he was compelled to put into slaves, he could till a farm three times as large as the one he held, using free labor—if it was to be had. Because cotton required Negroes and the price of Negroes was exorbitant, he predicted that all the rich level lands of the lower Mississippi Valley would soon fall into the hands of the great planters, the small holders being driven to the hills where they would live by growing corn and livestock. He knew, as Godkin knew, that this tendency meant social retrogression. In large areas, the whites would almost disappear, the land would be given over to slaves and their overseers, all importation of goods beyond the scanty fare and clothing of negroes would end, and education, cultural pursuits, good morals, and religion in all its higher characteristics would disappear before the advance of a blind exploitation of soil and slaves. In one Mississippi county the Negroes numbered six thousand, the whites two hundred and fifty, and in some other localities of the cotton kingdom (by no means all) the disproportion between the two races was growing.[46]

Hundreds of thousands of Southerners, too, knew in their hearts (and not a few said openly) that slavery was doomed, that it could not survive much longer except as a transitional institution, and that it must therefore be ameliorated. The ideas of Washington, Madison, and Jefferson were not so easily eradicated as the positive-good school supposed. When the Southern Central Agricultural Society was established in 1846, it avowed as one of its purposes the cultivation of the negro's aptitude for Christianity and civilization, so that by the time slavery had fulfilled its beneficent mission in the South, the social condition of

45 *Seaboard Slave States,* 210 ff., 572, 573, etc.
46 London *Daily News,* March 25, 1857. The census of 1850 did show one Mississippi county where 93 percent of the people were slaves; another with 91 percent. But Blanche Clark in *The Yoeman Farmer of Tennessee* proves that the small farmer in that State was quite holding his own; and see Frank L. Owsley, *Plain Folk of the Old South.*

the race might permit of a system which would relieve the colored race from servitude, without sinking it to the sad condition of free negroes in the North. The society lasted until 1857.

In 1855 some unidentified reformers in North Carolina—the State of Helper, B. S. Hedrick, Daniel R. Goodloe, and a large Quaker group—offered a plan for a triple change in the institution. They called for legal protection of marriage among slaves, preservation of the parental relation by outlawing all sales of minor children, and repeal of the statute forbidding the education of slaves. Their project received noncommital notice outside the State. In Mississippi, the Port Gibson *Reveille* remarked that most planters of that area had at least partially adopted the main features of the program, which was worth serious consideration. It weakly added, however, that evils might lurk in the scheme.[47] Robert Toombs, in his address on slavery in Boston in 1856, declared that to protect marriage and other domestic ties by laws forbidding the separation of families would be wise, proper, and humane. He, too, however, added the weak reservation that the evil of separation was much exaggerated, for Negroes in Africa knew no marriage, and more families had been separated by migration from Ireland than by the Southern slave trade.[48]

Other Southerners of prominence advocated amelioration. The sociologist Henry Hughes, insisting on the progressive character of the Southern labor system, declared that it should be called not slavery but warranteeism, the principle of which was justice; and he advocated a diminution of "the accidental abuses of our system." [49] J. F. H. Claiborne, editor, historian, and Unionist politician, penned an undated memorandum declaring that if the South were let alone, slavery would conform to the liberal ideas of the age by steadily improving its character. How? "Not towards the abolition of slavery, but towards its gradual improvement—to servitude—field labor—domesticity—mechanical apprenticeship—city drudgery. A steady progress, first physical, next mental and moral, is the upward tendency of a sound social policy." [50]

The very fact that many masters allowed slaves to purchase their freedom was a tacit acknowledgment of the weakness of the institution; since, as Booker T. Washington pointed out, the slave who could purchase his own freedom was one whom it was less profitable to hold in servitude. Even in the eighteen-fifties, many slaves, particularly in towns and among the skilled or semi-skilled, continued to buy their liberty.[51] Negroes sometimes earned their freedom in ingenious ways; one by hawking poems in manuscript, and one by migrating to California, with his master's sanction, where he made enough money to redeem

47 Quoted in *National Intelligencer*, June 7, 1854.
48 Brewton, *The Son of Thunder*, 243, 244.
49 November 5, 1858; Claiborne Papers, Miss. Dept. Arch. and Hist.
50 Claiborne Papers, Univ. of N. C.; probably between 1851 and 1855.
51 Matison, "Manumission by Purchase," *Journal Negro Hist.*, XXXIII, April, 1948.

his whole family. The majority simply showed unusual enterprise as carpenters, blacksmiths, shoemakers, and the like. As industrialization increased, opportunities for self-purchase should have multiplied. But the reactionary wave of 1830–60 interfered. John H. Russell, in *The Free Negro in Virginia, 1789–1865*, estimates that before 1800 the Virginia slave had about ten chances in a hundred of manumission in any of its forms; from 1800 to 1832 four or five chances; and after 1832 about two chances.

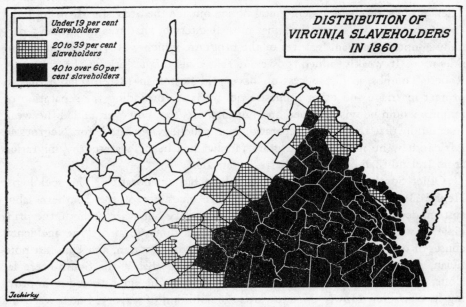

Another weak spot in slavery: western Virginia.

Many Southern churchmen felt like W. H. Barnwell, rector of St. Peter's in Charleston, who in 1848 earnestly desired two changes in the laws of his State: a repeal of the act prohibiting emancipation, and repeal of the law which severely punished anyone who taught a slave to read and write. Barnwell, who knew well "the old half-brute native Africans, of whom a few survive," saw that the difference between their lot and that of the healthy, lively, cheerful slaves who enjoyed Charleston life was a testimonial both to the educational value of slavery, and to the Negro's improvability. He recognized that some South Carolina legislation was bad—though he believed that the chief obstacle to its removal was the reckless agitation of the abolitionists. Many churchmen, like Alexander Campbell, boldly taught their slaves to write. When a Massachusetts clergyman wrote a pamphlet decrying colonization and advocating the amelioration of the lot of slaves where they were held, he received favorable answers from clergymen as far South as Natchez and New Orleans.[52]

Before the Southerners hardened their minds and spirits; before Governor Thomas Moore of Louisiana wrote that the institution of slavery had been completely vindicated and its perpetuity proved desirable;[53] before W. L. Yancey, reading Olmsted's pages, declared that if retrogression in the treatment of slaves had taken place, it was the fault of the abolitionists;[54] in short, before the middle fifties, a bold scheme for gradual compensated emancipation might have won, not a majority of Southerners, but a considerable minority. It might have been a minority sufficient, in alliance with a generous body of Northern opinion, to turn the scale in 1861 in favor of a new compromise and some improved scheme.

[VII]

The ablest, most passionate, and most industrious proponent of a plan of gradual emancipation was Frank P. Blair, Jr., on whom part of Benton's mantle had fallen. He rose to prominence in Missouri, where the movement for gradual emancipation had grown strong; where an emancipation candidate had been elected mayor of St. Louis in 1857, and where Carl Schurz would dare in 1860 to deliver an eloquent address on the imminent doom of slavery. Such leaders as Blair, Gratz Brown, and James O. Broadhead, a Unionist of Whig antecedents, emphasized both the moral and economic arguments for turning Missouri into a free State. Slavery was wrong; slavery was also unjust to white workers who had to compete with forced black labor. Blair held a noteworthy interview with Lincoln in Springfield, early in 1857. Entering Congress in December, 1857, he introduced a resolution to inquire into the expediency of acquiring territory in Central or South America for the colonization of free Negroes and liberated slaves; and he supported it in a careful speech which F. P. Blair, Sr., and Montgomery Blair had approved.

52 Letter to J. G. Palfrey, Charleston *Mercury*, August 11, 1848; W. W. Jennings, *Short Hist. Disciples of Christ*, 158; Everett MS Diary February 27, 1857. Colonization in Liberia was more and more regarded as a failure. Reports from Monrovia were discouraging. One Southern naval officer, who visited the capital in 1858 on the U. S. S. *Marion*, was horrified by the hardships suffered by Negroes from the United States in that unhealthy climate, and amused by the pompous talk of President Benson and other high officials at a state dinner. "I imagined myself among a collection of house-servants who were closely imitating their masters." June 19, 1858; C. C. Clay Papers, Duke Univ. The American Colonization Society lived to issue its sixtieth report in 1877; but by that time it had become largely a missionary society.

53 Address to Leg. 1860; Moore Papers, Univ. of La. Archives.

54 Yancey Papers, undated, Ala. Dept. Arch. and Hist. Frank Blair, Jr., wished early in 1857 to bring forward in Congress a bill granting to Missouri all the public lands in the State, amounting to about fifteen million acres, to be sold and the proceeds used to buy slaves and colonize them abroad. March 25, 1857, to his father; Blair-Lee Papers.

The background of Blair's speech was the raging debate on Lecompton, and the angry discussion of Commodore Hiram Paulding's seizure of Walker. He had been depressed by the wave of reactionary legislation on slavery in the South. He had also been struck by the proposal of Earl Grey, as Colonial Secretary, for importing into Trinidad large numbers of free colored people from America. He had learned that Honduras was anxious to enlist American capital in mining, railroad building, and commerce. African colonization was a failure, for climate, distance, and the barbarous state of society were against it. Central American colonization, however, as Britain had shown in sending Jamaican blacks to help develop Belize, was feasible. The time had come to realize Jefferson's great dream of so directing the process of emancipation and deportation that slavery would gradually disappear and the place of the negroes be *pari passu* filled up by whites.[55]

The voluntary removal of free Negroes to parts of Central America where the United States could establish homes for them, argued Blair, would benefit the emigrants, the people receiving them, and the United States. Central America was inhabited already by mixed races. Honduras, for example, had one hundred and forty thousand people called Negroes and mulattoes, one hundred thousand called Indians, and fifty thousand called whites—all showing great mixture of blood. Many Negroes and mulattoes had risen high in politics, commerce, and the church. Honduras and Guatemala, indeed, had been ruled by *mestizo* dictators. Poverty and insurrection fermented in Central America; but let the United States buy lands there for hundreds of thousands of Christianized, English-speaking, industrious negroes, and the little republics would make rapid progress toward wealth and stability. As Great Britain had colonized land after land, throwing a chain of dependencies around the globe, so the United States could colonize this neighboring region. Once Central America was thus opened up, benevolent masters in the temperate slave States would liberate their chattels, accepting a due recompense. The benefits would be immediate:

What a change would soon be wrought in the position of Maryland and Virginia, Tennessee and Kentucky, and in my own State, Missouri, if a smooth way were opened into the heart of the tropics—prodigal of wealth in the soil, in the mines, and in the forests; where the labor of the robust and skilful freedman, assisted by the capital and instruction, and inspired by the energy of enterprising American merchants, miners, or planters, would start everything into life. The mixed condition of the four different classes which, in our grain-growing States, obstruct each other; the masters dependent on the slaves, the slaves on their masters; the free negroes hanging on the skirts of both; while the great mass, the free white laborers, are cast out, in a great measure, from employment and all ownership in the soil; would be succeeded by the most useful of all the

55 *Cong. Globe*, 35th Cong., 1st Sess., 293–298.

tillers of the earth, small freeholders and an independent tenantry. The influx of immigrants from Europe and the North, with moderate capital, already running into Maryland and Virginia, would, as these States sloughed the black skin, fill up the rich region round the Chesapeake bay, the noblest bay in the world.

To proslavery Congressmen, Blair's proposal was a draught from the bitter waters of Marah, and they turned from it with revulsion. Lucius J. Gartrell of Georgia spoke for those who wanted slavery, more slavery, and slavery forever. The institution, he said, was not what Washington, Jefferson, Madison, and John Randolph had imagined it; the South now knew better. It was right in principle and practice; it was sanctioned by Holy Writ; it was a blessing to the colored man; it had developed the resources of the nation, and by its conservative influence had elevated Southerners in morality, wealth, enterprise, and intelligence to a point never attained by any other people.[56] Southern Democrats ranked Blair among the traitors to his party. Northern freesoilers, who had no faith in colonization, refused to come to his aid. Only one member gave him support, and that indirectly—Eli Thayer, who wanted to see Central America colonized by white Americans rather than blacks. His resolution did not come to vote.[57]

Yet the Blairs continued their drum-beating. The *Missouri Democrat*, Gratz Brown, and Frank Blair insistently pressed the demand for gradual emancipation in Missouri. With his brother Montgomery, Frank enlisted Senator Doolittle of Wisconsin in an effort to rally the Northwestern governors to the cause of colonization in Central America. The Blair family believed that if the Northwest spoke out boldly for such a policy, the border slave States, at least, could be brought into line; and they wished Governors Dennison of Ohio, Kirkwood of Iowa, and Randall of Wisconsin to press the subject simultaneously upon their legislatures. Let these governors come boldly up to their work, wrote Montgomery to Doolittle; let them say that the national government must provide passage for such free Negroes as will go voluntarily to some land where their capacities may be developed; let them give a vigorous leadership to Northern opinion. This would do more than ten thousand speeches to convince the great body of Southerners that the Republican Party did not wish to set the negroes free to be the equals of the Southern people, and hence their rulers in areas where they were more numerous than the whites.[58]

Frank Blair spoke for his plan during 1859 in various parts of the Northwest, in Missouri, and in New England. His most noteworthy address, delivered in Boston on January 26, was heard by Emerson, Governor Banks, and other distinguished men. To deal with slavery by emancipation and colonization, he said,

56 *Ibid.*, 391-393.
57 Smith, *Blair Family*, I, 405, 406; *Cong. Globe*, 35th Cong., 1st Sess., 227-229.
58 Smith, *Blair Family*, I, 443 ff.; *Mo. Hist. Rev.* XI, 136.

would require the joint action of State and Federal governments. Some Latin-American area should be acquired for a free negro state, dependent on the United States. Freedmen and their families should be persuaded to migrate thither by the same inducements which had persuaded settlers to move westward: financial aid, moral encouragement, and political protection. Why should the enterprise of Boston not take the lead in this new crusade? And why should the plan not be the principal undertaking of the Republican Administration to be elected in 1860? But he made few converts.[59]

"Has any person, of any party or opinion," inquired Edward Everett just after Harper's Ferry, "proposed, in sober earnest, any practicable method of wholesale emancipation?" Apart from Webster and Blair, the answer was no. "Has any person . . . ever undertaken to sketch out the details of a plan for effecting the change at once, by any legislative measure that could be adopted?" Not even Blair had done that. Everett pointed out how much emancipation would cost the South: a billion dollars in slave property, the outfitting of the emancipated millions for self-support, the derangement of the labor system, and an immense social turmoil. What contribution would the North make toward footing this bill? [60] Lyman Trumbull was suggesting the purchase of a great tract somewhere for the resettlement of the liberated colored people of both North and South; but he was careful not to speak realistically of costs, and his Illinois followers assumed that his main object was to exempt Republicans from the reproach that they wanted a large Negro body in the North.[61]

The fact was that all suggestions for compensated emancipation, whether in Elihu Burritt's plan of heavy taxation to buy slaves en masse,[62] or Webster's plan

59 Blair, March 1, 1859, Dana Papers; Smith, *Blair Family*, I, 448–450. Senator Doolittle believed that if the Republicans had embraced this scheme of Latin-American colonization, the hope it held out of ending the evils of slavery would have prevented John Brown's raid. Frank Blair, Jr., to his father, November 2, 1859; Blair-Lee Papers.
60 "Union Meeting in Faneuil Hall," December 8, 1859. Pamphlet.
61 McKibben, December 25, 1859, Wing, May 4, 1860, Trumbull Papers. See N. O. *Picayune*, August 18, 1860, for indignant comment on the unwillingness of Illinois to receive negroes while asking the South to set them free.
62 Elihu Burritt and others held a convention of friends of compensated emancipation in Cleveland on August 25–28, 1857, which scores of delegates attended. They resolved that it was highly desirable "that the people of the North should cooperate, in a generous and brotherly spirit, with the people of the South, and share liberally with them in the expense of putting an end to so great a moral and political evil as American slavery." Each slaveholder, they proposed, should be paid $250 for every slave freed, and each slave should be presented with $25; a sum which, the gathering hoped, would "go far toward supplying them with humble homes on this continent, or upon another, should they prefer so wide a removal." Abolitionists greeted the plan with hoots of derision. It received chilly disapproval from the N. Y. *Tribune*, which commented that while it was willing to devote the public lands to immediate emancipation, and to give twenty million dollars a year for fifty years from the Treasury for this purpose, it believed that it was both unjust and inexpedient for the country to pay the slaveholders for liberating their chattels. The slaves were entitled

for using the proceeds of the public lands, or Blair's plan of joint Federal-State effort, ran into three obstacles: radical opinion at the South, unwilling to part with slavery on any terms; radical opinion at the North, which held slavery immoral and therefore opposed paying slaveholders for giving it up; and the inertia of the majority, unwilling to do anything but drift. While national thought on slavery ran the gamut from Yancey to Garrison, most schools agreed on one thesis: that no drastic, costly, and painful plan need be made for the future. The abolitionists wanted no plan because they oversimplified the problem: free the slave, they said, and he will at once become an intelligent, self-governing citizen of high quality. The proslavery extremists wanted no plan because they believed that the *status quo* was the best possible situation. The Negro is just where he should be, said Charles O'Conor.[63] As for the great central mass of Americans, whether freesoilers or mildly proslavery, they were content to wait and hope. If slavery was doomed, they held, moral pressure and changing economic conditions would in time bring it to its appointed end.

The most thoughtful exponent of the policy of waiting upon time and economic change was Thomas Ewbank, English-born inventor, manufacturer, and author, who believed that the Age of the Machine would gradually conquer the Age of Slavery. Head of the Patent Office under Taylor and Fillmore, Ewbank returned to New York to write books and pamphlets on a wide variety of subjects. In the spring of 1859, he delivered a remarkable address before the American Ethnological Society of which he was a founder, entitled "Inorganic Forces Ordained to Supersede Human Slavery." His belief was that mechanical invention and industrialism would gradually extinguish all the baser forms of toil.

Neither the radical Northern nor the radical Southern attitude toward slavery seemed valid to Ewbank. He had no faith in the eradication of slavery by moral crusades or penal statutes; at the same time, he thought slavery an evil and rejected the doctrine of negro inferiority. The roots of the system, extending to the lowest depths of man's selfish nature, must—he declared—be deprived of nourishment before they would wither. As long as slavery paid in dollars, it would live. What would make it unprofitable?—the machine. Multiply machines, predicted Ewbank, and slavery would disappear; for a piece of fuel costing a

---

to freedom as a right, and by generations of unpaid labor they had earned it. This was the attitude of other freesoil journals. Southern newspapers, meanwhile, were hostile or contemptuous. The convention formed the National Compensated Emancipation Society, with Benjamin Silliman as president, Mark Hopkins as a vice-president, and Burritt as corresponding secretary. But the gathering was abortive, drawing fewer delegates and commanding less support than the radical abolitionist convention which met in Cleveland in the autumn. N. Y. *Weekly Tribune*, August 1, 1857; *National Intelligencer*, September 5, 1857; *Ann. Report Am. Antislavery Soc.*, 1858, 184.

63 Speech Academy of Music, N. Y., December 19, 1859 (pamphlet).

few cents would do the work of several rude hands.[64] Machine power, steadily advancing throughout the world, would eventually displace unskilled labor on the Alabama cotton plantation as it had done on the Illinois wheat farm. Already, machines ginned, spun, and wove cotton, "nor is there any insuperable obstacle to their planting and hoeing and picking it, or something equivalent to picking." Machines already ground the sugar cane; they would soon cultivate, reap, and transport it. When a proper combination of mechanical skills gave the South its needed inventions, predicted Ewbank, slavery would pass away amid the hosannas of proslavery as well as antislavery men. He might have quoted John Randolph's statement that once slave labor was proved unprofitable, the master would run away from the slave faster than the slave had ever run from the master. Societies to promote mechanical progress, said the lecturer, would achieve more than abolition societies. His pamphlet did not suggest, however, what was to be done with the displaced slave.

Lincoln had declared that if all earthly power were given him to deal with the institution, he would not know what to do with it. As a question of practical politics, Lincoln was right, for the subject bristled with difficulties which only a tremendous educational crusade could affect. The central perplexity had been stated long before by Jefferson: "Among the Romans emancipation required but *one effort*. The slave, when free, might mix without *staining* the blood of his master. But with us a second is necessary, unknown to history." The only place where the freed Negro could be colonized successfully was in the United States, North and South; and colonization at home by plan would cost the country far more in effort, money, and social friction than it had yet paid for any object— even independence. But the time had come when the country, however reluctantly, must face a plain fact: if the United States was really to be the last, best hope of mankind, it could not much longer remain a slaveholding republic.

[VIII]

While the American deadlock on slavery continued unbroken, the cause of human freedom was still advancing round the globe. Great Britain, in giving up her hold upon the Bay Islands, tried to stipulate that slavery should never exist in them. The Dutch colonies in America stood on the verge of emancipation. Year by year, outside Brazil and the Spanish possessions, the last vestiges of slavery died away in Latin America. And most impressive of all, the Russian movement for the liberation of serfs reached its climax.

64 Eli Thayer told the House in 1858: "Why, sir we can buy a negro power, in a steam engine, for ten dollars, and we can clothe and feed that power for one year for five dollars; and were we the men to give $1000 for an African slave, and $150 a year to feed and clothe him?" *Cong. Globe*, 35th Cong., 1st Sess., 229.

Provincial groups and an imperial commission had labored during 1859–60 on a practical scheme of emancipation. Finally, on the day before Lincoln was inaugurated, a decree of the Czar set all serfs free. With a stroke which rang throughout the globe, the hand on the world clock moved forward in a sudden leap. Nobody supposed that a white serf in Russia, his blood identical with that of the noblest families, occupied a position remotely comparable with that of a black slave in the South. Nevertheless, some circumstances connected with this emancipation were of direct significance to Americans.

The fact that the Russian authorities had enlisted the ablest men in the land, in a variety of national and local agencies, to work out a *plan*, was significant. So was the fact that Russia avowedly responded to a variety of pressures, among which world opinion, fear of a servile uprising, and a preference for long-term rather than short-term economic benefits were important. So, too, were the facts that once the reform was assured, land values rose; that when the spirit of idealism was given free rein, it proved unexpectedly powerful; and that the sobriety, industry, and ambition of the peasants immediately increased. The Czar paid tribute to the altruism of the landholders, actuated by Christian love of neighbor and philosophic respect for the dignity of man. From all parts of the realm came news of the opening of free schools, the progress of temperance, and the rise of a new social concord.

One incident of the emancipation seemed clothed with a certain meaning. John Brown's body lay mouldering in the grave. But far away in St. Petersburg, when the drafting of the final plan of emancipation was completed, the Czar's representative rose at a public dinner to offer four toasts: to the Czar; to the cause of emancipation; to the landholders; and to the memory of Emilian Pugatchev. Pugatchev was a serf who, heading a rebellion in 1774, had been caught and executed, his body being burnt. Now, by the changes of time, the work he had done was extolled by the very power which had put him to death.

The Russian emancipation, like John Brown's raid, was a lightning flash which illuminated the tragic predicament of America. While nearly the whole civilized world was moving in one direction, the South was moving in another. While even in Russia the movement for human freedom was scoring victories, *De Bow's Review* was announcing that no Southern movement had ever gained strength so fast as that for the revival of the slave trade. Abroad, believers in democracy looked to the shining principles of the Declaration of Independence. In Virginia itself the *Southern Literary Messenger* now repudiated those principles, and quoted Jefferson's statement that in any contest between masters and slaves, Divine Goodness must take the side of the downtrodden, only to stigmatize it as ignorant and erroneous. We may say that in setting the spasmodic Southern reaction against Northern attack 1850–1860 in contrast with the secular world movement 1776–1860, we do the slaveholding States a certain injustice. We may say that Southern retrogression was the natural outgrowth of a sense of peril. But these considerations do not exonerate a Southern leadership which might have clung to Jefferson's principles with that statesman's own vision and devotion; which might have appealed less to Southern fears and appetites, and more to Southern courage and idealism. The passion of John Brown, the patient, wise insistence of Lincoln that America must not evade its moral responsibilities, gained their deepest significance from a realization that the nation was losing its position of democratic leadership in the world. This realization that it was falling short of the objects of its founders was to give intensity to the final stand of the North for the restriction of slavery within its existing domain—a stand to which we now turn.

6

See the Front of Battle Lower

SOCIAL relations in Washington this winter of 1859–60 were sadly disrupted. "We shall *not* leave cards!"—so ladies from one side of the Potomac spoke of those from the other. In growing numbers, Southern and Northern Congressmen cut each other as they passed in the streets. Hostesses making up dinner lists had to bend with anxious care over the names. The feud between Buchanan and Douglas remained so bitter that the beautiful Adele Douglas never deigned to appear at a White House reception, and when she met Miss Lane on neutral ground they bowed with polite frigidity. Toombs and Henry Wilson had once been friends; now they glared frostily when their paths crossed.

To be sure, some accomplished hostesses counted good friends in both sections and among all party groups. The Pryors of Virginia, who loved to gather such fellow-Southerners as Lamar, Hunter, Muscoe Garnett, and Porcher Miles to their fireside, were also hospitable to Westerners and New Yorkers. Mrs. Horace F. Clarke, wife of a wealthy New York Representative, impartially entertained Yankees and men of the cotton kingdom. So did Mrs. Senator Thompson of New Jersey. The kindly intimacy between Seward and Jefferson Davis continued, while such border families as the Crittendens cultivated friendships in every quarter. As resentments deepened, however, even tactful matrons feared some sudden explosion.

Once, at the theatre, Mrs. Douglas entertained Mrs. Pryor in a box next that of Miss Lane. When Porcher Miles halted at the entrance, Mrs. Douglas turned upon him with glacial dignity: "Sir, you have made a mistake. Your visit is intended for next door!" And Miles haughtily retorted: "Madame, I presumed I might be permitted to make my respects to Mrs. Pryor, for whom my call was intended." [1]

Yet despite the tension, it was a busy social season. Never had more money been spent on dinners, receptions, and balls than in this year of returning prosperity. Even so plain a man as Seward felt it necessary, when he gave a dinner, to serve seventeen courses, changing the plates for each; and at the end, waiters

[1] Mrs. Roger A. Pryor, *Reminiscences of Peace and War*, Ch. 7.

handed around pyramids of iced fruits, oranges, French sweetmeats, and nuts.[2] A correspondent of the Charleston *Mercury* complained that dinners were not what they had been in the days of Clay and Webster, with ducks, oysters, and terrapin from the Chesapeake, shad from the James, venison from Virginia, and wines from the best Charleston or Philadelphia merchants; but, at any rate, entertainments were costlier. Secretary Toucey's grand evening party in February, graced by wealthy New Yorkers, was considered especially brilliant. As always, a contrast was visible between the quiet entertainments of the old Georgetown aristocracy and the affairs held by Southern grandees like Senators Slidell and C. C. Clay, with liveried servants, banks of flowers, music, and a superabundance of comestibles.

An ingenuous view of Washington is afforded by the letters of Susanna Keitt, bride of the South Carolina Representative, who saw everything through unspoiled eyes. Lawrence Keitt, now in his middle thirties, had faults enough, being hot-tempered, bombastic, and egotistical. But he was a very likable person, warm-hearted, impulsively affectionate, quick-witted, and of iron courage, as he would prove in dying at Cold Harbor for his principles. His romance with Susanna Sparks had been tempestuous enough. From Washington, he had written her on her South Carolina plantation long letters full of politics, gossip, and above all his personal philosophy. The young girl had been difficult and changeable after the manner of Southern belles; they became engaged, but she broke off the engagement; finally she consented again and they were married. She had extorted the promise of a long stay in Europe, where she wanted to live, study art, and travel extensively. They made a grand tour—and then the deepening crisis recalled him to Washington. She came reluctantly, and took quick alarm at the currents of passion swirling about them. A touching note is struck in her cry to her brother in the midst of the speakership contest—one of her repeated expressions of real fear:

"Oh, Alec, we are having frightful times here—war any moment, and no knowing who may fall. Mr. Pryor, Clingman, and Mann have just left the parlor, saying that all hope for a democratic speaker is gone, and that the Southerners are resolved a black Republican shall not take the chair. They are armed and determined to fight to the knife there on the floor of Congress. . . . Governor Wise has ten thousand men, drilled and armed, that would march to the Capitol at the first sound of war. Oh, Alec, I am so uneasy I can write no more."[3]

This sensitive girl, terrified by the violent talk, bored by the bigwigs and wistful for the quiet pleasures of plantation life, found the receptions, dinners,

---

2 *Harper's Weekly*, March 24, 1860.
3 Susanna Keitt to Alexander Sparks, undated; Keitt Papers, Duke Univ.

and balls exhausting. "It takes all your time to return the visits and all your money for the hire of hacks, and all this for people who care nothing for you." The city had too many rowdy Congressmen, importunate office-seekers, fast young women, and insipid dancing men to suit her. (Charles Francis Adams, Jr., mentions the fast young women; he sometimes hardly knew where to look when they talked to him.) It was a great place for dilly-dallyings, flirtations, and quasi-engagements. The men had better times than the women; on one occasion, when Porcher Miles gave the South Carolina Congressmen a dinner, wives were indignant over husbands returning at two A.M. half-tipsy. Buchanan insisted on seeing Mrs. Keitt, for Slidell said she was the handsomest woman resident in Washington, and after her visit he gave a dinner party for her. But though she thought Miss Lane very agreeable, she was not impressed by the President. "He has one of the most quizzical faces I ever saw—head and mouth twisted to one side, and then the erratic performance of that famous eye!" Moreover, he was full of prosy reminiscences: "I have no fancy for the story-telling old man."

At the White House receptions Susanna eyed some famous figures with amazement: Madame Bodisco, for example, still in her mid-thirties and good-looking despite her corpulence, wearing a court dress the diamonds and laces of which were whispered to have cost thirty thousand. Sometimes the Washington atmosphere, with its sectional hatreds, social rivalries, and malicious gossip, seemed stifling. She turned to close friends like the Crittendens and Hammonds for companionship. Particularly did she like Mrs. Crittenden, a lively woman who, though at least sixty, wore low-necked, short-sleeved evening gowns with lace flounces and tossed her curls, adorned with pink roses, like any debutante.

Chief place among the diplomats was taken by the new British minister, Lord Lyons, a bachelor of wealth, sagacity, and easygoing manners whose legation dinners were of statelier type than Napier's. His advent aroused talk of possible matches, with unfounded rumors of an engagement to Harriet Lane.

"The American women are undoubtedly very pretty," wrote the amused envoy, who was forty-two, "but my heart is too old and too callous to be wounded by their charms. I am not going to be married either to the fascinating accomplished niece of the President, nor to the widow of a late Foreign Minister, or to any other maiden or relict to whom I am given by the newspapers." [4] He noticed that Americans were pleased by courtesies from a man of title, and prone to think themselves slighted if little favors were omitted; "this quality may be sometimes turned to good account," he wrote Lord John Russell. Like others, he took care to avoid sectional collisions. Senator Clay's wife, driving to a legation dinner with her husband and the Crittendens, was perturbed lest the inex-

4 Lord Newton, *Lord Lyons,* Ch. 2.

perienced minister assign some Black Republican to take her in to dinner. "I will refuse to accept him!" she exploded. Her fears did not diminish when various Southern gentlemen, talking with her, revealed that they had to escort someone else to table. She was looking nervously at the Republicans when the massive doors slid apart and a voice announced dinner. Then, to her astonished relief, Lyons stepped to her side and took her arm with, "I have the honor, madam!"

Winter had brought the usual minor events: lectures by savants at the Smithsonian, attended by two thousand people, an exhibition of Indian dancing at the Navy Yard, an invasion by the New York Seventh, reviewed in glittering lines on Pennsylvania Avenue, and so on. Clark Mills's equestrian statue of the *pater patriae* was unveiled on Washington's birthday with a short discourse by Buchanan and a long one by Representative Bocock. Like Mills's other work, the statue tried to be exciting. It showed the magisterial-looking general in full regimentals, sword in hand, spurring his horse up to the cannon's mouth as he rallied his broken troops at Princeton.

Happily, no murder took place this season. But the capital quivered for a time over two threatened duels, Pryor calling out Potter of Wisconsin, and Robert J. Walker demanding satisfaction from Jeremiah Black. In the end, both disputes were adjusted bloodlessly; for when Potter proposed fighting elbow-to-elbow with bowie knives Pryor rejected the terms as barbarous, while Black refused even to consider Walker's challenge.[5]

After Lent came the visit of Japanese ambassadors carrying the recently concluded commercial treaty, and charged with cordial messages from the Emperor to the President. Installed in a large suite at Willard's, they endured cheerfully the inquisitiveness of the crowds. They were received in the East Room by the President, the Cabinet, leading members of Congress, and other dignitaries. Secretary Cass gave them a ball, attended by Miss Lane, Mrs. Douglas, and so many other ladies that reporters wrote of being engulfed in surging waves of silk and muslin. Then they left to accept honors in New York.

Their diminutive stature, dark skins, and dignified restraint; their half-shaved heads, surmounted by a boxlike headgear; their flowing robes of silk and brocade, with wide sleeves and crêpe belts; their straw sandals; their heavy swords, in chased and jewelled scabbards; their fans, and the pipes they carried at their sides for frequent whiffs—all this was amusingly fantastic. "They looked for all the world," wrote Major Jack Downing, "like little old ladies dressed up to kill, with queer little things tied on their heads, and two swords stuck in every fellow's belt, which reared up when they bowed down like the tail-feathers of a cockerel." The Japanese must have been equally astonished by the tail coats and stovepipe hats of American dignitaries, and the voluminous garb of the ladies,

5　*Harper's Weekly*, February 25, 1860.

Studying the hoop-skirts, they were impressed by the insubstantiality of Western costume; and one visitor, when jostled by a very fat Congressman, prodded the man twice in the abdomen, ejaculating with surprise—"Solid!"

[I]

The speakership contest ended, Congress turned to neglected tasks. This seven-month session was remarkable for the constant emergence of economic issues through the crust of slavery disputation, boiling up like lava propelled by irresistible internal forces. Morrill's tariff bill of the previous session was dead, but the Ways and Means Committee was busy with another predicated upon it. A bill was drafted to abolish Robert J. Walker's warehousing system—a system held to encourage excessive importations. The House made Morrill's bill donating lands for the establishment of agricultural colleges a special order for the third Tuesday in March. Improvement of communications came up in varied forms: the perennial Pacific Railroad bills, Gwin's proposal for a Government telegraph to California, Yulee's suggestion of a postal money-order system, and a Senate inquiry into the expediency of semi-weekly mails to San Francisco and El Paso. Homestead legislation, internal improvements, and the government of the future Colorado Territory could not be denied debate, for they touched the immediate interests of many millions.

Compared with such issues, the slavery question seemed barren. As one after another the new economic measures passed the House, Southern leaders of the Senate grew alarmed; they saw the national balance tipping against them, and centralization growing. As one after another the measures were stopped by Senate or President, Northerners dominating the House became more irritated. The alarm and the irritation reacted upon the slavery debate, which everybody knew would underlie the imminent Presidential campaign—and which indeed was plainly coming to a new crisis.

Next to this thrust of new economic demands, the session was made dramatic by the determination of radical Southern Democrats to subjugate the Douglas faction. Washington, and especially the Senate, was now the forum of something like a conspiracy to split the Democratic Party. Davis, Slidell, C. C. Clay, Iverson, Mason, and Benjamin were determined to dictate party policy in advance of the convention. With Buchanan's aid, they committed the Democratic caucus to their demands. This was a busy winter of subterranean activity. Many Southern Rights men believed that the slaveholding area was already in the labor pains of delivering a new nation.

Senator A. G. Brown of Mississippi had served notice on Douglas late in 1859: "The South will demand at Charleston a platform explicitly declaring that slave property is entitled in the Territories and on the high seas to the same protection that is given to any other and every other species of property and failing to get it she will retire from the Convention." [6] Governor Moore's address to the Alabama legislature late in 1859 had insisted upon positive territorial protection. From the Peedee to the Arkansas, voices were echoing the demand. It was inevitable that it should be raised in Congress as soon as that body began deliberations.

Just how far the Southern extremists, taking their courage in their hands, wished to proceed—just how much they hoped for party schism as opening the way to national disunion—just how ready they were for war—it is impossible to say except by examining one individual after another; and difficult to say even then. Jefferson Davis hoped to avoid even a party schism, believing that some neutral candidate like ex-President Pierce might yet be accepted by both Northern and Southern Democrats.[7] Judah P. Benjamin declared that he had never felt such an utter sinking of his whole being as when he learned that the party was being rent in twain. Toombs, J. L. M. Curry, Slidell, and even Yancey, all still posed as friends of the Union. But was not the use of party disruption to achieve secession contemplated by these men when, demanding that the South flatly refuse to accept either the nomination of Douglas or the election of a Republican, they strove to screw their States up to the pitch of their own temper? [8]

To a multitude of Southerners the slave-code demand appeared moderate enough. Memminger, appealing for concert of action between South Carolina and Virginia, told the legislature at Richmond on January 19, 1860, that the perilous position of the South rendered four guarantees necessary. The section was entitled to ask for an equal share in the nation's Territories; for the disbanding of all antislavery societies; for the repeal of all laws obstructing the return of fugitives; and for a bar against any amendment of the Constitution with respect to slavery. What was the slave-code compared with such sweeping requirements?

Virginia's new governor, the reasonable John Letcher, who loved the Union and was ready to support Douglas for President, was urging the South to demand Seward's exclusion from the White House on pain of secession. The irrepressible conflict doctrine, he told the legislature in his message of January 7, 1860, was an open declaration of war against slavery, and the election of its author ought to be resisted by all slaveholding States. "The idea of permitting such a man to have control and direction of the army and navy of the United States, and the appointment of high judicial and executive officers, postmasters included, cannot be entertained by the South for a moment."

6 Percy L. Rainwater, *Mississippi, Storm Center of Secession, 1856–61*, 109.
7 Davis to E. De Leon; De Leon Papers, South Caroliniana Library.
8 R. D. Meade, *Benjamin*, 139–141; Phillips, *Toombs*, 176–182; Yancey's Memphis Speech, August 14, 1860.

Yet many who supported the slave-code ultimatum knew that Northern Democrats, as Douglas had said, could never accept it; that if pressed, it would break the back of the party; and that its direct result would be the election of a Republican. The Alabama Democratic convention laid down its ultimatum in January. Is it conceivable that those who wanted secession, like E. C. Bullock of Eufaula, did not associate cause and effect? Is it conceivable that Alabama secessionists in Congress, led by C. C. Clay and J. L. M. Curry, did not do so? Plainly an ill-organized but very determined conspiracy was coming into existence.

That cultivated secessionist, Porcher Miles, had been given advice on strategy by another polished enemy of the Union, W. H. Trescot. The direst misfortune possible, Trescot warned him, would be a lull in the slavery discussion. If any such calm was threatened, a few strong men might act in concert to keep the agitation alive. They could arouse Southern emotions by some new policy which, while it preserved the color of a national system, should be based essentially on Southern principles and look to sectional effect. "Such a policy, whether it assumes an administration or an opposition character, might be made to form a Southern party which would either succeed and thus govern the country or fail and thus form a compact Southern party ready for action. I submit this would require subtlety in the leaders, and great skill in their tactics, but I am sure it is practicable." [9] This was the very definition of the policy behind the demand for positive protection.

Most Northern Democrats from New York to Iowa could assent to a call for guarantees to the South against invasion. Douglas himself quickly introduced a bill for that purpose. But when the Southern hysteria after John Brown was directed against the Douglas Democrats, and voiced demands which most Northerners interpreted as an attack on the right of freemen in new communities to exclude a pernicious institution (an attack threatening to ruin the Northern Democracy), it became in the eyes of millions quite unreasonable. The new Southern ultimatum was intolerable to Pugh of Ohio, Tilden of New York, Representative William S. Holman of Indiana, and countless others. They thought bitterly of the ground the party had lost because of Buchanan's weakness, the Lecompton folly, and Southern Rights threats. They all felt angered by the President's declaration in his message that no power whatever could interfere with slavery in any Territory, a statement which had given direct encouragement to slave-code radicals in the South.[10] Congressman Holman

9 December 29, 1858; Miles Papers, Univ. of North Carolina.
10 Evidence of this lies in the letter of J. L. M. Curry to Governor Moore of Alabama urging that the Democratic State convention come fully up to the State Rights standard. "Since Buchanan's message, our Convention can hardly hesitate upon our right to the Federal protection of our property in the Territories." January 3, 1860; Governors' Letters, Ala. Dept. Arch. and Hist.

wrote his Indiana friend, Allen Hamilton, that the Northern wing must make a stand:

The Charleston Convention will take the ground indicated by the Message unless there is a very decided popular expression to the contrary in the Northwest. . . . The chances are that we shall be compelled to face such a platform on the territorial question in 1860. And it is my private opinion (confidential) that we cannot carry a single Congressional district on that doctrine in the State. The South largely controls political sentiment here [in Washington], and the South can only be influenced by a bold and decided stand in the Northwest, the only part of the North for which they have any remaining regard.[11]

Not rule or ruin, but rule *and* ruin—such seemed the Southern demand to Northern Democrats. It appeared the more unreasonable because a slave-code, in the circumstances of the day, was a pernicious abstraction without the slightest practical value. Slavery was dead in Kansas; in Nebraska, Colorado, Utah, and other actual or potential Territories it had never been born or could not exist. Protected in New Mexico by a slave-code which many Northerners regarded as harsh, it had no real life there. Sensible Southerners admitted that a mere abstraction was not worth the sacrifice of Democratic unity.[12] Governor Magoffin of Kentucky, for instance, wrote sharply of the lack of realism in the demand. No individual in the Territories had yet complained of the want of legal protection or the impotence of the courts to protect slave chattels, he said; yet, though the issue would destroy the only national party in existence, it was suddenly dragged forth without any justifying grievance.[13] John Forsyth in the Mobile *Register* pointed out the the important distinction between the institution of slavery and property in slaves.[14] It might well be argued that Congress was bound to protect property everywhere under its jurisdiction. But was it bound to protect the institution of slavery? And if the Constitution enjoined any such duty, did it not apply to States as well as Territories?

These rational expostulations meant nothing to two groups: the small but resolute body which wished to destroy Democratic unity in order to clear the ground for a Southern Confederacy, and the great emotional mass of proslavery men eager to voice their irritations, injuries, and fears. This latter group was nettled when the lawmakers of Kansas and Nebraska, defying Taney and Buchanan alike, passed their bills to declare slavery forever abolished. Nebraska now had a capital town sprawling over the hills and ravines of Omaha, a population (such as it was, remarks one historian) of perhaps twelve thousand, and a new governor, Samuel W. Black, whose appointment had been opposed on the

11 December 28, 1859; Allen Hamilton Papers.
12 L. O. Branch in "Letters 1850-60," *N. C. Hist. Review*, X, 41 ff.
13 Beriah Magoffin in the Washington *Constitution*, February 10, 1859.
14 Mobile *Register*, December 4, 1859.

ground of intemperance, and who spent much time demonstrating that the charge was well founded. He vetoed the bill to abolish slavery, as Governor Samuel Medary did that in Kansas. In New Mexico, meanwhile, the legislature defeated a bill to wipe out slavery. These provocative Western nose-thumbings were probably intended by Republicans to emphasize the Freeport Doctrine, and in any event did so.[15]

The demands of the Southern radicals were quickly placed before Congress. On January 18, 1860, Senator A. G. Brown submitted resolutions declaring it the duty of that body, whenever any territorial legislature failed to pass adequate laws for the protection of slavery, to supply them.[16] A fortnight later, after more Southern conferences, Jefferson Davis introduced another set furnishing a more elaborate program. They declared that no State had a right, by itself or through a combination of citizens, to intermeddle with the domestic institutions of other States; that all attacks on slavery within the fifteen slave States were a breach of faith and a violation of the constitutional compact; that it was the special duty of the Senate to resist all discriminations with respect to property or persons in the Territories; and that the national government, through its courts and if necessary, Congress, should give slavery all needful protection in the Territories. His resolutions also asserted that the people of a Territory might not decide for or against slavery until admission; and finally, that all State laws interfering with the recovery of runaway slaves were hostile, subversive of the Constitution, revolutionary in effect, and, if persisted in, certain to lead to sharp counter-measures.[17]

Here was a grim sectional manifesto. At least five of its propositions were certain to be taken by all Northern Republicans as slaps in the face. Two—the demand for a slave-code and the denial of any right by territorial inhabitants to discourage slavery—were violently objectionable to all Douglas Democrats. It was given out that Buchanan supported them all.

This manifesto, the most aggressive step taken by any important Southern leader since Calhoun's day, stamped Davis as an aspirant for Calhoun's old position as the undisputed chieftain of the Southern Rights forces. Although he still believed himself an adherent of the Union, this was the platform of theories built to sustain the drama of secession. Davis asked for a full-dress debate, a rehearsal of the first lines of that drama, on February 8; but it was postponed and repostponed. The fact was that prescient Democratic leaders wished to avoid an irreparable party breach. Toombs, for one, sharply disapproved of the defiant demands of Brown and Davis; it was the very quintessence of folly to raise such

15 Morton and Watkins, *Nebraska*, 273–275; N. Y. *Weekly Tribune*, March 10, 1860. For denunciation of the antislavery bills see New Orleans *Picayune*, February 26, 1860.
16 *Cong. Globe*, 36th Cong., 1st Sess., 404.
17 *Idem*, February 2, 1860; 36th Cong., 1st Sess., 658.

issues on the eve of the election, he grumbled to Alexander H. Stephens.[18] Wigfall in his homely way derided the demand for a slave-protection bill applying to such Territories as Kansas. In the first place, it could not pass Congress; in the second place, if passed it could not be enforced—no territorial jury would sustain it. Then why cripple the Democracy on the eve of its great contest with the Republicans, whose victory would involve the destruction of the Union? [19]

Nevertheless, in March the Democratic Senate caucus voted that Davis's resolutions were the true interpretation of the Constitution. It was spurred to this action by the Directory, and that lesser part of the Administration, Buchanan himself. A year earlier, the President had been against the slave-code and for reliance on the courts; now he had moved forward to stand with Slidell and Davis. Naturally, Northwestern Democrats spurned the caucus action with contempt. Douglas declared that no mere Senate group could dictate party policy on any issue; only the national convention could do that. They must wait, he said, to see whether the Charleston gathering would abide by the Cincinnati platform or not. Davis retorted that no attempt was being made to prescribe a platform for the party, and that personally he would rather have an honest candidate on a rickety platform than an untrustworthy candidate on the best platform men could devise.[20]

Both wings of the party stated their position again and again, for the slave-code had a way of rearing its head in debate with disconcerting abruptness. At times, Davis, Mason, Curry, and others treated the issue as a matter of common honesty. If a man comes into a community avowing that he has a particular species of property which requires general aid for its preservation, they said, he has a right to get it. On other occasions they treated it as a matter of constitutional right, quoting Taney, and asserting that protection was the price paid by government for the support of its citizens.[21] On the other side, Douglas, Pugh, and their associates reiterated that if the people of New Mexico wanted slavery, they should have it; if the people of Kansas did not want it, it should not be forced upon them. Why these disruptive resolutions? Douglas demanded of Davis.

The Senator does not contend that there is any pressing necessity for them; he does not pretend that there is any great evil to be redressed; for, when asked by his colleague why he does not bring in a bill to carry out this right, he says there is no necessity for it. There is no necessity for legislation; no grievances to be remedied; no evil to be avoided; no action is necessary; and yet the peace of the country, the integrity of the Democratic party, are to be threatened by

18 February 10, 1860; U. B. Phillips, *Robert Toombs*, 184.
19 *Cong. Globe*, 36th Cong., 1st Sess., 1490.
20 *Idem*, p. 2155.
21 *Idem*, pp. 578, 1487, etc.

abstract resolutions. . . . The people will ask what all this is for; what it means; why it is so important to have a vote. . . . Why? There must be some purpose.[22]

[II]

Yet the main battle during winter and early spring was still between Republicans and Democrats, for most people believed that the Democratic Party would ultimately close ranks to meet its adversary. Wigfall's watchword, "Defeat them!" still seemed the natural rallying-cry as Lincoln and Seward defined the issues.

The New York Senator, returning from Europe in late December, had encountered a mixed reception. New York City and Auburn welcomed him with affectionate warmth. But powerful Democratic newspapers and Southern politicians were daily abusing him as the prime instigator of the John Brown outrage. The slave States seemed almost unanimous that his election as President would spell the end of the Union. Among the Republicans, his political future was poised in an uneasy balance, for many party members believed him too radical to make a good nominee. Received cordially in Washington by some and with icy restraint by others, he realized that weighty considerations, personal, party, and national, required from him a moderate and conciliatory course. As February ended, he delivered not so much to Congress as the country an eagerly awaited speech. Crowded galleries, a throng of House members, and a full corps of reporters heard a discourse of dulcet gentleness.

It would be an overwhelming source of shame and sorrow, he began, if thirty million Americans could not so combine prudence with humanity in dealing with the slavery question as to preserve their free institutions amid general harmony. He went on to expound Republican principles in the mildest terms. Not a hint of the higher law or the irrepressible conflict appeared. Instead, he declared that he knew of only one party policy, the exclusion of slavery from the Territories. And he invented placatory new terms to define sectional differences, speaking of the "capital States" of the South and "labor States" of the North.

No more slave States and free States; instead, capital States and labor States! Whereas moral considerations had long mingled with the distinction between slave and free, Seward now suggested that the difference in systems was merely economic. The capital States of the South were easy to unite, he said, while the labor States of the North stood dissevered. The capital States threatened disunion, while the labor States were devoted to the national fabric. But the capital States misunderstood the situation; they failed to distinguish between

22 *Idem*, p. 2156.

constitutional resistance to the extension of slavery in the Territories and unconstitutional aggression against slavery in the States. Seward condemned John Brown's raid in language emphatic enough to suit Wise himself, terming it sedition and treason, justly punished by death. The South, he declared, misapprehended Republican policy, which was in no sense hostile. His party represented simply a popular reaction against a measure fastened upon the nation by surprise (here Douglas's scowl deepened), the introduction of slavery into the new lands of the West. It was merely defensive against that measure; it wished to save the boundless plains from slavery or polygamy.[23]

At some points, Seward lifted his speech to the level of eloquence. It might be inferred from circumstances, he remarked, that his party would protect freedom of speech and the press, favor speedy improvement of the public domain under a homestead law, encourage mining, manufacturing, and internal commerce, and promote a Pacific railway. But free Territories being its prime aim, it would meet other contingencies cautiously, for "already it feels the necessity of being cautious in its care of the national health and life." And in a passage of notable force, he repelled the charge that the party was sectional.

Come if you will into the free States, he invited, into New York anywhere from Lake Erie to Sag Harbor, into my own Owasco valley. Hold your conventions, nominate your candidates, address the people as freely as at home; you will have hospitable welcome and appreciative audiences, with ballot boxes open for all the votes you can win. Are you less sectional than this? Extend us the same privilege, and you will soon have as many Southern Republicans as we have Northern Democrats. Suppose a Republican Congress and President elected, he went on, they would be friendly to all sections; and how could they practice tyranny under a Constitution so full of checks? Expressing incredulity at the idea of disunion, he closed with an eloquence anticipatory of the peroration he was soon to attach to Lincoln's first inaugural:

The earth seems to be heaving under our feet, and the pillars of the noble fabric that protects us to be trembling before our eyes. But the appointed end of all this agitation comes at last, and always seasonably; the tumults of the people subside; the country becomes calm once more; and then we find that only our senses have been disturbed, and that they have betrayed us. The earth is firm as always before.

23 Douglas had an explanation for Seward's newly minted terms. Some strikes had occurred among Massachusetts shoemakers, and the New Yorker, he thought, was playing for the votes of the laboring masses. Actually a great "free labor" movement was under way. Men interested in it said that free labor was to be encouraged in the West by a homestead law, and made prosperous in the East by tariffs. Bowles, Greeley, Medill, and other editors chanted the praises of free labor. The Republican (People's) State convention in Pennsylvania was shortly to hail its candidate for governor, Andrew G. Curtin, as a man who had "given a lifetime of earnest, untiring effort to the interests of Free Labor." *Cong. Globe,* 36th Cong., 1st Sess., 915; N. Y. *Weekly Tribune,* June 16, 1860.

A politic speech which, in its contradiction of Southern bogey-raising, was much needed. Many proslavery men in Congress were giving a wildly exaggerated picture of the Republican objects. Anderson of Missouri, for example, told the House that they embraced not merely the restriction of slavery, but its abolition in the District of Columbia, repeal or emasculation of the Fugitive Slave Law, prohibition of the interstate slave trade, and remodeling of the Supreme Court to sustain these acts.

The major Republican newspapers reprinted Seward's speech with editorial commendation, Raymond's *Times* declaring that it would remove unfounded prejudices from the public mind. The New York *Tribune*, boasting on March 1 that it had already printed two hundred and fifty thousand copies of the speech, prepared to sell a pamphlet edition of a million within the month. That the address strengthened Seward and his party in doubtful areas of the North and West, where both were feared as too radical, there could be no question.[24] It is unlikely, however, that it did much to diffuse reassurance throughout the South, which was in no frame of mind to accept it. And was the speech that of a man of firm principle? Might not the disclaimers of all aggressive intent have been combined with a certain constructive quality?

Very different in tone, and a far greater landmark in the thought of the period, was the speech which Lincoln had delivered two days earlier, February 27, in Cooper Union.

Despite his debates with Douglas, to most easterners Lincoln remained just what the New York *Times* called him, a lawyer of some local Illinois reputation. The *Tribune* had spoken of him as one of the secondary group of aspirants for the Republican nomination: "Banks, or Fessenden, or Dayton, or Cameron, or Lincoln." [25] The previous October, he had been invited to give a lecture in a popular course in Beecher's Plymouth Church in Brooklyn, with an offer of $200 and expenses. Advised by friends to seize the opportunity to speak on politics, he had obtained the consent of the church committee. At almost the last moment, the lecture was transferred to the Young Men's Central Republican Union of New York, and the place changed to Cooper Union. For several days in advance the speech was prominently announced in the metropolitan press, the *Evening Post* assuring readers that it would be a powerful assault upon the principles of the proslavery party and an able vindication of the Republican creed. The Young Men's Union was being adroitly used by Bryant, Greeley, Hamilton Fish, and David Dudley Field, opponents of the Weed organization, to bring forward important Republican alternatives to Seward; and it had already presented Frank P. Blair, Jr., and Cassius M. Clay to the city.[26]

24 Bancroft, *Seward*, I, 518, Merriam, *Bowles*, I, 301, 302; Pike, *First Blows of the Civil War*, 501 ff. Raymond's *Times* was now regarded as a Seward organ.
25 N. Y. *Weekly Tribune*, February 25, 1860.
26 Baringer, *Lincoln's Rise to Power*, 154.

Lincoln had prepared himself carefully. His discourse (and it is strange that chis has never been pointed out) was in great measure a refutation of Douglas's labored historical article in *Harper's,* and was largely inspired by that performance. We can picture him, the previous fall, stretched on the sofa in his cluttered law office, absorbed in Douglas's essay; we can imagine the emphasis with which, talking to Herndon, he repudiated Douglas's thesis that popular sovereignty was a time-hallowed tradition of the republic; we can picture him, as he paced between house and office, resolving to make the eastern speech a demolition of Douglas's argument. Spending weary hours in the State Library, he had toiled over Elliot's *Debates on the Constitution,* early Congressional reports, and newspaper files, until he had an exhaustive reply ready.

Arriving on Sunday at the Astor House, he was doubtless somewhat astonished to find many Republican politicians seeking him out, and to learn that elaborate preparations had been made to give him a distinguished audience. Tuesday night came, chill and snowy. As yet Cooper Union, the building less than two years old, seemed fairly well uptown. But fifteen hundred people tramped through the massive doors and downstairs to the great, round, subterranean hall with its many pillars, long, square stage, and flaring gas lamps. William Cullen Bryant, spare, bearded, and dapper, presided; David Dudley Field escorted the speaker to the platform; Peter Cooper, radiating pride in his shining structure, was benignly attentive; and among others in the audience were Greeley, the publisher G. P. Putnam, Abram S. Hewitt, and ex-Governor John A. King. As the *Tribune* remarked, no man since the days of Clay and Webster had spoken to a larger assemblage of the city's brains and character. Lincoln knew that he was under inquest; the two great editors and others, remembering his house-divided speech and his skill in bringing Douglas into the Freeport net, regarded him as a Presidential spar and were eager to measure his stature.

Seldom has a speaker risen with such quiet mastery to his opportunity. His gaunt height, shaggy hair, and ungainly awkwardness in managing his long limbs and huge hands and feet, the bad cut and wrinkles of his new broadcloth suit, the shrillness of his voice, all combined at first to make a questionable impression.[27] Then, as he warmed to his theme, as the glow of his earnestness lighted

27 G. H. Putnam, *George Palmer Putnam,* 274, 275.

The passage shown in the illustration on the facing page illuminates Lincoln's basic attitudes. This fragment, the conclusion of his speech at Springfield, October 30, 1858, was not published until long after his death. The original was owned by Oliver R. Barrett. Paul M. Angle, printing it in "New Letters and Papers of Abraham Lincoln" (1930), writes that it is probably only a small part of what he said on the occasion. It is inserted here as defining the assumption on which he reared his Cooper Union Address.

Lincoln's Last Speech

In the Campaign of 1858

My friends, today closes the discussions of this canvass. The planting and the culture are over; and there remains but the preparation, and the harvest.

I stand here surrounded by friends – some *political*, all *personal* friends I trust. May I be indulged, in this closing scene, to say a few words of myself. I have borne a laborious, and, in some respects to myself, a painful part in the contest. Through all, I have neither assailed, nor wrestled with any part of the constitution. The legal right of the Southern people to reclaim their fugitives I have constantly admitted. The legal right of Congress to interfere with their institution in the states, I have constantly denied. In resisting the spread of slavery to new territory, and with that, what appears to me to be a tendency to subvert the first principle of free government itself my whole effort has consisted. To the best of my judgment I have labored *for* and not *against* the Union. As I have not felt, so I have not expressed any harsh sentiment towards our Southern brethren. I have constantly declared, as I really believed, the only difference between them and us, is the difference of circumstances.

I have meant to assail the motives of no party, or individual; and if I have, in any instance (of which I am not conscious) departed from my purpose, I regret it.

I have said that in some respects the contest has been painful to me. Myself, and those with whom I act have been constantly accused of a purpose to destroy the Union; and bespattered with every imaginable odious epithet; and some who were friends, as it were but yesterday have made themselves most active in this. I have cultivated patience, and made no attempt at a retort.

Ambition has been ascribed to me. God knows how sincerely I prayed from the first that this field of ambition might not be opened. I claim no insensibility to political honors; but today could the Missouri restriction be restored, and the whole slavery question replaced on the old ground of "toleration" by *necessity* where it exists, with unyielding hostility to the spread of it, on principle, I would, in consideration, gladly agree, that Judge Douglas should never be out, and I never *in*, an office, so long as we both or either, live.

up his craggy face, as men caught the force of his ideas and language, he carried his audience with him. The tenor of his speech was as soberly conservative as Seward's. It fell into two halves; the first addressed to Douglas and a refutation of his arguments, the second to the South and a correction of its misconceptions. Its spirit throughout was calm and philosophic, employing historic facts to meet the popular sovereignty fallacy, and a sweet reasonableness to allay Southern fears. But whereas Seward had tended to blur moral principle, Lincoln emphasized it.

Turning to the national record, he reviewed it far more searchingly than had Douglas. To show that the early leaders of the Union had legislated for the restriction and, wherever possible, exclusion or elimination of slavery, he carefully scrutinized the action of the Federal Convention, of the Continental Congress as it had drawn up the Northwest Ordinance, and of the early sessions of the Federal Congress. Nowhere, he showed, had they fixed any line dividing national from local authority in the Territories, or laid down any rule forbidding the national government to exercise authority over slavery therein. Douglas had said of slavery at Columbus: "Our fathers, when they framed the government under which we live, understood this question just as well, and even better, than we do now." Lincoln ironically declared, "I fully endorse this." The fathers of the republic had marked slavery as an evil to be halted and contained; they had tolerated and protected it only insofar as its actual presence in the nation made toleration and protection a necessity. To that attitude the country should return.

The Southern people, Lincoln remarked in the second and more important half of his address, were as reasonable and just as any. What were their accusations against the Republican Party? They termed it a sectional party, when actually it was the Southerners who made it so, for they would give it no hearing. They declared it revolutionary, whereas it merely clung to Washington's doctrine that slavery ought to be restricted. They accused it of stirring up slave insurrections; yet such revolts had been just as common before the Republican Party was organized—everyone recalled the Southampton rising. No Republican had been connected with Harper's Ferry, which Lincoln roundly condemned, and for aught the Republicans said or did, the slaves would scarcely know there was a Republican Party. How much would it really avail the South if that section could break up the party? The sentiment against slavery in the United States commanded at least one and a half million votes, and if the party disappeared, that feeling would simply break into new and perhaps less peaceful channels. Would destruction of the party lessen or increase the number of John Browns?

The South, continued Lincoln, was asserting through numberless speakers and newspapers that it would end the Union if a Republican President were elected. This, in effect, was holding a pistol at the head of the Northern voters and demanding that they give up their ballot. To such a threat no self-respecting men could yield. Nevertheless, he said in conclusion, the Republicans ought to concede to the Southern people as much as their sense of duty permitted. The difficulty was that duty forbade a surrender of principle:

All they ask, we could readily grant, if we thought slavery right; all we ask, they could as readily grant, if they thought it wrong. Their thinking it right and our thinking it wrong is the precise fact upon which depends the whole controversy. Thinking it right, as they do, they are not to blame for desiring its full recognition, as being right. . . . Wrong as we think slavery is, we can yet afford to let it alone where it is, because that much is due to the necessity arising from its actual presence in the nation; but can we, while our votes will prevent it, allow it to spread into the national Territories, and to overrun us here in these free States? If our sense of duty forbids this, then let us stand by our duty fearlessly and effectively. Let us be diverted by none of those sophistical contrivances wherewith we are so industriously plied and belabored—contrivances such as groping for some middle ground between the right and the wrong: vain as the search for a man who should be neither a living man nor a dead man; such as a policy of "don't care" on a question about which all true men do care; such as the Union appeals beseeching true Union men to yield to Disunionists, reversing the divine rule, and calling, not the sinners, but the righteous to repentance; such as invocations to Washington, imploring men to unsay what Washington said and undo what Washington did.

The crowd, which had grown steadily more enthusiastic, gave Lincoln an ovation, shouting, clapping, and waving hats and handkerchiefs. Noah Brooks, the *Tribune's* reporter, exclaiming that Lincoln was the greatest man since St. Paul, hurried to his office to write that no description could do justice to the tones, the gestures, the kindling eye, and the mirth-provoking look of the speaker; that the assemblage had frequently rung with cheers and shouts; and that "no man ever before made such an impression on his first appeal to a New York audience." Hiram Barney, a veteran politician, was equally enthusiastic. "The *Tribune* has a good report of the *words* of your speech," he wrote Lincoln. "What a pity it cannot give the *manner* of it."

Lincoln's and Seward's addresses went to most of the reading public at the same time. Greeley's *Weekly Tribune* carried Seward in six columns of fine print on its first page, Lincoln in five and a half columns on its second and third. Both speeches were promptly issued by various presses in cheap pamphlet form for wide distribution; both were commended by all Republican editors. Seward's speech had in certain passages a nobler eloquence. But in bold candor, intellectual vigor, and positiveness of moral conviction, Lincoln was clearly the superior. He brought forward more ideas. He stated the case of the South with more complete honesty. Unlike Seward, he did not treat the disunionist threats as so unnatural that no hand would execute them; he implied that the peril was real. He did not gloss over the great divisive issue, but explicitly defined it; and instead of appealing to an expedient patriotism which would ignore issues, he appealed to a patriotism of principle which would face them.

"It has produced a greater effect here than any other single speech," one young New Yorker presently wrote Lincoln. "It is the real platform in the eastern states and must carry the conservative element in New York, New Jersey, and Pennsylvania." [28]

[III]

Immediately before the Seward-Lincoln broadsides, the House had placed the first of the pending economic issues—the homestead bill—before the country. This measure was the work of Galusha A. Grow, who brought to it two principal impulses. One was derived from his early experiences in the Tunkhannock Valley, a semi-frontier region of northern Pennsylvania, where, first as a farm boy and later as an active lumber trader operating down the Susequehanna, he had observed the voracities of land speculators. The other came from the land-reform ideas of George H. Evans and similar writers.

When he entered Congress in 1851 as its youngest member, Grow had been full of fire for his cause. In his first important speech he had taken a ground very different from Andrew Johnson's. Repudiating all ideas of state help and state paternalism, he asserted that men who would occupy and work the common lands had an inborn right to own them. In the ten years that followed, he stuck to his own broad proposals: no more public land to be sold, all surveyed lands not reserved for special purposes to be opened to settlers, and no distinctions to be allowed among groups or classes. The stalwart Grow (he was six feet two, with muscles hardened by woodchopping and bark-peeling) made an ideal champion. He was indefatigable, combative, and all devotion to his grand object. Most cool-headed when dealing the hardest blows, he loved the rough and tumble of debate with hot-tempered Southern members. When he had risen in mid-February to reintroduce his bill, House passage was assured, and to obtain quick action, debate was almost entirely cut off. He made one speech interesting for its economic principles. Free homesteads, he said, would shut out from land-investment a great deal of capital which would then flow into industrial undertakings. The rapid colonization of the West would not only create agricultural wealth but furnish avid new markets for manufacturers.

28 Once more Lincoln took pains to see his speech correctly presented, going late in the evening to the New York *Tribune* office to read proofs. Amos J. Cummings, who gave him the proofs, thinks that the original manuscript was tossed into the waste paper bin.

Thus farming, transportation, and industrial activity would all receive benefits. The measure passed the House early in March by a vote of 115 to 65.

Only one free State member, Montgomery of Pennsylvania, voted no, and he said he was for homestead legislation but wished the bill amended; only one slave State member voted yes. The alignment was completely sectional. At once the issue was transferred to the Senate, where debate that had crackled and sputtered on the slavery question swung to economic problems. Andrew Johnson, who represented the spirit of Jacksonian democracy as well as any man living, had said years earlier that the homestead issue would soon control elections; and it was now certain that it would play a great part in the campaign of 1860.[29] Petitions for passage rained upon the Senate table.

The Senate had its own bill, a substitute which Johnson proposed when it became evident that the House measure could not pass. It contained various conservative features. It gave homesteads only to heads of families, not to any man over twenty-one; it required a nominal payment of twenty-five cents an acre instead of granting the land free; it gave farms to the alien-born only when they became fully naturalized; and it was stricter than the House bill in its residential requirements.[30] Even in this modified form, however, the proposal aroused the antagonism of most Southern members. They were convinced that it would restrict slavery (for slaves were seldom profitable on a one-hundred-and-sixty-acre holding), encourage a flood of European immigration to the North and West, and increase the preponderance of the free States.[31] One Southerner alone, A. G. Brown, spoke warmly for the legislation. It was outrageous, he said, to compel the hardy pioneer to pay $200 within a year for the one hundred and sixty acres upon which he settled. The man and his toiling family reared a cabin, cleared some ground, and fenced it in; then if drought or flood ruined the crop, if sickness smote them, or if panic and depression brought prices to a ruinous level, they were without money, and lost everything to some land shark who possessed capital. Every settler taken from urban poverty to go and dwell upon a homestead would be lifted from the consumers and placed among the producers.[32]

The ablest of the slave State opponents, Green of Missouri, called the legisla-

29 *Cong. Globe*, 36th Cong., 1st Sess., 1114, 1115.
30 Robbins, *Our Landed Heritage*, 180; Winston, *Andrew Johnson*, 138.
31 When Doolittle of Wisconsin dropped an incautious remark that the homestead legislation was "a measure of empire," indignant Southerners caught this up as proof of a sinister intent. It reveals, said Mason, the Northern determination to take "command and control of the destinies of the continent." In the eyes of many Southern Senators, the North intended to fill the West with small farmers as a means of promoting abolition. They also arraigned the legislation as a political stroke, a baiting of the Republican trap for German, Irish, and Scandinavian voters. Mason called it a powerful political engine for battering down the last walls that protected Southern institutions. Cf. Matthews, *Grow*, 212, 213.
32 *Cong. Globe*, 36th Cong., 1st Sess., 1553.

tion unnecessary, because, under the graduation law, public land was already selling for as little as twelve and a half cents an acre. He argued that it was unwise because it would destroy an annual revenue of from two to two and a half millions from the sale of public lands, requiring a higher tariff revenue, and because it would cripple further land grants for railroads and thus impede the growth of transportation facilities. It was unjust because it would render worthless the bounty land warrants held by veterans, would encourage rich speculators to hire perjurers to go upon the public lands and swear to occupancy, and would take property belonging to all citizens in common and parcel it out to the very poorest, thus subsidizing the lazy and raffish. You cannot go to Richmond or Charleston and hire men to colonize the West, said Green; you might beat your drum and wave your flag for six weeks without getting five settlers. But go to New York and Boston, and men will flock forward by thousands. "Who are they? Men intent on destroying the institutions of the South—men determined to destroy the rights of the South." [33]

Green and such other Southern Senators as Wigfall would willingly give the public lands to the States in which they lay, letting Tennessee, Arkansas, or Minnesota pass homestead laws if they liked. Both frankly stated their sectional motive: We are under no obligation to provide for your paupers, they told the North. It was clear that the history of Kansas lay painfully in the Southern consciousness. The bill means more emigrant aid societies, growled Mason. On the other side, Douglas and Pugh, rehearsing familiar arguments for the measure, protested that opposition to it must not be made a test of Democratic regularity. The first men to bring such a bill into Congress had been Democrats; a homestead bill had passed the same Democratic House which enacted the Kansas-Nebraska bill. Andrew Johnson, pursuing a higher line of exposition, declared the measure essentially Jeffersonian and Jacksonian. The nation had a mighty patrimony of land, amounting to some seven million quarter-sections. It could give each of its four million voters a farm, and have a tremendous domain left over. It was sound Jeffersonian policy to build up the rural areas as a balance to the great cities, to fill these vacant spaces with virtuous, hard-working men of a type to sustain the government. Critics talked of encouraging radicalism, but who ever heard of a government being overturned by people having property? It was want of independence that created discontent. Rome had decayed because a few men had monopolized the land, shutting the poor servile masses out of all hope of prosperous homes. [34]

After much obstruction, the Senate bill came to a vote on May 11. It was then evident that no party which defeated it could carry critical Northern and

33 *Ibid.*, 1556.
34 *Ibid.*, 1650-1655.

border States. Passing 44 to 8, the measure went to the House. After two conference committees had failed, a third finally whipped a compromise bill into
shape, which in mid-June passed both chambers by overwhelming vote: 115 to
51 in the House; 36 to 2 in the Senate. Political expediency made its passage a
necessity.[35] The large number of abstentions told a significant story, however—
and the South had its ace card still to play. The bill really suited nobody. It was
a changeling, stripped of most of its homestead features. Abolishing the old
price of $1.25, it allowed heads of families, after five years of occupancy, to
purchase quarter-sections at twenty-five cents an acre. One reason it passed so
easily lay in the universal expectation that Buchanan would kill it.

By this date the Presidential campaign had begun; and partly to strike a
heavy new blow at Douglas and other Northwestern Democrats, partly to meet
the wishes of the South, and partly to express his own strict-constructionist
views, Buchanan vetoed the bill. The Constitution, he wrote, gave Congress no
power to make such a huge donation; it would be unjust to earlier settlers who
had paid $1.25 an acre and to veterans with bounty warrants; it would hurt the
old States by reducing the value of their lands and tempting their people to
emigrate; it would open a vast field for speculation, as rich sharpers settled poor
men on the land under secret agreements to divide their homesteads; and it
would diminish the public revenues and so increase taxation. These objections
were succinctly riddled by Senator Harlan of Iowa, who had been reared in a
log cabin on the Illinois prairie. They irritated Andrew Johnson, who recalled
that Buchanan in his inaugural had promised lands to actual settlers at moderate
rates. But the bill failed by three votes to pass the Senate over Buchanan's veto.
The South, for the last time, had balked a measure which it saw would give
enhanced population and power to the freesoil States.[36]

Homestead legislation had become enormously popular in the Northwest.
A typical Illinois country newspaper, the Warsaw *City Bulletin*, published in
the boyhood home of John Hay, dwelt in every issue upon its importance. It
would cure the evils of the existing laws, under which vast tracts fell into the
hands of speculators; would give work and shelter to the unemployed and homeless surplus population of the cities; would fill the West with a thrifty race of
producers; would restore the equilibrium between capital and labor; and would
bring a flood of Northern and European settlers to secure every mile of the
West to freedom. If defeated in Washington, it would be a plank of the Republican platform and would win a multitude of voters to the party. Many a Northern farm youth at his plow, many a casual laborer—and many a land speculator
too—cursed the interests that killed the homestead bill.

35 *Ibid.*, 3159, 3179.
36 *Ibid.*, 3267–3272; Brigham, *James Harlan*, 142–144.

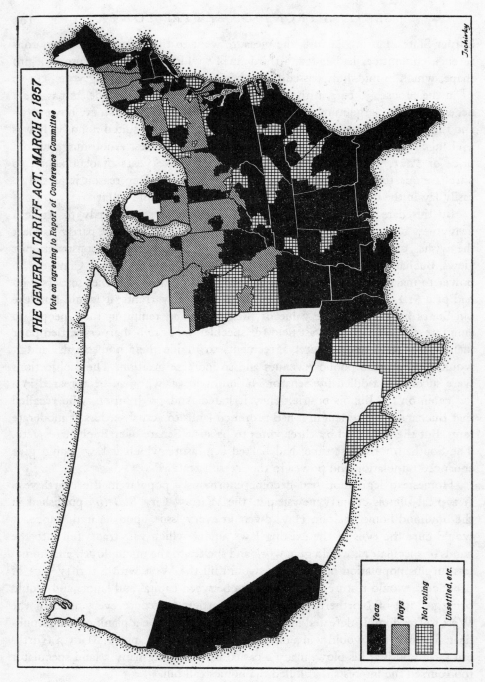

THE GENERAL TARIFF ACT, MARCH 2, 1857

Vote on agreeing to Report of Conference Committee

Tchivsky

Yeas

Nays

Not voting

Unsettled, etc.

A different kind of legislation interested the factory owner nervously watching prices and profits. "While you, gentlemen of the South, are protecting your peculiar institutions," cried Simon Cameron in the Senate, "you ought, at least, not to forget that we of the North have a peculiar institution to protect and encourage—our free white labor." He pointed to the fact that the annual value of the manufactured products of Philadelphia alone was $250,000,000.[37]

The Republican House this spring, by rapid effort, carried a bill for a slight upward revision of duties. Justin S. Morrill, the sharp-eyed, sharp-nosed, sharp-witted Yankee at the head of Ways and Means, believed in protecting Vermont wool and much besides. The bill promised the country the means to meet its deficit, to ease the cramped departments, and to pay off nearly fifty millions of debt which the Administration had contracted. At the same time, it would stimulate the metal, textile, and other industries. Its friends declared that within four years it would double the nation's annual output of coal and iron. The measure passed the House by a nearly solid vote of Republican and Opposition members, with half a dozen Democrats concurring.[38] In the Senate, however, it was blocked by the South and the Democratic low-tariff tradition.

Southern antagonism was voiced in extreme terms. Senator Hunter, denouncing it as monstrous, suggested that it be engrossed on vellum and sent to the Tycoon of Japan as a suggested method of improving upon the historic exclusiveness of his nation. Toombs declared that the true basis of taxation was property, and that an indirect tariff tax would lead to gross extravagance, the government plundering the people without their realizing it. Yulee agreed that the measure was an effort to benefit the North at the expense of the South. Jefferson Davis pronounced for a system of free trade, applied not merely to raw materials but to the woodman's axe and the farmer's plow and scythe.[39]

In the final Senate vote, every Republican present cast his ballot against postponement, while every Democrat but two followed Hunter's leadership in deferring action. The dissenters were Bigler of Pennsylvania and Latham of California. An indignant chorus rose from the eastern press. Greeley's *Trib-*

37 *Cong. Globe*, June 15, 1860, 36th Cong., 1st Sess.
38 *Ibid.*, May 10, 1860; the vote was 105 to 64.
39 Stanwood, *History of the Tariff*, II, 99; *Cong. Globe*, 36th Cong., 1st Sess., 3013, 3188, 3189.

The map on the facing page shows how the low tariff bill passed the House in 1857 by a vote that was mainly non-sectional and non-partisan. The mildly protectionist bill passed in the spring of 1860 received a very different support. Every representative from Massachusetts, Connecticut and Pennsylvania present and voting supported it; every representative from Alabama and Mississippi present opposed it. The vote of Illinois and Indiana was divided.

une spoke for scores of other papers when it said that the issue was made up, and that a multitude of Northern Democrats would now be converted to the Republican Party.[40] As that party entered the campaign, it planned to scatter broadcast the incisive tariff speeches of Morrill, Thaddeus Stevens, and Senator Simmons. Dogberry's axiom, "When two ride a horse, one must ride behind," seemed to countless Northerners to apply to the situation created by the failure of the homestead and tariff bills. The rear rider, as the slave States guided the steed, was growing restive.

Two other economic issues aroused special irritation in the Northwest. One was the failure of legislation to improve the navigation of the Great Lakes. All commerce from the west into Lake Erie had to pass through the River St. Clair, at whose mouth lay extensive shoals. After the opening of the Soo Canal, these shallows were the chief impediment to a fast-developing inland commerce. Republicans complained bitterly that since 1857 the Senate Commerce Committee, a body of seven, had only two members to represent New England, New York, and the Northwest, the South completely dominating it. Chandler's bill of 1858 to deepen the St. Clair channel was first blocked in committee by the chairman, C. C. Clay, and then on the floor by Judah P. Benjamin. When he got an appropriation for $55,000 worth of work added to the civil appropriation bill, Buchanan threatened a veto and the item was removed. Never a patient man, Chandler was roused to intense wrath. In demanding a yea-and-nay call on the appropriation, he uttered a peal of defiance. "I want to see who is friendly to the great Northwest, and who is not—for we are about making our last prayer here. The time is not far distant when, instead of coming here and begging for our rights, we shall extend our hands and take the blessing. After 1860 we shall not be here as beggars." He returned home to Michigan with a blazing tale of wrong.[41] In the winter session of 1858–59 a renewed effort was killed by Buchanan.

Now, early in 1860, Chandler offered his St. Clair legislation once more. This time Buchanan met it with a special message explaining his previous pocket veto, his main ground being that the Constitution made river and harbor improvement the function of the States, and that Michigan and Upper Canada should jointly remove the obstruction. Jefferson Davis, Toombs, Wigfall, and other Southern Senators stoutly defended Buchanan's position. Northern Senators, with Crittenden of Kentucky, assailed it. As all of Chandler's efforts to lift the bill from the table met defeat, the debate aroused strong feeling. "Wait until after the election!" declared Republicans.

Some observers discerned a deeper peril in Buchanan's veto. He had adopted

40 N. Y. *Weekly Tribune*, July 14, 1860.
41 Detroit *Free Press* staff, *Zachariah Chandler*, 169, 170.

Calhoun's mischievous idea that every State and town on the inland waters might pay for their betterment by local tonnage dues, thus denationalizing these arteries (they said) and allowing State and local authorities to clog trade by a multitude of vexatious duties. "I see," exploded Samuel B. Ruggles of New York in a letter to Chandler, "that Mr. Slidell has introduced a bill giving the consent of Congress in advance to any tonnage duties any State adjacent to the Mississippi may lay for the improvement of the river, real or intended—in other words, a bill to denationalize that national river. It is the beginning of the end, and the greatest blow with which the Union has yet been menaced. . . . It should be resisted *to the death*." [42]

The Pacific Railroad was another point at which the South appeared to countless Northerners to be blocking the legitimate demands of a growing nation. Sixty thousand people were now going to the West Coast annually, and some military men estimated that a railroad would have saved ten million dollars in fighting Indian wars. Such an empire was rising beyond the Rockies that it was manifestly imperative to provide rail communications. A select House committee under S. R. Curtis of Iowa, fairly representing every section, reported in May a bill for the private construction of a railroad starting from two points, one on the western border of Missouri and the other on that of Iowa; the two converging lines bearing westward and uniting within two hundred miles of the Missouri River, thence proceeding by a single trunk line to the Sacramento or San Francisco. This was essentially a bill for a railroad on or near the forty-first parallel. A generous land grant and other aids were to be provided by the United States.[43] In vain did Phelps of Missouri, a member of the committee, continue his ten years' battle for a railroad following generally the thirty-fifth parallel. Once more opposition appeared, both to the route chosen and to the financial provisions. By a narrow vote, 101 to 87, the House, as May ended, sent the bill back to committee, while the Senate did nothing.[44]

The central route, however, had won a moral victory in the committee report. Public sentiment seemed swinging in favor of that line. While emigrants plainly preferred it, mineral discoveries were fortifying its position. We have noted that Denver was now plainly destined to become a Western emporium; and meanwhile the winter and early spring of 1860 beheld another tumultuous exodus to Virginia City and the silver camps of Washoe. These rushes, with the steady growth of Kansas, Utah, and San Francisco, appeared to establish the superiority of the central route. It was generally believed that the government could afford to assist only one railway; and if two were built, Minnesota stood

42 S. B. Ruggles, March 19, 1860; Chandler Papers.
43 See Curtis's discussion, *Cong. Globe*, 36th Cong., 1st Sess., 2439–2452.
44 *Cong. Globe*, 36th Cong., 1st Sess., 2452.

ready to argue that a St. Paul-Puget Sound road would find a shorter, easier, richer, and better-wooded route than a New Orleans-El Paso-Gila Valley road. The West was eager for action and impatient of Southern obstruction.

Nor would the Kansas question disappear. The settlers had elected a constitutional convention, which, sitting at Wyandotte during the summer of 1859, had drawn up a serviceable instrument. This had been ratified on October 4 by a majority of nearly five thousand in a total vote of about sixteen thousand, and just as Congress opened, Charles Robinson had been elected governor. The House quickly passed a bill for admission, but the Senate was adamant. Wigfall declared that virtuous Texas would never associate with such a State of outlaws and land pirates as Kansas would make. Meanwhile, Morrill's bill for aiding agricultural colleges was also doomed.

In short, the familiar deadlock of the Thirty-fifth Congress was extending itself into the Thirty-sixth. Legislation which increasingly powerful blocks of voters regarded as urgent was being defeated by a more or less rigid sectional alignment. As one after another these economic measures were hurried through the House, the Southern managers of the Senate became more incensed; for the South believed its position entirely defensible—a position in harmony with the older traditions of the republic. Southern leaders wanted the government of Jefferson and Madison: a government that would not overshadow and weaken the States, that would not expand its activities and its expenditures, and that would guard against conferring economic favors on one section at the expense of the others. They held that it would be fatally easy to build up a great centralized power in Washington, and that, once created, this power could readily be used against them. On grounds both of theory and practice they had forcible arguments. Yet as one after another the new economic measures were stopped by the Senate or President, the Northern Congressmen felt a deepening resentment.

[IV]

Meanwhile, a House committee under "Honest John" Covode, appointed under a resolution of March 5, was inquiring into the Executive use of money, patronage, or other improper means to influence Congress or the administration of the laws. The primary object was to expose the pressures notoriously used by Buchanan in behalf of Lecompton and the English amendment.

Covode, a big-boned, awkward Pennsylvania German, part owner of the Westmoreland Coal Company, had distinguished himself in the Keitt-Grow affray by his rush into the melee brandishing a heavy spittoon. Republicans hoped for campaign ammunition from the inquiry, while the chairman was vengefully eager to repay Buchanan for a charge of bribery in the Pennsylvania Congressional elections of 1858. The President, deeply wounded by the implied accusation, sent the House a solemn protest. "Amid all the political storms through which I have passed," he declared, "the present is the first attempt which has ever been made, to my knowledge, to assail my personal and official integrity." Though his friends tried to obstruct the inquiry, it was relentlessly pressed.

Indeed, Covode's friends extolled, and his foes denounced, the inexorable thoroughness of his work. Buchanan in a second protest to Congress declared that the committee was more tyrannical than the Star Chamber, while the Democratic minority report asserted that the chairman had usurped all its powers, summoned a weird variety of witnesses, and pursued every type of suspicion and allegation.[45] Hearings continued from March 22 until the beginning of June. The first witness, Cornelius Wendell, onetime owner of the *Union*, was discontented with the Administration because it had failed to let him keep most of his perquisites. He talked freely. He was followed by such politicians as Augustus Schell, James C. Van Dyke, and George Plitt, by Attorney-General Black, prominent Senators and Representatives, and two Democratic haters of Buchanan, Robert J. Walker and John W. Forney. The complete testimony filled eight hundred pages; but the gist of it was summed up in the final majority report of thirty pages which the Republican press spread broadcast before the end of June.

Seldom in our history has a Congressional investigation furnished material more damaging to a President and his coadjutors. Its most disturbing evidence was the disclosure of Buchanan's weak timidity, and of the consistent skill of Cobb, Jacob Thompson, Slidell, and Jeremiah Black in overawing him. Forney told how Buchanan had first promised him the editorship of the Washington *Union*, and then under Southern pressure had withdrawn the pledge. "Sir," Forney told him, "you have surrendered me." Buchanan rejoined: "I have been compelled to do so." Later Buchanan had been "compelled" to give way on Lecompton, the Directory coercing him by pointing to the threats of certain States to secede or fight. Evidence was introduced by Ellis B. Schnabel, a friend of Douglas and Walker, to show how directly Jeremiah Black controlled the Washington *Constitution* when it made its fight for Lecompton. His details angered Black, who sat in the committee room, and the two men left the hall exchanging epithets and threats of criminal prosecution.[46]

The inquiry brought out the full text of Buchanan's letter to Walker of July 12, 1857, fully endorsing the very Kansas policies which he shortly repu-

45 Buchanan, *Works*, X, 402, 438; 36th Cong., 1st Sess., H. Rept. 648, 29 ff. The hearings were nominally secret, but the best bits were published; *Covode Report*, 31.
46 *Covode Report*, 296.

diated. It made a profound sensation as Douglasite and Republican organs all over the land gleefully reprinted it. The rash Jeremiah Black had called a clerk a liar for certifying to the existence of the letter; Walker then humiliated both the President and Attorney-General by producing it. Buchanan had not only written that "the point on which your and our success depends is the submission of the constitution to Kansas"; he had repeated that on "the question of submitting the constitution to the *bona fide* resident settlers of Kansas, I am willing to stand or fall." [47] Why had he receded from this high ground? Walker's emphatic statement left no doubt as to the way in which the Southern group had manipulated Buchanan. Secretary Thompson's despatch of his clerk Martin to Lecompton at the time the constitution was being written in that town was thoroughly aired. Plainly, a great deal of subterranean intrigue had accompanied the drafting of that document and the effort to get it through Congress.

The Covode Committee also revealed how Buchanan had employed the patronage to gain support for controversial measures and to destroy Douglas. Forney related that, after he had founded the Philadelphia *Press,* Black had sent an agent to offer him printing contracts worth $80,000 if he would abandon his opposition to Lecompton. "You can get all that post-office printing," said the man, "if you will write an editorial article as long as your hand." [48] Evidence showed that the Administration had frequently interfered in local elections, particularly in Pennsylvania. Equally disturbing was the testimony as to the misuse of public printing in both Pierce's and Buchanan's day. The profits had been enormous. Wendell and others furnished data indicating that they had aggregated nearly two million dollars in six years. In return for liberal government contracts, Wendell had diverted part of these profits into the hands of men conducting Buchanan's State organ, the *Pennsylvanian,* and the official Administration paper, first the *Union* and later the *Constitution.* Another part had been used to help contest close election districts. At one point, corruption was exposed. Wendell testified that he had distributed between thirty and forty thousand dollars to obtain passage of the Lecompton and English bills; and much of this went in plain bribery, for he admitted drawing checks to bearer or to fictitious names and he had used much loose cash, employing two newspapermen as almoners.

While the committee was at work, the East was startled by a report of heavy defalcations in the New York post office; and on the heels of this came news that Postmaster Isaac V. Fowler had absconded leaving his accounts short by some $155,500. The episode presented mysterious aspects. Fowler, a genial, warm-hearted man, universally liked, had no bad habits, did not speculate, and

47 *Ibid.,* 112, 113.
48 *Ibid.,* 291–304.

was not extravagant. He had held for seven years a position which, with its perquisites, paid at least $15,000 a year; his place in the local Democratic organiza-
tion could have been made to produce additional revenues; and he had borrowed about $50,000 from friends. One New York writer calculated that alto-
gether during the past seven years he had received at least $400,000—and yet he
had fled with only a few thousands. Where had the money gone? Why had he
escaped arrest and why was so little effort made to pursue him? Years later it
was revealed that his shortages had originated in heavy campaign contributions
and party gifts and that promises of reimbursement had not been kept. While
John A. Dix took over the post office to straighten out its affairs, the Republican
press naturally played fortissimo on the theme of Democratic corruption.[49]

Equally shocking was the exposure of an incompetence amounting to be-
trayal of duty on the part of Secretary Floyd. Incapable of taking dishonest
money himself, the Virginian was willing to protect men who did. At Fort
Snelling, the government owned a beautiful military reservation of about eight
thousand acres overlooking the junction of the Mississippi and the Minnesota.
Floyd decided to sell it, even though it had recently been declared essential.
Rapidly advancing in value, at auction it would probably have brought hundreds
of thousands. Instead, the Secretary permitted a combination of Virginia friends
and New York politicians to buy it through quiet inside bargaining for only
$90,000. The purchasers defaulted after the panic, but proof of Floyd's care-
lessness remained, and even the Democratic majority of an investigating committee pronounced the management of the sale injudicious and improper. Just
as malodorous was the Willett's Point affair. This Long Island peninsula was
wanted by the government for a fortified post. As late as the summer of 1856
it was priced at only $45,000. The next spring, Floyd authorized Augustus
Schell, the slippery Collector of the Port in New York, to ascertain its value.
A group was hurriedly organized under Prosper H. Wetmore to get hold of the
tract; Schell notified the Secretary that it was worth $200,000; and the govern-
ment paid that sum. A House committee reported that Schell was the chief instigator of a fraudulent arrangement to cheat the government—with Floyd holding the door wide open.

Nor was this all. Floyd had treated contracts, pay rolls, and appointments
with a disregard for economy, efficiency, and the public welfare, and a readiness
to assist political and personal friends, which were sometimes positively illegal.
The alarmed Democrats at one time thought of conducting an investigation
themselves to forestall Republican inquiry.[50] His purchases for the army were
bad enough; his management of the work on public buildings in Washington

49 N. Y. *Tribune*, May 19, 1860; Nichols, *Disruption of Democracy*, 313.
50 Nichols, 329.

was worse. The Capitol had to be completed; wings were being added to the Treasury and Interior buildings; a new Post Office building was going up; and the Great Falls aqueduct was being prosecuted. An admirable army engineer, Captain Montgomery C. Meigs, was in charge of these works. Since he was as vigilant as Floyd was lax, the two men came into sharp conflict; and early in 1860 Floyd actually tried to banish him to the Dry Tortugas, where some fortifications were being constructed. This was temporarily blocked. But the quarrel continued, and as Davis, Toombs, and other prominent Democrats came to Meigs's aid, the Secretary's shortcomings were brought before the public. It was shown that he had bought building materials from favorites in violation of statute, and had let an important contract for heating the Capitol to a Virginian who knew nothing of the business and was going to farm out his concession.

Floyd was disgraced. The Republican press, in impassioned editorials, connected his acts, Fowler's thefts, and Wendell's exploitation of public printing with other shady occurrences of the day. The sharp practice by which Indiana Democrats had seized a seat in the Senate, the election frauds of 1857 in Minnesota, the unfortunate act of Buchanan himself in helping a Philadelphia firm obtain a naval contract in order to secure its aid in an important local election— all this was lumped together. To a country which believed honesty a high Federal tradition, these revelations came as a heavy shock.

[V]

By mid-April, the eyes of the nation were bent upon Charleston, where the Democratic Convention was about to assemble. The whole weight of the Administration was being exerted against Douglas's candidacy. He reiterated again and again that he attacked no man, that he wanted party unity, and that he asked only for adherence to the Cincinnati platform. But deeply resenting the course of the Administration in promoting a convention at Springfield on January 10 which elected anti-Douglas delegates in Illinois, he spoke of Buchanan with a personal animosity which the President returned.[51] Howell Cobb and other Directory heads were assuring the Northern politicians who trooped into Washington on their way south that Douglas could get few votes in the slave States. Slidell, Jefferson Davis, C. C. Clay, and others were making it clear that they would accept no Northern Democrat whatever, save some impossible anti-Douglas figure like Dickinson of New York, who would ruin the party in the free States.

Had Douglas been more fairly treated in recent months by the Administration, he would probably have been willing to withdraw in the interests of

51 N. Y. *Weekly Tribune*, May 19, 1860. The Buchaneer convention in Springfield is described by an eyewitness in the Warsaw *City Bulletin*, January 16, 1860.

harmony. But his deposition from the Committee on Territories rankled; the venomous attacks by Jere Black and others seemed to him unforgivable; and he was not going to let proslavery men read him out of the party. He was the champion of the Northwestern Democracy, which was lost if he should be defeated.

January of 1860 brought Douglas an avalanche of Northwestern delegates. A heavy majority of the party in this region was devoted to him and his principles; and, quite apart from this, the leaders knew that his nomination would give them their best chance of carrying State and local offices. Ohio, Illinois, Indiana, Michigan, Iowa, and Wisconsin all chose Douglas men for Charleston and bound them to the unit rule. In several of these States the Administration groups suffered a humiliating debacle. In Illinois, everyone knew that the Douglas forces mustered all but a few thousands of the party membership. The Danite convention, with Isaac Cook as ringmaster and Federal pensioners largely furnishing the rank and file, was regarded from Chicago to Cairo as an absurdity. It talked of a State ticket, but did not venture to name one. The Douglas convention, on the other hand, was full and enthusiastic, speaking authoritatively for the State as it bound its delegates for the Little Giant. In Ohio, the convention declared unanimously for popular sovereignty, and by a vote of 242½ to 94½ instructed the delegation to support Douglas. Wisconsin and Iowa fell into line with enthusiasm.

The keystone of the Democratic arch in the Northwest was Indiana, and here the Buchanan men attempted a stubborn stand. According to the Washington correspondent of the Cincinnati *Enquirer*, nine prominent gentlemen who hated Douglas met, after visiting the White House, and subscribed $8,000 each to control the Indiana delegation. The money, said the *Enquirer* story, was to be used in buying up delegates to the State convention.[52] This body met in Indianapolis on January 11–12. A huge crowd of onlookers, tense with excitement, gathered in and about the Metropolitan Theatre. The Administration coterie, led by Senator Bright, Governor Willard, and Marshal J. L. Robinson, was on hand to threaten, cajole, and offer Federal jobs to the office-hungry. But the Douglas men immediately took control; they nominated a future Vice-President, Thomas A. Hendricks, for governor; and by a vote of 265 to 129, they instructed all delegates at Charleston to work for Douglas to the end. Senators Bright and Fitch were routed in their own counties. This was a blow to the Directory; and so was the action of the Minnesota convention, which expressed a warm preference for Douglas and adopted a popular sovereignty platform.

As spring approached, Douglas, toiling in Washington to strengthen his lines, sought the favor of the delegates who gradually thickened in the capital. He took the field in person, canvassing with his usual energy. "He may be seen in

52 Cincinnati *Enquirer*, Jan. 3, 1860.

the Senate lobbies, in the hotels, and on the sidewalks," reported Greeley's correspondent, "talking earnestly with his friends and by looks, word, and gesture stimulating them to action. Probably no other candidate for a presidential nomination ever played his hand so openly and boldly." [53] His hopes were high. Even in the Lower South he had his supporters. In Louisiana, Soulé was trying to organize anti-machine Democrats and Know-Nothings for him; [54] in Alabama, John Forsyth of the Mobile *Register* continued to laud his ability; in Florida, Senator Yulee was more than willing to make him the nominee. Even in South Carolina the Edgefield *Advertiser* laid down several reasons why his nomination might be desirable. He was the most available candidate, it argued; he was the only man upon whom Northern Democrats could effectively concentrate; his powers were unquestioned, and the South could be sure of just dealing from him.

As the date for the convention approached, however, all haters of Douglas redoubled their opposition. The Administration never rested; all over the land its officeholders abused the Senator and contrived plots to thwart his nomination. The incessant barking and snapping of even its meanest curs had some effect. But the harshest antagonism was that found among the radical slaveholders of the cotton kingdom. Since Jackson's day, no Democratic candidate had been named without their consent, and they intended to make their veto effective against the popular sovereignty leader. Slidell spun his webs with unresting, spidery skill. "Not a prominent politician of the North and West arrives here," wrote the *Tribune* correspondent early in April,[55] "but instantly he is approached by some emissary of the anti-Douglas cabal, of which the Louisiana Senator is the cogitating brain and the animating soul." Equally determined, if less bitter, was Jefferson Davis, a man who placed his opposition upon public grounds, and who labored adroitly to strengthen the Southern front against the Freeport Doctrine.

Like another Herne the Hunter, the shade of John Brown stalked the Windsor Forest of party affairs, frightening all peaceloving folk. The Harper's Ferry raid had gravely injured both Douglas's chances and the hope of Democratic harmony. Alarming large areas of the South, it had caused many citizens to take the view that safety demanded the nomination of a Southerner, and many more to assert that at any rate it required the selection of a man whose *friendliness* to slavery was more fervent and unbending than Douglas's. It had confirmed the hysteria now epidemic in much of the South, and thus strengthened the divisive demand for a slave code. As the convention opened, the Democratic Party was in a state of internecine war.

53 N. Y. *Weekly Tribune*, April 14, 1860.
54 Slidell to Buchanan, May 2, 1859; Buchanan **Papers**.
55 N. Y. *Weekly Tribune*, April 10, 1860.

7

The Democratic Rupture

CHARLESTON, heedlessly selected four years earlier as the scene of the Democratic convention of 1860, roused herself in April to write a new page in American history.[1] In this balmy season, perfumed with the last azaleas and first roses, the little city of some fifty thousand people offered many physical attractions. Perceptive Northern visitors were charmed by the eighteenth-century houses, prodigal of verandahs and piazzas; the old gardens, rich with tamarisks, camelias, and poppies, half-concealed behind wrought-iron gates and red-brick walls; stately St. Michael's, its tower lifting the four-faced clock that had told Charleston's time since George III ruled the Province, and the English chimes that had rung for so many great events; St. Philip's, guarding the plain brick tomb of Calhoun; the quaint shops of King Street, and the high sea wall of the Battery. They were delighted by the swishing palmettoes, the jargon of the Gullah darkies, the calls of street vendors, and the liquid accents of the citizens. Prosperity—the prosperity of King Cotton's subjects at the height of that monarch's pride and power—stamped the lineaments of the town: fine carriages in the ways, fine raiment on the women, fine silver and mahogany in the houses.

Those admitted to the more exclusive homes (many Southern but few Northern delegates had that honor) quickly realized that sharp social lines were drawn, and that the residents below Broad Street and along the Battery possessed a special distinction. They discerned, too, that this city of old English and Huguenot stock, with its memories of the Rutledges and Pinckneys, of Audubon and Alexander Garden, of the architect Robert Mills and the jurist Hugh S. Legaré, possessed a fine if slightly antique culture. The Charleston Hotel, where eight years earlier Thackeray had made a pencil sketch of colorful lobby scenes, the old Planters' Hotel whose courtyard had for half a century been the favorite resort of cotton and rice growers, and Russell's bookshop, were centers of cultivated talk. The college, the Citadel school, and the Society Library were proof that Charleston by no means neglected education.

1 In the Cincinnati Convention the special committee on national conventions had been headed by a New Yorker, T. C. McCreery. After considering New York and Charleston as meeting places, it chose Charleston as an incentive to party harmony. *Proceedings Reported for the Cincinnati Enquirer*, 42.

Nevertheless, the city was ill-chosen for the convention. It was difficult of access, and those who came by rail arrived exhausted. Already the heat was becoming uncomfortable. The hostelries, all too few and too small for convention crowds (though not so many spectators arrived as had been expected), had agreed upon the high rate of five dollars a day for bed and meals. At the best-known hotels, four or five delegates were sometimes stuffed into a single room. The Northwestern men supporting Douglas had hired Hibernian Hall, where the ground floor was equipped with chairs, writing tables, and campaign materials, including a large supply of Sheahan's life of Douglas, while the second story was crammed with several hundred cots. Fernando Wood's contesting delegation from New York had similarly taken St. Andrew's Hall, where a portrait of Queen Victoria looked down on a confusion of improvised beds. At night the visitors, tortured by noise, poor ventilation, and thirst, tried to snatch a few hours' sleep, and in the morning made rough toilets with washbowls, pitchers, and a few hand mirrors.

The atmosphere of the town was hostile to Northern men and ideas, and the tone of its press, parlors, hotel lobbies, and counting rooms was antipathetic to conciliation. Any large border city would have been a far better choice. The local hostility to Northerners was the more serious in that it was generally agreed that if the Democratic Party could remain united, its chances of victory were bright. The whole number of electoral votes would be 303, with 152 necessary to a choice. The Democrats would almost certainly carry the Southern States with 120 votes and Oregon and California with 7 more. Then New York alone (35 electors), or Pennsylvania alone (27), or Indiana and Illinois with any one of the less populous States, would be sufficient. It was obvious, however, that New York and Pennsylvania could never be carried on a slave-code platform. Neither could any other Northern State. Admit a slave-code plank into the platform, and defeat was practically sure.[2]

[I]

The delegates and their friends came in droves from Wednesday to Saturday, April 18–21, days bright, hot, and dusty. The Massachusetts men, with a brass band which began playing on the Battery every night, arrived by boat, as did the New York and Pennsylvania delegations. Barrooms, with bowls of iced punch and a weird variety of cocktails, did a rushing business; gamblers, unmistakable in their flashy dress and manners, were hard at work; pickpockets engaged the attention of the mounted and armed police.

Reporters mingling with the crowds were struck by the violent temper of

2 Cf. Chicago *Times*, March 13, 1860.

many delegates. While Illinois and Michigan men were denouncing Jeff Davis
as a fire-eating fanatic, Alabamians were calling Douglas a traitor only less
vicious than Seward. The Northwestern representatives made the Mills House
their principal place of resort. Here, in the humming lobby and corridors, the
principal Illinois leaders, John A. Logan, John A. McClernand, and William A.
Richardson, a formidable trio, could be seen talking with such other adherents
of Douglas as George Sanders, the burly, piratical-looking Navy Agent in New
York who had placed his office in peril by coming to work for the popular
sovereignty cause, and Pugh of Ohio, determined not to yield an inch to the
demand for a slave-code. Most Southerners could be sought in the parlors of
the Charleston Hotel. Waiting delegates enjoyed excursions up the Cooper and
Ashley, or down to islands in the bay.

One by one, the great men of the party arrived.

W. L. Yancey, a compact, erect man of medium height, with a square head
and face, his bland, quiet manner belied by his quick, expressive eyes, came with
a cohort of Alabamians who predicted that his oratory would sweep the Douglas forces away like chaff. He kept aloof from the swirling crowds. But he was
soon conferring with his fellow radicals on the ground, the A. B. Rhetts,
father and son; men who hoped rather than believed that the party and the
nation could be rent in twain, and who meant to work closely with other
extremists.

Caleb Cushing, delegate-at-large from Massachusetts and supposedly a supporter of Jefferson Davis, impressed onlookers by his high, full forehead,
straight, sharp nose, and strong jaw—a leader obviously of intellectual power,
Lowell's "dreffle smart man," surprisingly youthful-looking for his sixty years.
The best Charleston families threw open their doors to him. Everyone knew of
his recent activities: his defense of the Dred Scott decision, his futile efforts to
obtain a repeal of the Personal Liberty Act in Massachusetts, his attacks on the
abolitionists as a band of drunken mutineers, his laudation of Davis in Faneuil
Hall, and his candid avowals of a desire to annex not only Cuba, but all of
Mexico. As a result of close association with Davis and other Southern leaders,
he no longer believed that the Union must be preserved at all hazards; instead,
he had written after John Brown's raid that if the Southern States did not receive
guarantees that such offenses would not be repeated, it was their duty as well as
right to form a separate republic. In fine, Cushing would support the Southern
extremists.

Slidell arrived, his long, thin, white hair framing his cherry-red countenance,
harder and craftier than ever. Among other Administration spokesmen were
Ben Butler, short, bald-headed, cross-eyed, hook-nosed, his every movement
showing his sleepless energy, and his harsh voice (like a file on a crosscut saw,

wrote one reporter) suiting his combative temperament; Jesse D. Bright of Indiana, who wore the aspect of an oily businessman, a yellow vest setting off his portly frame; and Bayard of Delaware, a handsome patrician whose long, brown, curly hair parted in the middle.

The radicals of the Lower South included the aggressive Barksdale brothers, Ethelbert and William, two Mississippians of fiery temper (William had stood beside Brooks when he assaulted Sumner, and had lost his wig in the House fracas with Grew); and Leroy P. Walker of Alabama, who was Yancey's best aide. Of various spokesmen for business, the most conspicuous was Dean Richmond, vice-president of the New York Central, owner of Buffalo elevators and lake shipping, and head of his State delegation; a well-built man of bulging brow and shrewd eyes, who believed in moderation and unity.[3]

The captaincy of the Administration forces was in the hands of Senators Slidell, Bright, and Bayard, who had done so much to accomplish Buchanan's nomination at Cincinnati four years earlier. They had quarters (hired as in 1856 by S. L. M. Barlow) in an old Charleston mansion.[4] The diversity of opinion among Southern and Administration delegates, however, forbade their union on any single candidate. Senator Hunter, Vice-President Breckinridge, and former Secretary James Guthrie were all possible nominees, while many believed that Davis might make the best candidate. The opposed group of Northwestern leaders included Henry B. Payne and Daniel P. Rhodes of Cleveland; the former a lawyer and railroad-builder, the latter a successful coal and iron capitalist. They, with Pugh, Stuart, Logan, and McClernand, followed the general guidance of Douglas's veteran lieutenant, Richardson, whose robust physique, loud voice, and quick tactical eye made him a doughty floor leader.

Douglas himself professed great confidence. He had written Peter Caggner of New York on February 19: "There will be no serious difficulty in the South. The last few weeks have worked a perfect revolution in that section. They all tell me and write that all will be right if our Northern friends will fearlessly represent the wishes and feelings of the Democracy in their own States."[5] But if these professions were sincere, he was grossly mistaken.

The atmosphere of Charleston grew more bitterly hostile to Douglas and to any idea of union under his leadership as the delegates from the Lower South thickened. They gathered in knots to declare that they would permit no equivocation in the platform, such as the readoption of the hazy Cincinnati plank on the Territories, and that the nomination of Douglas would precipitate the dis-

3 Cf. portrait in Stewart Mitchell, *Horatio Seymour*, 246; Richmond favored Seymour.
4 Nichols, *Disruption*, 294.
5 February 19, 1860; Lanphier Papers.

ruption of the party.[6] They met in larger groups to make unavailing attempts to agree upon a candidate. In the lobbies of the Charleston and Planters' Hotels, men talked defiantly of secession and a new republic, and when any moderate Democrat tried to answer the Southern nationalists, he was jeered into silence. Douglas men were shocked by the black looks they encountered. The fire-eaters called them abolitionists, and told them they had better join their own kind at the Republican convention.[7] Even so warm a sympathizer with the South as Caleb Cushing was both shocked and alarmed, and resolved to use every resource to effect a compromise on some such candidate as Guthrie or Franklin Pierce.[8] But intransigence continued to grow. "There is going to be an explosion," said sagacious men.

Before the end of the week, word flew about that Yancey, who had induced the Alabama convention to instruct its delegates for withdrawal if they did not obtain a slave-code plank, had scored a major victory. A meeting of Southern delegations had been held. Those of seven States—Georgia, Alabama, Florida, Mississippi, Louisiana, Arkansas, and Texas—had agreed to withdraw in a body unless the platform pronounced for the Congressional protection of slavery in the Territories.[9]

[II]

The Douglas leaders, who had planned their strategy more shrewdly than the Administration elements, were hopeful that they could write an inoffensive platform and gain a two-thirds vote for their candidate. They were elated by their general success in inducing the Northwestern States to elect Douglas delegates, and to bind them to the unit rule. Each State had as many votes in the convention as in the electoral college; as the college now numbered three hundred and three, Douglas must have two hundred and two delegates to win

6 The readiness of Southerners to talk of Douglas as a disguised abolitionist (Stephen A. Douglas and Fred Douglass are just the same, said some) did not rest alone on Lecompton and the Freeport debate. Greeley boasted privately that the *Tribune's* praise of Douglas was injuring the man in the South. "Don't you see that they all believe already that he and I are in *cahoots,* as they say—secretly leagued to humble and ruin 'the South'?" February 28, 1860; Greeley-Colfax Corr. The fiercest hatred guided plans to stop the Little Giant. George W. Paschal of San Antonio had written Douglas that he knew on indisputable authority that the Texas delegates were secretly pledged to withdraw from the convention if they could not otherwise defeat the Little Giant's nomination. April 17, 1860; Douglas Papers. What another correspondent called "the clique at Washington" had been pulling wires to break up the convention rather than let Douglas win. I. I. Jones. Raleigh, April 18, 1860; Douglas Papers.
7 Milton, *Eve of Conflict,* 429.
8 Fuess, *Caleb Cushing,* I, 247.
9 Nichols, *Disruption,* 295.

the traditional two-thirds. But did not many Democrats hold that any man who attained a clear majority ought then to be given the requisite two-thirds as a matter of courtesy? And would not office-hungry delegates flock to the band wagon of a prospective victor? [10] The five States of the Old Northwest would furnish Douglas a solid bloc of fifty-eight delegates; Iowa and Minnesota would supply seven or eight more; of the nine Missouri delegates, shrewd observers thought he would have five.[11] This would give him at least seventy western votes, a good start. Ten or eleven from Pennsylvania and four from New Jersey would bring his column up to eighty-five, while Maryland, where Reverdy Johnson had labored devotedly for him, should add two or three.[12]

New York, after its habit, had sent two delegations to the convention. But here—though not as clearly as in Illinois—the Senator's group had the better title. Dean Richmond's body of Douglas men asserted that they had been regularly elected; they declared that Fernando Wood's anti-Douglas group had been chosen before the legal hour for the State convention by a minority of its members. The businessmen and politicians who clustered about Richmond—August Belmont of New York, Erastus Corning and Peter Cagger of Albany, Sanford E. Church of Albion—would stand behind the Little Giant as long as victory seemed possible. They included a former member of the Free Soil Party, John Cochrane, whose ringing voice, aggressive manner, and proficiency in parliamentary law made him a great asset in Charleston.[13] Douglas was strong also among the New Englanders. He could count on the fourteen votes of New Hampshire, Vermont, and Rhode Island, and would divide those of Massachusetts, Connecticut, and Maine with other aspirants. He knew, too, that nearly all the Southern delegations held members who, after an initial vote for favorite sons, would be ready to turn to him; some of them, like Joseph R. Bradley of Alabama and T. B. Flournoy of Arkansas, ready even to make a spirited fight for him.

Altogether, before the gavel fell in Charleston, the Douglas lieutenants—their chief remaining in Washington—were confident of a majority. This, they thought, should give them control of the platform, even though the resolutions committee, with one member for each State, might divide closely against them. After all, they asked only for a noncommittal stand; a reiteration of the Cincinnati platform or something like it. And from a majority they hoped that, like Buchanan in 1856, they could vault to two-thirds.[14]

10   Milton, *Eve of Conflict*, 430 ff.
11   Cf. Senator Rice in *Cong. Globe*, 36th Cong., 1st Sess., 2245.
12   Milton, *Eve of Conflict*, 415.
13   Alexander, *Pol. Hist. N. Y.*, II, 270–273.
14   Jefferson Davis had completely failed to gain strength. He recognized this himself, writing Edward De Leon: "My opinions as you know them would be sufficient to defeat

The Little Giant was resolved never to give up. His health was now poor. He was financially embarrassed. He was heartily tired of fighting on two fronts. But, stung by slurs upon his honor, he believed the fate of party and nation hung on his battle; only popular sovereignty and non-intervention could yet save the Democracy from destruction and the Union from disruption. "I do not intend to make peace with my enemies nor to make a concession of one iota of principle," he had written.[15] Pains had been taken to send considerable bodies of spectators from the Northwest, Douglas himself urging the appointment of consulting delegates; "the more the better." [16] Richardson and Stuart were prepared for a fight to get their New York and Illinois delegations seated. They had also laid plans to carry an astute motion: while the unit rule must apply to all delegations upon whom the State conventions had imposed it, in other delegations each member should have the right to cast his vote as he pleased. Because the Northwestern delegations were bound, and most of the border and Southern States were not, this motion would enable Douglas to pick up scattering votes. Finally, the Senator's managers were ready to offer Federal appointments right and left to ambitious men.

[III]

The strength, aggressiveness, and skill of the Douglas forces accentuated the readiness of the Lower South to use extreme measures. The senatorial triumvirate, Slidell, Bayard, and Bright, were at a heavy disadvantage for want of a single dominant candidate. From January onwards, attempts to place Hunter or Breckinridge in command of the stop-Douglas element had run into insuperable obstacles. Kentucky's delegates were for ex-Secretary Guthrie rather than Breckinridge. Tennessee was for Andrew Johnson. While Hunter could count on Virginia and most of North Carolina, with scattering votes elsewhere, he had never approached a clear preeminence. Hammond thought him the best candidate, and Bayard had predicted his nomination if the convention did not break up. But of late he had lost ground.[17] The South Carolina Convention had voiced a preference for ex-Speaker Orr, who was a Union man.[18] Had the oppo-

---

any efforts of my friends to nominate me at Charleston and should do so as they would impair the ability of the Democratic Party to succeed in the next presidential canvass." He thought that sentiment had moved toward the Southern Rights creed ("We are now all powerful at the South, but are still in a minority at the North"); it could best be promoted by someone acceptable to both sections, such as Franklin Pierce or Dallas. January 21, 1860; De Leon Papers, South Carolinian Lib.

15 March 31, 1859, Douglas Papers, Ill. State Hist. Lib.
16 Douglas to C. H. Lanphier, January 1, 1860.
17 Senator Hammond to Harry Hammond, April 27, 1860, Hammond Papers; James Bayard to T. F. Bayard, March 24, 1860, Bayard Papers.
18 Charleston *Courier, Mercury*, April 17-19, 1860.

sition to Douglas rallied about a single magical name, it might have taken strong ground—but no Merlin had found an Arthur. In talents, experience, and magnetism, the Little Giant loomed above all rivals.

The Gulf State delegations were in the main implacably hostile to Douglas. Nevertheless, many citizens of those States held that he had been traduced by Buchanan and the Directory; that the delegates had been unfairly elected; and that the people, if they knew his true character, would gladly support him. Soulé charged that the election for the Louisiana State convention had been controlled by placeholders, and that the delegates sent to Charleston were creatures of trickery and fraud.[19] In Texas, Douglas men described the Galveston convention as a pack of secessionists, totally unrepresentative of Union sentiment in the State. In Mississippi, wrote R. D. Shropshire, editor of the Aberdeen *Mississippi Conservative*, the delegation chosen to Charleston by no means voiced the real views of the State. It included fire-eaters of the most rabid description. They had been selected after the Buchanan Administration had done everything possible to whip up anti-Douglas feeling; after a violent campaign of deception by men who hoped that a break-up of the Union would give them prominence and office which they could never otherwise attain; after wire-pulling and manipulation. Yet he was sure that the Mississippians would cast an overwhelming vote for Douglas if he were nominated.[20]

Gideon Pillow of Tennessee described a similar campaign of calumny in part of the press of that State. Yet he too was sure that Douglas could carry every Southern State.[21] In Alabama, an observer thought that the voters who had chosen the Charleston delegates did not form one one-hundredth part of the population:

We all know how meetings of this kind are gotten up—one or two leading men in each county propose a call for a public meeting. A few youths, ambitious of distinction, and of their spouting qualifications, take the matter in hand. Chairmen, committees, and resolutions are manufactured beforehand. A few meet! The committee are formed, and as a matter of course withdraw to consider resolutions, long before cut and dried for the occasion. . . . Five or ten casual spectators, lolling over the railing of a dirty courtroom, are microscoped into a numerous body of the bone and sinew of the county. Resolutions are adopted; delegates, anxious to show off, are appointed. They attend the convention. They take to this or that aspirant for fame or office, as accident or favor influences. They vote for this or that set of resolutions, as this or that particular interest is to be served, or is in the ascendent. Here is the whole machinery of the plots by which national and State movements are regulated.

With respect to the late [State] convention, I have attended a great many

19 *State Rights Louisianian*, April 8, 1860, clipping in Douglas Papers, U. of Chicago Lib.
20 April 16, 1860; Douglas Papers.
21 April 3, 1860; Douglas Papers.

meetings for the appointment of delegates, and so far as the people are concerned, I could never discover but a single idea moving them; this was to
appoint delegates to the Charleston Convention to join with the Democrats of
the entire Union in nominating a President.[22]

And John Forsyth wrote that Douglas had not a few friends even in the
Alabama delegation, though they were helpless; that he was a thousand times
stronger than the superficial currents set in motion by the politicians would
indicate; and that he had the sympathy of the entire Union feeling of the South,
prodigiously strong both within and without the party. Bradley of Alabama
actually thought of protesting to the credentials committee that his entire delegation had been improperly chosen and should be excluded.[23]

The one hope of defeating Douglas lay in using the resolutions committee to
draft the type of platform which he had sworn he would never support. Of the
thirty-three members of this committee, seventeen (the fifteen slave States and
the Administration catspaws from California and Oregon) would bow to the
wishes of the anti-Douglas leaders. A majority report on the platform might,
by threats, bribes, and eloquence, be forced through the convention. If it were
defeated, the Gulf States could withdraw. Before they would let Douglas be
nominated on an equivocal platform, they *would* withdraw.[24]

For different reasons, the threat of a party schism did not terrify either the
Northern or Southern delegates as it should have done. As Murat Halstead and
other expert journalists soon reported, the Douglas men were not averse to a
minor schism; if Alabama and Mississippi left the convention, it would be easier
to roll up a two-thirds vote for their candidate. Many good Unionists in the
South believed that two Democratic tickets, one headed by Douglas and one
by Breckinridge or Hunter, would throw the election of a President into Congress and ultimately into the Senate, where the South could choose a trusted
son. These men showed a singular myopia and levity in contemplating the disruption of the last great organization uniting the two sections. For a petty
temporary advantage, for a chance of contingent benefits, they were willing to
run the gravest risks not merely to the party but the nation. Far more penetrating was the vision of disunionists like Rhett and Yancey, who saw behind
schism their goal of two American republics.

22 Letter by B. F. Porter of Sidney, Alabama, signed "John Smith" in *Southern Advocate*, n.d.; Douglas Papers.
23 April 5, 1860; Douglas Papers.
24 "There would have been no trouble about the platform . . ." wrote "Tiber," the
Washington correspondent of the New Orleans *Picayune*, when the convention was over,
"had the New York delegation offered to support any nominee selected by the South. But
the South was and is determined that Douglas should not be nominated." *Picayune*, May
9, 1860. The New York delegation was in many ways the key group.

[IV]

On Monday, April 23, after a delightful eleven-o'clock shower had broken the heat and quenched the dust, the delegates trooped into the hall of the South Carolina Institute on Meeting Street. Though a spacious structure for Charleston, it was ridiculously inadequate for the gathering. A platform just large enough to hold the presiding officer and twenty or thirty others; a level floor set with plain wooden chairs, bolted by the half dozen to planks under the seats; narrow galleries on each side, occupied at first by male onlookers whose expectoration greatly troubled delegates beneath; high rounded windows of church-like aspect, admitting more than enough of the brilliant Carolina sunshine—such was the hall. Below the platform, and in front of the delegates, was an enclosure occupied by the press. When three thousand people crowded the room, it soon become so stifling that coats came off and palm-leaf fans were lustily plied.

The first two days proved not only that the followers of Douglas constituted a phalanx stronger than all the adverse groups, but that they enjoyed a superior leadership. Two committees were appointed, one on organization and one on credentials—New York and Illinois being excluded from the latter. Much cheering and excitement marked the discussions. The organization committee promptly selected Caleb Cushing for permanent chairman. Though he was hostile to Douglas, his qualifications were so preeminent (for he had prestige, force of personality, a quick mind, and a thorough training in parliamentary law) that he was accepted with general acquiescence. On taking the chair he delivered a spread-eagle speech in which, after referring to the eastern hills, the Mississippi basin, and other geographical glories, he denounced the Republicans for a traitorous conspiracy to set section against section.

A hot debate then began on the question whether uninstructed State delegations should vote as units or according to the individual preference of delegates. This was a matter of considerable moment, for a number of delegations whose majorities stood against Douglas contained men who wished to vote for him. Even Alabama, it was thought, had a member or two on his side, and North Carolina certainly had one. Several Southern delegates, with one angry Pennsylvanian, spoke against giving uninstructed individuals full liberty. When William A. Richardson responded with a personal indictment of the Pennsylvanian, a wild uproar ensued; but standing on a chair, his sleeves rolled above his elbows, his voice as cacophonous as the screech of a fire-engine, he finished his speech. By a heavy majority, the convention decided that votes might be cast individually unless a delegation was bound by specific State instructions; and thirty or forty

Douglas men were thus freed to act as they liked. To many Southerners the new rule, for which no strict precedent existed and which gave the popular sovereignty forces a decided advantage, seemed a bit of sharp practice.

As ill-feeling thus increased, the convention determined, practically by acclamation, that the platform should be adopted before balloting for candidates began. In this action, Yancey's extremists and the Douglas column for once agreed. The decision was not so nearly unavoidable as it seemed—and it contained the seeds of disaster.

To be sure, Douglas was pledged not to accept a nomination if the platform contained a slave-code plank, and the whole Northwest stood with him. To be sure, Alabama and some sister States were pledged to withdraw if the platform did not meet *their* demands. Superficially, the issues of the platform apparently had to be resolved before the convention could proceed. Whenever the desire for party unity is strong, however, platforms have usually been subordinated to candidates—who interpret them much as they please anyway. If in this instance a candidate (whether Douglas, Hunter, Breckinridge, or someone else) had been nominated, then no quarrel need have taken place over the platform; a compromise would have been possible. The decision to grant the platform priority gave the South and the Administration men every incentive to fight for a set of resolutions which would debar Douglas, and it gave the platform an unwonted prominence. From that moment all hope of unity disappeared.

On the night of the second day, reporters were sending word over the country that Douglas was certain of a majority of delegates, that the struggle to give him two-thirds would be tremendous, and that the convention, rent by irreconcilable feuds, was heading for disruption.

The third day, Wednesday the twenty-fifth, brought the South a new blow and Douglas a fresh victory. The convention, as good judges had predicted, excluded the Danite contestants from Illinois and the Fernando Wood group from New York. The first decision was certainly just, and the weight of evidence supported the second. Inevitably, however, it aroused deep feeling, for the New York votes were of almost crucial importance. Fernando Wood, emphasizing the riotous character of the Syracuse convention, had made out a case which impressed many. The South felt a deep injustice in the fact that although Dean Richmond's delegation contained thirty anti-Douglas men to forty Douglas men, under the unit rule the entire vote of the State would be cast for the Illinoisan.[25] Nine slave States, with California, had mustered fifty-five votes for dividing the New York seats between the two sets of claimants, but they were overwhelmed by two hundred and ten noes. The New Yorkers might vote, before the end, for Guthrie, Hunter, or some other slave State man, but they would

25 See Ben Butler's speech, N. Y. *Herald*, May 19, 20 or 21, 1860.

certainly stand as rocklike as the Illinois delegates against any slave-code demand. Once more, on this third day, Murat Halstead reported to his newspaper that an explosion was certain, and that the only question now was the extent of the Southern defection.

Marking time on the fourth day, for the platform committee was still at work, the convention waited breathlessly for the great battle on resolutions. It knew that the future of the party, perhaps even the future of the nation, was being decided in that committee room. As they waited, the delegates let their animosities break into the debate. Douglasites and slave-code men baited each other. Several Southerners offered motions favorable to their own radical position and made speeches which Northern Democrats regarded as threatening the ruin of the party throughout the free States. As night closed in, everyone agreed that the platform committee must bring forward either a subterfuge, or a bombshell.[26]

At ten o'clock on Friday morning the delegates (many shivering, for the weather had changed to cold rain and blustering wind) gathered anew, and after routine business recessed to give the platform committee additional time. Parts of the floor as well as the galleries were now occupied by women, whose merry laughter furnished an incongruous note. At about eleven-thirty the committee, pale and careworn, filed into the hall. Printed copies of minority and majority reports were being excitedly passed from hand to hand

The majority report, signed by the fifteen slave States, with Oregon and California, declared that Congress had no power to abolish slavery in the Territories, and that the territorial legislature had no power to abolish slavery, exclude slaves, or impair the right of property in slaves by any legislation whatever. It further asserted that it was the duty of the national government to protect, when necessary, the rights of persons and property on the high seas, in the Territories, or wherever else its constitutional authority extended.

The minority report stood in sharp contrast. It reaffirmed the Cincinnati platform of 1856, with a preamble declaring that, since differences of opinion existed as to the rights and duties of territorial legislatures and Congress with respect to slavery in the Territories, the party would abide by the decisions of the Supreme Court on the questions of constitutional law. W. W. Avery of North Carolina, speaking for the committee majority, made the first argument. He represented, he said, the seventeen trustworthy Democratic States of the nation. Inevitably, Mexico, Cuba, and Central America would become part of the republic; and if the popular sovereignty doctrine, as interpreted by the Douglas faction, were accepted, no slaveholder would dare to enter these an-

26 Murat Halstead, *Caucuses of 1860.*

nexed domains with his slaves. He appealed to the Northern Democrats to prove that they would stand courageously by the Southern slaveholders. It was an outrageous speech, which many border men would have repudiated; but the Lower South cheered it to the echo.

Thereupon H. B. Payne of Ohio, a man of distinguished bearing, rose to speak for the committee minority. His address, logical, clear, and beautifully phrased, was worthy of one of the leaders of the Ohio bar. All those who signed the minority report, he declared, were deeply impressed with the belief that upon the action of the convention probably hung the fate of the party and the destiny of the Union. They were convinced that the national government should not interfere with slavery in the Territories, but permit the people themselves to determine their institutions. He could show, he continued, that every eminent Southern leader since 1850 had at some time planted himself upon the doctrine of non-intervention by Congress. Hunter, Toombs, Mason, Calhoun— he quoted them all. The Northern mind was too thoroughly imbued with the principle of popular sovereignty to abandon it. Northern Democrats asked for nothing but what the Constitution allowed them, for they promised to abide by the decision of the courts, the interpreters of the Constitution. Why should the South for a mere abstraction, he asked, throw away the chance of party success? If the Northern Democracy were allowed to run its race unhampered, it would do its full duty in the contest. But the North would not be coerced: "We cannot recede from this doctrine without personal dishonor, and so help us God, we never will abandon this principle. If the majority report is adopted, you cannot expect one Northern electoral vote, or one sympathizing member of Congress from the free States." [27]

Ben Butler then took the floor to plead for his own report from a minority of one, which proposed that the convention simply reaffirm the Cincinnati platform. Before he sat down, he engaged in a brisk skirmish with a Maryland delegate who acridly remarked that his State had never encouraged resistance to the Fugitive Slave Law. Recalling the recent Baltimore mobs, Butler retorted that Massachusetts had never submitted to a regime which frightened men from the polls with bludgeon and knife. After a recess for luncheon, Barksdale of Mississippi made a violent ultra-Southern speech, to which Austin A. King, former governor of Missouri, replied that the slave-code platform carried the sting of death to the party; that it would lose them all the Northern electors and all the border States except Missouri itself. Then the convention turned to the two principal contestants of the day: Yancey for the South, Pugh for the Northwest, both eager for battle. The very crisis of the gathering had arrived.

27 Halstead, *Caucuses; Official Proceedings;* N. Y. *Weekly Tribune,* May 5, 1860.

[V]

Yancey, a truly great orator and nothing more—not a constructive legislator, not a party organizer, not an administrator, not an able writer—held views which require a discriminating assessment. While men like Rhett, Porcher Miles, and Ruffin believed in disunion as a benefit in itself, Yancey(at least ostensibly) demanded disunion only because he thought it no longer possible to obtain the constitutional rights of the South within the Union. Rhett and Ruffin gloried in the name of disunionist; Yancey, whenever that epithet was fastened upon him,

Mr. Yancey, through his friend, William Barksdale, asks for the floor in the Charleston Convention.

protested indignantly. He said repeatedly that loyalty to the Constitution was the lodestone of his policy. He talked in Calhoun's terms of the compact among the States and the compact between North and South. He held that the position of Douglas and that of the Republicans were substantially identical, in that both would abolish the sectional compact and abrogate the Constitution. In short, he was for maintaining the Union—if only the rest of the country would accept the extreme Southern position. Within a few months he was to appeal to voters to "save us from Lincoln and so save the Union." [28]

Already, his opponents were charging that he was the head of a conspiracy to break up the party as a prelude to disruption of the Union, but this charge he angrily repelled. The South, in his opinion, should stand firm; show first the Northern Democrats, and later the Northern Republicans, what would be the result of their folly, and then, if they persisted in tyrannous courses, act to protect itself. It was the opponents of the South who were disunionists! [29]

Rising amid a storm of applause, Yancey spoke with characteristic quiet geniality, uttering the most uncompromising sentiments in the most musical and

[28]   Speech at Florence, Kentucky; Cincinnati *Gazette*, October 20, 1860.
[29]   George Petrie, "W. L. Yancey," in *Transactions Ala. State Hist. Soc.*, IV, 307–312.

ingratiating tones. The Southerners, he declared, had come to Charleston to save their constitutional rights. If they lost and the popular sovereignty platform prevailed, they would be bankrupted. They must let the Democracy go down to defeat if necessary, for defeat on principle was glorious defeat. He upbraided the Northern Democrats for treating slavery as an inherited evil; they should boldly pronounce it a positive good! If they had taken the position that slavery was right by the laws of nature and of God, they would have triumphed. With more force than logic, he appealed to Southern emotions on the issue of basic rights. "Ours is the property invaded; ours are the institutions which are at stake; ours is the peace that is to be destroyed; ours is the honor at stake—the honor of children, the honor of families, the lives, perhaps, of all—all of which rests upon what your course may ultimately make a great heaving volcano of passion and crime, if you are enabled to consummate your designs. Bear with us, then, if we stand sternly upon what is yet that dormant volcano, and say we yield no position here until we are convinced we are wrong." [30] He charged the Southern delegates to stand true to their constitutional duties, for if recreant they would merit defeat and eternal ignominy.

The gas lamps had now been lit. The deep feeling of Southern delegates and of the throng of Charleston spectators, excited by Yancey's rolling periods, found expression in wild handclapping and shouting. It was in an atmosphere glacial with hostility that Pugh, at seven in the evening, began his reply. He was glad, he declared, to hear a Southern leader speak out so plainly and boldly. Reading the resolutions which Yancey himself had presented to the Alabama Democratic convention four years earlier in favor of non-intervention, he pointed out that Alabama did not then ask what she now demanded, and that Yancey's mind was not then what it was now. His remarks on Southern inconsistency and intransigency became scathing. Must the Democratic Party be dragged at the chariot wheel of three hundred thousand slave-masters? A more fearless speech had never been heard in any party convention. It was as if Douglas himself were confronting the angry crowd. This Southern demand that the long-suffering Northern Democrats should avow slavery to be right, and its extension to be desirable, Pugh pronounced intolerable. "Gentlemen of the South," he declaimed, "you mistake us—you mistake us! We will not do it!" [31]

The convention adjourned that evening in an uproar. Everyone knew that a party split would probably take place on the morrow. Delegates stalked the streets with dripping umbrellas, or huddled in anxious consultation. Some Douglas men, knowing that they could muster a majority but not a two-thirds vote, were still cheerful in facing a disruption. They would let three or four State

30 "Speech of W. L. Yancey of Alabama," April 28, 1860; pamphlet.
31 Halstead, *Caucuses*, 50; Charleston *Courier*, April 30, 1860.

delegations leave the convention—just enough to give them control! Many Southern Unionists, too, still hoped complacently that a break-up might throw the election into Congress. But the anxiety of reflective men was growing, and not a few Democrats were haggard with worry.

Telegrams flew between Washington and Charleston. Various Southern members of Congress were advising their State delegations to withdraw alongside Alabama. Robert Toombs wired the Georgia delegates that if they could not get a sound platform with a Southern man on it they should bolt. The South Carolina delegation, asking the advice of their Congressmen, were told to leave.[32] George Sanders in a long telegram (sent collect at a cost of $26.80) had already implored the President to intervene. After denouncing Slidell and Bright for trying to break up the convention, he declared that most of the Northern delegates, with half of those from Kentucky, North Carolina, Maryland, Missouri, and Alabama, and a number from Florida, Tennessee, Georgia, and Arkansas, had agreed to accept certain changes in the old Cincinnati platform. The two most important amendments left all questions respecting the rights of property in States and Territories, arising under the Constitution, to the Supreme Court. But Buchanan was in no mood to carry out a type of intervention that would probably result in Douglas's nomination.[33]

Dawn broke on Saturday with rain still falling, and the air chill and clammy. A grave calamity stared the Kentucky and Ohio delegations in the face; their private stock of whiskey was almost exhausted. Everybody growled at the weather, the high prices of hotels and restaurants, and the gloomy party outlook. The only persons who looked cheerful were the Rhett-Yancey extremists, and supporters of such secondary aspirants as Hammond, Andrew Johnson, and Franklin Pierce, who hoped that the confusion over the platform could be manipulated to their advantage.

A dozen different crosscurrents of ambition and sentiment swirled through the convention as it reopened. Once more the proceedings became tumultuous— but almost miraculously, an immediate break was averted. The platform was sent back to committee, and when late in the day it reemerged, the Southern delegates made a brave stand against the Douglas majority by staging a filibuster.

32 *Toombs, Stephens, Cobb Correspondence*, 468, 469; B. F. Perry, *Biographical Sketches*, 188. A letter had been exhibited on the third day from Jefferson Davis, advising Mississippi to withdraw if Douglas were nominated; Charleston *Courier*, April 26, 1860. Some other men in Washington had already decided for a breach. "The plan for breaking up the convention is said to have been formed here some weeks ago," wrote "Tiber" from Washington on May 1. "The scheme was first announced in the N. Y. *Leader*." New Orleans *Picayune*, May 9, 1860.

33 Sanders to Buchanan, telegram, April 27, 1860; Buchanan Papers. It was widely reported that Hunter telegraphed the Virginia delegation not to withdraw. W. H. Trescot, May 8, 1860; Miles Papers, Univ. of N. C.

At one moment the disorder became so great that Cushing threatened to leave the chair.[34] Finally, after weary wrangling, the assemblage adjourned over Sunday—a Sunday to be spent in plots, discussion, and efforts to negotiate a peace.

[VI]

For several reasons the New York delegates stood in the best position to effect a compromise. Their metropolis and State had an immense stake in the maintenance of the Union; the feeling of New York City was notoriously moderate; August Belmont and Dean Richmond had a host of Southern friends; and the persuasive John Cochrane had been prominent in national conventions for a quarter of a century. On Sunday, several New Yorkers, with at least one Southern peacemaker in the person of Richard Taylor, son of the former President, approached Slidell and Bright. These Senators assured them that under certain circumstances and conditions the unity of the party could be preserved. They sent for Yancey, and some evidence exists that he promised to try to persuade the other Alabama delegates not to bolt the convention immediately. Perhaps, in characteristic fashion, he merely uttered uncompromising words in such soothing tones that they seemed to suggest compromise. At any rate, while the conciliators labored, the Southern lines were actually being drawn tighter, and Virginia was coming to the side of the Lower South in insisting upon a slave-code plank. The New Yorkers went to bed that night hopeful. Richard Taylor, Slidell, Bright, and Bayard sat up till nearly dawn in the vain hope that Yancey would return with encouraging news. He never came. The border State men talked of concord and victory—but in reality the situation had grown worse.[35]

On Monday morning, the seventh day, it was evident that the atmosphere of Charleston had become implacable. The *Mercury*, edited by the younger Rhett, appeared with an eloquent plea for the vindication of Southern rights. Alabama and Mississippi were resolved to leave if their demands were ignored, said the journal, and the other slave States should follow. Greater crowds than ever pushed into the convention hall, and trains and boats having carried many Northerners back home, South Carolinians rushed into their seats.

At ten o'clock, the platform was taken up. The minority, or Douglas, version was swiftly carried, 165 to 138, but amid a clamor of voices raising points of order. The Douglas forces then consented to separate votes on the component planks. The first resolution, reaffirming the Cincinnati platform of 1856, was carried by a heavy majority—the border States and Virginia giving it sixty

34 Charleston *Courier*, April 30, 1860.
35 Richard Taylor, *Destruction and Reconstruction*, 11, 12; N. Y. *Weekly Tribune*, May 5, 1860; Alexander, *New York*, II, 274.

votes. Thereupon a member of the New York delegation moved that the remaining part of the Douglas platform be laid on the table so that the convention might proceed immediately to the nominations. But some of the Douglas leaders, anxious to show their strength and possibly ready to court a limited defection, shelved the motion. A vote was then in order on the second part of the minority platform, declaring that the party would abide by the Supreme Court's decisions. But a number of Southerners uttered impassioned warnings that if this plank carried their States would leave; they insisted on a slave code; and no fewer than seven Southern delegations refused to vote at all upon the plank.

As it thus became clear that a large-scale schism would follow adoption, the Douglas men became frightened. A wild din had broken out; Richardson of Illinois was on his feet bellowing to be heard; the New England delegates were plainly anxious not to drive out the Southern men; the Northwestern delegates were hurriedly conferring. Dean Richmond withdrew the New Yorkers to a rapid conclave, in which they decided to vote against the plank. They returned to find the Douglas column beating a disorganized retreat. The roll call showed a perfect rout, the second resolution losing, 238 to 21. It was a humiliating result for the Northwestern men.

The convention might now have contented itself with restating the Cincinnati platform, have left the slave-code abstraction to time, and have gone on to name a man satisfactory to both sections. Unfortunately, Southern passions had been too deeply aroused. As the tumult over the critical Douglas plank had risen to frenzy, Yancey had been observed smiling as happily as a child at a Christmas feast. He knew well what was coming next. Several speakers rose to make conciliatory remarks. Stuart of Michigan attempted an explanation of the concessions which the Douglas men had made in helping vote down the principal plank of their own platform, but he was so hurt by the forced surrender that his remarks became bitterly offensive. Various observers surmised that perhaps he wished to make sure that the slave-code men would leave the convention.[36] Had he been sweet as honey, however, that would have availed nothing. The Southern radicals now knew that they could keep a popular sovereignty plank out of the platform, but they also knew that they could never force a slave-code plank into it, and on this issue many were ready to revolt. The echoes of a sharp exchange between Stuart and Yancey had hardly died away when L. P. Walker, chairman of the Alabama delegation, gained Cushing's recognition and declared that he had an announcement to make. As he walked to the front, a profound hush fell upon the gathering. The fateful moment had come!

The Alabama convention at Montgomery, said Walker, had directed its delegates to withdraw if they could not obtain a slave-code resolution, and as

36 Charleston *Courier*, May 1, 1860; Halstead, *Caucuses*, 9.

their demand had been denied, they must now follow their instructions. As the Alabamians rose to leave, Barry of Mississippi was on his feet. He and his associates, he announced, were also departing. One of them insisted on a final speech; and D. C. Glenn, in a powerful valedictory, prophesied that within sixty days the world would see a united South—a statement hailed with resounding cheers. In quick succession, Mouton of Louisiana and Simmons of South Carolina announced that their delegations too were withdrawing—although in fact two Louisianians and two South Carolinians remained. Milton of Florida presented the protest and withdrawal of his State, and another spokesman did as much for part of the Arkansas representation. The Texas representatives left in a body. Of the cotton States, only Georgia remained undecided, and as her delegates retired to consult, their secession was certain.[37]

That night, excitement ran high in Charleston, its streets thronged with men not merely excited but jubilant. A great crowd, gathering at eleven o'clock in front of the courthouse to listen to Yancey and L. Q. C. Lamar, wildly cheered an independent Southern republic. The city was mad with a passion not felt since Nullification days. "Perhaps even now," declared Yancey, "the pen of the historian is nibbed to write the story of a new revolution"—and Charleston hoped so. The withdrawn delegates, among whom Bayard and his Delaware associate Whiteley took their places, hesitated over their action. After much discussion, they resolved not to adopt a platform or a distinctive party name, and to adjourn to Richmond on June 11 for separate action.[38]

Meanwhile, on Tuesday, May 1, the regular convention met again; this time in an atmosphere of dejection, for few could still hope for a Democratic victory. Theoretically, about two hundred and fifty of the original three hundred and four delegates should still have been present, but the heat, confusion, hostile atmosphere, and high expenses were driving many to the homeward trains. The first decision taken by the convention was that no man should be nominated

37 Dumond, *Secession Movement 1860–61*, 52; *Proceedings*, 118–125. Next day 26 of the 34 Georgia delegates, followed by the remaining Arkansas men, withdrew. Halstead, 76.

38 Fuess, *Caleb Cushing*, II, 254. The South Carolina delegation, a moderate body, had no instructions to withdraw. Public sentiment in Charleston forced its action. When the delegates arrived, wrote Rhett, they had no more idea of going out than of flying. "If they had not retired, they would have been mobbed, I believe." May 12, 1860; Porcher Miles Papers, Univ. of N. C. The fact was that Yancey, having taken out his extremists, did not know what to do with them. Trescot thought that if Hunter had not telegraphed the Virginia delegates to stay in regular convention, Yancey might have nominated him. May 8, 1860; Miles Papers, Univ. of N. C. Louisiana and Delaware delegates opposed any nomination or even recommendation, and Yancey and his Alabama delegation yielded to this. He thought that Davis was the favorite for the Southern nomination, though Lane, Guthrie, and Breckinridge were urged by some. At once, Yancey took steps to scatter copies of his speeches at Charleston throughout the South, and wrote C. C. Clay—and doubtless others— in Washington urging them to stand by the radicals. Prompt and efficient action was necessary to back up the bolters, he stated. May 4, 1860; C. C. Clay Papers.

without a two-thirds vote of all elected delegates. This was a blow to the Douglas men, who contended that two-thirds of the delegates present ought to suffice. But Caleb Cushing ruled against them; the remaining Southern delegates threatened to withdraw if he were not upheld; and he had the support of various Northern groups, including the powerful New York delegation, which did not wish to cut its members off from a possible Presidential nomination. One participant remarked that the ballot had the sound of clods falling on Douglas's coffin. From that moment, all hopes of a rapid victory for him at Charleston were dead, for he could never obtain two-thirds of all the seats. While this rule had not been followed in earlier Democratic conventions, it could be said that the circumstances this time were unprecedented.[39]

Six men were formally but briefly nominated for the Presidency: Douglas, Guthrie, Hunter, Daniel S. Dickinson, Andrew Johnson, and Joseph Lane of Oregon. With 202 votes necessary for a choice, the first ballot gave Douglas 145½; Guthrie 36½; Hunter 42; and 30 for other men. Twelve ballots were taken that day and forty-five more the next without result. Strive as they might, Douglas's followers were unable to push his vote above 152½. This was a clear majority of all the seats, and they were quick to point out that four years earlier he had withdrawn the moment he learned that Buchanan had attained a majority. His enemies contended, however, that his vote included many delegates bound by the unit rule who were really against him. The strongest rival was James Guthrie, but even after Andrew Johnson was formally withdrawn in favor of the Kentuckian, Guthrie obtained only 64½ votes. With the convention hopelessly deadlocked, nothing remained but to vote an adjournment. Cushing, whose encouragement of Southern intransigency in years past had contributed not a little to the catastrophe, closed the proceedings by a rhetorical appeal for a restoration of harmony. His words could not assuage the bitterness with which most of the delegates, and particularly the Northwestern men—some of whom had shed tears over Douglas's failure—turned their backs on the flowers and rancors of Charleston.[40]

Something more than the convention had come to an end when the delegates of the cotton kingdom walked out of the hall. The Democratic Party had been riven asunder, and the stage set for secession and disunion. The melancholy words which a veteran leader of the South, ex-Senator Foote, wrote decades later, were all too true; the Southern extremists who had declared that they would never tolerate a Republican President had taken the very steps to make

---

39 Charleston *Courier*, *N. Y. Tribune*, May 3; Halstead, *Caucuses*, 85; E. D. Fite, *Presidential Campaign of 1860*, pp. 110, 111.
40 *Official Proceedings*; Fuess, *Caleb Cushing*, II, 253; Milton, *Eve of Conflict*, 447-449.

Republican victory certain, and had thus deliberately sealed the destruction of the national fabric.[41]

The word "deliberately" requires a gloss; levity, hot-blooded precipitancy, a stupid confidence that party schism would soon be healed, and other factors played a part. But that Rhett, Yancey, and others substantially foresaw the main events of the next nine months can hardly be questioned, and Slidell, Bright, and Bayard coolly dealt cards that gave these men their trumps. Alas, that nobody looked further ahead than the next nine months! The cheers that grew thunderous when Glenn of Mississippi predicted a united South before midsummer were cheers for the closing of the bright page on which all the glories of the old fraternal Union were inscribed. The bright smiles and handclappings which Charleston ladies bestowed upon the receding delegates were applause for an irrevocable step toward war; the bouquets which they brought next day to fill the empty seats of the seceders were symbolic of the flowers soon to be cast upon multitudinous Southern graves.

[VII]

Before the convention adjourned, the stubborn South Carolina Unionist, B. F. Perry, who had remained when his brethren departed, insisted upon being heard. Refusing to let the hissing galleries be cleared, he stood until silence reigned; then, erect, with outstretched arm and warning finger, he combined an appeal for reconciliation with an indictment of Southern radicalism. It was suicidal, he declared, for the South to demand Congressional intervention, which it had been resisting so many years. The South should instead yield as much as possible to the Northern Democrats who had sacrificed themselves in protecting slave State rights. Why insist on a "mere abstraction" at the hazard of breaking up the party? The recent South Carolina Democratic convention, he correctly said, had been controlled by moderates, anxious for party harmony. It had mentioned no contingency which would justify the South Carolina delegation in leaving the national convention. He was confident that his colleagues had contemplated no such step when they came. They had been swept into folly by a storm of emotion carefully prepared by intrigue.[42]

No question can exist that the main responsibility for the disruption, both immediate and remote, lay with the Southern extremists and the Administration men. The program of the disunionists had been outlined months before by Rhett in a letter to Porcher Miles. Revolutions, he wrote, are made by deter-

41 H. S. Foote, *Casket of Reminiscences*, 121, 122.
42 Charleston *Courier*, May 2, 1860; Perry, *Biographical Sketches*, 145-150, 188, 602.

mined minorities.[43] The War of 1812 had been effected by a mere handful of patriotic, fearless Southern men when a cowardly spirit was rife throughout the land. The South must now dissever itself from the rotten Northern element. There was no hope that the State Rights men could control the Charleston convention. "Hence the importance of obtaining the secession of the Alabama and Mississippi delegations on the issue of squatter sovereignty and the construction of the Dred Scott decision. If they will but do it, the people I am sure will come up to the scratch, and the game will be ours." This was the fire-eaters' own plan to precipitate the Southern States into revolution.[44] It had been realized to the letter; some steps remained to be taken, but so far it had operated well. The Administration men under Slidell and Bright made their indispensable contribution to the debacle by refusing to accept Douglas as a candidate and using the slave-code demand to exclude him.

To be sure, if Douglas had withdrawn, the South would doubtless have yielded to a compromise candidate and compromise platform, and the party would have marched into the campaign with united ranks. But Douglas had three excellent reasons for not withdrawing. The first was that by every available index a majority of Democratic voters, and probably a heavy majority, wanted him as their candidate. The second was that after the Administration effort to force him, the champion of the Northwest, out of the party, and especially after the culminating blow of his deposition from the chairmanship of the Territorial Committee, honor required him to fight to the end. The third was that he represented a principle which Northern Democrats simply could not give up.[45]

What had happened was that a minority of the gathering, who spoke for a minority of the party, had undertaken to dictate to the majority what they should put into the platform. By decisive vote, after full discussion, the convention had pronounced against the slave-code demand. Few sane observers could doubt that two-thirds of the Democrats of the country were against such a plank. Yet the minority had tried to coerce the majority by threats of a bolt,

43 "The bolt at Charleston," wrote J. H. Clay Mudd to Alexander H. Stephens on May 22, "was the result of prearranged action outside of the delegates, in advance of the Convention. The struggle over the platform was a mere sham; the real contest was about the candidate. Douglas out of the way, and the platform was of no consequence to the central managers who combined for his destruction. Slidell and Bright openly confessed before they went to Charleston that their action was governed by personal hostility to the man. The Administration labored and still labors diligently to the same end." Stephens Papers, LC.
44 January 29, 1860; Miles Papers, Univ. of N. C.
45 Douglas in a Senate speech of May 15 made an explicit statement that his honor was involved. "My name never would have been presented at Charleston, except for the attempt to proscribe me for a heretic, too unsound to be the chairman of a committee in this body, where I have held a seat for so many years without a suspicion resting on my political fidelity. I was forced to allow my name to go there in self-defense; and I will now say that had any gentleman, friend or foe, received a majority in that convention over me, the lightning would have carried a message withdrawing my name from the convention."

and, when they achieved only partial success, had bolted. In the matter of a candidate, the position was equally clear. Had all delegations remained, Douglas would certainly have had a heavy majority, and might have approached two-thirds. After the split, he not only had a majority of the votes cast on every one of the fifty-seven ballots, but on several ballots had a majority of *all* delegates. His agents were accused of sharp practice in passing the rule for individual voting by unbound delegates. He could reply to this charge that although the votes of New Jersey, Delaware, California, Oregon, and nearly half of Massachusetts were cast against him, most Democrats of those States were heartily for him. The New York *Tribune* remarked that he assuredly had two-thirds of the Democratic voters of the Union behind him.[46]

Looking back over the unhappy sequence of events, we can fix upon certain crucial moments. The first was the deposition of Douglas from the Senate Territorial Committee; a notice that his political life was sought and that he must conquer or be slain.

The second was the adoption by the Alabama State Democratic Convention in January, 1860, of Yancey's program. In 1856, the delegates to the national convention had been positively instructed to withdraw if they did not obtain a plank stating the principle of Congressional non-intervention in the Territories; in 1860, they were positively instructed to withdraw if they did not obtain a plank making it the duty of Congress to protect slave property in the Territories.[47] This Alabama convention had been far from unanimous. While Yancey led the slave-code wing, John Forsyth and J. J. Seibels led a militant wing willing to leave the status of property in the Territories to the courts, and eager to nominate Douglas. Outvoted two to one, Forsyth and others contended that the convention expressed the views of the politicians rather than the people. Our best evidence indicates that it really did reflect the majority will, but with a large dissenting minority.[48] By the beginning of 1860, Douglas had thus been compelled to fight to the end for popular sovereignty; while one Southern State was committed to disruption of the party if it did not get a plank which made popular sovereignty into mincemeat. Another, Mississippi, was ready to follow. Jefferson Davis's resolutions had determined its course. The Texas delegation, too, according to word sent to Douglas before the Charleston gathering, had secretly determined to bolt if he were nominated.

46 Much evidence on the methods by which the choice of delegates in various States was controlled by Administrative officeholders is to be found in the Douglas Papers. See, for example, the letter by John D. Stranahan of Le Boeuf, Pennsylvania, on the way in which the customs collector and postmaster in Erie manipulated the county convention against the will of the people; May 7, 1860.

47 Denman, *Secession Movement in Alabama*, 80, 81.

48 Murphy, "Alabama and the Chicago Convention of 1860," *Transactions Ala. State Hist. Soc.*, 1904, V. 224 ff.

The third crucial turning point was the midnight conference of Southern delegates which, just as the convention opened, decided that Mississippi, Louisiana, Arkansas, Texas, and Florida, with the South Carolina delegates cooperating "in a certain contingency," would stand by the Alabama demand: a slave-code, or withdrawal. Our best account of this conclave is that given by the special correspondent of the New Orleans *Picayune*, who, returning from it at one A.M. April 24, dashed off a full dispatch.[49] The caucus met in the hall of the Meagher Guards, with Governor Alexander Mouton of Louisiana presiding. Resolutions upon Southern rights were reported by Milton of Florida as the basis for demands in the convention. Yancey sustained them in what the correspondent termed a most powerful argument, and was vigorously seconded by Glenn of Mississippi, who dilated upon the Jefferson Davis resolutions. Rousing speeches were also made by L. P. Walker of Alabama, an old Nashville Convention man, and Burroughs of Arkansas. When a North Carolina delegate expostulated, denying the right of Congress to legislate upon slavery in the Territories, the majority laughed at him. Resolutions were adopted by acclamation for a Southern ultimatum: The platform must be written before a candidate was nominated, and the platform must contain the essential features of the Jefferson Davis-Mississippi program, including a slave-code.

The final turning point occurred on the night of Sunday, April 29, when the effort of leaders to avert the now imminent bolt broke down. Slidell, Bright, Bayard, and others were frightened by the impending ruin of the party. They made a last-minute effort to hold the cotton kingdom delegates. Their plan was to reaffirm the Cincinnati platform, table the remaining minority resolutions, and proceed to ballot for candidates. They told Southerners that a careful nose count showed that without slave State votes Douglas could get little if any more than a majority; that New York, with a majority of Pennsylvania delegates, was ready to swing to Guthrie; and that if the South remained, Guthrie could be nominated. Richard Taylor's story that Yancey vainly tried to get Alabama to consent may be correct. Southerners thought the count too close for safety. They knew that some slave State men *would* vote for Douglas, and they hence refused to change front (as Northerners were willing to do) and take up nominations before the main part of the platform. Until the very end, however, the managers and mediators retained hope. When, on Monday, the convention by a large majority reaffirmed the Cincinnati platform, six border slave States (Maryland, Delaware, Virginia, Tennessee, Kentucky, and Missouri) voted for it. The Douglas men gave way on the next resolution leaving territorial property to

---

49 N. O. *Picayune*, April 28, 1860. The South Carolina delegates did not attend this caucus; the phrase as to cooperation in a certain contingency (later verified by events) is in a Charleston dispatch to the N. Y. *Tribune* of April 23, 1860.

the court. Then it was dramatically revealed that the midnight attempt at an arrangement had failed.

Why did it fail? "The seceding States came to the convention," wrote Robert H. Glass, editor of the Lynchburg *Republican,* in a letter from Charleston dated May 1, "with a deliberate purpose to break up the convention if they failed to get, as they knew they would fail to get, their extreme ultimatum, and their ultimate design is to break up the Union by breaking up the Democratic Party." We have noted that Virginia on that fateful Sunday temporarily came to the support of the cotton kingdom in insisting on a slave-code plank. Glass believed that if his State had stood staunchly by its original position and upheld the Cincinnati platform, it would have become the ruling factor in the convention and would have drawn all the Northern States to its standard. His fellow-delegate Barbour also believed that Virginia made a fatal error when it temporarily followed Yancey's lead. "For myself," concluded Glass, "I have no great admiration for the Union . . . but I have no idea of assisting in bringing about such a serious result by insisting upon a mere abstraction which is not worth the paper upon which it is proposed to be written." His general conclusions were supported by the Washington correspondent of the Cincinnati *Enquirer,* who wrote May 1: "The secession movement [that is, from the convention] is universally regarded as a concerted plan for the dissolution of the Union."

Essentially, as we have said, the disruption came because Southern extremists, abetted until too late by Slidell and other Administration men, tried to force into the platform a slave-code plank which the majority would not accept. The motive of some in this attempt was disunion; the motive of the majority was their wish to stop Douglas. They wished to stop Douglas because they realized that the Freeport Doctrine meant the containment of slavery (so far as the existing domain of the United States went) just as surely as Republican doctrine meant it. Yancey was absurd when he said that the position of the Northern Democrats might convert the South into a great heaving volcano of passion and crime. The refusal to enact a slave-code for Territories opposed to slavery would not excite servile insurrections. But Yancey was right when he said that basically two different assumptions were in conflict. The South contended that slavery was a good and should be protected in any possible expansion. Most Northern Democrats held that slavery was an evil and should be restricted. Republican restriction by Congress and Douglasite restriction by popular sovereignty came to the same practical result. The cotton States men would not accept either type of containment.

Containment—or disunion! It had at last come to this naked issue. This was the fundamental question which underlay the Charleston schism. The South had refused to let the Wilmot Proviso be applied to lands won from Mexico, for that would have meant containment. It had blocked the organization of Kansas Territory without the free entry of slavery, for that would have meant containment. It was now rejecting the Freeport Doctrine as another name for containment. When Yancey called upon Pugh, Stuart, and other Douglas leaders to accept his assumption that slavery was a positive good, he was appealing to the bar of history. When Pugh declared that the Northern Democracy would never do it, he too was appealing to the bar of history. No question whatever exists as to the verdict which history, in the light of man's advancing concepts of social morality, has passed upon the two rival assumptions.

But disaster and twilight for the Democratic organization spelled opportunity and morning radiance for its great rival the Republican Party.

Sunrise in Chicago

THE DELEGATES and spectators who poured into Chicago in the third week of May, 1860, came with a spirit and to a scene which stood in startling contrast with Charleston. The spirit was one of complete confidence. When the chairman of the convention lifted the gavel, made of oak from Commodore Perry's flagship at the battle of Lake Erie, he remarked: "All the auguries are that we shall meet the enemy and they shall be ours." The scene was typical of the rough, exuberant, progressive outlook of the West. A city of a hundred and ten thousand people, of a dozen busy railroads, of meat-packing plants, grain elevators, foundries, and farm implement factories, suddenly swarmed with literally tens of thousands of visitors, full of gaiety, energy, and enthusiasm. They had a Western earnestness, too. "What seems a brilliant festival," wrote one journalist, "is but the rally for battle; it is an army with banners."

Across the page of party history falls the light of a great name, illuminating every recoverable detail. We know much more about the Republican convention and campaign of 1860 than about any similar events of the era, for they brought into power one of the nation's immortal leaders. But to the delegations which arrived by special trains and Lake boats, to political clubs which paraded with flaring torches, to the crashing bands and excited throngs, Lincoln's name was only one of a dozen under consideration—and not the most important. One reason for the sanguine mood of the party lay in its wealth of chieftains—Seward well in front, but a group of strong men behind him. All that the host which met in Chicago knew at first was that this convention was unlike any thus far known in national history. It was greater in size, in enthusiasm, in noise, in wire-pulling, in self-righteousness, in lust for office, and in its blend of mass hysteria with idealistic fervor.

The gathering multitude—thousands from Wisconsin, from Indiana, from Ohio, six hundred on one train from Pennsylvania, as many on another from New York—could afford to be uncertain about the candidate. They were starting their campaign with many advantages. They could thank their foes for half a dozen great vote-winning issues; free homesteads, tariff revision, internal improvements, adequate Pacific communications, and departmental honesty. They could point to needed measures obstructed by Southern Democrats. They could assert that Buchanan's Administration was more inefficient and inept than even Pierce's. They could shake their heads over the corruption of Fowler and the laxity of Floyd. And, as a crowning gift, their opponents had torn the Democracy in twain! [1]

The Republicans, far better organized than in 1856, were ready to make the most of their advantages.[2] Delegates from every Northern State could tell of growing strength. They and their allies had twice swept Pennsylvania, where their doctrines continued to infiltrate Philadelphia and other populous centers. They had three times won the governorship in Ohio, where Salmon P. Chase, going to the Senate, was giving way to William Dennison. In Illinois, the party had not only put a Republican in the governor's mansion but had carried Chicago, Rockford, and Quincy, all normally Democratic, at the last city elections.[3] Indianians in Chicago recalled how Frémont might have carried that State in 1856 but for the votes of several thousand Irish railway workers, and predicted that the party would win in 1860. The national committee, led by Governor Morgan of New York, had learned much in recent years. It had displayed shrewdness in choosing Chicago as a salute to the West; in advancing the convention date to mid-May to yield an extra month for campaigning; and in raising money. In its official call it had included members of the People's Party of Pennsylvania and the Opposition Party of New Jersey, along with all others who were ready to uphold the Republican nominee.[4]

The party was fortunate, again, in that the Republican press was reaching the height of its influence. It possessed an array of editors—Bryant, Greeley, Bowles, Medill, Schouler—which the Democrats could not match, and it was steadily gaining adherents. Raymond's *Times* had veered to catch the Republican breeze. Bennett's *Herald* could seldom resist the temptation to choose the victorious side. Similar journals of the North, whether they felt the moral groundswell of the

1 An admirable general treatment of the convention is found in William E. Baringer, *Lincoln's Rise to Power*; see also Reinhard H. Luthin, *The First Lincoln Campaign*; P. O. Ray, *The Convention That Nominated Lincoln*; Murat Halstead, *Caucuses of 1860*; O. H. Oldroyd, *Lincoln's Campaign; or, The Political Revolution of 1860*; Thomas H. Dudley, "The Inside Facts of Lincoln's Nomination," *Century Magazine*, 1890, 477 ff.

2 Lyman Trumbull and Zachariah Chandler had been active during 1859 in an organized plan of Republican publicity, furnishing prepared articles to the press, and franking out large quantities of documents. For this work a Mr. Dodd had raised funds. Lyman Trumbull to Chandler, April 4, 1859; Chandler Papers. The chief authors of the articles, which dealt with the tariff, homestead, slavery, and Democratic extravagance and corruption, were Frank P. Blair, Montgomery Blair, and George M. Weston. Trumbull wrote friendly editors asking them to publish the articles, which were then reissued in pamphlet form. See Trumbull to Thurlow Weed, April 11, 1859; Stuart Collection, HL.

3 Cole, *Era of Civil War*, 182.

4 MS Journal, NYHS.

Friends of Republicanism:

This town is the County Seat, with about 1,400 inhabitants, and is destined to be a city of first rank. Upon the opening of the Illinois Southern Railroad, its natural advantages for manufacturing purposes, which are not surpassed by any place in our land, will be developed, and thus hasten a rapid growth. Capitalists predict this will be a Western "Lowell," in the "Eden," of our nation. All who are acquainted with Southern Illinois say that no part of the country offers such inducements to the enterprising emigrant as this. Ere long, this beautiful section of our Republic will be filled up with representatives of many nations.

The above facts as regards our town, are stated only to impress upon the reader that we are a centre of influence, and ought to be in a position to do all we would like to for the cause in the midst of "Egypt," and could, had we the pecuniary ability. It must be remembered that this is the District represented by John A. Logan in Congress, who claims it (and with truth) as the Banner Democratic District of the Union. Is any other statement necessary to prove that we are in great political darkness, when John A. Logan can boast of 13,000 majority? We will reduce it some four or five thousand this Fall, we hope. "Old Abe," has many friends in Southern Illinois, yet there is a great want of ordinary political intelligence among the masses. One specimen, of many I could give, will suffice to show who hurrah for Douglas and boast of their Democracy. A few weeks after the Chicago Convention a prominent person in the community (in a position to pre-suppose ordinary intelligence upon the current matters of the day,) asked who the Republicans had nominated? Abraham Lincoln, was the answer. Well, who is He? The man who contested the State in 1858 with Douglas? Well, who is Douglas?

I ask, how are we to overcome such stupidity except by constant, patient laboring—"Here a little and there a little," &c. There are many Third Party men who will be with us in November, if we can reach them, meanwhile, by the Press and Documents, and School District laboring. The masses are honest, but often deluded by designing demagogues. Judge Bates' letter is doing much good where it is read; but is a fact that we have only three Republican papers south of the Ohio and Mississippi Railroad, with an aggregate circulation of not over 1,500. Now, do we not need help? Please remember that most of our present Republican strength we have obtained within a year or two, and of course does not know *how to do*, as we might wish it would; so we must have the aid of outside friends—if we have it betimes, we shall, ere long, redeem "Egypt" to light and political purity.

For our encouragement, I will state that in this precinct, in 1856, we had but 8 votes, now we have over 150—in some of our counties not a vote for Fremont, now we can count over 400—and so on all over Southern Illinois. Is not this a hopeful field? We ask that whoever can, will send forward all the documents possible pertaining to Republicanism and our Candidates. I *earnestly* request that every person who reads this, will at least send me a number of each paper published in his section, of every party, that we may, by reference to their fallacies, learn their fallacies, and use those of our party as campaign documents. It is astonishing how many will read a newspaper before it is worn out—often we can reach our most bitter opponents by giving them a paper, when a document they will reject.

If you can do nothing more, send Fifty cents to George Harrington, Secretary of the Republican committee, Washington, D. C., and ask him to send its worth in documents, for "Egypt." Also, you may send to the Young Men's Republican Union, 659 Broadway, New York—Charles T. Rodgers, President—to forward the value of documents of their publications, to the amount you may remit them, as we would like to have at least,not less than 100,000 of the right documents.

You will see that unless we are aided by our friends, we will be greatly hindered in the good work. Any of the campaign documents published by the New York *Tribune* would be greatfully received, as they are *very good*. Any one who will repay by correspondence

Induce your Republican Editors to send for the campaign a copy or more of their papers, and we will repay by correspondence from our field. Let it be known that this place is the largest in Southeastern Illinois, and about ten counties can be reached through us. If this be represented to Republican organizations where our cause is strong, they will feel inclined to subscribe for clubs of the *Tribune*, *Evening Post* or any good paper to enlighten "Egypt."

I have shown how any one who may wish to *do* something for "Lincoln and Hamlin," "Free Press, Free Speech, Free Soil, and Liberty and Union, can, *if he will.*

We would be happy to have a personal reply from you, sir, in regard to the prospects in your field of operations. It will serve to encourage our friends here to hear from elsewhere the "Nation o'er."

GEORGE P. EDGAR, *Corresponding Secretary.*

A Republican Organizer Uses Greeley and Bryant to Convert "Egypt."

231

freesoil movement, or were disgusted with the Pierce-Buchanan record, or wished to stand with the winners, were enlisting with the party of the future. What gave power over opinion to the great Republican journals—the New York *Tribune* and *Evening Post*, the Springfield *Republican*, the Philadelphia *Press*, the Cleveland *Leader*, and the Chicago *Tribune*—was the homogeneity of their audiences, the vogue of their weekly editions in village and country, and the power with which they combined editorial argument and news-gathering vigor.

Typical of them all in some ways and uniquely distinguished in others, was Greeley's *Tribune*—a splendidly equipped fighting unit. It covered the events of each day thoroughly; its Washington correspondence, by Dana, J. S. Pike, or "H. G." himself, was expert, colorful, and stingingly antislavery; its western intelligence was full and firmly agrarian in tone; its editors displayed a keen instinct for events and documents—a Congressional affray, a Tammany demonstration, a London *Times* leader—which served their ends; and the editorial page, written by Greeley, Dana, George Ripley, C. T. Congdon, and others, was a magnificent combination of argument, invective, and news. The issue of the *Weekly Tribune* which opened its twentieth year (April 14, 1860) was a typical production. Its front page contained, along with Albany and European news, a three-and-a-half-column article on the antislavery excitement in North Carolina and the trial of Daniel Worth for circulating Helper's book. Other contents included a House committee report in defense of the Covode investigation, London comment on a speech by Seward, a manifesto of Cassius M. Clay to Kentuckians, a speech by Congressman Lovejoy, and a Washington letter on Douglas's effort to win delegates. The editorials ranged from foreign policy and the homestead issue to sarcasm at the expense of Pollard's book on the Negro, *Black Diamonds*. Miscellaneous news articles dealt with the Pennsylvania oil fields, the Nevada silver mines, the Japanese mission to Washington, Illinois farming, and the author James K. Paulding, just dead. Such a newspaper was valuable enough to be passed from hand to hand and read from end to end, and could not but influence opinion.[5]

Systematic efforts were made by party organizers to augment the circulation of Republican sheets, while many clergymen allied with the new party encouraged the reading of the *National Era* and the *Independent*, both now powerful organs. Lyman Trumbull's correspondence is sprinkled with letters

5 The N. Y. *Tribune*, April 10, 1860, boasted that more than twenty-five new Democratic campaign sheets had been started expressly to counteract its influence. The Philadelphia *Press* was still nominally a Douglas sheet; but Forney was confidentially advising Thurlow Weed, who sent his information on to Lincoln—as the Robert Todd Lincoln Papers show. The *Pennsylvanian* of October 2 spoke of the *Press* as in the Republican interest.

from adherents describing the growing strength of the press. One rural Illinois correspondent had boasted in the summer of 1857, for example, that he had obtained more than three hundred subscribers for the Chicago *Tribune*, with a telling effect upon county sentiment. "I asked a gentleman the other day who has been taking it for about six months, how he liked it, his answer was, 'about twice as well as I ever intended to,' and then further remarked that some of his [Democratic] neighbors had been reading his paper, and that it had converted them also." Another adherent wrote Trumbull that whereas in 1856 not a copy of the *National Era* had come to his county, the close of 1857 found forty-five or fifty being circulated. Still other workers in southern Illinois wrote of promoting that ably-edited freesoil journal the *Missouri Democrat*. Horace Greeley offered his *Weekly Tribune* to clubs of twenty or more subscribers, using one address, at a dollar a year each, and other editors imitated him. The late fifties, we repeat, saw the freesoil press at its very apogee of energy and prosperity. Raymond's *Times* moved in 1858 into a handsome new building on Park Row; Greeley's *Tribune* the next year passed the 200,000 circulation mark; the *Evening Post* was making John Bigelow and Bryant rich men; the Philadelphia *Press* had become the chief Pennsylvania daily, and the Chicago *Tribune* was soon to reach a quarter of a million readers. The German-language press, too, had become a potent force in New York and the Middle West.

Facing a divided enemy, supported by a broadening freesoil sentiment, possessing so much effective ammunition and such powerful batteries to discharge it, the Republicans felt sanguine. But it was essential to make no blunder in candidate or platform.

[I]

When the year opened, the primacy of Seward had been universally conceded. He was the first choice not only of New York and New England, but of Michigan, Wisconsin, and Minnesota.[6] His enthusiastic reception on returning from Europe, and the general praise for his politic Senate speech of late February, had strengthened the confidence of Weed and other managers. Cool, calculating, and realistically informed, Weed believed his nomination certain.[7] Even the hostile Greeley, writing from Davenport, Iowa, in January, declared

6 Chase could possibly wait for a nomination; Seward could not. "It is now or never with him," wrote John Bigelow, who thought a stronger man should be named. "He does not mean to return to the Senate and he is fast becoming an old man." Paris, January 25, 1860; Blair-Lee Papers. The elder Blair told a friend that Seward wished Frank P. Blair, Jr., to be candidate for Vice-President on his ticket, and it is possible that Seward did make such overtures to the great border family. J. D. Andrews, July 16, 1859; Banks Papers, Illinois State Hist. Library.

7 Bancroft, *Seward*, I, 522.

that Seward enjoyed the preference of the Northwest.[8] His claims to the nomination on grounds of governmental experience, long service to the freesoil cause, and tested ability, seemed to outweigh those of anybody else.

Nevertheless, the field was crowded with possible candidates, for the new party had appealed so strongly to idealistic young men and had drawn so heavily upon the best Whig and freesoil Democratic talent that it was rich in ability. In the Northwest, wrote Greeley, many wished Lincoln's name on the ticket; everywhere, the merits of Bates, Dayton, Cameron, Chase, Banks, and others were canvassed; and a few suggested Frémont. The editor, convinced that Bates was the strongest figure, labored to prove that he could carry the borderland as well as the North. The Blairs also continued supporting Bates, and with them stood Gratz Brown, Orville Browning, and Schuyler Colfax. Bates himself was sanguine. "The signs indicating my nomination are growing in number and strength every day," he wrote in his diary on February 26. He hoped to be the nominee of both the Republicans and Constitutional Unionists. Simon Cameron had the initial support of the fluctuating New York *Herald*, strong-stomached Pennsylvanians, and scattered protectionists elsewhere. While many New Englanders, including Samuel Bowles, gave lukewarm recommendation to Banks, most Ohioans stood behind the very smooth Chase or the very rough Ben Wade.

Had the nomination been bestowed for length and power of freesoil service or proved capacity in important office, only Seward and Chase would have been considered. Political expediency, however, had to be weighed. The party being young, in such States as Pennsylvania and New Jersey devotion to its principles was not yet well established; for these States were as conservative as New England and the upper Northwest were radical. Special predilections and antagonisms likewise had to be regarded: the dislike of many former Whigs for Chase as a former Democrat, the opposition of Greeley, Bryant, and Bowles to Seward, the belief of many German-Americans that Bates had once leaned toward the Know-Nothings, the desire of many Yankees for a radical antislavery man, and the insistence of most border men upon a moderate nominee. The Republican Party is beset with difficulties, wrote a brilliant young Connecticut Representative, O. S. Ferry. Without the radical Yankees and Germans of Michigan, Wisconsin, and northern Illinois it might lose the Northwest, while if it meets the wishes of this wing, it will repel voters in the Middle States.[9]

The more prominent the aspirant, the more numerous were the objections to him. Seward, as marshal of the Republican forces in the Senate, a longtime champion of the alien-born, and the leading advocate of internal improvements and higher tariffs, had a legion of friends. But he also had countless enemies. His

8 N. Y. *Weekly Tribune*, February 11, 1860.
9 To Gideon Welles, March 1, 1860; Welles Papers .

irrepressible-conflict speech still alarmed the conservatives.[10] His devious ways and fits-and-starts leadership had offended men of iron conviction. Former Democrats, remembering him as the principal lieutenant of President Zachary Taylor, distrusted him. Were he elected, prophesied Bryant, it would be a special favor of Providence if every honest Democrat in the new party were not driven into opposition within a year. His quarter-century partnership with Weed had long been hurtful, for everyone knew that Lord Thurlow's ostentatious show of unselfishness in declining office masked an insatiable appetite for other rewards. In the last legislative session, Weed had damaged the Senator fearfully by helping engineer the corrupt passage of six street-railway bills which gridironed half a hundred New York streets without conditions as to compensation, tenure, or fares. Raymond, Greeley, and Governor Morgan unsparingly denounced this scheme, the object being, Bryant wrote, to get the franchise-recipients "to furnish a fund of from four to six hundred thousand dollars, to be expended for the Republican cause in the next presidential election." [11] How could Seward be sent to the White House without sending Weed there too?

There was something deeply pathetic in Seward's position. He had toiled so long for the Presidency, first among the Whigs, then the Republicans. His expectations were so confident; he had spoken all spring as if his nomination were certain, throwing his house open in elaborate entertainments and keeping in touch with powerful economic interests in New York which desired his election. When he left the capital for Auburn on the eve of the convention, he told friends that he expected to return in a much higher capacity. The feeling among most Republican Congressmen was that he would almost surely be nominated—and that his nomination would be a disaster to the party.[12] It was not his fault that the legislature, with which he did not have even a Spenlow & Jorkins connection, had been corrupt. Yet many now believed that if the party nominated him it would lose the shining advantage which it drew from Covode's exposures of Democratic venality. Nor was it Seward's fault—altogether—that his radicalism with respect to slavery was grossly exaggerated. While his higher-law and irrepressible conflict speeches had been indiscreet, his usual temper was moderate; indeed, many who were truly radical distrusted him as a trimmer. Yet some of the mud thrown after the John Brown raid inevitably clung to his garments.

10 Numerous expressions of conservative Republican feeling in southern and central Illinois against Seward may be found in the Lyman Trumbull Papers. Even Stephen T. Logan did not know whether he could vote for him. Our people, wrote a Peoria citizen, are generally moderate men, opposed to extremes—neither abolitionists nor nullifiers. Seward's nomination, declared a Collinsville citizen, would place success beyond hope. Trumbull Papers, April–May, 1860.
11 W. C. Bryant to John Bigelow, December 14, 1859, Bigelow Papers; Nevins, Evening Post, 261, 262; Van Deusen, Weed, 245–248.
12 J. S. Pike in N. Y. Weekly Tribune, May 26, 1860.

And those who opposed him for mistaken reasons were reinforced by a good many whose reasons were quite definite. As Hamilton Fish wrote, for twenty years Seward had sown innumerable seeds of selfishness which were now springing up to choke his hopes.[13]

The Republican victory in Connecticut in April, 1860, had the curious effect of injuring Seward's chances—simply because it was so close. The little State had seethed with excitement; both sides had spent money by the bucketfull. Observers called the contest a Presidential election in miniature. Governor W. A. Buckingham was reelected—but by a plurality of only 541. Had he been a man of more extreme views, he would have lost. In Rhode Island, simultaneously, a wealthy young Democratic manufacturer was chosen governor over a Republican whose tenets came close to abolitionism. The Hartford *Courant* expressed the hope that the Republicans of the nation would take warning, and turn away from any "ultra" leader.[14]

Salmon P. Chase, a man of intellectual vigor, spotless character, and commanding physique, had been one of the first of the nation's leading statesmen to identify himself with the Republicans, and had done so when the step took courage. He possessed a clear head, an inflexible will, and a cultivation which impressed young William Dean Howells. If, like Seward, he seemed somewhat devious, it was not from any lack of conviction, but because he had too keen an eye to the main chance. He had flirted with the Know-Nothings when that seemed advantageous and with the foreign-born when that appeared helpful. Cold, dignified, aloof, he had never attracted hearty allies nor constructed an effective personal organization. Though burning with Presidential ambitions, he had no party managers, no important editors, and no Congressional friends to push him forward. We have seen that he made no secret of his hopes, and that in March, 1860, Carl Schurz had frankly told him they were impossible. Undiscouraged, Chase traveled to Washington the following month to seek friends among the easterners and to urge Ben Wade to withdraw his troublesome candidacy. He was received frigidly, got nowhere with Wade, and heard his friend, Dr. Gamaliel Bailey, urge him to withdraw in Seward's favor. Nevertheless, he remained hopeful. The fact that as a former Democrat he was distrusted on the tariff question was not enough in itself to disqualify him, but he lacked any advantages sufficient to offset that handicap.

One of Lincoln's Washington friends, J. M. Lucas, sent him a vivid picture of Chase bustling about on the floor of the House to enlist support; his usual cold and stoic aspect was replaced for the nonce by the cheeriest and most genial smiles, and the friendliest and most obliging manner. This struck Lucas and

13 Nevins, *Hamilton Fish*, 78.
14 Springfield *Republican*, March 26–April 7, 1860; Hartford *Courant*, April 7, 1860; S. G. Buckingham, *William A. Buckingham*, 43 ff.

others as hypocritical, for they knew that Chase was by nature chill, calculating, and selfish, uniting a powerful intellect with still more powerful ambition. It was not in the man to make devoted followers. One Ohio observer defined his shortcomings bluntly: "Chase is too supremely selfish to be popular or to have any devoted personal friends among men of sense who know him thoroughly but this is not his worst misfortune. I will not say that he cannot distinguish between a sycophant and a friend but I will say that he ever preferred the former and every one of his entire political helpers that I know belongs to the class of cheats or nincompoops." It is not strange that Ohioans looked to other men for a Presidential nominee—not a few of them to Lincoln. The proud, sensitive Chase was deeply wounded by the divisions in his own State, and by the plain disposition of many politicians there to prefer Joshua Giddings, Ben Wade, or some rank outsider.[15]

The dapper, adroit N. P. Banks, with his somewhat commonplace mind, the wealthy, unprincipled Simon Cameron, the ignorant, profane Ben Wade, and the drab septuagenarian John McLean were all receptive and all impossible. Banks, by failing to oppose an amendment to the Massachusetts constitution which unreasonably deferred the grant of the ballot to naturalized citizens, had destroyed what little chance he had ever possessed. To nominate Cameron would have been to select a crass businessman, a turncoat politician, and the head of one of the most notoriously venal of State machines. McLean, a legalistic old fogy, was obviously standing on the edge of his grave. As for Wade, a self-made man whose blustering egotism had carried him into a Senate seat which might better have gone to Joshua Giddings, he had great force and genuine ability; but he would have required schooling of several kinds to make him fit for the White House.[16]

For a time, at the beginning of 1860, it had seemed that the only leader likely to be strong enough to defeat Seward was Bates of Missouri. A former Clay Whig, as hostile to slavery as his great mentor, he would command the votes of many border State citizens who wanted a safe, tactful, and sagacious Unionist.[17] John Minor Botts, naked-sword enemy of secessionist "conspirators," had said

15 Lucas, May 6, 1860, Robert Todd Lincoln Papers; J. M. Root, May 26, 1860, Chase, May 10, 1860, Giddings Papers, Ohio Arch. and Hist. Soc.

16 Frémont was never seriously considered, even the Blairs, once his closest political friends, having dropped him. A story of a sort all too commonly alleged against prominent political leaders and probably not true was sometimes mentioned; see Preston King, March 3, 1860, Gideon Welles Papers, LC.

17 Some influential men thought that the Republican Party was moving to the right and hence could well take Bates. This was the view of James S. Rollins of Missouri, who wrote J. O. Brodhead of that State: ". . . the truth is, as you remark, the Republicans have greatly moderated their views; in fact, they differ in no very essential particular, on the subject of slavery, from the Whigs; they entertain now, almost the precise view, which Henry Clay reiterated hundreds of times, whilst living." This could indeed be said of Republicans like Lincoln; not of Republicans like Wade, Chandler, or Sumner. J. S. Rollins, February 1, 1860; Brodhead Papers.

in Virginia's Opposition convention early in 1859 that if the Republicans should nominate Crittenden, Bell, or Bates, the candidate would actually poll a large slave State vote. This was true. Western Virginia, for example, now had three good weekly Republican newspapers and one daily, while Wheeling had enough Republicans to justify a proposal that the Republican National Convention be held there.[18] If Bell and Crittenden were out of the question, Bates was not. Charles A. Dana was typical of many ardent young Republicans who believed their best chance lay with the grave Missourian. "It is either Bates or Seward," he had written James S. Pike. "I can't see any third chance. The Northwest won't have Chase. With Seward we are dead, beaten. He can't carry Ind., Ill., Penn., or N. J. With Bates we can carry Missouri certainly; Maryland and Tennessee probably. He may be elected. No one else can. That is the beginning, middle, and end of the story." [19] When Greeley returned from his Far Western tour in the fall of 1859, the *Tribune* adopted Bates with earnestness if not precisely enthusiasm. A flattering sketch of the public services of the sage of Grape Hill (Bates's residence four miles outside St. Louis) blossomed in the paper early in February; and thereafter, though refraining from explicit endorsement, it gave more space to his claims than to those of any other candidate.[20] The Baltimore *Patriot* gave him early support.

One difficulty was that, since Bates had for years given all his energy to legal and judicial work, he was little known in the East. At the time of Botts's speech, the New York press had felt it necessary to identify him.[21] But as newspapers by dozens from Massachusetts to Oregon gradually placed his name at their mastheads, his personality became known. Another difficulty was that he had long treated the slavery issue as a mere exciting device of politicians to keep themselves in power. Seeing that it was necessary to rectify this position, he published a letter to Missouri delegates to the Chicago convention which had the right freesoil ring. He made it clear that he detested slavery, opposed its extension, denied that the Constitution carried it into the Territories, and held that the Dred Scott decision had no validity beyond affirming the incapacity of a Negro to sue in the Missouri courts. Going further, he pronounced in favor of the

18 J. C. Underwood to Welles, April 9, 1859; Welles Papers, LC. Underwood, an officer of the American Emigrant Aid & Homestead Co., wrote that the operations of this company had produced a marvelous change in Western Virginia in the previous two years. "Instead of my blood or banishment being demanded as in 1856 I have been feasted and serenaded and invited to make public speeches in the principal towns."

19 Charles A. Dana to Pike, August 25, 1859; Pike Papers.

20 Crawford *Journal*, quoted in N. Y. *Weekly Tribune*, February 11, 1860. "If Bates cannot be nominated," wrote Greeley, whose political judgment was often deplorable, to Schuyler Colfax, "I think our next man is Dayton." Greeley reported from the West that Banks would not do: "The odor of Americanism without the support of Americans." February 3, 1860; Greeley-Colfax.

21 Cf. N. Y. *Weekly Tribune*, February 26, 1859.

building of a Pacific railroad, the passage of homestead legislation, and the immediate admission of Kansas.[22] These sentiments, as the Blairs and other friends exultantly remarked, were as unequivocally Republican as those of any leader.[23]

Yet Bates, too, had his weaknesses, and opponents thrust fiercely at the joints of his armor. While most Missouri Germans knew that he had supported Fillmore in 1856 for reasons quite unconnected with the Know-Nothing platform, many foreign-born voters outside the State viewed his stand in that year resentfully. When the Missouri Republican convention met in March, a German-American demonstration against him disturbed observers in far-away areas. Inasmuch as we depend on the Germans to help carry the western States, wrote E. C. Smith to the economist Henry C. Carey, this ebullition of feeling ought to be conclusive against his nomination.[24] Lyman Trumbull heard from well-informed politicians in the West, such as Gustave Koerner in Illinois and John G. Stephenson in Indiana, that the Germans and Scandinavians would never accept Bates.[25] Germans of Davenport, Iowa, held a meeting in March which formally resolved that his nomination would imply such a desertion of principle that it would compel them to forsake the party. At the same time, the conservatism of the Missourian chilled ardent Republicans who pronounced him an old granny or a wet blanket.[26] Fitz-Henry Warren of the New York *Tribune* spoke for many young men when he said that to carry Pennsylvania, New Jersey, and Indiana he would go almost anywhere for a leader, but not into a cemetery or catacomb.[27] The Chicago *Tribune* warned the party that the selection of Bates would estrange its entire radical wing.[28]

Thus, although on the eve of the convention Seward appeared the leading figure, he lacked the vital quality of "availability" in the conservative States, and although Bates was the chief secondary aspirant, he was equally deficient in "availability" in the radical States. Seward's confidence continued undiminished. On the day that the Chicago convention began its balloting, his friends placed a cannon on his lawn to roar the expected news of his triumph. Bates's hopes ran almost as high. His diary shows that he believed that he was the only man who could carry Missouri and other border areas for the Republicans.[29] Yet no aspirant had a really commanding lead.

22 *Missouri Democrat*, March 21, 1860.
23 N. Y. *Weekly Tribune*, March 31, 1860.
24 E. C. Smith to Carey, March 14, 1860; Carey Papers.
25 J. G. Stephenson, March 25, Gustave Koerner, April 16, 1860; Trumbull Papers.
26 G. A. Nourse, May 13, 1860; Trumbull Papers. E. L. Pierce, April 20, 1860; Sumner Papers.
27 Pike, *First Blows of the Civil War*, 484.
28 Chicago *Tribune*, March 15, 1860.
29 Bates, *Diary*, 105, 106, 122, 127.

[II]

It was this fluidity of the situation which gave opportunity for a new standard bearer whose armor was tighter than that of Seward, Chase, or Bates, and who stood midway between the radical and conservative wings of the party. The Democratic schism in Charleston had helped to make the outcome of the convention unpredictable. It opened up brilliant vistas of success, but it also left visible some menacing dangers. Most cool observers expected, to begin with, that the Democrats would reunite in Baltimore. In the second place, the Constitutional Union convention, meeting May 9, nominated John Bell and Edward Everett on a platform which seemed certain to appeal to the broad belt of border States. Obviously, the election might be thrown into Congress and thus lost to the Republicans. They must find a leader who would minimize the chances of such a catastrophe.

Without foreseeing the outlines of this situation, Lincoln throughout 1859 had done much to meet it. Although not flagrantly pursuing the nomination, he had prepared the Party to give him serious consideration.[30] During the year, he had traveled four thousand miles to deliver twenty-three political speeches, every one of which he might easily have avoided. His friends' plan, in which he acquiesced, was to make him the second choice of as many delegations as possible. He had written numerous letters to men of potential political usefulness. In December, he had sent a group of influential Ohioans a carefully prepared manuscript of the Douglas-Lincoln debates (mainly clipped and pasted reports) for immediate publication. That same month he had written his short autobiography for Jesse Fell, corresponding secretary of the Illinois Republican Committee, to use in promoting his ambitions. He was gratified when a Pennsylvania newspaper, the Reading *Journal*, declared that the West might successfully bring Honest Old Abe forward as its candidate; and when an energetic young newspaperman of West Urbana (now Champaign), William O. Stoddard, used his four-page weekly, the *Central Illinois Gazette*, to boom Lincoln as the man who could carry the Mississippi Valley in a rush of popular enthusiasm. As the *Illinois State Journal* took up the cry, Springfield in January witnessed the formation of a Lincoln Club.

The last week of that month found a number of the best lawyer-politicians of Illinois in the capital to plead before the Supreme Court and Federal Court. Under the guidance of Jackson Grimshaw of Quincy, a dozen of them, including secretary of state O. M. Hatch, Leonard Swett, and State Chairman Norman Judd, who had just returned from Washington, met with Lincoln to discuss

30 Baringer, *Lincoln's Rise to Power*, 159.

plans for gaining him the nomination. After a night and day of reflection,
ror modesty made him hesitate, he authorized them to place him in the
field.[31]

It was significant of Lincoln's sagacity that, when Grimshaw asked if his
friends might, on finding the Presidency unattainable, press him for the Vice-
Presidential nomination, he replied emphatically: "No!" He thus set his face
firmly against the kind of dicker that might end in a Seward-Lincoln or
Cameron-Lincoln ticket. It was the highest type of strategy to insist on first
place or nothing.[32] Actually, he was not very hopeful. He wrote Norman Judd
early in February: "I am not in a position where it would hurt much for me not
to be nominated on the national ticket; but I am where it would hurt some for
me not to get the Illinois delegates." [33] He meant that it would hurt his prospects
for a future senatorial seat. He was anxious to keep his path open in either
direction; to the Presidency if possible, to the Senate if not. Judd, conferring
with him, suggested an avoidance of controversial local efforts to get delegates
distinctly pledged to him, leaving it to State pride to carry resolutions of instruction through the Decatur convention.

While Buchanan was letting the Democratic Party be disrupted, Lincoln
had been worrying over the problem of maintaining Republican unity. "Massachusetts Republicans," he had written, "should have looked beyond their noses,
and then they could not have failed to see that tilting against foreigners would
ruin us in the whole Northwest. New Hampshire and Ohio should forbear tilting against the Fugitive Slave law in such a way as to utterly overwhelm us in
Illinois with the charges of enmity to the Constitution itself. Kansas, in her confidence that she can be saved to freedom on 'squatter sovereignty,' ought not to
forget that to prevent the spread and nationalism of slavery is a national concern
and must be attended to by the nation."

On February 16, the powerful Chicago *Tribune* came out editorially in Lincoln's behalf, as a man equal in ability to any yet named, and more nearly certain
than anybody else to carry Illinois and Indiana. Moreover, the *Tribune* urged
careful organization; Lincoln clubs should be formed in every precinct, town-
ship, and city ward in the State.[34] Though belated in its championship of the
Springfield attorney, the newspaper quickly struck some hard blows for him.
Young Joseph Medill, part owner and at this moment Washington correspondent, wrote a long letter from the national capital, published February 27, in
which he argued that as a leader midway between the radical Seward and the
conservative Bates, Lincoln could hew his way to party victory. The journalist

31 *Idem.*, 142, 143.
32 Jackson Grimshaw in Herndon-Weik, *Lincoln*, II, 366.
33 Lincoln, *Works*, I, 598; February 9, 1860.
34 Baringer, *Lincoln's Rise to Power*, 140, 150.

showed it to Republican politicians in Washington, and Seward, seeing it, expostulated vigorously.[35]

Then came the Cooper Union address, already described. The accident of its delivery immediately after Seward's long-studied Senate speech made it (in a sense) a trial of strength with him, as the debates of 1858 had been a trial of strength with Douglas. The millions—for literally they were millions—who read Seward's and Lincoln's efforts together could have no doubt that the prairie statesman, as Seward condescendingly called him, had the more sinewy mind, the surer touch on political realities, and the stronger moral impulse.

In the New England tour which followed, undertaken primarily because he wished to see his son Robert at Phillips Exeter Academy in New Hampshire, Lincoln made speeches in New Haven, Hartford, Providence, Concord, and other towns. At Manchester, New Hampshire, he was presented as the next President of the United States; at Norwich, Connecticut, as the next Vice-President. All his speeches were effective, and that at Hartford was very able. Gideon Welles was much impressed by Lincoln on his visit to the Connecticut capital. After talking with him for an hour in the *Evening Press* office, Welles wrote editorially that Lincoln had been caricatured—that if not Apollo, neither was he Caliban. "He was made where the material for strong men is plenty, and his huge, tall frame is loosely thrown together. He is in every way large, brain included, but his countenance shows intellect, generosity, great good nature, and keen discrimination. He is an effective speaker, because he is earnest, strong, honest, simple in style, and clear as crystal in his logic." That the New England speeches assisted the Cooper Union address in making the Illinoisan much better known in the East than before is unquestionable. Whether they did anything more—whether, for example, a New Hampshire writer is justified in stating that the Concord speech did much to mould sentiment throughout the State in Lincoln's favor—is dubious.

These New England speeches were devoted exclusively, as Lincoln's audiences expected, to the slavery issue. To be sure, he adverted to current troubles in the shoe industry, defending labor's right to strike. Even this, however, bore upon the problem of slavery: "I like the system which lets a man quit when he wants to, and wish it might prevail everywhere." More emphatically than ever before, he spoke of the economic importance of the Southern institution. Involving at least two billion dollars' worth of human property, he remarked, it naturally aroused a strong protective instinct among slaveholders. He also dwelt upon both the magnitude and the irrepressibility of the issue. With one-sixth of the population of the land held to forced labor, how could so great a problem

35 Philip Kinsley, *Chicago Tribune*, I, 105–110; H. I. Cleveland in *Saturday Evening Post*, Vol. 172, pp. 84, 85.

be ignored? Southerners said that if they were just let alone, they would quickly solve it. But essentially they *were* let alone, and they did nothing. Since the system touched the vital future of the nation and its standing in the world, the North simply had to discuss it. "If slavery is right, it ought to be extended; if not, it ought to be restricted—there is no middle ground." All previous efforts to deal with the issue, said Lincoln, had proved failures—partly because they had been small efforts, a plaster too tiny to cover the sore. The Republican plan of restriction, he implied, would be adequate.

Once more, fault could have been found with Lincoln for not saying what he wished done with slavery once it had been bound within an immovable ring— for he certainly hoped for some gradual type of national action. And once more, Lincoln could have replied that one step at a time was enough, and that if the South agreed to restriction it would by implication agree to reasonable further measures. He said he would not act rashly. If he saw a venomous snake crawling in the road, he declared, he would seize a club and kill it; but if he found the snake in bed with his children, that would be a different matter.

Even before Lincoln's eastern appearances, his swelling correspondence showed that he had become a national figure. Particularly after his speeches of 1859 in Ohio and other States, letters had come from political leaders all over the North. Tom Corwin wrote him repeatedly on national affairs. Lincoln exchanged confidential views with Frank P. Blair, Jr., who thought his Columbus speech the best answer yet made to Douglas. Thurlow Weed, for some obscure purpose of his own, had telegraphed Norman B. Judd on October 20, 1859: "Send Abraham Lincoln to Albany immediately." Of course Lincoln did not go. Horace Rublee, half-owner of the *Wisconsin State Journal* and head of the Wisconsin State Committee, sent messages indicating that he had become a warm admirer. From James Speed, a distinguished Louisville lawyer who would later become Attorney-General, came assurances that he would have been glad to see Lincoln in the Senate: "I feel that our rights and institutions would not have been in jeopardy in your hands." The prominent Ohio politician, Samuel Galloway, who felt that Chase would never do, urged the Illinoisan to be unobtrusive but receptive. "Your visit to Ohio has excited an extensive interest in your favor," he wrote on October 13, 1859. Long before the year 1860 began, State Chairman Judd and Editor Ray of the Chicago *Tribune* had concluded that Lincoln would probably be on the next Presidential ticket either in first or second place. And mixed with communications from all the men named we find in the long-sealed papers of Robert Todd Lincoln numerous complimentary letters from obscure people all over the map.

"If I have any chance," wrote Lincoln on March 15, 1860, "it consists mainly in the fact that the whole opposition (*to the Democrats*) would vote for me if nominated." This was in response to Samuel Galloway, who agreed with other Ohio leaders that Lincoln would best satisfy sentiment in their State. During March and April the correspondence of the Springfield attorney was filled with encouraging letters. James F. Babcock of New Haven wrote of the great impression he had made in Connecticut. "Since the [State] election I have heard your name mentioned more freely than ever in connection with the Chicago nominations, and by some who have had other views. . . ." Lyman Trumbull, remarking that Seward seemed very confident but that the situation was uncertain, added that Lincoln had made many friends by his eastern trip, and that nobody had spoken of his speeches but in the highest terms. In a subsequent letter of April 24, Trumbull reported that the Congressional delegations from Rhode Island, Connecticut, New Jersey, Pennsylvania (except Cameron), and Indiana all declared that Seward could never carry their States. David Davis described his conferences in Chicago with "Long John" Wentworth, both eager to see Lincoln named. And J. M. Lucas related that a gathering of fifteen men in a corner of the House of Representatives had taken a straw poll, with the result that seven proved to be for Lincoln, the rest for various aspirants.

It was now easier for the Chicago *Tribune* to declare that no man had ever risen so rapidly to political eminence as Lincoln; easier for scattered eastern sheets to speak of his nomination as a possibility. His principal strength remained in the Northwest, however, and the main result of the New York and New England successes was a reflex effect among more enthusiastic and hopeful Westerners.

As great a turning point in Lincoln's career as the Cooper Union address was the unexpectedy fervent and even riotous State convention in Decatur on May 8, an event which imparted to his cause all the political revivalism of Jackson's and Harrison's day. Thus far nothing had dramatized to the nation the heroic character of Lincoln's rise from backwoods poverty. His years of struggle, while taken as a matter of course in the West where such stories were common, were almost unknown in the East. A versatile Decatur politician named Richard J. Oglesby, a veteran of the Mexican War and a forty-niner, realized that some touch was needed to give their candidate the picturesque and stirring appeal of "Old Hickory" and "Old Tippecanoe." He talked with patriarchal John Hanks, with whom Lincoln had toiled in early days to clear land. When Hanks spoke of rail splitting, Oglesby had an inspiration. The two men plucked from an old fence, twelve miles east of Decatur, two rails which Hanks identified as his and Lincoln's handiwork; Oglesby took some friends into his confidence; and when the convention met he was ready for a spectacular *coup*. Three thousand men, including six hundred delegates, crowded into the improvised convention hall. Amid a tremendous demonstration, Lincoln was lifted over the heads of the mass to a seat on the platform. Then, at the moment when emotion ran highest, down the central aisle marched bearded old

Lincoln Becomes the Railsplitter Candidate.

John Hanks and a fellow pioneer bearing two weather-beaten rails, flag-bedecked, with a great banner inscribed:

"Abraham Lincoln. The Rail Candidate For President in 1860. Two Rails From a Lot of 3,000 Made in 1830 by John Hanks and Abe Lincoln—Whose Father Was the First Pioneer of Macon County."

The storm of cheering, with hats, canes, and papers tossed aloft as the crowd surged and shouted, literally brought down part of the canvas roof of the structure. The uproar, continuing for fifteen minutes, was heard by all the wondering citizens of Decatur. Lincoln, yielding to the demand for a speech, explained how, when he first entered Illinois, he helped fell timber, make fences, and erect a cabin on the banks of the Sangamon. These might or might not be his own rails; at any rate, he had made many better ones! As a matter of fact, John Hanks's brother Charles presently wrote the Decatur *Magnet* that the original Lincoln fence had been burned up and replaced by new material. "I think, and am almost certain, that the rails that are now worshipped all over the North as Lincoln rails, were made by poor Bill Strickland, who is now old, blind, and helpless in the Macon County poorhouse." [36]

It had been anticipated that Norman B. Judd, the railroad official and attorney who had written the first city charter of Chicago and who had angrily abandoned the Democratic Party when the Nebraska bill was introduced, would be nominated for governor. Two other candidates, Leonard Swett and Richard Yates, however, obtained respectable support on the first three ballots, and on the fourth Swett released his delegates to Yates, giving the nomination to the eloquent Jacksonville lawyer. Taking the stand, Yates in a brilliant speech declared that he strongly favored the nomination of Lincoln for President. A committee on delegates to the Chicago convention being appointed, it repaired to a neighboring grove to make out its list. This was submitted to Lincoln, who revised it.[37] Thus closed the first day.

The next morning, John M. Palmer leaped to his feet with a resolution instructing the delegates in the Chicago convention to vote as a unit for Lincoln. When a spokesman for Seward's followers in northern Illinois objected, Palmer crushed him in an able speech. The Lincoln instructions were carried unanimously; four notable delegates at large were appointed—Judd, Gustave Koerner, David Davis, and Orville H. Browning; and after adopting a platform, the convention adjourned. It had greatly advanced Lincoln's chances. For one reason, the genuine enthusiasm at Decatur attracted attention all over the Middle West. For another, the carefully selected body of twenty-two delegates would make a hard sustained fight for Lincoln instead of voting briefly for him and then going over to another man. But above all, Oglesby's little drama which brought Lincoln before the country as the Rail Splitter, and thus identified him with all the pioneer virtues and the rousing cause of Free Labor, had a great and fast-widening psychological impact.[38]

The two rails that went down that Decatur aisle proved to be mighty levers. Democracy must be reborn in every generation; and who was so fit to bring about a rebirth in 1860 as this son of the West, who had advanced so rapidly from the axe and maul to leadership in expounding the best principles of the

36 Decatur *Magnet,* quoted in Havana, Illinois, *Squatter Sovereign,* July 21, 1860. See R. P. Morgan, "Birth of the Rail-Splitter Legend," in R. R. Wilson, ed., *Intimate Memories of Lincoln,* 260–267.

37 Arnold, *Lincoln,* 163.

38 Baringer, *Lincoln's Rise to Power,* 180–186.

new party? All over the country, already, men were reading a short biographical article on Lincoln which a Pennsylvania editor had based upon the autobiographical paper sent to Jesse Fell—a paper full of humanly appealing matter:

My paternal grandfather . . . was killed by the Indians. . . . My father . . . removed from Kentucky to what is now Spencer County, Indiana, in my eighth year. We reached our new home about the time the State came into the Union. It was a wild region, with many bears and other wild animals still in the woods. There I grew up. . . . Of course, when I came of age I did not know much. Still, somehow, I could read, write, and cipher to the rule of three, but that was all. I have not been to school since. The little advance I now have upon this store of education, I have picked up from time to time under the pressure of necessity. . . .

At twenty-one I came to Illinois, Macon County. Then I got to New Salem, at that time in Sangamon, now in Menard County, where I remained a year as a sort of clerk in a store. Then came the Black Hawk War; and I was elected a captain of volunteers, a success which gave me more pleasure than any I have had since. I went the campaign, was elated, ran for the legislature the same year (1832), and was beaten—the only time I ever have been beaten by the people.[39]

[III]

If the choice of Charleston as meeting place had been the most unfortunate in Democratic annals, that of Chicago can always be regarded as one of the happiest in Republican history. It was a recognition of the fast-growing strength of the prairies and their increasing attachment to Republican principles. The city was easily accessible by rail or lake, still charming in its semi-rural aspect, with wide dooryards and gardens, and fascinating in the bustling evidences of incessant activity and rapid growth. It now boasted of fourteen miles of dock frontage. From the cupola of the courthouse the visitor could see wide, flat vistas of wooden shops, lawns, and houses (even the magnate William B. Ogden lived in a large white frame dwelling, surrounded by fine trees); long rows of lumber yards on each side of the north and south branches of the Y-shaped Chicago River; out in the blue lake the new lighthouse, and long piers that sheltered steamers and sailboats; the new customhouse and post office; the roomy North Side Market, with drays discharging vegetables, meat, and fish; warehouses, breweries, the city water-works, and imposing hotels; and line after line of glistening tracks leading south, west, and east, all alive with smoking trains. Some delegates visited the shops lining Lake Street, where Potter Palmer's jewelry store was already famous; some dropped into the rooms of the Library Association which Walter L. Newberry had been chiefly instrumental in estab-

39 Lincoln, *Works*, I, 596, 597.

lishing, or the newly founded Historical Society; some went to the Board of Trade rooms to see samples of wheat, corn, sorghum, lumber, coal, and other Illinois products. Many inspected the modish North and South Side residential districts, where not a few families had grounds covering an entire block each.

Chicagoans had a go-ahead spirit. They had raised five thousand dollars, put a little army of carpenters at work on an empty lot at Market and Lake Streets, and thrown up what they called the largest auditorium in the country. The "Wigwam" was useful in itself and valuable as a symbol. Republican leaders hoped to fill the country with big and little wigwams housing party headquarters. The Chicago building, a hundred and eighty by a hundred feet, enclosed a broad wooden platform, a huge rectangular floor facing it, and a spacious gallery running around three sides—the whole seating about ten thousand people. Women of the city, called upon to decorate the building, had festooned the upright beams with bunting, rosettes, and evergreens. A great gilt eagle, a dozen portraits of American statesmen, and six busts adorned the platform. Raw and ugly as the hall was, its abundant windows gave plenty of air and light, its large exits permitted free movement, and it had well-nigh perfect acoustics. Gas lights were ready to furnish a brilliant evening illumination.[40]

Though Wednesday, May 16, was the date fixed for Governor Morgan to call the convention to order, by the previous Sunday the city was bursting with delegates, political friends, and sight-seers. Party leaders and city newspapers had persuaded the railroads to offer cheap excursion rates, while hotels had kept their charges reasonable. A sense that the hour of destiny had struck for the Party and that national history was to be made, together with the eager rivalry of Seward men, Chase men, Bates men, and all the others, brought hosts of onlookers from all quarters of the country and filled them with excitement.[41] All the chief buildings of the city rippled with flags and bunting in the bright May sunshine. Bands had blared on Saturday as the Wigwam was dedicated, and at dawn on Monday drum and bugle again filled the air. Hotel lobbies hummed like hives. Up and down the planked streets, greeted by sporadic bursts of cheering, tramped campaign clubs with banners, transparencies, and emblems. Everywhere, notabilities were being pointed out. Thurlow Weed, flanked by veterans like Moses H. Grinnell and James Watson Webb, with two brilliant young lieutenants, William M. Evarts and George William Curtis, opened headquarters for Seward at the Richmond House. David Davis rolled his portly

40 Caroline Kirkland, ed., *Chicago Yesterdays*, passim; for a Southern impression of Chicago, see N. O. *Picayune*, August 10, 1860; for Isaac H. Bromley's memories, *Scribner's Monthly*, November, 1893.

41 Charles Leib, a man peculiarly gifted in making enemies, had attached himself to Cameron. A. H. Reeder, March 10, 1860; Cameron Papers.

frame about the Lincoln headquarters in the Tremont, grunting placidly or snorting angrily as good or bad news came in; while Judd danced around talking with delegates, and Oglesby, Stephen T. Logan, Leonard Swett, and Joseph Medill conferred on strategy.[42]

It was soon evident, amid this bedlamite confusion, that a critical role would be played by what Party leaders called outside influences; that is, by rival cohorts of shouting, arguing, buttonholing men. The New York managers had brought from their home State thirteen cars of boisterous merrymakers who, with the pugilistic Tom Hyer at their head (men jested about Seward's Hyer-law platform), raised a thunderous racket. The Cameron managers had fetched in an almost equal number of Pennsylvanians, with two bands.[43] Michigan and Wisconsin had large contingents on hand, shouting, pleading, and threatening for Seward. St. Louis trains disgorged a wild body of Bates enthusiasts. It was obvious, however, that in cheering-power the Lincoln hosts held the advantage. Word had been circulated throughout the State that if friends of Old Abe wished to see him nominated, they should be on hand to create the requisite atmosphere of enthusiasm for his name. By thousands they had poured in from Danville, from Bloomington, from Springfield, from Peoria, from Quincy, from Rock Island. Many thousands more had mustered from Chicago and the belt of surrounding towns—Elgin, Aurora, Kankakee, Waukegan. The plan of David Davis's group was to give Lincoln a hundred votes on the first ballot, increase his roster steadily, and meanwhile release an irresistible mass enthusiasm in the hall.[44]

Long before the convention opened, the leaders of the rival groups were exerting themselves frenziedly to convert the wavering, to intimidate the fearful, to bargain with the purchasable, and to outmaneuver, outbluff, and outswap their opponents. Long before it began, delegates were being detached here and corralled there. It was plainly Seward against the field—and the Seward managers, encouraged by the Charleston debacle, were redoubling their efforts. Yet among the arrivals in Chicago were a surprising number of men who believed that it would be fatal to nominate the New Yorker. Given a seat by proxy from Oregon, Horace Greeley was early on the ground to spread doubt and objection. Gideon Welles of Connecticut arrived, armed in hostility to Seward by letters from Senator James Dixon, who stated two emphatic reasons for another candidate. First, Seward could not be elected; and second, if by some miracle he was, his elevation to the Presidency would be a disaster, for

42 Clark E. Carr, *The Illini*, 276.
43 Thomas A. Scott of the Pennsylvania Railroad secretly provided free transportation to Chicago for the entire Pennsylvania delegation and its attached persons, three hundred and seventy-six in all. Cameron Papers, April–May, 1860.
44 O. H. Oldroyd, *Lincoln's Campaign*, 71.

he was surrounded by corrupt rascals demanding free access to the treasury.[45] George Opdyke came from New York convinced that party interest demanded the naming of anybody but Seward.[46] Hannibal Hamlin of Maine, while esteeming the New York Senator personally, believed that it would be unwise to nominate him; he had been impressed by Lincoln's power in the debates with Douglas, and after reading the Cooper Union speech began persuading other Maine delegates that Lincoln would be a happy choice.[47]

Amos Tuck of New Hampshire, who had named Lincoln for Vice-President at the convention in 1856, was in Chicago, actively laboring among the New England delegates. He wrote Lincoln on Monday that he was sanguine. David Davis and Jesse Dubois were full of confidence. "We are quiet but moving heaven and earth," they telegraphed Lincoln the day before the opening. "Nothing will beat us but old fogy politicians. The hearts of the delegates are with us."

Nevertheless, as the eve of the convention found Chicago bursting at the seams with its crowds (fifteen hundred people slept in the Tremont House that Tuesday night), Seward maintained his lead. He was sure of more than one hundred and fifty votes on the first ballot out of the whole four hundred and sixty-six, while no other aspirant could count on more than fifty. Samuel Bowles summed up the situation with fair accuracy. Seward was absolutely certain of New York, Michigan, Wisconsin, and Minnesota; fairly certain of Iowa, California, and the greater part of New England. Against him in solid column stood Illinois, Indiana, Pennsylvania, and New Jersey, the leaders stoutly insisting that he could carry none of these States, and that, if he were nominated, the Bell-Everett ticket would make heavy inroads among the Republicans, defeating the party's State and Congressional tickets as well as its Presidential nominee.[48] The States of Ohio, Connecticut, Oregon, and Rhode Island inclined

45 Dixon to Gideon Welles, April 26, 1860; Welles Papers, LC. Dixon liked Seward personally, but wrote: "My apprehension is his administration would be the most corrupt the country has ever witnessed."
46 Opdyke to F. P. Blair, Jr., May 10, 1860; Blair-Lee Papers.
47 C. E. Hamlin, *Hannibal Hamlin*, 339–344. Young James G. Blaine, sent to Chicago as a Maine delegate, agreed with Welles, and did his utmost to convert Lot M. Morrill on the journey westward. What Morrill saw and heard in Chicago quickly brought him over to the Lincoln side. As a result of the labor of Hamlin and Blaine, on the first three ballots Maine gave Lincoln six votes against ten for Seward. Louis G. Hatch, *Maine, A History*, II, 421, 422; David Muzzey, *James G. Blaine*, 31.
48 Weed had made every effort to reach an agreement with the Cameron men. He had written Cameron on April 27 asking for a personal conference in Philadelphia, New York, or Washington; Simon Cameron Papers. Six Pennsylvania delegates were in Chicago as early as May 10, making preparations for the contest to carry Cameron through. They wrote Cameron that they had resolved that when Curtin came, they would put the issue squarely to him; he must stand for Cameron or for Seward. C. Casey to Simon Cameron, May 10, 1860; Cameron Papers. A. K. McClure and A. H. Reeder had been working hard for Cameron, but their willingness to make a prolonged fight was questionable.

toward the opponents of Seward.[49] The votes of the border States, Delaware, Maryland, and Missouri, were confidently claimed for Bates, while Virginia's delegates would be divided between him and Seward. Bowles indicated that the day might be swayed by a group of doubtful States which, standing in the position of compromisers between the earnest supporters and stubborn opponents of Seward, did not wish to force an unacceptable candidate upon either.[50]

The border, it will be seen, was represented. The arriving delegations included groups from Kentucky, Maryland, and Virginia, where the existence of true Republican organizations was denied, along with a flagrantly bogus group pretending to be from Texas. All these questionable bodies were admitted, even "Texas" being allowed six votes. Meanwhile, much discussion dealt with the question whether the ticket should be nominated by a majority of all delegates seated, or merely of all the delegates present. In the end the majority-present rule won. Leaders of the party, anxious to preserve harmony, yielded to determined pressure in both these matters.

At noon on Wednesday, Morgan brought down his gavel before the largest, most brilliant, and most enthusiastic party gathering yet seen in the country. A galaxy of celebrities was present. The venerable Joshua Giddings, the battle-scarred David Wilmot, the dashing Frank P. Blair, Jr., the brilliant Carl Schurz, the crusading Eli Thayer—these were but a few of the well-known figures. Every corner of the building was jammed. The open doors showed crowds choking the streets. When Morgan moved that Wilmot, the first great battler for freedom in the Territories, be made temporary chairman, a tempest of applause swept the hall.

[IV]

For decades to come, participants were to retell the story of the convention until it became a part of the legendary lore of the republic. At the very outset, as Morgan, Wilmot, and the permanent chairman, George Ashmun, delivered brief speeches, a rapport was established between the thousand delegates and ten thousand spectators which seemed, as by an electric current, to fuse them into a single body in feeling and action. The stirring spectacle presented by the crowd, and its animated response to every appeal, created an irresistible temptation to oratory. While many delegates betrayed their uncertainty as to a

49 Ohio held a peculiar position. Ostensibly for Chase, it was really not with him. "The reason that Chase was so soon dropped," declared Giddings later, "was that his leading friends appointed by his request wanted to substitute Wade for him, and gave out notice as soon as we reached Chicago that we were to give Chase only a complimentary vote, and then go for Wade." See J. L. Sellers, "The Makeup of the Early Republican Party," *Trans. Ill. State Hist. Soc.*, 1930.
50 Springfield *Republican*, May 16, 1860.

nominee, the concourse inevitably began to express its preference; with the result that, in midafternoon of the opening day, correspondents were writing distant newspapers that although half the members seemed in doubt, and though the Blairs were still predicting Bates's nomination, with a Ben Wade movement in formation, Lincoln was rapidly assuming prominence as the head of the opposition to Seward.

Indeed, the New York *Tribune* told Easterners on Thursday morning that according to its regular correspondent, Lincoln seemed likely to be nominated. The Chicago *Tribune* had been striving amain to make converts. On Tuesday, it had carried a column editorial—"Abraham Lincoln, the Winning Man"— giving eight reasons why he should be named. Next day it reprinted the editorial. Its news stories on Wednesday and Thursday conspicuously favored Lincoln, and on Friday the seventeenth another editorial—"A Last Entreaty"— summarized the arguments for the Rail Splitter.[51] The marked antagonism arising between the New Yorkers and Westerners played into the hands of Lincoln's managers. While some of the best men of the Empire State were in Chicago, many rowdies, braggarts, and quarrelsome partisans were also present. As Greeley wrote, they used bad tactics. "Noisy barroom denunciations of anti-Seward men from this State as ingrates and traitors; claims for Gov. Seward not only of the exclusive leadership but even of the authorship of the Republican party; public boasts that ever so much money could be raised to carry Seward's election, and none at all for anybody else, with triumphant queries, 'If you don't nominate Seward, where will you get your money?'— these were the weapons only of the lowest stratum of New York politicians, yet they had a most damaging effect." Westerners replied that *they* had been the first to form a Republican organization, that they did not believe in carrying elections by money, and that they could earn what was needed by splitting rails at fifty cents a day. What was more effective, the Lincoln managers tried to make friends in all delegations, enemies in none.[52]

The principal event of the second day, the adoption of a platform, was lifted to high interest by the economic realism of the document and by a dramatic clash over the incorporation of Jeffersonian doctrine.[53] As an observant young Springfield lawyer, Shelby M. Cullom, later wrote, the platform of 1860 was in sharp contrast with that of 1856. While more conservative in phrasing, it was far more boldly constructive in content. Already, Republican action in Congress and State conventions had dictated a number of the planks;

51 Kinsley, *Chicago Tribune*, I, 115.
52 N. Y. *Weekly Tribune*, May 26, 1860.
53 The platform declared that the Constitution, the rights of the States, and the Union must be preserved. It asserted that every State had the right to determine and control its own domestic institutions, and denounced lawless invasions as the greatest of crimes.

free homesteads, tariff revision, internal improvements, a Pacific railroad, a daily overland mail, the immediate entry of Kansas. The subcommittee which put these doctrines into form included Austin Blair, Carl Schurz, Greeley, and John A. Kasson. Greeley, especially concerned over the homestead resolution, later boasted that he had written it exactly to his liking.[54] A plank assailing any abridgment of rights of citizenship which had heretofore been accorded to the alien-born, vigorous in tone, was the work of Schurz and Gustave Koerner.[55] The tariff plank was put in, one delegate wrote, to satisfy Pennsylvania, and was accepted with some hesitation outside the industrial States.[56] One by one, after midnight, most of the tired committee members retired, until at dawn Greeley and Kasson were left alone to finish. As the editor had to send a dispatch to his paper, Kasson put the last touches to the draft.[57]

The Pennsylvania delegation, traveling to Chicago determined to insist on a strong tariff plank, had been imperious in their demands. They took the attitude already expressed by the Philadelphia *North American*: The convention must understand that it could not carry Pennsylvania and New Jersey unless it stood squarely on protectionist ground. The largest gathering of iron men ever seen in Pennsylvania, representing nearly all ironworks in the eastern part of the State, had met in Philadelphia in March and appointed a committee which drew up stiff protectionist resolutions. Of this committee, three men were delegates to the Chicago convention. When they had found various leaders convinced that party harmony demanded caution, they were depressed. Western members of the platform committee were averse to any mention of the tariff at all, and had some support, apparently, from New England. A New Jersey delegate, Thomas H. Dudley, then made a determined battle in committee to obtain some action; and the result was a compromise plank, calling for a revenue tariff together with "such an adjustment of those imposts as to encourage the development of the industrial interests of the whole country." When the tariff plank was presented in Chicago, the Pennsylvania delegates indulged in a striking demonstration of joy. Privately, however, they were disappointed by the cooing-dove character of the resolution.

Lincoln, it may be noted, would have preferred no tariff plank at all. Just before the convention opened he wrote one Edward Wallace that he was and always had been a Henry Clay tariff man. "I now think," he went on, "the tariff question ought not to be agitated in the Chicago convention; but that all should be satisfied on that point with a presidential candidate, whose ante-

54 Greeley-Colfax Corr., June 20, 1860.
55 Gustave Koerner, *Memoirs*, II, 87.
56 W. C. Noyes foresaw no "serious mischief"; Lieber Papers, HL, no date.
57 A. B. Burk, ed., *Golden Jubilee of the Republican Party.*

cedents give assurance that he would neither seek to force a tariff law by Executive influence; nor yet to avert a reasonable one, by a veto, or otherwise."

The platform as a whole was generally regarded as admirable. It has been said that its mingled idealism and materialism represented the union of Jefferson and Hamilton—or Jefferson and Clay. Everyone liked its negative features—its denunciation of Lecomptonism, popular sovereignty, the movement to revive the slave trade, and disunion. Nearly everyone approved an innovation for which Eli Thayer later claimed credit, replacing the stereotyped Wilmot Proviso doctrine, out of date since the successful battle in Kansas, with a declaration that the normal condition of all Territories was freedom, and that legislation to maintain it was to be passed only when necessary.[58] Even Greeley agreed that Congress need not positively prohibit slavery in a Territory where it could not possibly exist. This was a conservative feature; and the conservatives also dropped the insulting and inaccurate phrase of 1856 about "twin relics of barbarism" from the platform. But Joshua Giddings discerned one fault. The resolutions failed to reaffirm those truths of the Declaration of Independence which had been quoted four years earlier. When he moved to add Jefferson's words upon life, liberty, and the pursuit of happiness to the preamble, conservative members objected that they were inappropriate, and the convention voted Giddings down. In humiliation, the venerable freesoiler rose to leave the hall. As friends clustered about to dissuade him, George William Curtis rose in the midst of the New York delegation. His tall form caught every eye and his rich, musical voice held every ear as he moved to amend the *second* resolution by the words of the Declaration. Chairman Ashmun, irritated, tried to pass on to other business. But Frank Blair supported the young editor and insisted upon a vote.

Will the convention, asked Curtis, go before the nation as rejecting the Declaration of Independence? "I rise simply to ask gentlemen to think well before, upon the free prairies of the West, in the summer of 1860, they dare to wince and quail before the assertions of the men of Philadelphia in 1776." A crash of cheers shook the rafters; the motion was unanimously carried; and ten thousand voices loosed a deafening salvo as Giddings, his snowy head radiantly erect, came back to his seat.[59]

[V]

The third day, Friday, brought the crisis of the struggle over nominations. At dawn, Seward's victory still seemed inevitable to most friends and many foes. Greeley, whose antagonism had become increasingly bitter as the excitement in

58 F. P. Rise, MS Life of Eli Thayer, Harvard Library.
59 Julian, *Giddings*, 372–375; *Harper's Weekly*, August 7, 1875.

Chicago mounted, had telegraphed the *Tribune* during the night that the failure of the opposing delegations to agree on any one man had made it almost certain. The Seward delegates, believing any concentration of the hostile forces impossible, breakfasted with triumphant faces. They made inquiries, in perfect good faith, as to the wishes of the supporters of Bates, Chase, Cameron, and Lincoln respecting a Vice-Presidential candidate. The convention was to open at ten. By eight o'clock the streets were full of people hastening to the Wigwam; by nine that structure was tightly packed, with a great concourse outside. Most of the delegates formed in procession, with bands playing lively airs, and as they trooped into the central area applause greeted every prominent figure. Several politicians were making speeches outside, and while the opening prayer was being offered the roars of their audiences came in recurrent gusts. An electric excitement seemed almost to make the air crackle as the chairman announced that the pending business was a nomination for the Presidency of the United States.

In reality, more had been done to achieve a last-minute union of forces against Seward than Greeley or other observers guessed. The astute leaders of the Illinois delegation, grasping the situation, had been busy all night, laying plans and moving from caucus room to caucus room. Such men as David Davis, Joseph Medill, John M. Palmer, and Dick Yates were a fair match, in energy, resourcefulness, and indomitable determination, for Thurlow Weed, Edwin H. Morgan, and Moses H. Grinnell of the New York delegation.[60] They were being aided by the Republican candidates for the governorship in Pennsylvania and Indiana, Andrew Curtin and Henry Lane, who were convinced that the nomination of Seward would be death to their hopes, while that of Lincoln would mean victory. At one in the morning, Murat Halstead, historian of the convention, saw the pale, haggard Lane racing from room to room in the Tremont House to rally the doubtful. The Illinoisans knew that Evarts, Schurz, and Austin Blair, floor leaders of the New York, Wisconsin, and Michigan delegations, hoped to plunge through to victory in the first two or three ballots. With two hundred and thirty-three votes necessary to nominate, Seward would come within seventy of that total on the first roll call. Could he then be stopped?

Lincoln's supporters believed he could. If to Illinois could be added Pennsylvania, Indiana, and New Jersey (these four States making what Greeley called

60 Arrangements for seating the delegates were in the hands of Judd and Medill. They saw to it that the New York delegation was at one end of the hall, with no State for neighbor that was not already for Seward; and that the doubtful Pennsylvania delegation was at the other end, with the Illinois men flanking it. Medill believed that this device weakened the power of Seward's lieutenants to apply pressure on wavering men. T. E. Strevey in Paul M. Angle, ed., *Papers in Illinois History*, 59, 60. See Leonard Swett's story in R. R. Wilson, ed., *Intimate Memories of Lincoln*, 292-298.

the Malakoff redoubt of the anti-Seward forces), and if enough scattered delegates could be recruited from New England and other areas, Lincoln might be made powerful enough to win. Let him make a strong showing on the first two ballots, and other States would respond.

During their sleepless night, the Lincoln enthusiasts left no measure neglected. They knew the importance of overwhelming the Seward gallery. Davis saw to the preparation of a thousand counterfeit tickets, which were issued to as many men drilled to cheer for Lincoln; and a Boanerges reputed to be able to shout clear across Lake Michigan, with a Stentor hurriedly brought in from Ottawa, were put in charge of this force. Lincoln had sent a paper to headquarters reading, "Make no contracts that will bind me." But as one lieutenant swore and others protested, Davis swept it aside with a curt: "Lincoln ain't here and don't know what we have to meet!" [61]

The Illinois leaders that night addressed two main pleas to the men of Indiana, Pennsylvania, and New Jersey. One was based on party expediency; the ultra-radical Seward could never carry these four crucial States. Curtin, David Wilmot—for some time favorable to Lincoln—and Henry Lane were ready to support this thesis. The other plea embraced an offer of post-election rewards. Necessarily, these offers were made orally and under circumstances of partial secrecy. The evidence is overwhelming, however, that David Davis virtually promised a Cabinet position to Caleb B. Smith, reputedly the most influential Indiana delegate. Smith was more than receptive; indeed, he seems to have laid a little trap to obtain the pledge, for, according to another Indianian, he made Davis believe that unless he got the promise of the Cabinet place, the delegation would plump for Seward—"when the truth was that none of us cared for Smith and after we got to Chicago and looked over the ground all were for Lincoln." [62] The precise moment when a majority of Indiana delegates (many of whom had at first leaned toward Bates) decided to vote for Lincoln cannot be determined. If we may judge from the statements of Carl Schurz, sensitive men immediately on arrival in Chicago found themselves attracted to Lincoln by the popular enthusiasm for him, and repelled from Seward by the low politicians, the champagne and cigars, the free money-spending, and the hole-and-corner whispering which characterized the New York headquarters as dominated by the stealthy-footed Weed.[63]

New Jersey was half won over that Thursday night by sheer force of argument—W. L. Dayton could not be nominated, Seward could not be elected. Pennsylvania presented a harder problem. Forcible Thad Stevens displayed a

61 So says Whitney in *Lincoln the Citizen*, 289. Weed, as spokesman for Seward, had obviously been making promises of future "recognition."
62 Gresham, *Walter Q. Gresham*, I, 110, 111.
63 Schurz, *Reminiscences*, II, 173 ff.

curious preference for the colorless McLean, while others liked Bates as a representative of old-fashioned high-tariff Whiggism. Launching themselves on this
uncertain sea, Davis, Koerner, and other Illinoisans used every available plea. It
was Koerner's task, aided by Germans in Chicago, to make it plain that Teutonic
voters could never stomach Bates, and Davis's part to deal in more substantial
considerations.

The Keystone delegates sat late discussing their duty. A special factor perhaps helped to bring the Pennsylvanians over to Lincoln's side. The Rock
Island bridge had been constructed by two Pennsylvanians, William L. Scott and
his brother-in-law John F. Tracy, men associated in railway building, shipping,
and coal mining. Tracy, in fact, had gone to Chicago in 1854, and taken over
the extension of the Rock Island Railroad, then a few miles west of Chicago,
across the Mississippi and into Iowa. Tracy employed as attorney for the railroad Norman B. Judd, and it was through Judd that Lincoln was made special
counsel in the famous bridge case. As it happened, the Chicago convention found
a partner of Scott's and Tracy's named Morrow B. Lowry (who had charge of
some of their Great Lakes shipping) a delegate from Pennsylvania. Lowry and
Judd were good friends. Moreover, Lowry knew Lincoln, and had consulted
with him in the bridge case. In after years, Lowry frequently boasted that he
had been the active agent in bringing the Pennsylvania vote over to Lincoln.[64]
At any rate, about midnight, Davis came down the stairs of the Tremont House
from the Cameron rooms, and exultantly told Medill: "Damned if we haven't
got them!" [65] As they had apparently been bought and sold once or twice before,
this was saying a good deal. He had promised Cameron a Cabinet position. According to A. K. McClure, this pledge also was unnecessary; the delegation had
already decided to support Lincoln when the Senator's friends maneuvered
Davis into giving the inducement! What is certain is that the promise was made.
It was given without authority, and to a man quite unfit for Cabinet position;
but in time it was duly honored.

The decision of the Indiana, New Jersey, and Pennsylvania men to support
Lincoln destroyed Bates's chances, and laid the foundation for Seward's defeat.
At a later date, the various factors entering into this decision were subjected to
diverse interpretations. Greeley believed that Indiana, the first to take the plunge,
did much to bring Pennsylvania with her. A. K. McClure held that Pennsylvania could never have acted until assured of Lincoln's soundness on tariff revision.[66]

64 John C. Blackford, son of an intimate friend of Lowry's, to author, Seattle, July 25,
1939.
65 T. E. Strevey in Angle, ed., *Papers in Illinois History*, 58, 59.
66 See Greeley's long signed letter, N. Y. *Tribune*, May 26, 1860. Cf. T. M. Pitkin, "The
Tariff and the Early Republican Party," MS Dissertation, Western Reserve Univ.

One other witness asserts that the critical moment came when committees from the Illinois, Indiana, New Jersey, and Pennsylvania delegations, meeting in David Wilmot's rooms on the fateful night, took a poll to decide which man, Lincoln, Cameron, or Dayton, had the most support. This is the story told by Charles Perrin Smith, in personal reminiscences deposited in the New Jersey State Library. Early in the week, he relates, a body of New England delegates, headed by John A. Andrew, had called upon the New Jersey delegation. They said that if Seward could not be elected, they would support anyone who could; but, pointing out that the opposition strength was divided among Cameron, Dayton, and Lincoln, declared that unless Illinois, Pennsylvania, New Jersey, and Indiana agreed on a single man, the New Englanders would go into the convention to vote for Seward. Smith states that on Thursday at noon the four doubtful States assembled at the Cameron rooms in an attempt to unite. Reeder presided. It was soon evident that nothing could be done by so large a body. The matter was therefore referred to a committee of three from each of the four States, which sat in David Wilmot's rooms from six until ten without reaching a decision. As a last recourse, one delegate proposed that it should be ascertained which of the three candidates had the greatest actual strength, and could carry the largest number of delegates from the four States, if the other two were dropped. This showed that Lincoln stood in the strongest position; and Pennsylvania and New Jersey then decided to turn to him after the first ballots.[67]

Many stories of these hectic hours are conflicting; many details confused. But the essential facts are clear: That Lincoln's managers fastened upon Indiana, Pennsylvania, and New Jersey as vital; that they established their Malakoff by a judicious combination of alarmist reports and promised rewards; and that they had perfected their position when the sun rose on May 18. It then remained for another factor to make itself felt—the great excited crowd, now an integral part of the convention machinery.

[VI]

The crowd was there; it had flooded into every nook of the Wigwam; it had invaded the stage, reserved for delegates and newspapermen; it milled

67 Some partially corroborative evidence is furnished by a dispatch to the Springfield *Republican* dated Chicago, May 16, afternoon session (Wednesday or first day). This recites that the Massachusetts delegation had organized under John A. Andrew as president. It was formally visited by the Pennsylvania, Illinois, and New Jersey delegations, which informed it that under no circumstances could they accept the nomination of Seward; for by that they would lose the State, Congressional, and local elections. E. H. Kellogg of Pittsfield then proposed that each of the three should submit the names of three men who could carry the State. Illinois presented the name of Lincoln alone; New Jersey those of Dayton, Lincoln, and Banks; and Pennsylvania those of Cameron, McLean, and Lincoln. Springfield *Republican*, May 17, 1860.

in a tumultuous throng about the building, communicating with its members inside by men posted on the roof. What pen, asks one who was present, could adequately describe this alert audience of ten thousand freemen; the low, wavelike roar of its ordinary conversation; the rolling cheers that greeted a popular favorite? There was something irresistibly stirring in its united voice.[68]

A thrill pervaded the concourse as it saw ballots being distributed, and as William M. Evarts rose to make his first nomination—then a process of unadorned simplicity. "In the order of business before the convention, sir," he said, "I take the liberty to name as a candidate to be nominated by this convention for the office of President of the United States, William H. Seward." Long-continued applause followed. Then Norman B. Judd was on his feet. "I desire, on behalf of the delegation from Illinois," he shouted, "to put in nomination, as a candidate for President of the United States, Abraham Lincoln of Illinois." [69] Instantly, the assemblage rose in a deafening response, wild with excitement; men shouting, women waving their handkerchiefs, and a tremendous roar echoing from the masses outside. This continued for several minutes. Then Dayton, Cameron, McLean, and Chase were nominated, each with much milder cheering, and various nominations were seconded. Smith of Indiana offered the second for Lincoln, and Schurz that for Seward.

The competition in applause was evident. "Abe Lincoln has it by the sound now," shouted one man. "Let us ballot!" And Judge Stephen T. Logan of Illinois vociferated: "Mr. President, in order or out of order, I propose this convention and audience give three cheers for the man who is evidently their nominee."

It was high noon as the balloting began. Nobody expected the first poll to do more than indicate the general trends. All the favorite sons received their due tribute—Collamer, Dayton, and others. Bates's following was lamentably small, for he trailed just behind Cameron and Chase, fifth in the whole roster. The two highest votes showed where the battle was to center: Seward, 173½, Lincoln, 102. As yet, the Seward managers did not lose their confidence. Some protesting delegate furnished a brief interruption. Eager for a full trial of strength, the audience growled its impatience, and "Call the roll! the roll!" came from a multitude of throats.

This time, the swing of the tide was unmistakable. The complimentary votes faded away, and the Lincoln column grew longer. Most of Cameron's delegates came to him; so did Collamer's ten; so did six from Chase and McLean. Seward's followers grew sick at heart as they saw their leader held at a practical standstill while Lincoln drew fairly abreast. The racing pencils quickly footed up the

68 Nicolay and Hay, *Lincoln*, II, 270, 271.
69 MS Proceedings, NYHS, 153–155.

totals: Seward, 184½; Lincoln, 181; Bates, 35; scattering, 42. If Lincoln could be kept immovable, there was still a chance that Seward's men might swing over to the other leader reputed to be radical, Chase. But the crowd, wilder than ever in its enthusiasm over Lincoln's gains, was shouting jubilantly. Then, without a pause, the third ballot began.

It had proceeded only to the fourth State, when Massachusetts suddenly changed four votes from Seward to Lincoln; and this heralded the avalanche. Rhode Island gave Lincoln two new votes; New Jersey for the first time gave him eight. Instead of forty-eight from Pennsylvania, he now received fifty-two. Instead of none from Maryland, he had nine—a token that the Blairs had given up Bates and were on Lincoln's side. Seward, losing one vote in Maryland and another in Kentucky, was actually dropping back. Once more the swift pencils of the spectators had the result before it was officially tabulated: Lincoln, 231½, Seward, 180. Some of the New Yorkers were in tears. If two delegates changed their votes, Lincoln was nominated.

"A profound stillness," writes one spectator, "fell upon the Wigwam; the men ceased to talk and the ladies to flutter their fans; one could distinctly hear the scratching of pencils and the ticking of telegraph instruments on the reporters' tables." An Ohio delegate jumped to his chair and announced four new Lincoln votes taken from the Chase column. A pause of one moment ensued; a teller waved his tally-sheet toward the skylight, and shouted a single word; the deep boom of the cannon on the roof threw echoes flying across the city; and from the crowd in the streets came a wild pandemonium of cheers, a wave of sound that mingled with the happy uproar inside the building.[70]

70 When the final total was announced, giving Lincoln 364 votes out of 466, Evarts rose and with a neat speech moved that the vote be made unanimous. The whole scene is described in the MS Proceedings, NYHS, 164–169.

9

The Four-Party Campaign

THE DISCORDS of Charleston and the enthusiasms of Chicago were both tokens that the country had been carried far along the course that led to sectional conflict. Midway between the two major gatherings, on May 9, the Constitutional Union Party met in Baltimore to try to turn time back; to demand that distracting sectional issues be banished from the national councils. Here Clay's despairing ghost was invoked for almost the last time.

The delegates cherished a momentary hope of playing a decisive role. As the candidacy of Douglas had provoked a Democratic schism, so they believed that Seward's candidacy might cause a Republican split; large sections of both parties then turning to their conservative organization. Nearly all the leaders of the promising Opposition movement of 1858–59 had joined in raising the Constitutional Union banner. Most of them came from the borderland: Crittenden of Kentucky, Rives and Goggin of Virginia, John P. Kennedy of Maryland, and Kenneth Rayner of North Carolina. In New York, a devoted group of adherents was led by Washington Hunt, D. D. Barnard, and James and Erastus Brooks; while in Massachusetts Edward Everett, Amos A. Lawrence, and Robert C. Winthrop lent their assistance. Winfield Scott sympathized with the cause. Clearly, the main strength of the party was among old-time Whigs. In still other respects it smacked of the past, many members being so venerable that opponents derided it as the Old Gentlemen's Party.

For a party of union, it at first showed a somewhat contentious spirit. While a Southern wing, largely survivors of the Know-Nothing organization, wished to nominate Sam Houston, most Northern and border men preferred a veteran Whig. On the second ballot the latter element swept through to victory, naming John Bell by a vote twice that of Houston. The strongest possible candidate, Crittenden, who had worked hard in Washington to organize the party, writing numberless letters and holding many conferences, emphatically insisted that he must not be considered. As he was well past seventy, this was reasonable. Bell, now in his sixty-fourth year, was universally acknowledged to be a man of character, ability, and patriotism, whose long public career had shown great

integrity if some vacillation. When Edward Everett was unanimously named
for Vice-President, not a few critics declared that he should have been placed
first; but actually the convention made no mistake in preferring Bell. Everett,
three years older, was a retiring, self-distrustful man, easily intimidated, and
lacking in popular appeal. The ticket, which had intellectual distinction, inspired
general respect—but no enthusiasm.

Everywhere conservative people, especially merchants, manufacturers, and
professional men of old Whig antecedents, expressed high satisfaction with the
Constitutional Union nominations, and almost everywhere they added that the
party was of no use. Most conservative men were by definition averse to
active labor in politics. The fervent unity of the Republicans in Chicago was a
body blow to the Bell-Everett group. "All New England is warmly in favor of
Old Abe and split rails," Amos A. Lawrence frankly wrote Crittenden.[1] Nor
did the Constitutional Union platform satisfy realistic men. Declaring merely for
the maintenance of the Constitution, the Union, and the laws, its evasion of the
real issues gave it a fossil look; it would have done better for 1824 than for 1860.
Nevertheless, the party, with at least some semblance of organization in most
of the North and all of the South except South Carolina, set earnestly to work.
Representative Boteler of Virginia was chairman of the national executive committee, which numbered John A. Gilmer of North Carolina, Marshall P. Wilder
of Massachusetts, and other able men. A scanty newspaper guard, made up of
surviving Whig or Know-Nothing sheets, rallied about Bell; the *National Intelligencer*, Louisville *Journal*, Nashville *Republican and Banner*, and the St.
Louis *Intelligencer* in the border area being prominent.[2]

[I]

Meanwhile, as the Charleston convention delegates returned home, all
responsible Democrats attached to the Union were filled with consternation.
"What do you think of matters now?" Richard Malcolm Johnston asked Alexander H. Stephens. "Why," rejoined Stephens, "that men will be cutting one
another's throats in a little while. In less than twelve months we shall be in a
war, and that the bloodiest in history."

He and many other Southerners would have been glad to see the party unite
behind Douglas and the Cincinnati platform.[3] To an apprehensive group at
Macon, he sent a long public letter urging that the slave-code demand be
dropped and that delegates be sent to the regular convention when it met again

1 May 25, 1860; Crittenden Papers, Duke Univ.
2 See pamphlet, "Bell and Everett," Washington, 1860.
3 Johnston and Browne, *Stephens*, 355, 356.

in Baltimore. Two other leading Georgians, Herschel V. Johnson and Governor Joseph E. Brown, took the same stand. From Democrats of all the border States, from the Soulé men in Louisiana, from the Forsyth forces in Alabama, from followers of Thomas B. Flournoy in Arkansas, and from numerous Texans, rose a demand for party reunion even if it meant accepting the Little Giant. In Washington, many of the fire-eaters were so visibly abashed by the disruption that Senator Hammond concluded that their big talk had been bosh.

Yet a swift-running tide was carrying the dissevered halves of the party further apart. The breach was essentially irreparable. The popular sovereignty Democrats of the North were vibrant with anger over what they termed party treason; the radicals of the South were equally savage over what they considered a threat to their sectional safety. While Dean Richmond, his blood up, declared he would stand or fall with the Northwest, the Dubuque *Herald* and other Douglas sheets of that section called the Yancey-Davis-Slidell crew a disunionist faction who should get out and stay out. Meanwhile, Robert Toombs heartily endorsed the bolt, and advised against any concession. Rhett's Charleston *Mercury* and Yancey's Montgomery *Advertiser* were declaring that the South would never accept a popular sovereignty candidate or platform. The Administration, with the *Constitution* chuckling over Douglas's failure, and Howell Cobb asserting that Southerners must never yield to the man, took the same ground. Both sides wanted to bring delegates from all the States together again in Baltimore. But while Douglas's managers wished to gain enough votes to nominate him, the Administration forces wished to nominate some other man on a platform embodying the Davis resolutions.

As soon as the convention ended, Washington boiled with political activity. A number of Southern extremists hoped that nothing whatever would be done to heal the schism; that the bolting delegates would meet in Richmond as practically a Southern convention; that they would present a united front for the slave-code demand; and that they would nominate Jefferson Davis and Joseph Lane, or two men like them.[4] A much larger body, backed (so far as we can determine) by dominant Southern sentiment, desired a general return of delegates to the Baltimore convention, where they might place such a man as Hunter on a platform acceptable to the South. Nine Southern Senators and ten Representatives signed an address advising the bolters to defer or abandon their Richmond gathering, go to Baltimore, and unite with other Southerners in procuring a satisfactory platform; and the *Constitution* applauded this plan.[5] They hoped that New York would assist in nominating a conservative man. Douglas's friends meanwhile strove to hold their old delegates and maneuvered to

4 Rhett, May 10, 1860; Porcher Miles Papers, Univ. of N. C.
5 "Tiber" in N. O. *Picayune*, May 16, 1860.

win new ones. Amid this jockeying, an acrimonious debate sprang up in the Senate.

It was begun by Jefferson Davis, who—ailing and haggard—spoke on May 8 for his long-pending resolutions. Containing no new ideas, his address was resolutely defiant. He would not surrender a comma of the radical platform. He asked for no immediate legislation, he said. (He knew well that he could not get it if he did ask, for the Democratic Senate no less than the Republican House would have refused to pass it. A. G. Brown, striving for several months to push forward a slave-code bill, had been unable to get a second for it, and Clingman of North Carolina avowed his belief that not a single Senator was willing to vote for it.) But Davis did ask that territorial legislatures be made to understand that Congress would not let them interfere with rights of persons or property guaranteed by the Constitution, and would apply a remedy if they did interfere. "We claim protection, first, because it is our right; secondly, because it is the duty of the general government." His arrogance grew more pronounced when he said that if safeguards, once demanded, were denied, Mississippi would secede. As for the Republican Party, its advent to power would be the signal for a break-up of the Union. They were asked, he scornfully remarked, to stand still and wait for an overt act. "Overt act! Is not a declaration of war an overt act?" We make no threat, he said; we only give the North warning.[6]

Douglas was waiting for him. He sought no quarrel, but when men urged him to "give the infernal scoundrels the devil," he said he would reply to Davis and Davis alone. Speaking again on May 17, the Mississippian declared that he would sooner have an honest man on a rickety platform than an untrustworthy candidate on the best platform possible. This was a thrust at the Little Giant. Douglas instantly saw the opening it presented. Indeed! he snorted. "Why break up the party on the platform, if you do not think that is of any consequence? . . . Why did you not tell us in the beginning of this debate that the whole fight was against the man, and not upon the platform?"[7]

Douglas's principal speech, delivered May 16-17, upheld his old thesis that non-intervention in the Territories was the historic Democratic doctrine, cherished until recently by all the chief party leaders. He too was ill and tired; during his recent disappointments he had begun drinking again; and, unsupported by any Senator except Pugh, he felt terribly alone. Going over familiar ground, he began less vigorously than usual. But he always gained new life from battle; and, as he went on, his ringing voice, his lucid argument, his energy

6 *Cong. Globe*, 36th Cong., 1st Sess., 1937-1942.
7 *Cong. Globe*, 36th Cong., 1st Sess., 2155, 2156. J. Hanly Smith sent Stephens his impression of Douglas's speech. "He has utterly demolished Jeff Davis—putting him under his heel and grinding him to powder. . . . As far as debate is concerned it is the grandest triumph of his life." May 19, Stephens Papers, LC.

fierce as a lion rending its prey, gave the address tremendous polemic force. He had arranged a dramatic effect. At intervals, he paused for a citation proving the adherence of some Democratic champion to non-intervention doctrine, and Pugh's crisp voice was heard reciting an apposite quotation from Daniel S. Dickinson, Franklin Pierce, Governor Winston of Alabama, the Florida legislature, a Georgia Democratic convention, President Buchanan, and even Yancey. This antiphonal chorus was impressive. Douglas made room for a frank revelation of personal feeling. He had been removed from his committee chairmanship in 1858, he said, because he had uttered statements identical with the public utterances of Buchanan and Breckinridge in 1856. A senatorial caucus had read him out of the party because he had espoused the Democratic platform of that year. He had fought that proscription until he had won a victory. "The Charleston convention affirmed the same platform. I am no longer a heretic. I am no longer an outlaw from the Democratic Party." [8]

In a rattling exchange of bitter personalities with Davis, Judah P. Benjamin, and others, the Illinoisan argued that he had been the choice of a majority in Charleston, declared the slave-code plank a novel invention brought forth for selfish purposes of the cotton kingdom leaders, and arraigned Yancey's avowed scheme "to precipitate the cotton States into revolution." Benjamin retorted that Douglas would not have had a majority but for the coercion of the unit rule in the New York, Indiana, and other delegations. In view of the Administration's use of patronage to capture delegates, this was not very impressive. When Davis declared that the seventeen certainly Democratic States were for the slave-code platform at Charleston, and that the sixteen States offering the Douglas platform did not include one that was surely Democratic, Douglas checked him resentfully. Maryland had opposed the Douglas platform at Charleston; was she surely Democratic? She had voted against Buchanan in 1856. Tennessee had opposed the Douglas platform; was she always Democratic? She had voted against Pierce in 1852, and of her ten Congressmen, only three were now Democrats. Kentucky was on Davis's list; yet Kentucky too had voted against Pierce in 1852. Illinois had never once failed the Democratic Party in a Presidential campaign. Could Davis say as much for Mississippi? He could not, for the Whigs had once carried the State.[9]

By these acrid defiances the gulf between the two factions was deepened and the failure of the impending convention at Baltimore rendered more probable. Various Southerners, including Benjamin, announced that the cotton kingdom delegates would arrive with unaltered instructions and a firm determination to wear the Northern Democrats into compliance. Mr. Benjamin is mistaken, re-

8 *Cong. Globe.*, 36th Cong., 1st Sess., App., 301–316.
9 *Cong. Globe.*, 36th Cong., 1st Sess., 1937; 1966; 2120–2122; 2143–2146.

torted Pugh, "if he supposes that the men who stood there at Charleston for two weeks in that atmosphere voting down your resolutions again and again, and voting for Stephen A. Douglas, are going to be tired when it comes to Baltimore, which is a much more agreeable atmosphere for them." [10]

[II]

The course of events inside the Southern States had meanwhile been highly interesting. Would the people support the bolters? Would they, even while supporting them, send them back to the new regular convention in Baltimore? Thus far the slave States stood divided. Delegates of eight of them had withdrawn at Charleston; delegates of seven, counting Delaware, had remained. It seemed evident that majority sentiment in the seven States and at least a strong minority sentiment in the others hoped for party reunion on a compromise basis; the Cincinnati platform, say, with a Southern nominee. Important Democratic journals of the upper South—the Richmond *Enquirer* and *Examiner*, Louisville *Courier*, and others—called for such a solution. The Nashville *Union and American* asked for the rejection both of the slave-code plank and the candidacy of Douglas.[11] Deep in the Lower South, such newspapers as the Montgomery *Confederation*, which declared that the issue of union or disunion was now drawn, implored all the Southern States to send delegations to Baltimore.[12] Stephens favored such action. To this course, Yancey, Rhett, and other extremists were strongly opposed. They declared the Cincinnati platform unacceptable because it was open to two interpretations; and they believed that the Douglas men would never yield but would try to force the Southerners in Baltimore to come to Canossa.

In the end, all of the bolting States but one decided to send delegates to the Baltimore gathering. South Carolina alone, swayed by Rhett, Porcher Miles, and

10 *Ibid.*, 2247.
11 The Wilmington *Weekly Journal* (May 3, 10, 17) was emphatic in condemning the bolters and in declaring its willingness to accept Douglas as candidate if justice were done the South. "Shall we leave the gallant barque to seek for safety in a cockboat? Are fifty-two seceders the 'Constitutional Democracy,' simply because they choose to assume that name? Not at all! Not at all!" It appealed to the Douglas men to withdraw the Illinoisan, and work for complete harmony at Baltimore. The New Orleans *Picayune* declared that Louisiana sentiment was overwhelmingly against a separate convention in Richmond, and for a return to Baltimore. Few were prepared to meet the issue presented by Yancey. "Louisiana will not sustain disunionism. However strongly she may feel the aggressions of a hostile Northern majority, she is true to the Constitution and the Union, and will continue so as long as she can maintain that position with honor. She will never secede, or cooperate with friends of secession, in view simply of threatened wrong, but will wait for overt acts." May 15, 1860.
12 *Weekly Confederation*, May 12, 1860; Phillips, *Toombs*, 191.

Gist, stood out, refusing to send representatives anywhere but to Richmond.[13] In Texas, the State committee reaccredited the former delegation to both Baltimore and Richmond. Similar action was taken by State conventions in Georgia and Florida, though about one-tenth of the Georgia convention withdrew and elected a separate, contesting, delegation for Baltimore alone. In Louisiana and Alabama spectacular fights developed. The opposition elements in these States, led by Pierre Soulé and John Forsyth, were outraged by what had happened in Charleston. When the Slidell forces reconvened the Louisiana State convention, commended the delegates, and sent them to Baltimore, Soulé flew to arms. Not intimidated by an enthusiastic Southern Rights mass meeting in New Orleans, he called an equally vociferous mass meeting of popular sovereignty men. This body convoked an opposition convention, which sent its own delegation to Baltimore.[14] Events followed much the same course in Alabama. The Yancey forces, dominating the State convention, approved the acts of the delegates in Charleston, and appointed a largely identical body to go to Baltimore and Richmond. On the same day, and in the same city of Montgomery, an opposing convention led by Forsyth and ex-Governor John A. Winston chose a contesting delegation for Baltimore.[15]

Most Douglas men, meanwhile, were adamant. They would yield nothing to seceders. The Charleston convention had declared the seats of the bolters vacant and called on the cotton States to elect new delegates. W. A. Richardson, who would be Douglas's floor manager again in Baltimore, said that if any seceders got into the convention without a reelection, his own self-respect would compel him to leave it. He had flatly told an agent of Secretary Cobb that the issue had been drawn between union or disunion, and that he was on the union side. Senator Pugh took the same attitude. These Southern dissidents have no business in Baltimore, he told the Senate, for they have left the party. "I will sit and vote until the fourth day of March, 1861, against allowing one man of them to come back again, unless he is newly elected as a delegate." [16] As most of the

13 The second Columbia convention in South Carolina was full of men of strong secessionist proclivities. The irreconcilables elected Rhett to Richmond, and the three other delegates at large. They were left in full control. But this was only after a vicious fight. Bitter feeling was aroused, and the State was left deeply divided.

14 Dumond, *Secession*, 65 ff.

15 Forsyth and Winston in Alabama were supported by J. J. Seibels of Montgomery, who was now certain that Yancey, Rhett & Co. aimed at breaking down the Union and creating a Southern Confederacy. He was much pleased by the opposition covention—"one of the most numerously attended, talented, and respectable bodies of men ever convened in Alabama." Our friends, he reported to Douglas on June 5, are in glorious spirits. Douglas Papers.

16 *Cong. Globe*, 36th Cong., 1st Sess., 2247. H. B. Payne wrote Douglas that the Northwestern delegates would stand firm to the last; "aut Caesar aut nihil." Regarding Virginia as of critical importance, he was anxious for Richardson to bargain with Hunter. "He can safely promise him anything from the Northwest in the future if he will now play the man." May 16; Douglas Papers.

cotton States were returning their original delegations, this question of readmission generated intense feeling.

[III]

It was a hot Monday morning, June 18, when the convention opened in the Front Street Theatre in Baltimore. Caleb Cushing, hearty, smiling, quick-witted, once more served as chairman. Howard of Tennessee no sooner offered a resolution that the sergeant-at-arms be instructed to admit all delegates of the convention as originally constituted at Charleston than a storm of mingled hisses and cheers arose. While Southerners applauded, the Douglas men manifested unalterable opposition. An angry quarrel seemed about to break forth. Sanford E. Church of New York proposed that the title of seceders be submitted to the committee on credentials, and that all delegates who were admitted be bound in honor to abide by the action of the convention and support its nominees.[17] This time, Douglas's followers loosed a burst of applause, while the cotton State men —who would submit to no conditions of loyalty—hissed. Clearly, the factions were at swords' point, and while Cushing rebuked the demonstrations, fierce words and gestures expressed the sectional bitterness. After a wrangle of three hours, the convention adjourned until five o'clock so that, as one member said, it might harmonize—a word which provoked an ironic laugh.

It was generally understood that the readopted Cincinnati platform could not be changed at Baltimore. The North could not yield on that point without dishonor; and the platform was fair to all sections. The real issue was the candidate. Ben Butler and other New England politicians hoped to have Horatio Seymour nominated for President, with Alexander H. Stephens for Vice-President. Some New York delegates shared this wish. But William S. Holman wrote his friend Allen Hamilton from Washington on May 15 that no Democrat could be elected except Douglas. "His friends and he himself count with absolute confidence on his receiving the nomination at Baltimore, and that the platform will remain unchanged."

From its bad beginning the convention went on to worse, as the committee on credentials fought and hesitated. In its first three days it did little except make the party ludicrous. Republican newspapers teemed with jeering articles. The people of Baltimore, who had hoped for a love feast followed by general jubilee, grew more and more disgusted. Twice or thrice a day, the convention would solemnly assemble; ladies in crinoline, newspapermen, prominent citizens, and idlers would fill the gallery; and then the delegates would adjourn. At noisy evening meetings rival groups listened to inflammatory speeches. Douglas men

17 *Proceedings, Charleston and Baltimore,* 160.

assailed the "disunionists" while Southerners attacked the "nigger lovers." Yancey, at hand to stir up trouble, declared that his opponents were ostriches, hiding their heads in the sand of popular sovereignty, all unaware that their great, ugly, ragged, abolition body was exposed.

By the third day, the shrewdest observers had divined the probable course of events. Greeley, or somebody equally perspicacious, inserted in the New York *Tribune* a remarkable forecast. New York delegates, he wrote, had been in a difficult situation; for if they voted to reject the seceders at Charleston they broke with the South, while if they voted to reject the new claimants under Soulé, Forsyth, and others, they broke with the Northwest. But a great light had just dawned upon them with the discovery that if they killed Douglas, his devoted friends were resolved to kill Horatio Seymour, so that they would lose the fruit of their meditated treachery. They were now resolved to go straight for Douglas, voting out the seceders and voting in the new Douglas delegates from the Lower South. Thereupon Cotton would bolt and make a ticket of its own, while Douglas would be nominated by the remainder of the convention.[18]

This was almost precisely what happened. On Thursday morning the credentials committee presented two reports. The Douglasite majority proposed to exclude the Louisiana and Alabama bolters, divide the Georgia seats evenly between seceders and new contestants, and admit a number of newcomers from Arkansas and other States; they were ready to let in all the original delegates from Texas and Mississippi, and most of those from Arkansas. The minority report, a document of great ability, provided for the admission of the original delegates from the Lower South. It argued that the convention had no right to declare seats vacant when a delegation withdrew, for bolting was not resignation; a valid resignation must be addressed to the appointing power. This statement produced a strong effect on a number of wavering delegates, and the New York delegation took time to confer. In the end, however, Dean Richmond and most others resolved to stand by Douglas, so that under the unit rule all thirty-five New York votes were cast for the majority report.

Friday, the twenty-second, after all the interminable waiting, witnessed a spectacular explosion. Amid intense excitement, the minority report was rejected by 150 to 100½.[19] The majority report was then taken up, part by part. The vote for replacing the Louisiana seceders by Pierre Soulé's contingent was emphatic—158 to 98. The vote to replace the Alabama bolters by Forsyth's group was 148 to 101½. Only in dealing with Georgia was the report altered, for here New York united with the Southern men in approving the admission of the

18 N. Y. *Tribune*, June 21, 1860.
19 Dumond, *Secession*, 86.

entire regular delegation. The convention then adjourned until evening. Since the New York delegates were perturbed and might vote for reconsideration, some hope for a reconciliation persisted. Dean Richmond had in his pocket a letter which Douglas, doubtless in anguish of spirit, had written at eleven o'clock on Wednesday night. The unity of the party and the maintenance of its principles, declared Douglas, were more important than the nomination of any man; and if his enemies were determined to destroy the Democracy and perhaps the nation rather than see him elected, he would withdraw in favor of some other reliable Union-loving Democrat of non-interventionist views. W. A. Richardson had a similar letter. The story had gone around Washington that after Douglas withdrew, Alexander H. Stephens would be brought forward and nominated.[20] But it was too late; resentments had again risen too high. Neither letter was made public. When the convention resumed work, it was in an atmosphere of doom.

The rattle of Cushing's gavel; the putting of the question; the steady march of the vote against the Southerners—and then the tall, spare form of Russell of Virginia, monotonously chanting "Mr. President!" caught every eye. Shouts of "Order!" and the frowns of the chair could not stop him. He announced in measured words that a large majority of the Virginia delegation had instructed him to say that they would no longer participate in the convention, and directed him to bid it a respectful adieu. This was the fateful turning point which all had feared, and the gathering listened in awe-struck silence. Then another voice broke the stillness, as Anderson of North Carolina gave notice that sixteen of his State's twenty delegates were withdrawing. Ewing of Tennessee succeeded him, announcing that his delegation was retiring to confer, and probably would not return. California and Oregon also departed. The Kentucky and Missouri delegations asked time to consult; some Marylanders declared they would share the fate of the South; and sixteen of the twenty-six Massachusetts men left to determine their course.

The disruption of the party was now complete. Other voices were heard— voices of confession, of explanation, of denunciation, of lamentation.[21] The members, wearied with excitement, adjourned at eleven. Thus ended all hope of Democratic victory, and, as many believed, of averting disunion.

The last day, Saturday, June 23, witnessed the resignation of Caleb Cushing,

20   J. Hanly Smith, July 6, 1860; Stephens Papers, LC.
21   Among those who spoke was W. B. Gaulden of Georgia, who said that he would remain in the convention. He added that he was a "nigger man," and gloried in the term. He had boasted at Charleston of the newly-imported Africans whom he owned. Now he praised Virginia as a nigger-breeding State, and when a Virginia delegate called him to order, he said that he meant no offence; he was a "nigger-breeder," Georgia was a "nigger-breeding" State, and he was proud of the business. N. Y. Tribune, Baltimore correspondence dated June 23.

whose agile departure by a side door was hailed with cries of "Good!" and "Now we shall have a fair chairman!" It witnessed much speechmaking, including Pierre Soulé's brilliant denunciation of the Slidell-Yancey men as an unscrupulous combination of politicians and traitors. This speech was the climax of Soulé's career, his last public service; for before him lay nought but disaster and final insanity. Above all, the last day witnessed the nomination of Douglas. On the first ballot, with 212½ votes cast, he received 173½; and on the second, 180½.[22] A deafening roar saluted the result. As the news was telegraphed over the country, followers organized celebrations in cities from Boston to Chicago and St. Louis. That evening in Washington, a procession marched to Douglas's house and elicited a brief speech. "Can the seceders," asked the Senator, "fail to perceive that their efforts to divide and defeat the Democratic party, if successful, must lead directly to the secession of the Southern States? I trust that they . . . will return to the organization and platform of the party before it is too late to save the country." Benjamin Fitzpatrick had been nominated for Vice-President, and when he declined, Herschel V. Johnson was chosen by the National Committee in his place.[23]

Meanwhile the bolters in Baltimore, with other Southern delegates who had not applied for admission or had been excluded, had gathered at noon Saturday in the Maryland Institute, and elected Caleb Cushing chairman of a new convention. Here Yancey was the ruling spirit. He had previously met in Richmond with something less than a hundred delegates to the Constitutional Democratic convention, a body which had accomplished virtually nothing. He had then pursued his way to Washington, where George Sanders made the preposterous suggestion that he accept the Vice-Presidential nomination on the Douglas ticket, reinforcing it with an intimation that Douglas's health was so bad that Yancey would soon succeed to the Presidency. He had been busy in the background at Baltimore. Now he was in his element as two hundred and thirty-one delegates from nineteen States (New York and Missouri represented by only two each) gathered for a briskly efficient session. A slave-code platform was unani-

22 The number of regularly elected and accredited delegates after the withdrawals was but 166½ votes, representing eleven States. Counting the irregular delegates seated from Louisiana and Alabama, the Soulé and Forsyth men who really had a certain title, thirteen States were represented with 182½ votes. Other irregulars and withdrawn delegates present as spectators were counted to bring the total up to 212½ votes. See Dumond, *Secession*, 89-91.

23 J. Hanly Smith states that Robert Toombs brought about Fitzpatrick's declination. "He got Mrs. Gwin and others to see Mrs. Fitzpatrick, who told her the Governor would be eternally ruined if he accepted—got her to crying until he promised to decline. I was at Brown's when the telegraph announced Fitz's nomination. I was beside Pugh of Alabama who went up to Fitz's room to find out what he was going to do. He came down and told me that Fitz accepted—he had just seen him and had it from his own mouth." August 18, 1860; Alex Stephens Papers, LC.

mously adopted, and on the first ballot the reluctant John C. Breckinridge and Joseph Lane were nominated for the Presidency and Vice-Presidency.[24]

Then on Sunday the tumult in Baltimore died away. During the turmoil and excitement, neither faction had been able to estimate the long-term effect of its own actions. As they caught the trains home, the delegates could quietly reflect upon their deeds and try sadly to calculate the result.

[IV]

Thus the campaign of 1860 began. It was a campaign full of color as "Wide Awakes" paraded and orators thundered; a campaign packed with emotion, especially in proud communities of the Deep South, but lacking all the ordinary excitements of close rivalry. The country had the sensation of watching one of the old double dramas of the Elizabethan stage, a play within a play; the outer drama determining whether Lincoln, Breckinridge, or Douglas should gain national leadership, while the far more fateful inner drama decided whether the republic should be torn in twain. The New York *World* remarked that the party battle was the tamest since Monroe had been sent to the White House. In one sense this was true; but in another sense men who watched the banners sway, the fireworks soar, and the fife-and-drum corps march, divined a crisis working yeastily beneath all this gaiety, a cataclysm almost ready to break. These observers could but watch, for events were getting out of control.

The campaign was quieter than the Frémont-Buchanan struggle for a variety of reasons: because the existence of four parties, with a constant effort to make alliances in various States, rendered it confusing; because no clear-cut practical issue (the fate of slavery in the Territories being certain anyhow) separated any two parties; because the Republicans had lost their first picturesque *élan;* and above all, because the result of the election was fairly certain from the outset—Lincoln would win. Nevertheless, Fate brooded over the scene.

Of the four candidates, three were familiar public figures. Douglas for ten years had been in the very center of the national stage. Bell, who had entered Congress while J. Q. Adams sat in the White House and had defeated Polk for the speakership in 1834, was a veteran scarred by many an engagement. As a Whig, he had held the secretaryship of war under Harrison, and had thereafter been in the Senate for a decade. As for Breckinridge, the fact that he was not yet forty did not mean that he was little known. He sprang from a noted family; his grandfather had been Attorney-General under Jefferson, his father a leader

24 Again J. Hanly Smith: "Mr. Toombs induced Breck to accept—asserted that he would carry the whole South like a storm, and that in less than forty days he would have the field clear for himself—Douglas being withdrawn." *Ibid.*

of rare promise whose career had been ended by death at thirty-four. He had made his political debut in dramatic fashion, reaching Congress in 1851 from Henry Clay's district by defeating a strong Whig opponent. A capable record in the House had prefaced his election as Vice-President in 1856.

Of this trio, Douglas alone, iron-willed, sleeplessly active, and holding a constructive vision of the nation's future, possessed great intellectual power and force of character. Bell was popularly assumed to be less impressive than his associate Everett, and, as Greeley suggested, Everett was respectable without being commanding. What most distinguished Bell was the judicial balance of his temper. Every American interested in public affairs knew that, though he and his wife were large slaveholders, he had always taken a conservative and nationalist position. He had supported Taylor's policy in 1850, had opposed the Kansas-Nebraska bill, and, in calm disobedience to the instructions of his home legislature, had voted against Lecompton. He had been reviled in the Lower South and applauded in the Northwest. But, while a man of principle, he was a lesser Clay in a time when not even a greater Clay could have succeeded. Breckinridge possessed far more fire and energy. More than six feet tall, straight as an oak, with a youthful dash that made him seem more a Highland chieftain than a serious legislator, he brought to the Senate debates a high-bred impressiveness of speech and manner. But he lacked originality, and, as a colleague later wrote, was to be grouped not with the constructors of institutions, but with those who fashion and polish what others design.[25]

The relatively unknown candidate was Abraham Lincoln. Although most literate Americans had read at least some fragments from his speeches, of the man himself the vast majority of Easterners and Southerners knew nothing. The initial tendency in hostile quarters was naturally to depreciate him, the Washington *Union* declaring that so insignificant a nominee could never carry New York and Pennsylvania, and the Albany *Atlas and Argus* saying that the first news of the choice in Chicago had been regarded as a hoax. But a fairer view quickly supervened. The great Know-Nothing organ, the New York *Express*, pronounced him a much better nominee than Frémont and a wiser selection than Seward. The New York *Sun*, Democratic but close to the masses, hailed him as a strong candidate, certain to make a good President. Although James Russell Lowell expressed regret in the October *Atlantic* that the more advanced New Yorker had not been named, Douglas was emphatic in telling a group of Washington Republicans that they had made no mistake: "Gentlemen, you have nominated a very able and a very honest man."

Curiosity regarding his personality and views was intense, and journalists and party leaders hastened to supply all the information they could find. That

25 H. L. Dawes, "Two Vice-Presidents," *Century Magazine*, July, 1895.

his self-made career, homely virtues, and original vein of thought had a broad potential appeal to the masses was evident to all. The Republican editors, led by Medill, Bryant, Greeley, and Bowles, at once emphasized the log cabin. flat-boat, and country store background; they all described the scanty schooling, the eager pursuit of knowledge, and the development of a tough, sinewy, intensely logical mind. On the morrow of the nomination, the New York *Tribune* struck the general keynote by hailing him as "a Man of the People, raised by his own genius and integrity from the humblest to the highest position, having made for himself an honored name as a lawyer, an advocate, a popular orator, a statesman, and a Man." [26]

"If Lincoln should be elected," said a highly respected Democrat, "he will be a mere nullity in the Administration." (So went a newspaper paragraph the week of the nomination.)

"It strikes me," answered a Republican who heard the observation, "that a man who by his own genius and force of character has raised himself from being a penniless and uneducated flatboatman on the Illinois river to the position which Mr. Lincoln now occupies, is not likely to be a nullity anywhere."

Springfield was forthwith invaded by reporters and political visitors who labored amain to diffuse a correct understanding of the country lawyer on whom fate had so suddenly laid her finger. George Opdyke, soon to be mayor of New York, published in Bryant's *Evening Post* a significant vignette. He found Lincoln living in a house that was handsome but not pretentious, its rooms neatly but quietly furnished, and its library holding long rows of books. The candidate received callers with an urbanity which Opdyke found surprising; for if awkward abroad, at home he appeared easy if not graceful, and his conversation was fluent, agreeable, and polite. What was of more importance, his talk reflected an acute, decided, and original mind; he had views of his own, founded in the main on sound common sense, though now and then a striking phrase revealed some original insight. [27]

Very similar was the letter which the New York *Herald* published from a Springfield correspondent. He, too, found Lincoln in a dignified, comfortable residence suitable to a gentleman of means. He thought the candidate far from ugly, for when engaged in earnest conversation his features lightened into a highly engaging expression. Learning that the townsfolk all admired him, he quoted a typical citizen. "He is honest, talks sense, and is not too proud to sit down upon his doorstep in his shirt sleeves and chat with his neighbors." [28] The correspondent of the Baltimore *Patriot* dwelt upon Lincoln's patient

26 N. Y. *Weekly Tribune*, May 26, 1860.
27 Nevins, *Evening Post*, 263, 264.
28 N. Y. *Herald* correspondence, dated August 8, 1860.

shrewdness in dealing with crowds of callers and floods of mail. His intimate friends, aware that he had a deep insight into human nature and a sound judgment of men and motives, remarked that he had astonished them by his dexterity in meeting these new burdens.[29] He concealed an impatience which "Billy" Herndon noted:

"Lincoln is well and is doing well—has hundreds of letters daily—many visitors every hour from all sections. He is bored—bored badly. Good gracious, I would not have his place and be bored as he is. I could not endure it." [30]

The honest newspaper material effectively counteracted malicious Democratic talk of Lincoln's Hoosier style of living, gauche manners, and essential ignorance. It destroyed such slurs as the New York *Herald's* editorial quip that the Republicans had passed over Seward, Chase, and other statesmen to take up a fourth-rate lecturer who delivered his hackneyed compositions at $200 apiece. A generous testimonial to Lincoln's talents came from Bates, who in a widely published letter to Orville H. Browning wrote that he had known the man for more than twenty years, and that his truth, courage, and candor, his powers and will to use them, abundantly qualified him for the Presidency.[31] Another came from John Bell, who generously mentioned in a speech the high impression which Lincoln had made in Congress upon himself and others.

Something was accomplished, too, by the campaign biographies of Lincoln. Party leaders called for a million copies of some cheap life to be put in the hands of indifferent, ill-informed, and secluded voters. William Dean Howells, then an editorial writer on the *Ohio State Journal*, was commissioned by Follett, Foster & Co. of Cincinnati, to write one, which appeared in abbreviated form in June and in full text in July. It enjoyed a wide sale. It would have been a better book had Howells not missed one of the opportunities of his career by failing to go to Springfield to interview Lincoln. Nearly half the text was devoted to the period preceding Lincoln's Congressional term. John L. Scripps, Chicago newspaperman, undertook a very hasty and very brief biography (he was required to compress it within thirty-two printed pages) on joint commission by the New York *Tribune* and Chicago *Tribune*; selling in large lots for two cents a copy, it had a wide circulation.[32] Lincoln, after protesting that his early life could be condensed into Gray's sentence on the short and simple annals of the poor, prepared some biographical material for it. Horace White wrote its account of the Douglas-Lincoln debates. Other biographies appeared—one by James Q. Howard, one anonymously issued by Thayer & Eldridge of Boston,

29 Quoted by N. Y. *Weekly Tribune*, September 22, 1860.
30 June 19, 1860; Trumbull Papers.
31 N. Y. *Weekly Tribune*, June 30, 1860.
32 Horace White, June 27, 1860, Robert Todd Lincoln Papers. See E. J. Wessen's essay on campaign biographies in Angle, ed., *Papers in Illinois History*.

SATURDAY, MAY 19, 1860.

"HONEST OLD ABE."

The People's Candidate for President.

"RAILS AND FLAT-BOATS."

Log Cabins and Hard Cider Come Again?

Biographical Sketch of Abraham Lincoln.

ABRAHAM LINCOLN is a native of Hardin county, Kentucky. He was born on the 12th day of February, 1809. His parents were both from Virginia, and were certainly not of the first families. His paternal grandfather, Abraham Lincoln, emigrated from Rockingham county, Virginia, to Kentucky, about 1781 or '2, where a year or two later he was killed by Indians, not in battle, but by stealth, while he was laboring to open a farm in the forest. His ancestors, who were respectable members of the Society of Friends, went to Virginia from Berks county, Pennsylvania. Descendants of the same stock still reside in the eastern part of that State.

Mr. Lincoln's father, at the death of his father was but six years of age, and he grew up literally without education. He removed from Kentucky to what is now Spencer county, Indiana, in 1816. The family reached their new home about the time the State was admitted into the Union. The region in which they settled was rude and wild, and they endured, for some years, the hard experience of a frontier life, in which the struggle with nature for existence and security is to be maintained only by constant vigilance. Bears, wolves and other wild animals still infested the woods, and young Lincoln acquired more skill in the use of the rifle than knowledge of books. There were institutions here and there known by the flattering denomination of "schools," but no qualification was required of a teacher beyond "readin', writin' and cypherin'," as the vernacular phrase ran, so far as the rule of three. If a straggler supposed to understand Latin happened to sojourn in the neighborhood, he was looked upon as a wizard, and regarded with an

of the prominence now given to the chief actor in that exciting event, it cannot fail to be interesting to all.

The affair came off on the fourth day of October, 1854. The State Fair had been in progress two days, and the capital was full of all manner of men. The Nebraska bill had been passed on the previous twenty-second of May. Mr. Douglas had returned to Illinois to meet an outraged constituency. He had made a fragmentary speech in Chicago, the people filling up each hiatus in a peculiar and good humored way. He called the people a mob— they called him a rowdy. The "mob" had the best of it, both then and at the election which succeeded. The notoriety of all these events had stirred up the politics of the State from bottom to top. Hundreds of politicians had met at Springfield expecting a tournament of an unusual character—Douglas, Breese, Kœrner, Lincoln, Trumbull, Matteson, Yates, Codding, John Calhoun, (of the order of the Candle Box,) John M. Palmer, the whole house of the McConnells, Singleton, (known to fame in the Mormon War,) Thos. L. Harris, and a host of others. Several speeches were made before and several after, the passage between LINCOLN and DOUGLAS, but that was justly held to be the event of the season.

We do not remember whether a challenge to debate passed between the friends of the speaker or not, but there was a perfectly amicable understanding between Lincoln and Douglas, that the former should speak two or three hours and the latter reply in just as little or as much time as he chose. Mr. Lincoln took the stand at two o'clock—a large crowd in attendance, and Mr. Douglas seated on a small platform in front of the desk. The first half-hour of Mr. Lincoln's speech was taken up with compliments to his distinguished friend Judge Douglas, and dry allusions to the political events of the past few years. His distinguished friend Judge Douglas had taken his seat, as solemn as the Cock-Lane ghost, evidently with the design of not moving a muscle till it came his turn to speak. The laughter provoked by Lincoln's exordium, however, soon began to make him uneasy; and when Mr. L. arrived at his (Douglas') speech pronouncing the Missouri Compromise "a sacred thing which no ruthless hand would ever be reckless enough to disturb," he opened his lips far enough to remark, "A first-rate speech!" This was the beginning of an amusing colloquy.

"Yes," continued Lincoln, "so affectionate was my friend's regard for this compromise line, that when Texas was admitted into the Union

The Chicago *Tribune* Offers a Brief Biography of Lincoln.

and so on. Much the best of them was D. W. Bartlett's *Life and Public Services of the Hon. Abraham Lincoln*, a three-hundred-and-fifty-four-page book, with steel portrait carefully wrought. The previous year, Bartlett had brought out a volume on twenty-one men regarded as possible Presidential candidates, including such minor figures as Orr and Dickinson but omitting Lincoln.[33] Howard's book possessed some fresh qualities, for it was largely the product of a visit he had paid to Springfield in order to collect material for Howells.

Lincoln alone of the major candidates made no speech during the campaign. As he confidentially explained to friends, his conservative opinions had been so often expressed that honest seekers of his views could easily find them, while any new expression would be misrepresented by bad men North and South. This was true; but it was also true that his silence permitted continuous attacks on him as an enemy of the South.[34] In that section, countless voters had no access to his past views. In the North, an edition of his debates with Douglas was in its fourth printing even before his nomination, and sold widely thereafter. His Cooper Union address had been circulated far and wide. The *Political Textbook* for 1860, which the New York *Tribune* scattered over the North in six editions before the end of August, contained his house-divided speech, part of the Freeport debate, the Cooper Union address, and three lesser utterances. These sufficed not only to present his views but to illustrate his intellectual qualities. Judicious Northerners doubtless agreed with the London *Critic*: "We collect from the speeches of Mr. Lincoln that he has a mind of the straightforward rather than the subtle order; that he rather seizes upon great and prominent facts and argues them to plain conclusions than builds up elegant but fragile theories . . . ; that he is earnest more than passionate, and persuasive more than commanding. Indeed, every one of his speeches which we have read bears upon it evidence that he is 'Honest Old Abe.' "

The caution that characterized Lincoln's part in the campaign was illustrated by an incident of the notification ceremonies in Springfield. For the eminent committee which arrived on a special train from Chicago, Mrs. Lincoln had provided champagne and sandwiches. Two Illinois politicians exclaimed that the champagne would never do—it would offend temperance people; and though

33 Lincoln refused to look at the proofsheets of Howells's life. "When," he wrote, "by the lessons of the past, and the united voice of all discreet friends, I am neither [to] write or speak a word for the public, how dare I to send forth, by my authority, a volume of hundreds of pages, for adversaries to make points upon without end? Were I to do so, the Convention would have a right to reassemble, and substitute another name for mine." To Samuel Galloway, June 19, 1860; Lincoln Collection, Ill. State Hist. Lib. But he did later make detailed private corrections in a copy.

34 When Zach Chandler made an effort to bring Lincoln to Detroit for a speech, Lyman Trumbull reported that the candidate thought that this would be departing from a fixed line of conduct which his friends had approved. Trumbull, September 3, 1860; Chandler Papers.

Mrs. Lincoln spiritedly defended her arrangements, Lincoln substituted ice water. His acceptance speech was a mere expression of thanks and of his high sense of responsibility. Caution was recommended not only by party leaders but by William Cullen Bryant, who as "an old campaigner" urged Lincoln to avoid making promises, expressing opinions, or forming any arrangements for the future. "The people have nominated you without any pledges or engagements of any sort; they are satisfied with you as you are, and they want you to do nothing at present but allow yourself to be elected." The vast majority of your friends, Bryant continued, "want you to make no speeches, write no letters as a candidate, enter into no pledges, make no promises, nor even give any of those kind words which men are apt to interpret into promises." [35] Lincoln declined to answer letters from strangers upon political topics, most correspondents getting nothing but an acknowledgment. But caution was not alone responsible for his refusal to make explanations which might reassure the South. He was sincerely convinced that Southern threats of secession were mere political gestures. Like nearly all Northerners, he failed to grasp the passionate fears and resentments of the Southern people.

While Herndon took sole charge of the law practice, Lincoln spent the summer in the governor's room at the State House. Assisted only by his secretary, John G. Nicolay, he took pains to see callers great and small, his mingled dignity and bonhomie making a happy impression on all. Some of his most interesting interviews were with Southerners who came full of prejudice, but left satisfied with his loyalty to the full constitutional rights of the South. He held no political conferences, and though he talked casually with visiting Republican leaders, he left the direction of the campaign to E. D. Morgan's national committee with scarcely a private hint of his wishes. As Southern alarm was increasingly fanned that summer by press and oratory, the demand for a counteracting pronouncement by Lincoln grew. But he continued to resist it, maintaining that in view of his repeated statements that the Republican Party would never molest slavery within the States, a new enunciation would but give an impression of weakness and cowardice.

"Why do not uneasy men *read* what I have already said? and what our platform says?" he asked. "If they will not read, or heed these, would they read or heed a repetition of them?" But his statement did not cover the whole ground. Had he realized the mental and emotional state of the South since Harper's Ferry, he would possibly have taken a different view. At the same time, his papers contain much evidence that he comprehended the rabid growth of Yanceyism in the cotton kingdom and pondered the means of meeting it. He saw no hope of arresting it by aught he could say; a conciliatory statement would not

35 June 16, 1860; Robert Todd Lincoln Papers, LC.

affect the South but would affect the North, creating division in his party and giving Douglas a powerful lever for prying away votes.

[V]

All four parties maintained busy headquarters. The Breckinridge campaign was managed by Governor Isaac Stevens of Washington Territory, with offices in the capital. Douglas fought his own battle with modest aid from an organization headed by Miles Taylor, a Representative of Louisiana, and the two Wickliffes, father and son. August Belmont as treasurer was never able to supply adequate funds. In managing the Bell-Everett campaign, Boteler had desultory help from some former Whigs and Know-Nothings. The most efficient organization by far was that of the Republicans. Their machine, strong in half the North in 1856, stronger still in every subsequent election, was now given a tremendous reinforcement by politicians eager to find room on a victorious ship. Village politicians, crossroads squires, country editors, and ward-workers from Maine to Missouri, the backbone of the party, were turning toward the holders of future power; while the tough-fibred managers at the top—E. D. Morgan, Norman B. Judd, Caleb Smith, Gideon Welles, Austin Blair, Simon Cameron, and the like —left no opportunity unused. Two Illinois leaders, David Davis and Leonard Swett, took immediate steps to conciliate the crestfallen Thurlow Weed, while Orville Browning hastened to St. Louis to enlist Judge Bates. As the Seward-Weed men began laboring heartily for the cause, Bates published a long letter in the St. Louis *Democrat* arguing for Lincoln's election. Republican unity was perfect.[36]

While the eagle of victory rode on Republican standards, croaking ravens of imminent defeat perched on all the opposition flags. The Constitutional Unionists and the Breckinridge forces, with some initial hope of victory, soon lost heart; and if Douglas waged a magnificent battle, it was not for the Presidency but for a larger object.

For the Constitutional Unionists, D. D. Barnard penned the ablest argument in a hard-hitting pamphlet, "Truths for the Times," directed primarily against Lincoln. The real object of the Republican Party, he wrote, was to effect the destruction of slavery; some wishing to do this at once, some in an indefinite future. He quoted Sumner's recent statement that the proslavery power must die, once the Republicans triumphed, as a poisoned rat dies of rage in its hole; and his declaration that the free communities must become a belt of fire about the South, within which slavery would perish. He quoted Seward's assertion in March, 1858, that the interests of the white race demanded the ultimate emanci-

36 Bates, *Diary*, 132 (May 31, 1860).

pation of all men. He quoted Lincoln's phrase about putting slavery in the course of ultimate extinction. Some men tried to pretend that the sole object of the party was the exclusion of slavery from the Territories. This was hypocrisy; there was no more chance of slavery going into any existing Territory than of its going into the land of the Eskimos. With the feeling over slavery what it was, and value of slaves so high, wrote Barnard, the migration of masters with their bondsmen to regions where soil, climate, and productions absolutely forbade the profitable employment of black labor was utterly preposterous. No, the real aim of the Republican Administration would be to hasten the extinction of slavery; and as soon as the Administration took power it could and would do a great deal to give effect to its hostility to the institution. It would be an Administration of Northern antislavery men; it would fill the Federal offices with antislavery appointees; and it would carry out Seward's pledge to reform the Supreme Court.[37]

The gravamen of Barnard's argument was that the triumph of such a party must inevitably give the signal for secession. Southern disunionists were always watching for an opportunity to be driven from the Union by Northern aggression. Nor did he doubt for a moment that Southern conspirators had planned the disruption of the Charleston convention and the organization of a separate party on extreme Southern ground as steps toward an independent republic. The one way, therefore, to defer the crisis, checkmate the conspirators, and save the Union, was to defeat Lincoln. Unquestionably Barnard was right about the real intent of the Republican leaders. Their aim was not primarily to keep slavery out of the Territories, for it could not go there, but to put it in the way of ultimate extinction everywhere. His pamphlet was a contribution to realism. But the Republican reply to his argument was simple. Lincoln had candidly avowed his desire to see slavery put in the way of ultimate extinction—and what of it? He had promised not to touch it in the States; no sudden, arbitrary, or unjust step was intended; none could or would be taken.

Though both Bell and Everett maintained for some time a belief that they might win, their cause was hopeless from the outset. As late as July 30, Bell was convinced that his ticket would carry all but two or three of the slaveholding States, and that if it could win in Pennsylvania, or New York, or Ohio, it would obtain a majority in the electoral college.[38] He was anxious for a coalition in the North with the Douglas Democrats on some terms of equality. The electors chosen on a combined ticket should have freedom to vote for whichever man they could elect to the Presidency—and as Douglas could gain no Southern electors, this would obviously be Bell. Since the prime object of both parties

37 Pamphlet, dated Albany, August 15, 1860.
38 Bell to A. R. Boteler, July 2, 30, 1860; Boteler Papers.

was to save the Union, the Tennesseean saw no violation of principle in such an arrangement. Everett, who had accepted his empty honor reluctantly, was more moderate in his hopes. For some years he had been wholly withdrawn from politics; feeling himself Bell's superior, he disliked taking second place on the ticket; and he feared that his fund for saving Mount Vernon would suffer heavily.[39] As the campaign progressed, to be sure, even his slow blood moved faster. With a little show of real strength in the North, he believed the ticket could sweep the entire South.[40] But the show never appeared, and realists like Amos Lawrence admitted the hopelessness of the cause.

The fact was that the Constitutional Union Party could not breast the tremendous tide of enthusiasm for Lincoln in the North, the deep surge of loyalty to Breckinridge and State Rights Democracy in the South. The conservative businessmen and planters who ought to have toiled amain for Bell were just the men most prone to indifference and apathy. They would vote, but they would not take off their coats and go to work.[41] Only a fervent crusade for the Union could have succeeded, and the whole Bell-Everett enterprise was too balanced, Laodicean, and timid. The platform pronouncement for the Constitution, the Union, and the laws meant nothing. Whose Constitution—Clay's? Calhoun's? Seward's? What laws? Bell refused to answer, referring inquirers to his past course on slavery issues. On examination, these proved highly equivocal; and while it was possible to quote his proslavery utterances in the South and his antislavery statements in the North, it was also possible to reverse the process. Everett, too, declined to interpret the party's doctrines. The Constitution is platform enough, he fatuously remarked, and the public character of the candidates sufficient guaranty of their fidelity to it. Their characters might be well enough, but what of their backbones? Before long it was shown that some of Bell's utterances on behalf of slavery were more extreme than any of Breckinridge's, while some of Everett's early excoriations of slavery were severe enough for an abolitionist. The party was thus left looking as two-faced as Janus; a party that appealed to principle while clinging to unprincipled equivocations.[42]

It was clear that despite all its noble intentions and intense "respectability," the Bell-Everett movement would do no more than poll a sizable protest vote against disunion. Its feebleness made the temptation to vote-trading and expedient alliances irresistible. Half the Northern States soon reported Bell-Everett men engaged in dickers and trades. In New Jersey, they were willing to fuse with the Breckinridge forces; in Georgia, with the Douglas men; and in New

39 To Kennedy, May 17, 1860; Kennedy Papers.
40 He believed so even after election; MS Journal, November 8, 11.
41 G. S. Hilliard, September 21, 1860; Boteler Papers.
42 Bell, July 30, Boteler Papers; Everett, May 7, June 2, Crittenden Papers.

York with almost anybody—so the reports ran. It was only in the border areas that the Constitutional Unionists mustered a dominating power.

[VI]

Not even Breckinridge could give much grace or dignity to the thrust of the Southern Democracy. The nominee, far from being identified with the slave-code extremists, had so recently as 1856 made a distinctly non-interventionist speech. Far from adopting the principles of Slidell, Toombs, and Cobb, he had shrunk during the Lecompton contest from throwing his weight into one scale or the other, and had been charged with absenting himself from the Senate chamber lest he might have to break a tie vote. His generous letter to Douglas during the senatorial contest of 1858 was well remembered, as was the fact that he had cordially taken Douglas's hand when the Illinoisan, amid Southern scowls, reentered the Senate chamber in January, 1859.

Breckinridge played his part in the canvass with gentlemanly decorum. But it was impossible to give moderation and perfume to a political effort so largely vengeful in character; for the Breckinridge-Lane ticket had been devised by Slidell, Buchanan, Cobb, and others to kill Douglas and other party rebels. It was impossible, too, to divest the Breckinridge party of a disunionist aroma which hung about it even while the candidate was protesting his devotion to national integrity. It was all too patent that Yancey, Rhett, Iverson, A. G. Brown, and others looked to the organization to make secession unescapable.

The essentially sectional character of the party could not be mistaken. To be sure, many prominent Northerners clung to it. Yancey boasted that three previous candidates of the Democracy, Cass, Pierce, and Buchanan, were upholding Breckinridge, while only Martin Van Buren stood with Douglas—and he very quietly. Eight of the ten Democratic Senators from the North, Bright, Fitch, Bigler, Gwin, and others, were for Breckinridge, as were four-fifths of the Representatives. So were such men as Caleb Cushing and Daniel S. Dickinson.[43] Against these men, Douglas's best champions in the South, Soulé, Forsyth, Foote, and Jere Clemens, were a feeble detachment. Yet somehow the Northern names were not really impressive. They meant simply that party regularity and the power of the Administration, joined in some instances with an inveterate sympathy for the slave States and in others with a timid desire to placate the men who threatened secession, had brought a large number of old party wheel-horses into harness. Everybody comprehended that Breckinridge could not carry a single free State. Everybody knew also that (as Douglas correctly said) while not all of Breckinridge's followers were secessionists, every secessionist was a

43 W. L. Yancey, speech at Memphis, August 14, 1860 (pamphlet).

CIRCULAR.

National Democratic Committee Rooms,

No. 28 Four-and-a-Half street, Washington, D. C.

WASHINGTON CITY, *June 30*, 1860.

The undersigned, Committee of Finance appointed by the Executive Committee, address you in relation to the collecting of funds for the expenses of the campaign. We need not urge the importance of the promptest action, with the view of efficient organization throughout the country. The preparation and circulation of documents which will place our cause before the great body of the American people on its just ground of nationality, devotion to the equal rights of all, and which will exhibit the pre-eminent qualifications of our candidates, BRECKINRIDGE and LANE, is of the first consequence. We feel, also, that all our friends will appreciate the necessity of untiring correspondence to perfect and consolidate the organization of our party throughout the country.

The Executive Committee is now prepared at once to enter upon the duties which have been devolved upon them; and they now appeal for efficient pecuniary aid. We have bold and desperate opponents to meet, and we need for the purposes mentioned a large amount of funds. We hope that no delay whatever will occur in answering this circular. Contributions should be forwarded to the Chairman of the Committee. It will be our purpose to see that the utmost economy be practiced in the use of funds.

With this determination on our part, we appeal again to the liberality of our friends to furnish us with the necessary means, to the end that our documents may go to every town and hamlet in the country.

Believing that an appeal for prompt action will be at once responded to by you and all our friends, we subscribe ourselves your friends in the cause of the great Democratic party of the country,

ISAAC I. STEVENS, *Oregon, Chairman.*
AUGUSTUS SCHELL, *New York.*
ISAAC H. WRIGHT, *Massachusetts.*
JOHN R. THOMPSON, *New Jersey.*
ROBERT W. JOHNSON, *Arkansas.*
JOHN W. STEVENSON, *Kentucky.*
JESSE D. BRIGHT, *Indiana.*
JOHN SLIDELL, *Louisiana.*
WILLIAM FLINN, *Washington City.*

Address—
HON. ISAAC I. STEVENS, M. C.,
Chairman of the National Democratic Executive Committee,
Washington City, D. C.

The Breckinridge Democrats Appeal for Funds.

Breckinridge follower. "Parson" Brownlow named twenty-six Southern leaders, all members of Congress, governors, or ex-governors, who in supporting Breckinridge were openly preaching disunion in the event of Lincoln's election.[44]

The unofficial headquarters of the Breckinridge forces, naturally, were in the White House. There Slidell, Bright, Bigler, Lane, and other managers conferred with the President and laid plans; thence patronage was manipulated, and a subtle venom sent coursing through all the veins of the party. The animosity which many Administration men expressed for Douglas recalled the bitterest warfare between Jeffersonians and Burrites, or Hamilton and Adams men. The *Ohio State Journal* remarked that the rival Democratic factions of that State displayed a violence, a vindictiveness, and a passion of hate to which it knew no parallel. In no Southern State would the Breckinridge faction consent to any compromise or coalition—not even in Virginia, where Governor John Letcher among others deplored the schism.[45] It held rigidly aloof even in those border States where an alliance with popular sovereignty Democrats offered the only hope of defeating Bell. "They do well to call us bolters," vociferated Daniel S. Dickinson at the "Hard" convention in Syracuse on August 7; "for we intend to bolt the door fast against all hucksters, auctioneers, and jobbers." [46] The nominee of the Breckinridge men for governor in New York, James T. Brady, had opposed Buchanan's Lecompton policy, but for a much longer period he had evinced his hearty distrust and dislike of Douglas.

Almost from the outset, and largely because of the stiff aversion to compromise, the Breckinridge Democrats anticipated defeat. There being three hundred and three electoral votes, they needed one hundred and fifty-two to win. If they could gain one hundred and twenty electors in the South, with the seven of California and Oregon (where Federal officeholders were mobilized in a powerful phalanx for Breckinridge), they would require only twenty-five more votes in the North. But this would mean carrying New York, or Pennsylvania, or Ohio plus either Indiana or Illinois—and most Southerners soon realized that the task was almost impossible. Only a complete fusion of the Douglas-Breckinridge-Bell elements would have offered a chance of clean-cut victory over Lincoln.

The obvious strategy for the National Democrats, any broad fusion being impossible, was to give the Douglas forces a free field in the Northwest and the Bell-Everett Party a full opportunity in the border area in the hope of throwing the election into the House. Then some compromise Democrat might well be chosen President. But strategy was precisely what the Breckinridge men

44 Fite, *op. cit.*, 186, 187.
45 Crenshaw, *Slave States in 1860*, 141.
46 N. Y. *Weekly Tribune*, August 11, 1860.

neglected. No evidence whatever appears that the candidate, the national committee, or the advisers who tramped in and out of Buchanan's office, ever formed a serious plan. Some leaders believed that the contest would, in the end, shake down to a close race between Breckinridge and Lincoln, the two other candidates falling into the background; and that national conservatism would elect the Democrat. Other leaders, including Buchanan, believed that the grand goal was the destruction of Douglas. Still others, the extremists like Rhett, Yancey, and A. G. Brown, whom Senator Hammond cursed as odious wreckers of the national temple, looked forward to party defeat as opening the door to a Southern republic.[47] Let the slave States have done with the whole wretched system; let the South, instead of scrambling to win a President in the House, turn to manly resistance! Still other Breckinridge men, the great majority, confused, helpless, and despondent, were content merely to drift. As the campaign wore on, less and less talk of a possible House contest was heard, and more and more pessimism was expressed. As Sam Houston remarked, the American people liked to have their Presidential elections settled at the polls and dreaded a remission of the question to the House. Even in the Lower South a feeling existed that, calamitous as the election of Lincoln would be, a ferocious contest in Congress, all the factions and sections clashing in embittered antagonism, might well prove more disastrous.[48]

One Southern Democratic leader alone, Jefferson Davis, attempted a stroke of bold leadership to defeat Lincoln. Seeing certain defeat ahead, as he wrote years later in his memoirs, he undertook to bring together all the opposition groups. His hope appears to have been that some such man as Horatio Seymour, devoted to the Union and standing outside old factional quarrels, might be named in the stead of Breckinridge, Bell, and Douglas. He made approaches to all three candidates.

Bell and Breckinridge, he tells us, promised him that they would withdraw if Douglas would do so.[49] This is plausible; for both knew that they had little if any chance, and Bell in particular had been eager for fusion arrangements by his party. Most of Bell's party, reconciled to defeat, would have been ready to fall in behind any moderate and able man who showed firm attachment to the Union. The plan was wrecked, however, on the rock of Douglas's refusal. He wanted no bargain with Southern radicals. He had denounced all schemes for carrying the election into Congress. "By God, sir," he told Representative Edward McPherson of Pennsylvania, "the election shall never go into the House; before it shall go into the House, I will throw it to Lincoln."[50] He informed

47 To M. C. M. Hammond, July 4, 1860; Hammond Papers, LC.
48 Cf. Crenshaw, *Slave States in 1860*, 70–73.
49 Davis, *Rise and Fall*, I, 52.
50 N. Y. *Weekly Tribune*, October 20, 1860.

Davis that the proposed plan was impracticable, because, if he withdrew, his Northern Democratic supporters would turn to Lincoln rather than to any substituted Democrat. "I am in the hands of my friends," he stated in effect, "and my friends will not accept such a scheme." [51] His own plan for the party was simple. If he dropped out, no other Democrat could be elected, for none could carry vital Northern States. But if Breckinridge resigned in his favor, then he would be confident of party and personal success.

By late summer, the question was no longer of Lincoln's election but of the results of his impending victory; and, in the play within the play, it was the inner drama—the radicals of the South fervently whipping up secessionist sentiment and one candidate alone, Douglas, dealing courageously with the issue—which held the gaze of shrewd observers.

51   Milton, *Eve*, 487; Wilson, *Slave Power*, II, 52; N. Y. *Weekly Tribune*, September 15.

10

The Election of Lincoln

HOT AS the summer of 1860 became, the breath of sectional passion grew hotter still. Early in August, the veteran Mississippi unionist Henry S. Foote, who had once exchanged blows with Jefferson Davis and had always opposed the Southern extremists, undertook to warn the country of imminent catastrophe. He was in New York at the time; he had been irritated by complacent Northern statements that the recent elections in Missouri, Kentucky, and North Carolina indicated the South would submit to Lincoln's election; and he wrote the *Herald* in contradiction. All prominent Southerners visiting the North, he declared, agreed with him that secession was certain if Lincoln won. Even moderates thought so—and he quoted a letter from a unionist who, while deprecating rash action, believed that on the morrow of Lincoln's victory the Southern States would indignantly strike for revolution. Foote might have pointed to the Southern newspapers. The Richmond *Enquirer* spoke for dozens of them when it appealed to the spirit of '76: "Resistance to wrong and injury—to tyranny, whether of one man or eighteen millions—is the cherished birthright of every citizen of the Federal Union." [1]

In parts of the South, as men heard such orators as Reuben Davis assert that war was inevitable, mob feeling boiled near the surface. George W. Cable describes an incident illustrating the excitement that sometimes flashed up in New Orleans. A crowd suddenly roared down Royal Street, fierce in pursuit of a pallid fugitive. "Hang him, hang him!" the mob thundered. Before rescue came he was almost lynched. He was a vendor of campaign medals (for half the population, men, women, and children, wore ribanded Breckinridge emblems) who in opening his stock had failed to notice that a Lincoln and Hamlin badge had crept in among his wares. As the mob dispersed an onlooker spoke up: "Didn't I tell you? Bound to have war. It's already begun."

The storm-cloud background of the Breckinridge campaign in the Lower South lay in a concerted if rather unsystematic effort to create emotions which would give that section a monolithic unity in facing the North. Many politicians

1 N. Y. *Herald*, August 13, *Enquirer*, July 10, 1860; Foote was now a Tennesseean.

like Keitt, Porcher Miles, and Yancey, many editors like the Rhetts, were eager for the early destruction of the Union. Many more, like Slidell, who had stood for secession in 1856 if Frémont were elected and had threatened it again in 1858, were not eager—but were ready. A large number, while wishing that the Union could be preserved, made defiant utterances and urged extreme measures in order to frighten the free States into concessions; they hoped that the crisis would end in writing guarantees for the South into the Constitution. Jefferson Davis and R. M. T. Hunter well represented this group. Still others indulged in harsh denunciations of cowardice and submission simply in order to shame voters out of the Constitutional Union Party. Raucous warnings of Northern plots, of new John Brown invasions, of servile revolts, and of a Lincolnian program of race equality filled the air. Since Harper's Ferry, the Lower South was in a mood to respond. Men who traveled through the cotton States with eyes and ears open found great numbers of men deeply, terribly aroused. As the political pot seethed at barbecues and rallies, many communities became gripped by a rising excitement. Garibaldi's triumphs in Italy, the civil war in Mexico, and the visit of the Prince of Wales seemed in comparison with the crisis only trivial events.[2]

A thousand Southern voices were raised to inform the North that Lincoln's election would be the signal for disunion. Such fire-eaters as Wigfall of Texas and Durant Da Ponte of New Orleans, speaking for Breckinridge, declared secession the only possible alternative. They drew lurid pictures of abolitionist armies invading the South, firing homes, and murdering women and children. Lincoln's Presidency would mean emancipation, declared the Charleston *Mercury*, and emancipation would mean a loss not merely of political ascendency, but of every vital interest. "It is the loss of liberty, property, home, country— everything that makes life worth having." The terrors of submission would be tenfold worse than the terrors of disunion. It is idle to deny, exclaimed Keitt, that the North is to the South a hostile community. "Shall we permit a party stained with treason, hideous with insurrection, and dripping with blood, to occupy the government?"[3] One Mississippian in a campaign speech described the Union as "fettered antipathies." Incendiary pamphlets were being scattered broadcast throughout the section. One, penned by William D. Porter of Charleston, was typical in its denunciation of present tyrannies and its evocation of a vision of still greater evils in the future. While we are now submitting to Northern rapacity, cruelty, and hatred, wrote the author, the worst is yet to come. "When new States are admitted; when Abolition becomes stronger and stronger;

2 White, *Rhett*, 163; Crenshaw, 295, 296; Reuben Davis, *Recollections*, 390.
3 Charleston *Mercury*, October 11; N. Y. *Weekly Tribune*, July 28, 1860.

when the power to amend develops the power to destroy—how are we to stem the torrent or avoid the cataract?" [4]

But it was significant that abler, saner men than these hotheads also predicted disunion. Former Speaker Orr, writing on July 23 to his constituents, declared that, since the election of Lincoln was a certainty, they would have to decide whether they would submit to the rule of a party whose fundamental principle was open, undisguised, and declared war on their social institutions. He believed that honor and safety would require prompt secession and that, if the North did not concede new and firmer guarantees of Southern rights, the slave States should form a new government. Henry W. Hilliard of Alabama, speaking in Cooper Union, predicted that Lincoln's success would be followed by a convulsion which would shake the institutions of the country to their deepest foundations. Alexander H. Stephens, who opposed secession, predicted that South Carolina would secede, that the Gulf States would follow, and that after some hesitation by the border region, war would begin. Later, talking with a correspondent of the New York Herald, he repeated that Lincoln's election, now certain, would usher in an attempt at secession and revolution. Robert Toombs, while less sober and responsible than these men, was never a wild radical. Yet he was quoted as writing privately from Washington that he would come home to raise ten thousand troops; and when he crossed the Potomac again it would be with drawn sword. He added that thirty members of Congress were pledged to that unflinching position. [5]

Not a few men in the cotton kingdom knew that the governors were exchanging letters on possible ways and means of secession. Gist of South Carolina, on October 5, sent a confidential missive to his colleagues, declaring that concert of action was essential, that South Carolina desired some other State to take the lead or at least move simultaneously in seceding, and that if none did so, she would in his opinion secede alone. The governors of North Carolina and Louisiana replied that, with public opinion much divided, their States would probably not regard Lincoln's election as justifying secession; and even Joseph E. Brown declared that Georgia, if acting alone, would probably wait for an overt act. But the governors of Mississippi and Florida believed that their States would join any other in secession; while Governor Moore thought that Alabama would cooperate with any two or more. [6]

It was the obvious duty of the Administration to rebuke these counsels of

4 "State Sovereignty and the Doctrine of Coercion," pamphlet.
5 N. Y. Weekly Tribune, August 11, September 22, 1860; Johnston and Browne, Stephens, 356; N. Y. Herald September 29, 1860; Sumter, Ga., Republican, quoted N. Y. Weekly Tribune November 3, 1860.
6 Nicolay and Hay, Lincoln, II, 306–314.

disruption with a stern voice. Buchanan should have combined his support of Breckinridge with a Jacksonian admonition to all secessionists. Being what he was, he kept silent. The Administration organ, the *Constitution*, enjoying a temporary boom as a campaign sheet and loosing all its broadsides against Douglas, actually encouraged disunion measures. It declared that if Lincoln were elected, his antislavery Administration would have antislavery officeholders quietly at work in every community, introducing the abolition virus as adroitly as possible, and gradually sowing disaffection among the slaves; while the post office would be converted into a machine for scattering Helper and Garrison publications broadcast, and the Federal marshals would menace, not protect, the public peace. Could the South be expected to wait until it had thus been undermined? "We think not. . . . Let Lincoln be President, and how many months' purchase would the Union be worth?" [7] While the Directory encouraged Editor Browne to write in this vein, Southern Cabinet members were talking intransigently. Secretary Cobb, according to Washington correspondents, went about freely threatening a revolutionary break-up of the Union.[8]

[I]

If Buchanan was supine, Douglas was not. Beginning his campaign as a battle for the Presidency, he shortly converted it into one for the Union. Only for the first two months was the Douglas branch of the Democratc Party able to cherish any hopes. Then it became clear that the ticket would run second to Lincoln in most Northern States, to Breckinridge in most Southern, and to Bell in the borderland—that the party was fated to a crushing defeat in the electoral college. But Douglas, indomitable, indefatigable, never so formidable as when meeting hopeless odds, turned to a far greater object than popular sovereignty—to the cause of national unity. This, even more than the Lecompton struggle, was his finest hour.

He alone of the candidates traveled widely and spoke industriously. When after his nomination a friend told him that the attacks of vindictive enemies and the momentous nature of the issues involved in the contest would compel him to take the stump, he showed reluctance.[9] But the pressure of friends, his wife, and above all of events, soon brought him to the front. One admirer was reminded of Napoleon at Lodi. His temper sternly aroused, he spoke during the summer and fall in nearly every free State; he invaded Virginia, North Carolina, and the Deep South; everywhere he held large crowds, and everywhere he

7 Washington *Constitution*, September 21, 1860.
8 N. Y. *Weekly Tribune*, November 3, 1860.
9 S. J. Anderson, September 2, 1860; Stephens Papers, LC.

took the offensive. Fiery, ready, and able as ever, he imparted his combative spirit to followers. At Concord, New Hampshire, and in Milwaukee, he denounced the Administration with passionate vigor, giving the country revealing glimpses of his personal encounters with the President and eliciting from Buchanan a public letter in denial of some of his assertions. Everywhere he spurned appeasement.

In Boston, the veteran machine politician B. F. Hallett called at the Revere House with oleaginous words, saying that the party would soon be reunited. "Never!" rejoined Douglas. "If you voted against me at Charleston on principle, being for intervention, we cannot act together. If you voted against me out of personal hatred, I know very well how to act toward you!" His denunciation of treasonable schemes was scorching.[10]

The Little Giant had quickly seen that all the omens were unfavorable to his election. Apart from his running mate Herschel Johnson, and Soulé, Forsyth, Dixon of Kentucky, and Alexander H. Stephens, he had no prominent Southern adherents; even his old friend Clingman of North Carolina deserted him. Nor was the list of his Northern friends impressive. In New York, he commanded the aid of Horatio Seymour and Dean Richmond, while August Belmont was chairman of the National Committee, and ex-Governor Washington Hunt eventually joined his column. Forney of Pennsylvania, Reverdy Johnson of Maryland, Pugh and Henry B. Payne of Ohio, W. W. Wick of Indiana, William A. Richardson of Illinois, and H. H. Sibley of Minnesota, were loyal and hardworking as ever. These names, however, nearly exhausted the roster.

His newspapers were a scattered and generally ineffective band. In New York City, the influential Oswald Ottendorfer brought the *Staats-Zeitung* to his side, but he had only the *Herald* among English-language dailies to give him its capricious and sometimes damaging aid—for Bennett's sword wounded friend and foe alike.[11] The Philadelphia *Press* was a wavering and unhappy adherent. In Chicago, he suffered a blow when, late in July, Cyrus H. McCormick paid about ten thousand dollars for the struggling *Times* and combined it with the *Herald*—the faithful James Sheahan losing his editorship. McCormick had en-

10 N. Y. *Weekly Tribune*, August 4, September 15, 1860.
11 Bennett, always with an eye to the main chance, was half for Breckinridge, half for Douglas, and ready to leap to the Republican chariot. Joseph Medill had a friend sound him out early in the campaign. This agent found Bennett not unwilling to bargain with the Republicans, and urged Medill and Norman B. Judd to go see him. As Medill started east, he wrote Lincoln: "We deem it highly important to spike that gun; his affirmative help is not of great consequence, but he is powerful for mischief. He can do us much harm if hostile. If neutralized a *point* is gained. We think his terms will not be immoderate. He is too rich to want money. Social position we suspect is what he wants. He wants to be in a position to be invited with his wife and son to dinner or tea at the White House occasionally, and to be 'made of' by the big men of the party. I think we can afford to agree to that much."

dorsed Buchanan's political policies, while he remembered that Douglas had opposed the extension of his patents; and the *Daily Times* henceforth gave the Senator only lukewarm espousal, trying at the same time to conciliate the Breckinridge Democrats. Its editor was anxious to heal the breach in the party. It may be surmised that if Douglas had not felt certain of his defeat, he would have taken steps to prevent this transfer.[12] The *Missouri Republican,* the most influential Douglas paper in the border area, was the only sheet regarded as at all likely to carry its own State for him. The Albany *Atlas,* Buffalo *Courier,* and a few others did what they could. The weight of the Northern press was for Lincoln, however, as that of the South was for Breckinridge.

Of unmistakable significance were the difficulties which the Douglas organization encountered in raising funds. Belmont, impaneling a weighty committee and making an initial gift of a thousand dollars himself, hoped for a generous response in New York. Yet despite urgent entreaty, the steamship magnate George Law flatly declined to contribute, and the New York Central men who in Belmont's opinion could well afford to pay $100,000 to help gain the State were almost equally indifferent. Important merchants were fearful lest they offend Southern customers by supporting Douglas. In midsummer, Miles Taylor, the energetic Louisiana Congressman toiling in New York for the cause, found the coffers so bare that it seemed hopeless to continue the battle unless fresh sums could be raised. He set up a financial committee of his own under Horace F. Clarke, but it too failed. Frantic appeals from the Northwest for financial assistance had to be given a stony answer, Belmont informing Sibley that his group could not raise for the whole country as much money as Minnesota alone demanded. A little money was scraped together for Maine, whose September election would be taken by many voters as a straw in the wind; but a call upon each Congressional district for a hundred dollars brought nothing into the treasury. To the very end, poverty laid a palsying hand on the Douglasite effort. Wealthy interests of the North saw no reason for aiding a party certain of defeat and a candidate hated by half of the South.[13]

But the obvious imminence of defeat did not daunt Douglas. His protracted tours were undertaken not for votes, but to vindicate his recent course, ensure the downfall of his enemies, and above all to rally men to the Union. His first speeches were at his birthplace in Brandon, Vermont, and in Concord, Boston,

12 Hutchinson, *McCormick,* II, 43 ff. Poor Sheahan, forced to sell, with the sheriff at the door, not a dollar in his pocket, and debts of perhaps four thousand, felt maltreated. He wrote a friend that Douglas had treated him cruelly—"in the matter of the book of which I had hopes, he wantonly interfered to my injury." This was perhaps the life of Douglas, perhaps a projected history of the Kansas struggle. Sheahan probably did not realize the gravity of Douglas's financial embarrassments. See his letters July 28, August 3, Lanphier Papers, Ill. State Hist. Lib.
13 Milton, *Eve,* 488–490.

Portland, Providence, and other New England cities. Meeting Henry Wilson in Boston, he predicted Lincoln's election and said he would go South to urge the people to submit to the result and sustain the national fabric. Making good his word, in Virginia and North Carolina he spoke more courageously upon secession than any other man in the land.

Behind this Southern tour of Douglas's, indeed, lay his conviction that a widespread and intricate conspiracy had been formed to bring about a *coup d'etat* as early as November or December, and that only hard campaigning in the border States could prevent it. He forcibly expressed his fears to Charles Francis Adams, who recorded them in his unpublished diary. According to Douglas, radical leaders of the cotton kingdom wished to form a powerful new slaveholding republic around the Gulf of Mexico, embracing Cuba and the Mexican and Central American states. The Illinoisan learned that when the dissolution of the Baltimore convention made it evident that the Democratic Party would lose the government, certain Southern fire-eaters had laid a plot. They helped to nominate Breckinridge with the idea that they would concentrate upon him the votes of every slaveholding State. They would make special efforts to carry Virginia and Maryland. Then, whether the Republicans won the election or no candidate emerged with a majority, they would declare Breckinridge the rightful President, use their control of the Cabinet to take possession of the Washington departments, and call upon the Southern States to recognize their *de facto* government. The slaveholding area could thus be used as a unit to overthrow the existing regime. It is certain that Douglas believed this conspiracy a grim reality; certain that he thought various high figures in Washington involved in it; and certain that he felt that it could be defeated only by carrying Virginia (and if possible her neighbors) against Breckinridge.

Hence the Little Giant's dramatic invasion of Maryland, Virginia, and North Carolina, denouncing disunion on every hand. He had no idea of carrying these States himself. But as he later told Adams, he did wish to help secure the borderland against the radicals, to break the Yancey-Rhett-Ruffin line, and to make impossible the plan for precipitating the entire South into rash action. In due time he was able to assert that he had succeeded. The Bell-Everett ticket carried Virginia and Douglas himself carried Missouri, while Breckinridge won in Maryland by only seven hundred votes. If the Southern conspirators, with Secretaries Cobb, Thompson, and Floyd, had planned to seize the capital, Douglas thwarted their scheme.

At Norfolk on August 25, standing on the City Hall steps to address seven thousand people, he announced that he wanted no vote except from men who desired the Union preserved by the faithful execution of every line of the Constitution. Two questions were handed him on slips of paper. One asked whether, if Lincoln were elected, the Southern States would be justified in seceding. He gave an emphatic no. The other inquired whether, if the South did secede, he would advise resistance by force to their withdrawal. "I answer emphatically," returned Douglas, "that it is the duty of the President of the United States and all others in authority under him to enforce the laws of the United States as passed by Congress and as the courts expound them. And I, as in duty bound by my oath of fidelity to the Constitution, am to do all in my power to aid the government of the United States in maintaining the supremacy of the laws against all resistance to them, come from what quarter it would. In other words, I think the President of the United States, whoever he may be, should treat all attempts to break up the Union by resistance to its laws as Old Hickory treated the Nullifiers in 1832." [14]

Though this forthright utterance provoked a Southern storm, Douglas stuck to his position. At Raleigh, on August 30, he used even stronger language. "I would hang every man higher than Haman who would attempt to resist by force the execution of any provision of the Constitution which our fathers made and bequeathed to us." He told North Carolinians that no Illinoisan would ever consent to pay duty on corn shipped down the Mississippi. "Never on earth! We shall say to the custom house keeper that we furnish the water that makes the great river, and that we will follow it throughout its whole course to the ocean, no matter who or what may stand before us." At Baltimore, he warned the country again, as he had done in the Senate, that the Yanceys and Rhetts had laid a plot to sunder the nation and that America stood in dire peril. Every disunionist, he said, was a Breckinridge man, and he would countenance no fusion of his party with secessionists. "I am for burying Southern disunionism and Northern abolitionism in the same grave." Speaking to an immense picnic concourse at Jones's Wood in New York City, he asserted that he would consent to no alliance with the Breckinridge Democracy until its leaders promised an enforcement of the laws against seceders. "I wish to God," he vociferated, "that we had an Old Hickory now alive in order that he might hang Northern and Southern traitors on the same gallows." [15]

And carrying the campaign to the Northwest, he repeated his warning to an enthusiastic multitude who welcomed him to Chicago at the beginning of October. A deadly peril hung over the Union, he said, and all lovers of the Consti-

---

14 N. Y. *Weekly Tribune*, September 8, 1860.

15 N. Y. *Herald, Tribune, Times*, September 17, 1860; Milton, *Eve*, 493; N. O. *Picayune*, September 16, 1860. Edmund Ruffin talked with Governor Magoffin of Kentucky about Douglas's threats of coercion. The governor declared that if Lincoln's election were followed by secession, and the United States sent an army which tried to march through Kentucky, "every night's encampment will be made a graveyard." Ruffin, MS diary, September 13, 1860.

tution should awake from their sleep. The head of the Breckinridge electoral ticket in Virginia had asked if he would fight secession. He had answered unequivocally, and had demanded that the elector propound the same question to Breckinridge. "We cannot get an answer from him, and the Republicans justify Mr. Breckinridge in concealing his opinions on that subject. . . . I believe the Union is in peril, and all good men, all true men . . . should rally to put down these sectional parties." [16]

Never did Douglas's claims to statesmanship stand higher than when he thus pointed to a danger which most Republicans were denying or minimizing, and defied the Southerners and border men who were attacking him on the ground that he was a brutal coercionist. He gloried, like Jackson, in upholding coercion. He was not so happy when, assailing the Republicans as advocates of Negro equality, he appealed to race prejudice. His Chicago speech indicted Seward, who had spoken there a few days earlier, for doctrines more extreme than the New Yorker really held. When he declared that Seward wished to make the Negro in Illinois and other States the equal of the white man—something that Sumner intended, but not Seward—the crowd raised an angry shout of "Never! Never!" The Northwest responded as of old to Douglas's unconquerable energy. Mass meetings were held all over the section and delegations of Douglas men streamed in from neighboring towns. Hickory poles were raised, and the Democrats called their local organizations "Hickory Clubs," "Little Giants," and "Invincibles." These were in fact militant Union organizations.

When at Cedar Rapids, Iowa, Douglas heard that the Republicans had swept the October elections in Pennsylvania (as they simultaneously swept Indiana), he immediately turned to his secretary. "Mr. Lincoln is the next President," he said. "We must try to save the Union. I will go South."

It was the Deep South this time that he invaded. Passing through Springfield, Alton, and St. Louis, where large crowds, five thousand people even in Lincoln's home city, cheered him, and speaking at Memphis, Chattanooga, and Nashville, he was soon in Georgia and Alabama. Never had he made a more heroic effort. He was worn out by constant travels and speeches, often two or three in a day. His devoted wife and the hard-working secretary, James B. Sheridan, who accompanied him, knew that his health had deteriorated. Southern radicals denounced his journey savagely; ruffians threatened his life, and several incidents convinced him that efforts were being made to wreck the trains on which he rode.[17] But he was encouraged by ovations in Memphis and Jackson, Tennessee, while in Nashville the enthusiasm of the greatest crowd collected there in twenty years contrasted with the chilly reception given

16 Havana, Ill., *Squatter Sovereign*, October 20, 1860.
17 Milton, *Eve*, 498, 499.

Yancey the same night. One planter who heard Douglas at Jackson returned exclaiming that the occasion was the most notable event of his life, and that Douglas was the greatest statesman of the age. This auditor, who pronounced his effort masterly, asserted that the Little Giant had utterly demolished both the Southern secessionists and Northern Republicans, and concluded by saying that Douglas could create more enthusiasm among the masses than any other man living. The impression in Chattanooga was equally great.[18]

Even in Georgia and Alabama Douglas found many friends. His visit was encouraged by Alexander H. Stephens, who clung to a faint hope that civil war might yet be averted if public sentiment could be aroused against the extremists. In a speech at Crawfordsville, Stephens had said that while Douglas was not his first choice for President, he admired the man. He declared that the Senator had shown greater moral courage in defending his convictions of right against prejudice and fanaticism at home than any other statesman living; that he had stood by the South in her perils, and was indeed the most powerful friend the South ever had; and that the war now waged against him by office-holders and office-hunters, by malicious and envious pettifoggers, reminded him of wolves hounding to death a lordly buffalo.[19] Many Georgians and Alabamians were as determined as Stephens to keep the flag afloat so long as the government survived.[20] In Atlanta, where Stephens introduced Douglas with warm praise, a great crowd cheered the Senator's speech. At Macon, Herschel V. Johnson and Douglas spoke together. In Montgomery, where the *Mail* had said that Douglas's political garments were dyed with Southern blood,[21] he was greeted by a torchlight procession; and, though ruffians tried to pelt him with fruit and eggs, he made an eloquent plea against secession from the steps of the capitol.[22]

Unhappily, not all Douglas's followers attained his elevated level. Reverdy Johnson warned that the break-up of the Union and the ruin of all its hopes for mankind were imminent, but, unlike his leader, he rather justified than denounced a Southern revolt. Republican ascendancy, he said in Faneuil Hall, would be followed by the barring of slavery from all Territories, the abolition of the domestic slave trade, and the reversal of the Dred Scott decision; and with all security for slavery torn away, disunion would be inevitable. And Herschel Johnson explicitly said at Atlanta that if the South did secede, he would follow her fortunes for weal or woe.[23]

---

18 Diary of Harrod C. Anderson, October 24, 1860; Univ. of La. Archives.
19 Augusta *Constitutionalist*, quoted in Washington *Constitution*, September 6, 1860.
20 See letter quoted in Wash. corr. N. Y. *Tribune* dated October 26, 1860.
21 Quoted in Washington *Constitution*, September 20, 1860.
22 Washington *Constitution*, September 6, 20, etc., 1860; N. Y. Weekly *Tribune*, October 26, 1860.
23 Reverdy Johnson, "Speech of June 7, 1860" (pamphlet); Dumond, *Secession*, 111.

The principal attempt of the Douglas Democrats to effect a profitable alliance with another party was made in New York. Horatio Seymour, Dean Richmond, and other leaders, holding their Soft convention in Syracuse in mid-August, nominated a palpably weak ticket. Their candidate for governor, a respectable merchant-farmer of Hudson named William Kelly, was markedly inferior in parts and popularity to the candidate of the Breckinridge men, the brilliant James T. Brady. But the Douglasites, after welcoming Fernando Wood and his followers into their fold, did accomplish one brilliant stroke. They made a compact on much their own terms with the Bell-Everett party. An electoral ticket was drawn up which allotted twenty-three of the thirty-three places to Douglas men, and the other ten to the Constitutional Union Party. The understanding of at least some Constitutional Union leaders was that if these ten votes were needed to make Douglas President, they would be cast for him. Of course the Republicans raised a jeer at the expense of the alliance. Washington Hunt and James Brooks, they sneered, had sold out to the highest bidder. "The Syracuse auction," Greeley called it. Since on matters of principle the Douglas and Bell-Everett parties were far apart, the transaction did have an immoral look, and it is certain that Douglas disliked it.[24]

This and other efforts at fusion had, in general, two main objects. One was to try to cut down Lincoln's vote sufficiently to throw the election into the House. The second, and more hopeful, was to promote the chances of State and Congressional nominees. All over the North, by September, knots of politicians were sitting up late in offices and taverns intent on some bargain that would save a governorship from the Republicans, and send three or four men to Congress. But these cabals, though resulting in a few alliances among Douglas, Bell, and Breckinridge forces, for two reasons accomplished little. While the national leaders, and particularly Douglas, frowned upon them, the people were for the most part equally hostile; for the plain voter wished to support the candidate and platform of his choice, and not a hybrid ticket. Even in New York, therefore, where fusion temporarily looked most promising, astute judges prophesied that the alliance would run from fifty to a hundred thousand votes behind Lincoln. A full history of these movements would be tiresomely complex.

In the end, fusion of at least a partial nature was achieved by the Douglas and Bell forces in New York, by the Douglas and Breckinridge factions in Pennsylvania and Rhode Island, and by Breckinridge, Bell and Douglas men in New Jersey. Various Senators in Washington were particularly active on the Democratic side, for they calculated that if the election went into the House and that body became deadlocked, the Senate choice for Vice-President, Joseph Lane, would become Chief Executive. A long shot that! However, little real harmony was

24 N. Y. *Weekly Tribune*, September 15, 1860.

achieved anywhere. In Pennsylvania, for example, Forney and the diehard wing of the Douglasites refused pointblank to vote for any but Douglas electors. In New York, all the efforts of such businessmen as August Belmont, William B. Astor, and A. T. Stewart to bring about a union of the two Democratic factions met the stony opposition of Administration adherents. Oil and water would not mix.[25]

[II]

Alas that Douglas's vigilance was not matched by Republican leaders! Confident of victory from the beginning, the young Party grew more exultant as the canvass advanced, exhibiting a blind optimism which took all too little account of the peril hanging over the nation. Lincoln himself was deplorably complacent. On August 15, he wrote John B. Fry that he had received from the South many assurances that "in no probable event will there be any very formidable effort to break up the Union."

The Republicans divided their appeal to the voters into four main segments. First, as a matter of course they gave emphasis to their immovable stand against any extension of slavery into any Territory at any time, coupling with this position appropriate attacks upon the appetite of many Southerners for Caribbean acquisitions. We have seen that it was now accepted Republican doctrine that the normal condition of the Territories was freedom, and that neither Congress nor a territorial legislature could give legal existence to slavery in them. Second, using the Covode Report (of which a hundred thousand copies had been printed for franking) and other evidence, they asserted that the Democratic Party which had governed the country for eight years was a corrupt, bickering organization with a record barren of aught but quarrels, bargains, and blunders, and that the hour had struck for a vigorous new Administration, animated by constructive ideals. In the third place, they laid their greatest stress upon their economic planks; and, varying their tune to suit local and regional desires, they argued persuasively for a protective tariff, agricultural colleges, the homestead law, internal improvements, and the Pacific Railroad. Finally, they held out to the alien-born assurances that they would permit no unfriendly legislation.

These bread-and-butter appeals were indispensable, for the party, only half a dozen years old, badly needed cohesive organization. "There is very little of Republican principle in Pennsylvania and New Jersey," O. L. Ferry had written Gideon Welles on March 1, "while the great foreign element of the Northwest is ultra in all its views and unable to understand the propriety of any concession." That is, the Middle Atlantic States were conservative; many Germans of the Middle West were radical. But organization was supplied with great vigor. Thurlow Weed raised what were then considered large sums of money. The Congressional Committee under Preston King, with Covode as treasurer, did as good work as the National Committee. W. H. Herndon wrote that in Sangamon County "we are organizing as we have never organized before"; and the same might have been said of numberless other counties all over the North. The party did its utmost, especially in the Northwest, to appeal to the foreign-born and to mobilize what Carl Schurz called a solid column of German and Scandinavian freesoilers. While the urban Irish and some settlements of German Catholics were doubtless Democratic, the Republicans by enlisting Schurz, Gustave Koerner, Friedrich Kapp, and other prominent German-Americans, and employing a phalanx of nearly a hundred German, Swedish, and Norwegian journals, made sure of a vote in the upper Mississippi Valley that was probably decisive in several States. Lincoln's letter to the *Staats Anzeiger* upon the Massachusetts proposal to withhold the ballot from fully naturalized citizens for two years was publicized to millions. He wrote:

I am against its adoption, not only in Illinois, but in every other place in which I have the right to oppose it. . . . It is well known that I deplore the oppressed condition of the blacks, and it would, therefore, be very inconsistent for me to look with approval upon any measure that infringes upon the inalienable rights of white men, whether or not they are born in another land or speak a different language from our own.

Flushed with hope, full of the energy of youth and inspired by reformative ardor, the Party indeed offered every attraction to progressive-minded Northerners. Nearly all the great editors, the distinguished men of letters, the leaders in law, theology, medicine, and learning, had been drawn into its ranks. In State after State it named gubernatorial candidates of shining ability and integrity: John A. Andrew in Massachusetts, Edwin D. Morgan in New York, Andrew G. Curtin in Pennsylvania, Richard Yates in Illinois, Oliver P. Morton in Indiana. To a great degree, the State campaigns carried the national ticket, and the combined effort of the future governors made Lincoln President. Meanwhile, in bright contrast with the stained, jaded veterans of the Buchanan-Breckinridge Democracy rode the champions who had swung to the saddle for Lincoln—Seward, making an admirable series of speeches in the Northwest; Charles Francis Adams, no stump orator, but so deeply aroused that he accompanied and aided Seward; Chase, redoubtable in Ohio and useful elsewhere; William M. Evarts, George William Curtis, John Sherman, Lyman Trumbull, Carl Schurz, and Francis P. Blair, Jr. The star of destiny seemed to sit visibly on the forehead of the organization.

When in August Missouri reelected the junior Blair, as the first Republican Representative from a slave State, a thrill of exultation ran through the ranks. This seemed one of the most important events of the campaign. Lyman Trumbull had gone to St. Louis to speak for Blair; so had Carl Schurz. The proslavery forces had denounced Blair as an abolitionist, using the foulest epithets. Such bitter feeling had been engendered that his life was in danger from ruffians, his public meetings provoked riots, and a heavy armed guard of Wide Awakes was needed to protect him. Carrying his district by nearly fifteen hundred votes, he proclaimed that his victory sealed the position of St. Louis as a Republican city. His Northern friends now felt that theirs was a Party not merely of defense but of invasion, which would yet win the whole borderland.

Pains were taken to disavow radical purposes and reassure the Southern people. Most Republican leaders deplored the course of Charles Sumner. That Senator, lately returned from Europe, broke his long silence on June 4 by delivering a four-hour harangue on "The Barbarism of Slavery," a stilted, schematic piece of invective, not lacking in literary polish or pedantic learning but abominable in taste. After listing five elements of barbarism in the slave system, he expatiated upon its practical results by the familiar method of comparing Northern and Southern manufactures, commerce, railroads, schools, and presses.[26] The speech was precisely what a Western editor called it, able, exasperating, and useless. Since Sumner denominated himself a Republican, it helped convince Southerners that the Party had a malevolent hatred of slavery as an institution, and of slaveholders as evildoers. Republican members of Congress generally agreed that it was vindictive and even brutal, that it pointed to no remedy for the evils it assailed, and that it simply impaired Sumner's influence, angered Southern leaders, and hurt the party.[27] Greeley's *Tribune* was obviously dismayed. A few other Republicans, such as Carl Schurz, went to unwise lengths in attacking slavery as a national evil. The general tone of speakers and press, however, was moderate and conciliatory.

It fell to Seward to make the most important effort to prove that the Party would be circumspect and rigidly constitutional in dealing with slavery, a task which brought out all his natural conservatism. In his western speeches he cooed as gently as any mourning dove of Auburn. The "irrepressible conflict" became, in his new interpretation, simply a phrase to signify a certain rivalry between slavery and free labor. The nation needed quiet, he said in Madison, Wisconsin, and the conflict between the slave and free States must end. "The time has come to repress it. The people will have it repressed. They are not to be forever disputing upon old issues and controversies. New subjects for national action will come up." The Republican Party would be the agent in this happy consumma-

26 But the speech had a strong appeal to antislavery radicals; Pierce, *Sumner*, III, 610–614.
27 William Salter, *Grimes*, 127.

tion, for once it was decided that slavery should never enter any Territory, "that will end the irrepressible conflict." [28] Thus manfully—and wisely—did Seward eat his rash words of two years earlier.

Pursuing the same theme, Republican editors and speakers labored to dissociate their party from the abolitionists, who, upon a budget of fifty dollars, had nominated Gerrit Smith for the Presidency. The noisier abolitionists like Wendell Phillips, who attacked Lincoln as a "knave" and "the slave-hound of Illinois," helped mightily in this dissociation. While the motives of antislavery extremists commanded respect, declared the New York *Tribune*, their methods had always been absurd and impractical. With such men the Republicans had no connection. The Party proposed to circumscribe slavery by prohibiting it in the Territories, but they did not propose to meddle with it in the States; for there they would use only moral implements. If slavery was ever to be overthrown in the South, it would have to be by the Southerners themselves—the other States could have no share in the work.[29] Greeley, too, it will be seen, had to eat a good many words.

Unfortunately, the prominence in the Party of a few such radicals as John A. Andrew (who at heart was an abolitionist, fierce in condemnation of the peculiar Southern institution) counteracted the bland terms of Seward and Trumbull, the *Tribune* and the *Evening Post*. Carl Schurz uttered words of folly, insulting the South and deriding the idea of secession. Many suspicious Democrats agreed with the New Orleans *Picayune* that as the Jacobin Clubs had triumphed over the Montagnards, so the Sumners, Andrews, Wades, and Zach Chandlers would triumph over the cautious Thurlow Weeds and Fessendens.[30] The fact was that the Republican Party already showed that sharp division between its moderate and radical wings which was to plague President Lincoln in years to come. The gulf between zealots like Giddings, Chase, Sumner, Julian, and Greeley, and such moderates as Weed, Cameron, Bates, Blair, and Corwin, was already wide and deep.

The main driving force of the Republican campaign was thrown behind the homestead issue in the Northwest, the tariff issue in Pennsylvania, New Jersey, and New England, the Pacific Railroad in the Mississippi Valley, and internal improvements everywhere.[31] A call went up for a campaign of education. Be-

28 *Works*, IV, 366.
29 N. Y. *Weekly Tribune*, September 8, 1860.
30 N. O. *Picayune*, September 11, 1860.
31 The fifth tract issued by the Republican Association of Washington (a series of great effectiveness) dealt with Administration policy upon the overland mail routes and Butterfield contract. It accused the Administration of illegal and improper acts to bring the overland mail down from St. Louis to the 32d parallel, thus traversing arid desert country merely to further the construction of a Pacific railroad along Southern lines. The argument had influence in the Middle West, including Missouri. St. Louis *Missouri Democrat*, August 16, 1859.

fore the end, it was estimated that not less than ten thousand set speeches had been made for the Party in New York alone, and fifty thousand in the Union.[32] Of books and pamphlets an abundance was provided. The *Campaign Textbook* prepared by Greeley and John F. Cleveland, a large volume in double columns of fine print, crammed with speeches, documents, and tables, and selling at sixty-six cents a copy in quantity lots, reached its fourteenth edition by the beginning of October. A pamphlet on the homestead bill, available in German as well as English, and a summary of the Covode findings were distributed by hundreds of thousands. In a typical rural county of Illinois—Madison—some six thousand campaign documents were distributed by the middle of June. Nor did the Republican managers confine themselves to their own party publications. Mid-Western communities reported a keen demand for disunion and proslavery speeches by Southern Democrats, which were used to win over shaky voters. Good use was made, too, of Cobb's report at the end of 1858 on the sad condition of the Treasury. The Republican press from Maine to Nebraska volleyed and thundered on those promises which seemed likeliest to capture votes.[33]

"This Homestead measure," a Minnesota delegate in Chicago had written Simon Cameron, "overshadows everything with us, and throughout the West." Everywhere from Ohio to Kansas the cry of free land had grown immensely popular.[34] People believed that it meant opportunity for the poor man and his children, rapid development of the country, and a growth in the wealth of the whole central valley. The sad situation of many settlers in Kansas and Nebraska, utterly destitute this summer and fall after a season of drought, was used to drive home the argument. Journalists pointed out that countless preemptors, unable to pay the government $200 in gold for a farm of one hundred and sixty acres, had obtained it by borrowing money to purchase a land warrant. A warrant for one hundred and sixty acres might be had as low as $150. But to get the $150, the borrower must pay interest at four and even five percent a month

---

32 N. Y. *Weekly Tribune*, November 10, 1860.

33 See scores of entries in Trumbull Papers, May-October, 1860.

34 Stephen Miller, April 2, 1860; Cameron Papers. This popularity is proved by the fact that Republican conventions in every Northern State and in Missouri and Kentucky this year adopted homestead planks; while Democratic conventions in every Northwestern State, four New England States, and New York and New Jersey, did the same. Files of N. Y. *Herald*, January-July, 1860. A change of one vote in twenty-seven would have given Douglas Iowa and Illinois; a change of one in twenty the whole Northwest. Without the homestead issue, or the vigorous appeal to the foreign-born, the Republicans would doubtless have lost important States. W. E. Dodd, "The Fight for the Northwest," *Am. Hist. Rev.*, XVI, 774–788; Donnal V. Smith, "Influence of the Foreign-Born of the Northwest in the Election of 1860," *Miss. Valley Hist. Rev.*, XIX, 192–204. Joseph Schafer in "Who Elected Lincoln?" in the *Am. Hist. Rev.*, XLVI, 51–63, reaches the conclusion that more Wisconsin Germans voted for Douglas in 1860 than for Lincoln, and that it was an upsurge of enthusiasm among old American groups which gave Lincoln the palm. But in Illinois and Iowa the Germans seem to have turned mainly to the Republican ticket. See Jay Monaghan's article, *Journal Ill. State Hist. Soc.*, XXV, 133–139.

REPUBLICAN
MASS MEETING.

A Grand Mass Meeting will be held at

ITHACA, ON FRIDAY, AUGUST 31, 1860,

AT NOON,

For the purpose of RATIFYING the Nomination of

LINCOLN AND HAMLIN
—AND THE—
STATE TICKET.

HORACE GREELEY,

OF NEW YORK.

GEN. B. F. BRUCE,

OF MADISON CO., AND

HON. C. L. BEALE

MEMBER OF CONGRESS FROM COLUMBIA CO.,

Have been POSITIVELY ENGAGED, and will address the meeting.

HON. DAVID WILMOT,

OF PENNSYLVANIA,

Has been written to and is expected to be present.

Republican Orators at Ithaca, New York.

—and attorney's fees in addition. If a settler met a crop failure the first year, he had the hard alternative of making a forced sale of his land and improvements or submitting to foreclosure. Kansas editors·furnished many poignant instances. One Burgett Thomas was notified early in 1860 that he must pay $200 with four percent a month interest from August 28, 1860, and fees of $40, or lose his farm. A settler named Gannon was called upon to pay $282 with interest at forty-eight percent a year from September 3, 1859, and $50 fees, or be sold out. One earnest pamphleteer got out a series of letters with such captions as: "Land Sales! Land Sharks! Forty-eight per cent for money! How Democracy Protects Workingmen, Starving Women, and Helpless Babes! Need of a Homestead Law." [35]

The record established by Republican Congressmen in support of the Morrill tariff bill was effective in parts of the East, and particularly so in Pennsylvania, where the conservatism of Philadelphia had to be combatted. Half the iron of the country was made in the Keystone State. The protectionists pointed out that only two Republicans in both houses had been against Morrill's measures, and one of these was an Ohioan who believed the wool schedule too low. Arguments were specially addressed to the workingmen—for ironmasters and manufacturers needed none. The laboring masses of Pennsylvania had been deluded in 1846 and 1857, declared Republican campaigners; would they cheat themselves once more by voting the Democratic ticket? Irish, German, and other immigrants, wrote a pamphleteer, "begin to see that a judicious tariff policy, on manufactured goods, sustains them at work in our factories; and therefore I have witnessed meetings of laborious Germans, Irish workmen, and of Frenchmen, and all of them meeting as Republicans, to sustain Mr. Lincoln for President." [36] As William D. ("Pig-Iron") Kelley, destined to become the staunchest pillar of protectionism, made a successful run for Congress in Pennsylvania, Representatives Morrill and John Sherman delivered stirring tariff speeches in the State. The trend of sentiment there was unmistakable.

Nor was the tariff plank without some support in the Northwest. In view of the oft-stated thesis that this section naturally stood with the South for low tariffs, the support which Medill of the Chicago *Tribune* gave the demand is significant. He sent Chase repeated pleas to make it clear that he was not a free trader. "Nobody is in favor of a high protective tariff or prohibitive tariff," he wrote. "But the present one is ruinous. It is taxation without even incidental protection. There must be a change; the country will not receive, will not enjoy solid safe prosperity until we supply more of our own wants and import less from abroad of those staples which we can so well make at home." [37]

35 Thaddeus Hyatt Papers, 1860. KHS.
36 Hotaling, *The Questions in the Canvass,* pamphlet.
37 Chase Papers, LC, July-August, 1860; Cf. T. E. Strevey, *Joseph Medill and the Chicago Tribune during the Civil War Period,* MS Doctoral Dissertation, Univ. of Chicago.

For all their emphasis on economic questions, the Republicans did not neglect emotional appeals. Their rallies, picnics, and mass meetings were as numerous as in '56, while the Wide Awake and kindred organizations, embodying and drilling hundreds of thousands of young men, were a spectacular feature of the contest. Hartford Republicans laid claim to originating these solid columns of marching men, who, in glazed capes of varying colors and smart military caps, bearing oil-burning torches and bright transparencies, swung down countless streets to the crash of brass bands and the roar of cadenced cheering. Nothing like them had been seen in America before. Their disciplined forces, lending fervor and enthusiasm to the Northern canvass, played no small part in the final result. They took pride in the military precision of their evolutions, and in developing a set of songs, salutes, and emblematic displays which were tumultuously stirring.[38]

Particularly picturesque were the well-advertised Wide Awake parades in Lincoln's home city and in New York. To the Springfield display streamed delegations from all over the Northwest, enlivening the little Illinois capital as never in its history. In the metropolis, the grand rally of the banners of light, as Republicans called it, was said to have marshalled ninety thousand well-trained Lincolnites into line. Broadway was packed to view the spectacle, which moved even cynical reporters to flights of ecstasy. From roofs along the route poured up a steady gush of rockets, roman candles, volcanoes, and other fireworks. The street itself seemed a river of fire. The martial swell of the music, the resounding tramp of the men, the fountains of flame and many-colored lights which shot upward on each side, the cheering of the spectators, answered by the sharp "one, two, three" of the Wide Awakes, all combined to produce an unforgettable impression. When, to the music of the bands, the tens of thousands of marchers took up the chorus of the song, "Ain't You Glad You Joined the Republicans?" the effect was tremendous.

[III]

The cardinal error of the Republicans was their failure to treat the now imminent danger of secession with the candor and emphasis which it required. That failure had various roots. It seemed to the Party's interest to minimize a peril which, if nakedly exposed, might drive many to vote for a candidate acceptable to the South; optimism is always easier than pessimism; and many honestly believed that the cry of "wolf, wolf!" would prove as empty now as before. Yet, however explained, the attitude was part of that national levity which we have identified as one key to the disaster which was about to befall the nation.

38 For the origin of the Wide Awakes, see N. Y. *Herald*, September 19, 1860.

When Henry W. Hilliard of Alabama said in Cooper Union that Lincoln's election would be followed by a terrible civil convulsion, he was derided by the New York *Tribune,* which declared that the stale Southern threats would appall nobody but fools, and that the diabolical mask did not frighten men who knew at what toyshop it was bought.[39] Seward, in his Northwestern speeches, was all reassurance. He told his Minneapolis audience that the menaces to the Union were absurd—nobody was afraid. At La Crosse, he said that the homogeneity of the American people furnished assurances for the future which enabled men to trample underfoot every threat of disunion, every apprehension of national dismemberment.[40] Edward Bates, who knew the Southern people better than most Republicans, was equally ready to pooh-pooh the rising storm. He dismissed what he called the idle fears of nervous people with the assertion that only a few conceited egotists were talking of a Southern confederacy, and that the Southern people as a whole could never be guilty of such wicked folly as rending the country in half.[41] These men should have listened more carefully to Southern leaders and paid closer heed to other plain indices of opinion. Perhaps Schurz made the most fatuous statement of all. Telling his St. Louis audience that secession talk was absurd, for "the mere anticipation of a Negro insurrection will paralyze the whole South," he struck the most painful nerve of slaveholders while adding to the foolish sense of Northern security.

In great parts of the South it was a summer of unprecedented excitement, with subterranean upheavals and rumblings. The Knights of the Golden Circle, a filibustering society organized a half dozen years earlier to promote the conquest of a wide crescent around the Gulf, was shifting its front to become a secessionist society. At the same time it clung to its filibustering designs, as was shown by a letter of its founder, George Bickley, in the Richmond *Whig.* Bickley, exhorting the South to rescue Mexico from the brigands who were pillaging and destroying the country, summoned an army of fellow rescuers to meet him on the banks of the Nueces with arms, wagons, mules, provisions, and $20 apiece.[42] As Lincoln's election became certain, a wave of apprehension regarding Negro insurrections again swept the South. Reports of a plot in upper Georgia ended in the arrest at Dalton of thirty-six Negroes accused of planning to burn the town and kill all its people. In Talladega, Alabama, two whites and eight Negroes were arrested, and one white man was summarily hanged. Bowling Green, Virginia, was thrown into fever by the mere arrival of a stranger who somehow looked like an abolitionist. A Louisianan traveling from Dallas to Crockett, Texas, to buy a farm, was almost lynched when his appearance ex-

39 N. Y. *Weekly Tribune,* September 22, 1860.
40 Bancroft, *Seward,* I, 549, 550.
41 Letter, September 15, to Keokuk Republicans, N. Y. *Weekly Tribune,* October 6, 1860.
42 Gray, *Hidden Civil War,* 70; N. Y. *Weekly Tribune,* June 28, 1860.

cited distrust. And during July and August the alarm and frenzy in other parts of Texas became almost a mass hysteria.

Incendiary fires were reported in nearly a dozen Texas towns. One excited editor wrote that the flames were no sooner put out in one settlement than they were lighted in another—all, of course, "kindled by the torches of abolitionists." This was taken as evidence of a diabolical plot to devastate all northern Texas. The Cameron *Sentinel* announced that during the summer the town patrol had found four guns, a pistol, and a dirk in the hands of Negroes. From another town came a report that colored people had collected a hundred bottles of strychnine to poison the inhabitants. Of valid evidence of any conspiracy or plan of concerted outbreak on the part of the slaves there seems to have been none. Some Northern observers suspected that the real object of this artificial panic was to check antislavery feeling among the Methodists and Germans of the State. Many people preferred the discipline and ministry of the Methodist Episcopal Church to that of the Methodist Episcopal Church South, for it was not sectional but national and its discipline seemed in better accord with Christian doctrine. Its precepts included a strong statement on the evil of slavery, a request that members should emancipate their slaves, and a rule forbidding any slaveholder to be a traveling preacher. The feeling against the church and its more outspoken ministers had engendered mob violence in Missouri and other places. The wave of hysteria in Texas, the worst thus far known, resulted in the lynching of a moderate antislavery man named Bewley, mild of speech and peaceful in demeanor; and it prompted strong protests in the church press of the North.[43] Various Southern observers meanwhile believed that the Texas furor was concocted primarily to weaken the Bell-Everett ticket and to destroy the influence of Sam Houston and his Union-loving friends. Alex and Linton Stephens spoke scornfully of the "pretended insurrections" in the Lone Star State.

Even at the time, the New Orleans *Picayune* declared of the Texas furore that "much of the apprehension may be unreal and some of the facts imperfectly proved," while no modern Texas historian credits the wild rumors of the time. They were of a piece with the reports in northern Georgia and other places. Yet the important fact was that the stories of insurrection, arson, and murder, sweeping the South, aroused deep emotions of fear and resentment. A Mississippi brother of Joseph Holt, writing that within three weeks he had read of twenty-three abolitionist agents being lynched, attributed their "hellish" activities to Northern organizations. Even John H. Reagan believed the excited tales, for he shortly told Congress:[44]

43 Cf. letter by T. M. Eddy September 7, 1860, in *Northwestern Christian Advocate*.
44 N. Y. *Weekly Tribune*, September 8, 15; N. O. *Picayune*, August 19, 1860; *Cong. Globe*, January 15, 1861.

We found, for the last two or three years, the members of the Methodist Church North, and others, living in Texas, were propagating abolition doctrines there. We warned them not to carry on their scheme of producing disaffection among our Negroes; but they persisted, and did not cease until they had organized a society called the Mystic Red. Under its auspices, the night before the last August election the towns were to be burned down and the people murdered. There now lie in ashes near a dozen towns and villages in my district. . . . The poisonings were only arrested by information which came to light before the plan could be carried into execution. The citizens were forced to stand guard for months. . . . A portion paid the penalty of their crimes; others were driven out of the country. These things had their effect on the public mind. They were the result of abolition teachings; a part of the irrepressible conflict; a part of the legitimate fruits of Republicanism.

As election day approached, the sense of defensive solidarity in the South became intensified.[45] Organizations of minute men, military bodies well trained in the simpler evolutions, were formed in Alabama, South Carolina, and Georgia. Yancey, wearing a suit of Southern homespun, reviewed in New Orleans a parade of semi-military clubs, including the Yancey Rangers. Several States were systematically buying arms. In many communities such a spirit of terrorism was abroad that out-and-out Unionists dared not raise their voices. While a growing body of Southerners avowed that they actually wished Lincoln elected so as to precipitate the crisis, sober men who, like B. F. Perry of South Carolina and Goggin of Virginia, asserted their readiness to abide by Republican victory, were angrily hooted down. The New Orleans *Commercial Bulletin* declared that secession would cause the steamboats to rot at the levee, cotton to sink to ruinous levels, and real estate to become unsalable. Not so, retorted the Charleston *Mercury;* secession will usher in a new age of prosperity for the South.[46] When on the eve of election the opening of the one-hundred-and-three-

45 This is Crenshaw's phrase; *Slave States,* 234. The South, said the Washington *Constitution* on September 13, is "in a blaze." Southerners staying at White Sulphur Springs had passed indignant resolutions calling on their people to fight rather than submit to Northern tyranny. Stories were flying around the section of insults offered to slaveholders who travelled above the Potomac. The *Constitution* on September 28 quoted a letter of James L. Orr to Alexander H. Stephens, the former Speaker writing that it would be fatal to let the Black Republicans take possession of the army, navy, and treasury. "If the South should think upon this subject as I do, no Black Republican President should ever execute any law within her borders, unless at the point of the bayonet and over the dead bodies of her sons." Like the Boston *Post* and other Administration papers, the *Constitution* was asserting that the Union could never be preserved by force.

46 The New Orleans correspondent of the Charleston *Mercury* (November 6) described the military character of the Breckinridge clubs in Louisiana. W. Doubleday of New York sent Lincoln two letters from Captain Abner Doubleday, of the small garrison in Charleston Harbor; "the last of a large number, all, until recently, pointing to the purpose of the Charlestonians to seize the forts in their harbor." Robert Todd Lincoln Papers. Yancey, touring the country from Boston to Mobile, declared the right of every State which objected to Lincoln's inauguration to secede.

mile Charleston & Savannah Railroad was celebrated in Savannah with a large Carolina delegation present, the company refused to honor a toast to the President of the United States.[47]

Northern tempers rose in response to Southern taunts and defiances. By early fall, many Republicans and Douglas Democrats were thoroughly angry, feeling that the time had come to test whether the Union could survive a fair and legal election. When the thickening tokens of Republican victory produced alarm in mercantile circles and a fall in stock prices, Zach Chandler angrily charged certain interests with trying to bring on a financial crisis to defeat Lincoln. "The West have put up with this attempt to bully, coerce, or frighten them out of their political convictions long enough," he stormed. Seward, speaking at Auburn, dropped his easy optimism and uttered a ringing appeal for Northern unity irrespective of party. "It is time, high time," he said, "that we know whether this is a constitutional government under which we live. It is high time that we know, since the Union is threatened, who are its friends and who are its enemies." [48]

[IV]

Ironically, while the political struggle held the nation in a grip of passion and apprehension, scattered newspaper reports of the early census returns of 1860 appeared, reflecting the unbounded vigor and spectacular growth of the past decade. Still the country grew—still the youthful sinewy race tramped forward:

We debouch upon a newer mightier world, varied world,
Fresh and strong the world we seize, world of labor and the march.

It was not merely that the returns showed a growth of more than eight and a half million people in the decade, to a grand total of 31,443,500. The features of a new American society were appearing. Thus, the value of manufactures had risen from a little over a billion dollars in 1849 to $1,886,000,000 ten years later, and the railroad system had expanded from 8,500 miles to more than 30,000. Although the nation was still primarily rural, tokens of the coming urban age could be discerned. In 1850, one-eighth of the people had lived in centers of eight thousand or more; now nearly one-sixth dwelt in such cities. New York, with Brooklyn, counted well over a million inhabitants, and Philadelphia well over a half-million. Baltimore held third place with 212,000, and Boston, Cincinnati, and St. Louis could boast of between 160,000 and

47 Charleston *Mercury*, October 5, November 5, 1860.
48 Greeley, *Amer. Conflict*, I, 327.

180,000 each. The South was plainly falling behind in the race for population. Of the eight and a half million increase during the decade, the States of the future Confederacy could lay claim to only about two million.

Most arresting of all the new census figures were those which disclosed the tremendous growth of the Northwest. The eleven States and Territories

The Center of Population Swings into Freesoil Territory

which stretched from Ohio to Dakota inclusive had contained but 5,403,000 people when President Taylor died; now they counted 9,100,000. The population of Illinois had almost doubled during the decade, that of Wisconsin had more than doubled, and that of Iowa had more than trebled. One striking fact could not escape even the casual analyst. Whereas in the North the old States grew vigorously alongside the new ones, in the South the old States were comparatively at a standstill. New York, for example, had enjoyed a population growth of nearly 900,000, and Pennsylvania of almost 600,000; but Virginia's population had risen by only 175,000, and that of South Carolina by a mere 35,000. A Southern historian speaks of the exhaustion of Virginia and her coastal neighbors; and though the word is too strong, it is true that North Carolina's population increase of 77,000 compared but ill with Massachusetts' of 237,000.

Some of the most striking figures were not publicized at the time, although they bore directly upon the election. These were statistics pointing to the remarkable shift of Northwestern trade from the Gulf to the North Atlantic. In 1850 the North Central area had sent two-thirds as much corn to the South as it sent to the East; but in 1860 it sent only one-fourth as much. In 1850 it had shipped four times as much pork to the South (1,200,000 barrels) as it shipped to the East; in 1860 it sent the South only 570,000 barrels, and the

East 930,000 barrels. The swing in wheat movements from South to East was still more notable. In 1850 the Northwest had sent roughly half a million bushels southward, and five millions eastward; ten years later it still sent only a little more than half a million bushels to the South, but it shipped nearly 28,500,000 bushels eastward. The building of an efficient railroad system had enabled the East to capture trade that formerly went down the Mississippi, and to exchange its manufactures for Western foodstuffs. These commercial ties had their political consequences.

We have evidence in newspaper comment that the census of 1860 was being watched with interest; and attentive Southerners unquestionably saw in it new omens of the day when their section would be hopelessly outstripped in population, wealth, and political power.

[V]

The early State elections all pointed to the certain result. In September, Maine chose a Republican governor by more than eighteen thousand majority, and Vermont by more than twenty-two thousand. October brought the Pennsylvania and Indiana elections. In both States the Republicans decisively triumphed, electing their governor in Pennsylvania by thirty-two thousand and in Indiana by nearly ten thousand majority. Thereafter, the principal anxiety of the party managers was not over Lincoln, but their remaining State tickets. In Illinois, for example, Lyman Trumbull sent out a call for leaders in other States to come and help, for a desperate fight was being waged by the opposition to win the legislature. In the South, the Pennsylvania and Indiana result had a stunning effect. Voters stampeded from both the Bell and Douglas parties to the Breckinridge fold; for they saw that their only hope of defeating the Republicans (if they had any) lay in giving the Kentuckian a solid Southern vote. It seems probable that the early State elections also affected Douglas adversely in the North. The St. Paul *Pioneer and Democrat*, a Douglas organ, turned to Lincoln, declaring that the Little Giant was out of the race; while another Douglas paper, the Toledo *Herald and Times*, likewise advised its readers to vote the Republican ticket.[49]

49 Pennsylvania Democrats also forsook Douglas. A. K. McClure, Republican State Chairman, wrote Lincoln after the State election that the Democrats had utterly abandoned the national contest. "The Douglas straight ticket has now no force, and will not be pushed with any energy. Many of that camp will not vote at all—others will vote for you, and some will vote for the Douglas electors on the Reading ticket and scratch the balance. Our own men will, notwithstanding, vote, and poll more than they did for Curtin." October 15, 1860; Robert Todd Lincoln Papers. One Democratic observer had the courage to tell Buchanan the truth. "The fact is, and there is no use in assuming any other, the State is freesoiled and abolitionized. The tariff did something toward the result, but not all, as the terrible frontier majorities show." W. S. Hirst, October 12, 1860; Buchanan Papers.

It was evident by mid-September that Lincoln would carry all New England, all the Northwest, Ohio, and Pennsylvania. The last, infinitesimal chance of his opponents rested upon New York, where a huge city poll might just conceivably throw the contest into Congress.

Election day fell on November 6. No violence marred the polling. By an early hour next morning it was known that Lincoln had swept New York and at least fourteen other States, giving him a clear majority of electors. As returns from the border States, the South, and the Far West gradually came in, his total electoral vote rose to one hundred and eighty—a majority of fifty-seven. Some unexpected results presented themselves. The most astonishing disclosure was that Douglas, despite his lion-hearted fight, had won only twelve electors—nine in Missouri, three in New Jersey. The fact that the Breckinridge nomination had been made to kill was plainer than ever, for if the popular vote for Breckinridge had been added to Douglas's, the total would have exceeded that cast for Lincoln by three hundred and fifty thousand. As it was, Breckinridge obtained the seventy-two electoral votes of eleven slave States, and Bell the thirty-nine electors in Virginia, Kentucky, and Tennessee.

The followers of Douglas, if disheartened by his weak showing in the electoral college, could take comfort in his popular vote, which was 1,376,957 as against 1,866,452 cast for Lincoln. Breckinridge obtained only 849,781 votes, and Bell only 588,879. What the result would have been had the Democratic Party avoided its tragic schism none can undertake to say. If the whole Douglas, Bell, and Breckinridge vote, as finally cast, had been consolidated for any one of the three candidates, Lincoln would still have won with one hundred and sixty-nine electors, a majority of thirty-five. But if the Democratic Party had remained united, doubtless the danger of disunion would have seemed far slighter; the Constitutional Union Party would then probably have played a much smaller role; and far more spirited efforts would have been made in the North to rally all conservative voters against the Republican ticket. Had Douglas been nominated at Charleston, Lincoln might well—in view of the different trend which the campaign would have taken—have lost.

The results of the contest obviously illuminated certain faults in the nation's machinery for electing its Presidents. A good deal could be said in criticism of a system under which a candidate who polled only a large third of the popular vote could carry the electoral college so decisively. Lincoln had not received a single ballot in nearly one-third of the States, and had not gained a single elector in the entire South, yet he was now to be head of the entire country. The election was nevertheless constitutional, legally fair, and not more undemocratic in character than others before or since. Lincoln had an unimpeachable title. It could be pointed out that he had received substantial support in five slaveholding States: about 17,000 votes in Missouri, where he carried St. Louis, 3,800 in Delaware, 2,300 in Maryland, 1,900 in Virginia, and 1,300 in Kentucky. There were Northern States in which Breckinridge had likewise polled a meagre vote; he had less than a thousand followers in Wisconsin, only a thousand in Iowa, and only 2,400 in Illinois. One of the remarkable features of the election was the closeness of the race in half a dozen States. It was by margins of only a few hundred votes over the nearest oppo-

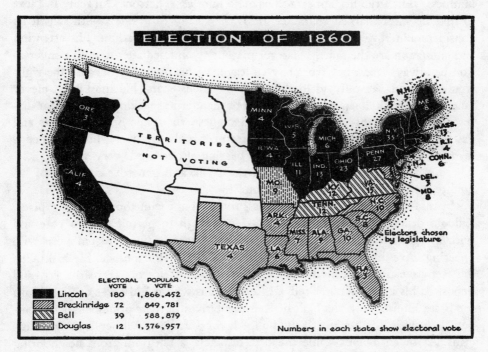

nent that Douglas carried Missouri, Bell carried Virginia, Breckinridge carried Maryland, and Lincoln carried Oregon and California. Altogether, it was a very curious, a very mixed, and except for its grand central result, a very inscrutable election.

[VI]

The most interesting scenes on election day naturally took place in Springfield. That pleasant prairie town, with its neat white-painted houses, its lines of maples, elms, box elders, and catalpas, their last leaves fluttering down in the chill winds, its central square surrounded by stores, hotels, and courthouse, and its dominating State Capitol, was tremulous with excitement as the polling began.

Strangers helped fill the streets—some of them "floaters," brought in as short-term residents to swell the normal vote of their party, more of them Republicans come to celebrate victory. Roving bands of music and occasional discharges of cannon enlivened the day. Lincoln, taking refuge in the governor's room of the State House, which commanded a full view of the courthouse opposite, settled himself in an armchair and chatted with numerous callers. The New York *Tribune* correspondent was struck by his winning manners and unaffected kindness. "His affability appears to have no limit as to persons. All share it. Next to this, his most marked characteristic is the steady earnestness with which he considers and reviews all subjects that are brought before him. His attention and animation are the same, whatever may be the immediate topic. In conversation he always leads, not from any endeavor of his own, but because the right is at once and naturally yielded to him by all listeners. He must be a clever talker who would keep even with him. His manner in speaking is somewhat different from what his appearance would suggest, for while his movements and gestures are quick, and the play of his features is always lively, his utterance is peculiarly measured and emphatic. His bearing altogether is very striking. . . . There is something beyond all art in the frank and generous sunshine of his countenance. It is full of fine expression." [50]

In mid-afternoon, after a cautious survey of the courthouse polling place, Lincoln decided that the crowd was thin enough to permit him to vote and with a few friends strolled across the way, where he was greeted with wild cheering. Five minutes later he was back in the governor's office. He had taken the Republican ballot, modestly cut his name and electors from the list, and deposited his vote. As night fell, all Republicans who could enter crowded into the State House, with the Hall of Representatives as their principal focus. Lincoln had with him Senator Trumbull, Mayor Litten, and other leading politicians. At seven o'clock came the first dispatch, a telegram from neighboring Decatur showing large Republican gains over 1856. [51]

The early news was overwhelmingly reassuring as to the Northwest, but left everyone uncertain of the East. Lincoln, anxious and elated by turns, decided about nine o'clock to walk to the telegraph office outside, where bulletins were coming in rapidly. Before ten, a telegram arrived from Simon Cameron: "Pennsylvania 70,000 for you. New York safe. Glory enough." But still there was no direct word from the crucial Empire State. The minutes ticked away until midnight. Lincoln proved the quietest of the watchers, manifesting quite as much interest in the local offices and the fate of fellow candidates as in his own fortunes. As the first Missouri news arrived, he straightened up, saying: "We shall

50 N. Y. *Weekly Tribune*, November 17, 1860.
51 Angle, *Here I Have Lived*, 251, 252; N. Y. *Tribune, Herald*, November 8, 1860.

now get some licks back"—but they were not severe licks. Then came a summons to his party to step over to a hall where Springfield women had prepared a supper. He walked through the door to see a gaily decorated room and a long table spread with food, while a hundred feminine voices chorussed: "How do you do, Mr. President?" The guests had hardly seated themselves when a messenger burst in waving a telegram from Simeon Draper which announced that New York was safe—that the fusion vote in the metropolis had been held to a mere twenty-seven thousand. This was almost too good to be true. A chorus of "You're elected now! It's all over!" shook the rafters, and the gathering burst into spontaneous song:

> Ain't you glad you joined the Republicans?
> Joined the Republicans—Joined the Republicans! [52]

Meanwhile, the same news had electrified the crowd at the State House. Men hugged each other, threw up their hats, hurrahed for Lincoln and New York, and even rolled on the floor in their delight. More dispatches poured in. Lincoln, back in the telegraph office, undoubtedly began to feel a sobering realization of his new burdens. When a late telegram—with which fat Jesse Dubois tore breathlessly into the State House—proclaimed that New York had gone Republican by fifty thousand, another scene of happy excitement took place. The old Capitol had never before heard such a roar. Then the President-elect, specially pleased by word of a party victory in Springfield, said good night and went home. The crowd began to break up, scattering over town the glad news: "New York fifty thousand for Lincoln!" All Springfield was agog; men shouting from housetops, from sidewalks, from buggies. Parties roamed the streets in the lightening dawn, chorussing: "Ain't I glad I joined the Republicans!" And as Lincoln closed the door of his house behind him, the boom of a cannon dragged into the square by young men of the town rolled forth to greet the morn.[53]

A very different scene took place that night in Mobile. Stephen A. Douglas had battled to the last; from Montgomery he had gone to Selma to speak, and then on election eve had told a great Mobile audience that their rights would be far safer in the Union than outside. He had spent election day quietly. After dinner he went with his secretary, Sheridan, to the office of John Forsyth's *Register* to await the news. The paper's telegraph service was good. Dispatches from the North and East soon made it plain that Douglas was overwhelmed and Lincoln victorious. This in itself was no shock to the Little Giant. Weeks before,

52 See the description by the correspondent of the *Missouri Democrat*, quoted in the Havana, Illinois, *Popular Sovereign*, November 7, 1860.
53 Springfield correspondence in N. Y. *Weekly Tribune*, November 16, 1860; Baringer, "Campaign Techniques in Illinois, 1860," *Trans. Ill. State Hist. Soc.*, 1932.

telling Anson Burlingame that Lincoln was sure of election, he had rejoiced in the weight that four Illinois men would soon have in Washington. "Won't it be a splendid sight, Burlingame," he had said, "to see McDougall returned Senator from California, Baker from Oregon, and Douglas and Old Abe all at Washington together?" [54]

But the news had to be accepted against the background of his recent observations. Completing his Southern tour, he had found new proofs that a conspiracy formed the previous spring to dissever the Union was nearing its climax. He had to interpret the news in the light of the intention of a hundred Southern leaders, from Slidell, Cobb, and Toombs down to Yancey and Rhett, to dissolve the Union once Lincoln won; in the light of the proclamation of even the friendly Atlanta *Confederacy:* "Let the consequences be what they may—whether the Potomac is crimsoned in human gore, and Pennsylvania Avenue is paved ten fathoms in depth with mangled bodies, or whether the last vestige of liberty is swept from the face of the American continent, the South will never submit to such humiliation and degradation as the inauguration of Abraham Lincoln." [55]

Forsyth asked his editorial associate to read Douglas an editorial for the *Register,* calling for a State convention to debate Alabama's course in the crisis. The best policy for Alabama Unionists, he explained to the Senator, would be to yield to the widespread demand for a convention, elect as many delegates as possible, and try to channel the proceedings into some safe outlet. Douglas dissented. If the Union men could not prevent a convention, he argued, they could not control it when it met. But Forsyth insisted on his view, and the editorial went to press. The Illinoisan, who saw more realistically than any leader except Stephens the disruption and bloodshed that lay ahead, left the office to return to the Battle House. As they walked through the desolate streets, his secretary observed that he was "more hopeless than I had ever before seen him." [56]

*　　*　　*　　*　　*

Men might, as always, dispute the meaning of the election. On the surface it seemed to offer no clean-cut national verdict for anything; certainly not for Lincoln and the Republican tenets. Yet its central import was actually plain: The nation had taken a mighty decision—the decision that slavery must be circumscribed and contained. Lincoln's 1,866,000 followers wished to contain the institution within existing limits by a flat Congressional refusal to recognize

54 N. Y. *Weekly Tribune,* September 8, 1860. James A. McDougall, who had been a Chicago lawyer and attorney-general of Illinois, was an intimate friend of Douglas.
55 Quoted in Dumond, *Secession Movement,* 104.
56 Wilson, *Slave Power,* II, 700; Milton, *Eve of Conflict,* 500.

it outside; the 1,375,000 adherents of Douglas wished to contain it by local-option type of popular sovereignty. But contained it would be, under either formula. No longer would a compact, determined Southern minority dictate national policy on the subject. The popular majority of the land had asserted itself, and a people's man, far stronger than the South supposed, stood ready to execute their will. Behind this decision that slavery had passed its flood tide and must henceforth stand still or recede, lay an implicit decision on the two rival assumptions that had divided South and North—one, the assumption that slavery was right and wholesome; the other, that it was wrong and deleterious. Slavery might persist indefinitely within the fifteen slave States, but as to its restriction, and as to the faith that it was in the path of ultimate extinction, the nation had come at last to an unavoidable determination.

From that decision there was but one appeal. Dreadfully clear now, to ears attuned to the future, sounded the drums and bugles.

11

The Lower South Secedes

THE MOMENT the election of Lincoln was certain, much of the Lower South gave way to a frenzy of excitement in which the clamor for secession of radical politicians and editors seemed to drown out the voices of conservative Unionists. Those who had been threatening the severance of the Union, and who had to make their threats good or confess impotence, united in a galvanic effort to revolutionize their States. Yancey, Iverson, Rhett, T. R. R. Cobb, Porcher Miles, and men of similar convictions had prepared to employ the first surge of resentment to carry a number of capitals into separate secession. In South Carolina, Alabama, and Mississippi the demand for action was so instant and aggressive that it took the North aback. Elsewhere, and especially in the broad border region, feeling was much calmer. While influential men called for separation, it was evident that the movement would be stubbornly resisted. As Northern opinion recovered from the first shock of dismay, it took heart from this division of sentiment and plucked up hope that even in the Lower South a national sentiment might, as in 1850–51, assert itself with effect. The swift events of the first month, however, proved that the new situation held grimmer perils than that of ten years earlier.

South Carolina was like a bed of charcoal suddenly leaping into flame. The legislature was sitting at Columbia to choose presidential electors. As the returns came in, Rhett, Milledge L. Bonham, Keitt, and Ruffin, all present in the city, delivered impassioned speeches. The State Rights flag, a red star on a white ground, was flung out over public buildings. In Charleston on Wednesday the seventh, crowds thronged the streets, the palmetto flag was hoisted over the *Mercury* office amid wild cheering, J. D. B. De Bow and others spoke, and the announcement that Federal Judge A. G. Magrath and Collector W. F. Colcock had resigned their offices inspired general enthusiasm. In the next few days a spate of news kept the people aroused. The legislature had authorized the governor to spend $100,000 for arms; Senator Chesnut had resigned his seat in Washington and Hammond had followed suit; telegrams from other States were tendering the support of volunteer corps. Everywhere the stars and stripes were coming down, and the red star or palmetto flags were going up. In Columbia,

Charleston, and other centers, militia units and minute men had redoubled their drilling. Bonfires, parades, and "resistance rallies" were the order of the day.[1]

The fever seemed to rage only less violently in Alabama and Mississippi, while in lowland Georgia it was intense. The night after the election, the largest mass meeting that Savannah had ever witnessed called for a State convention and rapid defensive measures. Another meeting, two nights later, amended the resolutions to demand immediate secession. In Augusta a similar assemblage cheered secessionist speeches. Toombs, T. R. R. Cobb (Howell's brother), and other radicals made bitter addresses; the colonial flag of Georgia was raised at various points; and citizens gathered at many county seats to organize minute men.[2] At Montgomery, where Yancey on the night of November 10 roused a crowd to wild emotion, people seemed almost unanimous for secession. Although dispatches from Mobile declared that commercial men opposed a separation, some observers reported that nine-tenths of the country districts in the lowlands were for disunion. Leaders of volunteers told the governor they would have eighty thousand men under arms by New Year's Day. All the prominent officers of Alabama—the governor, both Senators, all Representatives but one, the Supreme Court judges—were in favor of drastic action.

Meanwhile, in Mississippi an overwhelming demand had arisen for a special session of the legislature. The spirit animating much of the Lower South was voiced by the mother of E. Kirby Smith, writing from St. Augustine to that future Confederate general:

I never expected to see a revolution, to see our long cherished stars and stripes hauled down—but so it is—you are so far removed from the scene of these acts that you can form no idea of the excitement which prevails among all classes—all ages—women as well as men. Our Cause is a just one, and I fully believe Providence will smile upon it—if we can pass through it without a baptism of blood and fire, shall we not have reason to thank God with our whole hearts?[3]

[I]

For several reasons, South Carolina was in the best position to give the secessionist forces vigorous leadership. Since in that State alone presidential electors were chosen by the legislature, the two houses had met November 5; they would

1 Ruffin, MS Diary, November 7, ff., 1860; Schirmer, MS Diary; Charleston *Courier*, November 8, 10, 1860; Mrs. Mary B. Chesnut, *A Diary from Dixie*. A caucus of South Carolina leaders was said to have met, October 25, at Senator Hammond's house to make plans; Nicolay and Hay, *Lincoln*, II, 328.

2 Stephens, writing from Crawfordsville on November 8, makes the astonishing statement: "The people here are taken greatly by surprise at the result. They did not anticipate it and thought I was only indulging in unnecessary apprehensions when I told them months ago how it would most probably be." *Toombs, Stephens, Cobb Corr.*, 502.

3 St. Augustine, January 7, 1861; Kirby Smith Papers, Univ. of N. C.

reconvene again on the twenty-sixth for the regular session and to elect a governor. No legislature in the country was less representative of the masses. Seats were apportioned according to a ratio compounded of the white population and the amount of taxes paid, so that the wealthy lowlands, with their heavy slave properties, held a marked advantage over the poorer up-country where the whites so strongly preponderated over the Negroes. Governor Gist, a wealthy planter and veteran State Rights man, had already prophesied the secession which he wished to make a reality. A month before the election, he had sent the before-noted letters to various Southern governors declaring that South Carolina would secede if she had any assurance of similar action by another or other States, and would desire their cooperation. As soon as his legislature met, he had informed it that in view of the probability of a Republican victory, which would give the South the prospect of becoming a mere province in a consolidated despotism, it should remain in session, and if Lincoln were chosen, should call a State convention to consider modes of redress.[4]

The legislature was ready to act. Differences arose as to the time schedule, one party demanding immediate and separate secession while another urged delay until joint action with other States could be arranged; but the issue was quickly resolved. On November 9, a bill passed calling a secession convention, to which the various districts should send as many delegates as their quotas in the legislature—thus preserving lowland domination. The election was to be held January 8, and the delegates were to meet a week later. This would give time for ascertaining the temper of other States. But when Charleston heard of the movement for delay, a great mass meeting entered a vehement protest; it was seconded by a body of influential Georgians who had come for the before-mentioned celebration of the opening of the Savannah-Charleston Railroad; and a committee of three was hurried to Columbia by special train. The legislature then reversed itself, fixing the election for December 6 and the convention for the seventeenth. The members, caustically wrote J. L. Petigru, were afraid to "trust the second thought of even their own people." It seems probable, however, that a decisive majority of South Carolinians wished to express themselves without delay, and to point the road for their sister States.[5]

The people have taken the helm, exultantly wrote Judge Longstreet to the Richmond *Enquirer*. They have carried the politicians before them. South Carolinians feel a universal resolution never to submit to Black Republican rule.

4 Nicolay and Hay, *Lincoln*, II, 306 ff., gives Gist's corr. with the governors. The S. C. *House Journal* and *Senate Journal* for 1860 mirror the rush of the radicals, though Speaker James Simons of Charleston was a moderate, and many members opposed precipitate action.

5 Carson, *James L. Petigru*, 361; Lillian A. Kibler, "Union Sentiment in S. C. in 1860," *Journal Southern Hist.*, IV, August, 1938.

"You might as well attempt to control a tornado as to attempt to stop them from secession." He praised the high spirits of the populace. "All is smiles, joy, and good fellowship." [6]

Mississippi was prepared, though with less precipitancy, to fall into line. Governor John J. Pettus had already written Gist that if any State acted, he believed his own would go with her. He hastened (November 13) to call the legislature into session on the twenty-sixth. Lincoln's election, he wrote, demonstrated that men eager to "destroy the peace, property, and prosperity of the Southern section" had gained control of the government, and that Mississippi must provide surer safeguards for life and liberty than could be hoped for "from Black Republican oaths." He also privately arranged a meeting in Jackson of part of the delegation in Congress to advise him. Here the usual disagreement arose between advocates of joint and disjoint secession; but when Reuben Davis offered a resolution calling on the governor to propose immediate and separate State action, it was adopted—the governor voting for it.[7] Gist had telegraphed Pettus asking whether the South Carolina convention should make secession effective at once or on March 4, and, again at the suggestion of Davis, a majority of the gathering decided that Gist should be advised in favor of immediate secession. The Jackson *Mississippian* was arguing that it would be wisest to secede while the national government still was in friendly hands.[8] To wait for joint secession might mean waiting forever.

"We are no longer one people," wrote a representative Alabama secessionist. "A paper parchment is all that holds us together, and the sooner that bond is severed the better it will be for both parties." As we have noted, the legislature early in the year had provided for calling a State convention if the Republicans won the Presidency. But when did Lincoln's election really take place— on November 6, or when the electoral college cast their ballots on December 5? Governor Moore, who had assured Gist that he believed Alabama would secede with any two or more cooperating States, decided that the true date fell in December. He made it known at once, however, that he would designate December 24 for the election of delegates, and January 7 as the day for the convention to meet; so that the canvass began forthwith in most counties. Here, again, the secessionist party divided into two main elements—one favoring immediate and if necessary separate action, the other demanding group secession. As the passing days made it obvious that other States would go out, however, the latter element gave way. It became evident that the opponents

6 Longstreet's letter, dated December 6, is copied in Charleston *Courier*, December 13.
7 N. Y. *Weekly Tribune*, November 21, 1860.
8 Reuben L. Davis, *Mississippi and Mississippians*, 391; Jackson *Mississippian*, November 13, 1860; Jefferson Davis, *Rise and Fall*, I, 57 ff.

of secession would meet certain defeat—that Alabarna, like South Carolina and Mississippi, had sealed her determination.[9]

As for Georgia, keystone of the cotton kingdom arch, Governor Joseph E. Brown held aggressive disunionist views. He had urged his legislature, which met just before Lincoln's election, to adopt retaliatory measures against the North. He had also informed Gist that, in his opinion, Georgia would meet all the Southern States in convention, and might even take action without waiting for her sisters. The day after Lincoln's election, he sent the legislature a message recommending that it call a State Convention. Some delay took place, for opinion in Georgia was much more closely divided than in her neighbors. The hesitating legislators invited nearly a score of the strongest leaders of the State to address them. While Toombs spoke in fiery terms for immediate secession, Stephens argued for sober deliberation. In the end the legislature set January 2 for the election of a convention to meet a fortnight later.

Before November closed, the Mississippi and Florida legislatures had also called conventions, to be elected December 20 and 24. Thus, within three weeks of Lincoln's victory, five States had arranged for gatherings to pass upon secession—and nearly everyone assumed they would vote for leaving the Union. If nothing were done in Washington to halt the movement, South Carolina would assuredly withdraw before Christmas, and Mississippi, Alabama, Georgia, and Florida would probably do so before the end of January. Congress was to meet on Monday, December 3. The national government would have to act with celerity and wisdom in the next six weeks if it were to control the situation.

One hopeful factor was that all five States contained a Unionist party of no little strength and dignity. In the upper districts of South Carolina, many citizens—one observant minister thought them a majority—stood for maintenance of the Union. The able editor-politician, B. F. Perry, had published a strong attack upon secessionist scheme in the Charleston *Courier* of August 20, and he kept up his battle. Chief Justice John B. O'Neall, a nationalist since nullification times, believed that secession was madness and had the support of his associate, Judge Job Johnstone. Gabriel Cannon of Spartanburg was one of several State senators who counseled patience. "I am still for the Union," declared George S. Bryan of Charleston, "on the sole ground that the South has made Mr. Lincoln President." [10]

The respected jurist James L. Petigru, just entrusted with the codification of the State laws, protested to the last against the flowing tide. Charlestonians long remembered one dramatic moment of his career. Listening attentively to the

9 Denman, *Secession in Alabama*, 87 ff.
10 November 6, 1860; Kennedy Papers.

reading of Sunday prayers from the pulpit of his beloved St. Michael's, he started when he heard the usual invocation for the President of the United States omitted, and without hesitation walked up the aisle and out the door. It required all the varied excitements of the day, all the oratory of Keitt, Bonham, and Ruffin, all the urgings of Chesnut and Gist, and all the fiery editorials of the *Mercury* (whose normal paid circulation of five hundred and fifty compared badly with the three thousand circulation of the *Courier*) to convince Carolinians that the Unionist minority was too insignificant to be heeded.[11]

In Alabama, numerous merchants and professional men of Mobile, small farmers of the northern counties, and scattered lowland planters were insistent that the State should not secede without at least one final effort to secure redress of grievances within the Union. Yet national sentiment in Mobile, a city of thirty thousand with considerable trade connections with the North, found little effective expression. Such Unionists as John Forsyth of the *Register* and C. C. Langdon of the *Advertiser* (a journal established in 1833 to oppose nullification, and ever since then on the Union side) could accomplish nothing. Not until mid-December was a call issued for a meeting of men opposed to hasty action, and this gathering merely adopted a platform and nominated candidates favorable to cooperative secession. Alabama, ran its resolutions, should assert its independence only if the four neighboring cotton States did the same. In the ensuing election of convention delegates, advocates of separate secession swept Mobile County.

It was only in northern Alabama that the opposition made a formidable stand. This area, lying partly in the Tennessee Valley, sold much of its production across the Tennessee line, which it realized might soon become an international boundary. The last census had shown eight northern counties where the slaves were fewer than thirteen percent of the population. Cooperative secessionists here held a majority, while several counties were controlled by outright Unionists or men who at least wished secession delayed until it was proved that no other recourse existed. Before the national election, the Bell-Everett and Douglas men talked angrily of a conspiracy, pointing in proof to the legislature's provision for a convention in the event of a Republican victory, and to Yancey's successful efforts at Charleston to make that victory certain. The State, they had charged, was being railroaded into secession. Attacking the

---

11 The Charleston *Mercury*, while extensively copied outside the State, was not much read in it. It was supposed to cost the Rhett family $8,000 a year to maintain it. Charleston corr. N. Y. *Tribune*, dated November 7, 1860. See John B. O'Neall and John Chapman, *Annals of Newberry*, for the opposition. Petigru later was walking down Broad Street when a friend accosted him. "Have you heard the news, sir?" he asked. "Great news; Louisiana has seceded." "Good God, Williams," Petigru said in a tone of mild disgust, "I thought we had *bought* Louisiana." Undated sheet, Petigru Papers, S. C. Hist. Soc.

unfair ratio of representation in the legislature, they had accused the leaders of the conspiracy of being afraid to submit the issue of a convention to the whole people. A Huntsville friend of Governor Moore's wrote him:

By vehement denunciations of this fancied conspiracy, and unmeasured eulogies upon the Federal Union, the leaders of these opposition parties have gradually led their followers into the adoption of doctrines touching the theory of our government, which in 1799 would have stamped them as rank federalists —insisting that their first and highest allegiance is to the Federal government— that there can be no lawful resistance to the pressures of the Federal government or of a violation of the compact by other States; that the only remedy is the right of revolution on the part, not of the State but the people of the State, and that *success* alone can exempt those participating in the revolution from traitor's doom; many of them insisting that the States occupy the same relation to the general government that our counties do to the State. . . . But a few days ago I heard the most influential leader of the Douglas party in this part of the State declare that if the people of South Alabama should succeed in putting the State out of the Union he would be in favor of putting this valley out of the State; contending at the same time that a separation of the State from the Federal government would operate as an utter annihilation of all government within the State. . . .[12]

Of the first five States to arrange conventions, Georgia was that where the separate secessionists had to fight their hardest battle and where Union feeling proved strongest. Alexander H. Stephens, Benjamin H. Hill, and Herschel V. Johnson all maintained a staunch conservatism. Nor were they without important followers. Less than a fortnight after Lincoln's victory, Judge Wayne of the Supreme Court arrived in Washington reporting that he thought four-fifths of the people of Savannah opposed immediate secession. Savannah, like Mobile, had important trade links with the North. A considerable minority of lowland planters, chiefly men who had clung to the Whig Party until its death, were steadfastly opposed to what they called premature action. The hilly country at the north of the State and the upper pine-barrens, where slaves were few, were strongholds of Union sentiment. Of the six diehard delegates who, in the end, were destined to vote against secession, four came from the hill region and two from the pinelands. In the middle black belt, feeling was almost evenly divided between radicals and conservatives.

When Governor Brown sent the legislature his message justifying the right of secession, asserting that "the time for bold and decided action has arrived," and proposing a tax of twenty-five percent on all merchandise manufactured in or imported from Massachusetts, New York, Michigan, and other States which had passed unfriendly legislation, he met rigorous opposition. It was because

12 S. D. Cabaniss, October 29, 1860; Governors' Papers, Ala. Dept. Arch and Hist.

public sentiment was so manifestly unclarified that the legislature asked the lead-ing men of Georgia to debate the issues before it. Although the secessionists were, in Herschel V. Johnson's words, "impatient, overbearing, dictatorial, and intolerant," they did not dare to move precipitately.[13]

Toombs, in his rousing vindication of Southern rights delivered November 13 before the two houses, declared that the Republican Party patently intended to destroy the institution of slavery, and that guarantees from men already guilty of violating the Constitution would not be worth the paper on which they were inscribed. He was followed the next night by Stephens, whose appeal on behalf of Georgia's motto, "Wisdom, justice, and moderation," was one of the finest of his career. With haggard earnestness, Stephens argued that Lincoln, faced by hostile majorities in both House and Senate, could do nothing to jeopardize Southern security; that his bare election was no justification for destroying the institutions which generations of patriotic forebears had built up; and that, while the honor of Georgia must be maintained even if this meant eventual disunion, they should await an act of aggression before moving. He stood, he said, upon the Georgia platform of 1850 demanding equal rights in the Territories and enforcement of the Fugitive Slave Act. They should unite with the rest of the South in asking a repeal of unfriendly laws, and if the North refused a proper adjustment, "then let the consequences be with them."[14] Herschel V. Johnson, too, urged consultation with other slaveholding States and an appeal to the North for justice.

But despite all the evidence of scattered Union feeling, by December 6, the date of the South Carolina election, it was clear that the secessionists were over-riding all opposition in four of the five foremost States—Georgia alone being doubtful. The course of events under the palmetto flag was eloquent of the situation. November found the State full of secession meetings, while Union men hardly dared assemble. Even B. F. Perry, who was defeated in his own county for the first time in twenty years, confessed himself paralyzed. "The election was hurried on without giving time for discussion," he writes in his autobiography. "I did not go out at all to electioneer, and the people of the district did not turn out to vote. The secessionists all went to the polls and did not cast more than a thousand votes, whilst the district could vote more than twenty-four hundred. The Union men thought that it was a foregone conclusion that the State would secede, and it was not worth their while to go to the polls."[15] Chief Justice O'Neall and Judge Johnstone, speaking from the steps of Newberry courthouse, were a target for eggs and turnips; and, according to

13 See U. B. Phillips, *Georgia and State Rights*; "From the Autobiography of Herschel V. Johnson, 1856–1867," *Am. Hist. Rev.*, XXX; Dumond, *Secession*, 142–144.
14 Extracts in Pendleton, *Stephens*, 159–163.
15 Perry, MS Autobiography.

O'Neall, "the majority of those entitled to suffrage" in that area did not vote. In the last week before the election, some observers discerned a strong conservative rally. One wrote the New York *Tribune* that if a true vote on the issue could be taken, a majority of South Carolinians would refuse to leave the Union. But on election day, the secessionists won from sea to mountains. And on the morrow Governor Gist issued another stirring message, urging immediate secession so that South Carolina might not exercise "a blighting and chilling influence upon the action of the other Southern States."

An explanation of the comparative impotence of Union men is not difficult to find. They were scattered, and, in such areas as northern Alabama and the Georgia hill country, isolated. They were handicapped, especially in South Carolina and Alabama, by apportionment laws and districting which penalized the small farmers. They had little organization, for neither the Bell-Everett nor Douglas forces had set up an efficient party machinery in the Lower South, and a good many Bell and Douglas leaders yielded to the secession impulse. The disunionists, on the other hand, availed themselves of the well-articulated Breckinridge organization. Most moderates and conservatives were by disposition inert, and stayed at home cautiously waiting while the radicals acted, spoke, and wrote with ebullient fervor. All the excitement of the time, too, favored the party of action—and an inflammatory spirit was sedulously maintained. "People are wild," wrote Senator Hammond on November 12. "The scenes of the French Revolution are being enacted already. . . . God knows the end." [16] Or as the British consul in Charleston put it, a few weeks later: "The public excitement is kept alive by the constant arrival of telegrams, many of the most absurd and mendacious character." [17] The brevity of the campaigns for electing the State conventions, moreover, gave no time for coolheaded reflection.

Then, too, as seeming majorities asserted themselves, many moderates thought it right to contribute to the moral unity of the State, and filled up the phalanx. This was the easy course to take. Greeley was unable to understand why the Bell-Everett party did so little outside the border region to make good their fidelity to the Constitution and the Union. He might have turned to the history of the American Revolution for illustrations of the power of an active minority to carry a population into revolt. He need only have consulted Burke's Speech on the Unitarian Petition for an analysis. "The greater number," wrote Burke, "is generally composed of men of sluggish tempers, slow to act and unwilling to attempt; and, by being in possession, are so disposed to peace, that they are unwilling to take early and vigorous measures for their defense, and they are almost always caught unprepared. . . . A smaller number, more expe-

16 Hammond to his brother; Hammond Papers, LC.
17 January 4, 1861; FO 5/780.

Washington D.C.
Nov. 30. 1830

Eli Whitney Esq.

Dr Sir, when the Adj't. Genl.
of Mississ. consulted me as to the best mode
of obtaining rifles for the volunteer companies of that state, I influenced him against
a preconceived plan of action, to propose to
you a contract for the manufacture of the
number required: My advice was based upon
the confidence reposed in you as a manufacturer and as a man. Recently it has been
reported to me that you had after much time
had been lost by depending upon you, in accordance with an agreement entered into, for said
manufacture, you have notified the authorities
of Mississ. that you declined to make the arms as
stipulated. The circumstances induce me to ask
of you an explanation, & will I hope lead you to
give me such a statement as will relieve me
of the impression created and justify me in
the advice given when I referred the Adjt. Genl.
to you as the best person with whom he could
make a contract. I have the honor to be yr obs't.

Jeffn. Davis

Jefferson Davis Writes the Whitney Arms Works Concerning Rifles.

327

dite, awakened, active, vigorous, and courageous, who make amends for what they want in weight by their superabundance of velocity, will create an acting power of the greatest possible strength. When men are furiously and fanatically fond of an object, they will prefer it, as is well known, to their own peace, to their own property, and to their own lives. . . ." Toombs, Yancey, and Ruffin were furiously and fanatically devoted to their object.

Wherever opponents of secession attempted to use delay, the radicals resorted to social pressure, denunciation, and in sporadic instances to threats of violence. Volunteer companies, some old, some newly organized, all training lustily, tended to become centers of secessionist activity. The Knights of the Golden Circle, which under "General" George Bickley had held a convention at Raleigh in the spring of 1860, and which, as we have already seen, was actively recruiting an expeditionary force to take possession of Mexico and a home guard to serve Southern objects upon demand, uttered threatening growls. Bickley had boasted at the convention that his organization numbered nearly forty-eight thousand. According to F. A. P. Barnard, head of the University of Mississippi, Union men in his State had become targets for the harshest name-calling. When Governor Pettus took steps to have the convention called, the university professor of law, though a zealous secessionist, was aghast. Protesting that he knew the sentiment of people in all parts of the State, he declared the effort must fail. "I am perfectly satisfied," he said, "that it is impossible to take Mississipi out of the Union." Events quickly proved him wrong; and Barnard believed that it was largely because the opposition was cowed by taunting words like "poltroon," "submissionist," and "traitor" that it was quickly overcome.[18]

[II]

What hidden forces controlled this dramatic surge of Southern intransigence? Both at the time and later, many observers in the Northern and border States believed that an uprising so sudden and well-concerted could only be the fruit of a carefully matured plot. "The election of Lincoln is but a pretext," Douglas presently declared:

The present secession movement is the result of an enormous conspiracy which was matured a year ago. The conspiracy was formed by the leaders of the secession movement twelve months ago, and they have used every means to urge it on. They have caused a man to be elected by a sectional vote, to demonstrate that the Union was divided; and when the history of the country from the time of the Lecompton constitution to the date of Lincoln's election is written, it will appear that a scheme was maturing in the meantime which was for no end

18 See pamphlet, "Proceedings of the Convention of the Knights of the Golden Circle, Raleigh, May 7-11, 1860"; Fulton, *Barnard*, 272, 273.

except to break up the Union. They desired to break it up, and they used the slavery question as a means. They desired to create a purely sectional vote, to demonstrate that the two sections could not live together. The disunion card dictated that the South was to carry its own elections, and that the North was to elect Lincoln. Then a united South was to assail a divided North, and gain an easy victory. This scheme was defeated by the overthrow of the disunion candidates in Kentucky, Tennessee, and Virginia. Still the grand conspiracy existed, and the disunion movement was the result of it.[19]

This explanation was in time to be elaborated by Lincoln's secretary, John G. Nicolay, by John Minor Botts of Virginia, by the dashing commander of the Army of the Tennessee, John A. Logan, and other writers, all taking the view that secession was essentially the work of a small number of reckless, artful politicians whose plot carried six millions of reluctant or indifferent citizens into rebellion.[20] This conspiracy theory of secession furnishes no illumination of events. It is true that Rhett, Yancey, Wigfall, Porcher Miles, and others, bold, imperious, and in some respects unscrupulous men, had planned to make disruption of the Democratic Party a prelude to national disruption; and that numerous Southern extremists during 1859–60 were constantly corresponding and conferring, with disunion as their object. But it would have been impossible for even a far larger and better organized body of conspirators to have carried the South into this sweeping movement for independence had it not been that a large body of people in the cotton States had lost their old attachment to the Union, and had abandoned their old faith in the security it gave to their institutions and rights.

The central factor which made the secession movement possible, and which must be viewed as fundamental to the national schism, was a triple-fronted sentiment which, for a long generation, had been inculcated among the Southern people: A fervent belief in State Rights, including the right of secession, as the palladium of their liberties; an ever-deepening hatred for the freesoil movement in the North; and an increasing readiness to indulge the vision of a happy, opulent Southern republic. This sentiment had gradually sapped the once-powerful devotion of the Lower South to the Union. Alexander H. Stephens ranked preeminent as a Southern Unionist, yet he declared that if Georgia seceded he would bow to the will of the people. Such a declaration was worth little to the national bond.

Millions of Southerners felt much as Stephens did. They disliked secession for a number of reasons—because they revered the national concept established by the fathers, because they despised the fire-eaters (Rhett was never popular

19 Speech in Chicago May 1, 1861; Havana, Illinois, Post, June 13, 1861.
20 See Nicolay, The Outbreak of Rebellion; Botts, The Great Rebellion; Logan, The Great Conspiracy; Greeley, American Conflict, I, Chs. XXI–XXVI.

even in South Carolina), because they feared war and loss; but of militant, active Unionism, ready to give battle for the great ideal of Washington and Jackson, the majority of people in the Lower South had little. Their primary attachment was to their State or section. It was this lack of deep Union feeling, conjoined with the fear, irritation, and jealousy produced by Northern attitudes, and with a firm belief in the right of withdrawal, which made it possible for the extremists to bring about decisive action. The forces which had produced this psychology were all-important, and the so-called conspiracy, which was really a broad, groping, ill-coordinated impulse, was quite secondary.

The living social, economic, and intellectual interests of the Lower South, its sense of civic duty, its highest ambitions, had taken a turn divergent from the Union; and if Northerners had not learned what its state of mind was during the Congressional debate of 1859–60 and the Presidential compaign, a thousand men now informed them. Many voices, like that of Governor Gist, enunciated the right of peaceable secession. Many voices expressed a general prejudice. "I look upon the whole New England race," one Georgian had written, "as a troublesome, unquiet set of meddlers—their original stock a set of jailbirds, outlaws, and disturbers of the peace, who could not live among decent and civilized people in Europe; and this same intolerant and turbulent spirit has been transmitted to their posterity, and will cling to it to the latest generation." [21] Many voices expressed a resentment for past injuries, real and fancied. Northerners, declared Governor Pettus in his message of November 26 to the Mississippi legislature, have succeeded in educating a whole generation to hate the South. "They have attempted to degrade us in the estimation of other nations, by denouncing us as barbarians, pirates, and robbers, unfit associates for Christian or civilized men. They have excited our slaves to insurrection; advised them to burn our property and murder our people, and have furnished them with arms and ammunition to aid them in their bloody work." [22]

The secessionists also offered, however, reasoned and weighty if not coolheaded justifications of their cause. A belief that the outlook for the South would be hopeless in a Union no longer equal, just, and generous was stated with a thousand variations. Pettus wrote that the North had proclaimed that it would never rest satisfied until slavery was placed in a position ensuring its ultimate extinction; that these hard terms were offered fifteen States as if they were conquered and not coequal sisters; and that submission to such an ultimatum would establish a despotism under which the dearest rights of the South would be held at the sufferance of a hostile people. Governor Moore of Alabama similarly

21 J. Hanly Smith, Washington, April 3, 1860; Stephens Papers, LC.
22 Governor Brown of Georgia, harking back to Locke's ideas, wrote in his message of November 8 that the constitutional rights of Southerners had been violated by several free States to an extent justifying any measure necessary for their future protection.

insisted that safety demanded secession. The Black Republicans had elected a President; they would soon elect majorities in both houses; and then they would remake the Supreme Court. "Slavery will be abolished in the District of Columbia, in the dockyards and arsenals, and wherever the Federal Government has jurisdiction. It will be excluded from the Territories, and other free States will in hot haste be admitted to the Union, until they have a majority to alter the Constitution. Then slavery will be abolished by law in the States." Pamphleteers quoted leading Republicans in proof of their wish to end slavery. They pointed to Lincoln's words on ultimate emancipation, Sumner's statement that slavery must surely die, John Wentworth's assertion in the Chicago *Democrat* that the States must all be made free and the Republican Party would do it without bloodshed, the platform of 1856 which spoke of slavery and polygamy as relics of barbarism. Other writers warned the South that enemies like Sumner would rejoice in a revolution which made the slave the legal and social equal of the white man.

Even if the promise of Lincoln not to touch slavery within the States is taken at face value, declared some leaders, the South will be in dire danger. Senator Robert W. Johnson and Representative Thomas C. Hindman of Arkansas, addressing their constituents, foresaw disaster in the mere restriction of slavery. If the South submitted, the Republicans would limit slavery to its existing domain. This domain would be filled by the natural multiplication of colored people until the pressure of the blacks became intolerable. Finally, a conflict for racial supremacy would ensue; and either the Negroes would be exterminated, or the white man must abandon his Africanized country forever.[23] Meanwhile, asked other men, how much will slave property held under constant threat be worth? "The sole cause of the existing disunion excitement which is about to break up the government," wrote James A. Bayard to his son, "is the war which has been carried on for years past by all manner of devices by the antislavery fanatical sentiment upon more than $2,000,000,000 of property." [24]

It was in vain that Stephens reminded Southerners that they were no abject minority, and that for sixty out of seventy-two years they had controlled the government. In vain did men point out that the talk about a hurried admission of Nebraska, Washington, Dakota, Idaho, Nevada, and Arizona was nonsense, for these areas were far short of the population needed. In vain did moderates demonstrate that the Republicans could not possibly gain a majority in either house before March, 1863, and could not gain a sufficient majority to amend the Constitution under any circumstances.

23 January 8, 1861; E. L. Harvin, "Arkansas and the Crisis of 1860–61," MS, Univ. of Texas.
24 Washington, December 12, 1860; Bayard Papers, LC.

Apprehension for their future safety filled the minds of countless Southerners—and not without reason. Lincoln had said that a crisis must be reached and passed; that is, a critical decision be made *final*. This was the decision for the permanent containment of slavery, which meants its ultimate extinction. Southerners felt that if they assented to such a decision, they would have taken the first step on a road which could have but one ending. They could not guess how rapidly they might be hurried down the road, but they knew that much human history is a gloss on the text: "If ultimately, why not now?" They seemed safer against a premature revolution of their social and economic system outside the Union than in it. It probably did not occur to many Southerners, as it did to Buchanan, that the tide of world hostility to slavery was now so powerful that the South could better withstand it as part of the United States than as an isolated and exposed republic.

Then, too, many felt that it was not the old Union that they were leaving, for that was dead. "Equality and safety in the Union are at an end," Howell Cobb shortly informed his fellow Georgians. "The Union formed by our fathers was one of equality, justice, and fraternity. On the 4th of March it will be supplanted by a union of sectionalism and hatred." [25] So jangling had the national household become that not a few sincere lovers of concord believed that disunion would actually promote peace. The perpetual brawling over the slavery question was like some chronic dispute between husband and wife which only divorce could heal. The history of the Methodist Church seemed to illustrate the possibility of gaining harmony by a choice of separate ways. Before the church split, the General Conference was always a scene of disgraceful bickering; after the separation, Southern and Northern wings went forward peaceably and happily.

Next to the demands for safety and equality, the secessionist leaders emphasized familiar economic complaints. South Carolinians in particular were convinced of the general truth of Rhett's and Hammond's much publicized figures upon Southern tribute to Northern interests. Rhett had estimated that of the $927,000,000 collected in duties between 1791 and 1845, the South had paid $711,200,000, and the non-slaveholding States $216,000,000. Hammond had declared that the South paid about $50,000,000 and the North perhaps $20,-000,000 of the $70,000,000 raised annually by duties. In expenditure of the national revenues, the Senator thought the North got about $50,000,000 a year, and the South only $20,000,000.[26] These statistics were not the less persuasive because totally devoid of scientific quality. The theory that imports were paid

25 Address of December 6, 1860; *Toombs, Stephens, Cobb Corr.,* 505–516.
26 White, *Rhett,* 126–127; *Cong. Globe,* March 4, 1858. See Washington *Constitution,* November 13, N. Y. *Weekly Tribune,* November 17, 1860, for Southern economic complaints.

for out of exports was generally accepted in South Carolina. A widely distributed pamphlet published in Charleston, John Townsend's "The South Alone Should Govern the South," computed the total tribute of the section each year at $105,000,000, of which $20,000,000 was an exorbitant share of the tariff levies, $20,000,000 was profit on Northern manufactures, and $30,000,000 the profit of shipowners on the Southern export-import trade. What do we get in return for this? demanded Townsend. Nothing but insults and incitements to rebellion.[27]

Rhett, in his speech to the South Carolina legislature on November 10, touched the familiar chords anew. A generation earlier, according to his interpretation of history, the North had determined to live on the labors of the South. It had passed legislation to bring the whole carrying trade into American hands and lift the tariff to extortionate levels. When it had found its match in little South Carolina, it had changed its tactics. Northern leaders had resolved to increase the number of free States and unite them against the Southern people. They had forbidden the admission of any more slaveholding States, taken unfair measures to bring California into the Union, and bullied and shot the Southerners out of Kansas. How would he now meet the North? He would go to these plunderers, and tell them that the Union was dissolved. When the Yankees found their factories paralyzed and their shipping idle, they would come begging for the restoration of fraternal relations; but the Southern leaders should deal with the North as with any other foreign nation, and use their vast resources to enrich their own people. It is not likely that many readers accepted all of this statement. But it is certain that a great many Southerners believed at least part of it.

Other motives entered into the secessionist movement, some affecting one element and some another. Sheer pride counted for a great deal. The Lower South had been stung by derisive Northern comments upon its tendency toward gasconading threats and bombastic vaunts. The cotton kingdom could not let New York and Boston newspapers taunt it once more upon its windy resolutions and blustering manifestoes. Porcher Miles wrote that he was sick and disgusted with talk—he wanted action, and one State could "break up things generally." South Carolina newspapers and letters in the crisis repeated again and again the assertion that the State was too far committed, and must act or be disgraced. Allied with this pride was the feeling of many leaders that if they drew back once more, their last real opportunity would have vanished. Rhett said frankly that it would have been better to dissolve the Union in 1850, when the

27 Townsend, of St. John's Colleton, sums up a whole series of arguments for secession with great ability. The pamphlet, which quickly went into a third edition, must have had considerable influence. For a hostile response, see J. P. Kennedy's pamphlet of 1861, "The Border States: Their Power and Duty in the Present Disordered Condition of the Country."

States stood fifteen slaveholding, and fifteen free. What chance, he implied, would the South have in 1870 or 1880?

Many merchants of Charleston, Savannah, and Mobile, many railway promoters and other speculative men, hoped that with independence the cities, towns, and communications of their section might rise to larger opportunities. In Charleston, men pointed to maps showing what an immense region would soon export its produce and import its merchandise across their wharves. Interior Tennessee, they declared, could ship its crops more cheaply to them than to New York. They talked of flourishing lines of steamers, nurtured by free trade, plying via the Azores to England, France, and Italy. Not a few planters, too, believed that their fortunes would be bettered if the South gained independence. A Cooper River magnate with two thousand slaves declared that he favored secession in order to make more money. "Most of us planters are deeply in debt; we should not be if out of the Union. We should have a direct trade with Europe. We should get a better price for our cotton, and our goods would cost us fifty per cent less than now. . . . We must do it now or never. If we don't secede now the political power of the South is broken." [28]

As another consideration, a revolutionary movement always serves aspiring men, and many a Southern politician who had never achieved high office under the Union dreamed of eminence under a new Confederacy. Fame might be won by merely helping build the foundations of the republic. When the election was held for delegates to the South Carolina convention, a Charleston diarist commented: "there were a large number of candidates anxious to hand their names down to Posterity as actors in the Southern Drama." [29] The future glories of the new nation inspired enthusiasts. Rhett invoked the historian of 2,000 A.D. who would write of the brave Southerners who had thrown off the chains of their oppressors. "And extending their empire across this continent to the Pacific, and down through Mexico to the other side of the great gulf, and over the isles of the sea, they established an empire and wrought out a civilization which has never been equalled or surpassed—a civilization teeming with orators, poets, philosophers, statesmen, and historians equal to those of Greece and Rome—and presented to the world the glorious spectacle of a free, prosperous, and illustrious people."

The widespread belief that secession might and probably would be bloodless contributed mightily to the radical sweep. Yancey, returning from his Northern tour in the campaign, declared he had good reason to believe that the withdrawal of any State would be peaceable. A. B. Longstreet had told a baccalaureate audience at South Carolina College that he would stake everything he was

28 Quoted in N. Y. *Weekly Tribune*, November 17, 1860.
29 Schirmer Diary, December 6, 1860.

worth upon Northern acceptance of a general Southern secession. Even if the Yankees did resist, the South stood the better chance of winning. "Away with this notion of whipping us into the Union, or whipping us at all!" [30] Some politicians went about declaring they would drink all the blood that was shed. "You may slap a Yankee in the face and he'll go off and sue you but he won't fight!" De Bow, who had traveled widely and whose work as editor and supervisor of the census gave him authority, scoffed at the idea of a conflict. If one occurred, he assured F. A. P. Barnard, it would take place between the Northern factions, and blood would flow in the streets of New York and Philadelphia before it did in the South. He may have seen Franklin Pierce's letter to Jefferson Davis predicting that, if war began, the Northern cities would witness fighting between the fanatical antislavery men and those good citizens who respected their obligations, and that the Northern radicals would find occupation enough at home. But it is more likely that De Bow was simply one of those self-deluded men whom W. J. Grayson describes in his autobiography:

In both sections of the Union were shortsighted men striving to avoid slight or imaginary evils by rushing into others of incalculable magnitude. In both, were heated shallow partisans scoffing at dangers because their limited faculties were unable to perceive them. The carnage, the desolation, the destruction of property, the enormous public debt, the insupportable taxes, the standing army, the fortified frontier, the ruin that awaits all parties, were beyond the reach of their feeble vision.[31]

[III]

Northern opinion in the anxious weeks just after the election was a maelstrom of conflicting currents, in which a few dominant tendencies rapidly became visible. At first, the characteristic national optimism held sway. Till after South Carolina's withdrawal, millions believed that the Southern "rant" and "bluster" need not be taken seriously, while others clung to hope of a speedy compromise. A great part of the North vehemently maintained that nothing must be done to hector or threaten the South. Some argued that the cotton

---

30 Wade, *Longstreet*, 323, 324; E. J. Arthur, February 16, 1861, to E. De Leon, De Leon Papers; Fulton, *Barnard*, 272–274. Hodgson in *Cradle of the Confederacy*, 469, 470, quotes Yancey on Northern acquiescence, and writes: "That secession might be, and doubtless would be, a peaceable measure, was almost universally believed by the secession party of the South."

31 Grayson's remarks are the more notable because they were penned in Charleston in the midst of the Civil War. He wrote that both sections were to blame for the conflict. "There are men, South as well as North, who used slavery as a trumpet to excite sedition, who desired dissolution of the Union and found slavery as the readiest means to bring it about, who sought a cement for party union and found the Negro the strongest within reach." MS Autobiography, R. D. Bass, editor, 290–292.

States could yet be coaxed back; some declared that if no violence took place the border States could all be held; and some asserted that, in any event, coercion was improper, impracticable, or both. Still another group took the view that the primary task was to attempt a compromise. If it failed, and only then, firmer policies might be formulated.

Business difficulties deepened the general consternation. The election was followed by all the premonitory symptoms of a sharp business panic. The stock market staggered uncertainly, the banks contracted their credit, and borrowers fell into distress. The South was just completing its cotton harvest, for the growing of which it had incurred the usual debts at the North. Now, in view of possible departure from the Union, it tended to hold on to the crop, meanwhile letting obligations to Northern merchants and jobbers stand over. It also moved to withdraw its specie balances from Northern banks. Its talk of direct trade with Europe worried Northern exporters, importers, merchants, and shippers. Money became tighter, and business circles, looking forward to a dark winter, grew anxious.

On November 13, the New York money market would not buy paper at all. Next day, borrowers of the highest quality were able to obtain funds at eight and ten percent, but very good names still sold at twelve percent, while the notes of jobbers connected with the South went at eighteen and twenty-four percent. The following week brought news of the suspension of various banks in the South and West, and failures continued throughout the fall. Material amounts of Southern railroad securities and State bonds were held in the North, and, as they declined, the paper currency of Western banks issued upon them depreciated. The Federal Treasury was in such weak condition, with expenditures steadily exceeding receipts, that when December opened it was unable to pay Congressional salaries and many other demands. As political uncertainty increased, so did the business dislocation.

Yet this business recession did not daunt most Northern freesoilers. Lincoln was frankly scornful of it. "I am not insensible to any commercial or financial depression that may exist," he assured Truman Smith on November 10; "but nothing is to be gained by fawning around the 'respectable scoundrels' who got it up. Let them go to work and repair the mischief of their own making; and then perhaps they will be less greedy to do the like again." And he curtly rejected the suggestions of Truman Smith and Henry J. Raymond that he offer some reassuring statement to the South. He could say nothing that he had not already said, he wrote; and to press fresh statements upon those who had refused to listen would not only show a want of self-respect—it "would have an appearance of sycophancy and timidity which would excite the contempt of good men, and encourage bad ones to clamor the more loudly."

Of the three thousand and more Northern newspapers, hardly half a hundred were at this time outright defenders of slavery. Conspicuous among this corporal's guard were three New York journals, the *Herald*, the *Day-Book*, and the *Daily News*, the first exhibiting James Gordon Bennett's cynicism and moral obtuseness, the second enjoying a considerable Southern circulation, and the third appealing to the Irish laborers of the city; one moribund sheet in Philadelphia, Buchanan's old organ the *Pennsylvanian*, and another in Washington, the *Constitution*; and Cyrus H. McCormick's Chicago *Times*. These journals declared that slavery was neither an evil nor a crime, that it was the status best fitting the inferior nature of the Negro, and that it could not be overthrown without destroying the fabric of Southern society. Some of them, notably the *Herald*, espoused Grayson's doctrine that the slave possessed greater economic security and social contentment than the hireling.

For various reasons, however, this proslavery element in the press exercised a diminishing influence. Bennett, for all his memorable work in improving the news-range and widening the democratic appeal of the press, was regarded as an erratic and unprincipled adventurer, while his *Herald* combined lurid sensationalism with a readiness to change its opinions with every veering wind. Men read it while despising it. The *Day-Book*, edited by the notorious Negrophobe, Dr. John Van Evrie, who published pseudo-scientific works on white supremacy and black subordination, was an eccentric, prejudiced racial organ. Both the *Pennsylvanian* and the *Constitution* were subsidized sheets, which died as soon as they lost the Administration advertising. As for the Chicago *Times*, which had gained real prestige when edited by Sheahan for Douglas, it was now suspect because conducted by one former Virginian, and owned by another.[32]

The great majority of Northern journals disliked slavery, believed in respecting the rights of the Southern States, and abhorred disunion. They took a position equally distant from the *Day-Book* and the *Liberator*. While they hoped for the eventual extirpation of slavery, they wished to see this accomplished in a way which would not ruin the Southern economy, bring the races to social and political equality, or fill the North with a mass of needy freedmen. Whether they inclined to the view of Breckinridge, Douglas, or Lincoln as to the position of slavery in the Territories, they condemned the fanaticism of both abolitionists and secessionists. But slavery was not the immediate issue. When the five cotton States which led the van arranged before the end of November for conventions, it became necessary for the Northern press to abandon generalities and take a stand on the question of secession.

Acquiescence or coercion? The fifty proslavery sheets, of course, chose the

32 See H. C. Perkins, "Defense of Slavery in the Northern Press on the Eve of Civil War," *Journal Southern Hist.*, IX, November, 1943.

former. Bennett's *Herald* sneered at Lincoln, remarking that as he had once split rails he was now splitting the Union. All thought of coercion was outrageous, it said. That would precipitate "a fratricidal conflict, which will destroy the industrial interests of all sections, and put us back at least a hundred years in the estimation of the civilized world." Scolding Lincoln for not begging the South to come back, the *Herald* in the end, half mockingly, half seriously, suggested that the seceding States should arrange a constitutional convention for their section, adopt whatever amendments for safeguarding slavery they thought proper, and submit them to the North for ratification. It would be a happy result if all the States came under the new roof except New England, to which the country could bid good-riddance. Already, the nation had suffered too much from "the provincial meanness, bigotry, self-conceit, love for isms, hypercritical opposition to anything and everything, universal faultfinding, hard bargaining, and systematic home lawlessness . . . which are covering their section of the country with odium." [33] Not only the New York *Day-Book* and *Daily News*, but the *Journal of Commerce* and the *Express* were nearly as complaisant. Ben Woods's *Daily News* declared that while no State had the right to withdraw, nothing could be done if withdrawal took place. The Brooks brothers' *Express*, denouncing personal liberty laws, the underground railroad, and abolitionist publications, implied that secession was an act of desperation.[34] And Gerard Hallock's *Journal of Commerce*, speaking for conservative businessmen, was for letting the seceders go.[35]

A median position was taken by the *Tribune*, which disappointed a multitude of readers by its indecisive tone. Immediately after the election, it declared that while the right to secede might be revolutionary, it nevertheless existed—if the secession really represented majority opinion. "Whenever a considerable section of our Union shall deliberately resolve to go out, we shall resist all coercive measures designed to keep it in. We hope never to live in a republic whereof one section is pinned to the residue by bayonets. But we must insist that the step be taken, if ever it shall be, with the deliberation and gravity befitting so momentous an issue. Let ample time be given for reflection; let the subject be fully canvassed before the people; and let a popular vote be taken in every case before secession is decreed." [36]

Very different, and very heartening to all believers in stern Union principles, was the stand taken by the *Evening Post* of Bryant and the *Times* of Raymond. The Jacksonian principles of the poet-editor prompted an immediate thunderpeal under the title "Peaceable Secession an Absurdity," which declared that no

33 Nevins, *Evening Post*, 273–274.
34 N. Y. *Express*, November 12, 13, 1860.
35 Perkins, *Northern Editorials on Secession*; files, November–December.
36 N. Y. *Weekly Tribune*, November 17, 1860.

government could have a day of assured existence if it tolerated views which deprived it of credit or future. "No, if a State secedes it is revolution, and the seceders are traitors. Those who are charged with the executive branch of the government are recreant to their oaths if they fail to use all lawful means to put down such rebellion." Bryant next day expressed his faith that Lincoln would restore American unity and make it perpetual. The *Times* meanwhile exhorted citizens to stand by the Union and the Constitution first, and talk of guarantees to the South only when their safety was assured. "We would yield nothing whatever to exactions pressed by threats of disunion." The *World*, a penny paper established by some religious-minded businessmen, warned the secessionists that they faced resistance. "It is of no use to mince matters," it remarked; "this rampant cotton rebellion will haul in its horns or we shall have civil war." [37]

This confusion of voices in the metropolis was echoed by a similar medley outside. The Dubuque *Herald*, a Douglas journal, defended the right of secession. So did the Bangor *Daily Union*, a Breckinridge paper, which remarked that while a sovereign State might be conquered and held as a subject province, no aggregation of power could ever force it to be a member of the Union. The Brooklyn *Eagle*, denying any State the right to secede, also denied the nation any right to prevent one from doing so. To coerce an unwilling member would be to convert the government into a sanguinary and odious despotism. The Cincinnati *Press* held that the revolt of the colonies offered a fair precedent for secession, and that the general voice of the North was for letting South Carolina go or stay, as she wished. Other journals simply urged the government to wait upon circumstances.

Yet a considerable and growing number of editors were for iron measures. Samuel Bowles's Springfield *Republican*, while willing to grant reasonable concessions, exclaimed on December 17: "Oh, for one hour of Jackson!" [38] Morton McMichael's Philadelphia *North American* pronounced the nation indissoluble. The Providence *Daily Post* insisted that the Union should be maintained with all the powers held by the government, and J. R. Hawley's Hartford *Courant* was equally emphatic. In the Middle West, the Chicago *Tribune*, accompanied by most Republican and many Douglasite newspapers, was ready for coercion. The Madison *State Journal* declared positively that the new President would not and could not be less prompt and decided than the President who had forced nullifiers to yield. We might as well face secession firmly, asserted the Washington *National Republican*, which was established just after the election to support the new Administration; for to talk about consenting to it is only to encourage with false hopes the traitors who will have to be quelled.

37 Nevins, *Evening Post;* Elmer Davis, *Times;* Perkins, *Northern Editorials.*
38 Merriam, *Bowles,* I, 277, 278. But Bowles blew cold as well as hot.

A clear majority of Northern newspapers, and certainly a heavy majority of Republican journals, denied the right of secession as explicitly as a majority of Southern sheets asserted it. For the two midwinter months in which some hope of compromise remained, however, only a minority of editors emphatically expressed the judgment that coercion was indispensable. While Bryant, Raymond, Forney, Medill, and others were militantly outspoken, Greeley and others hung back. It was only as the cotton kingdom plunged forward, as plans of adjustment proved futile, and as tempers grew hotter, that sentiment for coercion increased. Amid the crowd of events, the maelstrom of currents and counter-currents, hopes and fears alternated. So intelligent and decided an anti-slavery man as Charles Eliot Norton wrote to George William Curtis on December 17 that war was "most likely" and to Arthur Hugh Clough on February 10 that it was only "a remote possibility." [39] Such was the confusion, North and South, that conscientious men, torn between hope and despair, anger and conciliation, caution and impatience, changed in mood from day to day.

[IV]

That in this crisis the President was beset by the most awful anxieties, that he was racked between his long love for the South on one side and his attachment to the Union on the other, that in his deep aversion to violence he was tortured by the prospect of a fratricidal war, need not be said. No President ever faced a more difficult task. None, it may be added, ever faced a terrible crisis with feebler means of dealing with it effectively.

For what was the situation of the government? The nation had a President who within a few months would enter his seventieth year, tired, so infirm that at times he could not move outside his upstairs rooms, and utterly discredited. It had a Cabinet which was sharply divided over the permissibility of secession; Secretaries Cobb, Thompson, and Floyd standing defiantly for that right, and Cass, Holt, and Black denying it. It had a Congress which had been elected two years earlier, and which was dissevered as completely as the Cabinet; the Senate being Democratic, the House Republican, while both chambers broke into numerous factions on the questions of secession, compromise, and coercion. It had a public opinion which, largely because of the refusal of Republicans to face the certainty that Lincoln's election meant secession, and the failure of Southern extremists to face the certainty that secession meant war, was to the last degree ignorant and fluctuating. All these elements fell within a framework of government which kept a repudiated President in office four months after his party had been defeated, and the new Congress out of power for at least

39 Norton, *Letters*, I, 215–218.

that period. Had the nation possessed a ministerial form of government, a new leader would have taken over the reins immediately, with a united Cabinet behind him, and a close working relation with a new legislature. The stiffness of the American system, at times an advantage, now served it ill.

The main objective of Buchanan, the preservation of peace until compromise and sober second thought could bring the two sections together, was entirely sound. Most indices of public opinion suggest that the country desired caution, delay, and conciliation. A rough Jacksonian threat of force would have been repugnant to it. Buchanan believed that forbearance and moderation would keep the Upper South in the Union, that it would give time for placatory measures, and that the Lower South, finding itself alone and gradually softening under the offer of new guarantees, would return to its old allegiance. This was a reasonable policy. The President's use of appeasement had been unwise when it operated to bolster Southern unreason in the Lecompton dispute, in dealing with Douglas, and in pressing the slave-code demand; he should have checked and rebuked the radicals when that was still possible. But now that matters had come to an extremity, peaceable action was an imperative. Buchanan was unquestionably right in thinking that a military and naval demonstration against South Carolina in November of 1860 would have precipitated war. That angry State would have struck back. He was doubtless right in believing that most, if not all, of the South would have moved to defend the Carolinians. His resolve to explore every reasonable path toward reconciliation was sagacious statesmanship.

To be sure, it struck many Americans then and later as a supine course. Winfield Scott, a week before the election, had advised that six forts in the South be immediately garrisoned so strongly that their seizure would be impracticable. Some secessionist leaders, even, pronounced it a feeble policy. Ruffin jubilantly described it as such in his diary:

January 31, 1861. . . . I had not expected war between the old government and the seceded states, as a necessary or even probable result, provided all the southern states should secede at once, or even six or eight of the more southern states, with the early sympathy and early concurrence of the remaining and more northern slaveholding states. But I had certainly also expected, in the other contingency, of one only, or a few states seceding, that the first and immediate action of the federal government (denying the right of secession) would be to attempt the coercion and conquest of the seceded portion by a prompt and vigorous military attack. Instead of this no such attempt has yet been made, and nothing beyond the very partial and inefficient strengthening and reinforcing three of the many forts in the seceded and other southern states.

The imbecility of the executive department, added to the want of funds and means by the federal government, have prevented anything being done to coerce the seceded states. This impunity from federal attack must now continue until the 4th of March. . . . This has given four months of unforeseen and almost undisturbed time for action for the seceding states. Thus there has been avoided, what I certainly counted upon, the interregnum of lawful powers, or transition state of disorder, or illegal rule and perhaps revolutionary anarchy, expected to attend the change of government of every separately seceding state, and of all from the rule of the old to that of the new confederacy.

But Ruffin assumed that secession was fixed, irrevocable, and enduring, and that war must result from any attempt to disturb it. Buchanan's whole policy was to induce the Lower South to revoke its steps toward secession, and to guide the nation past war.

The correctness of this general policy, however, does not enable history to acquit Buchanan of weakness, vacillation, and timidity, his inseparable faults. His course passed through three fairly clear phases. The first was a period during which Cobb, Thompson, Slidell, and other Southern leaders still exerted almost their full influence, and he seemed ready to admit the main claims of the secessionists. The Directory, in fine, maintained its control over the Administration. The second was a brief interval during which he moved forward to a denial of the right of secession, but also denied that the government had any power to obstruct it. This acceptance of paralysis obviously could not last long. The impetuous action of the Lower South and the pressure of Northern sentiment forced the reluctant President to take a stand against Cobb, Thompson, and Slidell. Then the third period, following the reorganization of the Cabinet, found a strong Unionist group—Jeremiah Black, Joseph Holt, E. M. Stanton, and John A. Dix—maintaining the duty of the government to hold the forts and other Federal property in the South even if that course led to war. It is in the first two phases, falling in November and December, that we are immediately interested.

[V]

The initial Cabinet discussion held after Lincoln's election revealed that its members were violently divided in opinion, and that the President, anxious to learn the opinion of each, was as yet without sure conviction on the cardinal issues of secession and coercion. The date was November 9, and every member was present. Buchanan announced that they confronted the most momentous problem they had yet met, that of the course to be pursued in relation to Southern, and especially South Carolinian, threats of withdrawal. He raised for debate a specific proposal: That a convention of the States, as authorized in Article V of the Constitution, be called to devise some plan of adjustment. "He said," according to Floyd's diary, "that if this were done, and the North or non-slaveholding States should refuse it, the South would stand justified before the whole world for refusing longer to remain in a confederacy where her rights were so shamefully violated." [40] Cass, Black, Thompson, and Toucey favored calling a convention, and the two former spoke warmly in support of coercion if needed. Black, moreover, advocated immediate reinforcement of the Charleston forts. Cobb was saturnine and Floyd noncommittal on a convention, both feeling that nothing could be done to rescue the Union; while Holt opposed such a gathering on the ground that if it failed the secessionists would be more determined than ever.

Buchanan was working amain on a state paper which he thought of using either as a proclamation to expound his policy or as part of his annual message to Congress; and when he read the first draft to his Cabinet on November 10 a battle instantly opened between the two wings. His paper called upon the South to acquiesce in Lincoln's election, attacked the doctrine of secession, and hinted at the use of force to maintain the national authority. Cobb protested passionately. He had said the previous day that he thought disunion both inevitable and desirable. An implacable hater of the Republicans, he wished Georgia to secede in concert with the other Southern States; and he hoped that they would all take steps to leave on March 4, electing delegates to meet on that date to form a new Confederacy. Jacob Thompson held much the same views. He was anxious for Mississippi to secede; he believed that his political future lay with a Southern republic; he, too, thought that united action on March 4 would be the best course. When he heard Buchanan's paper he flared up angrily, denouncing its plea for acquiescence and its condemnation of secession. Floyd took the side of his fellow-Southerners. Like most Virginians, he was at this time opposed to secession or other rash steps and deplored the course of the Lower South. He even published over his own signature in a Richmond paper an essay rebuking secessionist attitudes. But he upheld the abstract right of withdrawal, and could not now abandon his stronger associates. He therefore attacked Buchanan's paper as false to the true State Rights doctrine and unjust to the temper of the Southern people.

On the other side, Cass, Black, Holt, and Toucey spiritedly espoused Buchanan's views. They gave the paper "extravagant commendation," records Floyd. Cass and Black were firm believers in Union principles. So was Holt, a man who had come into national politics as a staunch Jacksonian and adherent of Richard M. Johnson, and who represented the Union feeling in Kentucky. Toucey was simply a weak echo of the President. Like Buchanan, he was highly antagonistic to Northern "fanatics" and "agitators," but when his chief took a stand for national principles, he meekly followed. The Cabinet meeting broke

40 A thorough search has failed to reveal any more of Floyd's diary than is quoted in Pollard's *Lee*, 791 ff. Cf. P. G. Auchampaugh, "John B. Floyd and James Buchanan," *Tyler's Quarterly Hist. and Gen. Mag.*, XV, 71–90.

up without making any decision; but a deep cleavage had been revealed between its secessionist and antisecessionist wings.[41]

At this point, a President of spirit and acumen would have reorganized his Cabinet to make it a unit in harmony with his view, and would have pressed hard for the convention of States. The Cabinet schism sorely crippled the government. It was particularly inexcusable for Buchanan to retain Cobb and Thompson; to keep in the government two ministers who favored breaking that government down. As for the convention, if it were to be held, an immediate appeal to the country was essential. It could be called only by Congress on application of two-thirds of the State legislatures. The five States about to secede would probably spurn the idea and it would take time to get the others in motion. Bell-Everett men in the border region particularly favored a convention. Large numbers of conservative Democrats, and indeed numerous journals of all parties, were ready to support the plan. If Buchanan had given the movement energetic leadership, the convention might have served as a focus for national interest and Union sentiment; a body of men who inspired general respect could have been chosen; and their decisions might have saved the day. Unfortunately, Buchanan drifted. Doubtless fearing that the dismissal of Cobb and Thompson would raise a storm of anger in the cotton States, he kept his Cabinet intact. Actually, the expulsion of these two men would have yielded rewards as well as penalties, for it would have heartened Southern Unionists. Deciding to shift his responsibility to Congress, he dropped the convention plan.

It was a fatal error. Not a day should have been lost in calling for the grand national assize. An urgent request should have been sent the governors to convoke special legislative sessions. The mere spectacle of such executive energy in Washington would have encouraged the host of Southern unionists. A widespread demand that the country await the decision of the convention of States would have impeded the labors of the radical secessionists. Voices of moderation and statesmanship would have gained resonance as from a great amplifying apparatus. But neither vision nor boldness was part of Buchanan's nature, and he let the objections of the Directory deter him.

In this failure to unify his Administration and press for a bold national plan, Buchanan was influenced by the same Southern intimates who had surrounded him from the beginning. Horatio King, the First Assistant Postmaster-General and a close observer of events, wrote John A. Dix on November 10 that the President was "beset by secessionists who are almost exclusively occupying his

---

41 Curtis, *Buchanan*, II, *passim*; Nichols, *Disruption*, 382 ff.; Nicolay and Hay, *Lincoln*, II, Chs. XVIII–XXII; P. G. Auchampaugh, *James Buchanan and His Cabinet*; Frank W. Klingberg, "James Buchanan and the Crisis of the Union," *Journal Southern Hist.*, IX, November, 1943.

attention." He informs us that these men, Cobb and Thompson at their head, importuned and badgered Buchanan nightly until he was almost exhausted; until it was only with painful effort that he performed his duties, while some Cabinet sessions had to be held in his second-floor library because he was too unwell to go to his more distant office.[42] Soon after the election, Secretary Thompson was discussing with other Southerners ways and means of preventing Lincoln's inauguration. Within a month of the election, Secretary Cobb was addressing to Georgia a long exhortation to leave the Union. Yet these men were not merely kept in the government, but made the means by which Southerners of like views gained Buchanan's ear. Slidell, states King, was "among the most determined conspirators in seeking to destroy the Union." He remained intimate with Buchanan till the end of January, carrying his arrogance so far that when the President at that time dismissed Slidell's secessionist protégé, Beauregard, from the superintendency at West Point, the Senator sent the White House an insolent letter of rebuke.[43]

To the intense disgust of Cass, King, and others, the *Constitution*, still fed on Administration patronage, published articles day after day justifying secession. The morning after election, it asked whether the Southerner would submit to a Chief Executive chosen for his hostility to the South, or "make a struggle to defend his rights, his inheritance, and his honor." Greeley's Washington correspondent reported that when the first article appeared, Buchanan gave orders that the offenses should not be repeated and rebuked the Cabinet officer responsible. This may or may not have been true—but they continued. Finally, on December 14, King's disgust found vent in a letter to Attorney-General Black. "Is it not possible," he asked, "to relieve the Administration from the *infamy* which must attach to it for all time, so far as it is made responsible for the course of the *Constitution*, and for keeping men in responsible positions who are known and avowed disunionists? For God's sake, let us see the government placed squarely and unequivocally on the side of the Union!" Not until Christmas Day did Buchanan, "mortified" by an editorial declaring that the country must recognize secession or face civil war, notify W. M. Browne, the editor: "I am deeply sorry that I must in some authentic form declare the *Constitution* is not the organ of the Administration." At the end of January the disloyal sheet ceased publication.

While under this Southern pressure, Buchanan continued work on his state

42 King, *Turning On the Light*, 27 ff, 56, 57. King writes, p. 69 ff., that the conspirators had their headquarters in Washington, that many of them were in the pay of the United States, and that their object was first to embarrass and then break up or get control of the government. He earnestly defends Buchanan's patriotism and fidelity, but laments the influences surrounding him.

43 King, *op. cit.*, 33, 34, 113.

paper, turning to Attorney-General Black as his principal counsellor.[44] This strong-minded jurist, always positive in opinion and forcible in utterance, prepared some paragraphs asserting the indissoluble nature of the Union. "It can meet, repel, and subdue all those who rise against it," he wrote. He gave space to a severe castigation of the political course of both Southern and Northern extremists. When Cobb and Thompson saw these paragraphs, they violently rejected them as inflammatory. Buchanan thereupon told Black that he had gone too far, that his language was provocative, and that he should rewrite his sheets, confining himself to the strictly legal aspects of the situation. The Attorney-General did so. Thus Black's contribution to the President's document was watered down lest it ruffle Southern tempers; and at the same time it was decided, Cobb, Thompson, and Black all agreeing, that this document should take the form not of a proclamation but of part of the annual message to Congress.

When Black's legal paper was finally ready on November 20, its tenor proved sufficiently mild to suit the timid Buchanan. To be sure, it denied the right of secession. It offered a telling series of arguments for the perpetuity of the Union under the Constitution. Thompson had searched the debates of 1787 to find counter evidence, but he was no match for the Pennsylvanian. Apart from this stand on the abstract question, however, Black's contribution had lost all its initial fire; he temporarily turned his back on that advocacy of coercion which, if we accept Floyd's diary, he had twice previously affirmed. We can only guess at the psychological conflict which was raging in the breast of the tough-minded, courageous Scotch-Irishman, torn between prejudice and patriotism. He hated Republicanism and sympathized with the South; but he felt a devoted allegiance to the Union. His irresolution in these November weeks was pitiable. It almost matched the irresolution of the chief whom he loved but was now beginning to regard realistically. Black, however, was a man of iron qualities. The iron was being tempered by his inner fires, and he was soon to emerge as a resolute champion of the national authority and national idea.

His report contended that the national government had every power except *the* power which seemed needed in this crisis. In South Carolina, nearly all Federal officers—judges, marshal, district attorney—had resigned, while the

---

44 For Buchanan's dependence on Black, see Auchampaugh, *James Buchanan and His Cabinet*, 132, with citations. Buchanan remarked that he wished to stand between the quarreling parties in the country as a moderator, "with my hand on the head of each, counselling peace." The papers of W. H. Trescot in the South Caroliniana Library contain an undated "memorandum of views submitted to Cass and the President," which enforce the opinion that Congress alone could decide what policy was to be taken with reference to secession; that the President could only submit the situation to them and await their decision. This view, which played into the hands of the secessionists, Buchanan adopted.

collector seemed likely at any moment to be driven from his custom house. How could the laws be executed in these circumstances? Black concluded that no State, while in the Union, could absolve its people from obedience to the constitutional demands of the national government; that the collector could pursue his legal duties even if driven aboard a vessel in the port; that the President had a right to take such defensive measures as seemed necessary to protect forts, arsenals, navy yards, and other public property; and that he had a right to enforce the decrees of the courts on individuals. But Black also concluded that if antagonism to the United States forced the resignation of all national officers, the government was helpless. The laws in such an event could not be executed. Under these circumstances, the dispatch of military forces into a State with orders to act against the people would be an act of war against them. He advised Buchanan to transfer the decision for or against such acts of war to other hands:

Whether Congress has the constitutional right to make war against one or more States, and require the Executive of the Federal Government to carry it on by means of force to be drawn from the other States, is a question for Congress itself to consider. It must be admitted that no such power is expressly given; nor are there any words in the Constitution which imply it.[45]

This, obviously, was not the view which Jackson had taken in nullification days. Nor is it the view which some of the best constitutional authorities of later times have laid down.[46]

[VI]

The four weeks between the election and the opening of Congress meanwhile found the President desperately worried by the situation in Charleston harbor. Here stood three of the nine coastal forts in the South: Castle Pinckney, with eighteen heavy guns and four howitzers, commanding the city; the incomplete Fort Sumter, with seventy-eight guns on hand, some unmounted; and Fort Moultrie, with fifty-five guns. Some seventy-two thousand muskets were stored in the Charleston arsenal, and a quantity of powder in Castle Pinckney. At Pinckney on November 11 was housed only an ordnance sergeant, and at Sumter only a lieutenant and a few regulars to control the workmen. Moultrie was garrisoned, however, by two small companies of the First Artillery.[47]

Late in October, Winfield Scott, general-in-chief, had sent the President the before-mentioned recommendations which became known as his "views." He

45 Full text in Curtis, *Buchanan*, II, 319–324.
46 Corwin, *National Supremacy*, 242, 243.
47 *Official Records*, Series I, Vol. I, 70–72.

wrote that one or more of the Southern States would probably secede, that danger existed of a seizure of all of the nine forts, and that they should immediately be garrisoned against surprise. While his interpolated political remarks were absurd, for he suggested an ultimate division of the nation into four confederacies, his military opinions were to be treated with respect. Buchanan pondered his proposal. It was evident that spirited action by the government might give hotheaded Southerners a deterring sense of the gravity of their undertaking.

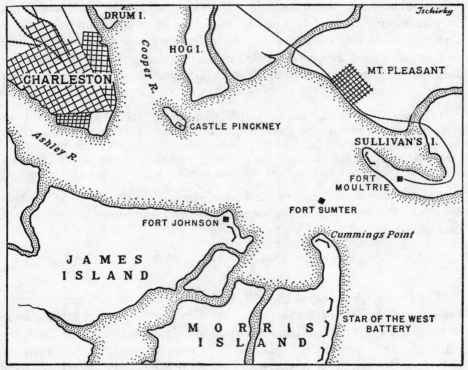

Charleston Harbor and the Forts

It was equally evident that to collect troops and throw them into the forts might exasperate other Southerners, intensify the excitement of the hour, and precipitate the very clash that the nation was anxious to avoid. Moreover, was the government justified in assuming that precautions were needed? With strong Union parties active in most Southern States, it seemed inadvisable to suggest that Washington anticipated their overthrow by men intent upon violent measures. Buchanan wisely put Scott's plan aside. But this left the question of strengthening the Charleston forts still acute.

The Charleston forts! Wearily pacing the library floor, dispiritedly cracking a few jokes at table for Miss Lane, lying awake hour after hour in the bedroom that looked out over the placid, moonlit Potomac, the aged President worried ceaselessly lest the hot South Carolinians make some lawless move against the three posts. The forts were so weak! Only a sergeant in Pinckney, with its guns dominating the city; only sixty-four men (of whom eleven were in arrest or confinement at last report) with a handful of officers, at Moultrie; only a tiny squad keeping order at unfinished Sumter! Daily, the fevered population uttered threats against them all. A storm might break at any moment. Every newspaper was discussing the question of reinforcements. Every time the Cabinet met, the quarrel on the subject broke out afresh—Cass and Black arguing for more troops, the Southern members vigorously protesting, and the President—with Toucey feebly seconding him—in the role of unhappy moderator.[48] It seemed certain that South Carolina would go out on December 20. What would happen to the forts then?

Buchanan's first instinct was to take the side of Cobb, Thompson, and Floyd in a scrupulous avoidance of any provocation whatever to the Carolinians. The day after Lincoln's election, Colonel John L. Gardner, commanding at Charleston, attempted a quiet transfer of ammunition from the city arsenal to Fort Moultrie, but was blocked by a hostile crowd. He was promptly transferred to Texas, and his place given to Major Robert Anderson.[49] This was a happy choice. Since Anderson was of Kentucky birth and Virginia ancestry, had married a Georgia girl, and displayed a friendly attitude toward slavery, he was fitted to play a conciliatory role in a Southern community. Yet he was thoroughly loyal to the Union, for which he had fought in the Black Hawk, Seminole, and Mexican wars. Hurrying to his post, he gave the three forts a close inspection. The result was dramatic. On November 24, again on November 28, and again on December 1, he called urgently for reinforcements.

It is not strange that the harassed President, never of decisive temper, presented a fluctuating front on this question of reinforcement. He had at first taken the Cobb-Floyd position, declining to send more troops. Anderson's first long dispatch, however, arriving November 27, put a new face on the matter. The South Carolinians evinced a settled determination, wrote the major, to leave the Union and seize Moultrie. They regarded Castle Pinckney as already practically in their possession. Nothing could be better calculated

<hr />

48 Black later remarked in Cabinet that there had never been a time in English history when a minister who proposed to give up to an enemy a defensible military post would not have been brought to the block. King, *Turning On the Light*, 123.

49 *Official Records*, Series I, Vol. I, 69–73.

to prevent bloodshed than to put the forts in such a position "that it would be folly and madness to attack us." Anderson asked at least two companies for Sumter and Pinckney at once, and a reinforcement for his own Moultrie garrison, with ordnance stores and ordnance experts.[50] If he were thus strengthened, he believed South Carolina would not attempt to take the forts; if he were not, the secessionists would soon demand their surrender and launch an attack. Cass and Black now insisted more forcibly than ever that Buchanan should send aid to Anderson. Although Cobb, Thompson, and W. H. Trescot, Assistant Secretary of State, labored still to persuade the President that no reinforcements were needed, Buchanan gave way. He directed Floyd to send the required force to Anderson.

But Floyd took refuge in delay. He induced the President to consent to talk with General Scott before making his orders final—and Scott was too ill in New York to come to the capital. While the delay lasted, Cobb, Trescot, and Thompson hurriedly arranged a bargain between the Administration and South Carolina. The President agreed to revoke his decision to send troops to Charleston, while Governor Gist promised that national property there should not be seized. This was a precarious arrangement, subject to sudden disturbance. Floyd felt it necessary to send personal reassurances to South Carolina. A Charleston paper shortly published a letter of December 5 from an unnamed officer of distinction in Washington, quoting a conversation with the Secretary of War. "You may say to the people of South Carolina," Floyd remarked, "there will be no more troops sent to the forts at Charleston. I will resign before it shall be done." [51]

Meanwhile, as Cabinet differences over the two immediate issues, the doctrinal content of the message and the strengthening of the Charleston posts, continued unabated, the Southern group moved to improve their position. Floyd and one other Cabinet member, probably Cobb, invited Senators Jefferson Davis, Mason, and Slidell to hasten to Washington well in advance of the sitting of Congress. Davis, who responded with alacrity, tells us that he was especially wanted for his influence on the message. When he called at the White House, Buchanan informed him that the rough draft was completed but was still open to revision, and he would read it aloud. "He did so, and very kindly accepted all the modifications which I suggested. The message was, however, afterward somewhat changed, and, with great deference to the wisdom and statesmanship of the author, I must say that, in my judgment, the last

---

50 *Idem*, 75 ff.
51 Quoted in N. Y. *Weekly Tribune*, December 22, 1860. For Buchanan's vacillation, see Nichols, *Disruption*, 387. The articles on Black's acts by Col. Frank Burr in the Phila. *Press* of 1881 and 1883 are inaccurate in many points, but illuminating if used guardedly.

alterations were unfortunate—so much so that, when it was read in the Senate, I was reluctantly constrained to criticize it." [52] Davis's recollections may be inaccurate in detail, for his book was not published until 1881, and Buchanan may have accepted his suggestions for consideration, not outright incorporation. But the picture he gives of Presidential uncertainty is correct.

Until the day Congress opened, the wrangling within the Administration went on. Cass still maintained that the forts should be strengthened; he was curtly overruled. Major Anderson was ordered to take no step that would provoke an attack, and to wait patiently, though he must defend the forts to the last extremity if attacked. To emphasize these orders, Major Don Carlos Buell was sent southward to repeat them both orally and in writing. The embittered Cass was contemplating resignation. In discussions of the President's forthcoming message, Black maintained that while the President had no power to take *offensive* action against a State, he had the fullest power of *defensive* action in holding possession of the public property and in clearing away all obstruction to the execution of Federal law. He argued also that if a State seceded, Congress or a convention of States must take "necessary and proper measures" to deal with it. He, too, was overruled.[53]

The message was completed on December 2. The final Cabinet session on it saw Black contending vainly for his views on defensive action and necessary and proper measures. Buchanan refused to accept them. He declared that the Executive had no power to clear away obstructions in a State where no judicial authority existed to issue process, where there was no marshal to serve it, and where, even if a marshal could be found, the entire population would join in resisting him. He also declared that Congress, far from having any latitude to take "necessary and proper" measures against a State, had been expressly denied the power to coerce, and that such power was at variance with the spirit of the Constitution. Thompson, citing evidence that in 1787 the coercive power had been proposed at Philadelphia and rejected, had convinced Buchanan of *this* point. Black accepted his defeat with bad grace, and said that he did not see how he could submit to the President's decision. But he had to submit. The Southern members, reinforced by Davis, were in control on every issue except the abstract right of secession, which Buchanan denied. On the main practical matters—the forts, the rejection of coercion, the retention of the divided Cabinet—they could feel satisfied that they had made the controlling decisions; they could feel that they still dominated the Administration.[54]

52 Davis, *Rise and Fall*, I, 59.
53 Curtis, *Buchanan*, II, 323, 324.
54 Burr, in Phila. *Press*, March 4, 1883.

[VII]

Congress reconvened in an atmosphere of uncertainty, confusion, and frustration. All the members were present except Senators Chesnut and Hammond of South Carolina. The other States of the Lower South were fully represented, for they had much to gain and nothing to lose by keeping their seats in Washington. They could frustrate any Republican designs for taking control of the Senate; they could prevent the adoption of any threatening measures; they could encourage anti-war Democrats in the North; and, most important of all, they could urge members from the Upper South to join the new slaveholding republic. Most of the thirty Representatives and twelve Senators from the Lower South were not interested in restoring the Union, but they were intensely interested in peaceable separation. At the other extreme, the majority of Republicans were concerned with saving the Union only on the basis of their main plank, the containment of slavery. The prospects of any compromise were thus exceedingly slender.

Noon of December 4 brought the anxiously awaited message; and it is safe to say that no American state paper in time of crisis ever produced a more disappointing impression. The South was left dissatisfied and irritated—though some members agreed with Jesse D. Bright that Buchanan was more conservative than they had expected. Feeling in the North ranged from explosive indignation in radical Republican circles to a resigned sense of futility and helplessness among many Douglas Democrats and to partial satisfaction among some future Copperheads.

The essence of the message was that the Federal government held certain authorities and also certain disabilities which, taken together, resulted in complete paralysis. Secession, declared Buchanan, was unconstitutional, but there was no power in Congress or the Executive to compel a State to remain in the Union. It was the duty of the President to enforce the laws, but in the existing situation in South Carolina it was utterly impossible for him to do so. The government was "great and powerful," and its framers had not been "guilty of the absurdity of providing for its own dissolution"; but even if it possessed the right to make war against a State (which it did not), any exercise of that right would be unwise, for the resulting loss of blood and treasure would make a future reconciliation impossible. "The fact is," Buchanan wrote, "that our Union rests upon public opinion, and can never be cemented by the blood of its citizens shed in civil war. If it cannot live in the affections of the people, it must one day perish."

To this statement of national helplessness he prefixed an indictment of the Northern antislavery agitation as primarily responsible for the predicament of the nation. The incessant attack on Southern institutions, he said, had produced such alarm in the South that many a matron retired to bed at night uncertain whether she and her children would see the next dawn. Several of his assertions went far toward justifying and encouraging the secession which he elsewhere denounced as unconstitutional, unnecessary, and futile. Should the apprehension of Southern peril from servile revolt become intensified and pervade the masses, he remarked, "then disunion will become inevitable"—for self-preservation is man's first law. He assailed the personal liberty laws of various States, saying that Southerners had a right to ask their repeal. If this were denied them, the North would have willfully violated the Constitution. "In that event, the injured States, after having first used all peaceful and constitutional means to obtain redress, would be justified in revolutionary resistance to the government of the Union." Such utterances were far more likely to stimulate hesitant secessionists than to restrain them.

To meet the crisis, Buchanan suggested that an explanatory amendment respecting slavery be added to the Constitution. It should recognize the right of property in slaves in States where it already existed, or might thereafter exist; it should guarantee the protection of slave property in all Territories until they were admitted as States; and it should reaffirm the title of masters to the restoration of fugitive slaves, and declare all State laws impairing or defeating this title null and void.

The general Northern verdict on the message was that Buchanan stood by his views on the wrongfulness of secession theoretically, but ran away from them practically. The Philadelphia *North American* found the treatment highly characteristic of the President, in that "with much soundness of argument we have singular inadequacy of results." The Buffalo *Courier*, which had supported Douglas, was shocked by the way in which an excellent vindication of the constitutional authority of the government was coupled with "an ill-timed confession of weakness." The Cincinnati *Enquirer*, another Douglas paper, pronounced it silly to argue against secession without applying the corollary of coercion. "Seldom have we known so strong an argument come to so lame and impotent a conclusion." In general, Republican newspapers condemned the partisanship of the message, which scolded extremists on the Northern side while soothing them on the Southern; its historical errors; and its suggestion that they give up their interdiction of slavery in the Territories. They did not fail to comment scornfully upon the President's renewal of his proposal for buying Cuba, a step which, said the New York *Tribune*, would at once strengthen the slaveholding interest by ten or twelve additional members of Congress and as many Presidential electors—and which, commented the Des Moines *State Register*, would tax the nation several hundred million dollars to buy an island that might secede with the Gulf States before the ink used in drawing the bill of sale had dried on the paper.[55]

Repugnant to most Northerners, the message irritated most Southerners by its condemnation of secession. No sooner had it been read in the Senate than Clingman of North Carolina rose to denounce it, and to declare that its proposed concessions came too late. His State, he said, would not be satisfied with the repeal of all personal liberty laws. He favored immediate secession, spurning further parley with Northern men. A. G. Brown, Wigfall, and Iverson spoke in similar terms. "There will be no war," said Iverson. "In less than twelve months, a Southern Confederacy will be formed; and it will be the most successful government on earth." Even Jefferson Davis and Mason, who spoke in favor of waiting upon further efforts at an adjustment, were sharply critical of the message.

Yet Buchanan, before sending it to Congress, had been so confident that it might arrest the secession movement that he had asked Assistant Secretary Trescot to go at once to South Carolina with a copy for Governor Gist. He had plaintively told Trescot that he thought the South ought to find the message acceptable, for "all he had declared was that with regard to the laws of the United States and the property, he would discharge all the obligations of his official oath." The honest Trescot emphatically informed the President that the message would produce no effect. South Carolina was in headlong movement toward secession, he declared, and he proved it by describing the excitement and exaltation of the people, and by reading a letter from Gist which predicted withdrawal as soon as the convention should meet.[56]

Newspaper men, mingling with Southern members of Congress, found that many of them favored an early convention of the Southern States in order to lay down terms on which the section would remain in the Union; others favored a convention to organize a separate Confederacy whose members might rejoin the Union when proper concessions were made; still others were determined that the new Confederacy should assert and maintain its independence. Southern members of the House and Senate began to hold almost continuous conferences. No informed observer believed that any event could prevent the immediate secession of South Carolina, Mississippi, and Alabama, and few believed that the withdrawal of Georgia and Florida could be halted. Joseph Holt was hearing from his brother in Mississippi that that State would never turn back. He heard from a friend in New Orleans under date of December 14 that the cotton States were determined on secession: "I do not believe that these States would accept Union, if the North was to give every constitutional guarantee."

55 Editorials December 4, 5, 6 in papers named; *State Register*, December 10.
56 "Narrative of William Henry Trescot," *Am. Hist. Rev.*, XIII, 528–556.

[VIII]

Upon Buchanan's message, Lincoln uttered no recorded comment. As events soon showed, however, he differed radically from the President on two issues of paramount importance. Whereas Buchanan was for conceding to the South all its demands respecting the Territories, including a slave-protection code, Lincoln was bound by personal conviction and party pledge to insist that the national domain should be forever barred against the intrusion of slavery. The young new commonwealths of the West must, he had said, be given a clean bed, with no snakes in it. And whereas Buchanan wrote that it was his duty to enforce the laws and protect the national property, but that he could not, Lincoln held that it was *his* duty to do this, that he could, and he would. He had maintained his silence as the crisis developed. To a correspondent of the New York *Evening Post* who interviewed him in Springfield on November 14, he had made it clear that he would say nothing that might be construed as a token of weakness. "I know the justness of my intentions," remarked the President-elect, "and the utter groundlessness of the pretended fears of the men who are filling the country with their clamor. . . . My declarations have been made to the world without reservation. They have been repeated; and now, self-respect demands of me and the party that has elected me, that when threatened I should be silent." But he also made it clear to his interviewer that he was determined to yield no part of his own or his party's principles. He intended to adopt a policy for the whole country, reported the correspondent, and pursue it firmly and even obdurately to the end.[57]

Other evidences of his attitude reached the nation. Lincoln viewed the situation at first with an excessive optimism, believing (as did many other Illinois Republicans, including Lyman Trumbull and the editors of the Chicago *Tribune* and *Illinois State Journal*) that the secession clamor was largely bluff.[58] Nevertheless, the demand of the New York *Herald* and other papers that he redefine his position brought him to make one interesting experiment in reaching public opinion. Illinois Republicans arranged a grand jubilee for November 20. Trumbull was to speak, with Lincoln present. This meant that anything Trumbull said would be regarded as authorized; and to make this fact plain, Lincoln told the press that the speech would reflect his views—the New York *Herald* announcing the "Forthcoming Semi-Official Exposition" of the opinions of the President-elect. Moreover, Lincoln secretly wrote two paragraphs for the Senator to include in his address. The speech was highly moderate in

57 Nevins, *Evening Post*, 269, 270.
58 For an impression of Lincoln's optimism, see Donn Piatt, *Memories of Men Who Saved the Union*, 31–34. The *Illinois State Journal* said, December 12, of the action of the Lower South: "We do not apprehend any serious trouble from these incipient movements." Lincoln's secretary expected no secession; Helen Nicolay, *John G. Nicolay*, 57.

tone. Lincoln's paragraphs implied, with wishful blitheness, that the Union men of every State would themselves overthrow the disunionists. At the same time, the address made no concessions. Trumbull explicitly said that any interference by South Carolina with the collection of Federal revenues would be revolution, and that if any man assailed with force of arms the national authorities, the great mass of Americans would echo Jackson's stern words and deal hardly with these "traitors." [59]

The address, widely published and discussed, did not make the impression for which Lincoln had hoped. He expressed aggrieved disappointment in a letter to Raymond of the *Times*. Did a single newspaper previously in opposition to the Republicans use that speech to quiet public anxiety? "Not one, so far as I know. On the contrary, the Boston *Courier* and its class hold me responsible for that speech, and endeavor to inflame the North with the belief that it foreshadows an abandonment of Republican ground by the incoming administration; while the Washington *Constitution* and its class hold the same speech up to the South as an open declaration of war against them." Referring both to Northern zealots and Southern doctrinaries, he expressed disgust with the "political fiends" who were still possessed by "party malice, and not public good." [60] His resolution to make no public statements became fixed more firmly than ever.

Nevertheless, dispatches from Springfield made it known that he was studying Jackson's utterances in the nullification crisis. And the *Illinois State Journal*, whose editor was regarded as his personal spokesman, and whose columns at least once contained matter which on internal evidence might well be Lincoln's, was sufficiently militant in tone. On November 14, after remarking that the new President's policy would be peace, it added that if nullification raised its head he would have no discretionary power but to execute the laws. "Should it come to the worst, we feel satisfied from what we know of Mr. Lincoln that those who would destroy the law will be dealt with by the strong arm of the law." After Buchanan's message, the *State Journal* spoke still more sternly:

South Carolina . . . cannot get out of this Union until she conquers this government. The revenues must and will be collected at her ports, and any resistance on her part will lead to war. At the close of that war we can tell with certainty whether she is in or out of the Union. While this government endures there can be no disunion. . . . If the overt act on the part of South Carolina takes place on or after the 4th of March, 1861, then the duty of executing the laws will devolve upon Mr. Lincoln. The laws of the United States must be executed—the President has no discretionary power on the subject—his duty is emphatically pronounced in the Constitution. Mr. Lincoln

59 For Trumbull's speech see W. E. Baringer, *A House Dividing*, 32 ff.
60 Lincoln, November 28. 1860; *Works*, I, 656.

will perform that duty. Disunion by armed force is treason, and treason must and will be put down at all hazards. This Union is not, and will not, and cannot be dissolved until this government is overthrown by the traitors who have raised the disunion flag. Can they overthrow it? We think not.[61]

In private conversation with visitors and in reply to certain Southern letters, Lincoln did not hesitate to give assurances of fair treatment to the South. He was anxious that men understand that he would be a conservative President, acting in the interests of the whole country and not of one section. To a Kentucky judge who asked him to place one or more Southerners of non-Republican ties in the Cabinet, he explained that the party could not give up the fruits of victory, but promised to consider the plea. To two callers in mid-November, he spoke of his wish to maintain "a government of fraternity." [62] But on matters of well-understood principle he was adamant.

We can have no doubt as to what Lincoln would have thought of a curious episode which took place in Washington on December 9—the episode of Buchanan's so-called pledge to secession leaders. That day, four members of Congress from South Carolina held a conference with the President. They and one other followed it by sending Buchanan a letter. In this they expressed their conviction that the forts would not be molested until the State convention met, and until an offer had been made by an accredited representative to negotiate for an amicable settlement of all questions between the State and the Federal government; "provided that no reinforcements shall be sent into these forts, and their relative military status shall remain as at present." The President declared that he would never make any agreement not to reinforce the forts. But, he stated, he had no design at the moment to alter their status. Representatives Miles and Keitt later reported to the State convention that Buchanan had promised he would return their letter to them if for any reason he changed his policy. They declared that "the impression made upon the delegation was that the President was wavering, and had not wholly decided as to what course he would pursue." [63]

Thus the President made no pledge not to reinforce the forts. But he did promise (or so the South Carolina members understood) that he would not change their status without notifying the Congressmen.

[IX]

In the last half of December, a swift rush of events carried the nation past old landmarks and beacons, and into a tempestuous sea of uncertainty. On

61 December 20, 1860.
62 Baringer, *A House Dividing*, 52, 53.
63 King, *Turning On the Light*, 162; Buchanan, *Works*, XI, 56, 57; Crawford, *Genesis of the Civil War*, 38, 39.

December 13, Cass made his last effort to compel Buchanan to reinforce the Charleston posts. "These forts must be strengthened," he said. "I demand it." Buchanan replied that he was sorry to differ. "I have made up my mind. The interests of the country do not demand a reinforcement of the forces in Charleston. I cannot do it, and I take the responsibility on myself." Next day Cass resigned. Uncertain health and the pressure of his son-in-law, Henry Ledyard, contributed to this impulsive decision which he immediately tried to revoke—asking Black and Thompson to tell the President that he was willing to withdraw his letter.[64] Buchanan appointed Black to the Secretaryship of State, and named to Black's place a highly able, forceful, and erratic attorney of Pittsburgh, destined to a great and dubious place in American history— Edwin M. Stanton. The retirement of Cass further lowered the President's prestige, radical Northern newspapers interpreting it as the refusal of a patriotic statesman to remain longer in the family of a President who paltered with, if he did not abet, treason. At the same time, it did not really place the Secretary himself in an heroic light. Men of Harz-rock principles like Charles Francis Adams, recalling that Cass had for decades pursued a flabby, time-serving course on the slavery question, believed that he had created a false impression of a highly courageous stand against the Administration so that he could live with greater credit among his freesoil neighbors in Detroit.

At the age of fifty-seven, Stanton had achieved a position of high distinction at the American bar, and a reputation for fiercely positive opinions on public questions. Born in Steubenville, Ohio, the son of a Yankee Quaker of staunch abolitionist convictions, he had learned hatred of slavery at his father's knee and at that of a valued family friend—Benjamin Lundy, whose journal *The Genius of Universal Emancipation* the father assisted with money and labor. While a student at Kenyon College and under the influence of its head, Bishop Philander Chase, the lad had been converted to the Episcopal Church; and a fervent religious faith, almost morbid in some of its tendencies, had strengthened his aversion from human bondage. At Kenyon, too, he had aligned himself with strong feeling on the side of Andrew Jackson in combatting the Nullification movement. Later he had supported the Wilmot Proviso. No stauncher believer in the idea of national union could be found in the land, no sterner antagonist of disunion schemers and plotters—and, we may add, no more excitable, suspicious, and apprehensive prophet of coming dangers. To every task that he undertook Stanton gave a passionate determination, a fierce intensity, a power of instant action, and a terrible industry. He had shown in a long list of famous cases, including the patent action of McCormick vs. Manny, where he so brutally snubbed Lincoln, that he was one of the best

64 McLaughlin, *Cass*, 344.

lawyers of his day. Jeremiah Black believed that his successful work as special counsel for the government in resisting fraudulent land claims in California proved him the best living lawyer. He brought to public office an aggressive (and capricious) temper, tremendous driving force, and remarkable powers of organization. It was a stalwart fighter for the national principle who now entered the cabinet room; a pugnacious "little black terrier," as Montgomery Blair called him.

Both the promotion of Black and the appointment of Stanton constituted a telling gain for the Union cause in Washington. Equally important was the resignation of Cobb on December 8. He believed that secession was imperative. Between the Black Republicans and the people of the South, he wrote in a manifesto dated December 6, there was now no feeling but of bitter and intense hatred. Responding to what he called the paramount demands of his State, he hurried to Columbia and Macon to incite the people to create their own republic. Buchanan made an unfortunate choice in his stead. To deal with the desperate Treasury problems he selected a mediocre Maryland politician of Southern sympathies, Philip F. Thomas, so unfit that he was destined to a very brief tenure.

And on December 20 came the electrifying news of the secession of South Carolina. The convention met in Columbia on the seventeenth, adjourned to Charleston next day to escape a threatened smallpox epidemic, spent the nineteenth in talking about procedure, and at 1:30 on the afternoon of the twentieth unanimously adopted the ordinance of secession. Buchanan had sent Caleb Cushing to expostulate, but he was ignored. That evening, all the delegates having signed the engrossed copy of the ordinance, South Carolina was proclaimed an independent commonwealth.[65] Few farsighted men could have doubted the implications of this act. Ben Wade, on the day the convention met, delivered to the Senate a militant speech in which he proclaimed that the only way for a State to leave the Union was by making and winning a war, and that he would sacrifice everything to keep the flag flying over an intact nation. "Half a million Wide Awakes," tauntingly observed Senator Iverson at a committee meeting, "cannot inaugurate Lincoln." "Well, then," coolly replied a Republican Senator, "we will send a million." South Carolina at once appointed three commissioners (one of them Trescot, who resigned his place in the State Department) to negotiate with Buchanan for the cession of

65 Dumond, *Secession Movement*, 139–142. Bonfires, fireworks, bands, a military parade, and general illumination of the city celebrated the event. The *Mercury* sold six thousand copies of its extra. Crowds cheered the transparencies: "One voice and millions of strong arms to uphold the honor of South Carolina." *Mercury*, December 22, 1860. Commissioners from Alabama and Mississippi, Governor Perry of Florida, and other prominent Southerners were present at the convention.

national property to the commonwealth; and the new governor, Francis W. Pickens, wrote the President demanding that he be allowed to put a small guard of his own in Fort Sumter.

The nation was now in sore extremity. Inside and outside Washington, talk of war was increasing. The Mississippi and Florida elections, on December 20 and 24, resulted in the choice of conventions which would be strongly dominated by secessionists. One State was out, and four or five others certain to follow! Great elements in the border area were asserting that if the national government made war on the Lower South, they would stand by their brothers of the new, slaveholding Confederacy. The division of opinion in the North, some for outright coercion, some for generous concessions with coercion in reserve, and some for peace at any cost, seemed likely to paralyze that section. Justice Grier of the Supreme Court wrote from Washington on December 29 to his friend W. H. Smith in terms of despair. He feared that he was receiving his last salary check from the United States:

Everything is getting *worse and worse* here. Buchanan is *wholly unequal* to the occasion. He is surrounded by enemies of the Union. The Secretary of War wished to recall and censure the commander of Fort Moultrie—but was fortunately overruled by the Cabinet—Black Stanton and Holt the *honest* members of the Cabinet will probably withdraw unless Floyd is dismissed. Poor Toucey is *nobody*. Thompson is honest but a *secessionist*. I should not be astonished if the Cabinet should be wholly dissolved before ten days—and the country without a government.

We dined with the President yesterday. He is getting very *old*—very *faint*—poor fellow he has fallen on evil times. He put his confidence [in] and gave his power to his enemies and not to his friends and now he is enjoying the fruits of his mistakes. He *knows* Floyd to be a traitor and one who has conducted his office in a manner to disgrace the administration and plunder the country, and who is now plotting its destruction yet he hesitates to dismiss him. I should not be astonished from what I have heard privately, if Floyd was arrested and Buchanan impeached before 60 days. Everything is going to ruin unless the people rise in their majesty and rebuke the scoundrels north and south who are working together to divide the Union. This [division] would be certainly followed by civil war—*servile* war and ruin and misery to both parties. We are governed by fools and knaves we have not a *man* for the occasion. I expect to be at home on Thursday the 10th if nothing happens— and perhaps *sooner*—if the hero *Wise* should take the capital with his army.[66]

To what extent had Buchanan's management of the government in the crisis been censurable? A later generation was to condemn him in terms almost as severe as those of his Pennsylvania friend, Grier. In great part, this condemnation was unjust. A clear distinction must be drawn, in reviewing his

66 Copy by courtesy of Carnegie Bookshop, New York.

acts, between his general policy, which was sound, and his mode of implementing it, which was weak, timid, and blundering.

The President was entirely right in determining upon a policy of peace, conciliation, and delay. This was the statesmanlike course, offering the one hope of preserving the Union without carnage, destruction, and hatred. But having chosen this policy, he showed all his characteristic feebleness, hesitation, and timidity in its execution.

At no fewer than four points did he fail to rise to the exigencies of the situation. (1) He should have lost no time after the election—not a day, not an hour—in preparing as eloquent and spirited an appeal to national sentiment, North and South, as he and his aides could pen. He should have rallied the patriotic feeling of the country as Jackson, Clay, and Webster had rallied it in the past. (2) He should have reorganized his Cabinet forthwith to give it unity and decision. It was something worse than a blunder to keep in the government two men, Cobb and Thompson, who were intent on the utter ruin of that government. No strong President would have hesitated to dismiss these marplots and give himself the support of a harmonious and truly Union-loving group of men.[67] (3) With a united Cabinet, he would certainly have reinforced Charleston as soon as Major Anderson set forth the facts demanding a stronger garrison. This would have angered many Southerners. But the government had every right to act; and action would have made it clear that secession meant war—dispelling an illusion which was giving secession sentiment one of its strongest supports. Either the government was going to fight to defend its forts, or it was not. Plainly it was, and the honest course was to show to all that disunion meant a fight. At this, many deluded men would have drawn back. (4) Most important of all, Buchanan should have pressed with instant vigor his plan for a national convention to formulate a scheme of adjustment. His weak decision to transfer responsibility to Congress was a choice of the easy path—but the wrong path. Congress was in the hands of the politicians, and mainly of small politicians at that. Two great groups of Congressmen, the radical secessionists and the radical Republicans, were committed to oppose any practicable scheme of accommodation. A national convention would have given the people an opportunity to choose their best statesmen and set aside small politicians; it would have been freer from party trammels than Congress; and

67 A New York friend of the President's niece, T. Bailey Myers, made bold to write her on December 8 urging a reconstruction of the Cabinet. If I were President, he stated, "I would resort to a change of ministers." He added that the chief difficulty of the country lay in "the want of a rallying point"; that "justly or not there is an utter want of confidence in the Cabinet on all hands"; that "New York will as a unit stand by the Union"; and that the actions of Cobb, Thompson, and Floyd "have shocked the public sense here and there is but one sentiment as to their course." Buchanan-Johnston Papers.

the memory of the great convention of 1787 could not but have given it an overwhelming sense of responsibility.

In the first six weeks after the election, great opportunities had been lost. The main responsibility for the future now lay with Congress. What would it do with its own opportunities?

12

The Administration Reorganized

CONFUSION NOW hath made its masterpiece, Americans might exclaim in Shakespeare's words as the old year gave way to the new. A clamor of discordant voices assailed the ear. Cave Johnson burst forth in a long Union letter to the Nashville *Banner*: Governor Thomas H. Hicks and Henry Winter Davis published appeals to the loyalty of Marylanders; and John Bell, while attacking Northern fanaticism, assured the South that the recent election gave no ground for secession. In New York, Mayor Fernando Wood was penning a sensational message to the aldermen, proposing that the city sever the bonds which placed it under up-State tyranny, declare its freedom, and levy a nominal duty on imports. At Norfolk, General John Tyler, son of the former President, fulminated: "Let the Union go to hell!" In New Orleans, the historian, Charles Gayarré, delivered a hot secession speech; in Missouri, the new governor, Claiborne F. Jackson, declared that all slaveholding States must stand united against oppression. While in Memphis a crowd burned in effigy Andrew Johnson, the Unionist Senator, in Philadelphia special police had to be used to protect Sumner in an intolerant speech. Ten thousand men all over the map, from Joseph Lane to Thurlow Weed, were presenting schemes of compromise.

As additional legislatures gathered, many State capitals became centers of fevered if rather aimless activity. Those of the North took up resolutions demanding strict enforcement of the laws, tendering support or swords to Major Anderson, and offering the government arms and recruits. Lawmakers of the South pealed defiance and authorized new purchases of weapons. In Massachusetts, Governor John A. Andrew ordered all the militia companies immediately filled up with trained and uniformed men. In Alabama, Governor Moore just after New Year's directed the occupation of Forts Morgan and Gaines. Coercionist resolutions were introduced in New England, and anti-coercionist resolutions in Virginia. While rumors of a servile revolt in southwestern Georgia worried Southerners, reports of Democratic disloyalty in New York City troubled Northerners. Everywhere, excited men were begging people to be cool. Everywhere outside of the Lower South, appeals were being made to

Union sentiment. *Harper's Weekly* published spirited pictures recalling the heroism of Nathan Hale and Sergeant Jasper. A hundred newspapers reprinted Longfellow's new poem, "Paul Revere's Ride."

But the drama of the hour was largely concentrated in three widely separated and curiously different cities, where political actors were simultaneously playing out three fateful scenes. One was Charleston, now filled with more excitement, effort, and hope than ever before in her eventful record. Her spires, domes, brightly painted houses, and massive warehouses seemed to rise with new pride over the sea and level, marshy land. The streets resounded with ruffling drum and calling bugle; darkies watched delightedly the drill of lads in gray jackets trimmed with black worsted braid; officers barked commands at working-parties building fortifications. A censor reigned at the telegraph office. The river fronts were carefully guarded, while at the Battery men prepared to obstruct the channels by sunken vessels. Here, looking out over the creaming waves, watchers found their eyes drawn to two points far down the seven-mile bay. One, just short of the throat leading to the open sea, was the square brick block of Fort Sumter rising gloomily from the breast of the waters. To the left of it, barely discernible on a low promontory of the mainland (Sullivan's Island), was Fort Moultrie. Great hopes and fears hung over these posts. Townspeople, startled at dawn by practice firing, thought of them with instant alarm.

Far to the north, under a darker sky and in a grimmer atmosphere, lay Washington, where action or inaction, wisdom or unwisdom, controlled the nation's destinies. An unusually inclement winter had set in. The white marble buildings were cold-looking, the ailanthus trees bare, the waters of the Potomac leaden-colored. As snow and rain smote the town, streets were alternately sheets of dazzling white, and stretches of viscid yellow mud. Social activities were at a low ebb; Northerners in particular, resenting the Southern inclination of the city, kept away from general gatherings. No one knew when some thunderbolt might fall. It was at a Congressional wedding that President Buchanan, hearing a disturbance in the entrance hall and sending to learn the reason, caught Mrs. Roger Pryor's whisper: "South Carolina has seceded. Mr. Keitt has a telegram." The police, fearing disorders—especially after the Richmond *Enquirer* recommended that Washington be occupied by force—were keenly alert. The hotels hummed with politicians and newspapermen; the public buildings blazed with light until after midnight; the committee rooms saw Democratic and Republican Congressmen in endless conferences; the Senate gallery filled up with curious crowds by ten or eleven in the morning. Yet despite this bustle the city lay in an aura of uncertainty and apprehension.

The third city was Springfield, that homely prairie agglomeration of ten thousand people, its checkerboard streets all unpaved, its wooden houses gauntly unattractive, its small business district affording but one decent hotel. The Illinois capital had grown busier and livelier. Flags and bunting were still in evidence. Every train discharged its deputations of advisers, office-hunters, and visitors, an average of perhaps one hundred and fifty a day. Men in frock coats and stovepipe hats hurried up the steps of the State House. Here, for two hours each morning and two each afternoon, the President-elect received all who came, from Senators in fine linen to farmhands in checked shirts. A ready "Come in" at every knock; a hearty handshake; an inquiry for names; a disposal of guests in the half-dozen armchairs that crowded the governor's small office; a running conversation—this was the regular order. As the days passed, Lincoln, burdened by callers, overwhelmed by mail, perplexed by questions of Cabinet and policy, grew more careworn. Yet he continued to impress newspapermen by the quaint originality and sagacity of his talk. "His phrases are not ceremoniously set," wrote Henry Villard, "but pervaded with a humorousness and, at times, with a grotesque joviality, that will always please. I think it would be hard to find one who tells better jokes, enjoys them better, or laughs oftener than Abraham Lincoln." [1]

Never in any public crisis, declared Greeley, had he seen such calmness, steadiness, and firmness as the masses now displayed. Was this true? On the contrary, every newspaper, every diary, every bundle of letters of the time, exhales bewilderment and anxiety. From the three million square miles of the country, from coastal plain, hill, and prairie, from the thirty million people, came an almost audible cry for rescue.

[I]

Inevitably, the secession of South Carolina on December 20 brought the situation in Charleston harbor to a new crisis. The position of Major Anderson seemed dangerous in the extreme. If Fort Moultrie had possessed the complement of some seven hundred men for which it had been designed, it could have been made almost impregnable, but its pitiful garrison of threescore were helpless. On the land side they were commanded by sand hills. If the South Carolinians took over Fort Sumter, a far stronger post, their seaward side would be equally exposed. The popular temper seemed ever more menacing. Governor Pickens wrote Buchanan on December 17 a confidential letter which he sent to Washington by hand, requesting that the President permit him to send a force not exceeding twenty-five men and an officer to take possession

1 Angle, *Here I Have Lived*, 253 ff.; Henry Villard, *Lincoln on the Eve of '61*, 13, 14.

of Sumter immediately.[2] He explained that this would give a feeling of safety to the highly excited community, and added the threat that if something of the kind were not done, he could not answer for the consequences. On the nights of the twentieth and twenty-first, steamers from Charleston kept guard around Sumter; and on the twenty-second, Anderson informed Washington that he felt no doubt the South Carolinians would seize the fort if and when they heard from Washington that it would not be turned over to the State.[3]

But would they hear this? Buchanan had removed Colonel Gardner from Fort Moultrie for trying to add to his ammunition supplies. He had stood out against the efforts of Cass, Black, and Holt to induce him to reinforce the forts. He had accepted the resignation of Cass, the ranking officer of his Cabinet, rather than send such reinforcements. He had just demonstrated anew in the "forty-musket affair" that he would go to great lengths to avoid offending the South Carolina authorities. On December 17, Captain J. G. Foster of Fort Moultrie, needing some muskets and being entitled to forty under an unfilled order of the Ordnance Department dated November 1, had drawn that number from the Federal arsenal in town. The city was instantly thrown into new commotion. The military authorities there, sending word to Foster that the governor had been promised that no arms should be removed from the arsenal, warned him that a violent demonstration was certain unless the muskets were returned. Angry dispatches were sent to Assistant Secretary Trescot. The President was informed that if the muskets did not come back, South Carolina might take them. On December 19, Secretary Floyd telegraphed Foster: "If you have removed any arms, return them instantly." He did so. Would so compliant an Administration deny Pickens his request for control over Fort Sumter?

Happily, it did. Pickens's emissary, carrying the letter to Washington, had Trescot obtain an interview at the White House on the twentieth. The two men were received in the library. Buchanan, after reading the message, promised a reply next day. As the South Carolinians were leaving, he called Trescot back and gave him the letter to read. The experienced diplomatist, whose brilliant talents, fine scholarship, and record of public service entitled him to this mark of confidence, easily detected that Buchanan was offended. Few men had quicker insight than Trescot, who had won the personal regard of Richard Rush, Edward Everett, and other superiors, had talked and walked with Macaulay, Hallam, and other eminent Britons, and, as Acting Secretary during Cass's illness in the past summer, had administered the State Department with skill. He at once saw that the governor's demand was egregious. If Pickens had

2 Full letter in Crawford, *Sumter*, 81–83.
3 *Official Records*, Series I, Vol. I, 105–107.

merely asked the President to instruct Anderson not to occupy Sumter, he might have obtained assurances to that effect. But what President could let the head of a seceding State, claiming separate and independent sovereignty, take over a national fort? Already, Republicans were muttering of impeachment, and such a capitulation would justify it.

Trescot, who knew that Black and Holt would never let Buchanan make such a surrender, went at once to Slidell and Jefferson Davis. They agreed that to press this demand would lead to a rebuff, and would release the President from his supposed pledge to the South Carolina Congressmen. A message flew to Charleston, and at once Pickens authorized Trescot to withdraw his ill-judged letter.[4] That same day Trescot talked with Secretary Floyd, who pledged him that the War Department would take no action which would injure South Carolina, or give any real ground for alarm. But the obliging Floyd spoke without knowledge of what his commander at Fort Moultrie was determining to do!

Major Anderson, meanwhile, was convinced that the South Carolinians were about to seize Fort Sumter.[5] He had abundant reason for so believing. The *Mercury* was insisting that it be taken. Resolutions had been introduced in the legislature for immediate possession of all the forts. While the secession convention sat, a party of Alabamians visited Sumter and gave it a careful inspection. On the twenty-sixth, the younger Rhett, warned from Washington that Anderson might remove to the fort, called on Pickens to urge him to take instant action. The city was full of talk of the imminent capture of both Moultrie and Sumter. Anderson, a man of resolute energy, knew that he had full liberty to transfer his force, for the orders received through Buell authorized him, whenever he had "tangible evidence of a design to proceed to a hostile act," to put his command into whichever post he deemed most defensible. By Christmas Day, when officers and citizens mingled pleasantly at a party given by Captain Foster and his wife, he had made up his mind.[6]

With great address, Anderson effected the transfer to Sumter under cover of darkness on the night of December 26. A small rearguard remained to hew down the flagstaff at Moultrie, spike the guns, and burn the gun-carriages. Charlestonians next morning, seeing the smoke of the fires rise above the deserted post, were deeply incensed. Believing at first that Washington had ordered the movement, and that Moultrie had been totally destroyed, men flew to arms. The people swarming on the piers and Battery, wrote one correspondent, showed chagrin, disappointment, and rage.

4 Crawford, *Sumter*, 83–86, gives Trescot's statement.
5 See his letter to his wife, Nicolay and Hay, *Lincoln*, III, 47, 48.
6 Doubleday, *Forts Sumter and Moultrie*, 47, 48.

Pickens immediately sent Major Anderson a peremptory demand that he return to Moultrie. The commander replied that he had a right to dispose his troops as he thought best, that he had removed to Sumter as the best means of avoiding bloodshed, and that he would stay there. At once the governor called upon ten military units to hold themselves ready for service, put a guard in possession of the national arsenal with its half-million dollars' worth of munitions, raised the palmetto flag over the custom house, postoffice, and branch of the Federal Treasury, and dispatched a small force to take possession of the totally unguarded Castle Pinckney. Late in the day, another force was sent against Moultrie, which the last national troops had just left; and at eight in the evening watchers in Charleston saw three rockets, the signal of occupation, soar aloft.[7]

[II]

News of Anderson's unexpected move produced consternation in Washington. Secretary Floyd, hearing of it early on the twenty-seventh, was taken aback. "It is impossible," he exclaimed. "It would be not only without orders, but in the face of orders."[8] Telegraphing Anderson for an explanation, he received a firm reply: "I abandoned Fort Moultrie because I was certain that if attacked my men must have been sacrificed and the command of the harbor lost." A Southern trio, Jefferson Davis, R. M. T. Hunter, and Trescot, carried the intelligence before noon to the White House. Cass had told a friend a few days earlier that the President was "pale with fear, for his official household is full of traitors, and conspirators control the government." The scene which now took place confirms this statement as to the President's perturbation. Buchanan, we are told by Trescot, was found by the three Southerners in a state of intense nervousness.

"Have you received any intelligence from Charleston in the last three hours?" inquired Davis. "None," responded the President. "Then I have a great calamity to announce to you," the Senator stated. He furnished his news. "And now, Mr. President," he melodramatically concluded, "you are surrounded with blood and dishonor on all sides."

"My God," wailed Buchanan, who stood at the mantelpiece crushing a cigar in his hand, "are misfortunes never to come singly? I call God to witness, *you*, gentlemen, better than anybody, *know* that this is not only without, but against my orders. It is against my policy."[9]

7 Nicolay and Hay, *Lincoln*, III, 61.
8 Crawford, *Sumter*, 143.
9 See Trescot's "Narrative and Letter," edited by Gaillard Hunt, *Am. Hist. Rev.*, April, 1908.

The Southerners urged him to lose no time in restoring the former position in Charleston harbor. If he would promise to do so, they said, the almost certain reprisals of South Carolina might even yet be stayed. But Buchanan agitatedly protested that he could not condemn Anderson until he had the full facts. "I must call a Cabinet meeting," he pleaded. The trio assured him that they did not wish him to condemn Anderson unheard. All they asked was that he promise to restore the old position, if, on inquiry, he found that Anderson had moved without being attacked. Three commissioners, R. W. Barnwell, J. H. Adams, and James L. Orr, had been appointed by the South Carolina convention to negotiate on the forts, and had arranged an interview with the President for that very afternoon. If Buchanan would give his promise, said Trescot, this meeting could take place, and amicable negotiations proceed. The President, however, refused to be rushed into action, and adjourned his talk with the commissioners until next day, the twenty-eighth.

It was fortunate that he insisted upon consulting his Cabinet, for that body now contained three strong men capable of fortifying his determination upon matters of vital principle: Black, Holt, and Stanton. The first fruits of the reorganization of the Cabinet were now to be garnered, and Buchanan's policy entered upon its second phase; that in which Southern influences ebbed and Northern potencies took their place.

The turning-point in Administration policy was reached in a swift series of unprecedentedly important Cabinet meetings. Trescot, Davis, and Hunter had hardly ceased their effort to drive the President into a humiliating submission when the Cabinet began to assemble. As Floyd came into the White House, he saw Major Buell there. He rapped out that Anderson had made a most unfortunate move. "It has made war inevitable!" he exclaimed. Buell defended his fellow-officer, but without avail. "It has compromised the President," added Floyd. When the Cabinet began its discussion, Floyd denounced Anderson in the same strident terms. The major had disobeyed instructions, he said, had taken a wholly unnecessary step in violation of a clear agreement between the President and South Carolina, and had brought the country to the verge of war. Black warmly interposed. Denying that Anderson had breached his orders, he called attention to the instructions of December 11 sent down by Buell. A messenger was hurried to the War Department for this paper, which was read aloud to the Cabinet, and was found to bear Floyd's endorsement. Either the President had never been shown it, or had completely forgotten it.[10]

At once Floyd shifted his ground; he could not deny his orders, but he

10 Buchanan, *Administration on the Eve of the Rebellion*, 187 ff.; Crawford, *Sumter*, 146; Nichols, *Disruption*, 428, 429; Nicolay and Hay, *Lincoln*, III, 66, 67.

did deny that Anderson had possessed "tangible evidence of a design to proceed to a hostile act." Stanton and Holt came to Black's assistance in defending Anderson, while Thomas (whose sympathies were with the South and whose son was soon to enter the Confederate armies) and Jacob Thompson assailed the officer. Black and Stanton asserted that it was impossible that the President had given any pledge to South Carolina, and demanded a specification of the time and place; both Floyd and Thompson insisted—in Buchanan's presence—that it *had* been given. The quarrel grew violent; tempers rose and words became hot. For purposes of his own, soon to appear, Floyd presented an extreme ultimatum.[11] He sat down and wrote out a demand that he be permitted to order the garrison withdrawn entirely from Charleston harbor. At this point, the feeling of Black and Stanton appears to have broken all bounds. Black threw in Floyd's face the statement that no English minister who supinely surrendered a fortified place to an enemy would have failed to reach the block. Stanton went further; he said that to accede to Floyd's demands would be a crime like Arnold's, that all the participants ought to be hanged like André, and that a President issuing such an order would be guilty of treason. At this Buchanan raised his hands in deprecation: "Oh, no! Not so bad as that, my friend—not so bad as that!" [12]

Excitement over the situation had filled the opposite end of Pennsylvania Avenue. When the Cabinet broke up without a decision, a determined body of Southern Senators—Yulee, Slidell, Mallory, Toombs, and others—gathered at the White House. They besought the President to revoke Anderson's movement. An equally determined band of Administration Democrats from the North also gained admittance and urged Buchanan to take no backward step. That weary, vacillating, alarmed potentate, the center of a paralyzing storm, was unable to make up his mind.

Night came on. After dinner the Cabinet met again. Newspapermen were eagerly awaiting word of the result. Until a late hour the debate continued. Midnight dispatches carried word to the country that by a vote of four to three, the members had decided against ordering Anderson back; that Toucey, under heavy Northern pressure, had joined Black, Stanton, and Holt.[13] Even yet, however, Buchanan had not definitely fixed his policy. "In this state of suspense," he tells us, "the President determined to await official information from Major Anderson himself. After its receipt, should he be convinced upon full examination that the Major, on a false alarm, had violated his instructions,

11   Text in Moore's *Rebellion Record*, I, 10.
12   Gorham, *Stanton*, I, 151 ff.
13   The N. Y. *Tribune*, December 31, carried a dispatch dated December 30 giving the four-to-three vote; other papers had the same news.

he might then think seriously of restoring for the present the former status quo of the forts." [14]

Next day, the three commissioners from South Carolina duly called to press a demand that all national forces be ordered out of Charleston waters. Barnwell, a Harvard graduate who had been Representative, Senator, and president of the South Carolina College, was chairman; Adams, a Yale graduate, was the former governor, and Orr the former Speaker. They were men of parts, and Barnwell could have figured much more lustrously in history but for his modesty.[15] Only Adams, an oldtime nullifier and a recent proponent of the African slave trade, was highly radical. They had a natural sense of their dignity in representing a new republic, and came not to sue for terms but to treat as equals. Buchanan had just heard of the seizures of Fort Moultrie, the Charleston arsenal, and the postoffice and customhouse. Nevertheless, he received the men courteously, not as diplomatic agents but as private gentlemen. To negotiate, they must appeal to Congress alone, he told them, and he could but communicate to Congress their proposals.

The discussion lasted two hours. Again and again, the three men told Buchanan that his pledge was dishonored, that he must withdraw the troops completely, and that if he refused a bloody issue was probable. When he resisted, they redoubled their efforts. Finally the President agonized aloud.

"Mr. Barnwell, you are pressing me too importunely," he expostulated. "You don't give me time to consider. You don't give me time to say my prayers. I always say my prayers when required to act upon any great state affair." [16]

The demands of the commissioners, reduced to writing, came before another tense Cabinet meeting that evening, Friday, the twenty-eighth. Southern Senators had maintained their pressure on the President, Toombs writing him that day that the evacuation of Sumter was imperative to prevent drastic and perhaps irrevocable action by some Southern States. Once more the atmosphere quickly became electric. Thompson argued pertinaciously in favor of a total evacuation of troops from South Carolina. Floyd lay on a sofa between the windows of the Cabinet room. At last, driven from various positions, Thompson took refuge in a tricky plea to national magnanimity. Carolina, he argued, was a tiny State with a sparse white population; the United States was a powerful nation with a vigorous government. The country could afford to say to South Carolina: "See, we will withdraw our garrison as an evidence that we mean you no harm."

14 Buchanan, *Administration on the Eve of the Rebellion*, 181. Cf. Davis, *Rise and Fall*, I, 215.
15 Jefferson Davis wished to make him Confederate Secretary of State; see letters of T. R. R. Cobb, *Papers So. Hist. Soc.*, XXVIII, and *Proceedings So. Hist. Assn.*, XI.
16 Letter of J. L. Orr, September 21, 1871; Crawford, *Sumter*, 148, 149.

At this Stanton's blood boiled. He knew that a storm of anger would sweep the North if Buchanan took such a step. "In every hotel and every street in this city," the Washington correspondent of the New York *Herald* had written, "we hear hardly anything but denunciation of the President for his course in refusing to strengthen Major Anderson." The sober, cautious *National Intelligencer* had just published an editorial of unparalleled severity. It had declared its belief that no loyal citizen could look with complacency on the Administration's easy tolerance of members and subordinates who were "avowedly and ostentatiously laboring for the destruction of the government." It had castigated Buchanan for not displaying in the restraint of traitors one-tenth the zeal he had shown in immolating luckless Democrats who had been so unfortunate as to believe in popular sovereignty. It had declared that if the President had no solid facts to support his refusal to reinforce the forts, the country would hold him to "a fearful responsibility" for the policy he had pursued.[17]

"Mr. President," Stanton exploded, "the proposal to be generous implies that the government is strong, and that we, as the public servants, have the confidence of the people. I think that is a mistake. No Administration has ever suffered the loss of public confidence and support as this has done. Only the other day it was announced that a million of dollars had been stolen from Mr. Thompson's department. The bonds were found to have been taken from the vault where they should have been kept, and the notes of Mr. Floyd were substituted for them. Now it is proposed to give up Sumter. All I have to say is that no Administration, much less this one, can afford to lose a million of money and a fort in the same week." [18]

To this burning arraignment Floyd dared make no reply, for his negligence, blundering, and general misfeasance, which at least bordered on malfeasance, had finally found him out. Year after year, he had permitted laxity and scandal in his department. The Fort Snelling and Willet's Point exposures were yet fresh in the public mind, Greeley's *Tribune* insisting that these affairs had cost the country $550,000.[19] The fact that Floyd himself had never been shown guilty of taking an unclean dollar did not clear him from the charge that he had assisted certain favorites to make many. Now he was floundering in a veritable Oke-fenokee Swamp of embarrassments. A dark and terrible story was just becoming public.

17 See N. Y. *Weekly Tribune*, December 29, 1860, for summaries of press criticism of the Administration.
18 Nicolay obtained this statement from Stanton; Nicolay and Hay, *Lincoln*, III, 74, 75. Cf. Stanton's full account of the crisis written October 8, 1863, in Gorham, *Stanton*, I, 151-159.
19 See editorial, "The National 'Cracksmen,'" N. Y. *Tribune*, December 27, 1860.

During and after the Mormon War, the Western contractors, Russell, Majors & Waddell, had furnished large quantities of supplies and transportation to troops. Congress had been tardy in passing some of the appropriations to meet government contracts. To aid the firm, whose credit was impaired by rashly ambitious operations and faulty management, Floyd had accepted a large amount of their drafts, some of them conditionally, others absolutely. Banks then advanced funds on this endorsed paper. In fact, Floyd *asked* banks to do so. In 1859, the President instructed the War Department to desist from such financial practises, but the Secretary continued. The most careful students of the papers of Russell, Majors & Waddell have concluded that while no direct, conclusive evidence exists that Floyd received money from Russell, "there is much to arouse suspicion that he did." The amount of the Secretary's acceptances ultimately reached a dizzy figure. Although the figure later given by a select House investigating committee, $6,179,395 of unconditional acceptances, and $798,000 of acceptances conditioned and payable out of the earnings of the firm, has been pronounced exaggerated, the sum was at any rate enormous. By July, 1860, William H. Russell knew that large amounts of these drafts, endorsed by Floyd, were about to mature. Since the banks refused to make him any further advances and insisted that he pay his endorsed notes, he was in terrible distress. If the paper went to protest, he would be ruined and Secretary Floyd disgraced.

In desperation, Russell turned to Goddard Bailey, an attorney, a South Carolinian, and a distant kinsman of Floyd's, now a clerk in the Land Office. Explaining that a protest of the acceptances would place Floyd in a terrible predicament, he induced Bailey to lend him $150,000 in Missouri and Tennessee State bonds. It appears that not until later did Russell learn that they belonged to the Indian Trust Fund of the Interior Department, of which Bailey was custodian. After he gained this information, however, the desperate contractor guiltily connived with Bailey in the embezzlement of further bonds, raising the grand total abstracted to $870,000. It was the old story; he hoped to make quick restitution, but his affairs grew worse and he could repay nothing.

In the closing weeks of 1860, when interest on the bonds had to be sent to the Indian tribes, the whole set of transactions was dragged to light. Bailey, on December 22, confessed to his friend Senator Rice and his superior Secretary Thompson. Black, Stanton, and the President were informed. On December 23, a Cabinet meeting subjected Bailey to a painful inquisition, and on the twenty-fourth the public was startled by an explicit announcement of the loss. Russell that day was arrested in New York, to be carried to Washington and jailed. Everyone was horrified—not least Secretary Thompson, who acted promptly and diligently to learn the truth. Just how much or little Floyd had known about Bailey's embezzlement of the bonds is not clear, though evidence exists that he had known something. When the House committee delved into the affair, a cheap adventurer named Robert W. Latham, who had worked for Floyd until 1859 and had been intimate with Russell, was examined. Many suspected him of having been a go-between who helped the Secretary to profit from the large Russell, Majors contracts. He proved a most refractory witness, and his constant refusals to answer questions bearing on such a connection did nothing to diminish public suspicion of Floyd. Instead, they left the impression that a secret arrangement of some kind had existed.[20]

It was immediately plain that Floyd would have to be dismissed. No Administration could let such a man continue to disgrace it. The House committee shortly termed the acceptances unauthorized by law, deceptive, and fraudulent. Any other President would have summoned the Secretary to a private interview, given him a bad half hour, and directed him to write his resignation. Not so Buchanan; heartsick to lose two old friends (for Mrs. Floyd had been much at the White House), he disregarded a strong Christmas Day letter from Black urging him to take peremptory action next morning,[21] and requested Vice-President Breckinridge to obtain the resignation. But Floyd refused to resign, declaring he must vindicate himself first. He wanted more time for several reasons; to continue resisting the Northern wing in the Cabinet, to make sure of some Southern berth, and to manufacture out of the South Carolina imbroglio a plausible excuse for his exit. Hence his written demand that the President allow him to evacuate all troops from the Charleston area. Black and Stanton were outraged by his conduct, and unhappy over the President's willingness to palter with the man.

It need not be said that much Northern sentiment, already inflamed by the President's message, the failure to reinforce the forts, and Cass's resignation, was raised to boiling point by the exposure of Floyd. "Why in the devil don't you present articles of impeachment against Buchanan and Floyd?" burst out Greeley in a letter of December 30 to Elihu Washburne. "People here are becoming frantic—absolutely frantic with rage at the treason. If Old Buck would show his countenance in these parts he would be hung so quick that Satan would not know where to look for his traitorous soul." Although this was outrageously unjust to the harried, overwrought President, it is understandable.

20 Full evidence on this affair is in 36th Cong., 2d Sess., House Doc. 78. Russell, whose indictment was quashed on a technicality in January, 1861, published a long explanatory statement in the press April 4, 1861. Facts in the case are carefully analyzed by Mary Lund Settle and Raymond Settle, *Empire on Wheels*, 95-131.
21 The matter should be settled "definitely, finally, and forever," wrote Black; Buchanan Papers.

[III]

But at any rate Floyd's dishonor produced one signal benefit in giving Union men full control of the Union's Cabinet. On Saturday the twenty-ninth the Secretary went out. He grounded his resignation on the statement that he could not countenance the President's violation of solemn pledges respecting Sumter, an excuse which failed to cloak his incompetence and perfidy. The comments of the Northern press were scorching. After giving brief testimony before the House committee on his acceptances, Floyd returned to Virginia, was banqueted, and made gasconading speeches. On January 25, 1861, he was indicted by a grand jury of the District of Columbia for malversation in office. Denouncing the action as a gross violation of principles of law and justice, and protesting his innocence, he visited Washington, gave bail, and called for a trial. A week after Lincoln took office, the Federal Attorney asked that the case be dropped for lack of evidence.

This was not the only complaint of the North against Floyd. Five days before Christmas he had given oral orders, later confirmed in writing, for the shipment of forty-six cannon from Pittsburgh to Ship Island, Mississippi, and seventy-nine cannon to Galveston, Texas. Angry municipal leaders had instantly organized to block the transfer, and by vigorous appeals had spurred the President to issue a Christmas Day order countermanding Floyd. Throughout half the North, a conviction now reigned that he was a dangerous traitor. He always maintained that his distribution of arms had been fair and legal. "My course," he wrote Wigfall, "was a proper one dictated by the true interests of the country, and I . . . am ready any moment to die for it if that be necessary." Subsequent official investigation indicated that his transfer in the spring of 1860 of one hundred five thousand muskets and ten thousand rifles from Northern to Southern arsenals was a correct transaction, designed to make room for more modern weapons in the North. Actually the Southern States did not ask for or receive their due quota of arms in 1860. It was only after Lincoln's election that Floyd's course with respect to arms shipments became—particularly in the order for the Pittsburgh cannon—censurable. He was a dangerous man—but rather from ineptitude than anything worse.[22]

22 Floyd's letter to Wigfall, February 3, 1861 (Wigfall Papers, LC), is written with fierce intensity. After assailing "the mean and sneaking malignity of some of those about the executive," he declares that Bailey, Russell, and Luke Lea know all about the bond affair and must exonerate him. "These men are all bound to swear in the most unequivalent [sic] manner that I did not and could not know anything whatever about the transactions." He added: "There has not during the time of my administration of the War Dept. been lost to the Govt. *one dollar*, either from accident or fraud, or embezzlement or theft, every dollar appropriated has been accounted for according to law. . . ." Jeremiah Black finally

The still unsettled question of Buchanan's reply to the South Carolina commissioners now provoked a final Cabinet crisis. On Saturday night the body met again. The President showed his six remaining ministers a draft answer. This paper has disappeared from his records. That it conceded much more than was proper is evident from the debate which it provoked. The flaccid Toucey approved it. Thompson and Thomas opposed it only because it did not yield South Carolina an instant removal of all bayonets. Black, Stanton, and Holt, however, condemned it as excessively complaisant, and Black and Stanton at least were wrought up to a high pitch of indignation.

"These gentlemen," exclaimed Stanton, "claim to be ambassadors. It is preposterous! They cannot be ambassadors; they are lawbreakers, traitors. They should be arrested. You cannot negotiate with them; and yet it seems by this paper that you have been led into doing that very thing. With all respect to you, Mr. President, I must say that the Attorney-General, under his oath of office, dares not be cognizant of the pending proceedings. Your reply to these so-called ambassadors must not be transmitted as the reply of the President. It is wholly unlawful and improper; its language is unguarded and to send it as an official document will bring the President to the verge of usurpation." [23] Once more, the heat of the exchanges produced much plain speaking. When the President reserved the subject for further consideration, Black went home to spend a sleepless night. He knew to what a degree the President was still under the influence of Davis, Mason, and other Southern leaders. He was told by both Stanton and Ben Butler, two men as clearheaded as they were aggressive, that any President who negotiated with Southern conspirators upon the segregation of government property and the alienation of American territory would be open to impeachment. He held this view himself. Before dawn on the thirtieth he had reached a determination.

That dawn was Sunday; the church bells were soon calling Washington to worship; but the Secretary of State had urgent business to dispatch. He informed Stanton, Holt, and Toucey that if the President sent the commissioners such a letter as that laid before the Cabinet, he would resign. Stanton declared he would follow. The agitated Toucey hurried to the White House with the news. Such resignations, coming after that of Cass, would utterly prostrate the Administra-

concluded that Floyd had been guilty only of reckless imprudence; *Essays and Speeches*, 13. But the House investigating committee unanimously termed his issue of acceptances "unauthorized by law and deceptive and fraudulent in character"; while the Supreme Court in 1868 held such issues illegal (7 *Wallace*, 666). Floyd's disposition of arms was treated, without explicit judgment, by the House Military Committee in a report of February 18, 1861; 36th Cong., 2d Sess., House Report 85.

23 Flower, *Stanton*, 88. This quotation has the ring of truth even if not literally accurate.

tion. Immediately, Buchanan sent for Black and bade him explain his views. We do not know the spirit in which they spoke to each other, but it seems probable that Black, always tempestuous, had betrayed such anger and chagrin the previous evening that an indirect approach to the President by Toucey was necessary. It is certain that he now freed his mind. He declared that the letter must be rewritten; he called for stamina, defiance, and the immediate reinforcement of Anderson.

In this stand, Black was buttressing an emphatic plea by General Scott, who had hurried a messenger to the White House door that morning with an urgent request that Buchanan listen to his views. "Will the President permit General Scott," he inquired, "without reference to the War Department and otherwise as secretly as possible, to send two hundred and fifty recruits from New York harbor to reinforce Fort Sumter, together with some extra muskets or rifles, ammunition, and subsistence stores? It is hoped that a sloop of war and cutter may be ordered for the same purpose as early as tomorrow." [24] Black was seconding also the expressions of a great part of the Northern press, now filled with indictments of the Administration as feeble and cowardly. From Maine to Iowa, tenterhook anxiety was felt for the safety of Anderson's tiny force.

Buchanan's weak stubbornness was not long in conflict with Black's inflexible resolution. The President handed the Secretary his draft letter for revision, saying, according to Black's son, that he might strike out what he thought objectionable and insert what he deemed necessary, if he only did it immediately.[25] The event proved that he really gave something like this blanket authorization. Black at once repaired to Stanton's office, talked over every point with him, and discussed the means of extricating the Chief Executive from his perilous situation. The pair then drafted a memorandum, of which Stanton seems to have written six paragraphs and Black two. Seldom if ever have the advisers of a President administered, even by implication, so severe a rebuke.

At no fewer than seven points did Black and Stanton traverse Buchanan's letter. They objected to his implied acknowledgment of the right of South Carolina to send diplomatic officers to treat with the United States. They objected to his expression of regret that the commissioners were unwilling to go on with the negotiation; there could be no negotiation, willing or unwilling. They objected above all to his intimated readiness to make some arrangement regarding the national forts; they were not subject to any arrangement whatever. They objected to his statement of belief that the government had no right

24 *Official Records*, Series I, Vol. I, 114.
25 Black, *Essays and Speeches*, 14.

to coerce a State to stay in the Union; the government certainly had a right to coerce those who attacked national property. They objected to his implied assent to the commissioner's statement that he had made an agreement on the forts; instead, he should make a flat denial of any bargain, pledge, or agreement. They objected to phrases casting doubt upon the propriety of Major Anderson's behavior. They objected to Buchanan's tolerance of the idea that the removal from Moultrie to Sumter did possible wrong to South Carolina. If these radical amendments were adopted, wrote Black and Stanton, the whole paper would have to be recast.[26]

The two heads concluded with some positive words upon the need for forceful action at Charleston. The warships *Brooklyn* and *Macedonian* should be ordered thither without delay. A messenger should be hurried to Anderson with word that the government would not desert him. Troops from New York or Old Point Comfort should immediately follow. "If this be done at once all may yet . . . be comparatively safe. If not, I can see nothing before us but disaster and ruin to the country." And the memorandum contained a stinging sentence upon "the fatal error which the Administration have committed in not sending down troops enough to hold *all* the [Charleston] forts."

Thus was finis written to appeasement. With Cobb and Floyd gone, with Thompson helpless, and with Black, Stanton, and Holt enforcing their views on the irresolute President by their readiness to resign if he retreated, the revolution in the executive branch was completed. As for ten years past, the United States had no President in the full sense of the word. A directory stood in the place of a single clear-sighted, strong-willed Chief Magistrate. But that directory was now made up of granite-constant Union men, aware of what the crisis demanded. Henceforth, Buchanan largely adopted the ideas of his stern-fronted fellow Pennsylvanians, Black and Stanton.

This was manifest in his courteous but firm reply to the commissioners, delivered December 30, essentially following Black's suggestions. He restated his desire to have Congress deal with the situation in such fashion as to avoid war over the Charleston forts. He explained away his alleged pledge to preserve the status of the forts. When he had learned of Anderson's transfer, he stated, his impulse had been to order him back to Moultrie; but the South Carolinians had immediately seized Moultrie, Pinckney, and other national property, radically altering the state of affairs. Now he was asked, under penalty of a possible attack on Sumter, to remove all the country's forces from the harbor. "This I cannot do; this I will not do," he wrote, in language at last befitting a successor of

---

26 Text of the memorandum in Black, *Essays and Speeches*, 14–17; for the relative parts played by Black and Stanton in drafting the "Written Objections," see Flower, *Stanton*, 90–93. As Buchanan's legal adviser, Stanton was nominal author.

Washington and Jackson. Major Anderson would be left where he was; his act would not be disowned; and Sumter would be defended "against hostile attacks from whatever quarter they may come." [27]

The remodeled executive department quickly showed its spirit in other ways. When the commissioners sent an insolent response to the President's letter, accusing him of breaking his pledge and choosing the path to war, it was returned with a brief endorsement that he refused to receive it. Jefferson Davis printed the response in the *Congressional Globe* with a cutting attack of his own on Buchanan, which several fellow-Senators echoed.[28] The moment he saw the commissioners' insulting note, Buchanan's hesitations over the strengthening of Anderson vanished. He exclaimed: "It is all now over and reinforcements must be sent." On December 31, he instructed the War and Navy Departments to take steps, under which orders were issued that day to send the sloop-of-war *Brooklyn* to Charleston with troops, ammunition, and stores.[29]

[IV]

The New Year's Day reception at the White House found Southern and Northern guests displaying a glacial hostility to each other, some secessionists, wearing blue cockades, ostentatiously passing the President without greeting him, and the general atmosphere as gloomy as a funeral. Slidell was not there. His sharp protest against the cancellation of Beauregard's appointment to West Point ("this crack of the overseer's whip over our heads," Holt termed it in speaking to Buchanan) would soon receive a tart rejoinder. Jefferson Davis wrote an editorial friend that Southerners no longer had any confidence in or respect for the President. "His weakness has done as much as wickedness could achieve." [30] No longer could the President have heart for his daily walk. His aspect of sad anxiety and illness inspired the compassion of many a beholder.

Reinforcements, as it turned out, were not to reach Charleston. When it was learned that the South Carolinians had sunk vessels to block the channel, General Scott decided to substitute for the *Brooklyn* the light-draught steamer *Star of the West*. Aboard her went two hundred well-trained recruits from Fort Columbus in New York. On January 5 she quietly sailed. Telegrams apprising Charleston of the fact were hastily sent by Senator Wigfall and Secretary

27 Too late, the South Carolina commissioners realized that they had overplayed their hand. On Sunday they backed water lustily; sending Trescot and Hunter to the White House, they suggested as a compromise that South Carolina should evacuate Moultrie, that Anderson be ordered back to that post, and that the Carolinians then promise to respect the *status quo* so long as Buchanan was President. Nichols, *Disruption*, 432.

28 January 9; *Cong. Globe*, 36th Cong., 2d Sess., 288 ff.

29 *Official Records*, Series I, Vol. I, 130 ff.; Curtis, *Buchanan*, II, 445, 446.

30 To E. D. De Leon, January 8, 1861; De Leon Papers, So. Caroliniana Library.

Thompson. The Carolinians had continued active in erecting batteries and preparing for a conflict. When the ship arrived off the port on January 9, Fort Moultrie and Morris Island fired upon her and drove her away. Happily, Major Anderson was for the moment in a fairly safe position. Washington had received from him a dispatch of December 31, which, after justifying his recent movement, concluded:

Thank God, we are now where the Government may send us additional troops at its leisure. To be sure, the uncivil and uncourteous action of the governor in preventing us from purchasing anything in the city will annoy and inconvenience us somewhat; still, we are safe. I find . . . only a small supply of soap and candles, and also of coal. Still, we can cheerfully put up with the inconvenience of doing without them, for the satisfaction we feel in the knowledge that we can command this harbor as long as our Government wishes to keep it.[31]

A new page had been turned. The third phase in Buchanan's policy, the phase in which he asserted the right to maintain possession of the forts and other property of the government even if this meant open war, and in which he turned a severe face upon secessionists, had been entered upon; and it was to continue until Lincoln came into power with a policy essentially identical.

And the Administration was now immeasurably strengthened when the two remaining Cabinet sympathizers with the South, seeing the utter impossibility of their position, resigned, and were succeeded by loyal men.

As the *Star of the West* was approaching Charleston, on January 8, Secretary Jacob Thompson indignantly left the Cabinet. He declared that it had been distinctly understood that no further troops should be ordered south without prior Cabinet consultation, yet he had first learned of the projected reinforcement of Sumter from outside sources. On the eleventh, Secretary Thomas, after just a month in the Treasury Department, also made his exit, announcing that he could not approve of the policy adopted toward South Carolina, and probably could not support the President in an attempted enforcement of the collection of duties there. He had been a hopeless misfit, for eastern financial circles had no confidence in him. The President made no sustained effort to find a new Secretary of the Interior, but allowed Chief Clerk Moses Kelly, an excellent executive, to fill out the term as Acting-Secretary. In Thomas's place, however, he made one of the happiest of all his appointments—John A. Dix. This former member of the Albany Regency and Senator from New York, more recently a railway president and an attorney in the metropolis, was an admirable selection from every point of view. A man of great ability, courage, and grasp, Dix for

31 *Official Records*, Series I, Vol. I, 120. When this dispatch to Adjutant-General S. Cooper was shown to the President, he attempted to countermand the *Star of the West* expedition, but it was too late.

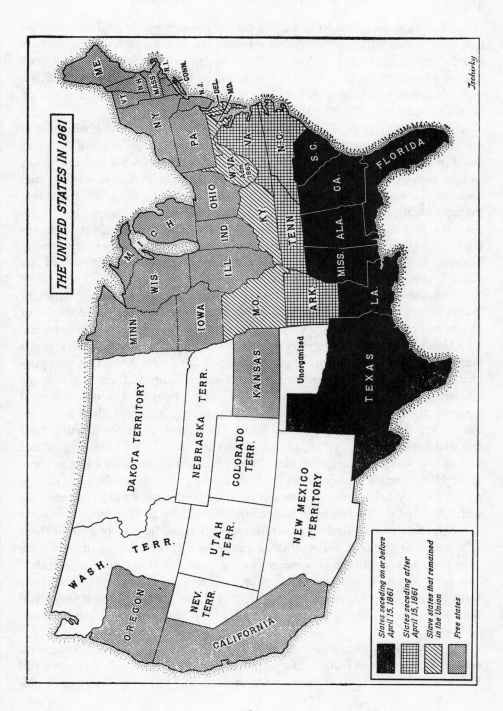

THE UNITED STATES IN 1861

Tschirky

Legend:
- States seceding on or before April 15, 1861
- States seceding after April 15, 1861
- Slave states that remained in the Union
- Free states

the past eight years had been denied his proper place in public affairs because he had been a Barnburner or antislavery Democrat, a supporter of the Wilmot Proviso, and in 1848 the Free Soil candidate for governor. He held the full confidence of eastern financial circles. Above all, he was a staunch believer in the maintenance of the Union, and was ready to put all his courage and power of decisive action behind his faith.

At Buchanan's request, Dix took up quarters in the White House, where from ten to eleven nearly every night for the next seven weeks he discussed the great issues of the time with the President. He found Buchanan timid and credulous, an easy prey for artful men. It was obvious also that the President was obsessed with the idea that the North, in the war now about to begin, must avoid shedding the first blood; an idea which had made him yield when he should have been firm. But he had now awakened to the true character of some of his old coadjutors, and as conscientiousness was a cardinal trait, he was anxious to show more firmness. Beyond doubt Dix did his full share in strengthening the will of the Chief Executive.

Thus the year 1860 closed and 1861 opened with an inspiriting series of events which restored the courage of all loyal Northerners. After weeks of gloom and almost of despair came a radiant sunrise of faith in the government. The Unionist press grew warm in praise of Secretary Holt as a Democrat and a Kentuckian who had thrown his great prestige behind firm Administration policies. News that he was in close touch with General Scott and was restoring the efficiency of the War Department, almost ruined by Floyd, aroused general enthusiasm. Men told anecdotes illustrating the determination of Black and Stanton. When Buchanan's reply to the South Carolina demand for a withdrawal from Charleston harbor appeared, his defiant words—"This I cannot do; this I will not do"—lifted the popular heart like a pealing trumpet. The letter of Governor Hicks declining to convoke the Maryland legislature had the same clarion note. "I firmly believe that a disunion of this government would produce civil war," declared the governor; he asserted that practically all Marylanders thought that no valid reason existed for immediate secession; and he was scornful of those who held that, "against our judgments and solemn convictions of duty, we are to be precipitated into this revolution because South Carolina thinks differently." The press was quoting Buchanan's reputed dismissal of Southern threats to use force in preventing Lincoln's inauguration. "If I live till the 4th of March," said Buchanan, "I will ride to the Capitol with Old Abe whether I am assassinated or not."

As newspaper dispatches came from Charleston and Major Anderson's brother Larz returned from a visit, people learned of the dramatic scene that had followed the occupation of Sumter. On the morning of December 27, two officers dispatched by Governor Pickens had waited upon Major Anderson. The commander explained that while his sympathies lay with the South, he was determined to adhere firmly to his duty to the national government. "Well, sir," said Colonel Johnson Pettigrew of the First South Carolina Rifles, "however that may be, the governor directs me to say to you, courteously but peremptorily, to return to Fort Moultrie." "Make my compliments to the governor, and say to him that I decline to accede to his request; I cannot and will not go back," rejoined Anderson. "Then, sir," said Pettigrew, "my business is done," and he turned on his heel.

As noon approached that day, Anderson ordered his command to parade. The band took its station on the parapet, sixty feet above the waterline; the troops were drawn up on one side of a square, facing the flagstaff; the 150 workmen were formed on the other sides; and Major Anderson stood erect beside the bare staff. The chaplain moved to the center of the square, and as the battalion came to "parade rest," all uncovering, he raised his voice in prayer. Giving thanks for the safe arrival of the force in its new post, he asked that the flag might never be dishonored and might soon float again over a united, peaceful, and prosperous nation. Anderson, who had knelt, then arose; the battalion presented arms; the band broke into the national air; and amid the fervent cheers of the troops, the flag rose swiftly to the top of the staff and whipped out in the strong sea breeze.

Patriotic Northerners breathed more freely after these events and the reorganization of the Cabinet. They had feared that not merely the Charleston forts, but the government in Washington itself might be yielded by traitorous hands to the arrogant forces of secession—for arrogance seemed a striking quality of the cotton kingdom. Their spirits rose, and Jackson Day was celebrated with toasts, speeches, and cannonades which expressed undying devotion to the Union. Buchanan, reported his friends, now realized that he had been deceived and betrayed by the Southern leaders to whom he had given so much trust and made so many concessions. Disillusioned at last, he was convinced that Cobb, Jacob Thompson, Slidell, Jefferson Davis, and others had tried to use him as a tool; that while he had looked to them to help him maintain the Union, they had conspired to ruin him and the republic. He was ready to be guided by the strong men about him, Black, Holt, Stanton, and Dix; to some extent even by Seward, who was in touch with these men. The President, like his advisers, believed that by prompt action a sectional compromise might yet be achieved. The powerful border States, and especially Virginia, seemed to him in a strategic position to bring the two extremes together. But whatever happened, he was determined not to recognize secession nor to give up national property while he remained in the White House.

"You do the President great injustice," Dix shortly wrote the critical James

Watson Webb. "There is no warmer friend of the Union. I know no instance in history in which the head of a government was more grossly deceived by those in whom a generous confidence had been reposed." [32] Dix himself made a memorable contribution to Northern morale. One of his first acts was to order an officer of the Treasury Department to go to New Orleans, take over the revenue cutters there, and send them to New York. A Southern captain refused to surrender his vessel. On hearing this Dix (January 29) ordered the man arrested and the cutter seized, adding: "If anyone attempts to haul down the Union flag, shoot him on the spot."

The country at last had an Administration in which lovers of the Union could repose full confidence. The focus of public anxiety passed from the Cabinet room in the White House to other and more dangerous points.

32 Dix to Webb, February 1, 1861; Webb Papers.

13

The Failure of Compromise

MEANWHILE, what of the efforts of Congress to deal with the crisis? It had set to work in a blundering and legalistic fashion, but even if it had acted efficiently and sagaciously in the use of its mechanisms, it would have been doomed to failure. Three principal reasons, which by no means exhaust the list, may be assigned to explain the futility of its labors. In the first place, the heart of the great national scission lay in burning hatreds, gnawing distrusts, and inveterate prejudices which no new laws or statutory amendments could reach. In the second, two compact, determined wings of opinion and leadership, the radical Republicans and the secessionists, were committed to mutually incompatible positions. Finally, Congress, a body of politicians too close to party and sectional objects, too prone to posturing for effect, and too little inclined to think nationally, was ill adapted for the statesmanlike labor required. A new national convention would have been far more effective. If a fourth reason were to be named, it would lie in the belief of many Northerners and Southerners alike that their section would profit from temporary disunion followed by a peaceable reconstruction.

[I]

Nearly all informed leaders knew that the chances of successful action by Congress were exceedingly slender. After all, what was the situation? By the time Congress was well organized, in mid-December, five States had committed themselves to secession. On December 6, Senators Brown of Mississippi, Iverson of Georgia, and Wigfall of Texas had made speeches implying that the heroic South would depart no matter what delusive concessions were made to her. Iverson declared that Alabama would undoubtedly go out on January 7, and Georgia on January 16, and three if not five other States before March 4. Describing the enmity between the two sections as "deeper than hell," he said that in his opinion nothing under heaven could prevent such a consummation. Howell Cobb had included in his address to Georgians on December 6 a condemnation of compromise; every hour that Georgia stayed in the Union after Lincoln came into power would be "an hour of degradation, to be followed by certain and speedy ruin." Governor Gist on December 8 told the Alabama commissioner that two members of Congress had just written him "that Gen. Davis, Gov. Brown and others *have abandoned all idea of compromising the difficulty* and say that they desire South Carolina to get out of the Union without delay." [1] Much the same statement was made by a bustling politician, S. F. Butterworth, who wrote from Washington on December 2 to the active New York Democrat and lawyer S. L. M. Barlow. After giving much accurate information drawn from Southerners, Butterworth (who had advance knowledge of the President's message, and wanted a stock-exchange operation carried out on the basis of this knowledge) reported: "Jeff Davis says that no human power can save the Union, all the cotton states will go, no amendment short of protection of the institution by Congress in the territories will now satisfy the South, says that ninetynine-one hundreths of the people of Missi. are determined to secede."

As early as December 7, John H. Reagan wrote a friend from Washington that all idea of another Congressional compromise was vain and foolish.[2] Representative David Clopton of Alabama, less than a week later, informed Senator C. C. Clay that efforts to compromise differences and patch up the rotten concern would prove bootless. His frank description of secession commitments bulwarked this opinion:

The old man [Buchanan] is very anxious to avoid a collision, and wants secession postponed until the 4th March. His message was referred, in the House, to a committee of one from each State. Several of us, Pugh, Curry, Moore, and myself (Stallworth not here, but has since come) and others from other cotton States, declined to vote, believing that we ought to keep ourselves clear of all compromises. . . . The Republicans are quiet, say nothing, promise nothing, threaten nothing.

In my opinion, Alabama, Mississippi, Florida, and Texas will secede with South Carolina. Georgia will necessarily follow; but there has to be an iron wedge driven to split her off from the Union. Crawford, Jackson, Underwood, and Jones are firm, Love a grade lower, and Hill and Hardeman for the Union. Reagan is with the most advanced, Hamilton for the Union. Garnett, De Jarnette, Jenkins, Leake, Ryan, Edmundson, Stephenson, Ruffin and Craigie of North Carolina, and Anderson of Mississippi are doing nobly; and whilst from policy, they do not openly advocate the secession of the States, yet they say to us, Secede! and they can carry the border States with us. The general impression now, with all parties, is that a dissolution of the Union is inevitable. I cannot see how a collision of arms can be avoided. Be that as it may, far rather die a freeman than live like a slave to Black Republicanism. I would be an equal, or a

---

1 J. W. Garrett, Columbia, December 8, 1860, to Gov. Moore, Governors' Papers, Ala. Dept. Arch. and Hist.; my italics.
2 O. M. Roberts Papers, Univ. of Texas.

corpse. The argument is exhausted, further remonstrance is dishonorable, hesitation is dangerous, delay is submission. "To your tents, O Israel," and let the God of battles decide the issue.[3]

This letter found an echo in an open address which thirty Southern Senators and Representatives on December 13, only ten days after Congress opened, sent their constituents in Alabama, Georgia, Florida, Arkansas, Mississippi, North Carolina, and Louisiana. "The argument is exhausted," they declared. "All hope of relief in the Union, through the agency of committees, Congressional legislation, or constitutional amendments, is extinguished. . . . The Republicans are resolute in the purpose to grant nothing that will or ought to satisfy the South. We are satisfied the honor, safety, and independence of the Southern people are to be found in a Southern Confederacy. . . ."[4] One of the signers was Judah P. Benjamin. However hotheaded at times, the Louisiana Senator was a man who shrewdly gauged the moment. Already, on December 9, he had written S. L. M. Barlow of New York that compromise was hopeless:

It is a revolution; a revolution of the most intense character; in which belief in the justice, prudence, and wisdom of secession is blended with the keenest sense of wrong and outrage, and it can no more be checked by human effort for the time than a prairie fire by a gardener's watering pot. I see not how bloodshed is to be avoided, and at a meeting of Southern Senators yesterday, I implored them all to devote all their energies to devising means for rendering the separation peaceful if possible, rather than to vain discussions about the practicability of a settlement now totally out of our power to accomplish. On a comparison of views it was ascertained that Mississippi, Alabama, Louisiana, Florida, Arkansas, and Texas would secede separately as quickly as the forms of proceeding could be carried out, that Georgia would probably be led by the example, and many believe that Virginia and Maryland will join them before the 4th March, thus preventing the inauguration of Lincoln in the Federal capital. How all this is to occur without collision I cannot foresee; but some indulge the hope that the Middle States will join the South, and that New England will be left out of the Union to enjoy by herself her fanaticism and the blessings of such freedom as she prefers.[5]

And Benjamin illustrated the fervor of Southern feeling by his close. "I sicken," he wrote, "to contemplate the ruin and desolation thus gratuitously inflicted on my country by the blind and insane fury of a fanaticism which contemplated with calmness and even with complacency the reduction of fifteen States where civilization now flourishes into a new Haiti."

Meanwhile, Republican extremists were equally irreconcilable. Such leaders as Sumner, Wade, Zack Chandler, and Chase disliked the very idea of con-

---

3 December 13, 1860; Clay Papers, Duke Univ.
4 McPherson, *Political Hist. of the Rebellion*, 37.
5 S. L. M. Barlow Papers, Columbia Univ.

cession as implying timidity and apology. So did such editors as Bryant, Greeley, Bowles, and Medill. Two milder publicists, Henry J. Raymond of the New York *Times* and Thurlow Weed of the Albany *Evening Journal*, had just before the election suggested oblations to the spirit of union; Raymond proposing a Federal indemnity for rescued fugitives from slavery, and Weed going much further by asking why the North should not restore the Missouri Compromise line. Already unpopular in wide Republican circles, the Albany boss drew down upon his head a storm of wrath. Even his friend Preston King scolded him fiercely.[6] Immediately after the election, Senator Doolittle of Wisconsin, speaking for Northwestern Republicans, reasserted their determination that slavery should never be extended into any Territory by any means whatever. Many of the leaders had come to Washington in a stiffly unyielding temper. "The Republican Party today," Seward had written Weed after the first Senate caucus, "is as uncompromising as the Secessionists in South Carolina." He hoped that tempers on each side might moderate.[7]

And when the problem was reduced to its basic elements, how much room for compromise really existed? Associate Justice John A. Campbell of the Supreme Court was right when he wrote that the grievances of which the South complained were either not material or not remediable. The loss from fugitive slaves, for example, was not truly material; Campbell believed that not one Southerner in ten thousand ever knew a man who had lost a slave by Northern rescue. What the South really wanted was a cessation of the agitation against slavery. It could never be granted, because the slavery question agitated itself. Slavery was in conflict with the spirit of the age, and even if ten thousand Garrisons and Ben Wades were muzzled, the agitation would continue. What the North wanted (for the moment) was a cessation of the pressure for the expansion of slavery. But this pressure depended on economic and social forces independent of all such men as Wigfall, Iverson, and A. G. Brown. To name but one, slavery seemed usually to yield its best profits upon cheap lands, and this meant expansion. No, the basic question could not be compromised; one section must yield its fundamental position.

Each side in Congress naturally exhibited a deep suspicion of its opponents. Southern leaders believed that the Republicans meant to sing a Lorelei song of compromise to delay and cripple the secession movement until, their object of dividing and paralyzing the South attained, they would trample on all real concessions. Conversely, many Republican leaders believed that the secessionists, determined to go out even if they were offered apples of gold on platters of

6 "You and Seward," wrote King, "should be among the foremost to brandish the lance and shout for war." Weed, *Memoir*, 308, 309.
7 *Ibid.*

silver, were using talk of compromise as a screen. Behind fair words in Washington they were executing fell deeds in the South. Some of the playing for delay was sincerely based on patriotic motives. Union men in the South earnestly besought their Northern friends to delay the hotheads by irenic speeches and measures. "Their prayer is for time as strongly as that of Ajax is for light," wrote Senator Dixon of Connecticut.[8] It must be admitted, however, that the suspicions of both Northerners and Southerners had a substantial basis. Both sides harbored members who dissembled their real intent.

Charles Francis Adams, a member of the House committee appointed to deal with compromise, was a man of high probity. Yet his object in this committee is stated by his son to have been to maneuver for position and to gain time. We are told that he instinctively sought to demonstrate to Northern opinion that compromise was impossible by driving the Southern Representatives from one position to another, until their irreducible demands were shown to be impossible of concession. While he thus united the North, the peaceable attitude adopted might temporarily paralyze the South, and permanently hold the border States in the Union. Adams justified the duplicity inherent in this policy on the ground that he was but stripping the Southern radicals of their mask.[9]

On the other side, the Virginia historian Pollard informs us that radical Southern Senators had no real heart in the discussion of compromise. Determined to secede anyhow, they wished merely to affect public opinion; and while professing to desire a pacification of the nation, they secretly intrigued against it.[10] A Christmas Day letter of Douglas proves that he thought many leaders of both parties dissemblers and tricksters. Under these circumstances, tempers tended to harden. As December closed, Representative William S. Holman, an Indiana Democrat who earnestly prayed for adjustment, wrote home:

We must expect to face all the consequences of a revolution that divides us into two nations on the slave line. I have not seen the slightest evidence of reaction since Congress met. Every *moment* and every *movement* tend to consolidate the Southern sentiment, and even the most conservative of the Southern men look to a united South as an inevitable result. In the midst of these contending elements there is no yielding on the part of the Republicans, not an inch to be given by the leaders, and in the main the Republican press sustain and back up their determination not to yield an inch. . . .[11]

Nevertheless, a few brave men, notable among them Crittenden and Douglas in the Senate and Tom Corwin and John Sherman in the House, were resolved

8 From Washington, December 22, 1860; Welles Papers, LC.
9 Charles Francis Adams, Jr., *Charles Francis Adams*, 128 ff. But there was more of a sincere desire for peace and settlement in the elder Adams than his son gives him credit for; his letters in the Dana Papers, Mass. Hist. Soc., show him working hard for agreement.
10 Pollard, *Jefferson Davis*, 68.
11 Allen Hamilton Papers, Ind. State Lib.

to struggle to the last for a fair settlement. Conspicuous among the battlers for compromise was the rudely eloquent Andrew Johnson, an anxious champion of peace and an impassioned defender of the Union. His speech of December 18, exhorting the Southerners to battle for their rights on the vantage-ground of the Constitution, and warning them that in the storm of civil war slavery would be cut down by the sword of destruction, was one of the memorable orations of the winter.

[II]

The action of the Senate, delayed by much ugly wrangling, did not begin until December 18, when it voted to form a Committee of Thirteen on the crisis. Two days later, Vice-President Breckinridge named a strong group who met for the first time that day. Two men of transcendent ability represented the Lower South, Jefferson Davis and Robert Toombs; three stood for the borderland, R. M. T. Hunter of Virginia, and Lazarus W. Powell and John J. Crittenden of Kentucky. The Northern Democrats were given spokesmen in Stephen A. Douglas, William M. Bigler of Pennsylvania, and Henry M. Rice of Minnesota. This left five places for Republicans. Breckinridge naturally named William H. Seward, and with him the quiet, moderate, industrious Jacob Collamer of Vermont, adding three Northwestern radicals—Ben Wade of Ohio, James R. Doolittle of Wisconsin, and James W. Grimes of Iowa. At first, Davis declined to serve because of the position he and his State were known to occupy, but under the advice of friends he changed his mind.[12]

It will be noted that the committee was named on the day that South Carolina seceded. Time was running out, and it would have to act rapidly. It is also to be noted that not one of the committee leaders was in close working relations with the President, especially after Davis broke with him, and that in this terrible convulsion all too little liaison existed between the executive and legislative branches. The astute and adroit Seward, curiously enough, became the principal intermediary between the Thirteen and the staunch Unionists of the Cabinet.

Leadership of the committee lay with Crittenden, who, though unhappily lacking the force, charm, and eloquence of Clay, had something of his breadth of vision. On the day the body was born, he made a speech presenting a well-rounded plan of adjustment quite in the Clay tradition. He proposed six amendments to the Constitution. The first would extend the line of 36° 30′ to California, prohibiting slavery in all Territories north of it, but recognizing and protecting the institution south of it; future States to be admitted with or with-

12 *Cong. Globe,* 36th Cong., 2d Sess., 158, 182.

out slavery as the people might decide. The second amendment would forbid Congress to abolish slavery in any place of national jurisdiction inside a slave State. The third would prohibit abolition in the District of Columbia so long as either Virginia or Maryland had slavery, or without the consent of the people of the District, or without compensation to those who asked it. The fourth amendment would protect from Federal interference the interstate transportation of slaves. The fifth would enable Congress to furnish compensation to owners of fugitive slaves rescued by force, this indemnity to be collected from the county responsible. The last amendment would forbid any future tampering with the Constitution as it applied to and shielded slavery. Annexed resolutions called for strict observance of the Fugitive Slave Law, repeal of the personal liberty laws, and efficient enforcement of the laws against the African slave trade.[13]

It need not be said that Crittenden had consulted with colleagues North and South before offering his broad scheme, and had received hopeful assurance of support.[14] Four Democratic members of the committee, Douglas, Powell, Bigler, and Rice, were ready to give general support to his plan. The vital question was whether Republicans, pledged to the exclusion of slavery from all new Territories, could consent to an amendment which, if the nation expanded southward, might permit great slaveholding accessions. Crittenden was aware of Republican sensitivity on this head. But he believed that the revival and extension of the Missouri Compromise line would prevent any expansion whatever; for while the North would stand adamant against all annexations southward, the South would forbid any acquisitions northward. Practically, therefore, the division on 36° 30' would settle the slavery issue in the Territories for all time. Of course many Republican leaders held the alternative view, that the plan would simply inaugurate a new contest for the balance of power: The free States would fix their covetous gaze on Canada and Alaska, the slaveholding States on Mexico and Cuba, and strife would be intensified rather than quieted.

The Committee of Thirteen commenced work on December 22. Davis shortly moved that no proposals should be reported to the Senate unless they had the support of a majority of both the Republican and the Democratic members of the body; that is, they must have four Democratic and three Republican votes. This seemed reasonable, for a one-sided recommendation would carry

13 Text in McPherson, *Pol. Hist. Rebellion*, 64, 65.
14 Crittenden wrote Larz Anderson March 20, 1861, of his resolutions: "They were the result of the joint labor of and consultation with friends, having the same object in view, and I believe that if those measures thus offered had been at a suitable time promptly adopted by the Congress of the United States, I would have checked the progress of the rebellion and revolution and saved the Union." Crittenden Papers, Duke Univ.

little weight. The rule was adopted. Thereupon the two leaders of the Lower South both submitted plans.[15]

Toombs, speaking for Southern extremists, asked for constitutional amendments granting recognition and protection to slave property in all Territories; providing for the surrender of fugitive slaves without writ of *habeas corpus* or jury trial; forbidding the passage of any law by Congress pertaining to slavery without the consent of a majority of slaveholding States; and stipulating that these and other constitutional provisions upon slavery (except that on the African slave trade) should not be altered without the consent of every slaveholding State. Davis made just one comprehensive suggestion. It was that the Constitution be amended to declare slave property on the same constitutional footing as any other species of property, and exempt from any impairment by the local law of any State, or by any enactment of the United States or of a Territory. This would establish slavery in all Territories and entitle it to full protection therein, while it would also estop the Northern States from passing any law limiting the recovery of fugitive slaves, or restricting the right of a slaveholder to bring his Negroes to free soil in transit or for a sojourn. Obviously, the Republicans could not accept either Toombs's or Davis's formula.

Douglas also had a plan, the chief features of which were that the status of each existing Territory should remain unchanged until, on attaining a population of fifty thousand, it should be admitted as a State with or without slavery; and that no further expansion of the nation should take place except with the consent of two-thirds of each house. He proposed to forbid any abolition of slavery in the District of Columbia except upon the same general conditions laid down by Crittenden; to prohibit any interference with the domestic slave trade, or any opening of the franchise or of office to the African race; and to furnish Federal compensation for rescued slaves. Very interestingly, he added a notation that land might be acquired at Federal expense for the colonization of colored people. His suggestions got little consideration, since his chief proposal, based on popular sovereignty principles, was repugnant to Republicans and Southern radicals alike. Indeed, the Crittenden plan alone out of seven offered in committee received really earnest attention.[16]

That Crittenden's scheme had wide and enthusiastic public support there could be no question. John A. Dix, Edward Everett, and Robert C. Winthrop no sooner saw it than they wrote strongly approbatory letters. Martin Van Buren declared that the amendments would certainly be ratified by three-

15 The Journal of the Committee is in the 36th Cong., 2d Sess., *Senate Committee Reports*, No. 288. For an analysis of its work, see Potter, *Lincoln and His Party in the Secession Crisis*, 171 ff.
16 A competent digest of all plans submitted is in Nicolay and Hay, *Lincoln*, III, 220–222.

fourths of the States. The Senator received hundreds of assurances from all over the North and the border States that his policy had reached the popular heart. It took time to hold meetings and get memorials signed, but before long resolutions and petitions were pouring in upon Congress. In New York City, sixty-three thousand people signed an endorsement of the plan; another document bore the names of fourteen thousand women, scattered from North Carolina to Vermont. From St. Louis came nearly a hundred foolscap pages of names, wrapped in the American flag. Greeley, who had as good opportunities for knowing public sentiment as any man in the country, later wrote that supporters of the Crittenden Compromise could claim with good reason that a large majority of people favored it.[17]

But the five Republicans in the committee were influenced not by general opinion but by personal conviction, party principle, and the voice of freesoil leaders and editors. The four minor Senators were to some extent inclined to wait for guidance on the preeminent Seward, who was expected by most people to be the controlling force in the next Administration. Seward, for his part, was disposed to be silent for the time, from a conviction noted in his journal that "concession, or solicitation, or solicitude would encourage, and demonstrations of firmness of purpose would exasperate." He preferred, also, to await a statement of policy from Lincoln. A week before the committee was appointed, he had learned that the President-elect desired him to be Secretary of State. He wrote at once to ask time for consideration, and left next day, December 14, with the intention of spending the holidays at home. Halting in Albany to talk with Thurlow Weed and others, he heard that on an invitation from Lincoln's friends, Weed was about to pay his second visit to Springfield. It seemed wise to see Weed on his return and find out what Lincoln had said on a variety of subjects.[18]

At this point a somewhat confusing incident occurred. Already, as we have seen, Weed had come out in favor of restoring the Missouri Compromise line. On Monday, the seventeenth, after talking with Seward, he renewed the proposal in his *Evening Journal*. His object, he tells us in his autobiography, was to do something to hold the border States in line, thus reducing the extent and strength of the "rebellion," and to keep the Northern people clearly in the right, so that if and when war came they would have greater unity. Of course he also hoped to do something for peace. Many people inaccurately leaped to the conclusion that his stand had been inspired or at least supported

17 Coleman, *Crittenden*, II, 237–258, presents detailed information on public support; see also Potter, *Lincoln and Secession Crisis*, 195 ff.
18 Weed, before visiting Springfield, suggested that a conference of governors be arranged and that Lincoln send it his views. Baringer, *House Dividing*, 204, 205; Weed, *Memoir*, 310; Nicolay and Hay, III, 252, 253.

by Seward. The fact was, however, that the Senator had a position all his own—a position which rendered him much more likely to follow Lincoln than to try to revive the old 36° 30′ line.

[III]

Lincoln had already made up his mind. Indeed, that central phalanx of the Republican Party which, comprehending not only all radicals but many moderates, believed that the doctrine of the exclusion of slavery from the Territories must be defended as their supreme citadel, was never for a moment moved by the Crittenden Compromise. Lincoln was less likely than anyone else to abandon a principle which he held vital.

On December 10 he had written Lyman Trumbull, who could tell the next Republican caucus: "Let there be no compromise on the question of extending slavery. If there be, all our labor is lost, and ere long, must be done again. . . . The tug has to come, and better now than at any time hereafter." Next day, in response to an inquiry from William Kellogg of the House committee on the crisis, he wrote again: "Entertain no proposition in regard to the extension of slavery. The instant you do they have us under again: all our labor is lost, and sooner or later must be done over." On the thirteenth he sent a similar letter to Elihu B. Washburne: "Prevent, as far as possible, any of our friends from demoralizing themselves and our cause by entertaining propositions for compromise of any sort on 'slavery extension.' There is no possible compromise upon it but which puts us under again, and leaves all our work to do over again. Whether it be a Missouri line or Eli Thayer's popular sovereignty, it is all the same. Let either be done, and immediately filibustering and extending slavery recommences. On that point hold firm, as with a chain of steel." [19]

This was one of the most fateful decisions of Lincoln's career. The reasons why he made it so quickly and emphatically, without consulting others, require a brief analysis.

"They will have us under again; all our work will have to be redone." By this Lincoln meant a good deal more than the naked words assert. It seems

[19] The letter to Trumbull is in Tracy, *Uncollected Lincoln Letters*, 171; those to Washburne and Kellogg in the Thomas-Tandy edition of Nicolay and Hay, *Lincoln's Works*, VI, 77, 78. Lincoln's reply to Weed on December 17 was in the same vein. If the convocation of governors should meet, he wrote, Weed might tell them that "you judge from my speeches that I will be inflexible on the territorial question; that I probably think either the Missouri line extended, or Douglas's and Thayer's popular sovereignty would lose us everything we gain by the election; that filibustering for all south of us and making slave States would follow, in spite of us, in either case; also that I probably think all opposition, real and apparent, to the fugitive slave clause of the Constitution ought to be withdrawn." Weed, *Memoir*, 310, 311.

safe to say that he had two important ideas in mind. First, he meant that the whole work of his party in winning the election would have to be redone if the victorious candidate immediately surrendered the central tenet of the party. He could yield on peripheral points—not on the expansion of slavery. And Lincoln believed that the expansion of slavery was implicit in the Crittenden Compromise. He told Duff Green that the adoption of the line would still the controversy for the moment, but the quarrel would be renewed by the seizure and attempted annexation of Mexico.[20] Was this unlikely? The South had forced Pierce and Buchanan to take extreme attitudes on Cuba and Mexico. Not only the Knights of the Golden Circle, but a large clandestine organization in California had an eye on Sonora and other territory to the southward.[21] And what if Hawaii were annexed? The Republican Party had been born from a great principle—and now it was asked to sacrifice it under threat and menace. If it did so, how could it face honest Northern voters again?

More fundamentally, Lincoln had in mind his statement that "a crisis must be reached and passed," and the country brought to a completely new resolution respecting slavery. He had said explicitly that the nation as a whole must be persuaded to accept the containment of slavery within existing bounds as a prelude to the blest goal of ultimate extinction. His election on the principle of nonextension constituted the crisis; if the South accepted the election, realizing its import, the crisis *would* be passed; the nation could go on to consider slavery from a more constructive point of view. Its psychology on the great question would rapidly alter. But what if the nation backed away from a decision, and refused to accept the only principle on which a permanent solution, in keeping with nineteenth century progress, could be based? What if it turned back to the old policy of drift? Europe in 1848 had given the world the tragic spectacle of nations coming up to a healthy turning-point—and refusing to turn. Could the United States afford to do so? Could the one leader who had demanded that the country face the crisis now flinch and bid his party recede? To this question, Lincoln said *No*.

Talking with one of his Springfield friends, Lincoln partially summed up his view in a characteristically pungent sentence: "Well, we have got plenty of corn and pork and it wouldn't be exactly brave for us to leave this question to posterity." This was the report of his words sent to Washburne.

His letters to Kellogg, Trumbull, and Washburne were shown to leaders

20 Duff Green, December 28, 1860, to Buchanan; Buchanan Papers.
21 "We hope that Uncle Sam will soon own Sonora. . . . We have an organization here of about 4,000 men, and when they start I have a Captain's Commission, if it is not owned by the Government by 1862, we are going to take it from the cussed Mexicans. . . ." V. H. Claiborne, San Francisco, November 1, 1860, to "Dear Charles"; Brock Papers, HL.

and newspapermen. On December 22, his determination was revealed to the public in the New York *Tribune*, by an authorized statement in the editorial columns. Lincoln, announced the journal, "is utterly opposed to any concession or compromise that shall yield one iota of the position occupied by the Republican Party on the question of slavery in the territories, and. . . . he stands now, as he stood in May last, when he accepted the nomination for the presidency, square upon the Chicago platform."

Thurlow Weed, in his conference with Lincoln on December 20, discussed the question of compromise, though in his twelve-page record he confines himself almost entirely to the Cabinet slate.[22] He found Lincoln still possessed by an apparent cheerfulness, declaring that despite the threats of the cotton States, serious trouble might be averted by wisdom and forbearance. This, on the day South Carolina departed! Yet by this time Lincoln's optimism was probably more feigned than real. His strong, clear mind undoubtedly gauged the intentions of the cotton kingdom leaders accurately. But he could not talk of war without exposing himself to the accusation of exaggerating the crisis and fanning the flames. And whatever his fears, he did not intend to budge on the central issue.

When Weed showed him the new editorial in the *Evening Journal* advocating the Missouri Compromise line, he betrayed annoyance. Remarking that it was an attack on friend and foe alike, and would do "some good or much mischief," he inquired whether Weed thought Republican sentiment in New York would sustain it. The boss had to admit that it would not. Doubtless Lincoln spoke emphatically against opening the door to any extension of slavery. He had his own ideas as to how far concession might go in other matters, and embodied them in three resolutions which he asked Weed to show to Trumbull and Hannibal Hamlin, and to get Seward to introduce: [24]

Resolved: That the fugitive slave clause of the Constitution ought to be enforced by a law of Congress, with efficient provision for that object, not obliging private persons to assist in its execution, but punishing all who resist it, and with the usual safeguards to liberty, securing freemen against being surrendered as slaves—

That all state laws, if there be such, really or apparently, in conflict with such law of Congress, ought to be repealed; and no opposition to the execution of such law of Congress ought to be made—

That the Federal Union must be preserved.

22 Weed, *Autobiography*, 602–614.
23 Others also assumed an optimistic attitude. Henry J. Raymond had all the facilities of an editor for knowing the situation. He wrote from the *Times* office on January 21, 1861: "I think this crisis will work out gradually and leave things in much better condition than they were before—*provided* it is managed with firmness as well as forbearance." J. R. Hawley Papers.
24 Text in Bancroft, *Seward*, II, 10.

While this was all that Lincoln wrote at the time, he would not have objected to other assurances to the South. He had not the remotest thought of recommending that slavery be abolished in the District of Columbia, even under safeguards, or touched in Federal reservations within the slaveholding States. He had no idea of interfering with the domestic slave trade. He would not object to the confirmation of slavery in New Mexico, if further extension were prevented. He had said repeatedly that, far from harassing Southerners, he would give them a friendly Administration.[25] But on the containment of slavery he was adamant. Weed, returning east, met Seward on December 22 at Syracuse, for the Senator had been summoned back to Washington; and as the two rode together to Albany, they discussed all that Lincoln had said.

[IV]

The first committee vote on the Crittenden Compromise was taken that day in Seward's absence, and the proposal was defeated by the Republican majority. In a discussion of nearly seven hours, Douglas, Bigler, and Crittenden supported the plan. Hunter, Toombs, and Davis, speaking for Southern Democrats, declared they would accept it if the Republicans gave sincere assent, but not otherwise. On the vital point, the reestablishment of the Missouri Compromise line, Collamer, Doolittle, Grimes, and Wade all voted no. Thereupon Toombs and Davis cast negative votes, and the resolution failed, six to six. Returning to the sessions on December 24, Seward recorded a negative vote. Four days later, the committee reported to the Senate that it could reach no conclusion.[26]

This report, it must be kept in mind, almost coincided with the revolution in the Cabinet which placed Buchanan under staunch Union influence, and which made it certain that the demand for evacuating Sumter would be brusquely dismissed. It almost coincided with the action of Buchanan, under the stimulus of Horatio King and other Unionist advisers, in repudiating the Washington *Constitution* and its semi-treasonable utterances. Within a few days after the Thirteen reported their failure, Floyd was out and the Cabinet was fully revolutionized. In short, the Republican leadership was proving itself adamant on slavery extension at nearly the same time that the Administration became adamant on the issue of the Charleston forts.

It would be erroneous to say that these two events made continued secession certain; it was certain anyway. Ignoring compromise talk, Florida, Mississippi, and Alabama, on December 18, 20, and 24 respectively, had elected conven-

25 See Randall, *Lincoln the President*, I, 234–237, for a masterly statement on this head.
26 *Committee Journal*, 4, 8, *et seq.*

tions with decisive secessionist majorities. But the events did convince Southern radicals that they must push faster, further, and harder. Toombs, on December 23, telegraphed his State that the people of Georgia should thunder secession by unanimous voice in the election to be held on January 2. On January 5, a momentous caucus of Southern Senators was held. It is said that it took place in a room of the Capitol itself. Members from Alabama, Arkansas, Georgia, Louisiana, Florida, Mississippi, and Texas determined that immediate secession was imperative, that a convention should meet in Montgomery before February 15 to organize a Confederacy, and that they should temporarily hold their seats in an effort to protect their movement and impede hostile legislation. On January 8, Jefferson Davis wrote a friend:

We are advancing rapidly to the end of "the Union." The cotton States may now be regarded as having decided for secession. South Carolina is in a quasi war, and the probabilities are that events will hasten her and her associates into general conflict with the forces of the federal government. The black republicans exultant over their recent successes are not disposed to concede anything, and the stern necessity of resistance is forcing itself upon the judgment of all the slaveholding States. The Va. Legislature met yesterday and took promptly and boldly the Southern ground.[27]

In rejecting the Crittenden Compromise, the Republicans had taken what history later proved to have been a fearful responsibility, just as in thrusting secession steadily forward the Southern extremists were taking the same responsibility. Some Republicans, after war came, made an effort to divest themselves of the burden by contending that the true blame for the rejection fell upon Davis and Toombs, whose votes in the affirmative would have carried the compromise eight to four—or with Seward voting, eight to five. (Even then the measure would have died under the rule requiring a majority of both parties.) Edward Everett argued that the supposed willingness of Davis and Toombs to support the compromise was purely illusory, and that if the Republicans had come out for it, the two would have gone over to the opposition.[28] But we have unimpeachable evidence that the pair were sincere, and much additional evidence that, as Breckinridge told the Senate, "the leading statesmen of the lower Southern States were willing to accept the terms of settlement" proposed.[29] At any rate, Stephens, Toombs, Herschel Johnson, and Davis were ready to do so; though probably not Slidell, Howell Cobb, A. G. Brown, Iverson, Wigfall, or Benjamin.

Whether the secession of Florida, Alabama, Mississippi, and Georgia could

27 To E. De Leon; De Leon Papers.
28 "Address at Inauguration of Union League Club, Boston, April 9, 1863"; pamphlet.
29 See Potter, op. cit., 204-207; Rhodes, United States, III, 154, 155; Cong. Globe, 27th Cong., 1st Sess., 142.

under any circumstances have been arrested is another question, doubtless to be answered in the negative. Seward had written Lincoln just after Christmas that in his opinion the offer of the Missouri Compromise line would be utterly inutile in stopping them. Be it remembered that the address of various Southern Senators and Representatives declaring the argument exhausted and demanding a separate Southern Confederacy had been issued as early as December 14; that when Seward voted on the Crittenden proposal, four States were already committed to secession.

Since Lincoln and other leaders had said no, it was necessary for the Republicans to offer an alternative. The resolutions written by the President-elect were not presented, because Senators in Washington decided that the ground had been covered elsewhere and that the form of his proposal on the recovery of fugitives would excite party dissension. Seward now stepped to the front. On January 22, after Mississippi, Florida, and Alabama had all gone out, he rose in the Senate before an audience said to be unprecedented in size for one of his most telling efforts. The country rang with the shots just fired at the *Star of the West*. The Southern States were seizing one Federal post after another: The day before, Louisiana had taken over the arsenal at Baton Rouge and Forts St. Philip and Jackson, while, as he rose, Florida forces were occupying Fort Barrancas and the Pensacola navy yard. Yet his tone was bland as May.

He spoke of meeting prejudice with conciliation, exaction with concession, and violence with the right hand of peace. Never had he shown more literary felicity. Specially effective was the contrast he drew between a puissant warship of the United States, hailed with awe as she entered a foreign port flying her thirty-three stars, and a warship steaming in with a palmetto flag, to be greeted with the contemptuous words: "She comes from one of the obscure republics of North America. Let her pass on."

On the fundamental question of fresh extensions of slavery, Seward yielded nothing; but he went far in other respects, and his proposals were practical as well as patriotic. If Kansas were admitted under the Wyandotte constitution, he would consent to the consolidation of all remaining Territories into two States, to be organized under enabling acts similar to those of Oregon or Minnesota; the right to a future subdivision of each into several States being reserved. This would take the territorial question out of politics for all time. Presumably New Mexico-Arizona would come in as a slaveholding State, and certainly the region north of it would be a free State. Second, Seward proposed to satisfy the South on the sore point of efficient enforcement of the Fugitive Slave Law, while safeguarding the liberty of free blacks. In the third place, he was willing to write into the Constitution an amendment affirming the permanent exemption of slavery in the States from Congressional control. Fourth, he would support laws to prevent such invasions as that of John Brown. And finally, regarding physical bonds as the most powerful of all links, he wished to see both a northern and a southern railroad built to the Pacific with national help. His eloquent closing appeal for peace left more than one Senator in tears.[30]

In sober reality, Seward had little faith in Congressional schemes of compromise. He said so in his speech, frankly expressing his wish that, when the excitements of the hour had subsided, a new Constitutional convention could chisel out a settlement enduring as granite. By this time, his selection as Secretary of State had become public, and he expected to be one of the chief directors of the nation's destinies. "I will try to save freedom and my country," he had exuberantly written his wife on accepting. While he believed that secession could not be halted, he also believed that the Union might in time—perhaps in two years, he wrote Weed—be reconstructed. He trusted that he could be the chief architect of this reconstruction, this noble new edifice.

At about the time he wrote Lincoln that he would undertake the State Department, Seward approached Senator Gwin of California, who deplored secession, and said that he had a policy which he wished Gwin to understand he would pursue as head of the Cabinet. It was a plan for avoiding civil war and ultimately rebuilding the Union. Gwin writes:

His policy was, that if the separation of States could not be prevented, let the separation be a peaceful one; and to lead the public sentiment of the people of the North and South in the future, and especially of the South, in such a direction that they might see what a grand error that section had committed, and to reestablish the Union without the intervention of civil war. To carry out this policy, Mr. Seward's appointment as Secretary of State was an indispensable necessity, and to secure that appointment it was important that Mr. Lincoln should know that Mr. Seward's long services with the great leaders of the South in the Senate would inspire them with confidence that his appointment as Secretary of State would inaugurate a policy for the peaceable separation of the two sections, leaving it to be determined by the people in the future whether or not the two sections should be kept separate.[31]

This statement to Gwin ran parallel with the extempore speech which he had made to the New England Society in New York on December 22, when he laid heavy emphasis on the healing effects of time. The necessities which made the Union were enduring, he said, while the passions of men were short-lived and ephemeral; if the country kept calm, a discussion would ensue which, kindly in character, would soon show which side was in the wrong; and on

30 Bancroft, *Seward*, II, 16; Seward, *Seward at Washington*, II, 494.
31 MS Memoirs, Bancroft Library; cf. *Overland Monthly*, May–November, 1891.

the basis of concessions to correct this error, the discontented States would "come back into fraternal relations with us." That this was Seward's view is corroborated by the British minister, Lord Lyons, a warm friend, who wrote Lord John Russell on February 4, 1861:

Mr. Seward's real view of the state of the country appears to be that if bloodshed can be avoided until the new government is installed, the seceding States will in no long time return to the Confederation. He seems to think that in a few months the evils and hardships produced by secession will become intolerably grievous to the Southern States, that they will be completely re-assured as to the intentions of the Administration, and that the Conservative element which is now kept under the surface by violent pressure of the Seces-sionists will emerge with irresistible force. From all these causes he confidently expects that when elections are held in the Southern States in November next, the Union party will have a clear majority and will bring the seceding States back into the Confederation. He then hopes to place himself at the head of a strong Union party, having extensive ramifications both in the North and in the South, and to make "Union" or "Disunion" not "Freedom" or "Slavery" the watchword of political parties.[32]

Making this unrealistic analysis of the situation, Seward was little worried by the rejection of the Crittenden Compromise or his own proposals. Why pay a heavy price for keeping the Lower South in the family when it would soon repent separation? He believed that any hostile external pressure, any foreign attack, would quickly restore a spirit of national solidarity; and in his speech to the New England Society he pictured the gallant South Carolinians, the moment they heard that New York was being attacked by the French, the Russians, or the British, rushing in a body to her defense. This was an idea which was to bear strange fruit early in Lincoln's Administration.

[V]

Early in January, Crittenden rose in the Senate to make the remarkable proposal that his compromise should be submitted to the people of the entire nation for their solemn judgment, as expressed by a popular vote. His reason for suggesting so novel a step, as he frankly confessed, was that he had come to fear he could never obtain a two-thirds vote for his plan in the Senate. The proposal inspired widespread enthusiasm. Douglas declared in the Senate on the same day it was made, January 3, that he ventured to prophesy that the Republicans themselves would approve the proposed amendments. Horatio Seymour wrote Crittenden that he was confident New York State would give the measure a majority of a hundred and fifty thousand. Horace Greeley later

---

32 *British Blue Book, United States,* 1862, pp. 62, 63.

declared that in a popular referendum, the compromise would have prevailed by "an overwhelming majority." But neither radical Northerners nor radical Southerners liked the plan. Because of Republican obstruction, interposing delay after delay, it never came to a vote in the Senate. The objection of men like Wade, Chandler, and Sumner, and of journals like the New York *Tribune*, was candidly stated. They said (1) that in the Lower South the secession elections had been unfair and fraudulent; (2) that the naked submission of the Crittenden Compromise alone was not enough—the entire controversy should be taken before the proper tribunal, which Greeley pronounced to be a Constitutional Convention; and (3) that some guarantees should be given in advance that the Southern States would accept the result of the election. Whether these were good or bad reasons, and whether it was for good or for ill that the American people were never given a chance of passing on this crucial compromise scheme, are questions on which no historian can pronounce a light judgment, and on which few would care to pronounce at all. But for Crittenden himself the repeated refusals of the Senate to vote on his referendum constituted a great tragedy.

The second critical decision on the Crittenden Compromise proper took place in open Senate on January 16. Crittenden had introduced his resolutions on the third, and had made a long argument in their behalf on the seventh— followed by a fierce disunion speech from Toombs. A motion to consider the resolution was now defeated by the adoption of a meaningless substitute, 25 to 23, with six Southern Democrats not voting. While the twenty-five adopting votes were all Republican, the six Democrats—Johnson of Arkansas, Iverson of Georgia, Benjamin and Slidell of Louisiana, and Hemphill and Wigfall of Texas—by their stubborn silence helped seal the fate of the measure. Crittenden, Andrew Johnson, and Douglas all severely censured the abstentionists.

While the vote was being taken Andrew Johnson, wrung with anxiety, hastened quietly to the side of Judah P. Benjamin, and whispered to him with tense earnestness: "Mr. Benjamin, vote! Let us save this proposition and see if we cannot bring the country to it. Vote, and show yourself an honest man." Making a scornful reply, Benjamin remained silent. More than a fortnight earlier he had delivered a speech announcing Louisiana's determination to secede, and threatening a bloody war. Obviously he wanted no compromise. As Johnson recrossed the Senate floor he saw Crittenden's venerable face pale with anguish and disappointment, the very image of gloom.

Had the six Southerners voted, the Crittenden resolutions would have had a majority of four. If the Senators from four seceding States had been in their seats, the majority would have been increased to twelve. Six of them were in Washington, but chose not to consider themselves competent to attend. According to Andrew Johnson, as soon as the vote was declared, Judah P. Benjamin sent a telegram to Louisiana, where the issue of secession was still undecided, notifying his State that the Crittenden scheme was lost, and the Black Republicans were carrying everything before them.[33] Provoking though the conduct of the six secessionists was, the fact remains that the chief responsibility for the defeat of the compromise falls upon the twenty-five Republicans who voted to slay it. A combination of Republicans and Northern Democrats could easily have carried the resolutions.

That responsibility the Republicans should squarely have accepted, and unquestionably Lincoln and his principal associates did so accept it. Once more, we must bear in mind that the central tenet of the Republican Party, ever since its foundation, had been the exclusion of slavery from all new Territories. We must also bear in mind that to Lincoln this doctrine of the containment of slavery represented much more than an objective, a goal. It represented rather a beginning, a new start. It represented, that is, the point at which one phase in the consideration of the great problems of slavery and race adjustment ended, and another phase began.

Once containment was tacitly accepted by the South, that section must also accept the corollary that slavery was a transitional and not a permanent institution; that the nation must look forward to a time, however distant, when it would be ended; that the country must take some initial step toward gradual abolition, perhaps combined with colonization abroad, and certainly combined with a fair plan of compensation. By arduous labor and heroic sacrifices, beginning in 1846 with the Wilmot Proviso and running through the spasmodic thrust of the Free Soil Party, the organization of the Republicans, their four Congressional campaigns, their two Presidential battles, and a tremendous mobilization of newspapers, orators, and pamphleteers, an Administration had been elected on a platform of containment. It had reached the end of the beginning. And now it was asked to begin all over again!

Such a surrender would have been endurable had it meant only a formal waiving of the interdiction of slavery in the West. After all, a mere handful of slaves could be found in all the Territories of the land. Nobody in his senses supposed that Negroes would ever be carried in any numbers into Nebraska, Dakota, Colorado, and Washington. In all New Mexico, despite favorable legislation, census-takers this year found only twenty-two slaves. On any practical basis, the issue of slavery in the Territories was empty. Nor was it likely, though it was certainly possible, that the Southern expansionists who had signally failed to gain any Cuban, Mexican, or Central American soil during the eight years of Pierce and Buchanan would be able to do so in the near

33 *Cong. Globe*, 37th Cong., 2d Sess., 587.

future. Northern opposition would be too dogged and powerful. So far as the actual diffusion of slavery went, the Republicans could have afforded to swallow the Crittenden Compromise—for the possibilities of slavery expansion were near their end.

The psychological and political effects of such an acceptance, however, would in Lincoln's eyes have been disastrous in the extreme. At one blow, all hope of lifting the slavery discussion, so long a futile debate between the positive-evil and positive-good schools and so totally out of key with the aspirations of civilization, to a new, enlightened, and constructive plane, would be ended. For what would be the moral result of accepting the Missouri Compromise extension? Forthwith, the hopes of the slavery extremists would rise anew. They would *toil* to make New Mexico a slave State; they would redouble their filibustering efforts; they would dream, however hopelessly, of Cuba, Lower California, Sonora, and Ceneral America. Instead of changing the climate of opinion, the recent Republican victory would leave it unaltered; instead of seeing a "crisis reached and passed," the country would see the perennial crisis lengthened.

No, the time had come to make a stand. The old American policy of drift, postponement, and politic evasion of fundamental issues would have to be stopped somehow, some day, in some fashion—and the Republican Party was pledged to stop it now. It was committed, in Lincoln's words, to placing the institution of slavery in a position where its ultimate extinction would be generally taken for granted.

To Lincoln, therefore, and all who shared his views, it seemed wise to stand on principle, hoping that it could be peaceably maintained. For great causes, great risks have to be taken. For some high causes, it is well that nations will fight and men gladly die. But Lincoln did not mean to make war in defense of his principle. He would coerce nobody to accept it. He would attack no slave-holding State, in the Union or out of it. Bound by oath to enforce the laws and protect the property of the government, he would not even do this in a needlessly offensive fashion, as, for example, by sending Federal officers where they would be resisted. To him the revival of the Missouri Compromise line did not mean assured peace; rather, it meant a temptation to war against Mexico and a certainty of continued bickering at home. He would not surrender the bright ideal he had so cogently stated in June, 1858, of a nation brought again to regard slavery as Washington, Madison, and Jefferson had regarded it. He meant to make good, if Providence permitted him, the great hope which some anonymous versifier in *Punch* had just forcibly expressed:

> Thus far shall Slavery go, no farther;
> That tide must ebb from this time forth. . . .

This is America's decision;
Awakening, she begins to see,
How justly she incurs derision
Of tyrants, while she shames us free;
Republican, yet more slaves owning
Than any under Empire groaning. . . .

Come, South, accept the situation;
The change will grow by safe degrees.
If any talk of separation,
Hang all such traitors if you please.
Break up the Union? Brothers, never!
No, the United States for ever,
Pure Freedom's home beyond the seas!

[VI]

While compromise was failing in the Senate, it was doing little better in the House, which was even worse adapted to the task of peacemaking; a body too large, too contentious, and too strongly Republican for mediatorial effort.

On motion of Boteler of Virginia, the House had agreed on December 4, by a vote of 145 to 38, to create a special committee of one from each State to consider the perilous condition of the country. The opposition was all Republican; but a number of Southern members refused to vote, Porcher Miles saying that South Carolina was already out of the Union in everything but form, and Pugh declaring that Alabama intended to follow South Carolina. Two days later, Speaker Pennington appointed the Committee of Thirty-three. His choices were maladroit. At a time when the fate of the nation hung in the balance, Pennington (a "dolt," an "old owl," wrote one observer) was showing a pitiful inability to control the chamber or drive public business ahead.[34] He could be credited with apportioning the Committee fairly among the parties, with sixteen Republicans, fourteen Democrats, and three Opposition members, while in Tom Corwin he chose an excellent chairman. But he failed to name a single Douglas man from the North; most of his Southerners were unrepresentative of public opinion in that section; and he chose too many radical Republicans. The body was far more likely to quarrel than agree.

On December 11 the Thirty-three held their first meeting. S. R. Curtis, an Iowa Republican, writes that they "seemed cordial conciliatory and deeply impressed with the importance of our position." [35] But on the twelfth, when Reuben Davis of Mississippi made a long speech on the causes of Southern

34 Charles Francis Adams, Jr., *Autobiography*, 44, 92.
35 MS Journal, Ill. State Hist. Lib.

disaffection, painting a most sinister picture of Republican objects, discord reared its head. Next day the situation grew worse.

The Committee passed a resolution written by Dunn of Indiana, expressing regret for Southern discontent, and declaring that whether this was without just cause or not, "more specific and effectual guarantees of their peculiar rights and interests" should be "promptly and cheerfully" granted. This was a handsome gesture, and went even further than a similar resolution which Rust of Arkansas had proposed. Yet at this very time it was announced that some of the Southern members had been collaborating with other Representatives and with Senators on the firebrand circular issued on December 14 with thirty signers—a manifesto declaring to the South that argument was exhausted and the Republicans would offer nothing that the section could accept. Reuben Davis declared that the Committee resolution was mere eyewash designed to mislead the South. While the resolution was telegraphed over the South with the design of restraining precipitate action, the manifesto was being just as assiduously telegraphed about with the object of promoting it.[36]

On the fourteenth Chairman Corwin made a long conciliatory speech (though he pronounced secession treason), proposing to take up issues *seriatim* and to seek, one by one, an adjustment. He suggested beginning with Henry Winter Davis's resolution calling upon the States to repeal all laws which conflicted with the Fugitive Slave Act. At once, unhappily, the wrangling recommenced. When Curtis introduced some coercionist resolutions, the Southern members protested in great indignation, and Reuben Davis declared that persistence in such a course would compel him to leave the Committee. From the beginning, two other Southerners, Hawkins of Florida and Boyce of South Carolina, had refused to serve. Curtis withdrew his motion. Thus the Committee pursued its stormy way. A weird variety of proposals was suggested to it, some reasonable, some hopeless, some fantastic. The Republicans were quite willing to give the South satisfaction on the question of fugitive slaves, and to urge the North to abandon its personal liberty laws. But the proposal to revive and extend the 36° 30' line was defeated by a solid Republican vote, with Henry Winter Davis, Opposition member from Maryland, assisting; a vote, that is, of 17 to 14.[37]

By Christmas, the once-hopeful Curtis had lost faith in the possibility of any effective result. "I see no way of uniting even Republicans on any terms of compromise," he wrote.

No member of the Thirty-three offered a plan which caught the national

36 The *Journal* of the Committee of Thirty-three is in 36th Cong. 2d Sess., *House Reports* No. 30. Reuben Davis's statement is in McPherson, *Pol. Hist. Rebellion*, 37.
37 *Committee Journal.*

attention like the Crittenden Compromise; but two distinguished Republicans did present schemes possessing great interest. One was John Sherman. This tall, spare, incisive Ohioan, now closing his third term in the House and about to open a great career in the Senate, had gained increased caution and moderation from his recent defeat as Speaker. He was eager to do anything to sustain the Union short of writing into the Constitution guarantees of the protection and extension of slavery. On December 12 he offered the House a resolution instructing the Committee of Thirty-three to divide all the Territories into States of convenient size with a view to their prompt admission. This would abolish the strife over slavery in the Territories by simply abolishing the Territories themselves. As they became States, the slavery issue would be settled by constitutional conventions and legislatures. Sherman's scheme quickly dropped into oblivion, but not before he had published a burning appeal to reason. The burden of his message was that the country could never huckster into fragments its nationality, its flag, its history.

"Disunion is war!" he wrote. He would not threaten it; he would indeed do almost anything to prevent it; but what honest man could deny that it would be inevitable? "If war results, what a war it will be! Contemplate the North and South in hostile array against each other. If these sections do not know each other *now*, they will *then*."

Still more striking was the role played by Charles Francis Adams. As a veteran observer of affairs, Adams was convinced that South Carolina and other cotton States were determined to erect a separate confederacy, and that nothing could stop them. The all-important object, he believed, was to hold Virginia, Maryland, Kentucky, and the other border States which stood shivering on the brink of secession. For this purpose, he would go to the outer verge of conciliation, standing firm only on principle. He felt certain that when a generous conciliatory offer was made to the cotton kingdom men, they would spurn it; for they meant to have a separate republic, and expand it around the Caribbean. Thus they would openly put themselves in the wrong. The border region, seeing them do so, would cling to the Union. If Virginia, Kentucky, Missouri and the rest could be held for even a year, their people would learn that Lincoln's Administration was fair and mild, and would realize once and for all the folly of secession.

In refusing to countenance the extension of slavery or to offer pledges of its territorial protection Adams, gratified to find Lincoln in full agreement with himself, stood firm as Monadnock. He would not affront the spirit of nineteenth century civilization by doing in 1860 what the nation's founders had refused to do in 1787. Delivering a trenchant speech to the Committee on December 20, he made it plain that he would prefer civil war to any such surrender. But he had a positive program to urge; a program which he shared with Henry Winter Davis, the handsome and eloquent Marylander. Both believed that everything depended on holding Virginia, Maryland, and other border States; both unhesitatingly opposed the Crittenden resolution; both saw that if they rejected the Crittenden proposals, they had to make an offer of their own.

The resulting Adams-Davis plan, hammered out—apparently with some aid from Seward—in protracted caucuses of Republican members of the Committee December 21–26, had for its central feature a bold proposal for the immediate admission of New Mexico (including present-day Arizona) as a State, letting her people decide for or against slavery. Adams waved aside all suggestions for giving statehood to the area north of 36° 30′; it was understood that Kansas must soon come in as a free State, but he believed that the rest of the region was unready. New Mexico, he argued, was the only area sufficiently populated to become a State, and the only area where slavery was an issue. At first most Republicans were shocked by the suggested admission of New Mexico, and Seward told Adams that party members on the Committee of Thirteen opposed it. Before long, however, they realized that the step was as adroit as it was bold.

In the caucus discussions of December 24–25 Adams and Davis explained that their plan had one advantage which was not visible at first glance. Whereas New Mexico, with her slave code, might enter the Union as a slave State, she must soon become free. Her terrain, climate, products, and traditions were hostile to slavery. Though peonage unhappily flourished there, slavery had never gained a real foothold. On the 25th John S. Watts of New Mexico, a former Federal judge of nine years' residence in the Territory, soon to become its Delegate in Congress, explained that slavery was impossible. His clear and decided testimony converted most of the Republicans. As Senator Crittenden privately said, the admission of New Mexico would simply give the Union another free State!

And Southerners perceived this too. When the proposal was introduced in the Committee, slave State members were as startled as if a bomb had exploded. They whispered nervously together, withdrew into an adjoining room to consult, and finally came back to announce that they could not entertain the plan. The Republicans were accepting the main part of Crittenden's proposal; they were offering the South a delusive possibility of one more slave State; but they were adamant against permitting slavery in "lands hereafter to be acquired" south of 36° 30′. The Adams-Davis plan thus cut through the nascent alliance between the border States and the cotton States as with a Saladin blade. It was acceptable to the former, repugnant to the latter. Miles Taylor of Louisiana and Warren Winslow of North Carolina, both extremists, announced that if the road was barred against slavery in lands thereafter acquired south of 36° 30′, they would no longer vote in Committee. When the Committee passed the New

Mexican proposal twelve to ten, only one slave State member, F. M. Bristow of Kentucky, voted alongside Adams and Davis for it.

These two adroit leaders could say they had compelled Southerners to admit that they did not want New Mexico as a new State. More than that, they had exposed some Southern members—in full view of the borderland—as willing to break up the Union because the Committee would not guarantee slavery in areas which the nation did not yet possess!

Early January found the Committee of Thirty-three so thin, because of Southern abstentions, that it could hardly keep a quorum. It found the rising excitement North and South powerfully affecting the body. Such Northern radicals as Sumner and Preston King had been painfully fearful that Adams might yield too much. Indeed, Sumner displayed a vindictive temper which made his associates feel that he looked forward to civil war almost with grim complacency. Meanwhile, Southern fire-eaters were equally fearful lest their Representatives concede too much. It is not strange that in the end the Committee wrote a record of too little, too lukewarm, and too late.

The Committee meeting on January 14 presented a remarkable spectacle. With twenty-nine members present (Houston of Alabama had seceded with his State), the body was unwilling to act either for or against the pending set of resolutions. No majority could be found to pass them; no majority could be found for adjournment without a report. Rust of Arkansas wished the Committee to break up without result, but was impotent to bring this about; other members wished to carry certain resolutions, and were equally impotent. Finally, Millson of Virginia offered a resolution directing Chairman Corwin to report the main proposals with his own opinions upon them. When this was carried 16 to 13, the Committee was left without responsibility, yet its chief suggestions were brought before the nation.[38]

In accordance with this resolution, Tom Corwin at once reported to the House, in addition to a series of declaratory resolutions, five specific "propositions." The first, which called for a repeal of personal liberty laws and a faithful execution of the Fugitive Slave Act, was passed by the House on February 27, 1861, by a vote of 137 to 53. The second, a constitutional amendment, providing that the Constitution should never be altered in such a way as to abolish or interfere with the domestic institutions of any State, including slavery, was carried in the House on February 28 by a vote of 133 to 65, and in the Senate on March 2 by 24 to 12. The third proposition, for the immediate

38 See John Sherman's letter in Rachel Sherman Thorndike, ed., *The Sherman Letters,* 92–104; McPherson, *Pol. Hist. Rebellion,* 52–62; *Committee Journal;* Henry Adams, "Secession Winter," Mass. Hist. Soc. Proc., XLIII, 674 ff.; W. C. Ford, ed., *Henry Adams Letters, 1858–1891;* Charles Francis Adams, Jr., *Autobiography.* For a fuller and kindlier view of Sumner, see Laura White's paper in the *W. E. Dodd Essays.*

admission of New Mexico, was defeated 115 to 71, though a number of Republicans, including Charles Francis Adams, Roscoe Conkling, and Eli Thayer, supported it. The fourth, granting to fugitive slaves a jury trial in the State from which they had fled, passed the House alone by the close vote of 92 to 83. Finally, the fifth proposition, to strengthen extradition procedure—an echo of Harper's Ferry—was decisively rejected.

It was the constitutional amendment which was most important; a self-denying amendment, which in theory would forever have chained the country in dealing with slavery inside the States. That it should have received sixty-six Republican and Opposition votes in the House, including those of Adams, Colfax, Corwin, Morrill, and John Sherman, and nine Republican or Opposition votes in the Senate, was a striking fact.

Nevertheless, when Corwin's report was submitted on January 14, Charles Francis Adams struck a pessimistic note. He stated in a separate document his melancholy conviction that no adjustment would suit the recusant States which did not fix in the Constitution an obligation to protect and extend slavery; that on this condition alone would they recognize the constitutional election of Lincoln. "He can never," he wrote, "give his consent to the terms demanded." [39] Six other minority reports were submitted. Inasmuch as, at the end, a considerable number of cotton kingdom members had systematically absented themselves from the Committee, the so-called majority report really emanated from a minority. Chairman Corwin was as bleakly discouraged as Adams. Ten days after the document went in, he wrote Lincoln that his month of toil had been a sad revelation.

"If the States are no more harmonious in their feelings and opinions than these thirty-three representative men," he wrote,[40] "then, appalling as the idea is, we must dissolve, and a long and bloody war must follow. I cannot comprehend the madness of the times. Southern men are theoretically crazy. Extreme Northern men are practical fools. The latter are really quite as mad as the former. Treason is in the air around us everywhere. . . . God alone, I fear, can help us."

But if these men were gloomily certain that the cotton kingdom could not be halted, they and Seward rejoiced that the borderland yet stood loyal, and hoped that with its aid the Union could yet be restored.

[VII]

It was the border States which, torn in sentiment and fearful of becoming a battleground, watched the drift toward disruption and war with the most

39 McPherson, *Pol. Hist. Rebellion*, 57.
40 Robert Todd Lincoln Papers.

harrowing anxiety. The Old Dominion, so long the leader in the American sisterhood and so prolific of great men, felt a commingled sorrow and fear of the liveliest character. Governor John Letcher ably expressed this emotion in his message of January 7 to the legislature. He declared it "monstrous to see a government like ours destroyed, merely because men cannot agree about a domestic institution, which existed at the formation of the government." Bitterly rebuking the governors of Mississippi and South Carolina for their disunionist proposals, and sternly indicting the North for its intolerant agitation, he proposed a national Peace Conference. The legislators, attached alike to the South and the Union, immediately took up the subject. On January 19, they invited all the States to send delegates to a convention which should meet in Washington on February 4, and whose members, with the Crittenden Compromise as a basis for discussion, should strive earnestly to adjust the unhappy controversy.

Thus was born the last sad effort to avert war. The gathering opened on the appointed date with a highly distinguished but somewhat superannuated roster of delegates.[41] John Tyler, who presided, David Wilmot, William C. Rives, Caleb B. Smith, Stephen T. Logan, and Thomas Ewing, with a number of others, belonged too plainly to the past. The New York *Herald* remarked that many of them were political fossils who would not have been disinterred but for the shock given the country by the crisis. They began by excluding reporters, which was wise, for the speechmaking was diffuse and aimless. The seven States of the Lower South, with Arkansas, boycotted the gathering; they were busy forming their Confederacy, and they thought compromise a game to hoodwink the border area. Michigan, Wisconsin, and Minnesota, with the two Pacific Coast States, were also unrepresented. This left twenty-one States with delegates. Republican radicals scoffed at the "venerable" conclave and predicted its total failure. According to John Bigelow, some of these radicals had a double object in their opposition: to prevent the adoption of anything like the Crittenden Compromise, and to keep Seward out of the Cabinet by discrediting the compromise idea.

A revealing incident illustrated the attitude of Northern extremists toward this gathering. The Michigan Senators were at first opposed to the participation of their State in the Conference; but both of them, on February 9, telegraphed the governor to send delegates. They did this on the ground that moderate members of the assemblage seemed likely to gain the day, and that more obstructionists were needed. "I hope you will send *stiff-backed* men or none," Zack Chandler wrote the governor on the eleventh, callously adding

41 For the Proceedings of the Peace Convention see L. E. Chittenden, ed., *Report of the Peace Convention*.

that he had no patience with those who were afraid of civil strife: "Without a little bloodletting, this Union will not, in my estimation, be worth a rush." This cynical letter Jefferson Davis was later to reprint in his memoirs—forgetting how many fiery Southerners were speaking in similar terms.

The dark prophecies of failure, although Rives, Reverdy Johnson, and former Secretary of the Treasury James Guthrie made strenuous exertions, were in the end fully realized. Such radicals as J. A. Seddon of Virginia, David Wilmot of Pennsylvania, and Lot M. Morrill of Maine did their utmost to obstruct the gathering. It was in vain that Rives made an eloquent appeal. "Virginia steps in to arrest the progress of the country on its road to ruin," he said. "I have seen the pavements of Paris covered . . . with fraternal blood! God forbid that I should see this horrid picture repeated in my own country. . . ." Ex-President Tyler told the delegates that they had a task as grand as that of the godlike fathers. "If you reach the height of this great occasion, your children's children will rise up and call you blessed." But it was all too late. The absence of thirteen States was too great a handicap; the fact that the convention possessed nothing but a thin moral authority was too evident; and the clash of radicals from each side was too savage. In the last days of the Buchanan Administration, the Conference agreed to resolutions resembling the abortive Crittenden plan. When they were laid before a Senate committee, that body rejected them 28 to 7,[42] while the House on March 1 refused to suspend its rules in order to consider them.

Virginia was the mother of the Peace Conference. Yet in the final House discussions five Virginia Congressmen opposed the plan it offered, and only three gave it support. It was an ironic fact that the failure of the gathering lent added strength to secession in Virginia.

All along the line, in the Senate, the House, and in Tyler's conclave of minor statesmen, efforts at compromise had proved futile. Had a Constitutional Convention, with the very ablest leaders of the nation in charge, been convoked at an early date, it is barely possible that the story might have been different. As matters stood, lovers of the Union could comfort themselves in February, 1861, with only one major consideration—the fact that although seven slaveholding States were leaving in anger, eight remained. In Virginia, Tennessee, Arkansas, Missouri, and North Carolina, the secessionist forces had thus far met repulse. The boasted Southern Confederacy was as yet but a fragment of the South. This fact gave encouragement to those who believed that the Union might yet be peaceably reconstructed on a sounder basis. Even in the cotton kingdom, this belief was still cherished by many. Jefferson Davis has recorded that a considerable number of men as late as February held the

42 The Senate action is in *Cong. Globe*, 36th Cong. 2d Sess., 1254, 1255.

hope, which he pronounced not unreasonable, that by the offer of suitable guarantees the North would make possible a reunited nation. Seward, a firm believer in voluntary reconstruction, looked at the matter a little differently. Young Henry Adams found him early in February in high spirits, chuckling himself hoarse with his stories. "He says it's all right. We shall keep the border States, and in three months or thereabouts, if we hold off, the Unionists and Disunionists will have their hands on each other's throats in the cotton States."

The realities, reflected in the drill of volunteer companies North and South, were far darker than these views indicated. Later generations find it hard to believe that many Southerners, like Judah P. Benjamin, thought that the North might actually agree to reconstruct the Union with the New England States thrust into outer darkness. They find it hard to believe that many Northerners, including Lincoln and Seward, indulged the fantasy that Southern Unionists might actually overpower by force of arms the Southern secessionists. It is depressing to recall with what continued levity many men spoke of civil war. The New York *Tribune*, on February 21, declared that if conflict came: "It would only be necessary for the Government of the North to concentrate at New York a small fleet of seagoing steamers and an army of 20,000 to 30,000 men to hold the entire South in perpetual check." Edmund Ruffin had written in the Richmond *Index* of January 13 that there was "not the slightest danger of war from the Northern States," for they could not win such a contest "without the sacrifice of fifty thousand lives of the Northern invaders, and one hundred million of dollars." From such fantastic misconceptions of the situation, self-deluded men in both great sections were to have a swift and harsh awakening.

14

The Rival Republic

WHILE COMPROMISE was grinding to a standstill, the dramatic process of creating a new Southern republic was attracting general attention. It might be viewed with all the eager hope of Yancey or Toombs, with the amused cynicism of W. H. Russell, the British correspondent who travelled to Montgomery to witness its birth, or the scornful hostility of Sumner, Wade, and countless other Northerners. But that it was an event of the first magnitude, none could doubt. It was necessarily built upon the completion of secession in the Lower South.

[I]

Mid-January found Milledgeville, on the Oconee River in central Georgia, filling up with delegates for the State convention. The eyes of most Southerners were fixed on the gathering, for the adherence of Georgia was essential to sectional unity. Jacob Thompson was writing Howell Cobb: "I have all along felt that as goes Georgia, so goes the whole South." The little town, with its capital, its cluster of four substantial churches, and its handsome residences, for it was much liked by wealthy Georgians, was soon crammed to bursting. One visitor, secretly a correspondent for the New York *Tribune*, found himself in such an incessant jostle that he dared take no written notes. On Tuesday the fifteenth, the two camps, the separate secessionists and co-operative secessionists, held caucuses and anxiously counted noses. During the next two days, crowded galleries watched the convention elect officers, give the South Carolina and Alabama commissioners a hearing, and do other preliminary work. Then a seal of secrecy was clapped on the session. Nothing could be picked up, grumbled newspapermen, but a few crumbs moistened by the prevailing whiskey.[1]

The tide of popular feeing in Georgia had been setting steadily toward an early abandonment of the Union. Alexander H. Stephens had written at the

1 N. Y. *Weekly Tribune*, February 2, 1861.

close of November that while large numbers would sustain his conservative position, the odds were against them. It was all too true, he thought, that most leading Georgians did not wish to remain on any terms. "They do not wish any redress of wrongs; they are disunionists *per se,* and avail themselves of present circumstances to press their objects; and my present conviction is that they will carry the State with them by a large majority." He kept reiterating these despondent statements.[2] Howell Cobb's long argument for secession issued simultaneously with his resignation had much effect; so did Toombs's public letter in the Savannah *Republican* of December 17, and his admonition to Georgians just before Christmas to thunder secession from the ballot box. The two men differed on one point, Cobb wishing secession immediately and Toombs preferring it on March 4; but on the need for a severance they stood together.

The election of delegates on January 2, held as a terrible storm smote Georgia, apparently resulted in a decisive victory for the separate secessionists. Only about two-thirds of the voters went to the polls and their verdict was roughly four to three for immediate action. Stephens, who struggled through the storm to vote and make a speech, believed that the weather had cost his side ten thousand ballots, for it favored the town dwellers and planters who had the best means of getting to the polls. "It really appears as if Providence was on the other side," he ejaculated.[3] As he prepared to leave for the convention, he wrote his brother that he had known for weeks that secession was certain, for the currents of the day were irresistible.

Yet the convention battle between the advocates of immediate and of postponed secession proved closer than had been anticipated. The gathering was one of remarkable ability. The radical leaders included Toombs, T. R. R. Cobb, and Francis S. Bartow, along with Governor Joseph E. Brown and Howell Cobb, who were invited to seats on the floor; the cooperationist leaders were Stephens, his brother Linton, Benjamin H. Hill, and Herschel V. Johnson. The latter group were handicapped by the lack of any preconcerted plan of action, by an old enmity between Stephens and Hill, and by the defeatist temper of Stephens. When the ordinance of secession was offered, Hill offered a substitute plan which Johnson had hurriedly drawn up. This series of resolutions declared the South in danger, proposed a convention of slaveholding

2 Cleveland, *Stephen,* 159, 160; Johnston and Browne, *Stephens,* 369 ff.

3 Johnston and Browne, *op. cit.,* 378, 379. Election figures vary; one set is 50,243 for immediate-action delegates and 37,123 for cooperationists. Pendleton, *Stephens,* 178. It should be noted that group attitudes were complex. The cooperationists included (1) those who wanted immediate secession but only by united State action; (2) those who wished to attempt compromise, and secede only when that failed; (3) those who desired to await an overt act of aggression by Lincoln before seceding; and (4) strict Unionists playing for delay. For a full elucidation see Dumond, *Secession Movement,* 113 ff.

States at Atlanta the next month, suggested some needed amendments to the Constitution, and deferred Georgia's decision until the North could be given an opportunity to reply. The substitute was lost 164 to 133. A change of but sixteen votes in the total of two hundred and ninety-seven would have reversed the result. Hill and others then joined in passing the secession ordinance 208 to 89, and all but half a dozen delegates signed it.[4]

Analysis of the vote showed that, like other Southern States, Georgia divided largely on economic and regional lines. The radical secessionists came from the Savannah River valley, the seacoast, and the tier of counties behind it, extending into southwest Georgia. Here dwelt most of the wealthy planters and large slaveholders. The townspeople, whether in Savannah, Augusta, Columbus, Macon, or Atlanta, were predominantly sympathetic with the planting interest. They included the merchants and factors who handled cotton and merchandise, the professional men who sprang largely from the planter class, and many retired or absentee landholders. It was noteworthy that all fifteen of the delegates from these five cities were immediate secessionists. On the conservative side, the great strongholds were, as we have noted, the pine barrens and the northern hill country. Here lived a population of small farmers, stockmen, and others with a pioneering tradition, whose immediate forebears had conquered the wilderness and fought the Indians. They liked the Union; their instinct was for the doctrines of Jackson, not Calhoun; they had little direct interest in slavery; and their concern for a peculiar Southern culture was slighter still. While exceptions to these generalizations were numerous, the convention decision was broadly a victory of plantation and town over the small farmer.[5]

When secession was announced, Milledgeville sprang into a spasm of illuminations, bonfires, Roman candles, cannon salutes, and speechmaking. Yet many were heavy-hearted. "I never felt so sad before," Herschel Johnson later wrote. "The clustering glories of the past thronged my memory, but they were darkened by the gathering gloom of the lowering future."[6] Georgia's action was widely regarded as decisive for the whole Lower South. With her great production of cotton, wheat, corn, and rice, her flourishing seaport of Savannah, her textile factories, her key railroad system, and her energetic population, the State was vital to a new republic. The step was described then

<hr>

4 A. D. Candler, ed., Confed. Records of Ga., I, 213 ff.; I. W. Avery, Hist. Ga., 149 ff.; Hill, Joseph E. Brown, 44, 45; Pearce, B. H. Hill, 49–53.

5 A. J. Cole, "Sentiment in Ga. Toward Secession, 1850–61," MS, Univ. of Ill.

6 Flippin, Johnson, 192. Johnson always thought that "a fair and energetic canvass" would have shown a large majority of Georgians against secession; he always believed that ambitious Southern leaders wanted disunion as a means of establishing their personal power. Idem. 168–170.

and thereafter as one that electrified the cotton kingdom and determined the revolution; and while this is an overstatement, it is certain that it cleared up a great area of doubt and hesitation.

The Lower South was now swiftly completing its withdrawal from the Union. Already, on January 9, the Mississippi convention, sitting at Jackson, had passed its secession ordinance 84 to 15. On the tenth, Florida had followed, 62 to 7. On the eleventh the Alabama convention, its temper fired by Yancey, the Patrick Henry of the new cause, had decided upon withdrawal by a vote of 61 to 39. The Louisiana convention passed its secession ordinance on January 26 by a vote of 113 to 17, and on February 1 Texas took the same step, 166 to 8. Seven States were not as many as Ruffin and Yancey had hoped for, but they were regarded as sufficient for a viable new confederation.

[II]

On their face, the heavy convention majorities for secession seemed to point to an overwhelming disunionist strength. Actually, however, in every State the division of opinion ran deep, the forces opposing immediate secession were formidable, and, while the question defies settlement, perhaps a majority of citizens were Union men in the sense that they opposed secession altogether, or wished it deferred until other remedies had been exhausted, or hoped for a reconstruction of the nation on better terms within a few years. Certainly in the fifteen slave States taken as a whole, a heavy majority were against a permanent severance of ties. The apparently crushing victory of the immediate secessionists in the Lower South was accomplished by skillful use of the advantages before enumerated; their driving energy, superior organization, success in making action so rapid that the opposition could not mobilize, effective use of shibboleths and epithets, and capitalization on the demand for moral unity. They were aided in some States by favorable apportionment systems, and in nearly all by the excessive influence wielded by the planting class and its various allies.[7]

Public opinion in every such crisis necessarily moves like a great pendulum, gathering momentum. It was inevitable that the bright vision of a Southern republic should catch the imagination of multitudes of men and women. The spirit of nationalism, with its heady, volatile appeals—to traditionalism, to ancestral reverence, to folklore, to pieties of hearth and home, to the ideal of sacrifice—and its demand that the individual lose himself in a mass solidarity,

7 On this insoluble problem of the real sentiment of Southerners toward secession, see Potter, *Lincoln and Secession Crisis*, 208 ff.; Rhodes, *United States*, III, 273 ff.; Dumond, *Secession Movement*, Ch. X.

had already made impressive progress. As volunteer companies marched to the "Southern Marseillaise," as crowds began singing "The Bonnie Blue Flag," as slogans of freedom and justice ran through the press, a kindling sense of sectional patriotism swung even the dubious from their old allegiances. To join the new movement seemed (especially to youth) an affirmative, progressive, heroic act; to resist it seemed negative and timid. Every day, militancy grew. And as one step after another was taken, more doubters yielded to State loyalty, and to their feeling that the hard-pressed Southern people must at all hazards stand together.

All the standard agencies for moulding opinion were brought to bear upon conservatives. In Mississippi, for example, the Jackson *Mississippian*, Vicksburg *Sun*, and Natchez *Free Trader*, with other newspapers, spoke of moderation as a policy of imbecility, of delay as abject submission, and of Union men as enemies of the South. Many churches throughout the cotton kingdom preached resistance. The Thanksgiving sermons of the Rev. B. M. Palmer, head of the largest Presbyterian church in New Orleans, and the Rev. W. T. Leacock, his Episcopal colleague, two stirring exhortations to secession which were scattered broadcast in pamphlet form, were long remembered. "I warn my countrymen the historic moment once passed never returns," rumbled Palmer. "Sapped, circumvented, undermined, the institutions of your soil will be overthrown; and within five and twenty years the history of San Domingo will be the record of Louisiana." [8] The official journal of the powerful Baptist denomination in Mississippi urged citizens to insist upon their full rights within the old nation, or win them outside in a new.[9]

Plangent effects were produced by a steady reiteration of inflammatory news items from Washington and other centers. The Congressional leaders of secession had long been in close touch with the Washington correspondents of Southern newspapers, and many of the fire-eaters knew the art of manufacturing and coloring press intelligence. Many Southern editors, for their part, made a one-sided selection of the news. "Every morning for the past three or four weeks," complained A. H. Arthur of Vicksburg on January 10 to Joseph Holt,

---

[8] The two sermons were printed together in "The Rights of the South Defended in the Pulpits," and were notable for their violent tone. Palmer declared that it was the South's duty under God "to conserve and perpetuate the institution of domestic slavery as now existing," and that "the abolition spirit is undeniably atheistic." Leacock was even fiercer. Who could hesitate, he asked, "when we consider the treatment we have received from the hands of our enemies; our character they have defamed; our feelings they have lacerated; our rights they have invaded; our property they have stolen; our power they have defied; our existence they have threatened? Murderers and robbers have been let loose upon us, stimulated by weak or designing or infidel preachers, armed by fanatics, and sustained by a band of assassins out of the very wealth which they have accumulated by their connection with us."

[9] *Mississippi Baptist*, cited in Rainwater, *Mississippi*, 173, 174.

"we have been inundated with fresh dispatches from your region to keep up the courage of the leaders at home, and still further inflame the public mind." A week later another of Holt's correspondents, J. O. Harrison of New Orleans, wrote that the South was flooded with dispatches describing the unjust and coercive policy of the government. Censorship and intimidation meanwhile suppressed much news favorable to the cause of compromise and the Union. One Southerner after another, hearing indirectly of Andrew Johnson's great Union speech but unable to find any of it in the press, wrote him for copies, and spoke bitterly of the suppression of facts and opinion.

The companies of minute men, too, placing graybeards alongside striplings, were active propagandist agencies. State flags and badges helped win the wavering. When in Eufaula, Alabama, an enthusiastic lady flung from her window a banner of fifteen stars and fifteen stripes, the Eufaula Rifles promptly paraded and fired a fifteen-volley salute.[10] Such incidents were incessant and they had a cumulative effect.

In some areas, the secessionists frankly capitalized upon the illiteracy or apathy of the many voters who, as Helper and others had noted, knew all too little of public measures. In South Carolina, one radical exulted that ignorance played into the hands of his party. Secession had to be achieved by a select minority, he wrote. "I do not believe that the common people understand it; in fact I know that they do not understand it. . . . We must make the move and force them to follow." [11] The use of threats was not infrequent. Senator Iverson set a bad example when he suggested that the loyal Sam Houston was a Caesar who might yet find his Brutus. A Georgia secessionist, speaking of such men as the Stephens brothers, growled: "When the State goes out and we are on our own hook, those fellows will have to walk straight and keep quiet." The Savannah correspondent of the New York *Tribune* wrote in December that conservatives did not dare express their views with any force and warmth. A wealthy planter had confessed that he would be ejected from the State if he spoke his mind. "For," he said, "when a man once falls under the hand of the mob, though they only threaten him today, they will doubtless return tomorrow and burn his property, and the next day they will bring a rope with them." [12]

The extremists have taken our positions by storm, lamented one conservative of the Lower South. Nevertheless, Stephens was unjust in asserting that the people had run mad, and were "wild with passion and frenzy, doing they know not what." [13] The number who struggled to the last for delay, or yielded

10 Denman, *Secession in Alabama*, 89.
11 A. P. Aldrich, November 25, 1860; Hammond Papers.
12 *Weekly Tribune*, January 19, 1861.
13 Johnston and Browne, *Stephens*, 369, 370.

in the hope that the Union could yet be rebuilt, was formidable. Just how equivocal the character of the decision really was in some States will become evident from a brief examination of the secession struggle.

[III]

Although the Louisiana convention voted more than six to one for immediate departure, the true will of the people must always remain in doubt, for this result was attained by highly undemocratic means. The State had obvious reasons for exhibiting caution. It was closely linked with the Northwest by the commerce rolling up and down the Mississippi. Through the port of New Orleans passed every year a hundred million dollars' worth of cotton, and sixty-five millions in corn, wheat, pork, and other products; while importers distributed merchandise of all kinds through the upper valley. Enjoying an unprecedented prosperity, Louisiana feared that she would be separated from her rich Northern connections, and that a new nation built on slavery would foster the commerce of Norfolk, Charleston, and Savannah at her expense. Just after the election, Douglas, visiting New Orleans, spread a long letter in the press. Regrettable as Lincoln's election was, he wrote, it had been gained by constitutional means and offered no ground for secession; while the Democratic majority in both houses and the Democratic control of the Supreme Court rendered the new President powerless for evil, even if he had the disposition. This letter had attentive readers. A prominent citizen wrote that he believed that ninety-nine in a hundred people sincerely hoped for some adjustment to end the national dissension.[14]

The widespread notion that Louisiana was exclusively a land of opulent sugar and cotton plantations was a myth. More than two-thirds of the free population owned no slaves; three out of five agricultural holdings were farms; almost a third of all the cultivated land was tilled in units of less than a hundred acres.[15] Our best evidence is that the slavery system was economically injurious to a majority of the population. "Farmers were actually hurt by slavery and the plantation economy, which gradually deprived them of all opportunity to acquire Negroes and fertile land, or to participate on a large scale in the production of profitable staples."[16] The State had cast a much larger vote for the Bell and Douglas tickets combined than for Breckinridge.[17]

Yet the secessionists, directed by Slidell and his creature Governor Moore,

14 Quoted in *Ann. Cyc.*, 1861, p. 428.
15 *U. S. Census, 1860, Agriculture*, 202 ff.
16 Shugg, *Origins of Class Struggle in La.*, 78, 79; but F. L. Owsley and others dissent.
17 The figures were Breckenridge, 22,687; Bell 20,205; Douglas 7,625.

managed to carry everything before them. They did everything possible to stimulate disunionist sentiment. When South Carolina went out, they fired a hundred guns in New Orleans and displayed the pelican flag. Moore quickly summoned the legislature, dominated by the planter oligarchy and its allies of the New Orleans machine. Seats in this body were apportioned on the basis of total population, including slaves, so that the black belt of rich alluvial land and big plantations held a clear majority, while the white belt, with two-thirds of the free population, was in a minority. The system was one in which property, rather than white people, ruled the State.[18] On December 11, the legislators called for a State convention to be elected less than four weeks later, on January 7. Although the constitution stipulated that a referendum be held on the question of any such convention, this requirement was ignored; for the times, said the radicals, were too revolutionary.

Fraud was an old story in Louisiana elections, and this one seemed no better than others. To the last, the conservatives had hoped to carry the twenty-five delegates of New Orleans. Instead, it was announced that the city had gone for the immediate secessionists by a plurality of three hundred and eighty in a total vote of eight thousand three hundred and thirty-six—about half of the registration; while the whole State had elected eighty-three immediate secessionists against forty-seven cooperationists. Rumors sprang up that the cooperationists had really carried Louisiana by about three hundred votes. When the *Picayune*, which held that the separate secession of one State was a species of dictation to her Southern sisters, insistently demanded publication of the official returns, they were kept suppressed. Not until more than three months had passed and the whole subject had become academic, was the New Orleans *Delta* allowed to publish a tabulation of parish votes, and this was in a form which aroused suspicion of manipulation.[19]

The convention, meeting just after Governor Moore had seized the national forts and arsenals on his own authority, was as much under the sway of the planter oligarchy as the legislature; and it acted in what the historian Gayarré called a spirit of "sublime imprudence." [20] An effort to refer secession to a general Southern convention was defeated 73 to 47. An attempt to obtain a

18 For full treatment of representation, see Shugg, *Class Struggle*, 139 ff. The MS Diary of Alexander F. Pugh (Univ. of Texas Library) gives a good picture of the secessionist sentiment of one wealthy Louisiana planter. He thought that to ask cooperation was "humiliating;" January 9, 1861. The Liddell Papers, La. Univ. Library, contain letters showing how leaders of the planting interest worked for concert of action, and how confident they were that a few men could take control.

19 *Picayune*, January 8, et seq.; Shugg, *Class Struggle*, 162 ff. The city vote was given as 4,358 to 3,978; the State vote as 20,448 to 17,296. The N. O. *Picayune* had anticipated fraud. It stated on November 6 that the radical leaders were thoroughly ruthless, and frequently repeated this warning.

20 *Hist. La.*, IV, 692.

plebiscite on the secession ordinance was then voted down 84 to 43,[21] The majority displayed a joyous insouciance which depressed such of its own members as Richard Taylor.[22] A scrutiny of the convention vote and of the parish returns shows that, although no class voted as a unit, the wealthier slaveholding parishes were strongest for immediate action, while the small farmers elected most of the cooperationists. In Louisiana, as in South Carolina, the long-established domination of a planting and commercial aristocracy had made it easy to take the State out of the Union; not as part of a conspiracy, but by the use of powers always exercised when the economic, social, and political philosophy of the ruling group was imperilled.[23]

In Alabama we encounter a different pattern, and the victory of the immediate secessionists was more fairly won; yet the result was exceedingly close. North Alabama took a firm stand for delay, and won supporters in other areas. Had it not been for unexpected reverses in Mobile and Autauga Counties, the cooperationists would actually have gained control of the State convention. The outcome in Mobile was particularly remarkable. Although that county had given both Douglas and Bell much larger votes than Breckinridge, immediate secession gained the day nearly two to one. In this State, as in Louisiana, the vote for convention delegates was only seventy or seventy-five percent that given in the recent presidential election. A good deal of confusion enveloped the precise stand taken by some candidates, and the returns are not complete; but the radicals seem to have polled about 35,700 votes to the conservatives' 28,200, and the delegates stood fifty-four for immediate secession, forty-six for cooperative action. On the theory that conservative men were more likely to stay at home than the radicals, a full vote might have given them the victory.[24]

And the convention battle proved sternly exciting. Ex-Senator Jeremiah Clemens helped lead the cooperationist minority.[25] It showed such a stubborn

21 The *Picayune* had insistently asked for a referendum, but the *Delta* and *Crescent* replied that in such a crisis questions of form sank into insignificance.

22 Taylor, *Destruction and Reconstruction*, 13. Yet the *Picayune* had steadily warned of impending agony. It had said as early as November 4: "If the fires of civil war be kindled—and kindled they must be by any formidable movement in hostility to the Federal Government—they will burn until all is consumed that is perishable, and the land becomes a waste over which shall brood the silence of another and hopeless desolation."

23 Cf. Shugg, *Class Struggle*, 169.

24 It is roughly fair to say that of the fifty-two counties represented in the convention, twenty-nine were for immediate secession, twenty-three for some type of delay. The Montgomery *Weekly Post* of January 9, 1861, accused Governor Moore of taking high-handed steps, including seizure of the national forts, suspension of specie payments, and sending of commissioners to other States, in order to hurry Alabama into secession.

25 The cooperationists, discovering they were only eight fewer than the immediate secessionists, issued a public statement that Yancey could save the State for the Union by a wave of his hand; but of course Yancey's intention was just the opposite. On the first day, he and a longtime opponent, Thomas H. Watts, walked to the platform arm in arm, a token of unity against Northern "oppression." See G. M. Wrenn, "Ala. and the Formation of the Confederacy," Univ. of Texas Library.

spirit that Yancey, losing his temper, declared that any resistance to an ordinance of secession would be treason to the State. Nicholas J. Davis of Hunts-

VOTES FOR DELEGATES TO THE SECESSION CONVENTION

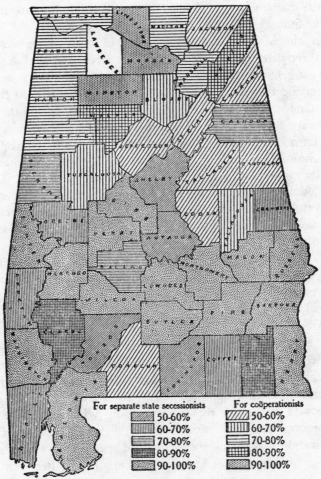

Cherokee County divided—three delegates for coöperation and one for separate state secession. No returns available for Lawrence County other than that a coöperationist delegate was elected.

Opinion in Alabama

ville, a Douglas man, instantly defied him. His constituents, he said, denied the sovereignty of the convention because of the way in which it had been called; they would sustain it only if it reflected the popular will, and the way to ascertain that was to hold a plebiscite on secession. He and his people were ready to meet Yancey at the foot of their mountains and settle this question of treason with the bayonet. In the end, the effort to refer secession to a general Southern convention to be held at Nashville on Washington's Birthday and the effort to gain a popular referendum on the subject were both voted down. But a change of a mere half dozen votes would have defeated the immediate secessionists in Yancey's own State.[26]

Moreover, the Alabama decision left great bitterness in its wake. No fewer than thirty-three delegates out of the hundred refused to sign the ordinance of secession on the ground that the State had not been allowed to consult her sisters before acting, and that the measure had not been submitted to the people for ratification. One county burned Yancey in effigy.[27] "In South Carolina the people have very little to do in politics but choose their own masters," angrily exploded Thomas M. Peters of Moulton, Alabama, in a letter of January 15 to Andrew Johnson. "And outside of South Carolina in the Cotton States politicians are trying the experiment of getting along without the people. Thus far they have succeeded. But in the end, unless we resort to a military government, there will be a revulsion, and as the Negro is the sole cause of our present troubles, the fury of the non-slaveholders will be turned on him and his masters; and we will have another tragedy of Actaeon and his dogs."

In Florida and Mississippi, by contrast, large secessionist majorities were obtained. The leading figures in Florida affairs were Senator Yulee, wealthy planter and railroad promoter, and Governor Perry, both warm secessionists. The State had been easily carried by Breckinridge. Immediately on Lincoln's election, nearly all the Democratic newspapers called for the disruption of the Union and the formation of a Southern Confederacy. When the legislature met, Perry appealed for separation from the faithless, perjured States of the North, and a convention bill passed both houses unanimously. One old Jacksonian, General Richard K. Call, opposed hasty action and distributed in pamphlet form a passionate address to the State, pleading with the people to await an overt act of wrong. The convention, however, sitting at Tallahassee, voted down a series of amendments which were designed merely to keep Florida waiting until the action of Georgia and Alabama was certain, and then formally seceded.

26 W. R. Smith, *Hist. and Debates of the Ala. Convention, passim.*
27 Hugh Lawson Clay of Huntsville had written C. C. Clay on January 11 that northern Alabama was ready to revolt. A meeting there had instructed the delegates to leave the convention if secession was not submitted to popular vote; one leader had made a violent speech, denouncing secession, assailing Governor Moore, and saying he "would have his neck stretched three feet and spend his money to the last dollar before he would consent to the dismemberment of the Union." Clay felt certain that "there will be a successful attempt made to excite the people of N. Alabama to rebellion vs. the State and that we will have civil war in our midst." Clay Papers, Duke Univ. Library. Cf. W. R. Smith, *Hist. and Debates,* 445–447; Denman, *Secession in Ala.,* 149.

According to the St. Augustine *Examiner*, which had recently been moderate, a large majority of the State held that "our grievances are not longer to be tolerated." [28]

In Mississippi also, most leaders were radical in outlook. "The Union is dead and in process of mortification," declared A. G. Brown, "and nothing now remains but to bury the rotten carcass." [29] Only three weeks were allowed in that State for the pre-convention campaign, and many voters learned so little of the issues that, feeling totally confused, they stayed away from the polls. The vote was only about sixty percent of that in the presidential election. About three-fourths of the delegates were immediate secessionists, motions for a special plebiscite and for cooperative action being defeated 74 to 25, and 70 to 29.[30] The gathering, which then voted secession by nearly six to one, was apparently a true reflection of the people: "Entirely representative of the social, economic, and political life of the State," concludes one student. At least three-fifths of the members belonged not to the class of rich planters, but to that of farmers, shopkeepers, and professional men, holding few slaves. In this State even more than in others, the cooperationists were not against secession if other means failed but hoped for an attempt to exhaust these means; they wanted time, as one member said, "for deliberation while we stood on the brink of the abyss."

Some Mississippians, nevertheless, realizing that disunion meant almost certain war, regarded any step on that road with dark foreboding. Two opposing members ventured into prophecy. The able planter-lawyer, James L. Alcorn, recalled many years later: "Judge J. S. Yerger was especially eloquent in picturing the workings of Conscription (which would of necessity be resorted to) upon the non-slaveholding classes of the South. I undertook to give a picture of the South when the Northern soldier would tread her cotton fields; when the slave would be free and the proud Southerner struck to the dust in his presence." [31]

In Texas, behind an outwardly overwhelming decision for immediate separation, we again meet factors which create grave doubt as to the real will of the people. Then, as later, the spirit of Texan life was more largely Western than

28 D. Dodd, "Secession Movt. in Fla., 1850–1861," Pt. II, in *Fla. Hist. Quarterly*, XII, October, 1933; C. M. Brevard, *Florida*, II. Call, who had been territorial governor, published an able letter in the Tallahassee *Sentinel* of December 22, 1860, and tried to hold public meetings.

29 Speech at Jackson in late November; Rainwater, *Mississippi*, 173.

30 *Journal of the State Conv.* (1861), pp. 9, 10.

31 Quoted by Rainwater, *Mississippi*, 213. This author's analysis of economic, geographic, and social factors is illuminating. He finds that many solid, conservative men of property, who had moved from the Whig into the Opposition Party, were against separate secession. The aggressive cutting edge of the secession movement was furnished by the petty planters, the lawyer-politicians, and the country editors, men still on the make. We shall later see a somewhat similar situation in another semi-frontier State, Arkansas.

Southern. The population comprehended a large German element, numerous traders and mechanics from the North, and a heavy sprinkling of stockmen, farmers, and planters of free-State origin. Everyone knew that Texas specially depended for her growth upon Northern capital, immigration from Europe and the North, and Northern mercantile credit. The six hundred and two thousand four hundred and thirty-two people registered by the census this year included the rather modest number of one hundred eighty thousand six hundred and eighty-two slaves. While Lincoln's election was at once followed by an outcry for dissolution of the Union, large moderate groups urged Texans to stand beside the border States in a conservative position. They pointed to the Federal moneys spent to win Texas, to the Federal troops guarding the Indian and Mexican frontiers, and to the millions which the Treasury annually paid Texas stockgrowers and farmers in maintaining defense and communications. The weekly *Alamo Express* of San Antonio predicted "untold evils" from secession, and it was abetted in its stand by the Dallas *Herald*, the Austin *Southern Intelligencer*, the San Antonio *Ledger* and *Herald*, the *Northern Standard*, and the German press.[32]

At the head of the opposition to immediate secession stood the rugged governor, Sam Houston, who for some stormy weeks withstood the demand for a special session of the legislature. When he yielded and called one to meet January 21, it was in terms indicating his desire to delay separate State action as long as possible. His utterances were outspoken. "You may," he said, "after the sacrifice of countless thousands of treasure and hundreds of thousands of precious lives, as a bare possibility, win Southern independence, if God be not against you; but I doubt it."[33] At the outset, the influential John H. Reagan was for cooperative secession, proposing that all the slaveholding States meet in convention, that they submit certain demands (including guarantees of equal Southern participation in the settlement of the common territory) to the free States, and that if these were denied (which he did not expect), they should then secede in a body. Just before Christmas, however, he wrote a public letter announcing that he had reached the conclusion that the North would never give adequate guarantees, and that his chief hope now was for a peaceable separation.[34] Not a few Texans thought of reestablishing a Lone Star republic; and certain of Houston's utterances squinted in that direction. Unlike some other States, he wrote the Alabama commissioner, Texas feels a spirit of imperial expansion, and expects to carry her institutions westward and southward.[35]

32 John H. Reagan also lists the Harrison *Flag*, Quitman *Clipper*, and McKinney *Messenger* among "submission sheets;" letter in *Texas Republican*, January 12, 1861. C. W. Ramsdell's brief treatment of secession in *Reconstruction in Texas* is excellent.
33 Marquis James, *Houston*, 409, 410.
34 December 23, 1860, to O. M. Roberts, et al., in Texas *Republican*.
35 January 7, 1861, to J. M. Calhoun; Smith, *Hist. and Debates*, 425 ff.

Ignoring Houston, many radical leaders had signed a call for a convention to meet in Austin on January 28. At once a violent campaign began. "The whole State was in a blaze of excitement," writes one Union observer. "Arbitrary arrests, broils, murder and hanging were the order of the day, and under the pressure large numbers of Union men were giving way, and the secessionists were receiving daily accessions to their strength. The people were either deceived into secession, led into it, or forced into it." [36] The Knights of the Golden Circle, whose active organizer Bickley was now a resident of Texas, played some small role, later much exaggerated, in the movement.[37] Moral intimidation was probably much more freely used than physical. One important citizen, William Pitt Ballinger, who feared that secession was a fatal step, found himself "excommunicated" from public affairs and shunned by old friends. "Thomas Harrison wrote me that the children of those not in the front of the present secessionists would be ashamed of their fathers," he records in his diary. "I am willing to bide the test of time on that subject." [38]

Because of the irregularity of the convention call, the vote for delegates was very light; in many well-settled counties only a third or fourth of the voters went to the polls. Nearly half of the one hundred twenty-two counties held no election and sent no delegates to the convention. The passage of the ordinance of secession, one hundred sixty-six to seven, was obviously no index of public sentiment whatever; and realizing this, the convention submitted the measure to the voters. The election was held February 23, when six other States were already out. Little over two weeks were allowed for the campaign. Pressure upon the conservatives was at once redoubled. Vigilance committees sprang up in various towns. In Waco, one such body proclaimed its intention to hang every "Lincolnite" who did not stop talking, and warned leading conservatives to shut up or leave town. Numerous Union men, we are told, left the State.[39]

On election day, eighty counties gave a vote of thirty-four thousand seven hundred and ninety-four for secession and eleven thousand two hundred and fifty-five against. Charges of fraud and unfair dealing at once came from all parts of the State. The machinery of election was in the hands of the secession-

36 James Pike, *Scout and Ranger*, 145.
37 James P. Newcomb, *Secession Times in Texas*, states that the perfect organization and secrecy of the K. G. C. made it a powerful instrument in the hands of the radicals. H. H. Bancroft in *Texas*, II, 435, takes the same view. But this is not the best judgment. See two essays in the Univ. of Texas Library; Julia L. Hering's "Secession Movement in Texas," and M. L. Arnold's "Later Phases of the Secession Movement in Texas."
38 December 31, 1860; MS Diary, Univ. of Texas Library.
39 Houston defiantly faced hostile audiences. At Waco his life was threatened, and at Galveston the crowd was so menacing that friends begged him not to appear. Here it was that, speaking the words on the cost of civil war quoted above, he warned Texans that the Northerners were determined to maintain the Union. They are not a fiery, impulsive people, he said, but "they move with the steady momentum and perseverance of a mighty avalanche, and what I fear is, they will overwhelm the South." Williams, *Houston*, 354.

ists, who were accused of refusing to receive opposition ballots or miscounting them; and for years afterward Union men declared that a true vote would have shown a majority against secession. Doubtless they were mistaken—but the whole course of events in Texas had certainly been such as to prevent a cool consideration of the issues and a fair popular verdict upon them.[40]

[IV]

All in all, we may wonder if the result in the Lower South would not have been different if South Carolina had not acted in such haste; if there and in Louisiana the governmental system had not been weighted heavily on the side of the wealthy planting interest; if in Georgia men like Stephens had exerted themselves more vigorously and the election had been held in sunny weather; if conservative Alabamians had been given more time to rally their forces in the northern counties and Mobile; and if a fair and calm election of delegates had been held in Texas. The amount of thick-and-thin Union sentiment in this section was not impressive. But the sentiment for delay and cooperative action might well have won the day; and a deliberative Southern convention, offering reasonable conditions to the North, might well then have furnished a solid foundation for compromise.

It will be seen that certain common features stamped the action of these seven States on secession. No really effective plebiscite on immediate as against cooperative action was held in any of them. In all except Georgia, the period allowed for discussing the issues and selecting delegates was deplorably short; usually but three or four weeks, and in Florida less than three. In all of them the vote for convention delegates fell surprisingly short of that just cast in the presidential election, being less by two-fifths, one-third, or one quarter. In a number of States (though not in Mississippi), the slaveholding aristocracy and its allies profited by advantages running even beyond those written into laws and constitutions. In Louisiana, for example, much of the slaveless population was too unstable in residence to qualify for voting, even if it cared to vote; in 1859, scarcely seven percent of the whites of New Orleans were registered

---

40 Analysis of the result in Texas shows a fairly close correlation between secession and slavery. In only three areas did this break down. A line of counties along the Red River boundary voted against secession apparently because they feared attack from the North (through Indian Territory) if Texas went out, and because the population was largely from the border States, Illinois, and Indiana; a group of slaveholding counties about Austin went against secession because of the influence of Houston and other leaders, of several able Union newspapers, and of German communities; and a group of six western counties (Hamilton, Brown, Young, and others) with almost no slaves voted for secession in apparent disgust over the failure of the government to give them adequate protection against the Indians. See Arnold, "Later Phases," 51 ff.; Ramsdell, *Frontier and Secession, passim.*

voters, and immigrants among them were subject to intimidation at the polls.[41]
In all these States, too, observers agree on the emotional power and kinetic
force of the spirit of Southern solidarity, speaking of it as a torrential current,
an irresistible wind, carrying all before it.

It will also be noted that in their formal declaration of the reasons for secession, the seven States almost completely ignored any questions but those which
pertained to slavery. Even South Carolina, in the clearheaded, dignified "Declaration of Immediate Causes" written by Memminger, made no mention of tariffs
or other economic grievances. In Georgia, both the hot secessionist Toombs and
the reluctant secessionist Stephens were old-time Whigs who had believed in
the justice of moderate tariffs. The ablest statement of Alabama's reasons for
secession, made by E. S. Dargan of Mobile, rested the action squarely on fear
of emancipation. The South, he argued, had more than four million slaves; the
removal of such a host was impossible; and if they were liberated without
restraint, the result would be utter disaster. "They would either be destroyed by
our own hands, the hands to which they look, and look with confidence, for
protection, or we ourselves would become demoralized and degraded." [42]

All the seceding States held for a time an anomalous position. They were in
their own eyes independent republics, yet they patently lacked the full governmental equipment of republics. Were the Federal laws dead within the States?
Was the national coinage still valid? Should the national government continue
to deliver mails? A. P. Calhoun told the South Carolina convention that having
pulled down a temple which it had taken three-quarters of a century to erect,
they must clear away the rubbish and erect another. "We are now houseless
and homeless, and we must secure ourselves against storms." [43] The simple
method of meeting the situation was to adopt the whole body of United States
laws, and take over the whole corps of postmasters. In various States, as the
conventions continued to sit and pass ordinances, a murmur arose against the
doctrine that all powers were now lodged in a revolutionary group brought together under circumstances of intense excitement. Much fluttering of the pages
of old histories for Revolutionary precedents took place in the weeks while men
waited for a new Southern Confederacy to replace the United States with an
indispensable central authority.

Meanwhile, the problem of relations with the Upper South and borderland
raised anxious questions. Many hotheads of the cotton kingdom would have

41 Shugg, *Class Struggle*, 130.
42 Smith, *Hist. and Debates*, 93, 94.
43 N. Y. *Tribune*, December 20, 1860. Although Governor Pickens of South Carolina
assumed charge of postal affairs and appointed a head of the postal department, Postmaster
Alfred Huger of Charleston informed Joseph Holt that he would continue to account to
Washington for the finances of his office; Holt Papers.

preferred to create a new nation without including the border States. The small number of men eager to reopen slave importations, and the much larger number intent upon establishing a free-trade republic, knew that Marylanders, Virginians, and Missourians would obstruct their aims. In Charleston, Savannah, and parts of Alabama and Mississippi in particular, a cotton republic thus seemed desirable. "We must beware lest the Border Slave States overslaugh us," William Gilmore Simms wrote Porcher Miles. "Their destiny involves more rapid changes than ours. . . . They will become manufacturing." [44] Moreover—and this is important—radical leaders were well aware that the Upper South and border would probably quit the Union (if at all) only with the expectation of reconstructing it. That seemed to be the dominant sentiment in North Carolina, Virginia, and Tennessee as well as in the slaveholding areas north of them. Hostile to any such policy, and taking "once out, always out," as their motto, many of the fire-eaters wanted nothing to do with States which hoped to reknit the old ligaments. Not a few of them denounced the border men as fainthearts, Laodiceans, and skulkers.

The more sober view, however, which all cooperationists strongly preached, was that the Lower South was bound both by duty and self-interest to gain the adherence of other slaveholding States. The erection of a mere cotton republic would do great wrong to the borderland, and irreparable injury to the institution of slavery. It was the Upper South which suffered most from Northern injuries and abolitionist propaganda; and could this region be left alone in resisting Yankee encroachment? Already, Northern writers were computing that for a little over ninety million dollars every slave in Maryland, Delaware, and Missouri could be purchased at the generous average price of five hundred dollars a head, and set free. For the Lower South to maintain its separate republic, many urged, would be a base and cowardly desertion of slaveholders in the sister States. Nor was this all. A cotton republic would not be strong enough to conquer Cuba or overrun Mexico in the teeth of European hostility. Slavery there, confined within narrow bounds, faced with world reprobation, and, as the blacks multiplied, operating to "Africanize" large districts, would in Seward's image eventually sting itself to death. [45]

In the chaotic situation which had developed by the beginning of February, many Gulf State men clearly perceived a terrible dilemma. They could probably not gain the accession of the Upper South, which they required, without striking a blow, and to strike a blow would precipitate all the horrors of a fratricidal war. Meanwhile, opinion in the great region from North Carolina and Virginia to Missouri was racked and torn by a thousand currents and counter-

44 February 26, 1861; Porcher Miles Papers, Univ. of N. C.
45 N. Y. *Weekly Tribune*, February 2, 1861; Rainwater, *Mississippi*, 182–185.

currents; and the idea that this populous area might soon be dragged into war by the impulsive cotton kingdom, while pleasing some, gave others the deepest anguish.

[V]

In Washington, the hope of compromise still existed. Charles Sumner saw Buchanan on February 2. "What, Mr. President," he inquired, "can Massachusetts do for the good of the country?" "Much," responded Buchanan, "no State more." "What is that?" "Adopt the Crittenden proposition," said the President.

"Is that necessary?" asked Sumner. "Yes." The Senator made an emphatic gesture. "Mr. President, Massachusetts has not yet spoken directly on these propositions. But I feel authorized to say—at least I give it as my opinion—that such are the unalterable convictions of the people, they would see their State sunk below the sea and become a sandbank before they would adopt these propositions."

Such an explosive statement was to be expected of Sumner, who, according to Edward Everett, was laboring under a morbid excitement which approached insanity. He had a magnificent project for acquiring Canada, and gladly accepting the secession of such slaveholding States as would not live in the Union under the tenets of the Republican platform.[46] But while the Crittenden Compromise was dead, other schemes of conciliation were not. Seward and Charles Francis Adams, whose opinions were fairly in unison, believed that by concessions on every point but territorial extension, they might yet save the Union. Both believed that the slavery issue had been substantially settled by the election. Both believed that to let this settlement be followed by a dissolution of the Union would be a terrible blunder as well as a catastrophe. Seward had written Lincoln on January 27 that a generous and hopeful attitude was indispensable; that the new Administration must collect the revenues and regain the forts; but that "every thought that we think ought to be conciliatory forbearing and patient, and so open the way for the rising of a Union Party in the seceding States which will bring them back into the Union." [47] Adams wrote to

46 Sumner stood at one extreme as Howell Cobb stood at another. On January 10, Cobb had written Porcher Miles that all the threat of coercion was attributable to the false position of Southern men talking of adjustment in Washington. "We ought to let it be distinctly understood, that we will accept no settlement—and if that position had been firmly taken at Washington from the beginning, the trouble would now be all over, and the country engaged in the discharge of the only remaining duty to be performed and that is, the terms of a *peaceable* and *perpetual* separation." Miles Papers, Univ. of N. C. Sumner narrates his talk with Buchanan in a letter of February 3, 1861, to John A. Andrew; Andrew Papers, MHS.

47 Robert Todd Lincoln Papers.

R. H. Dana in much the same terms. The first duty of the government, he thought, was to reestablish confidence by conciliatory language, to encourage the loyal Southerners, and to deprive the conspirators of the materials with which they had worked. Men in the Upper South were plucking up hope, the efforts to reject secession were growing more systematic, and if a fair understanding could only be reached in Congress or the question postponed until after Lincoln came in, "I think we shall have won the day." [48]

It was assuredly of good omen that neither the firing on the *Star of the West* nor the seizure of scattered forts and arsenals had enraged Northern opinion. While few Northerners were ready to admit that every outgoing State was entitled to all the national property within her limits, to be taken whenever a revolutionary agency chose, these "aggressive acts" had been accepted calmly. Even Horace Greeley spoke of them merely as highhanded.[49] The forbearance of Major Anderson in not returning the fire of the Charleston batteries on the Federal vessel was generally applauded, and Secretary Holt sent him the formal commendation of the President.[50]

Of calming psychological effect, too, in these last weeks of the Buchanan Administration, was the quasi-truce respecting Fort Sumter reached at Charleston between Major Anderson and Governor Pickens, and that respecting Fort Pickens at Pensacola arranged between various Southern Senators and President Buchanan. The attorney-general of South Carolina and one of Anderson's officers travelled jointly to Washington to initiate negotiations for determining the status of Sumter. The resulting parley came to nothing. South Carolina again demanded the surrender of the fort; the Administration again sharply refused it.[51] Secretary Holt delivered a grave warning to the State. "If with all the multiplied proofs which exist of the President's anxiety for peace and of the earnestness with which he has pursued it," he wrote, "the authorities of that State shall assault Fort Sumter, and peril the lives of the handful of brave and loyal men shut up within its walls, and thus plunge our common country into the horrors of civil war, then upon them, and those they represent, must rest the responsibility." This was a just anticipation of the verdict of history. An unwritten understanding continued, however, that the United States would not reinforce the fort without notice, and that South Carolina would meanwhile not yet attack it; an understanding the easier to respect because Anderson did not want reinforcements. Secretary Holt had told Anderson, nevertheless, that whenever

48 February 9, 1861; Dana Papers.
49 Signed article, N. Y. *Tribune*, January 8, 1861.
50 January 11; *Official Records*, Series I, Vol. I, 140.
51 Buchanan, *Administration*, 194 ff.; Curtis, *Buchanan*, II, 452; Crawford, *Sumter*, 222 ff.

he needed supplies or men, a prompt and vigorous effort to forward them would follow.[52]

The Fort Pickens truce was ampler and stronger. It was agreed that the government might provision the post but not disembark troops, and that in return the Florida authorities would make no attack. Buchanan gave firm orders through Holt to the provisioning force, which included a small body of troops: "The *Brooklyn* and other vessels of war on the station will remain and you will exercise the utmost vigilance and be prepared at a moment's warning to land the company at Fort Pickens and you and they will instantly repel any attack on the Fort." This was a display of proper vigor. He was anxious to maintain the truce while the Peace Convention under ex-President Tyler labored, and while other efforts at reconciliation were being made. But he was emphatic that the national forces should be ready to meet an attack on Pickens or preparations for an attack. "In either event, the *Brooklyn* and other vessels will act promptly." Had such a clear truce been made respecting Sumter, worry over the future would have been greatly lessened.

[VI]

Three days after the secession of Texas, and on the very day that the Peace Convention opened in Washington, February 4, delegates from six States met in Montgomery to launch their hopeful new Southern republic. South Carolina had proposed the gathering a month earlier. Delegates had in general been chosen by the various State conventions, in proportion to the number of electors each State possessed under the Constitution. They made up a distinguished body of men. Alexander H. Stephens asserts, indeed, that he was never associated with one of more ability; that nobody in it failed to rank above the average of the House in any of the sixteen Congresses in which he had served; and that several of the delegates might justly be placed among the first of the land.[53] Jefferson Davis, Yancey, Slidell, and Judah P. Benjamin were not present. But Toombs, the two Cobbs, Rhett, Memminger, Reagan, J. L. M. Curry, and Benjamin H. Hill were. The spirit in which they met was one of high enthusiasm and optimism. A patriotic harmony prevailed, and many of the wisest believed that their future was one of assured peace.

With Howell Cobb as presiding officer, and with each State given one vote, the convention moved with great celerity. Only four days after assembling, it adopted a Constitution for the provisional government of the Confederate

52 *Official Records*, I, I, 134–190.
53 Stephens, *War Between the States*, II, 325.

States of America; and on the fifth day it elected Jefferson Davis as provisional President. The choice necessarily had to be conservative in character, for while Rhett and Yancey were both highly receptive, their elevation to the leadership of the new nation would have frightened Virginia and the other hesitant States. At the outset, it was the general impression that the palm would be awarded to Toombs, who in the eyes of Stephens seemed far better equipped for the place than any rival. Davis would have preferred a high military post for himself. Unfortunately for Toombs, the Georgia delegation was divided, some members supporting him, some Howell Cobb; the veteran Democrats in the convention distrusted him as an old-time Whig; Yancey, when forced to withdraw, did so in favor of Davis; and after a good deal of complicated maneuvering, the Georgia Senator himself agreed to the austere Mississippian. Some small part may have been played in the rejection of Toombs by his well-known weakness for drink. By another unanimous vote, Stephens was selected for Vice President.[54]

No stronger pair of men could have been selected. Here were one representative of the older South, and one of the new frontier South; one of the old-time Whigs and one of the old-time Democrats; one of the Breckinridge men, and one of the Douglas men. Both were capable orators and parliamentarians. Davis had shown his skill and energy as an administrator in one of the most difficult of the government departments. Their election pleased cautious elements in the borderland; and the fact did not escape the North that, while the convention professed to be adamantine in spurning the old Union forever, both Davis and Stephens had followed a policy which made them seem not totally averse to its reconstruction.

The provisional Constitution had been drawn up by a committee of two from each State, with Memminger its chairman; and by general consent the Federal instrument was accepted as its basis. Within a few weeks a permanent Constitution was drafted. It differed from the old national model chiefly in its emphasis on State Rights, its careful guarantee of slavery (which it named without any cimcumlocution), and a number of interesting reform provisions. The general welfare clauses were omitted. Any Confederate official acting within the limits of a State might be impeached by the State legislature, though the Constitution, laws made under it, and treaties were declared "the supreme law of the land." The central government was forbidden to pass any law denying the right of property in slaves, and although the African slave trade was prohibited, the interstate rights of slaveholders were safeguard. Provision was made for a judicial system like that of the United States, including a Supreme Court. The restrictions upon the States followed in general the old pattern; they

54 See *So. Hist. Assn. Pubs.*, XI, 163 ff.; Johnston and Browne, *Stephens*, 389-391.

might not coin money, make alliances, form compacts with other States, or grant titles of nobility.

The most remarkable features of the new instrument sprang from the purifying and reforming zeal of the delegates, who hoped to create a more guarded and virtuous government than that of Washington.[55] The President was to hold office six years, and be ineligible for reelection. Expenditures were to be limited by a variety of careful provisions, and the President was given a budgetary control over appropriations which Congress could break only by a two-thirds vote. Subordinate employees were protected against the forays of the spoils system. No bounties were ever to be paid out of the Treasury, no protective tariff was to be passed, and no post office deficit was to be permitted. The electoral college system was retained, but as a far-reaching innovation, Cabinet members were given seats in Congress for the discussion of departmental affairs. Some of these changes were unmistakable improvements, and the spirit behind all of them was an earnest desire to make government more honest and efficient. The process of ratifying the new Constitution by the people of the respective States was destined to be slow; and the permanent government of the Confederacy was not to be inaugurated until Washington's birthday in 1862. Meanwhile, the provisional Administration served with all the authority that its leaders could give it.

On the evening of February 16, Jefferson Davis arrived in Montgomery, to be met with a storm of cheers as his erect figure was discerned emerging from the train. To the crowd at the station, he spoke a few sentences. "Our separation from the old Union is complete," he declared. "No compromise and no reconstruction can now be entertained." Two companies of Georgia militia, with a committee of the Confederate Congress and a deputation representing the city, escorted him to the Exchange Hotel, where a greater crowd awaited him. Their exultant shouts soon brought him out upon the balcony. Prominent among the distinguished men who surrounded him was William L. Yancey. He stepped forward, gesturing for silence that he might introduce Davis, and his voice rang out with clarion vibrance: "The hour and the man have met!"

55 We speak here of the permanent Constitution, adopted early in March. Texts of the Confederate and Federal Constitutions are given in parallel columns in Davis, *Rise and Fall*, I, 640–675.

15

Lincoln Takes the Helm

AS THE President-elect left Springfield for Washington on February 11, it was evident that the national crisis was gathering itself to some mighty climax; but no man could say what that climax would be. A complex web of intertwined and fateful questions would have to be decided within the next ten weeks.

Lincoln had as yet fully determined upon only two members of his Cabinet. Though compromise by the Missouri line was dead, lesser concessions to the South hung in balance in Washington; the House did not receive the report and proposals of the Committee of Thirty-three until three days after Lincoln's departure, while, for that matter, the Senate still had to take its final vote on the Crittenden scheme. Major Anderson had not determined when his garrison would need provisions and other stores, the South Carolina authorities marked time while the *Mercury* exhorted them to take the forts, and the new Confederate government remained without a policy as to Sumter and Pickens. The people of the border States still anxiously debated their future, and although Stephens told a Montgomery audience that the new nation might soon have more stars than the thirteen of the original Union, the battle of conservatives and radicals continued to rage in North Carolina and Virginia, in Kentucky and Tennessee. Seward believed the general excitement was abating, but Seward was always optimistic. To most people, the public bewilderment, apprehension, and irritability seemed as great as ever.

So great was the uncertainty that Lincoln was vastly relieved to learn at Columbus, Ohio, on the evening of the thirteenth, that the counting of the electoral votes had been safely completed in Washington that day. The country shared his feeling. Circumstantial stories of plans for a Virginia attack had been afloat. Joseph Medill had written Lincoln on New Year's Eve that the disunionists expected to have an army in the capital within five weeks.[1] Elihu B. Washburne had informed the President-elect on February 3 that a wide and powerful conspiracy to seize Washington undoubtedly existed. But Winfield Scott had

1 Robert Todd Lincoln Papers.

gathered troops and taken precautions. "I have said," he thundered to a New England visitor, "that any man who attempted by force or unparliamentary disorder to obstruct or interfere with the lawful count of the electoral vote should be lashed to the muzzle of a twelve-pounder and fired out of a window of the Capitol. I would manure the hills of Arlington with his body!" The New York attorney and civic leader, George Templeton Strong, noted in his diary that the metropolis was glad to have the critical day passed. "A foray of Virginia gents with Governor Wise at their head and Governor Floyd at their tail could have done infinite mischief by destroying the legal evidence of Lincoln's election (after they had killed and beaten General Scott and his Flying Artillery, that is)." [2]

[I]

The man who was journeying east to grapple with the crisis possessed more qualifications than men dreamed, but great public prestige he sadly lacked. Douglas had told a New Orleans audience, just after the election, that Lincoln, faced with hostile majorities in Congress, was entitled to commiseration rather than envy. While the adverse majorities were now melting away, the question of his power to push through such a thickening jungle of difficulties remained. Outside Illinois he was generally regarded as a secondary leader of commonplace gifts. A typical verdict of the hour characterized him as a fair Western lawyer, a good stump-speaker, and an adroit hand at electioneering, but a politician and not a statesman. C. H. Ray, who knew him well, wrote Governor Andrew that one reason for getting Chase into the Cabinet was that Chase's "great ability in affairs will give the force to Mr. Lincoln which nature has denied him." [3] The men who interviewed him during the winter—Weed, Chase, Cameron, Duff Green—had struck no note of pleased surprise over unexpected talents. His task was made harder by the general supposition that, like the four Presidents preceding him, he would be controlled by his intimate advisers.

But his Illinois intimates knew that he had plenty of backbone. C. H. Ray of the Chicago *Tribune*, stationed in Springfield, assured Elihu Washburne on January 7 that the Party leaders might trust Old Abe implicitly. "He is rising every day in the estimation of all who know him best. He is wiser and more sagacious than I thought he would prove to be. Our cause is dearer to him than anything else; and he will make no mistakes. Depend on that." And Horace White bore the same testimony: "There is no backdown in Old Abe, nor any toleration of that element in others."

2 L. E. Chittenden, *Recs. of President Lincoln*, 38; Strong MS Diary, Columbia Univ.
3 John Rutherfoord, December 19, 1860, Rutherfoord Papers, Duke Univ.; Ray, January 17, 1861, Andrew Papers, MHS.

Since election, he had been incessantly busy seeing politicians, answering letters, discussing Cabinet selections, paying a short visit to Chicago and conferring with Hannibal Hamlin there, tidying his personal affairs, and preparing his inaugural address. He had named John G. Nicolay, a Bavarian-born newspaperman of twenty-eight, frail-looking, wispy-bearded, and ceaselessly industrious, as secretary. Nicolay, overwhelmed with work, had presently suggested that John Hay—an active, brilliant young man from western Illinois, a Brown graduate of literary tastes—be retained as well, and Lincoln, after humorously demurring that he couldn't take the whole State to Washington, had consented.[4] Under the remorseless attack of job-hunters, Lincoln told Herndon that he was sick of his office before he got into it.

It is impossible to overemphasize the fact that his twin tasks of Cabinet-building and policy-making were inextricably entangled; that the stark battle being waged in Washington between the Seward-Adams moderates, who wished to show a conciliatory front toward the South in the hope of holding the border States and eventually rebuilding the Union, and the Sumner-Wade-Chandler implacables, who agreed with Greeley that the very word concession was hateful, was directly connected with efforts to manipulate the new President in the choice of his official family. The struggle on both these closely-linked fronts was to continue until the hour he entered the White House.

As Lincoln moved on toward Cleveland, Buffalo, and New York, Charles Francis Adams wrote Richard H. Dana that the negotiation between North and South was complicated by difficulties growing out of rival approaches to the new chief. "It is not to be disguised that two distinct lines of policy advocated by opposing parties within our ranks are developed. The index of one of them is Mr. Seward. That of the other [is] Mr. Chase. As yet there is no evidence before the public which will be adopted. Until it appears, there will be no firmness here. As yet I can form no opinion of the character of the chief. His speeches have fallen like a wet blanket here. They put to flight all notions of greatness. But he may yet prove true and honest and energetic, which will cover a multitude of minor difficulties."[5]

Antagonism between the moderate and the "iron-back" wings of the party, long jealous and suspicious, grew more bitter as each reached for power. Sumner was now ranting about Sewardism as a fatal policy of cowardice. To Congressional friends he orated, declaimed, and issued ukases after his wont, saying that the path of duty was plain as Washington Monument. Adams set him down as "crazy—actually frantic." He said he would give up nothing, not even the Personal Liberty law of Massachusetts. Characteristically, he denounced Seward

4 Thayer, *Hay*, I, 87; Helen Nicolay, *John G. Nicolay*, 1–65.
5 February 18, 1861; Dana Papers.

to his face. Just before the New Yorker made his great Senate speech on conciliation, Sumner went to his house, heard it read, and angrily protested. "I pleaded with him," he told friends, "for the sake of the cause, the country, and his own good name, to abandon all his propositions and simply declare that Mr. Lincoln would be inaugurated on the 4th March President of the United States, and to rally the country to his support." [6] Seward, laughing at Sumner as he seemed to laugh at everybody, was aware that he faced one of the most desperate battles of his life. For all his effervescent show of cheeriness, he looked thin, worn, and older than the previous summer. "The majority of those around me are determined to pull the house down," he said, "and I am determined not to let them." He was willing to risk his reputation in various ways to save the country. Not merely did he preach compromise where it was unpopular; he kept in close touch with Dix, Holt, and Stanton, encouraging and advising them as they managed the Administration.

Next to Weed, the ablest and most loyal of Seward's helpers was Charles Francis Adams, who possessed a weight of character that Weed lacked. The old family friendship of Seward and the Adamses had been reinforced the previous summer, when they stumped the Northwest together. The Senator hoped that Adams would be New England's representative in the Cabinet. Adams, for his part, believed that the destiny of the nation rested with the New Yorker. "All depends upon Lincoln *and the power of Seward in influencing his policy*," he wrote.[7] Like many others, Adams was annoyed by what he deemed the vacillating course of the President-elect, believing that he had begun well but failed to carry his policy through. Lincoln, thought Adams, should be like Seward—firm on the principle of non-extension of slavery, but conciliatory on other points, and suave in avoiding talk of coercion.

[II]

Lincoln's initial steps in forming his Cabinet had been taken before differences over policy could develop. The day after election, smitten with a crushing sense of the burden he was to take up, he made a tentative Cabinet slate. "It was almost the same that I finally appointed," he said later. But the problem was too difficult to be rapidly solved. His guiding principle, from which he never deviated, was to give places to the major leaders of the party, thus forming a ministry of all the talents—what Seward called "a compound Cabinet"—and reducing the danger of factional revolt against himself. If it could be kept in harmony, it would harmonize the party. Leaders and groups held such divergent

6 So he wrote Andrew, January 17, 1861; Andrew Papers.
7 February 28, 1861, Dana Papers; my italics.

views, however, that at times he despaired of realizing his object. An additional complication lay in the commitments his managers had made at the Chicago convention.

With the basic initial selection, that of Seward, we have already dealt. His position as the foremost leader of the party, his preeminent abilities, his long experience, and his genial personal qualities combined to make his appointment to the first position in the Cabinet almost imperative. With great friendliness toward the man, Lincoln could not be completely happy about the choice. He knew that Seward's undeserved reputation for radicalism made the South suspicious of him, that many Republicans disliked him for his real moderation, and that the Weed machine association was a handicap. Nevertheless, on the whole Seward's acceptance greatly strengthened his position. Another selection, that of Edward Bates as Attorney-General, was made without hesitation or difficulty. Not only was the Missourian fully equipped for this post by his legal erudition, fidelity to constitutional principles, and assuasive temper, but his appointment would gratify Union men in the border area. In December, Lincoln paid him the compliment of proposing to call on him in St. Louis. "I thought I saw an unfitness in *his coming to me*," writes Bates, "and that I *ought to go to him*." When they talked in Springfield on the fifteenth, Lincoln, discussing his whole Cabinet problem with candor, remarked that he thought Bates's participation in its work essential to his complete success. There was no refusing such an invitation.[8]

It was a weirdly unhappy comedy of errors which brought the wily Simon Cameron into a position where (though his appointment was still undecided when Lincoln left for the capital) a Cabinet assignment seemed almost a necessity. This drama, at times almost farce but in the end almost tragedy, began when David Davis and Swett promised Cameron's followers at the Chicago convention that he would be given a Cabinet seat. It was an unauthorized and disreputable bargain, but David Davis insisted that it be honored. So did Cameron's loyal Pennsylvania clansmen, and a number of old-time opponents, like David Wilmot, who had an eye on his senatorship. Seward was distinctly favorable to Cameron, and went so far as to urge Weed—unsuccessfully—to make a special trip to Springfield to press the nomination. Cameron himself, while protesting to various men that he did not want a post, left no wire unpulled and no stone unturned, until by extracting from Swett an invitation to visit Springfield, he was able late in December to push himself into Lincoln's presence. He faced a deeply troubled President-elect.[9]

Precisely what passed at this interview we do not know, and some have sur-

8　*Diary of Edward Bates*, 164–167; Nicolay and Hay, *Lincoln*, III, 351, 352.
9　Gideon Welles states that Swett's invitation was unauthorized; *Diary*, II, 390.

mised that the unwilling Lincoln let himself be browbeaten into offering an appointment. Cameron's own statement, now available in the papers of S. W. Crawford, would indicate that this is not true—that Lincoln had already yielded to Davis and others. Cameron writes:

At that interview a tender of the Secship of the Treasury was made by the President to Genl C. who replied that he was then in the Senate of the U. S. and satisfied with that position and that he was not seeking any other. But it was repeated by the President, who considered as arranged and then said "Now what am I to do with Chase." Why not offer him the War Dept. said Genl C. it is the most important department now as there is no doubt that a war is imminent. Will you take the War Dept. yourself, said Mr. Lincoln. I offer it to you. But I am not seeking for any position replied Genl C. and I would not decline of course what I had recommended to another. Genl C. returned at once to Harrisburg having remained but one day in Springfield. . . .[10]

It is unnecessary to accept this memorandum at face value. What is certain is that Cameron received from Lincoln a letter dated December 31, 1860, stating that "by your permission I shall at the proper time nominate you to the United States Senate for confirmation as Secretary of the Treasury or as Secretary of War—which of the two I have not yet definitely decided." Even if the President-elect did not believe that the unholy compact at Chicago had to be redeemed, he must have felt that to rebuff Cameron and the powerful Pennsylvania machine behind him would be politically dangerous.

The vituperative resources of the English language are large, but they were almost exhausted by the storm of condemnation which beat upon this selection as soon as it was suspected or known. William Cullen Bryant wrote Lincoln on January 3 that all observers of Cameron's career felt "an utter ancient and deep seated distrust of his integrity—whether financial or political." [11] Thaddeus Stevens went further; he pronounced Cameron "a man destitute of honor and honesty." [12] Matthew Carey informed the President-elect that Cameron stood charged in the courts of Pennsylvania with serious crime, that most good citizens "look upon him as the very incarnation of corruption," and that his appointment would be "a signal to all the vultures of the Union to flock around the Treasury." The fact that Cameron on January 21 made a conciliatory speech in the Senate, saying that Pennsylvania would do anything consistent with honor to save the Union, deepened the antagonism of the "iron-backs." [13] Governor Andrew G. Curtin and his faction expressed violent opposition, the State Chairman in Pennsylvania, A. K. McClure, telegraphing that the appointment

10 Undated memorandum in S. W. Crawford Papers, Ill. State Hist. Lib.
11 Robert Todd Lincoln Papers.
12 To E. B. Washburne, January 19, 1861; *Ibid.*
13 L. F. Crippen, *Cameron*, 229, 230.

would mean the destruction of the Party in that State. Lincoln, taken aback, summoned McClure to Springfield and listened to a circumstantial account of all Cameron's derelictions. The chairman bore letters from various men supporting his charge that, in view of "the notorious incompetency and public and private villainy" of the Pennsylvania boss, the selection would disgrace the republic.[14]

Lincoln now saw that he had acted prematurely. His proper course would doubtless have been to revoke his offer, drop Cameron completely, and keep him dropped. Instead, he followed a hesitant policy. First, he wrote the Senator on January 3 an abrupt letter, saying that "things have developed which make it impossible for me to take you into the Cabinet"; that this was partly because of McClure's interposition but more largely because of "a matter wholly outside Pennsylvania"; and that he wished Cameron to yield tacit assent by sending him a telegram reading, "All right." Unfortunately, McClure at the same time returned to Pennsylvania with loud and positive statements that no final decision had been reached on any Cabinet appointment for that State. This put Cameron, who had talked boastfully of Lincoln's offer, in an impossible predicament. If he sent the President-elect the desired telegram and kept quiet, the public would believe that he had lied about his selection, and that, after his lie, McClure had summarily put him in his place. He refused to budge.[15]

Not only that, but he employed all his varied political resources to bring fresh pressure upon Lincoln. Springfield was deluged with letters, telegrams, and signed memorials in Cameron's behalf. The Pennsylvania legislature passed resolutions of eulogy and endorsement. A stream of emissaries, including Senator-elect Edgar Cowan, was hurried to Springfield to expostulate. David Davis and Swett were rallied to return to the charge. Various Pennsylvania newspapers, led by the Philadelphia *Inquirer*, gave Cameron their support, some because they were allied with his machine, and some because they saw in him a pillar of protection. Under this bombardment, Lincoln wavered—for, after all, the allegations against the Senator were mainly vague, and McClure, when asked to document them, had declined to do so. The endorsements of Cameron soon outnumbered the protests three to one, and Lincoln was able to declare that "he is more amply recommended for a place in the Cabinet than any other man." [16]

In vain did various men, East and West, strive to resist this pressure. Horace White, declaring that Cameron's appointment would be positively

14　McClure, *Lincoln and Men of War-Times*, 41, 42, 141–143.
15　Burton J. Hendrick, *Lincoln's War Cabinet*, 108 ff.; Carman and Luthin, *Lincoln and the Patronage*, 39, 40.
16　To Lyman Trumbull; Tracy, *Uncollected Letters of Lincoln*, 173, 174.

awful, did so. So did C. H. Ray. So did Elihu Washburne. From New York came a deputation of three, George Opdyke, Hiram Barney, and Judge Hogeboom, supported by Greeley's *Tribune* and Byrant's *Post*, who in a three-hour interview told Lincoln what they thought were plain home truths. "If this goes on, and Thurlow Weed and Cameron get the reins," they declared, "no course will be left but a disgraceful compromise with the South. After that, the Administration will forfeit the confidence of the country, and the Democratic Party will regain its strength in all the free States." Some Springfield men hoped that the trio had given Lincoln an eye-opener; but Old Abe had a way of making up his own mind.

The upshot was that Lincoln sent Cameron a gentler letter, contritely disclaiming any intention of giving offense, or any doubt as to the Senator's ability and fidelity in a Cabinet post. He stuck to the withdrawal of his offer. At the same time, he made it clear that he was still considering Cameron's name. "If I should make a Cabinet appointment for Pennsylvania before I reach Washington," he wrote, "I will not do so without consulting you, and giving all the weight to your views and wishes which I consistently can." David Davis remained certain that Cameron would get a place, and assured him of the fact. Moreover, strong economic interests entered the contest in the Senator's behalf. The iron and coal men of Pennsylvania, hungry for tariffs, set to work and persuaded Curtin and McClure to withdraw their opposition. As Lincoln passed through Philadelphia, they had a spokesman there, the ironmaster James Milliken, to tell the President-elect that practically all elements wished Cameron appointed to the Treasury. The astute and tireless boss had succeeded! The New York *Times* on February 25 declared that although one of the bitterest political fights in all American history had been waged against him, he had won a complete victory, and it was a settled fact that he was to represent Pennsylvania in the Administration.[17]

One other promissory note of the Chicago convention was presented for payment, and in the end was met. Davis and Swett had pledged a Cabinet position to Caleb Blood Smith in return for Indiana delegates that Smith did not really control. This lawyer, politician, newspaper owner, and promoter of railways and canals, a commonplace contriver of Whig antecedents, had seconded Lincoln's nomination and spoken industriously during the campaign. It seemed important that Indiana receive some reward; Smith's interest in internal improvements suggested that he might do for the Interior Department; and Lincoln, after hesitating between him and Colfax, took the older man. You "are sure of a bright future in any event," he wrote Colfax; "with Smith it is now or

[17] Crippen, *Cameron*, 239–242; Baringer, *op. cit.*, 288–291. He was to get the War post.

never." Corwin praised Smith as industrious, well-informed, and firm—but he was to prove firm in some wrong directions.[18]

[III]

As Adams remarked, the two opposed poles in the Party leadership were represented by Seward and Chase. Each man had followers in Lincoln's immediate entourage. While such moderate Illinoisans as David Davis heartily liked Seward and his policies, radicals like Norman B. Judd and the editors of the Chicago *Tribune* espoused Chase. Lincoln's choice of Seward for the State Department had no sooner been disclosed than the milk-of-the-word Republicans, the true-blue implacables, rallied for their own champion. "We," wrote C. H. Ray of the *Tribune* (meaning radical Chicagoans), "are doing what we can to get Mr. Chase into the Cabinet as a counterbalance to the schemers who hang upon the skirts of Mr. Seward." [19] To men like Sumner, Preston King, Wilmot, and Zack Chandler, the idea that Seward would dominate the Administration was horrible; just as to Weed, Charles Francis Adams, and Cameron, the idea of domination by Chase was ghastly.[20]

The drive to make certain that Chase would be offered one of the best Cabinet positions and would accept it (for as a newly-elected Senator he might prove coy) was entirely successful. By invitation, he visited Springfield on January 3. As in other interviews of the sort, Lincoln was candor itself. He first inquired if Chase would accept the Treasury if it proved possible for him to offer it; and then, as his visitor hesitated, explained that Seward was to be Secretary of State (for Chase could hardly stand second to any less important man), and that if Seward had declined, Chase would have been his second choice. This statement largely disarmed the touchy Ohioan of any pique. He felt a little offended that Lincoln did not approach him with the same prompt definiteness as Seward, but he could not deny that the New Yorker had superior claims to first place. The two separated with a quasi-understanding. While Lincoln, his fingers just badly burnt in the Cameron fire, did not quite commit himself to an

---

18 Corwin to Lincoln, January 18, 1861, Robert Todd Lincoln Papers. One aspirant for the Interior Department, Norman B. Judd, was pushed aside. Mrs. Lincoln, who was in Washington in mid-January, wrote David Davis on the 17th asking him to warn Lincoln against that appointment. She had heard people at a neighboring table that morning laughing at the idea of Judd for the place. "Judd would cause trouble and dissatisfaction, and if Wall Street testifies correctly, his business transactions have not always borne inspection." David Davis Papers, Ill. State Hist. Lib. The letter is interesting as evidence of Mrs. Lincoln's participation in political affairs.

19 January 17, 1861; Andrew Papers, MHS.

20 For Lincoln's own early ideas of Cabinet-making, see Welles, *Diary*, I, 82.

offer, he almost did so; and while Chase said he must consult friends, he almost promised to accept.[21]

At once, Chase and his friends bestirred themselves to give firmer outline to this understanding. It is impossible to detect an iota of hesitation in Chase's attitude. He wanted the Treasury because it was more important than a senatorship, because it would put him as a low-tariff man in a place that might otherwise go to the high-tariff Cameron, and above all, because it would enable him to checkmate Seward. He wrote a number of friends, hinting to George Opdyke of New York that he would like a deputation to visit Lincoln and press his nomination, and plainly telling J. S. Pike that the support of Greeley and Dana would be much appreciated. He probably wrote to Bryant, for that editor shortly sent a highly significant letter to the President-elect. It was important to nominate Chase to the Treasury Department, he stated, as a man of wisdom, rigid integrity, and force of character—"not to speak of the need of his presence as a counterpoise to another member who, to commanding talents, joins a flexible and indulgent temper, and unsafe associations." It was also important to hurry his nomination, for it was nearly certain that he would not take the place "unless it were offered him early." [22] Sumner was hot to see Chase safe in the Cabinet; "it is our only chance," he exclaimed.

As Congress labored throughout February, Seward and Adams still cherished the idea of conciliation, while Chase and Sumner steadily opposed all compromise. One of Chase's phrases gained wide currency: "Inauguration first, adjustment afterward"—by which he meant that unconditional submission by the South must precede any concessions. Seward, who believed it imperative to hold Virginia and the borderland and to build a groundwork of fraternal feeling for ultimate reconstruction, regarded such an attitude as calamitous. He had been intensely worried lest a secessionist victory in Virginia, which held elections for her convention on February 4, might precipitate an attack by Governor Wise upon Washington and open a war. The victory of the Union men heartened him enormously, for it seemed to indicate that his policy might well succeed. When the middle of February came without disturbance, he was still more relieved. Every day, he believed, was bringing the people nearer the tone, temper, and ideas that he hoped would prevail. Knowing that Lincoln was at work on his inaugural, he had written him a long letter in the hope of influencing its tenor:

21 R. B. Warden, *Chase*, 365 ff.; Schuckers, *Chase*, 201–203. Chase wrote Elihu Washburne on January 14: "Should he conclude it is desirable that I take the position, he will let me know; and then I shall decide with just as little reference to personal considerations as possible." Washburne Papers.

22 January 22, 1861; Robert Todd Lincoln Papers.

The appeals from the Union men in the Border states for something of concession or compromise are very painful since they say that without it those states must go with the tide. . . . In any case, you are to meet a hostile armed Confederacy when you commence. You must reduce it by force or conciliation. The resort to force would very soon be denounced by the North, although so many are anxious for the fray. The North will not consent to a long civil war. . . . For my own part I think that we must collect the revenues, regain the ports in the gulf, and if need be maintain ourselves here. But that every thought that we think ought to be conciliatory, forbearing, and patient, and so open the way for the rising of a Union Party in the seceding states which will bring them back into the Union.

It will be very important that your Inaugural Address be wise and winning.[23]

With every passing week the antagonism of the two factions became more acidulous, and more threatening to the harmony of the new Administration. Early in February, Greeley opened all the *Tribune* batteries upon Seward. He had reserved his fire for a time, merely because a severe struggle was raging at Albany for the senatorial seat soon to be vacated. The Seward-Weed forces had united behind the brilliant young William M. Evarts; the opposition, rallying against Weed with the cry, "Down with the dictator!", had divided its votes between Greeley and Ira Harris. The outcome left Greeley half-elated, half-frustrated. When Weed, sitting in the executive chamber nervously smoking, learned that Greeley was leading and Evarts was about to be overwhelmed, he suddenly transferred his votes to Harris, thus robbing the editor of the prize. Nothing was now too harsh for Greeley to say about the humiliating surrender of Seward to the compromise spirit. "Mr. Seward Renounces the Republican Party," ran one of the *Tribune* headlines. Bryant's *Evening Post* was equally virulent, for neither man could reconcile himself to the prospect of four years of government by what Samuel Bowles called "the New Yorker with his Illinois attachment." [24]

[IV]

The policies of the new President were as yet but adumbrations projected against two jutting principles, as rising mist might cling to two mountain crags. One principle was inflexibility on the territorial question. "I am for no compromise," Lincoln had written Seward, "which *asserts* or *permits* the extension of the institution on soil owned by the nation. And any trick, by which the nation is to acquire territory, and then allow some local authority to spread slavery over it, is as noxious as any other." The other principle was an anxious desire

23 January 27, 1861; Robert Todd Lincoln Papers. Punctuation slightly altered.
24 N. Y. *Weekly Tribune*, February 9, 1861; Merriam, *Bowles*, I, 318.

to maintain peace, first by taking no aggressive step, and second by making concessions on all points but that of new slaveholding territory. "As to fugitive slaves, District of Columbia, slave trade among the slave States, and whatever springs of necessity, from the fact that the institution is among us, I care but little; so that whatever is done be comely, and not altogether outrageous. Nor do I care much about New Mexico, if further extension be hedged against." [25]

One evidence of his desire to woo the South lay in his effort to find a Southern leader who could and would enter his Cabinet. Various men suggested that he retain, as head of the War Department, the capable Joseph Holt, who was not merely a native of Kentucky but a former resident of Mississippi. The Lower South, however, now hated Holt. Seward sat down on Christmas Day to propose Randall Hunt of Louisiana, and John A. Gilmer and Kenneth Raynor of North Carolina, while he later added Robert E. Scott of Virginia to the list.[26] Of these, Gilmer, a strong antagonist of secession and advocate of compromise, seemed the most promising. On Lincoln's authorization, the Senator wrote Gilmer (they were warm friends), inquiring as to his willingness to serve, but received only a hesitant, evasive answer. Lincoln himself had meanwhile invited him to come to Springfield; and he could not have been pleased when Gilmer not merely declined the visit, but called upon the President-elect to restate his policy toward the South in more satisfactory terms. When Seward talked with Scott of Virginia late in January, it appeared that he too would not do; he was too exacting in his demands on behalf of the slave States.

The fact was that, as even Seward was compelled to admit, such men as Gilmer, Scott, and W. C. Rives were now halfway secessionists, holding that their States could and should depart unless the government executed sweeping guarantees—guarantees that the North would find abhorrent. Lincoln's early belief that no really able and influential Southerner could be found except on terms that would mean hopeless future friction thus appeared justified, and the quest was abandoned.

In one respect the pathway ahead of the incoming President seemed to grow clearer. The departure of many Southern members from Congress gave a coalition of Republicans and Northern Democrats an opportunity to carry through some long-thwarted measures. On January 21, in a scene which thoughtful men found affecting, Senators Yulee and Mallory of Florida, Clay and Fitzpatrick of Alabama, and Davis of Mississippi had formally withdrawn from the Senate. All of them reproached the North, Clay's speech being a bitter indictment; all, and particularly Yulee, defended secession as springing from a profound sense

25 Seward, *Seward*, II, 504.
26 Senator Doolittle suggested Major Anderson, a Kentuckian, for the War Department; January 10, 1861, Robert Todd Lincoln Papers.

of duty to the Southern people and to posterity; and all voiced their regret at leaving old friends. Mallory spoke with horror of civil war—"imbrue your hands in our blood, and the rains of a century will not wash from them the stain"; but Davis expressed a magnanimous good will toward the North—"I wish you well; and such, I am sure, is the feeling of the people I represent towards those whom you represent." [27] Other members from seceding States, at appropriate times, uttered their farewells.

On the very day the five Senators departed, the bill to admit Kansas passed the Senate 36 to 16, with nine Northern Democrats joining the Republicans in its support. Much the same alliance carried legislation organizing the Territories of Dakota, Colorado, and Nevada. In accordance with the Republican platform statement that the normal condition of all Territories was that of freedom, it was assumed that no explicit exclusion of slavery was necessary. Since Lincoln would appoint the territorial officers, and since no sane Southerner would carry a slave into such regions, the assumption was quite sound. Nevertheless, Douglas did not miss his opportunity to point out that the organizing acts left slavery in the three Territories, so far as Congressional interference was concerned, precisely where his law of 1854 had left slavery in Kansas; that the Wilmot Proviso was relegated to oblivion.[28] His taunt did not disturb his opponents, who knew that the three Territories in 1861 stood in a very different position from that in which Kansas had stood when Pierce was in the Executive Mansion, and when Missouri was full of men eager to carry slavery into the valley of the Kaw.

The mild tariff bill of the preceding session, amended after a fashion which we shall discuss later, was carried through Congress with the aid of Democratic votes from Pennsylvania, New Jersey, and New York, and President Buchanan signed it as one of his last official acts.[29] Once more, the Pacific Railroad died amid unhappy wrangling over routes—but in the certainty of an early resurrection. Impressed by the popular interest in reform, Congress stopped the subsidy for the carriage of mails to the Pacific by steamship, revised the patent laws, and created a Government Printing Office to do the work heretofore farmed out on the scandalous terms exposed in the Covode Report.

---

27 *Cong. Globe.*, 36th Cong., 2d Sess., 484–487.
28 *Ibid.*, p. 1391. The fact was that Republicans did not need or want positive prohibition in these Territories; and sensible Southerners did not want positive protection of slavery, which would have been useless.
29 Lincoln dealt briefly with the tariff in his speech at Pittsburgh on February 14. Saying that "it is a question of national housekeeping," and that "it is to the government what replenishing the meal-tub is to the family," which was then true, he pledged himself to support the Chicago plank on the tariff; but he admitted that it was subject to varying interpretations, and said frankly that "I have by no means a thoroughly matured judgment upon this subject, especially as to details." N. Y. *Herald, Tribune*, February 15.

Although the cry of sectional legislation might be hurled against some of these enactments, they actually contained little of which the South could legitimately complain. The population in the three Territories obviously needed a governmental machinery near at hand. A higher tariff revenue had become exigent, and the new duties were moderate by any standard. In one field, too, sober Congressional leaders conspicuously avoided any provocative action. Buchanan having asked Congress for increased power to deal with disorders, the House spent days in discussing various proposals to enable the President to use the militia and accept volunteer forces to maintain the peace in Washington and to protect or recover Federal property elsewhere.[30] Among other steps, it set up a committee of five to investigate certain alleged plots, backed by subversive organizations, to prevent Lincoln from taking power. All this pother came to nothing, however, when the Democrats and the cooler Republicans in the House, fearful of offending Virginia and of closing the door to reconciliation elsewhere, refused to help carry any new measure looking to the employment of armed forces. Various leaders, including Charles Francis Adams, were anxious for the Northern States to arm and drill troops, without fuss or undue publicity, for the protection of the national government, and they wrote urgent letters to the State capitals.[31] But no force bill was allowed to pass. Lincoln, after reaching Washington, used his influence against any such measure.

Fort Sumter, where Major Anderson and Captain Abner Doubleday were energetically bossing laborers and soldiers who sweated to strengthen the post, was still the danger point. A host of South Carolinians burned to seize it. Governor Pickens was eager to attack as soon as he felt strong enough. Reports that he was about to strike had led Robert Toombs and ex-President Tyler to beseech him to stay his hand; and as he continued to breathe threats the Confederate Congress, much alarmed, passed a resolution on February 12 taking control of the question of the forts. At once Pickens sent a vehement protest to the president of Congress, Howell Cobb. It was vital, he wrote, to seize Sumter before Buchanan left office, so that the incoming Lincoln Administration would face the

30 There were in fact three principal measures. One, reported from the select committee on the President's message of January 8, empowered the President to accept the services of volunteers in protecting or recovering the forts and other national property. A second, from the same committee, gave the President such additional powers in collecting imports as he seemed to need in the port of Charleston. The third, reported from the House Military Affairs Committee, gave the President power to call out the militia in dealing with insurrections against the Federal authority; the existing laws covering only the use of militia against foreign invasions, or when the State governments asked for aid in quelling revolts against their peace and order. *Cong. Globe*, 36th Cong., 2d Sess., January 30–March 1, *passim*.

31 See Adams's letters, Andrew Papers; Medill's letters, Robert Todd Lincoln Papers. The steps which Northern and Southern State governments had been taking will subsequently be covered in detail, as will the situation in Virginia and the border States.

question of a declaration of war separated from any hostile act occurring since it held power! Radicals in Montgomery also wanted bold action. The Confederate Congress therefore made an aggressive move on February 22. It passed a resolution declaring that steps should be taken to obtain Forts Sumter and Pickens, by negotiation or force, as early as possible, and authorizing President Davis to make all necessary military preparations. Davis for his part wrote Pickens on March 1 that he wished to see Sumter in Confederate hands as quickly as possible, but that they must make sure of victory at the first blow; and the same day he ordered Brigadier-General Beauregard to take command at Charleston. In Washington, meanwhile, Acting-Secretary Holt warned Southern leaders again and again that the government could not give up Sumter, that it had as much right to reinforce it as to occupy it, that if Anderson required reinforcements they would be sent, and that any attack on Sumter would mean war. The stage had been set for a grand battle tableau—but still men waited.

[V]

"Lincoln is making little speeches as he wends his way toward Washington," wrote George Templeton Strong in his diary of February 18, "and has said some things that are sound and creditable and raise him in my esteem." It was true that he had said some good things. Standing on the balcony of the Bates House in Indianapolis, with the mayor and Governor Oliver P. Morton beside him, while a crowd of twenty thousand waited in the cold February twilight, he had said that maintenance of the Union depended upon the people. He had said that the word coercion needed definition: "If the United States should merely hold and retake its own forts and other property, and collect the duties on foreign importations," would that be coercion? He had said that the secessionists had a queer idea of the country: "In their view the Union, as a family relation, would seem to be no regular marriage, but rather a sort of free-love arrangement, to be maintained on passional attraction."

In Cincinnati, where he was greeted by an imposing procession and an enthusiastic crowd, he flung a pledge across the river to the Kentuckians: "We mean to treat you, as near as we possibly can, as Washington, Jefferson, and Madison treated you. We mean to leave you alone, and in no way to interfere with your institutions." In Pittsburgh and again in Albany, he had explained that he did not wish to speak prematurely on the issues: first, "I should see everything, hear everything, and have every light that can possibly be brought within my reach." Some of his extempore utterances were less felicitous. His repeated assertions that the crisis was all artificial, and that if tempers were restrained the trouble would soon come to an end, jarred on anxious citizens.

His rather clumsy attempts at wit were inappropriate to the tension of the hour. When at Westfield, New York, he asked for Grace Bedell, the little girl who had written him suggesting a beard, and said, "You see I let these whiskers grow for you, Grace," most people thought the episode undignified; as undignified as his invitation to a coal-heaver at Freedom, Pennsylvania, to clamber up on the train platform and measure heights. He did find private opportunity, however, to tell governors and local leaders that they must all stand firm in defense of the Union. On the nineteenth, he reached New York, where Strong had a glimpse of him:

Lincoln arrived here yesterday afternoon by Hudson River Railroad from Albany. I walked uptown at 3:30. Broadway crowded, though not quite so densely as on the Prince of Wales's Avatar last October. The trottoir well filled by pedestrians (vehicles turned off into side streets) and sidewalks by patient and stationary sightseers. Above Canal Street they were nearly impassable. At St. Thomas's Church I met the illustrious cortege moving slowly down to the Astor House with its escort of mounted policemen and a torrent of ragtag and bobtail rushing and hooraying behind. The great rail-splitter's face was visible to me for an instant and seemed a keen, clear, honest face, not so ugly as his portraits.

Four days later, on Saturday, newsboys at noon were crying extras in all the eastern cities. They told how a plot for Lincoln's assassination had been revealed to him at Harrisburg the previous evening; how he was to have been attacked as he rode from one station to another in Baltimore the next day; and how he thereupon left privily, disguised "in a Scotch cap and long military cloak," and by traveling all night reached Washington early in the morning. Though the alleged conspiracy sounded like a sensational piece of romancing, much evidence upon its reality has been preserved; and Lincoln's reluctant secret journey, made under the pressure of worried advisers, was wise. It was unfortunate that it detracted from the effect of his impressive short address at Independence Hall the previous morning.[32]

The eastward trip had taken eleven days; nine more were to be spent in Washington before the inauguration. Lincoln, housed in the best suite of Willard's Hotel (vacated for the time being by the wealthy William E. Dodge),

32 The Scotch cap and military cloak were fictions, and despite newspaper gibes, Lincoln's journey was entirely dignified. One element in the situation was distrust of George P. Kane, head of the Baltimore police, later arrested by General Banks and in time a Confederate officer. See Norma B. Cuthbert, *Lincoln and the Baltimore Plot, 1861*, which furnishes evidence from the Pinkerton files; R. W. Rowan, *The Pinkertons*, 82–118; Seward, *Seward*, II, 508–511. The story of the plot was temporarily discredited by W. H. Lamon in his *Life of Lincoln* because Lamon had a spiteful quarrel with Pinkerton; but it may now be regarded as valid. Nevertheless, the midnight journey did not add to Lincoln's prestige. Strong wrote in his diary for February 23: "It's to be hoped that the conspiracy can be proved beyond cavil. If it cannot be made manifest and indisputable, this surreptitious nocturnal dodging or sneaking of the President-elect into his capital city . . . will be used to damage his moral position and throw ridicule on his Administration."

was under the special guidance of Seward, who entertained him at breakfast and dinner the first day, took him to church the second, and escorted him on his visit of courtesy to President Buchanan. But Chase had taken quarters on the same floor of Willard's as Lincoln, and saw as much of him as possible. The President-elect had to receive everyone: the Illinois delegation in Congress headed by Douglas; the chief of the army, Winfield Scott; the Blair family, both father and sons, and an endless round of political callers. On his first Sunday in Washington he gave Seward a copy of his inaugural address, and that very evening the New York Senator indited a list of suggested emendations. Every observer was struck by the worn, haggard, troubled aspect of Lincoln's sensitive face.

About the incoming President, whose primary task was the completion of his Cabinet, swirled deep and murky currents of intrigue. To Seward, a perfect Cabinet would be one which included Charles Francis Adams for New England, Cameron for Pennsylvania, and Henry Winter Davis for Maryland—and which did not include Chase. Weed was in Washington, ably abetting his chieftain. To leaders of the radical wing, an ideal Cabinet would be one which included Gideon Welles for New England, someone like Wilmot for Pennsylvania, and Montgomery Blair for Maryland [33]—and which did not include Seward. Every motion that Lincoln made was watched by the rival forces with hope, dread, and suspicion. Greeley, who had come to the capital to do what he could, was almost frantic with anxiety. He wailed, on February 28, that Seward kept the incoming President perpetually surrounded, and that the compromisers would have full swing. "Old Abe is honest as the sun, and means to be true and faithful; but he is in the web of very cunning spiders and cannot work out if he would. Mrs. Abe is a Kentuckian and enjoys flattery—I mean deference. And God is above us, and all things will be well in the end. Life is not very long, and we shall rest by and by." [34]

But Lincoln intended, come what would, to be master in his own house. He meant to rule by a balance of factions and forces, in which he would hold pivotal authority. From the outset he had been determined, if possible, to have

33 Montgomery Blair, and indeed the whole Blair family, were at this moment radical with a fine Jacksonian fervor. They believed that if Buchanan had shown the nerve of Jackson, the Southern movement might have been checked at once. Montgomery wrote Governor Andrew on January 23 that he would not much care to serve in the same Cabinet with Seward and Cameron. "Neither of these gentlemen seem to me to appreciate the crisis or to comprehend what action it demands from the government. Violence is not in my judgment to be met with peace. Men intent on crime are not to be stopped from committing it by the promise of impunity, and it is my deliberate opinion that if such a policy is acted on we shall have a long and bloody war and permanent disunion. The truth is my dear friend that these gentlemen are wholly unfitted by mental and moral qualities for bearing sway in times of difficulty." Andrew Papers, MHS.
34 Greeley Papers, LC.

both Seward and Chase in his Cabinet and to give the direction to neither. He had no intention of yielding on the one side to Seward's objections to a "compound" Cabinet, nor on the other side to the last-minute battle of Chase, Greeley, and other radicals to close the door against Seward's ally in a policy of moderation, Cameron. As his biographers tell us, he listened patiently for a week to the voices of contending leaders, and found his original judgment as to the need for a balanced combination of talents unshaken.[35] He would not let Seward carry out the alleged agreements of a conference at Saratoga with David Davis the previous summer; he would not let the Chase-Sumner group be equally proscriptive on the other side. In the end, he decided to appoint Cameron to a place—which gave deep offence to the radicals or "iron-backs"; but also to appoint Welles and Montgomery Blair—which gave deep offence to Seward and his backers.[36]

By March 2, the heat generated by this battle had become so intense that informed Washingtonians looked for an explosion. Seward, the previous day, had presented an ultimatum: If Blair, Welles, and Chase all went in—and he particularly objected to Chase—he would go out. "There are differences between myself and Chase which make it impossible for us to act in harmony," he said. "The Cabinet ought, as General Jackson said, to be a unit." Lincoln expressed astonishment that at so late a day, after all the pains he had taken, and after all the negotiations that had taken place, he—facing so terrible a national upheaval—should be met with such a demand. He calmly asked Seward to reconsider the matter. Before he would yield, he was ready to part with the temperamental New Yorker. His friend Judd, hearing the gossip that was flying about, burst late one night into Lincoln's suite and asked whether he intended to put Henry Winter Davis in Blair's place as Postmaster-General. "Judd," replied Lincoln, "when that slate breaks again, it will break at the top."[37]

---

35 Nicolay and Hay, *Lincoln*, III, 368; Welles, *Diary*, II, 391.

36 Young Charles Francis Adams accepted the shelving of his father philosophically. Seward, he wrote R. H. Dana on February 28, had to drop the elder Adams and concentrate his energies on getting Cameron into the Cabinet; otherwise Lincoln would have fallen under the influence of the "iron-backs." To checkmate Chase, so violently pressed by the "ramwells," and to maintain his own peace-seeking policy, "Seward was obliged to abandon his wish to have my father in the Cabinet, and to throw his influence in favor of Cameron as a counterbalancing conservative force." But this was only one facet of the truth. Dana Papers, MHS.

37 Much light purports to be thrown on this Cabinet crisis by the mysterious *Diary of a Public Man*, attributed by Dr. Frank M. Anderson to Samuel Ward; and while its authenticity cannot be completely accepted, it bears some inner marks of veracity. See the editions by F. Lauriston Bullard and Dr. Anderson, with their introductions. Full treatment of all the complexities of the crisis would require much greater space than is here available. See Sandburg, *Lincoln*, I, 140–160; Randall, *Lincoln the President*, I, 256 ff; Nicolay and Hay, III, Ch. XXII; Hendrick, *Lincoln's War Cabinet*, 113–123; Carman and Luthin, *Lincoln and the Patronage*, 11–52; T. Harry Williams, *Lincoln and the Radicals*, 19–23, and the many biographies of Cabinet members.

Lincoln was actually ready to break his slate at the top—or to use the threat of such action to bring Seward to terms. Meeting George G. Fogg, who as secretary of the campaign committee had won his confidence, the morning after Seward's ultimatum, he described the situation. With a humorous twinkle, he remarked: "We must give up both Seward and Chase, I reckon; and I have drawn up here a list of the Cabinet leaving them both out." He showed Fogg a new slate which assigned the State Department to William L. Dayton of New Jersey and the Treasury to a New Yorker hostile to Seward. "I am sending this to Mr. Weed," dryly announced Lincoln.

That same day, Saturday, March 2, a New York deputation headed by Seward's friend Simeon Draper called to protest against Chase. They argued that Seward could never work with him. Lincoln, after listening patiently, remarked that the prime need of the nation was a hearty cooperation of all good men and all sections. At this the delegation pricked up hopeful ears, thinking he might say he would drop Chase. The President-elect drew a paper from a drawer. This, he explained, contained both his careful choice of Cabinet members, and an alternative list—the second list being in his opinion the poorer. As his hearers still radiated hope, he paused dramatically. Then he exploded his stick of dynamite! Mere mortals cannot have everything they like, he moralized. "This being the case, gentlemen, how would it do for us to agree on a change like this? How would it do for Mr. Chase to take the Treasury, and to offer the State Department to Mr. William L. Dayton?" He added that he could make Seward minister to Great Britain. And he bowed the stupefied delegation from the room.

In short, Lincoln made it plain that if Chase went, Seward must go too. And Seward had no mind to let the Administration be dominated by his rivals and enemies. He still hoped that time would justify the editorial prophecy just made by the New York *Herald*: "The destinies of the country are in Mr. Seward's hands. He will be the master spirit of the incoming Administration." He had embodied his oral ultimatum of Friday in a letter of March 2, informing Lincoln that circumstances seemed to make it his duty to withdraw his acceptance of the State Department; perhaps Draper's deputation had carried this with them. But when he heard from both Weed and Draper that if he persisted in his stand he would be shut out in the cold, he prepared to recede. On Sunday, Lincoln told Gideon Welles that although some difficulty still existed, he was satisfied that he could arrange the matter. He knew that his counter-ultimatum, "No Chase, no Seward," would be effective. "I can't afford to let Seward take the first trick," he told Nicolay.

On the morning of Monday, March 4, while the notes of the bands in the assembling procession drifted into the windows at Willard's, Lincoln penned a note, kindly but firm in tone, asking the Senator to countermand his withdrawal. "Please consider and answer by 9 o'clock tomorrow," he wrote. And that afternoon Seward, after a talk with Lincoln, came to terms. The New Yorker admitted to his wife that he had yielded. "The President is determined that he will have a compound Cabinet," he wrote; "and that it shall be peaceful, and even permanent." But even yet Seward did not begin to comprehend Lincoln's strength. After telling of his withdrawal and subsequent consent, he added: "At all events I did not dare to go home, or to England, and to leave the country to chance." Any Cabinet without himself was abandonment of the nation to chance! [38]

On the morning of the 5th Lincoln sent the Senate the names of his department heads. They were Seward as Secretary of State; Chase as Secretary of the Treasury; Cameron as Secretary of War; Gideon Welles as Secretary of the Navy; Caleb B. Smith as Secretary of the Interior; Edward Bates as Attorney-General; and Montgomery Blair as Postmaster-General. Four of the seven had been identified with the Whig Party before becoming Republicans; the other three had once been Democrats. Bates at sixty-seven was the oldest, and Montgomery Blair at forty-seven the youngest. Four members had a large national reputation, and Blair and Welles were quickly to earn one. Radical Republicans rejoiced that Chase had gained a place at Lincoln's right hand.

"Yes," exulted Greeley, "we *did*, by desperate fighting, succeed in getting five honest and noble men into the Cabinet—by a fight that you never saw equalled in intensity and duration. Gov. Chase, the ablest Republican living, who (as Gen. Dix said) was almost indispensable to the Treasury, got it at last, by the determined courage and clearheaded sagacity of Old Abe himself, powerfully backed by Hamlin, who is a jewel." Moderates also rejoiced, for their leader was head of the Cabinet. In reality neither of the two great factions of the party had won; the victory lay with the courage and wisdom of Abraham Lincoln.[39]

Meanwhile, a lesser struggle had been taking place over the contents and tone of the inaugural address. This paper had been written and set in type in Springfield, where David Davis and other intimates had read it. On the way east Lincoln showed it in Indianapolis to Orville H. Browning, who, while thinking it admirable, suggested one change. Lincoln had declared that he intended to *reclaim* the public property and national places lost to the South; Browning

38 For this Cabinet struggle, see Seward, *Seward*, II, 518; W. H. Lamon, *Recollections of Lincoln*, 49–51; Baringer, *A House Dividing*, 328, 329; Frank B. Sanborn, *Recollections of Seventy Years*, I, 26, 27; Welles, *Diary*, II, 391, 392; Nicolay and Hay, *Lincoln*, III, 370 ff.; N. Y. *Herald, Tribune, Times*, March 1–5, 1861.

39 March 12, 1861, Greeley Papers, LC. For criticism of the Cabinet, see Parker, *Morrill*, 124.

thought this too much of a threat; and Lincoln struck out the word. The most sensitive question remaining was whether, in addition to condemning secession as unconstitutional and unallowable, he should announce his purpose of protecting the property of the United States, South as well as North, executing all laws, and collecting the revenues. Any such statements will have a coercive look, said many; they will make it impossible for the Union men to hold Virginia, Maryland, Kentucky, North Carolina, and Tennessee; they will throw the border into revolution.

On this main point Lincoln stood his ground. Seward thought that instead of saying flatly that he would hold the forts and other public property, he should take refuge in an ambiguous statement that he would employ "the power confided to me" with efficiency but also with discretion. But Lincoln was adamant. He kept in his message a determined assertion: "The power confided to me will be used to hold, occupy, and possess the property and places belonging to the government, and to collect the duties and imposts." The one important change in content Lincoln made primarily on his own deeper reflection. In his original document he had spoken slightingly of any amendment of the Constitution, writing that he was not much impressed with the belief that it could be improved. Seward proposed a noncommittal statement. But Lincoln rewrote the passage, reversing his position. Stating that he would himself propose no amendments, he recognized the authority of the people over the question of constitutional change, concluding: "and I should, under existing circumstances, favor rather than oppose a fair opportunity being afforded the people to act upon it."

In lesser matters of style and tone, Seward was responsible for some marked improvements. When he objected to references to the Republican Party and Chicago platform, Lincoln, recognizing that they were improperly partisan, left them out. Lincoln elsewhere had written, "The Government will not assail you, unless you first assail it"; on Seward's advice, he omitted the last clause. Particularly did Seward improve the close of the document. Lincoln had ended with a prosaic statement that his oath required him to preserve, protect, and defend the government, and that it was for the secessionists and not himself to answer the question of peace or a sword. Seward, feeling the importance of sounding a higher note, and of concluding with words of affection and confidence, penned two paragraphs, and suggested that the President-elect take his choice. The second was truly inspired. Lincoln seized on it and gave it a perfection which has placed it among the nation's treasures of speech.[40]

40 On the inaugural address, see Browning, Diary, I, 455; Nicolay and Hay, Lincoln, III, 318 ff., 327–343; Randall, Lincoln, I, 297–310; and the well-informed Washington correspondence of the N. Y. Herald, March 2–5, 1861. David M. Potter in Lincoln and the Secession

[VI]

As a solemn public pageant, the inauguration ceremonies left nothing to be desired. The early morning was chill and cloudy, with a sharp northwest wind which swirled clouds of dust through the streets; but noon brought calm and a bright, cheerful sun. The usual host of visitors had surged into the capital, but with one sharp difference from previous years—few Southerners had come. Both Buchanan and Lincoln were busy at an early hour: the President signing bills at the Capitol, for the Senate had sat all night, and the President-elect giving a final touch to his address and receiving Bates, Welles, Cameron, Trumbull, David Davis, and other visitors. By nine o'clock crowds were filling the downtown streets, gazing at the volunteer soldiery who had begun to march and counter-march, and listening to the bands play patriotic music. Gradually the throng thickened; gradually the mounted marshals under B. B. French, with blue scarves, white rosettes, and blue-and-gold batons, got the procession into line. By noon double columns of troops flanked Willard's Hotel, and at 12:30 rolling cheers announced Buchanan's arrival in his open carriage.

General Scott had taken full precautions. As the procession to Capitol Hill got under way, riflemen were concealed on the roofs of scattered houses along Pennsylvania Avenue; platoons were stationed every hundred yards; cavalry guarded the side streets; and a guard of honor from the regular army and marines surrounded the presidential carriage so closely that it was often hard to see the occupants. Sharpshooters in the windows of the Capitol bent hawk-like eyes upon the crowd, and a battery of flying artillery was posted just north of that building. But the public saw little of all this. Its gaze was fixed on the fluttering flags and bunting, the gaily-dressed military corps, the pounding bands, and the float of thirty-four pretty girls representing as many States. Lincoln, entering the Capitol through a heavy plank passage-way, found Congress, the Supreme Court, and the diplomatic corps assembled in the Senate chamber. As attendants beat the dust of the avenue from his clothes, a reporter noted that he looked pale, fatigued, and anxious. Well he might, after the incessant conferences, interviews, dinners, receptions, and toils of the past ten days! He shook hands with friends. Then the march to the platform at the east portico began; and he was soon taking his place on that flag-dressed structure, the

---

Crisis holds that in declaring that he would not force unwelcome Federal officers upon any reluctant interior community, that he would exercise his authority "according to circumstances actually existing," and that he looked toward "a peaceful solution of the national troubles and the restoration of fraternal sympathies and affections," Lincoln was laying down both a formula and a plan; 327 ff. The mails would be delivered "unless repelled"; the duties would be collected, if at all, at sea. In short, Lincoln did not contemplate coercion, though he did insist that the Union "will constitutionally defend and maintain itself."

army and navy officers and uniformed diplomats splashing the black-coated groups about him with color.

Observant members of the great crowd (estimated at twenty-five thousand or more) facing the platform and the unfinished dome enjoyed some moments of drama. If we may believe Carl Schurz, Henry Watterson, and the author of *The Diary of a Public Man* (whose recollections, however, are not substantiated by any contemporaneous evidence) they saw Douglas, when Lincoln awkwardly sought a place for his tall hat, seize it and hold it on his knees as a symbolic act. They saw Lincoln's well-loved friend, the English-born Senator from Oregon, E. D. Baker, step forward and introduce the President-elect. They saw Lincoln lay down his manuscript, clap his hands in his pockets, and pull out a pair of steel-bowed spectacles—a surprise to those who knew him only through his pictures. As he read in his clear, shrill voice, which carried well to the outskirts of the assemblage, all listened in a solemn silence, as if moved by a conviction that the hour was big with their own fate and that of the nation. The sun shone down brightly on the gay dresses of the ladies, the uniforms and glittering weapons of the volunteer companies standing at rest on the outskirts, and the waving flags. Lincoln closed amid an intent hush. Then the crowd saw the bent, shrunken Chief Justice Taney, tottering with age and emotion, administer the oath to an incoming President whose views he deeply distrusted.[41]

The inaugural address had been awaited with feverish anxiety throughout the North, where nearly everyone felt that the nation was on the verge of its final decision for peace or war. Bulletins appeared in New York at noon: "Great excitement in Washington. The new President up all night. Great efforts to make him alter his inaugural. The President firm." This was a canard. Extras appeared there and in other cities at two o'clock, announcing that the ceremonies were safely under way; and multitudes of citizens, reading them, fervently exclaimed, "Thank God!" Evening editions carried first half and then all of the address. The comment of George Templeton Strong doubtless represents the first response of countless intelligent men. "I think there's a clank of metal in it," he wrote of the speech. "It's unlike any message or state paper of any class that has appeared in my time, to my knowledge. It is characterized by strong individuality and the absence of conventionalism of

41 The hat episode is also mentioned in J. G. Holland, *Lincoln*, 278 (1866). For a discussion of the authenticity of *The Diary of a Public Man* see James G. Randall in *Amer. Hist. Rev.*, XLI, 277-279. For the organization of volunteer companies in the District of Columbia to ensure the protection of the national capital and an orderly inauguration, see the interesting essay by Colonel Charles P. Stone in *Battles and Leaders of the Civil War*, I, 22, 23. Stone accuses Floyd of treasonable intentions. The N. Y. *Herald, Tribune,* and *Times* give full accounts of the inaugural ceremonies.

thought or diction. It doesn't run in the ruts of Public Documents number one to number ten million and one, but seems to introduce one to a *man*, and to dispose one to like him."

There was indeed a clank of metal in the address. Reciting the constitutional and historical arguments for deeming the Union perpetual, Lincoln declared: "It follows from these views that no State, upon its own mere motion, can lawfully get out of the Union; that laws and ordinances to that effect are legally void; and that acts of violence within any State or States against the authority of the United States are insurrectionary or revolutionary, according to circumstances." He proceeded:

I therefore consider that, in view of the Constitution and the laws, the Union is unbroken, and, to the extent of my ability, I shall take care, as the Constitution itself expressly enjoins upon me, that the laws of the Union be faithfully executed in all the States. . . . In doing this there needs to be no bloodshed or violence; and there shall be none, unless it be forced upon the national authority. The power confided to me will be used to hold, occupy, and possess the property and places belonging to the government, and to collect the duties and imposts; but beyond what may be necessary for these objects, there will be no invasion—no using of force against or among the people anywhere.

But the address was also full of expressions of a conciliatory spirit. Lincoln once more, and emphatically, declared that he had no purpose to interfere with slavery in the States where it existed. He asserted that in the matter of reclaiming fugitive slaves, Congress must make good the unanimous oath of its members to support the Constitution. He promised that where hostility to the United States in any interior community should be so great as to prevent resident citizens from holding Federal office, "there will be no attempt to force obnoxious strangers among the people for that object." Asking the nation to take time and think calmly, he appealed directly to the people of the South. "In your hands, my dissatisfied fellow-countrymen, and not in mine, is the momentous issue of civil war. The government will not assail you. You can have no conflict without being yourselves the aggressors. *You* have no oath registered in heaven to destroy the government, while *I* shall have the most solemn one to 'preserve, protect, and defend' it." And he ended, in poetic phrases for which Seward had supplied the framework of ideas:

I am loth to close. We are not enemies, but friends. We must not be enemies. Though passion may have strained, it must not break our bonds of affection. The mystic chords of memory, stretching from every battlefield, and patriot grave, to every living heart and hearthstone, all over this broad land, will yet swell the chorus of the Union, when again touched, as surely they will be, by the better angels of our nature.

I close.. We are not we must not be aliens or enemies but ~~countrymen~~ fellow countrymen and brethren. Although passion has strained our bonds of affection too hardly they must not be ~~broken~~ ~~they will not~~, I am sure they will not be broken. The mystic chords which proceeding from ~~every~~ ~~to~~ so many battle fields and ~~fields~~ so many patriot graves ~~and~~ pass through, all ~~the~~ hearts and ~~hearths~~ all ~~the~~ hearths in this broad continent of ours will yet ~~reason~~ again harmonize in their ~~ancient~~ music when ~~touched in the~~ ~~only~~ breathed upon ~~again~~ by the ~~better~~ ~~angel~~ guardian angel of the nation

Seward wrote the paragraph above and submitted it for the close of the inaugural address, to read: "I close. We are not we must not be aliens or enemies but fellow countrymen and brethren. Although passion has strained our bonds of affection too hardly they must not, I am sure they will not be broken. The mystic chords which proceeding from so many battle fields and so many patriot graves pass through all the hearts and all the hearths in this broad continent of ours will yet again harmonize in their ancient music when breathed upon by the guardian angel of the nation." Lincoln revised this, shortened, transmuted it into slightly different meaning and a distinctly changed verbal music, adding it to the printer's proof text brought on from Springfield, as below:

You can have no conflict, without being yourselves the aggressors. You have no oath registered in Heaven to destroy the government, while I shall have the most solemn one to "preserve, protect and defend" it. ~~...~~

☞ I am loth to close. We are not enemies, but friends— We must not be enemies. Though passion may have strained, it must not break our bonds of affection. The mystic chords of memory, stretching from every battle field, and patriot grave, to every living heart and hearth stone, all over this broad land, will yet swell the chorus of the Union, when again touched, as surely they will be, by the better angels of our nature.

It was natural that public response to the inaugural should be governed largely by party lines. The Chicago *Tribune*, the St. Louis *Democrat*, the New York *Evening Post* and *Tribune*, the Springfield *Republican*, all praised it warmly. So did such Republican leaders as Greeley, Sumner, Preston King, Hale, and Trumbull. On the other side, the Philadelphia *Pennsylvanian* called it a weak declaration of war on the South, a tiger's claw concealed under the fur of Sewardism; the Albany *Atlas and Argus* predicted that the attempt to collect revenues must lead to collision and war; and the New York *Herald* condemned it as bearing "marks of indecision, and yet of strong coercion proclivities." In the now all-important border States the secessionists regarded it as warlike, while many Union men seized on its mild phraseology as ground for hope. Thus in Virginia the fire-eating Richmond *Enquirer* declared that peace was now impossible—"Virginia must fight"; yet Governor John Letcher thought that it strengthened the hands of the conservatives. Many North Carolinians attacked it as a war message; but John A. Gilmer held that it offered cheering assurances which justified the South in waiting for the sober second thought of the North. Douglas said in the Senate on March 5 that after a careful analysis he had come to the conclusion that it was a peace and not a war speech; and John Bell declared that the South should accept it as a peace offering until by some act the North proved it otherwise.[42]

In the Lower South, however, it was generally treated as a justification of armed secession. The Charleston *Mercury* denounced Lincoln's "insolence" and "brutality"; Mobile and New Orleans journals grew inflammatory; and dispatches from Montgomery on the 5th universally construed the address as meaning that war was inevitable.

Far more important than the outward pageantry of the day were certain events of which the public knew nothing. On that historic March 4, the outgoing Secretary of War received from Major Anderson a disturbing dispatch, stating that the supplies of Fort Sumter were running low; intimating that he could not hold out much longer without help; and declaring that in his and his officers' opinion it would take at least twenty thousand troops to force their relief.[43] The South Carolinians had so strengthened the surrounding batteries, he wrote, that the fort might easily be reduced at any time. On that March 4, Martin J. Crawford of Georgia, Commissioner of the Confederate States, who had arrived in Washington only the previous day, held eager conferences with

---

42 Strong's comment on the inaugural is his MS Diary of March 5, 1861. The N. Y. *Herald* of March 5 and 6 contained an excellent resume of editorial opinion; the N. Y. *Times* of March 6 a number of excerpts. Jubal A. Early told the Virginia Convention that Lincoln's words showed he would perform his duty in moderate spirit; Munford, *Virginia's Attitude Toward Slavery and Secession*, 266. For a general survey see Randall, *Lincoln*, I, 303–308.

43 *Official Records*, Series I. Vol. I, 188 ff.

such Southern leaders as remained in the capital; and he mailed to Robert Toombs, Secretary of State in the Confederate Government, a long letter describing the situation. He wrote that Chase and Blair would compose the element in the Cabinet standing for coercion; that John Bell was in Washington, and was urgent in his entreaties to Lincoln not to disturb the Confederate States, but that he would not be heeded if the new Administration believed that it could act vigorously without losing the border States; and that "whatsoever the Republican Party can do without driving out Virginia it will do, and such coercive measures as the new Administration may *with safety* adopt it will most certainly." [43a] Ex-Senator Wigfall telegraphed from Washington that night to Charleston: "Inaugural means war. There is strong ground for belief that reenforcements will be speedily sent. Be vigilant."

Lincoln, as a matter of fact, wished to do everything within the limits of his duty to avoid a collision. When Scott, after studying Anderson's dispatch, reported to him that "evacuation seems inevitable . . . if indeed the wornout garrison be not assaulted and carried in the present week," he calmly instructed the general to give the subject further study. Nevertheless, the situation had become highly inflammable. Edward Everett, reading Lincoln's inaugural address, believed that its conciliatory tone was more than offset by the pledge to hold the forts and to collect the customs. "Either measure," he wrote in his diary, "will result in civil war, which I am compelled to look upon as almost certain." [44] Had he known what Major Anderson was reporting to Washington and what Commissioner Crawford was reporting to Montgomery, his forebodings would have been darker still.

*   *   *   *   *   *   *

Great and complex events have great and complex causes. Burke, in his *Reflections on the Revolution in France,* wrote that "a state without the means

43a Robert Toombs Letter-Book, Trescot Papers, South Caroliniana Library. Crawford's letter was dated March 3. His fellow Commissioners, John Forsyth and A. B. Roman, had not yet arrived. Bell, wrote Crawford, had assured Lincoln "that any attempt to reinforce the Forts, collect the revenue, or in any way whatever to interfere with your Government would be the signal for every border State to secede from the Union and join the Southern Confederacy. He advises an *indefinite* truce; the withdrawal of the troops from the Forts (except a sergeant with a nominal force); the flag of the U. S. to be kept floating on the fortifications to satisfy the war party North; in the meantime the Confederate States are to be left alone, to do as they may choose, prepare for war, strengthen defences, in short to do whatever may seem good to them. The advantages to the U. S. being, that the more we may do, looking to independence and safety, the greater will be the amount of taxation upon the people and the sooner will a current of dissatisfaction and discontent set in, resulting at last in a reconstruction upon the most permanent and durable basis." Crawford thought that part of the Administration was receptive to these ideas—but they would not prevail.

44 MS Diary, March 4, 1861.

of some change is without the means of its conservation," and that a constant reconciliation of "the two principles of conservation and correction" is indispensable to healthy national growth. It is safe to say that every such revolutionary era as that on which the United States entered in 1860 finds its genesis in an inadequate adjustment of these two forces. It is also safe to say that when a tragic national failure occurs, it is largely a failure of leadership. "Brains are of three orders," wrote Machiavelli, "those that understand of themselves, those that understand when another shows them, and those that understand neither by themselves nor by the showing of others." Ferment and change must steadily be controlled; the real must, as Bryce said, be kept resting on the ideal; and if disaster is to be avoided, wise leaders must help thoughtless men to understand, and direct the action of invincibly ignorant men. Necessary reforms may be obstructed in various ways; by sheer inertia, by tyranny and class selfishness, or by the application of compromise to basic principles—this last being in Lowell's view the main cause of the Civil War. Ordinarily the obstruction arises from a combination of all these elements. To explain the failure of American leadership in 1846–1861, and the revolution that ensued, is a bafflingly complicated problem.

Looking backward from the verge of war in March, 1861, Americans could survey a series of ill-fated decisions by their chosen agents. One unfortunate decision was embodied in Douglas's Kansas-Nebraska Act of 1854. Had an overwhelming majority of Americans been ready to accept the squatter sovereignty principle, this law might have proved a statesmanlike stroke; but it was so certain that powerful elements North and South would resist it to the last that it accentuated the strife and confusion. Another disastrous decision was made by Taney and his associates in the Dred Scott pronouncement of 1857. Still another was made by Buchanan when he weakly accepted the Lecompton Constitution and tried to force that fraudulent document through Congress. The Northern legislatures which passed Personal Liberty Acts made an unhappy decision. Most irresponsible, wanton, and disastrous of all was the decision of those Southern leaders who in 1858–60 turned to the provocative demand for Congressional protection of slavery in all the Territories of the republic.[45] Still other errors might be named. Obviously, however, it is the forces behind these decisions which demand our study; the waters pouring down the gorge, not the rocks which threw their spray into the air.

At this point we meet a confused clamor of voices as various students

45 We stated in an earlier chapter that Southern leaders in 1857 had time for a few more decisions, but they had to think fast and think straight. This slave-code demand represented their most flagrant error. It has been said that Jefferson Davis adopted it because his blatherskite rival A. G. Brown took it up. But a true statesman does not let an irresponsible rival force him into courses he recognizes as unwise.

attempt an explanation of the tragic denouement of 1861. Some writers are as content with a simple explanation as Lord Clarendon was when he attributed the English Civil War to the desire of Parliament for an egregious domination of the government. The bloody conflict, declared James Ford Rhodes, had "a single cause, slavery." He was but echoing what Henry Wilson and other early historians had written, that the aggressions of the Slave Power offered the central explanation. That opinion had been challenged as early as 1861 by the London *Saturday Review,* which remarked that "slavery is but a surface question in American politics," and by such Southern propagandists as Yancey, who tried to popularize a commercial theory of the war, emphasizing a supposed Southern revolt against the tariff and other Yankee exactions. A later school of writers was to find the key to the tragedy in an inexorable conflict between the business-minded North and the agrarian-minded South, a thrusting industrialism colliding with a rather static agricultural society. Still another group of writers has accepted the theory that the war resulted from psychological causes. They declare that agitators, propagandists, and alarmists on both sides, exaggerating the real differences of interest, created a state of mind, a hysterical excitement, which made armed conflict inevitable.

At the very outset of the war Senator Mason of Virginia, writing to his daughter, asserted that two systems of society were in conflict; systems, he implied, as different as those of Carthage and Rome, Protestant Holland and Catholic Spain. That view, too, was later to be elaborated by a considerable school of writers. Two separate nations, they declared, had arisen within the United States in 1861, much as two separate nations had emerged within the first British Empire by 1776. Contrasting ways of life, rival group consciousness, divergent hopes and fears made a movement for separation logical; and the minority people, believing its peculiar civilization in danger of suppression, began a war for independence. We are told, indeed, that two types of nationalism came into conflict: a Northern nationalism which wished to preserve the unity of the whole republic, and a Southern nationalism intent on creating an entirely new republic.

It is evident that some of these explanations deal with merely superficial phenomena, and that others, when taken separately, represent but subsidiary elements in the play of forces. Slavery was a great fact; the demands of Northern industrialism constituted a great fact; sectional hysteria was a great fact. But do they not perhaps relate themselves to some profounder underlying cause? This question has inspired one student to suggest that "the confusion of a growing state" may offer the fundamental explanation of the drift to war; an unsatisfactory hypothesis, for westward growth, railroad growth, business growth, and cultural growth, however much attended with "confusion," were unifying factors, and it was not the new-made West but old-settled South Carolina which led in the schism.

One fact needs emphatic statement: of all the monistic explanations for the drift to war, that posited upon supposed economic causes is the flimsiest. This theory was sharply rejected at the time by so astute an observer as Alexander H. Stephens. South Carolina, he wrote his brother on New Year's Day, 1861, was seceding from a tariff "which is just what her own Senators and members in Congress made it." As for the charges of consolidation and despotism made by some Carolinians, he thought they arose from peevishness rather than a calm analysis of facts. "The truth is, the South, almost in mass, has voted, I think, for every measure of general legislation that has passed both houses and become law for the last ten years." The South, far from groaning under tyranny, had controlled the government almost from its beginning, and Stephens believed that its only real grievance lay in the Northern refusal to return fugitive slaves and to stop the antislavery agitation. "All other complaints are founded on threatened dangers which may never come, and which I feel very sure would be averted if the South would pursue a judicious and wise course." Stephens was right. It was true that the whole tendency of Federal legislation 1842–1860 was toward free trade; true that the tariff in force when secession began was largely Southern-made; true that it was the lowest tariff the country had known since 1816; true that it cost a nation of thirty million people but sixty million dollars in indirect revenue; true that without secession no new tariff law, obnoxious to the Democratic Party, could have passed before 1863—if then.

In the official explanations which one Southern State after another published for its secession, economic grievances are either omitted entirely or given minor position. There were few such supposed grievances which the agricultural States of Illinois, Iowa, Indiana, Wisconsin, and Minnesota did not share with the South—and they never threatened to secede. Charles A. Beard finds the tap-root of the war in the resistance of the planter interest to Northern demands enlarging the old Hamilton-Webster policy. The South was adamant in standing for "no high protective tariffs, no ship subsidies, no national banking and currency system; in short, none of the measures which business enterprise deemed essential to its progress." But the Republican platform in 1856 was silent on the tariff; in 1860 it carried a milk-and-water statement on the subject which Western Republicans took, mild as it was, with a wry face; the incoming President was little interested in the tariff; and any harsh legislation was impossible. Ship subsidies were not an issue in the campaign of 1860. Neither were a national banking system and a national currency system. They were not mentioned in the Republican platform nor discussed by party debaters. The Pacific Railroad was advocated both by the Douglas Democrats and the Republicans; and it is noteworthy that Seward and Douglas were for building both a Northern and a Southern line. In short, the divisive economic issues are easily exaggerated. At the same time, the unifying economic factors were both numerous and powerful. North and South had economies which were largely complementary. It was no misfortune to the South that Massachusetts cotton mills wanted its staple, and that New York ironmasters like Hewitt were eager to sell rails dirt-cheap to Southern railway builders; and sober businessmen on both sides, merchants, bankers, and manufacturers, were the men most anxious to keep the peace and hold the Union together.[46]

We must seek further for an explanation; and in so doing, we must give special weight to the observations of penetrating leaders of the time, who knew at firsthand the spirit of the people. Henry J. Raymond, moderate editor of the New York *Times*, a sagacious man who disliked Northern abolitionists and Southern radicals, wrote in January, 1860, an analysis of the impending conflict which attributed it to a competition for power:

In every country there must be a just and equal balance of powers in the government, an equal distribution of the national forces. Each section and each interest must exercise its due share of influence and control. It is always more or less difficult to preserve their just equipoise, and the larger the country, and the more varied its great interests, the more difficult does the task become, and the greater the shock and disturbance caused by an attempt to adjust it when once disturbed. I believe I state only what is generally conceded to be a fact, when I say that the growth of the Northern States in population, in wealth, in all the elements of political influence and control, has been out of proportion to their political influence in the Federal Councils. While the Southern States have less than a third of the aggregate population of the Union, their interests have influenced the policy of the government far more than the interests of the Northern States. . . . Now the North has made rapid advances within the last five years, and it naturally claims a proportionate share of influence and power in the affairs of the Confederacy.

It is inevitable that this claim should be put forward, and it is also inevitable that it should be conceded. No party can long resist it; it overrides all parties, and makes them the mere instruments of its will. It is quite as strong today in the heart of the Democratic party of the North as in the Republican ranks; and any party which ignores it will lose its hold on the public mind.

Why does the South resist this claim? Not because it is unjust in itself,

46 South Carolina's Declaration of immediate causes of secession ignored economic issues, and concentrated upon slavery. Rhett's Address to the other slaveholding States did charge the North with gross injustice in tariff legislation; but the whole body of South Carolina's Representatives and Senators had voted for the existing tariff of 1857, and Rhett in defending his Address declared that to win the sympathy of Britain and France, a protest against protective tariffs would be more useful than a protest grounded on the slavery question. McPherson, *Political History*, 12-20.

but because it has become involved with the question of slavery, and has drawn so much of its vigor and vitality from that quarter, that it is almost merged in that issue. The North bases its demand for increased power, in a very great degree, on the action of the government in regard to slavery—and the just and rightful ascendency of the North in the Federal councils comes thus to be regarded as an element of danger to the institutions of the Southern States.

In brief, Raymond, who held that slavery was a moral wrong, that its economic and social tendencies were vicious, and that the time had come to halt its growth with a view to its final eradication, believed that the contest was primarily one for power, and for the application of that power to the slave system. With this opinion Alexander H. Stephens agreed. The Georgian said he believed slavery both morally and politically right. In his letter to Lincoln on December 30, 1860, he declared that the South did not fear that the new Republican Administration would interfere directly and immediately with slavery in the States. What Southerners did fear was the ultimate result of the shift of power which had just occurred—in its application to slavery:

Now this subject, which is confessedly on all sides outside of the constitutional action of the Government, so far as the States are concerned, is made the 'central idea' in the platform of principles announced by the triumphant party. The leading object seems to be simply, and wantonly, if you please, to put the institutions of nearly half the States under the ban of public opinion and national condemnation. This, upon general principles, is quite enough of itself to arouse a spirit not only of general indignation, but of revolt on the part of the proscribed. Let me illustrate. It is generally conceded by the Republicans even, that Congress cannot interfere with slavery in the States. It is equally conceded that Congress cannot establish any form of religious worship. Now suppose that any one of the present Christian churches or sects prevailed in all the Southern States, but had no existence in any one of the Northern States,—under such circumstances suppose the people of the Northern States should organize a political party, not upon a foreign or domestic policy, but with one leading idea of condemnation of the doctrines and tenets of that particular church, and with an avowed object of preventing its extension into the common Territories, even after the highest judicial tribunal of the land had decided they had no such constitutional power. And suppose that a party so organized should carry a Presidential election. Is it not apparent that a general feeling of resistance to the success, aims, and objects of such a party would necessarily and rightfully ensue?

Raymond and Stephens agreed that the two sections were competing for power; that a momentous transfer of power had just occurred; and that it held fateful consequences because it was involved with the issue of slavery, taking authority from a section which believed slavery moral and healthy, and giving it to a section which held slavery immoral and pernicious. To Stephens this transfer was ground for resuming the ultimate sovereignty of the States. Here we find a somewhat more complex statement of James Ford Rhodes's thesis that the central cause of the Civil War lay in slavery. Here, too, we revert to the assertions of Yancey and Lincoln that the vital conflict was between those who thought slavery right and those who thought it wrong. But this definition we can accept only if we probe a little deeper for a concept which both modifies and enlarges the basic source of perplexity and quarrel.

The main root of the conflict (and there were minor roots) was the problem of slavery *with its complementary problem of race-adjustment;* the main source of the tragedy was the refusal of either section to face these conjoined problems squarely and pay the heavy costs of a peaceful settlement. Had it not been for the difference in race, the slavery issue would have presented no great difficulties. But as the racial gulf existed, the South inarticulately but clearly perceived that elimination of this issue would still leave it the terrible problem of the Negro. Those historians who write that if slavery had simply been left alone it would soon have withered overlook this heavy impediment. The South as a whole in 1846–61 was not moving toward emancipation, but away from it. It was not relaxing the laws which guarded the system, but reinforcing them. It was not ameliorating slavery, but making it harsher and more implacable. The South was further from a just solution of the slavery problem in 1830 than it had been in 1789. It was further from a tenable solution in 1860 than it had been in 1830. Why was it going from bad to worse? Because Southern leaders refused to nerve their people to pay the heavy price of race-adjustment. These leaders never made up their mind to deal with the problem as the progressive temper of civilization demanded. They would not adopt the new outlook which the upward march of mankind required because they saw that the gradual abolition of slavery would bring a measure of political privilege; that political privilege would usher in a measure of economic equality; that on the heels of economic equality would come a rising social status for the Negro. Southern leadership dared not ask the people to pay this price.

A heavy responsibility for the failure of America in this period rests with this Southern leadership, which lacked imagination, ability, and courage. But the North was by no means without its full share, for the North equally refused to give a constructive examination to the central question of slavery as linked with race adjustment. This was because of two principal reasons. Most abolitionists and many other sentimental-minded Northerners simply denied that the problem existed. Regarding all Negroes as white men with dark skins, whom a few years of schooling would bring abreast of the dominant race, they thought that no difficult adjustment was required. A much more numerous body of Northerners would have granted that a great and terrible task of race adjustment existed—but they were reluctant to help shoulder any part of it. Take a million or two million Negroes into the Northern States? Indiana, Illinois, and even Kansas were unwilling to take a single additional person of color. Pay tens of millions to help educate and elevate the colored population? Take even a first step by offering to pay the Southern slaveholders some recompense for a gradual liberation of their human property? No Northern politician dared ask his constituents to make so unpopular a sacrifice. The North, like the South, found it easier to drift blindly toward disaster.

The hope of solving the slavery problem without a civil war rested upon several interrelated factors, of which one merits special emphasis. We have said that the South as a whole was laboring to bolster and stiffen slavery—which was much to its discredit. But it is nevertheless true that slavery was dying all around the edges of its domain; it was steadily decaying in Delaware, Maryland, western Virginia, parts of Kentucky, and Missouri. Much of the harshness of Southern legislation in the period sprang from a sense that slavery was in danger from *internal* weaknesses. In no great time Delaware, Maryland, and Missouri were likely to enter the column of free States; and if they did, reducing the roster to twelve, the doom of the institution would be clearly written. Allied with this factor was the rapid comparative increase of Northern strength, and the steady knitting of economic, social, and moral ties between the North and West, leaving the South in a position of manifest inferiority. A Southern Confederacy had a fair fighting chance in 1861; by 1880 it would have had very little. If secession could have been postponed by two decades, natural forces might well have placed a solution full in sight. Then, too, the growing pressure of world sentiment must in time have produced its effect. But to point out these considerations is not to suggest that in 1861 a policy of procrastination and appeasement would have done anything but harm. All hope of bringing Southern majority sentiment to a better attitude would have been lost if Lincoln and his party had flinched on the basic issue of the restriction of slavery; for by the seventh decade of nineteenth century history, the time had come when that demand had to be maintained.

While in indicting leadership we obviously indict the public behind the leaders, we must also lay some blame upon a political environment which gave leadership a poor chance. American parties, under the pressure of sectional feeling, worked badly. The government suffered greatly, moreover, from the lack of any adequate planning agency. Congress was not a truly deliberative body, and its committees had not yet learned to do long-range planning. The President might have formulated plans, but he never did. For one reason, no President between Polk and Lincoln had either the ability or the prestige required; for another reason, Fillmore, Pierce, and Buchanan all held that their duty was merely to execute the laws, not to initiate legislation. Had the country possessed a ministerial form of government, the Cabinet in leading the legislature would have been compelled to lay down a program of real scope concerning slavery. As it was, leadership in Washington was supplied only spasmodically by men like Clay, Douglas, and Crittenden.

And as we have noted, the rigidity of the American system was at this time a grave handicap. Twice, in the fall of 1854 and of 1858, the elections gave a stunning rebuke to the Administration. Under a ministerial system, the old government would probably have gone out and a new one have come in. In 1854, however, Pierce continued to carry on the old policies, and in 1858 Buchanan remained the drearily inept helmsman of the republic. Never in our history were bold, quick planning and a flexible administration of policy more needed; never was the failure to supply them more complete.

Still another element in the tragic chronicle of the time must be mentioned. Much that happens in human affairs is accidental. When a country is guided by true statesmen the role of accident is minimized; when it is not, unforeseen occurrences are numerous and dangerous. In the summer and fall of 1858, as we have seen, the revival of a conservative opposition party in the upper South, devoted to the Union, furnished a real gleam of hope. If this opposition had been given unity and determined leadership, if moderate Southerners had stood firm against the plot of Yancey and others to disrupt the Democratic Party, if Floyd had been vigilant enough to read the warning letter about John Brown and act on it, the situation might even then have been saved. Instead, John Brown's mad raid fell on public opinion like a thunderstroke, exasperating men everywhere and dividing North and South more tragically than ever. The last chance of persuading the South to submit to an essential step, the containment of slavery, was gone.

The war, when it came, was not primarily a conflict over State Rights, although that issue had become involved in it. It was not primarily a war born of economic grievances, although many Southerners had been led to think that they were suffering, or would soon suffer, economic wrongs. It was not a war created by politicians and publicists who fomented hysteric excitement; for while hysteria was important, we have always to ask what basic reasons made possible the propaganda which aroused it. It was not primarily a war about slavery alone, although that institution seemed to many the grand cause. It was a war over slavery *and* the future position of the Negro race in North America. Was the Negro to be allowed, as a result of the shift of power signalized by Lincoln's election, to take the first step toward an ultimate position of general economic, political, and social equality with the white man? Or was he to be held immobile in a degraded, servile position, unchanging for the next hundred years as it had remained essentially unchanged for the hundred years past? These questions were implicit in Lincoln's demand that slavery be placed in a position where the public mind could rest assured of its ultimate extinction.

Evasion by the South, evasion by the North, were no longer possible. The alternatives faced were an unpopular but curative adjustment of the situation by the opposed parties, or a war that would force an adjustment upon the loser. For Americans in 1861, as for many other peoples throughout history, war was easier than wisdom and courage.

RESPONSIBILITY OF McLEAN AND CURTIS FOR THE DRED SCOTT DECISION

The evidence available does not warrant dogmatic statements on the prime responsibility for the annulment of the Missouri Compromise restriction; but there are reasons why we may entertain doubts as to the sole burden of McLean and Curtis. The truth seems rather to be that the responsibility falls upon a number of the judges, and that Wayne must be included among those whose share in bringing about a broad decision was greatest.

To begin with, we have the knowledge that, from the outset, Southern leaders like Stephens and Democratic journals like the *Union* were urging the slave State judges to write a broad decision. We have Catron's statement as early as February 6 that Daniel was prepared to deliver his opinion "at length." We have Judge Campbell's testimony that Wayne, at a conference February 14, prior to the reading of Nelson's judgment, moved that his limited decision be put aside and that Chief Justice Taney write another of sweeping character— a motion which carried. Campbell not only made this statement to Taney's biographer Tyler, but repeated it in a letter of October 30, 1879, to George Ticknor Curtis. After accurately reciting many details, Campbell wrote: "Judge Wayne made the motion. . . . He stated that the case had been twice argued with thoroughness; that public expectation had been awakened and a decision of the important question looked for; that the Court would be condemned as failing in a performance of its duty, and that his own opinion was decided that the Chief Justice should prepare the opinion of the Court, and discuss all of the questions in the cause. There was no debate about this. It seemed to be acquiesced in, though some did not approve it." [1] Wayne, according to G. T. Curtis, made public boast of his achievement the day it was won.

Senator Yulee of Florida also asserts that Wayne had accepted primary responsibility for the broad verdict. From two sources we have proof that Judge Benjamin R. Curtis identified Wayne as the prime mover in substituting a broad for a narrow judgment; for Judge Curtis told his brother this, and he also told Clement H. Hill, one-time Assistant Attorney-General of the United States, that Wayne not only persuaded the Chief Justice to recall the case from Judge Nel-

[1] Campbell to George T. Curtis, October 30, 1879; Campbell Papers, courtesy of Charles Warren.

son, but busied himself to induce the other judges to concur in Taney's decision.[2] For that matter, Wayne states in the first sentence of his own brief concurrence with Taney that *before* the Chief Justice wrote his opinion he had prepared one which he subsequently laid aside as superfluous.[3]

In the second place, the question of motive enters. What possible reason had Curtis and McLean for provoking a judgment that Congress possessed no power over slavery in the Territories? They knew that all freesoilers dreaded such a pronouncement, which would be hailed as a resounding triumph for slavery. To be sure, McLean has been accused of a political motive in wishing to strengthen himself with the Republican Party. But this accusation is unconvincing in view of the facts that since the convention of 1856 he was politically dead; that in 1860 he would be seventy-five and within a year of his grave; and that the first weeks of 1857, with the Democrats assuming power for another four years, were no time to think of political chances. Moreover, to take a step seemingly certain to strengthen the new Administration would be perverse political tactics. On the other hand, Southern members of the Court knew that a decision annulling the Missouri Compromise restriction would be hailed with joy in all slavery areas. Press, politicians—and President-elect—were telling them that it would unify their party and give it enduring advantages. They had a motive for acting, while the two freesoil members had none. It was with reference to this Southern and Democratic attitude that Montgomery Blair, accurately writing Martin Van Buren on February 5, 1857, that the Missouri Compromise would be invalidated, stated his belief that the decision would be influenced by *outside pressure* on the judges (Van Buren Papers).

The majority of the Court, moreover, had special reasons for deeming this an opportunity not to be lost. The Dred Scott case, the first which had permitted a clear-cut decision on the Compromise, might also be the last to occur in many years. Chief Justice Taney was now old and ailing. Kindly Judge Curtis wrote his brother in February: "Our aged Chief Justice, who will be eighty years old in a few days, and who grows more feeble in body, but retains his alacrity and force of mind wonderfully, is not able to write much." The outcry against the partisan and sectional character of the Court was making a sharp impression. Before a similar case occurred, the character of the panel might be altered completely. Taney, his patriotism alloyed by sectionalism, indubitably wished to use the Court to bulwark his own people and their institutions. His most acute biographer writes: "First and foremost it is necessary to remember his devotion to the South, of which he was a product, and his belief that, if the trend of events continued, the South was doomed. . . . His deepest fear seems

2 Curtis, *Const. Hist. U. S.*, 266–278; Curtis, *Benjamin R. Curtis*, I, 234–236.
3 19 *Howard*, 454.

to have been that when a northern political party assumed the reins of government the South would not act with sufficient unanimity to make rebellion effective." [4] Now was the moment, if ever, to strike a judicial blow for Southern rights in the Territories.

Still another consideration may be noted. While the statement of Grier and Catron as to the provocative stand of the two dissentients might seem credible with respect to McLean (whose opinion took up the issues in a curious inverse order, dealing with Congressional power before he considered in detail the action of the courts below), it is quite incredible as regards Judge Curtis. That conservative Whig of the Daniel Webster school, who had protested against Sumner's election, who had endorsed the Seventh of March speech, who had long represented the views of State Street business circles, was one of the last men in the country to act a radical part. The abolitionists attacked him as a "doughface." [5] His son's biography expressly states that every word of both his and McLean's opinions was written only *after* they had heard Taney's judgment read in conference.[6] Moreover, his judgment protested against the Court's sweeping action. He declares in it that after the Court had decided that Dred was a slave under Missouri law, it could not properly proceed to larger issues. "I dissent . . . from . . . the opinion . . . that a person of African descent cannot be a citizen of the United States; and I regret I must go further and dissent . . . from what I deem their assumption of authority to examine the constitutionality of the act of Congress commonly called the Missouri Compromise. . . . I feel obliged to say that, in my opinion, such an exertion of judicial power transcends the limits of the authority of the Court."

How could a justice who denied the Court's right to examine the issue of Congressional power, and rebuked it for doing so, have insisted upon discussing that issue when the Court first proposed to avoid it? To be sure, Judge Curtis argued that his own position was different; that since he held that the Federal courts possessed jurisdiction, he was bound to consider the merits of the case to ascertain if the judgment of the lower court were correct; and that he must declare the Supreme Court of Missouri wrong in its judgment, which conflicted with the weight of judicial opinion in the slave States and with its own

4 Swisher. *Taney*, 503–504. Curtis has been accused of taking the broad ground to curry favor with Boston, where he would later practice law. But (1) it is not clear that at this time he had determined to resign from the Court; (2) his legal eminence would have given him a lucrative practice no matter what his political views; (3) conservative Boston businessmen would have warmly approved if he had refused to rouse new sectional issues; and (4) his lifelong integrity makes such a charge absurd. As for McLean, he would certainly have been glad to pen a ringing dissent at the time of the first argument, in the December term of 1855, when it would have helped his chances in the Republican Convention of 1856. But that time was now past, and the situation was completely altered.

5 October 22, 1854, et seq.; Quincy Papers.
6 Curtis, *Benjamin R. Curtis*, I, 238.

previous decisions. His argument up to this point rested upon the validity of the eighth section of the Missouri Compromise Act. But the whole tenor of his opinion bears out the statement of his son and biographer that "every word" was written as a dissent from an opinion of the Chief Justice which he "had heard read in conference," and which had "elaborately maintained" the unconstitutionality of the Compromise.

It is not necessary, in setting aside the statements of Grier and Catron, to question the veracity of these men; we may merely question their accuracy. While we must not be dogmatic in passing upon this murky question of responsibility, it would seem that they give a partial and partisan view of a complex transaction.

Admittedly, when the judges began considering the case in conference a series of angry discussions ensued. Tradition states that one session grew so violent that Taney had to use his authority to restore order. As the debate became heated, judges on both sides doubtless manifested a desire to set down certain views on paper. Justice McLean would tell Wayne that if he expressed his erroneous ideas publicly, McLean would voice contrary opinions; Wayne and Daniel would retort in kind. Emerging from such a debate, when Catron and Grier wrote to Buchanan they would naturally describe the dissentients as the provocative members, just as McLean would naturally place the blame at a Southern door. We can go further; we can imagine several Southern judges discussing the case after a heated conference, agreeing that the views of Curtis and McLean were pernicious, and coming to regard the pair as trouble-makers, even if they wished to voice their conclusions only in private. In short, the letters of Catron and Grier can be explained simply as a distortion of the painful controversy then raging.

It is an indisputable fact that during the consultations of the court in the spring of 1856, on the first argument of the case before it, radical opinion both South and North had hoped for a decision on the Missouri Compromise question. The Washington correspondent of the New York *Tribune*, James Harvey, expressed the hope that with "aid from the Southern members of the court" a broad decision would be rendered. When Nelson at that time moved a re-argument of the issues, it was (as Father Vincent C. Hopkins, S.J., shows in his monograph *The Dred Scott Decision*) both because he was uncertain of the proper scope of the decision, and because he doubted the wisdom of bringing the court "in collision with a popular election." After the victory of Buchanan, the desire of Republicans for a broad decision naturally abated, while that of Democrats outside the popular sovereignty school remained keen. It is significant that the critical motion on February 14, 1857, was made by Judge Wayne. He made it abruptly. As we have seen, he pointed to the public interest and expectation that the case had aroused. He declared that the court would fail in meeting the anticipations of the country if it did not render a broad decision. These are not the words of a man reluctantly spurred to action by two opponents; they are the words of a man speaking his own wishes and keenly conscious of outside pressures. A majority of other judges (Nelson being absent) readily assented; and thus the die was cast. From all the evidence, it seems clear that responsibility must be widely distributed, and that while McLean may have been a prime mover, Wayne—and probably Daniel—did not lag behind him.

It remains to say a few words about President-elect Buchanan's intervention. While no "conspiracy" was concocted between him and Taney, he did let key members of the Court know just what kind of decision he wanted, and just why he wanted it; so that the Court would save him from the peril of independent action on the disputed interpretation of popular sovereignty, quiet that disruptive question, restore unity to the party, and strike a crushing blow at the basic doctrine of the Republicans.[7] He moved the hesitant Grier to act. If Grier had not done so, Congressional power over slavery in the Territories might not have been adjudged null. Buchanan assumed a heavy partial responsibility for the Dred Scott decision. He had always taken a realistic view of the bench. He had long thought that politics should govern it. Six years earlier, he had written that the Democrats must control the Pennsylvania Supreme Court:

The mind that is strongly imbued with Democratic principles will naturally and necessarily take a different view of great constitutional and other highly important questions involving the rights and liberties of the people from that taken by a mind which has all its life delighted in high-toned federal doctrines. I agree that upon questions of mere *meum* and *tuum*, the politics of the judge could make no difference, but upon important questions involving the first principles of our government the difference might be very great. No Whig President has ever appointed a Democratic Judge of the Supreme Court of the United States, nor has a Democratic President appointed a Whig.[8]

It may be added that the Dred Scott decision was interestingly reviewed in one of the Insular Cases, *De Lima vs. Bidwell* (1901); and that the able argument of Frederic R. Coudert in this case contains much illuminating matter (182 U.S. 1).

7 See Grier's revealing phrase, "The cause of our anxiety to produce this result." Philip Auchampaugh considers Buchanan's note at length in "James Buchanan, the Court, and the Dred Scott Case," *Tenn. Hist. Mag.*, IX, January, 1926.
8 Buchanan to Mr. Hemphill, July 18, 1851; Buchanan Papers.

Appendix II

THE MORMON WAR

Almost no secondary account of the collision in Utah does justice to the Mormon position. This is presented with some fullness in H. H. Bancroft's *History of Utah* (1890) and B. H. Roberts's six-volume *History of the Church of Jesus Christ of Latter Day Saints* (1902–12), as well as in the writings of Brigham Young and the files of the *Deseret News*.

The conflict is incomprehensible without some grasp of a number of facts. (1) The Mormons at no time expected to establish an independent republic in Utah. They manifested their eagerness to become a member of the Union when early in 1849 they petitioned Congress to give them a government with the least possible delay; and they were pleased by Millard Fillmore's appointment of Young as governor of the Territory, September 28, 1850. (2) From an early date Gentiles had some valid complaints against the Mormons. When Young and other leaders found the overland trail pouring many emigrants through their community they were disturbed; and the result was non-intercourse regulations which greatly restricted trade with non-Mormons. Moreover, Mormons tended to regard the territorial government as applying primarily to Gentiles, for the church government controlled their own people. A dual system grew up, one civil and one religious, with two sets of courts. When litigation arose over chance affrays, trespass by emigrant cattle, marriages outside the church, and other matters, non-Mormons often felt treated with injustice. (3) From an early date the Mormons had valid complaints against the United States. Their land-titles were not secure; their memorials asking for statehood were treated with contempt; Congress gave Utah stingier appropriations than other Territories. (4) While all Territories suffered from the bad character of some Federal appointments, Utah had special reason to complain. Chief Justice George P. Stiles and Associate Justice W. W. Drummond were inefficient, tactless, and guilty of personal misconduct; and both deliberately fomented trouble by baseless accusations. (5) The turmoil over slavery in the East contributed to the discord; for especially after the Republican platform of 1856 denounced polygamy, attacks on the Mormons became politically popular.

In the end, provocative conduct by Federal officeholders was matched by provocative conduct on the part of Mormon leaders. Both sides, as Levi E. Young writes in *The Founding of Utah* (1923), were frequently rash and hotheaded. Buchanan did not sufficiently comprehend the special character of the Mormon community, which is vividly portrayed in Richard F. Burton's *The City of the Saints* (1861). They had an exceptional body of skilled artisans from the East and England; they were specially careful of education; they were a highly disciplined community. Brigham Young, for his part, did not sufficiently comprehend the American detestation of polygamy, the fear that Western travel routes would be blocked, or the eastern suspicion that he was trying to keep Utah an unassimilated enclave. Both men learned a lesson.

B. H. Roberts in the fourth volume of his comprehensive work on the Latter Day Saints attributes the Utah expedition to the mistaken impression of the national government that the Territory was in rebellion; to the influence of contractors who expected fat pickings from Secretary Floyd; and to the rivalry of the Democrats and Republicans in using the anti-Mormon issue to gain votes. He emphasizes the prejudice of the troops employed, quoting Captain J. R. Murdock: "All the way from the States to Laramie it was G—d d—n the Mormons." It is clear from his narrative that both the leadership in Washington and that in Salt Lake City altered its policy as events developed. Buchanan was at first determined upon rigorous measures; later, under pressure of American and European opinion, he became more forbearing. As for the Mormons, they were originally bent on armed resistance; then, after a council on March 18, 1858, they resolved on flight; and finally they made terms. Roberts's history is dry and one-sided, but accurate and extremely detailed. Naturally he pays warm tribute to Kane and Cumming. H. H. Bancroft's *Utah* is equally partisan, and bears evidence of having been compiled under Mormon aspices (see the *Nation*, February 27, 1890). For a corrective of the bias displayed in these books, general readers may consult William Alexander Linn's *The Story of the Mormons* (1902), which is strongly critical in tone. In this careful volume, based largely on the Helen Gould collection of Mormon materials, the sixth chapter deals with "Brigham Young's Despotism"; the eighth with "Some Church-Inspired Murders"; the eleventh with "Mormon Treatment of Federal Officers," Linn speaking of "the practical nullification of federal law"; and chapters 12–15 inclusive with "The Mormon War." Another work hostile to the Mormons, but more valuable than Linn's, is F. J. Cannon and G. L. Knapp, *Brigham Young and his Mormon Empire* (1913). Bernard De Voto includes in *Forays and Rebuttals* (1936) an admirable essay on Young and his achievement.

Official sources on the conflict fortunately provide a great mass of material. The annual report of the Secretary of War for 1858 contains documents on the Utah expedition by A. S. Johnston and other officers; that for 1858 gives more than two hundred pages to correspondence and reports on Utah affairs; and that for 1859 again includes a large body of official data on developments in the Department of Utah.. As noted in the text, House Exec. Doc. 71, 35th Cong., 1st Sess., treats of the expedition, its 215 pages being invaluable to students. Senate Exec. Doc. 2, 35th Cong., 2d Sess., covers the Mountain Meadow massacre and related matters. The National Archives contain much unpublished matter on the Utah expedition and Mormon affairs. Among the holdings may be mentioned a bound volume of general orders from New York headquarters relating to Utah; a volume of copies of headquarters letters 1857–59; a volume docketing the letters received by the Army of Utah 1857–59; and volumes containing copies of all letters written from headquarters of the Utah Forces or Department of Utah 1858–60. The Archives also have a package of letters and reports on the Mountain Meadow massacre, with a valuable map of the area.

For a general illumination of the Utah scene, no book compares with Richard F. Burton's *The City of the Saints*. Its tone is highly favorable. While the despotic tendencies of the theocracy and the crudities of Utah society did not escape the acute Englishman, he was impressed by Brigham Young's robust strength of mind and will, and still more by the miracle which Mormon industry had wrought within a dozen years in a wilderness waste. Burton had the insight to see that the conflict between the Mormon church-state and the nation grew out of an underlying social and economic conflict.

Appendix III

PRESIDENT BUCHANAN AND FOREIGN AFFAIRS

In most important diplomatic matters, President Buchanan was inclined to disregard Secretary Cass, who was infirm of health, timid, and deficient in vigor. "He brought many questions to me which he ought to have decided for himself," later wrote Buchanan, adding that Cass also relied heavily on Cobb and Black.[1] The President prided himself upon his own success in the foreign field. Particularly did he gain much for the United States in dealing with Great Britain, as the British themselves acknowledged. "We have yielded to the Americans in some of our recent disputes," remarked the London *Times* in 1859, "but it is because they were right and we were wrong." The newspaper was doubtless referring to the controversy over the Mosquito Coast and Bay Islands in Central America, and to the dispute over the right of maritime visitation and search. On these issues Great Britain gave way completely and in good temper. But Buchanan's achievements were not as completely creditable as most American diplomatic histories, excessively nationalistic in tone, have implied.

Anglo-American relations when he entered office were a good deal better than men might have expected in view of recent events. President Pierce in 1856 had dismissed the British Minister, J. F. T. C. Crampton, and three British consuls, for their activity in enlisting Americans for Crimean War service. This was done after the British Government had disavowed any intention of violating American neutrality laws, and had expressed sincere regret if any violation had taken place. Many Americans thought the action excessively harsh. Senators Toombs and Butler deplored it; so did a number of newspapers, led by the Washington *National Intelligencer* and New York *Journal of Commerce*. Britons took credit for patient endurance of the American rebuke. The government, stated Delane's *Times*, on July 31, 1856, had done well to show meekness. "A few more strokes of the pen, a few more blustering speeches on the one side and a little dogged obstinacy on the other, and at this moment 28,000,000 of British subjects would have been equipping the materials for carrying destruction among 27,000,000 of kindred people on the other side of the Atlantic."

The British government and people were aware that in the Crimean War the United States had not shown a marked sympathy for the Allies. W. H.

1 *Works*, XI, 59.

481

Trescot, for example, who was to become Assistant Secretary of State in June, 1860, wrote a pro-Russian pamphlet on the subject. London knew how violently anti-British were the speeches constantly uttered by many leading American politicians. Douglas, at the Washington dinner to Kossuth, had gone out of his way to denounce "proud, haughty England," and to say that if American institutions triumphed she must "give up her monarchy, her nobility, her Establishment, the whole system of machinery by which she has been able to oppress her own people." Even Seward was addicted to twisting the lion's tail. Speaking in the Senate on January 31, 1856, he had threatened war, talked of overwhelming Britain, and painted a vision of Canada joining the United States in the struggle. British consuls kept their government informed of the anti-British activities of Irish clubs, and of the constant drilling of Irish organizations calling themselves Emmet Guards, Phoenix Rifles, and like names.

Happily, the British also knew that the Anglophobe utterances of the New York *Herald* and Stephen A. Douglas were not representative of dominant American feeling. Buchanan expressed the view of nearly all sensible men when he said of British and America: "No two countries have ever existed on the face of the earth which could do each other so much good or so much harm." Emerson's *English Traits* (1856), full of praise both for the English people and English civilization, was one of his most successful books. "After all," wrote Richard Rush to Trescot, "What a glorious old country it [Britain] is. . . . In some things it shoots ahead faster than even we do. In others of course it cannot. Next to our own country, why should we not love our mother country better than any other?" [2] When Consul Bunch in 1857 addressed a gathering of Southerners in Charleston to celebrate the opening of the Memphis & Charleston Railroad, the reception of his speech electrified him. The mayor of Memphis rose excitedly to shout: "Three cheers for old England!" The Charleston *Mercury* printed an extra edition to meet the demand for Bunch's speech, while he had more invitations to visit Southern communities than he could fill in a year. The greeting given the Prince of Wales in 1860 was largely a tribute to Britain. The New York *Times* declared that Americans, well aware that they drew their language, literature, laws, and political spirit from England, found in her "the type of everything cherished and endeared." [3] Just after Buchanan's Administration closed the New York *Evening Post* paid the general policy of the British Government a warm tribute:

Whatever the English people may have said or thought of us, nothing is plainer than that our people have looked with growing admiration at the brave stand of England, in Europe, for liberty. Foreign writers have assured us again

2 July 30, 1853; Trescot Papers, South Caroliniana Library.
3 May 21, 1861.

and again that the liberal policy of England in continental Europe was only a measure of annoyance to her rival powers, and that when she encouraged Garibaldi in Italy, or defended Turkey against Russia, she was moved simply by considerations of interest, and not principle. But we have denied the imputation, and our people have been firm in the belief that Great Britain was strong because she was right. . . . It is not too much to say that a great part of England's strength has lain in this conviction, that she was a great moral power.[4]

Buchanan had a valuable asset in handling Anglo-American affairs in his personal familiarity with British leaders. Lord Clarendon was an old friend to whom he wrote with candor on many subjects: the importance of keeping a strong British minister in Washington, the desirability of a British acceptance of the American construction of the Clayton-Bulwer Treaty, and the weakness of the dull Sir William Gore Ouseley as a special envoy to arrange matters with Nicaragua and Honduras. When Richard Cobden visited Washington in April, 1859, Buchanan frankly declared his preferences as to British leadership. "In the course of conversation in the evening," writes Cobden, "he expressed the hope that Lord Palmerston would not again become Prime Minister, as it would be unfavorable to the maintenance of friendly relations between England and America; that although personally partial to Lord Palmerston he (the President) regarded him as hostile to the United States and of belligerent character; that he (Lord Palmerston) was unpopular with the people of America, who considered him dictatorial; and that he (the President) could in any negotiations make concessions to Lord Aberdeen which he would not dare to make to Lord Palmerston." [5]

The Buchanan Administration gained much that was highly creditable; had it not been for the complicating factor of slavery, these gains would have been offset with less that was discreditable. Slavery entered strongly into Central American affairs.

The British Government had made pretensions in Central America which the United States declined to recognize, its claims to a protectorate over the Indians of the Mosquito Coast of Nicaragua and Honduras, and to ownership of the Bay Islands off the Honduran shore, being quite unacceptable to Washington. The United States held that the Clayton-Bulwer Treaty was retroactive in debarring Britain from these areas; London at first held that the treaty was merely prospective and hence recognized Britain's earlier acquisitions. However, yielding to the American argument, Great Britain agreed to give up all claim to the disputed areas. In 1859 she negotiated treaties with Nicaragua and Honduras granting them full sovereignty over the territory, and late in 1860 Buchanan announced to Congress that the United States was satisfied with the

4 May 28, 1861.
5 MS Diary, April 28, 1859, Midhurst, Sussex.

arrangement. Before ceding the Bay Islands to Honduras, however, Great Britain attempted to incorporate in the treaty a provision excluding slavery from them. This offended Southern Senators, and the clause was dropped.

In Central American affairs, moreover, sauce for the goose was by no means sauce for the gander. While Washington was warning Britain from the Mosquito Coast, a citizen of the United States, William Walker, was possessing himself of the government of Nicaragua, becoming president in July, 1856. In several Southern States his agents collected supplies and arms and enlisted recruits with a boldness which furnished an interesting commentary upon the American dismissal of Crampton. They kept recruiting offices open in New Orleans, Mobile, and other seaports, with offers posted of free land grants to every volunteer.

A Central American coalition, by a tremendous effort which the republics still count among their glories, overthrew Walker, who on May 1, 1857, took refuge with the United States Navy. Organizing a new expedition and easily evading the Federal authorities, he was soon back in Nicaragua again. His agent W. R. Henry meanwhile took open steps to organize a regiment of Texas Rangers and concentrate it at Galveston. The New Orleans *True Delta* made merry over the "vigilance" of Federal officers who did not notice the wonderful pile of coal on one of Walker's ships, with articles of strange character under it, and the curious presence of artillery and medical staffs among the crew. Walker's second invasion was cut short when late in 1857 Commodore Hiram Paulding arrested him and sent him back to the United States. Southern members of Congress fiercely denounced the commodore; Buchanan in a special message of January 7, 1858, accused him of a grave error. When the President also seized the occasion to condemn lawless military expeditions which had aroused the suspicion and dread of Latin America, his words offended many Southerners.

Walker, always and increasingly an opportunist, utilized his final residence on American soil to pen a book, *The War in Nicaragua*, which was published early in 1860, and which combined a remarkably interesting and accurate record of his campaigns with an appeal to the South to reestablish slavery in Central America. The section, he wrote, must break through all barriers and "get her institution to tropical America" before restrictive treaties were made. He had planned a new descent upon Central America. But only a handful of men rallied to his standard; and, falling into the hands of the Honduran forces soon after he began his summer invasion of the little republic, he was shot on September 12, 1860. A blow to filibustering, his death was also a blow to schemes for the forcible expansion of slavery southward.

Slavery affected Anglo-American relations still more importantly when in 1859 a bitter dispute arose over the issue of maritime visit and search. Mr. Lewis

Einstein writes that Great Britain was trying to revive an offensive claim of the power of search "in the name of virtue," and that "to a great extent the slave trade was only the excuse." [6] How far this statement diverges from the facts will be plain to anyone who studies the published records of the Foreign Office, the best newspapers of the day, and William Law Mathieson's engrossing book *Great Britain and the Slave Trade, 1839–1865.*

It is a fact that the illegal carriage of slaves from Africa to Cuba was largely conducted under the American flag, by vessels sailing from American ports, and with capital from American sources. It is also a fact that while Britain and America kept squadrons off the African coast, the vigilance of the British warships had contrasted strikingly with the inefficiency of the American vessels —especially those under Southern officers. It is a further fact that in most instances no mode of detecting a suspected slaver existed except boarding her. Some of the slave-trading was done by foreigners in America, like the New York firm of Cunha, Reis & Co.; much of it was managed by Americans. The New York *Leader* of May 26, 1860, declared that an average of two vessels a week cleared the port bound for Africa and a slave cargo, and the New York *World* endorsed the figure. This was doubtless an exaggeration. Nevertheless, an informed writer in the New York *Evening Post*, under date of July 25, 1860, listed thirty-nine American ships known to have been in the slave trade during the Buchanan Administration, and the same paper a few days later gave a further list of eighty-five slave-trade ships fitted out from New York between February, 1859, and July, 1860. The British consul in New York, Archibald, had corroborative information from a secret informer. The inhumanity of the business defied description. The British naval commander on the West African station wrote in 1859: [7]

This expensive, cruel system is accompanied by the most terrible, most heart-rending loss of life that can well be conceived. In chained gangs the unfortunate slaves are driven by the lash from the interior to the barracoons on the beach; there the sea-air, insufficient diet, and dread of their approaching fate produce the most fatal diseases; dysentery and fever release them from their sufferings; the neighboring soil grows rich in the decaying remains of so many fellow-creatures, and the tracks are thick-strewn with their bones. On a short march of six hundred slaves, a few weeks back, intended for the *Emma Lincoln,* one hundred and twenty-five expired on the road. The mortality on these rapid marches is seldom less than twenty percent. Such, sir, is the slave trade under the American flag.

Soon after Buchanan became President, British warships seized several American vessels, suspected of being in the slave trade, off the African coast.

6 See his monograph on Cass in Bemis, *Amer. Secs. of State,* VI.
7 Quoted in Mathieson, *Great Britain and the Slave Trade,* 164.

The *Panchita* was arrested and sent in to New York. Inasmuch as the Anglo-American treaty of 1842 provided that the two nations should maintain naval units to enforce "separately and respectively" the laws prohibiting the slave trade, Secretary Cass made repeated protests. Soon afterward, in the spring of 1858, instances were reported of the British detention and search of American vessels in the Gulf of Mexico. A storm sprang up in Congress. Much of it represented a sincere desire to vindicate the old and fundamental American devotion to the principle of the freedom of the seas. But not a little of it was fomented by men who, like Keitt of South Carolina and Israel T. Hatch of New York, wished to use the incidents to destroy the Clayton-Bulwer Treaty and embark on Carribbean conquests. This bad treaty, declared Keitt, has bound "our feet while standing in the very porch of tropical power and wealth." "Cuba will be ours," declaimed Hatch; "England must surrender Roatan [British Honduras]." Reuben Davis of Mississippi said he abhorred the word negotiation—he would negotiate at the cannon's mouth.[8] A few men, like Garnett of Virginia, condemned the agitation for war as food for demagogues and stockjobbers. On June 15, 1858, the Senate unanimously voted a resolution pledging the United States to maintain the immunity of its merchantmen on the high seas.

President Buchanan ordered every naval vessel within reach to the Gulf with instructions to protect American ships from detention or search. A collision there might have had disastrous consequences. Happily, Lord Malmesbury, the Foreign Minister, quickly assented to the American position. At the same time he suggested that Cass might propose some method of meeting the fraudulent use of the American flag by slavers. Cass in return declared himself ready to receive any suggestion that Great Britain might be ready to make. At this point Mr. Einstein halts his narrative, and most histories of our foreign relations say little more on the subject.

The discreditable sequel is actually worth careful attention. It was now possible for any slaver to hoist the American flag, and no non-American warship might touch it. The profits of a successful voyage might be enormous. One trader named Mitchell boasted in New York in 1860 that by landing 1300 Africans in Cuba at $1,000 a head he had cleared a million dollars. The British Government proposed that American and British cruisers patrol the African coast in pairs so that one could deal with ships using the American flag, the other with ships flying no flag at all. Washington withheld its assent to the plan, though as previously noted, the American squadron was increased and given a more effective base. The importation of slaves into Cuba in 1859, still largely under American auspices, was estimated by the British authorities at about 30,000; in 1860, thanks to better naval dispositions and to a new Captain-General

8 *Cong. Globe*, 36th Cong., 1st sess., 2860 ff.

in Cuba, Serrano, the number was reduced to 18,000. Lord John Russell, in a debate in the Commons on February 26, 1861, summarized his fruitless expostulations with Secretary Cass:

I said, "If your national pride will not allow an English officer to search vessels belonging to the United States, employ cruisers of your own. If you will not allow British cruisers to put down the slave trade, put it down yourself, and take all the credit and glory which will attach to the successful extinction of the slave trade. Do it effectually—do it for the sake of your own character, for the sake of that great republic which I hope may still remain the United States of America." The President of the United States directed the Secretary of State to tell me that the American Government had already heard enough of these remonstrances on the part of the British Government, and hoped that they would not be continued.

Southern pressure largely accounted for the uncooperative attitude of the Buchanan Administration; pressure like that of Jefferson Davis, who told the Senate that he favored abrogating the article of the treaty which required maintenance of a squadron on the African coast, and the concentration of national attention on an armed force to protect the American flag.

Mexican policy was handled in the main by Buchanan, not Cass, and it too showed distinct marks of Southern pressure. The treatment in James Morton Callahan's *American Foreign Policy in Mexican Relations* offers an excellent summary. That the turmoil and disorder in Mexico were almost intolerable, and that American rights were flagrantly violated, there can be no question. The President's proposal in December, 1859, to enter Mexico with military force to obtain indemnity for the past and security for the future had some resemblances to President Theodore Roosevelt's subsequent proposals respecting Santo Domingo. Buchanan was correct in pointing to the danger of European intervention if the Mexican chaos continued: "It would not be surprising should some other nation undertake the task [of pacification], and thus force us to interfere at last, under circumstances of increased difficulty for the maintenance of our established policy." This was prophetic of French action. But American policy was suspect in that Buchanan's concept of indemnity for the past, like that of many Southerners, embraced the cession of Lower California, and if possible part or all of Sonora and Chihuahua. The complete failure of the two able ministers, John Forsyth and Louis McLane, to gain Buchanan's objects, makes a story which contrasts strikingly with his successes in dealing with Great Britain.

POPULATION RETURNS AS AMERICANS READ THEM IN 1860–61
(From *Appleton's Annual Cyclopaedia*, 1861)

STATES	CENSUS OF 1860			
	White	Free Colored	Slave	Total
Alabama	526,534	2,630	435,132	964,296
Arkansas	324,186	137	111,104	435,427
California	376,200	3,816	.....	380,016
Connecticut	451,609	8,452	.....	460,151
Delaware	90,697	19,723	1,798	112,218
Florida	77,778	908	61,753	140,439
Georgia	591,638	3,459	462,232	1,057,329
Illinois	1,704,684	7,069	.....	1,711,753
Indiana	1,340,072	10,869	.....	1,350,941
Iowa	673,925	1,023	.....	674,948
Kansas	106,487	623	.....	107,110
Kentucky	920,077	10,146	225,490	1,155,713
Louisiana	357,642	18,638	333,010	709,290
Maine	627,081	1,195	.....	628,276
Maryland	516,128	83,718	87,188	687,034
Massachusetts	1,221,611	9,454	.....	1,231,065
Michigan	742,289	6,823	.....	749,112
Minnesota	171,793	229	.....	172,022
Mississippi	353,969	731	436,696	791,396
Missouri	1,064,369	2,983	114,965	1,182,317
New Hampshire	325,622	450	.....	326,072
New Jersey	647,084	24,947	.....	672,031
New York	3,831,730	49,005	.....	3,880,735
North Carolina	631,489	30,097	331,081	992,667
Ohio	2,303,374	36,225	.....	2,339,599
Oregon	52,343	121	.....	52,464
Pennsylvania	2,849,997	56,373	.....	2,906,370
Rhode Island	170,703	3,918	.....	174,621
South Carolina	291,623	9,648	402,541	703,812
Tennessee	826,828	7,235	275,784	1,109,847
Texas	421,411	339	180,682	602,432
Vermont	314,534	582	.....	315,116
Virginia	1,047,613	57,579	490,887	1,596,079
Wisconsin	774,392	1,481	.....	775,873
	26,727,512	470,716	3,950,343	31,148,571
TERRITORIES				
Colorado	34,153	44	.....	34,197
Dakotah	4,839	.....	.....	4,839
Nebraska	28,755	71	10	28,836
Nevada	6,803	54	.....	6,857
New Mexico	93,447	70	24	93,451
Utah	40,236	30	29	40,295
Washington	11,548	30	.....	11,578
Dist. of Columbia	60,788	11,107	3,181	75,076
	27,008,081	482,122	3,953,587	31,443,790

THE NUMBER OF FUGITIVE SLAVES

According to the Seventh Census, the number of fugitive slaves in the year ending June 1, 1850, was 1,011; according to the Eighth Census, the fugitives for the year ending June 1, 1860, totalled 803. These were out of a slave population of 3,200,000 in 1850 and 3,950,500 in 1860. Both tables of fugitives include all absconding and hiding slaves—those, for example, who took refuge in swamps or mountain areas near home. Indeed, the Eighth Census explicitly declares: "it is not pretended that all missing in the border states, much less any considerable number escaping from their owners in the more Southern regions, escaped into the free States." The census returns showed that the borderland (which complained little) had the most fugitives; the Lower South (which complained bitterly) had the least. Delaware suffered the highest proportionate losses in both 1849–50 and 1859–60; South Carolina and Georgia suffered little. In total numbers of missing slaves, Maryland and Kentucky stood at the head of the list.

No other statistics on the number of fugitive slaves possess any factual basis whatever. It is impossible to determine their number by examining the increase of Negro population in the North, or in Canada. Estimates by politicians and editors of the period are contradictory and unconvincing. Senator James M. Mason of Virginia put the annual loss of his State at about $30,000 in a speech of January, 1850, and above $100,000 in a speech the next August! He was obviously guessing. When J. F. H. Claiborne declared in 1860 that the South had lost 100,000 fugitive slaves in the past fifty years, and the New Orleans *Commercial Bulletin* of December 19, 1860, asserted it had lost 75,000, they were obviously guessing. Most Northern estimates of the fugitives ran below the census totals, and most Southern estimates well above. Senator Walker Brooke of Mississippi supported the census totals for his State when he assured the Senate in 1852 that slaves there seldom if ever escaped to the North.

The whole subject has been carefully studied by Mr. Claude Bragdon in a monograph deposited in the Columbia University Library. His conclusion is that the monetary loss in fugitive slaves, which according to the census may have reached $800,000 in 1860, but which really cannot be calculated with any accuracy, provoked the South much less than the bad faith attributed to the North in refusing to execute the Fugitive Slave Act. Mason told the Senate on December 11, 1860: "The loss of property is felt, the loss of honor is felt still more."

Bibliography

I: MANUSCRIPT COLLECTIONS

(MHS denotes Massachusetts Historical Society; HL denotes Huntington Library; LC denotes Library of Congress. In all its sections, this Bibliography is but partial and suggestive. A full list of sources would far transcend the space here available.)

Anderson Papers, La. State Univ. Archives; Diary of Harrod C. Anderson, La. State U. Archives; John A. Andrew Papers, MHS; Appleton-Sumner Correspondence, Boston PL; Bagby Papers, Univ. of N. C.; Bayard Papers, LC; "Bill of Sale Book 1853" (actually 1848–57), S. C. State Archives; Jeremiah S. Black Papers, LC, Pa. Hist. Soc.; Blair-Lee Papers, Princeton Univ.; Borden Papers, Univ. of Texas; Boteler Papers, Duke Univ.; L. O. Branch Papers, Duke Univ.; Briggs, Samuel, MS Journal; Brodhead Papers, Mo. Hist. Soc.; John Brown Papers, Chicago Hist. Soc., LC, Ohio Arch. and Hist. Soc., Boston PL., etc.; Bryant Papers, NYPL; Buchanan Papers, Pa. Hist. Soc., N. Y. Hist. Soc., LC; Buchanan-Johnston Papers, LC; A. Burt Papers, Duke Univ.; Cameron Papers, LC; Chamberlain Papers, Boston PL; Zachariah Chandler Papers, LC; Chase Papers, LC, NYPL, Ohio Arch. and Hist. Soc., etc.; Claiborne Papers, Miss. Dept. Archives and Hist.; Claiborne Papers, Univ. of N. C.; C. C. Clay Papers, Duke Univ.; Clay, Mrs. C. C., MS Recollections, Duke Univ.; Clayton Papers, LC; Colfax Papers, Indiana State Lib.; S. W. Crawford Papers, Ill. State Hist. Lib.; Francis P. Corbin Papers, NYPL; Thomas Corwin Papers, LC; John J. Crittenden Papers, LC; S. R. Curtis, MS Journal, Ill. State Hist. Lib.; Cushing Papers, LC, MHS; Dana, R. H., Jr,. Papers, MHS; Davis Papers, Duke Univ.; De Leon, Daniel, Scrapbook, South Caroliniana Lib.; De Leon Papers, South Caroliniana Lib.; Stephen A. Douglas Papers, Univ. of Chicago, Ill. State Hist. Soc., LC; Du Bose Family Papers, Ala. State Dept. Arch. and Hist.; Duff Green Papers, LC; Duyckinck, Evert, MS Diary, NYPL; W. H. English Papers, Indiana State Lib.; Everett Papers, MHS; Ewing Papers, LC; Fish Papers, LC, Columbia Univ.; H. F. French Papers, LC; Gaillard, S. Porcher, Journal, 1856–1858, South Caroliniana Lib.; Garrison Papers, Boston PL; Giddings Papers, Western Reserve Hist. Soc.; Gould, W. P., MS Diary, Ala. State Dept. of Arch. and Hist.; Governors' Papers, Ala. State Dept. of Arch. and Hist.; Governors' Letter Books, Va. State Lib.; William A. Graham Papers, Univ. of N. C.; Gratz, Henry H., MS Reminiscences, Mo. Hist. Soc.; Greeley-Colfax Papers, NYPL; Greeley Papers, LC; Gregg Account Book, 1854–1855, South Caroliniana Lib.; Allen Hamilton Papers, Indiana State Lib.; Hammond, Edward S., MS Plans . . . Views of Agriculture, South Caroliniana Lib.; Hammond, James H., MS Journal, South Caroliniana Lib.; James H. Hammond Papers, LC; Hoge, Dr. J. D., MS Journal, HL; Hopkins, Kate, and Carolina, MS Poems, 1850, South Caroliniana Lib.; Houston Papers, Texas State Hist. Lib.; Richard J. Hinton Papers, Kan. State Hist. Lib.; R. M. T. Hunter Papers, Va. State Lib.; Thaddeus Hyatt Papers, Kan. State Hist. Lib.; G. W. Julian Papers, Indiana State Lib.; Keitt Papers, Duke Univ.; Kennedy Papers, Peabody Institute; Charles Lanman Papers, LC; Lanphier Papers, Ill. State Hist. Lib.; Liddell Family Papers, La. State Univ. Archives; Lieber Papers, HL; Lincoln Papers, LC; Robert Todd Lincoln Papers, LC; Lincoln Collection, Ill. State Hist. Lib.; Bulwer Lytton Papers, Duke Univ.; Robert McClelland Letter Book, LC; McClernand Papers, Ill. State Hist. Lib.; Maury Papers, Univ. of N. C.; Charles S. May Papers, Detroit Public Lib.; Memminger Papers, Univ. of N. C.; Minor Family Papers, La. State Univ. Archives; Moore Papers, La. State Univ. Archives; Moran, B., MS Diary, LC; E. D. Morgan

Papers, N. Y. State Hist. Lib.; Franklin Pierce Papers, LC; New Hampshire State Hist. Soc.; Pierpont Papers, Brock Collection, HL; J. S. Pike Papers, Calais (Me.) PL; Porcher Miles Papers, Univ. of N. C.; Pruyn, John V. L., MS Diary, New York State Hist. Lib.; Pugh Collection, Univ. of Texas Archives; Edmund Quincy Papers, MHS; Rives Papers, LC; Charles Robinson Papers, Univ. of Kansas, Kan. State Hist. Lib.; Edmund Ruffin Diary, LC; Rusk Papers, Univ. of Texas; Schirmer MS Diary, Charleston Hist. Soc.; George R. Smith Papers, Mo. Hist. Soc.; Gerrit Smith Papers, Syracuse Univ.; Kirby Smith Papers, Univ. of N. C.; Alexander H. Stephens Papers, LC; George Templeton Strong Diary, Columbia Univ.; Stuart Collection, HL; Charles Sumner Papers, Harvard Univ. Lib.; Swain Papers, N. C. Hist. Commission Lib.; Thayer, William W., MS Autobiography, LC; Judge Samuel Treat Papers, Mo. Hist. Soc.; William Trescot Papers, South Caroliniana Lib.; Lyman Trumbull Papers, LC; Wade Papers, LC; Thurlow Weed Papers, Univ. of Rochester; Weehaw Plantation Book, Charleston Hist. Soc.; Welles, Edward E., MS Diary, Miss. Dept. Arch. and Hist.; Gideon Welles Papers, LC, NYPL; Winthrop Papers, MHS; Daniel Woodson Papers, Kan. State Hist. Lib.; Yancey, W. L., MS Address to the Erosophic and Philomathic Societies, Ala. State Lib.; Yancey Papers, Ala. State Lib.

II: CONTROVERSIAL BOOKS, PAMPHLETS, AND REPORTS

Anon., "Five Years' Progress of the Slave Power" (pamphlet); Anon., "Letters for the People on the Present Crisis" (pamphlet, dated October 1, 1853); *The Abolition of Slavery in Cuba and Puerto Rico* (pamphlet, 1865); American Anti-Slavery Society, *Reports*, 1850–1861; Baines, Rev. Albert, *The Church and Slavery*; Barnes, Gilbert H. and Dumond, Dwight L., *Letters of Theodore Dwight Weld, Angelina Grimké Weld and Sarah Grimké, 1822–1844*, 1934; Barnard, F. A. P., Tuscaloosa Oration, July 4, 1851 (pamphlet); Birney, James G., *The American Churches the Bulwarks of American Slavery*; Bowen, Francis, *The Principles of Political Economy Applied to the Condition . . . of the American People*, 1856; Brown, G. G., Speech on Gradual Emancipation in Missouri (pamphlet, 1857); Cairnes, John E., *The Slave Power*, 1862; Christy, David, *Cotton is King*, 1855; Cobb, T. R. R., *An Inquiry into the Law of Negro Slavery*, 1858; De Bow, James D. B., *Industrial Resources of the Southern and Western States*, Three Vols., 1852–53; Dewees, Jacob, *The Great Future of Africa and America*, 1854; Donnan, Elizabeth, ed., *Documents, Illustrative of the History of the Slave Trade to America*, 1930–1932; Fisher, Ellwood, "The North and The South" (pamphlet, 1849); Fitzhugh, George, *Sociology for the South*, 1854; Fitzhugh, George, *Cannibals All! or, Slaves Without Masters*, 1857; Grayson, W. J., *Letters of Curtius*, 1851; Grayson, W. J., *The Hireling and the Slave*, 1854; Helper, Hinton R., *The Impending Crisis of the South: How to Meet It*, 1857; Hildreth, Richard, *The Slave: or, Memories of Archie Moore*, 1840; Hopkins, John H., *The American Citizen, His Rights and Duties*, 1857; Humphrey, Rev. Heman, *The Missouri Compromise* (pamphlet); Kettell, T. P., *Southern Wealth and Northern Profits*, 1860; Lowell, James Russell, *Anti-Slavery Papers*, Two Vols., 1902; May, Samuel J., *Some Recollections of Our Anti-Slavery Conflict*, 1868; Martineau, H., *Society in America*, 1837; Noyes, John H., *History of American Socialisms*, 1870; Parsons, D. D., *Inside View of Slavery*; Proceedings of the Convention of the Knights of the Golden Circle, Raleigh, May 7–11, 1860 (pamphlet); *The Pro-Slavery Argument, as Maintained by the Most Distinguished Writers of the Southern States*, 1853; A St. Louisian, "Letters for the People in the Present Crisis" (pamphlet); Stevens, C. E., *Anthony Burns, A History*, 1856; Townsend, John, *The South Should Govern the South* (pamphlet, 1860); Trenholm, W. L., *The South: An Address*, April 7, 1869 (pamphlet); Turner, Lorenzo D., *Anti-Slavery Sentiment in American Literature Prior to 1865*, 1929; Wolfe, S. M., *Helper's Impending Crisis Dissected*.

III: TRAVEL

Ampère, J. J., *Promenade on Amérique*, Two Vols., 1855; Ashworth, Henry, *A Tour in the United States, Cuba, and Canada*, 1859; Audubon, Marian W., and Hodder, Frank H., *Audubon's Western Journal, 1849–50*; Baxter, W. E., *America and the Americans*, 1855; Bishop, Mrs. I. L., *Aspects of Religion in the United States*, 1859; Bremer, Fredrika, *Homes of the New World*, Two Vols., 1853; Buckingham, James S., *America: Historical, Statistical, and Descriptive*, Three Vols., 1841; Buckingham, James S., *The Slave States of America*, 1842; Burns, Rev. Jabez, *Tour of the United States and Canada*, 1848; Caird, James, *Prairie Farming in America*, 1859; Chambers, William, *Things As They Are in America*, 1854; Cunynghame, Arthur, *A Glimpse at the Great Western Republic*; Dana, Richard A, *To Cuba and Back: A Vacation Ramble*, 1859; Dicey, Edward, *Six Months in the Federal States*, 1863; Gladstone, T. H., *Englishman in Kansas*, 1856; Grattan, T. C., *Civilized America*, Two Vols., 1859; Greeley, Horace, *An Overland Journey from New York to San Francisco in the Summer of 1859*, 1859; Ingraham, Joseph H., *The Southwest, by a Yankee*, 1835; Lyell, Sir Charles, *Travels in North America in the Years 1841–42*, 1845; Lyell, Sir Charles, *A Second Visit to the United States*, Two Vols., 1849; Mackay, Alexander, *The Western World*, Three Vols., 1849; Mackay, Charles, *Life and Liberty in America*, 1859; Martineau, Harriet, *Retrospect of Western Travel*, 1838; Monaghan, Frank, *French Travellers in the United States, 1765–1932: A Bibliography*, 1933; Nevins, Allan, *American Social History Recorded by British Travellers*, rev. ed., 1931; Olmsted, Frederick L., *A Journey in the Back Country in the Winter of 1853–54*, 1860; Olmsted, Frederick L., *A Journey in the Seaboard Slave States*, 1856; Olmsted, Frederick L., *A Journey Through Texas*, 1857; Pierson, George W., *Tocqueville and Beaumont in America*, 1938; Raumer, Ludwig von, *America and Her People*, 1846; Reid, H., *Sketches in North America, with some Account of Congress and the Slavery Question*, 1855; Russell, Robert, *North America: Its Agriculture and Climate*, 1857; Schaff, Philip, *Sketch of the Political, Social, and Religious Character of the United States of North America*, 1855; Sullivan, Sir E. R., *Rambles and Scrambles in North and South America*, 1853; Torrielli, Andrew J., *Italian Opinion of America as Revealed by Italian Travellers, 1850–1900*, 1941; Tremenheere, Hugh S., *Notes on Public Subjects in the United States and Canada*, 1856; Tuckerman, Henry T., *America and Her Commentators*, 1864; Wilson, James Grant, *Thackeray in the United States*, Two Vols., 1904.

IV: BIOGRAPHIES, DIARIES, REMINISCENCES; A SELECTED LIST

(Arranged alphabetically by *subject*. The *Dictionary of American Biography*, edited by Allen Johnson and Dumas Malone, furnishes a comprehensive guide to biographical data and sources.)

Charles Francis Adams, Jr., *Charles Francis Adams* (American Statesmen Series), 1900; *Charles Francis Adams, 1835–1915, An Autobiography, With a Memorial Address by Henry Cabot Lodge*, 1916; *The Education of Henry Adams: An Autobiography*, 1918; Worthington C. Ford, ed., *A Cycle of Adams Letters, 1861–1865*, two volumes, 1920; Worthington C. Ford, ed., *Letters of Henry Adams 1858–1891*, 1930; Harold Dean Cater, *Henry Adams and His Friends*, 1947. The first of these volumes is tantalizingly brief, and its chapter on the secession winter is by no means satisfactory. We need a full publication of the diary and principal letters of the elder Charles Francis Adams for the years 1850–1861. The autobiography of the younger Charles Francis Adams has an enlightening chapter entitled "Washington, 1861," which in the famous autobiography of Henry Adams is matched by a chapter called "Treason (1860–1861)." The letters of the two sons show well what they did and thought, but leave the course of the elder Adams only partially elucidated. That he labored valiantly to preserve peace there can be no doubt.

Henry Greenleaf Pearson, *The Life of John A. Andrew, Governor of Massachusetts 1861–1865*, two volumes, 1904. A pedestrian compilation, in which the chapter "First Months as Governor" contains useful letters and documents on Andrew's prompt preparations for war.

M. A. De Wolfe Howe, *Life and Letters of George Bancroft*, two volumes, 1908; Russel B. Nye, *The Biography of George Bancroft*, 1944. These lives of the eminent historian, of which Mr. Howe's offers the fuller quotations from letters and Mr. Nye's the greater detail, show how a Jacksonian Democrat reacted against the policies of the proslavery men.

Howard K. Beale, ed., *The Diary of Edward Bates, 1859–1866*, 1933; Floyd E. McNeil, *Lincoln's Attorney-General, Edward Bates*, MS doctoral diss., University of Iowa. The diary is invaluable for the borderland opposition to Buchanan, the Republican campaign of 1860, and the making of Lincoln's cabinet.

Thomas Hart Benton, *Thirty Years' View*, 1854–1856; Theodore Roosevelt, *Thomas Hart Benton* (American Statesmen Series), 1886; William M. Meigs, *Life of Thomas Hart Benton*, 1905. The *View* is an elaborate survey of American politics from 1820 to 1850. Roosevelt's life, though a hasty piece of work, shows grasp of character; Meigs's biography is detailed, careful, and dull.

John Bigelow, *Retrospections of an Active Life*, five volumes, 1909–1913; Margaret Clapp, *Forgotten First Citizen: John Bigelow*, 1947. The first volume of the *Retrospections* covers Bigelow's career from youth to the spring of 1863, and offers interesting letters and comments on public affairs. Miss Clapp's fine biography covers the Frémont campaign, the panic of 1857, and the crisis of 1860–1861.

William Birney, *James G. Birney and His Times*, 1890; Dwight L. Dumond, *Letters of James G. Birney, 1831–1857*, two volumes, 1938. These works, besides throwing general light on the antislavery movement, contain a corrective of much writing by and about the Garrisonian school.

W. N. Brigance, *Jeremiah S. Black*, 1934; Chauncey F. Black, ed., *Essays and Speeches of Jeremiah S. Black, With a Biographical Sketch*, 1885. The essays include Black's replies to Douglas on territorial sovereignty, and a very hostile examination of the character and career of Seward. The biography furnishes a discriminating estimate of Black as Attorney-General. On his career as Secretary of State see the essay by Roy F. Nichols in S. F. Bemis, ed., *American Secretaries of State and Their Diplomacy*, VI, 387–406 (1928).

R. J. Hinton, *John Brown and His Men*, 1894; Franklin B. Sanborn, *The Life and Letters of John Brown*, 1885; Oswald Garrison Villard, *John Brown 1800–1859: A Biography Fifty Years After*, 1910; Robert Penn Warren, *John Brown, The Making of a Martyr*, 1929; Hill Peebles Wilson, *John Brown, Soldier of Fortune: A Critique*, 1913. Of these books Villard's massive biography is the ablest and most thorough. Its final chapter on Brown's influence, "Yet Shall He Live," is worth special attention. Wilson goes over the evidence with the object of showing that "the story reveals little which is creditable to Brown or worthy of emulation and much that is abhorrent"; Warren attempts a balanced view. Most other books on John Brown should be avoided as inaccurate and confusing. Among magazine articles Alexander R. Boteler's "Recollections of the John Brown Raid" in the *Century*, July, 1883, is specially interesting. Brown's life to the age of fifty deserves a careful book.

Parke Godwin, *A Biography of William Cullen Bryant, With Extracts From His Private Correspondence*, two volumes, 1883; Parke Godwin, ed., *Complete Prose Writings of William Cullen Bryant*, two volumes, 1884; John Bigelow, *William Cullen Bryant* (American Men of Letters Series), 1880. Bryant was a greater editor than is commonly realized, and has been more fortunate in his biographers than Greeley. The four volumes given us by Parke Godwin throw much light on the history of the times.

George Ticknor Curtis, *The Life of James Buchanan*, two volumes, 1883; John Bassett Moore, ed., *The Works of James Buchanan*, twelve volumes, 1908–1911; Philip G. Auchampaugh, *James Buchanan and His Cabinet on the Eve of Secession*, 1926. Curtis's work is stiff, unrevealing, and full of gaps; Auchampaugh's, though showing careful scholarly research, is ill-organized and partisan. A good modern biography of Buchanan based on the extensive collections of his papers remained in 1950 to be written.

Gaillard Hunt, *John C. Calhoun*, 1908; W. M. Meigs, *Life of John Caldwell Calhoun*, two volumes, 1917; Hermann Von Holst, *John C. Calhoun* (American Statesmen Series), 1882; R. K. Crallé, *Works of John C. Calhoun*, six volumes, 1851–1855; J. Franklin Jameson, ed., *Correspondence of John C. Calhoun*, 1900. All previous biographies of Calhoun are now being supplanted by the large work of Charles M. Wiltse, of which the second volume was published in 1949. The three older biographies all possess merit, though Von Holst was too unsympathetic to understand the man.

Salmon P. Chase, *Diary and Correspondence* (Ann. Report Am. Hist. Ass., 1902, II); Albert B. Hart, *Salmon Portland Chase* (American Statesmen Series), 1899; J. W. Schuckers, *Life and Public Services of Salmon Portland Chase*, 1874; Robert B. Warden, *Private Life and Public Services of Salmon P. Chase*, 1874. The life by Warden was undertaken at Chase's own request; that by Hart is the most scholarly and readable.

Carl Schurz, *Henry Clay*, two volumes, 1887; George R. Poage, *Henry Clay and the Whig Party*, 1936; Glyndon G. Van Deusen, *Life of Henry Clay*, 1937; C. Colton, *Life and Times of Henry Clay*, revised edition, six volumes, 1864. A full biography of Henry Clay by Bernard Mayo has been begun. The volumes by Schurz in the American Statesmen Series constitute a masterly work, interpreting the man and his times with insight. New facts and ideas are added by Van Deusen's biography. The work by Colton contains speeches and correspondence.

Rowland Dunbar, ed., *Jefferson Davis, Constitutionalist: His Letters, Papers and Speeches*, ten volumes, 1923; Jefferson Davis, *The Rise and Fall of the Confederate Government*, two volumes, 1881; Mrs. Jefferson Davis, *Jefferson Davis, A Memoir*, two volumes, 1890; Edward A. Pollard, *Life of Jefferson Davis, With a Secret History of the Confederacy*, 1869; William E. Dodd, *Jefferson Davis*, 1907; Hamilton J. Eckenrode, *Jefferson Davis, President of the South*, 1923; Allen Tate, *Jefferson Davis, His Rise and Fall: A Biographical Narrative*, 1929. Other biographies of Davis, including the two volumes by Robert M. McElroy, might be added. It is perhaps the fault of the subject that none seems satisfactory. The chapters on this period by Varina Howell Davis in the first volume of her life of her husband are more interesting and more genuinely informative than the *Rise and Fall* by Davis himself.

George Fort Milton, *The Eve of Conflict: Stephen A. Douglas and the Needless War*, 1934; Allen Johnson, *Stephen A. Douglas*, 1908; William Garrott Brown, *Stephen Arnold Douglas*, 1902; Clark E. Carr, *Stephen A. Douglas, His Life, Public Services, Speeches and Patriotism*, 1909. Based on the voluminous Douglas Papers, Milton's biography is one of the indispensable works on the period. But the volume by Brown is a keen-minded study of personality, and that by Allen Johnson offers an accurate and fair survey. A collection of Douglas's own letters would be highly useful. No student should neglect Frank E. Stevens's monograph on Douglas in Volume 16 of the *Journal of the Ill. State Hist. Soc.*, 1924, with its many facts not available elsewhere.

James E. Cabot, *A Memoir of Ralph Waldo Emerson*, two volumes, 1887; Van Wyck Brooks, *Emerson and Others*, 1927; Ralph L. Rusk, *Ralph Waldo Emerson*, 1949; Edward Waldo Emerson, ed., *Complete Works of Ralph Waldo Emerson* (Centenary Edition), *With a Biographical Introduction and Notes*, twelve volumes, 1903–1904. The literature on Emerson is vast; see the bibliography in the *Cambridge History of American Literature*, I, 551–566, complete to 1917. The Centenary Edition is the best collection of the works, but should be supplemented by the ten volumes of the Journals. Rusk's biography, built in part on his complete edition of Emerson's letters, is the best life.

W. P. and Francis J. Garrison, *Life of William Lloyd Garrison, 1805–1879*, four volumes, 1885–1889; John Jay Chapman, *William Lloyd Garrison*, 1913. The great four-volume biography is indispensable to all students of the antislavery movement, while Chapman's admiring memoir is a penetrating estimate of a remarkable personality.

L. D. Ingersoll, *Life of Horace Greeley*, 1873; W. A. Linn, *Horace Greeley, Founder and Editor of the New York Tribune*, 1903; James Parton, *Life of Horace Greeley, Editor of the New York Tribune*, 1868, 1872, etc.; F. N. Zabriskie, *Horace Greeley, the Editor*, 1890; Horace Greeley, *Recollections of a Busy Life*, 1868. None of the more recent biographies has quite the value of the books by Linn and Parton, themselves journalists of distinction. Greeley's *Recollections* has the frank graphic qualities of Franklin's autobiography, and should be widely known.

Thomas W. Higginson, *Cheerful Yesterdays*, 1898; *Letters and Journals of T. W. Higginson, 1846–1926*, 1921. These volumes give a good view of a radical antislavery leader who had the courage of his convictions.

William Dean Howells, *Years of My Youth*, 1916; *Literary Friends and Acquaintance*, 1900; Mildred Howells, *Life in Letters of William Dean Howells*, two volumes, 1928. These books, invaluable for the social and literary life of the time, also throw some illumination on political affairs.

C. H. Ambler, ed., *Correspondence of Robert M. T. Hunter, 1826–1876*, Ann. Report Am. Hist. Assn., 1916, II. Very useful for one school of Virginia thought.

George Fort Milton, *The Age of Hate: Andrew Johnson and the Radicals*, 1930; Robert W. Winston, *Life of Andrew Johnson, Plebeian and Patriot*, 1928; Lloyd P. Stryker, *Andrew Johnson: A Study in Courage*, 1929. Three excellent books on the self-made popular leader of Tennessee. That of Milton is fullest on the period before 1861.

Percy S. Flippin, *Herschel V. Johnson of Georgia, State Rights Unionist*, 1931; Percy S. Flippin, ed., "From the Autobiography of Herschel V. Johnson, 1856–1867," *Am. Hist. Review*, XXX, 1925.

Horatio King, *Turning on the Light*, 1895. One of the indispensable books for the secession winter of 1860–1861.

John G. Nicolay and John Hay, eds., *Abraham Lincoln, Complete Works*, two volumes, 1894; Nicolay and Hay, *Complete Works* (sometimes called Tandy or Tandy-Thomas edition), twelve volumes, 1905; Gilbert A. Tracy, *Uncollected Letters of Abraham Lincoln*, 1917; Paul M. Angle, ed., *New Letters and Papers of Abraham Lincoln*, 1930; Rufus Rockwell Wilson, *Uncollected Works of Abraham Lincoln*, 1947; Nicolay and Hay, *Abraham Lincoln: A History*, ten volumes, 1890; Albert J. Beveridge, *Abraham Lincoln, 1809–1858*, two volumes, 1928; Carl Sandburg, *Abraham Lincoln: The Prairie Years*, two volumes, 1926; Sandburg, *Abraham Lincoln: The War Years*, four volumes, 1939; William H. Herndon and Jesse W. Weik, *Abraham Lincoln, The True Story of a Great Life*, 1892 (reissue from the rare original three-volume work of 1889 called *Herndon's Lincoln: The True Story of a Great Life*); Ida M. Tarbell, *The Life of Abraham Lincoln*, two volumes, 1909, etc.; William E. Barton, *The Life of Abraham Lincoln*, two volumes, 1925; Lord Charnwood, *Abraham Lincoln*, 1916; James G. Randall, *Lincoln the President, Springfield to Gettysburg*, two volumes (American Political Leaders Series), 1946. These are among the most important works on Lincoln. For the huge library which has grown up about him and his career, see Jay Monaghan's *Lincoln Bibliography, 1839–1939*, two volumes, 1945, which is supplemented by the valuable bibliography in Randall's second volume. The ten volumes by Nicolay and Hay, an official life, are rather a history of the time than a strict biography. Beveridge's work is notable for its fairness and even sympathy in treating Douglas; Sandburg's for its fine poetic spirit and mass of detail; and Randall's for its analytical quality and profound scholarship. The best edition of the Herndon-Weik life is the one-volume edition with introduction and notes issued by Paul M. Angle in 1930, since reprinted. Those interested in appraising the biographical work done on Lincoln should not fail to read David Donald, *Lincoln's Herndon*, 1948, which has much valuable material on the history of the time; Benjamin P. Thomas, *Portrait for Posterity: Lincoln and His Biographers*, and Paul M. Angle, *A Shelf of Lincoln Books: A Critical Selective Bibliography of Lincolniana*.

Samuel Longfellow, *Life of Henry Wadsworth Longfellow*, three volumes, 1891; Charles Eliot Norton, *Letters of James Russell Lowell*, two volumes, 1893; H. E. Scudder, *James Russell Lowell: A Biography*, two volumes, 1901; Ferris Greenslet, *James Russell Lowell. His Life and Work*, 1905; Sara Norton and M. A. DeWolfe Howe, *Letters of Charles Eliot Norton*, two volumes, 1913. These books throw much light on American life, letters, and public affairs as seen from the area of Boston. They are also delightful to read. The Riverside edition of Lowell's works, ten volumes, 1890, is useful.

Theodore Parker, *Collected Works*, fifteen volumes, 1907–1913; John Weiss, *Life and Correspondence of Theodore Parker*, two volumes, 1864; Octavius B. Frothingham, *Theodore Parker*, 1874; Henry Steele Commager, *Theodore Parker: Yankee Crusader*, 1936. These are the more important materials for understanding a leader who summed up much of the reform spirit and crusading ideology of the time.

Roy F. Nichols, *Franklin Pierce: Young Hickory of the Granite Hills*, 1931; P. Orman Ray, ed., "Some Papers of Franklin Pierce, 1852–1862," *Am. Hist. Review*, X. The biography by Nichols embodies an excellent history of the Pierce Administration.

Laura A. White, *Robert Barnwell Rhett, Father of Secession*, 1931; Avery O. Craven, *Edmund Ruffin, Southerner: A Study in Secession*, 1932. Two admirable biographies, both compact, of leaders in the movement for Southern independence.

William H. Russell, *My Diary North and South*, two volumes, 1863. Reprinted in various editions. A graphic and honest piece of reporting by one of the great journalists of the century. Its sketches of Washington and the South in the secession winter and spring are excellent.

Carl Schurz, *Reminiscences*, three volumes, 1907–1908; Frederic Bancroft, ed., *Speeches, Correspondence and Political Papers of Carl Schurz*, six volumes, 1913; Joseph Schafer, *Intimate Letters of Carl Schurz, 1841–1869*, 1928. A keen observer and a delightful writer, Schurz shows great accuracy—despite his strong freesoil bias. Claude M. Fuess, *Carl Schurz, Reformer* (American Political Leaders Series), 1932, has good chapters on the fifties and the campaign of 1860.

Frederic Bancroft, *The Life of William H. Seward*, two volumes, 1900; Frederick W. Seward, *Seward at Washington as Senator and Secretary of State*, three volumes, 1890, 1891. These, with Seward's works published in five volumes by order of Congress, cover the political career of the New Yorker with great detail; but room remains for the full critical life now being written by Harry Carman and R. H. Luthin (Amer. Political Leaders Series).

John Sherman, *Recollections of Forty Years in the House, Senate, and Cabinet. An Autobiography*, two volumes, 1895; William Tecumseh Sherman, *Memoirs of General William T. Sherman*, two volumes, 1875; Rachel S. Thorndike, *The Sherman Letters*, 1910; M. A. DeWolfe Howe, ed., *Home Letters of General Sherman*, 1909; Theodore E. Burton, *John Sherman* (American Statesmen Series). John Sherman's *Forty Years*, though dull in style, has useful chapters on the birth of the Republican Party, the panic of 1857, the Congressional conflicts during the Buchanan Administration, and the beginning of Lincoln's Administration. William Tecumseh Sherman's *Memoirs* is much more entertaining, but often wildly inaccurate. Its impressions of the South just before the war are particularly good. A really adequate biography of John Sherman is being prepared by Jeanette Paddock Nichols and Roy F. Nichols.

Louis M. Sears, *John Slidell*, 1925. A useful biography of a man who seems doomed to remain little known because of the destruction of his papers.

George C. Gorham, *Edwin M. Stanton*, two volumes, 1899; Frank A. Flower, *Edwin McMasters Stanton*, 1905. Neither of these works approaches a satisfactory standard. They are supplemented by A. H. Meneely's *The War Department, 1861*, 1928. But an adequate study of Stanton and his work remains one of the great desiderata in the field of American history.

R. M. Johnston and W. H. Browne, *Life of Alexander H. Stephens*, 1878; Louis Pendleton, *Alexander H. Stephens*, 1908; Rudolph Von Abele, *Alexander H. Stephens*, 1946; J. Z. Rabun, *Alexander H. Stephens, 1812–1861*, MS diss., University of Chicago; M. L. Avary, ed., *The Recollections of Alexander H. Stephens*, 1910; Alexander H. Stephens, *A Constitutional View of the Late War Between the States*, two volumes, 1868–1870; James D. Waddell, *Biographical Sketch of Linton Stephens*, 1877. The best of these works are the old book by Johnston and Browne, rich in letters, and the new study by Rabun, based on a full examination of various collections of Stephens papers. *The Constitutional View* is to the historian a most disappointing work.

Charles Sumner, ed., *The Works of Charles Sumner*, fifteen volumes, 1870–1883; Edward L. Pierce, *Memoir and Letters of Charles Sumner*, four volumes, 1877–1893; Moorfield Storey, *Charles Sumner*, 1900; George H. Haynes, *Charles Sumner*, 1909. The compendious memoir by Pierce, though eulogistic and formal, is full of useful matter. It exhibits Sumner as an admirable letter-writer. A full and scholarly new biography is being prepared by David Donald.

Carl B. Swisher, *Roger B. Taney*, 1935; B. C. Steiner, *Life of Roger Brooke Taney*, 1922; Samuel Tyler, *Memoir of Roger B. Taney*, 1872. Tyler's volume includes an autobiographical fragment. Each of these books has materials of value, but Swisher's is the fullest and most scholarly.

Holman Hamilton, *Zachary Taylor, Soldier of the Republic*, 1945. This first half of a projected two-volume work brings Taylor to the eve of his Administration.

Ulrich B. Phillips, ed., *The Correspondence of Robert Toombs, Alexander H. Stephens, and Howell Cobb*, Ann. Report. Am. Hist. Ass., 1911, Vol. II; Ulrich B. Phillips *The Life of Robert Toombs*, 1913; Pleasants A. Stovall, *Robert Toombs*, 1892; W. W. Brewton, *The Son of Thunder: Robert Toombs*, 1936. The correspondence of the three Southern leaders covers the years 1844–1882, and contains a frank and able presentation of the Southern standpoint. Phillips's life of Toombs is careful, critical, and thorough. W. P. Trent's *Southern Statesmen of the Old Regime*, 1897, contains an acute estimate of Toombs; and John C. Reed, *The Brothers' War*, 1905, is built mainly about the man.

John D. Wade, *Augustus B. Longstreet: A Study of the Development of Culture in the South*, 1924. A work as valuable in its field as W. P. Trent's *William Gilmore Simms* (American Men of Letters Series), 1892.

Edward Everett, ed., *Works of Daniel Webster*, six volumes, 1851; J. W. McIntyre, ed., *Writings and Speeches of Daniel Webster*, eighteen volumes (National Edition), 1903; George Ticknor Curtis, *Life of Daniel Webster*, two volumes, 1870; Claude M. Fuess, *Daniel Webster*, two volumes, 1930; C. H. Van Tyne, ed., *Letters of Daniel Webster*, 1902.

Harriet A. Weed, ed., *Life of Thurlow Weed (Autobiography)*, 1883–1884; Thurlow Weed Barnes, *Memoir of Thurlow Weed*, 1883–1884. These form the two volumes of a set. The autobiography is particularly valuable. The best biography is Glyndon G. Van Deusen, *Thurlow Weed, Wizard of the Lobby*, 1947.

John T. Morse, ed., *Diary of Gideon Welles*, three volumes, 1911. This contains a useful introduction. It is beyond price in the light it throws on American history 1860–1869. But it should be read in the light of Howard K. Beale's article in the *Am. Hist. Review*, XXX, 547 ff., 1925, "Is the Printed Diary of Gideon Welles Reliable?"

Barton H. Wise, *The Life of Henry A. Wise of Virginia, 1806–1876*; Henry A. Wise, *Seven Decades of the Union*, 1871; John S. Wise, *The End of an Era*, 1899. *The Seven Decades* contains interesting matter on the Peace Convention and Virginia's secession; and the book by Governor Wise's son gives a really vivid impression of an old era ended and a new one begun.

V: GENERAL LITERATURE: A SELECTED LIST

The principal comprehensive works on the period 1846–1861 are the following:

Adams, James Truslow, *America's Tragedy*, 1934. A thoughtful sketch of the conflict of North and South from the seventeenth century to the end of Reconstruction. The author finds the chief root of the Civil War in slavery; but he adds that "the South was not fighting from 1820 onward merely against the North but against the time spirit, the course of modern life and thought."

Burgess, John W., *The Civil War and the Constitution, 1859–1865*, two volumes, 1901. An outline history, now considerably outdated, by a native of Tennessee who fought on the Union side and later became one of the moulders of Columbia University.

Chadwick, French E., *Causes of the Civil War, 1859–1861* (American Nation Series), 1906. In the main an excellent book, though its research is not deep, and it has more than its share of errors.

Channing, Edward, *A History of the United States*, Vol. V, *The Period of Transition*, 1921, Vol. VI, *The War for Southern Independence*, 1925. Taken together, these cover the period 1815–1865. Full treatment is impossible in such limited compass, and Channing lacks literary quality. But as a series of monographic investigations of select topics, with excellent footnote bibliographical references, the volumes are useful and stimulating.

Cole, Arthur C., *The Irrepressible Conflict, 1850–1865* (History of American Life), 1934. Excellent treatment of social and cultural forces.

Craven, Avery, *The Coming of the Civil War*, 1942. In his account of slavery ("a very ancient labor system, drastically adjusted to local American conditions") and the antislavery movement, and in his handling of specific issues like Lecompton and Sumter, the author leans to the Southern side. More than half of the book deals with the period before 1849. The treatment of sectional self-consciousness and sectional antagonisms, and of the frequent triumph of emotion over reason, is especially able. At the end Craven condemns Lincoln for "double-talk," failure to see clearly, and refusal to adopt a clear-cut program. An unconventional, opinionated, stimulating, and exasperating volume.

Dodd, William E., *The Cotton Kingdom: A Chronicle of the Old South*, 1919. A brilliant sketch of the planter civilization of the cotton States; best read in conjunction with William Garrott Brown's *The Lower South in American History*, 1902, and the books of Ulrich B. Phillips and Frederic Law Olmsted.

Hart, Albert Bushnell, *Slavery and Abolition* (American Nation Series), 1906. Still the best single volume on the subject.

Holst, Hermann Von, *Constitutional History of the United States*, eight volumes, 1885–1892. More detailed on some subjects than any other treatment; valuable for its full use of official documents, pamphlets, and Northern periodicals; greatly impaired by Von Holst's abolitionist leanings, ignorance of Southern conditions, and unsympathetic attitude toward many American ways and institutions.

Hosmer, James K., *The Appeal to Arms, 1861–1863* (American Nation Series), 1907. A useful outline history.

Macy, Jesse, *The Anti-Slavery Crusade: A Chronicle of the Rising Storm* (Chronicles of America Series), 1919. A good brief account of the abolitionist movement, underground railroad, Kansas struggle, and John Brown.

McMaster, John Bach, *History of the People of the United States*, eight volumes, 1883–1913. The seventh and eighth volumes are particularly useful for this period; good on public opinion, especially as reflected in the press, and on many aspects of social change.

Nichols, Roy Franklin. *The Disruption of American Democracy*, 1848. An exhaustive, scholarly, and interesting book on the Democratic Party and its disruption, 1857–1861, and on the Buchanan Administration.

Randall, James G., *The Civil War and Reconstruction*, 1937. Impartial, thorough, and able; based on a comprehensive knowledge of source materials and monographs, yet admirably digested. Indispensable to all students of the time. The full bibliography is the best general guide to the literature of the period 1850–1877.

Rhodes, James Ford, *History of the United States From the Compromise of 1850*, seven volumes (to 1877), 1893–1906. One of the great road-breaking works of American historiography, and a narrative history of broad swinging interest. Many separate sections have been left outdated by the progress of research; but taken as a whole the first three volumes, which cover the period 1850–1862, deserve careful reading.

Schouler, James, *History of the United States Under the Constitution*, seven volumes, 1894–1913. The fifth volume covers the Mexican War and the years down to Lincoln's inauguration. Good as an outline guide, though badly organized, inadequately documented, and full of Northern freesoil bias.

Smith, Theodore Clarke, *Parties and Slavery, 1850–1859* (American Nation Series), 1906. Shows in brief compass how sectional antagonism "came to permeate law and politics, literature and social intercourse."

Stephenson, Nathaniel W., *Abraham Lincoln and the Union: A Chronicle of The Embattled North* (Chronicles of America Series), 1918. Mainly on the Civil War.

Wilson, Henry, *History of the Rise and Fall of the Slave Power in America*, three volumes, 1872–1877. The last work of the rugged Massachusetts Senator and Vice-President, left incomplete at his death, this shows less prejudice than its title would indicate. Its superficiality and lack of perspective are obvious, but it embodies the special knowledge which Wilson gained from his long official career.

Most of the general and monographic works used by the author of the present volumes are in the list below, arranged alphabetically under authors; dates are not invariably given.

Abbott, Edith, *Historical Aspects of the Immigration Problem: Select Documents*, 1924; Adams, Grace & Hutter, Edward, *The Mad Forties*, 1946; Adams, James Truslow, *America's Tragedy*, 1934; Affleck, Thomas, *The Cotton (or Sugar) Plantation Record & Account Book*; Albion, Robert G., *Rise of New York Port, 1815–1860*, 1939; Alexander, DeAlva S., *Political History of the State of New York*, Vols. 1 and 2, 1906; Allen, James Lane, *Blue Grass Region of Kentucky*, 1892; Ambler, Charles H., *Sectionalism in Virginia from 1776 to 1861*, 1910; *The American Textbook for the Campaign of 1856*, 1856; Anderson, Galusha, *A Border City During the Civil War*, 1908; Anderson, Godfrey T., "The Slavery Issue as a Factor in Mass. Politics from the Compromise of 1850 to the Civil War," unpublished Univ. of Chicago doctoral diss.; Andrews, E. H., *Slavery & The Domestic Slave Trade*, 1836; Anon., *The Attaché in Madrid*, or, *Sketches of the Court of Isabella II*, 1856; Anon., *The Five Cotton States and New York*, 1861; *Appleton's Cyclopedia of American Biography*; *Appleton's Railway Guide, 1855–1861*; Aptheker, Herbert, *American Negro Slave Revolts*; Ardrey, R. L., *American Agricultural Implements*; Auchampaugh, P. G., *James Buchanan and His Cabinet on the Eve of Secession*, 1926; Bailey, T. A., *Diplomatic History of the American People*, revised ed., 1950; Bancroft, Frederic, *Slave Trading in the Old South*, 1931; Ballagh, J. C., *A History of Slavery in Virginia*, 1902; Barnes, Gilbert H., *The Anti-Slavery Impulse, 1830–1844*, 1933; Baringer, William E., *A House Dividing: Lincoln as President Elect*, 1945; Baringer, William E., *Lincoln's Rise to Power*, 1937; Bassett, John S., *Slavery in the State of North Carolina*; Becker, Jeronimo, *Relaciones Exteriores de España*; Beecher, Henry Ward, *New Star Papers, or Views & Experiences on Religious Subjects*; Belcher, Wyatt, *Economic Rivalry of Chicago & St. Louis, 1850–1880*, 1947; Bemis, S. F., ed., *The American Secretaries of State and Their Diplomacy*; Benjamin, J. G., *The Germans in Texas*; Benton, Thomas H., *Historical and Legal Examination of the Dred Scott Case*, 1857; Bettersworth, John K., *Confederate Mississippi*, 1943; Bidwell, P. W. and Falconer, J. I., *Agriculture in Northern United States, 1620–1860*, 1925; Biesele, R. L., *History of the*

German Settlements in Texas, 1831–1861, 1930; Bigelow, John, Jamaica in 1850, 1851; Billington, Ray A., The Protestant Crusade, 1800–1860, 1938; Billington, Ray A., Westward Expansion: A History of the American Frontier, 1949; Bogen, Jules, The Anthracite Railroads, 1927; Botts, John M., The Great Rebellion, 1866; Boucher, Chauncey S., The Secession & Cooperation Movements in South Carolina, 1848–52, Washington U. Studies, pt. 2, no. 2, 1918; Boudin, Louis B., Government by Judiciary, Two Vols., 1932; Bowen, Francis, Principles of Political Economy, 2nd ed., 1859; Boyd, M. C., Alabama in the Fifties, 1931; Brearly, H. C., Time-Telling Through the Ages, 1924; Brisbane, Albert, Association; or a Concise Exposition of the Practical Part of Fourier's Social Science, 1843; Brooks, N. C., History of the Mexican War, 1849; Brooks, Van Wyck, America's Coming-of-Age, 1915; Brooks, Van Wyck, The Flowering of New England, 1815–1865, rev. ed., 1941; Brown, George W., False Claims of Kansas Historians; Brown, Herbert R., The Sentimental Novel in America, 1789–1860; Bruce, P. A., The Economic History of Virginia in the Seventeenth Century, Two Vols., 1896; Bruce, P. A., The Plantation Negro as a Freeman; Buckham, John W., Progressive Religious Thought in America, 1919; Burgess, John W., Civil War and Constitution; Burlingame, Roger, March of the Iron Men, 1938; Caffin, Charles H., The Story of American Painting, 1907; Cairnes, J. E., The Slave Power, 1863; Caldwell, R. G., The Lopez Expedition to Cuba, 1848–1851, 1915; Calkins, Ernest E., They Broke the Prairie; Capers, Gerald M., The Biography of a River Town; Carr, Lucien, Missouri; A Bone of Contention, 1894; Cash, W. J., The Mind of the South, 1941; Catterall, Helen T., Judicial Cases Concerning American Slavery & the Negro; Channing, Edward, A History of the United States, Vol. VI, 1925; Clark, T. D., A Pioneer Southern Railroad; Clark, Victor S., History of Manufactures in the United States, 1607–1860, 1916; Cleland, Robert S., From Wilderness to Empire: California 1542–1900, 1944; Cochran, T. C. & Miller, William, The Age of Enterprise, 1942, etc.; Cole, A. J., "Changes in Sentiment in Georgia toward Secession 1850–1860," Univ. of Ill. M.A. thesis; Cole, Arthur C., Era of the Civil War, 1848–1870 (Centennial History of Illinois), 1919; Cole, Arthur C., The Irrepressible Conflict 1850–1865, 1934; Cole, Arthur C., The Whig Party in the South, 1913; Coleman, J. W., Jr., Slavery Times in Kentucky, 1940; Cooke, George W., Unitarianism in America: A History of its Origin & Development, 1902; Commons, John R. & Associates, History of Labor in the United States, Three Vols., 1921; Cooley, T. M. et al., Constitutional History of the United States, 1889; Corwin, Edward S., National Supremacy, 1913; Corwin, Edward S., Twilight of the Supreme Court, 1934; Cotterill, R. S., The Old South, 1936; Coupland, Reginald, The British Anti-Slavery Movement; Cox, Samuel S., Three Decades of Federal Legislation 1855–85, 1885; Crallé, R. K., ed., Works of J. C. Calhoun, 1851–1855; Craven, Avery, The Coming of the Civil War, 1942; Crawford, Col. Samuel W., Genesis of the Civil War, 1887; Crenshaw, Ollinger, Slave States in the Presidential Election of 1860, 1945; Cubberley, E. P., Public Education in the United States, 1919; Curtis, George T., Constitutional History of the United States, 1896; Dana, E. S. and others, A Century of Science in America, 1918; Dana, R. H., Jr., Two Years Before the Mast, 1840; Davenport, F. G., Cultural Life of Nashville, 1825–60, 1941; Davis, Elmer, History of the New York Times, 1921; Davis, Charles S., The Cotton Kingdom in Alabama, 1939; Davis, Edwin Adams, Plantation Life in the Florida Parishes of Louisiana, 1836–1846; Davis, Jefferson, The Rise & Fall of the Confederate Government, Two Vols., 1881; Davis, Reuben, Recollections of Mississippi & Mississippians, 1889; Denman, Clarence P., Secession Movement in Alabama, 1933; Dixon, Mrs. Archibald, True History of the Missouri Compromise and Its Repeal; Dodd, William E., The Cotton Kingdom, 1919; Dodd, William E., Statesmen of the Old South, or From Radicalism to Conservative Revolt, 1911; Dollard, John, Caste and Class in a Southern Town; Dorfman, Joseph, The Economic Mind in American Civilization, Three Vols., 1942–1949; Dorman, Lewey, Party Politics in Alabama from 1850 through 1860, 1935; Dumond, D. L., Anti-Slavery Origins of the Civil War, 1939; Dumond, D. L., The Secession Movement 1860–1861, 1931; Easterby, J. H., The South Carolina Rice Plantation as Revealed in the Papers *of Robert F. W. Allston*, 1945; Eaton, Clement, *Freedom of Thought in the Old South;* Eskew, Garnett L., *The Pageant of the Packets;* Ettinger, Amos A., *The Mission to Spain of Pierre Soulé, 1853–1855,* 1932; Fairchild, Henry P., *Immigration,* 1913; Faust, Albert B., *The German Element in the United States,* 1909; Fish, C. R., *Rise of the Common Man 1830–50,* 1927; Fite, Emerson D., *Presidential Campaign of 1860,* 1911; Flanders, Ralph B., *Plantation Slavery in Georgia,* 1933; Follett, M. P., *The Speaker of the House of Representatives,* 1896; Foner, Philip S., *Business and Slavery,* 1941; Foote, Henry S., *War of the Rebellion,* 1866; Franklin, John Hope, *The Free Negro in North Carolina, 1790–1860;* Garber, P. N., *The Gadsden Treaty,* 1923; Gates, P. W., *The Illinois Central Railroad & Its Colonization Work;* Gihon, Dr. John H., *Geary and Kansas,* 1857; Gilbert, E. W., *Exploration of Western America, 1800–1850,* 1933; Gildersleeve, Basil, *The Creed of the Old South, 1865–1915,* 1915; Gohdes, Clarence, *American Literature in Nineteenth Century England,* 1944; Gray, Lewis C., *History of Agriculture in the Southern States to 1860,* Two Vols., 1933; Gray, Wood, *Hidden Civil War: The Story of the Copperheads,* 1942; Greeley, Horace, *The American Conflict,* Two Vols., 1865; Grund, Francis J., *The Americans in Their Moral, Social, and Political Relations,* 1837; Guillet, Edwin C., *The Great Migration,* 1929; Halstead, Murat, *Caucuses of 1860,* 1860; Hamer, P. M., *The Secession Movement in South Carolina, 1847–52;* Hazard, Lucy L., *The Frontier in American Literature,* 1927; Hansen, Marcus Lee, *The Atlantic Migration, 1607–1860,* 1940; Harper, James H., *The House of Harper,* 1912; Harris, N. D., *History of Negro Servitude in Illinois;* Havighurst, Walter, *Long Ships Passing;* Harvin, E. L., "Arkansas and The Crisis of 1860–1861," MS, Univ. of Texas; Hendrick, Burton J., *Lincoln's War Cabinet,* 1946; Hendrick, Burton J., *Statesmen of the Lost Cause,* 1939; Hesseltine, William B., *Lincoln and the War Governors,* 1948; Hesseltine, William B., *A History of the South, 1607–1936,* 1936; Heyward, Duncan C., *Rice From Madagascar,* 1937; Hilliard, H. W., *Politics and Pen-Pictures,* 1892; Hodgson, Joseph, *Cradle of the Confederacy;* Homer, William, *The Higher Law in its Relations to Civil Government: with Particular Reference to Slavery & the Fugitive Slave Law,* 1852; Howard, Robert W., *Two Billion Acre Farm;* Howe, M. A. De Wolfe, *The Atlantic Monthly and Its Makers,* 1919; Hume, John, *The Abolitionists;* Hundley, D. R., *Social Relations in our Southern States,* 1860; Hungerford, Edward, *The Story of the Baltimore & Ohio Railroad,* Two Vols., 1928; Hungerford, James W., *The Old Plantation;* Ingle, Edward, *Southern Sidelights: A Picture of Social and Economic Life in the South a Generation Before the War,* 1896; Jackson, Luther P., *Free Negro Labor and Property Holding in Virginia, 1830–1860,* 1937; Jenkins, William S., *Pro-Slavery Thought in the Old South,* 1935; Johnson, Guion G., *Ante Bellum North Carolina, A Social History,* 1937; Johnston, J. H., "Race Relations in Virginia and Miscegenation in the South, 1776–1860," MS dissertation, Univ. of Chicago; Kahn, Morton E., *Djuka, The Bush Negroes of Dutch Guiana,* 1931; King, Horatio, *Turning on the Light: A Dispassionate Survey of President Buchanan's Administration,* 1895; Kinsley, Philip, *The Chicago Tribune: Its First Hundred Years,* Vol. I, 1847–1865, 1943; Kirkland, Caroline, *Chicago Yesterdays,* 1913; Klingberg, Frank J., *The Anti-Slavery Movement in England: A Study of English Humanitarianism,* 1926; *Know-Nothing Almanac, or True Americans' Manual,* 1850; Krout, John A., *The Origins of Prohibition,* 1925; Langston, B. H., "The South and the Kansas-Nebraska Bill," MS, Univ. of Texas; *Letters Relating to a Collection of Pictures Made by Mr. James Jackson Jarves* (privately printed 1859); Lewis, Lloyd, and Smith, Henry J., *Chicago;* Lewis, Oscar, *The Big Four,* 1938; Lunt, George, *Origin of the Late War,* 1866; Luthin, Reinhard H., *First Lincoln Campaign,* 1944; MacGill, Caroline E. & others, *Transportation in the United States Before 1860,* 1917; McGregor, J. C., *The Disruption of Virginia;* Macy, Jesse, *The Anti-Slavery Crusade,* 1919; Malin, James C., *John Brown and the Legend of '56,* 1942; Mansfield, E. D., *History of the Mexican War,* 1849; Martin, Edgar W., *The Standard of Living in 1860,* 1942; Mathieson, W. L., *Great Britain and The Slave Trade, 1839–1865;* A Mechanic, *Elements of Social Disorder: A Plea for the Laboring Classes in the U. S.,* 1844;

Mott, E. H., *Between the Ocean & the Lakes: the Story of Erie*, 1902; Mott, Frank L., *A History of American Magazines*, Three Vols., 1930–1938; Mott, Frank Luther, *American Journalism: 1690–1940*, 1941; Munford, Beverly B., *Virginia's Attitude toward Slavery and Secession*, 1910; Neuhaus, Eugen, *The History and Ideals of American Art*, 1931; Nevins, Allan, *The Evening Post: A Century of Journalism*, 1922; Nevins, Allan, *America Through British Eyes* (revised ed.), 1948; Nicholas, Roy F., *The Democratic Machine, 1850–54*, 1923; Nichols, Roy F., *The Disruption of American Democracy*, 1948; Nichols, Thomas Low, *Forty Years of American Life*, Two Vols., 1864; Nicolay, Helen, *Our Capitol on the Potomac*, 1924; Nicolay, John G., *The Outbreak of the Rebellion*; Nordhoff, Charles, *Communistic Societies in the U. S.*, 1875; O'Brien, Frank M., *The Story of the Sun*, 1918; Oldroyd, O. H., *Lincoln's Campaign, or the Political Revolution of 1860*; Osterweis, R. G., *Romanticism and Nationalism in the Old South*, 1949; Overdyke, Darrell, "The American Party in the Old South," MS doctoral dissertation, Duke Univ.; Overton, Grant, *Portrait of a Publisher and the First Hundred Years of the House of Appleton*, 1925; Owsley, Frank L., *King Cotton Diplomacy*, 1931; Page, Thomas N., *The Old Dominion: Her Making and Her Manners*, 1908; Parrington, Vernon L., *Main Currents in American Thought*, Three Vols., 1927–1930; Parson, G. C., *Inside View of Slavery*; Pattee, Fred Lewis, *The First Century of American Literature, 1770–1870*, 1935; Paxson, F. L., *History of the American Frontier, 1763–1893*, 1924; Perkins, Howard, ed., *Northern Editorials on Secession*, Two Vols., 1942; Petersen, William J., *Steamboating on the Upper Mississippi . . . Commerce & Navigation*, 1847; Peto, Sir S. Morton, *The Resources & Prospects of America*, 1865; Phillips, U. B., *The Course of the South to Secession*, 1939; Phillips, U. B., *Georgia and States Rights*, 1902; Phillips, U. B., *History of Transportation in the Eastern Cotton Belt, 1860*, 1908; Phillips, U. B., *Life and Labor in the Old South*, 1929; Phillips, U. B., *American Negro Slavery*, 1918; Phillips, William, *The Conquest of Kansas*; Pike, James S., *First Blows of the Civil War*, 1870; Pitkin, T. M., "The Tariff and the Early Republican Party," MS diss., Western Reserve Univ.; Pollard, Edward A., *The Lost Cause: A New Southern History of the War*, 1866; Quinn, Arthur H., *A History of the American Drama From the Beginning to the Civil War*, 1923; Randall, J. G., *The Civil War and Reconstruction*, 1937; Rainwater, Percy L., *Mississippi: Storm Center of Secession 1856–61*, 1938; Rantoul, Robert, *Letter to Robert Schuyler on the Value of the Public Lands of Illinois*, 1851; Ray, P. O., *Repeal of the Missouri Compromise*, 1909; Reed, John C., *The Brothers' War*, 1905; Rennick, S. G., *Report on Cattle Transportation*, 1856; Rhodes, James Ford, *History of the U. S. from the Compromise of 1850*, Vols. 1–3, 1892–1895; Richardson, James D., ed., *A Compilation of the Messages & Papers of the Presidents, 1789–1897*, 1896–1899; Richardson, R. N., *Texas, The Lone Star State*; Riegel, O. W., *Crown of Glory: The Life of J. J. Strang*; Rice, M. H., *American Catholic Opinion in the Slavery Controversy*, 1944; Rives, G. L., *The United States and Mexico 1821–1848*, Two Vols., 1913; Robbins, Roy M., *Our Landed Heritage*, 1942; Robinson, Charles, *The Kansas Conflict*, 1892; Robinson, Harriet H., *Early Factory Labor in New England*; Rodriques, J. I., *Estudio . . . sobre . . . la idea de la Anexion de la isla de Cuba a los Estados Unidos de America*; Russell, Robert R., *Economic Aspects of Southern Sectionalism, 1840–61*; Savage, William S., *The Controversy Over the Distribution of Abolition Literature*, 1938; Sawyer, W. E., "Evolution of the Morrill Act of 1862," MS doctoral diss., Boston Univ., 1948; Schafer, Joseph, *Social History of American Agriculture*; Schlegel, Marvin, *Franklin B. Gowen*, 1948; Schlesinger, Arthur M., Jr., *The Age of Jackson*, 1947; Schultz, Harold, "South Carolina & National Politics, 1852–1860," MS diss., Duke Univ.; Schweitzer, Albert, *On the Edge of the Primeval Forest*; Scroggs, W. O., *A Century of the Banking Progress*, 1924; Scrugham, Mary, *The Peaceable Americans of 1860–1861*; Shanks, Henry T., *The Secession Movement in Virginia 1847–1861*, 1934; Shippee, Lester Burrell, *Hist. Canadian-American Relations, 1849–1879*, 1939; Shugg, Roger W., *Origins of the Class Struggle in Louisiana*, 1939; Siebert, Wilbur H., *The Underground Railroad from Slavery to Freedom*, 1898; Simms, Henry H.,

A Decade of Sectional Controversy, 1942; Smith, J. H., *The War with Mexico*, Two Vols., 1919; Smith, Theodore C., *Liberty and Freesoil Parties in the Northwest*, 1902; Smith, William E., *The Francis Preston Blair Family in Politics*, Two Vols., 1938; Somers, Robert, *The Southern States Since the War*, 1871; Spring, Leverett W., *Kansas: The Prelude to the War for the Union*, 1907; Stanwood, Edward, *History of the Presidency from 1788 to 1920*, rev. ed., Two Vols., 1924; Stanwood, Edward, *Tariff Controversies in the Nineteenth Century*, Two Vols., 1903; Starr, John W., Jr., *One Hundred Years of American Railroading;* Stephens, Alexander H., *A Constitutional View of the Late War between the States . . .*, Two Vols., 1868–1870; Stephenson, N. W., *Lectures on Typical Americans and Their Problems;* Strevey, T. E., "Joseph Medill and the Chicago Tribune During the Civil War Period," MS doctoral diss., Univ. of Chicago; Stroupe, Henry S., "The Religious Press in the South Atlantic States 1802–1865," MS doctoral diss., Duke Univ., 1942; Sweet, W. W., *Religion on the Frontier; Vol. 1, The Baptists, 1783–1830*, 1938; Sweet, William W., *The Story of Religions in America*, 1930; Sydnor, Charles, *Slavery in Mississippi*, 1933; Tannenbaum, Frank, *Slave and Citizen: The Negro in the Americas;* Taylor, Richard, *Destruction and Reconstruction;* Thayer, Eli, *A History of the Kansas Crusade, Its Friends and Its Foes*, 1889; Thompson, Edgar T., ed., *Race Relations and the Race Problem*, 1939; Tilby, A. Wyatt, *Britain in the Tropics, 1527–1910;* Trexler, Harrison A., *Slavery in Missouri, 1804–1865*, 1914; Trollope, Anthony, *The West Indies and the Spanish Main;* Turner, A. J. *Genesis of the Republican Party;* Tyler, Alice F., *Freedom's Ferment;* Vance, Rupert B., *Human Geography of the South*, 1935; Van Oss, S. F., *American Railroads As Investments;* Vilá, Herminio Portell, *Historia de Cuba;* Walker, William, *The War in Nicaragua*, 1860; Wallas, Graham, *Human Nature in Politics* (third ed.), 1921; Warren, Charles, *The Supreme Court in United States History*, Two Vols., 1926; Weeks, S. B., *Anti-Slavery Sentiment in the South;* Whitfield, Theodore M., *Slavery Agitation in Virginia, 1829–32*, 1930; Wender, Herbert, *Southern Comercial Conventions 1837–1859*, 1930; Wertenbaker, T. J., *Patrician and Plebeian in Virginia*, 1910; Williams, T. Harry, *Lincoln and the Radicals*, 1941; Williams, M. W., *Anglo-American Isthmian Diplomacy, 1815–1915*, 1916; Wilson, Henry, *History of the Rise and Fall of the Slave Power in America*, Three Vols., 1872–77; Wilson, W. B., *History of the Pennsylvania Railroad Company;* Winsor, Justin, ed., *Memorial History of Boston*, Four Vols., 1881; Wise, John S., *End of an Era*, 1899; Woodson, Carter G., *Education of the Negro Prior to 1861*, 1915; Woodson, Carter G., *A Century of Negro Migration*, 1918; Woodson, Carter G., *The Negro in our History*, 1922; Zahler, Helene, *Eastern Workingmen and National Land Policy, 1829–1862*, 1941.

VI: ARTICLES IN PERIODICALS AND PAMPHLETS

Anon., "Prospect and Policy of the South, as seen by a Southern Planter," *Southern Quarterly Review*, Oct., 1854; Anon., *The New 'Reign of Terror' in the Slaveholding States, 1859–60* (pamphlet); Auchampaugh, P. G., "The Buchanan-Douglas Feud," *Journal Ill. State Hist. Soc.*, XXV, 5–48; Baltimore and Ohio R. R., *Annual Reports*, 1855–1861; Barnard, F. A. P., *Improvements Practicable in American Colleges* (pamphlet); Bauer, R. A. and A. H., "Day to Day Resistance to Slavery," *Journal Negro Hist.*, 27:388–419; Bean, W. G., "Anti-Jeffersonianism in the Ante-Bellum South," *North Carolina Hist. Rev.*, 12:103; Binckley, W. C., "The Question of Texan Jurisdiction in New Mexico under the U. S., 1848–50," *Southwestern History Quarterly*, 24:1–38; Bining, Arthur, "The Glass Industry of Western Pennsylvania," *Pa. Mag. Hist. and Biog.*, Dec., 1936; Botts, J. M., *A Letter to the Opposition Members . . .* (pamphlet); Letters of L. O. Branch, *N. C. Hist. Rev.*, 10:47; Cady, E. H., "William Dean Howells and the Ashtabula Sentinal," *Ohio Arch. and Hist. Quarterly*, 53:40–41; Cade, John B., "Out of the Mouths of Slaves," *Journal Negro Hist.*, 20:294–337; Calhoun, A. H., MS, "Vindication of John Calhoun," *Kan. State Hist. Lib.; Presidential Campaign of 1856, The Election and the Candidates* (pamphlet); Carman, Harry J., "Eng lish Views of Middle Western Agriculture, 1850–1879," *Agr. Hist.*, Jan., 1934; Carman, Harry J., and Luthin, R. H., "The Seward-Fillmore Feud and the Crisis of 1850," *New York Hist.*, 24:163–184; Carnathan, W. J., "The Proposal to Reopen the Slave Trade," *South Atlantic Quarterly*, 25:410–430; *Speech of Cass on Religious Freedom Abroad; Letter of the Most Rev. Archbishop Hughes on the Madai; Letter of Hughes in Reply to Lewis Cass* (pamphlet); *Case of Dred Scott in the Supreme Court of the United States* (pamphlet); Catterall, Helen T., "Some Antecedents of the Dred Scott Case," *Am. Hist. Rev.*, XXX, 56–71; Cotterill, R. S., "James Guthrie, Kentuckian," *Ky. State Hist. Soc. Reg.*, Sept., 1922; Cole, A. H., "Wholesale Commodity Prices in the United States, 1843–1862," *Rev. of Econ. Stats.*, Feb., 1929; Corwin, Edward S., "The Dred Scott Decision in the Light of Contemporary Legal Doctrines," *Am. Hist. Rev.*, XVII, 1911; Craik, E. L., "Southern Interest in Territorial Kansas," *Kan. Hist. Colls.*, 25:348; Craven, Avery, "Agricultural Reformers of the Ante-Bellum South," *Am. Hist. Rev.*, 33:302–314; *Speech of John W. Crisfield, 1856* (pamphlet); Dodd, W. E., "The Fight for the Northwest," *Am. Hist. Rev.*, XLV, 774–788; Donelson Papers, *Tenn. Hist. Mag.*, 3:259–291; Eaton, Clement, "The Resistance of the South to Northern Radicalism," *New England Quarterly*, VIII, 215; *Facts for the People of the South, or Know-Nothingism Exposed*, 1856 (pamphlet); Flanders, R. B., "Free Negro in Ante-Bellum Georgia," *North Carolina Hist. Rev.*, 9:1932; Fleming, W. L., "The Buford Expedition to Kansas," *Am. Hist. Rev.*, 6:38–48; Fleming, W. L., "Jefferson Davis, the Negroes and the Negro Problem," *Sewanee Rev.*, 16:407–427; "The Free School System of South Carolina," *Southern Quarterly Review*, Nov., 1856; Fraser, Jesse M., "Louisa C. McCord," *Bulletin No. 91*, Univ. S. C.; Galpin, W. F., "The Jerry Rescue," *New York Hist.*, Jan., 1945; "Letters of Governor John W. Geary to President Pierce," *Am. Hist. Rev.*, 10:124 ff., 350 ff.; Govan, Thomas P., "Was Plantation Slavery Profitable?" *Journal Southern Hist.*, 8:513–535; Haar, C. M., "Legislative Regulation of New York Industrial Corporations, 1800–1850," *New York Hist.*, April, 1941; Harmon, G. D., "Douglas and the Compromise of 1850," *Journal Ill. State Hist. Soc.*, 21:453–499; Harrington, Fred H., "The First Northern Victory," *Journal Southern Hist.*, 5:186–205; Hesseltine, William B., "Some New Aspects of the Pro-Slavery Argument," *Journal Negro Hist.*, 21:5; Hitchcock, Henry, "Modern Legislation Touching Marital Property Rights," *Journal of Social Science*, March, 1881; Hodder, F. H., "The Authorship of the Compromise of 1850," *Miss. Valley Hist. Rev.*, 22:525–536; Hodder, F. H., "The Genesis of the Kansas-Nebraska Act," *Wis. State Hist. Soc., Bull, No. 60*, 1912; Hodder, F. H., "Some Phases of the Dred Scott Decision," *Miss. Vall. Hist. Rev.*, XI (1929), 3–22; Hodder, F. H., "The Railroad Background of the Kansas-Nebraska Act," *Miss. Valley Hist. Rev.*, XII; Johnson, H. B., "German Forty-eighters in Davenport," *Iowa Journal Hist. and Politics*, XLIV, 3–53; Johnson, Hadley D., "How the Kansas-Nebraska Line Was Established," *Trans.* Neb. State Hist. Soc., 2:85; Jordan, H. D., "A Politician of Expansion: Robert J. Walker," *Miss. Vall. Hist. Rev.* (1918); Julian, George W., "The First Republican National Convention," *Am. Hist. Rev.*, 4:313; Kennedy, John P., *The Border States: Their Power and Duty in the Present Disordered Condition of the Country* (pamphlet, 1861); Kibler, Lillian A., "Union Sentiment in South Carolina in 1860," *Journal Southern Hist.*, IV, Aug., 1938; Klem, Mary J., "Missouri in the Kansas Struggle," *Miss. Valley Hist. Assn. Proc.*, 9:393–413; Klingberg, Frank J., "James Buchanan and the Crisis of the Union," *Journal Southern Hist.*, IX, Nov., 1943; Landon, F., "Negro Migration to Canada," *Journal Negro Hist.*, 5:30; Learned, H. B., "Relation of Philip Phillips to the Repeal of the Missouri Compromise," *Miss. Vall. Hist. Rev.*, 8:303–317; Levermore, C. H., "Henry C. Carey and His Social System," *Pol. Sci. Quart.*, 5:555; Linthicum, Gordon, "Autobiography," *Miss. Hist. Soc. Pubs.*, IX; Lippincott, I., "History of River Improvement," *Jour. Pol. Economy*, XXII, 644; Loomis, N. H., "Asa Whitney, Father of Pacific Railroads," *Miss. Valley Hist. Assn. Proc.*, VI; "Literary Prospects of the South," *Russell's Magazine*, June, 1858; Luthin, R. H., "Lincoln Becomes a Republican," *Pol. Sci. Quart.*, LIX, No. 3; McCormac, E. I., "Justice Campbell and the Dred Scott Decision," *Miss. Vall. Hist. Rev.*,

XIX (1933), 565–571; McCulloch, M. C., "Founding the North Carolina Asylum for the Insane," *N. C. Hist. Rev.*, 13:185:July, 1936; Malin, J. C., "Beginnings of Winter Wheat Production," *Kan. Hist. Quart.*, X, No. 3; Moore, J. B., "A Great Secretary of State: Wm. L. Marcy," *Pol. Sci. Quart.*, Sept., 1915; Myers, C. M., "Rise of the Republican Party in Pa.," MS diss., Univ. of Pittsburgh; Nichols, Roy F., "Some Problems of the First Republican Presidential Campaign," *Am. Hist. Rev.*, 28:492; *North and South: Impressions of Northern Society Upon a Southerner* (pamphlet, 1853); Ordway, S. F., "John Bell," *Gulf States Hist. Mag.*, II, No. 1, 41, 42; Owsley, Frank L. and Harriet C., "The Economic Basis of Society in the Late Ante-Bellum South," *Journal Southern Hist.*, 6:21–45; Owsley, Frank L. and Harriet C., "The Economic Structure of Rural Tennessee," *Journal Southern Hist.*, 8:161–182; "The Peculiarities of the South," *North Amer. Rev.*, Oct., 1890; Perkins, Howard C., "A Neglected Phase of the Movement for Southern Unity, 1847–1852," *Journal Southern Hist.*, 12:153–203; Perkins, H. C., "Defense of Slavery in the Northern Press on the Eve of the Civil War," *Journal Southern Hist.*, IX, Nov., 1943; Persinger, C. E., "Bargain of 1844," *Oregon Hist. Quart.*, 24:137–146; Pierce, E. L., *Important Statistics in Regard to the Foreign Vote in the Presidential Election*, 1857 (pamphlet); Porter, William D., *State Sovereignty and the Doctrine of Coercion* (pamphlet); Phillips, Ulrich B., "The Central Theme of Southern History," *Am. Hist. Rev.*, 24:30; Ramsdell, C. W., "The Natural Limits of Slavery Expansion," *Miss. Valley Hist. Rev.*, 16:151–171; Ray, P. O., "Genesis of the Kansas-Nebraska Act," *Am. Hist. Assn. Report*, 1914, 1:259–280; Reagan, J. H., *Address to the Voters of the First Congressional District* (pamphlet); Rice, William G., "The Appointment of Governor Marcy as Secretary of State," *Mag. of Hist.*, Feb.-March, 1912; Sanger, D. B., "The Chicago *Times* and the Civil War," *Miss. Vall. Hist. Rev.*, 17:557–580; Savage, W. S., "Abolitionist Letters in the Mails," *Journal Negro Hist.*, 13; Schafer, Joseph, "Some Facts Bearing on the Safety Valve Theory," *Wis. Mag. Hist.*, Dec., 1936; Schafer, Joseph, "Who Elected Lincoln?" *Am. Hist. Rev.*, XLVI, 51–63; Sellers, E. M., "The Pittsburgh and Cincinnati Packet Line Minute Book, 1851–53," *Western Pa. Hist. Mag.*, Dec., 1936; Shannon, Fred A., "The Homestead Act and Labor Surplus," *Am. Hist. Rev.*, July, 1936; "A Slave Trader's Note Book," *North Amer. Rev.*, Nov., 1886; Smith, D. V., "Influence of the Foreign-Born of the Northwest in the Election of 1860," *Miss. Vall. Hist. Rev.*, XIX, 192–204; *Speeches in the Assembly of the State of New York in Exposition of the Know-Nothings* (pamphlet, 1855); Spring, L. W., "The Career of a Kansas Politician," *Am. Hist. Rev.*, Oct., 1898; Stenberg, Richard R., "The Motivation of the Wilmot Proviso," *Miss. Vall. Hist. Rev.*, 28:535–541; Stephenson, W. H., "Political Career of General J. H. Love," *Kan. State Hist. Pubs.*, III, 1930; Stone, Alfred H., "The Cotton Factorage System of the Southern States," *Am. Hist. Rev.*, 20:557; Sydnor, C. S., "The Free Negro in Mississippi," *Am. Hist. Rev.*, 32:769; "Narrative of William Henry Trescot," *Am. Hist. Rev.*, XIII, 528–556; Van Alstyne, R. W., "British Diplomacy and the Clayton-Bulwer Treaty, 1850–1860," *Journal Mod. Hist.*, 9; Wesley, C. H., "Lincoln's Plan for Colonizing the Emancipated Negroes," *Journal Negro Hist.*, 4:7; "Bunyan in Broadcloth, the House of Weyerhaeuser," *Fortune*, April, 1934; White, Laura A., "The South in the 1850's as seen by British Consuls," *Journal Southern Hist.*, 1:29–48; Wilkey, H. L., "Infant Industries in Illinois," *Journal Ill. State Hist. Soc.*, 32, No. 4; Woodson, Carter G., "History Made to Order," *Journal Negro Hist.*, 12:330–348; Yancey, W. L., *Speech at Memphis, August 14, 1860* (pamphlet).

Index

INDEX

A

B